19th Edition

WRECKS & RELICS

Ken Ellis

CONTENTS

Front Cover: *Just Jane*, Lancaster VII NX611 at full pelt down the East Kirkby runway during the filming of *Night Flight* in February 2001. NX611 also 'starred' on the front cover of *Wrecks & Relics: The Album* from its days on the gate at Scampton, so the opportunity has been seized to show just how far *Jane* has come!
Duncan Cubitt – FlyPast Magazine

Rear Cover: Moment of history for the ultimate 'Hot-Rod' as Concorde G-BOAF touches down at its birthplace, Filton on November 26, 2003. After that, all Concorde movements will be at even greater expense! *Tony McCarthy*

A waste of a rare and fabulous aircraft, Harrier GR.3 in fanciful scheme inside the Trocadero in London, August 2002.
Andy Wood

Title Page: One of two superb tributes to jet pioneer Sir Frank Whittle, a Gloster E28/39 full-scale model soars skyward at Lutterworth, June 2003. *Ken Ellis*

Copyright 2004 © Ken Ellis

This nineteenth edition published by Midland Publishing
(An imprint of Ian Allan Publishing Ltd)
4 Watling Drive, Sketchley Lane Industrial Estate,
Hinckley, Leics, LE10 3EY.

ISBN 1 85780 183 0

Printed in the UK by Ian Allan Printing Ltd, Riverdene Business Park, Molesey Road, Hersham, Surrey KT12 4RG

PREFACE

For a long, long time, the writer has felt that this book has a life all of its own... It certainly seems to be able to play tricks with time. No sooner has one edition come out and I begin to wallow in the idea that it is aeons before I'm called on again than the publishers are banging on the door asking for the next one!

Last year the knocking was as loud as ever but it really *did* seem to be early. And it was... It was Midland Publishing suggesting a cunning plan. The first edition of *Wrecks & Relics* with muggins here at the helm was the fourth one, which appeared in the summer of 1974. That makes this year my 30th anniversary. (The book itself is 43 years old this year.) It seemed that three decades of tenacity and/or stupidity needed celebrating and the plot was to 'do' a colour pictorial. That would be a physical impossibility alongside the 19th Edition, so in May 2003 the anniversary was marked early with *Wrecks & Relics - The Album*.

I was just recovering from this as the 19th Edition loomed above me. The opportunity was taken to show Lancaster NX611 'in action' on the cover by way of contrast to its slow decay on the gate at Scampton as shown on the front of *The Album*. It is as well to remember that the fortunes of some aircraft can get turned around. (Without trying to sound at all commercial (!), if you ain't got *The Album* yet, you should do! And there's a page near the back giving you more details, should you feel so moved.)

Inside this edition, readers will find I take more than a few pot-shots at the recent scattering of Concordes across the realm. Sexy as they may be, this sudden influx will take a lot of time and money to assimilate correctly and one wonders what other aviation heritage use these scarce resources could have been put to. Concordes were delivered to customers 1976-1980 and there were *no* exports. Likewise, in the type's twilight in 2003 it is my opinion that *not enough* of them were exported!

Just before this book closed for press a unique survivor of air transport from a different era seemed to be going *down* the food chain, when it had a chance to move *up* it. And the 'aviation heritage movement' seemed powerless to influence its course. Also, two museums are under threat of closure as these words are typed. One seems destined for oblivion, the other is richly deserving of a new venue and an injection of investment. We shall have to wait and see...

Those who have read (or borrowed!) *The Album* may have noticed that the Ellis household has two cats, named Rex and Relics. The names seemed a good idea at the time. On the two-legged front, as ever, Pam stoically views the mania that goes with compiling a book that has a life of its own...

Deadlines for the next edition are **31st January 2006** for illustrations and **1st March 2006** for information and comments. If you plan to send 'electric' illustrations (jpeg do-dahs etc) I pledge to have the technology to receive them, but please e-mail *beforehand* for image size and density. Who knows, I may even have found out what that all means by then!

Ken Ellis
April 2004

Myddle Cottage, Welland Terrace, off Mill Lane, Barrowden,
Oakham, Rutland, LE15 8EH

wrecksandrelics@compuserve.com

Dedicated with the fondest of memories to
Brian Billington
1956-2004

Acknowledgements

This book relies on the inputs of a huge spectrum of contributors, each making their mark on the contents in different ways. My many thanks to them all.

Overseeing the draft, adding to it and refining it were **Alan Allen**, **Dave Allport**, **David J Burke**, **John Coghill** and **Nigel Price**. I'm proud that Dave Allport and Nigel Price are not just mates, but colleagues, working on *Air International* and *FlyPast* respectively. Also on the 'daytime' front, Jarrod Cotter (*FlyPast*) and Mark Nicholls ('Specials') have provided much support. Major photographic input came from **Tim R Badham**, **Ian Haskell**, **Alf Jenks**, **Tony McCarthy**, **Roger Richards**, **Brian** and **James Roffee**, **David S Johnstone**, **Phil Whalley**. Thanks also to master lensman **Duncan Cubitt** and Key Publishing for the cover.

The following subject and area specialists made vital inputs: **Gary Adams**, Ulster Aviation Society for Northern Ireland; **Andy Appleton**, Filton; **Peter R Arnold**, Spitfires; **Roy Bonser**, a font of answers!; **Michael R Cain**, Southend and others; **Alan Crouchman**, North Weald; **Peter Green**, a constant guiding light!; **Mark Harris**, for notes from his travels; **David S Johnstone**, Scotland; **Tony** and **Brenda McCarthy** for extensive notes of equally extensive travels; **Chris Michell**, Isle of Wight: **Seamus Mooney**, Ireland; **Watson J Nelson**, museum policies; **Alistair Ness**, Central Scotland Aviation Group for Scotland; **John Phillips**, rotorcraft; **Mike Phipp**, Bournemouth; **Geoffrey Poole**, Bruntingthorpe; **Col Pope** Duxford warbirds and others; **Allen Stacey**, gliders; **Stephen C Reglar**, Coventry; **Mervyn** and **Andrew Thomas**, St Athan and Cardiff; **David E Thompson**, north of England; **Andy Wood**, Humberside, Lincolnshire and Yorkshire

A mail-shot is made to the wide array of organisations working within the heritage movement. Thanks to the following for taking the time to update items and for their constant help and support: **Air Defence Radar Museum**; **Cliff Aldred**, Blyth Valley Aviation Collection; **Andy Allen**, Cessna EI-BAG; **Peter Amos**, The Miles Aircraft Collection; **Bill Baker**, BB Avaition; **Philip Baldock**, Robertsbridge Aviation Society; **Jenny Beard**, Imperial War Museum North; **Alan Beattie**, Yorkshire Helicopter Preservation Group; **Frank Beckley**, Brenzett Aeronautical Museum Trust; **Philip Bedford**, South East Aviation Enthusiasts, Ireland; **Dave Blackburn**, Jetstream Club; **Haydn Block**, Terrington Aviation Collection; **Mick Boulanger**, Wolverhampton Aviation Group; **Bournemouth Aviation Museum**; **Kevin Bowen**, Trident Preservation Society; **Alec Brew**, Boulton Paul Aircraft Heritage Project and the Black Country Aircraft Collection; **Ben Brown**, Sywell Aviation Museum; **Flt Lt Kevin Burchett**, Sea Vixen Preservation Group; **Ray Burrows**, Ulster Aviation Society; **James Campbell**, Highland Aviation Museum; **Glenn Cattermole**, Buccaneer XT284; **Graham Chaters**, Lincolnshire Aviation Preservation Society; **Chatham Historic Dockyard Trust**; **Ron Clarke**, Harrington Aviation Museum Society; **Richard Clarkson**, Vulcan Restoration Trust; **Roy Coates**, Sea Hawk WV838; **Doug J Cockle**, RAF Manston History Museum; **David Collins**, De Havilland Hornet Project; **Croydon Airport Society**; **Pete Davies**, Montrose Aerodrome Museum; **Lewis Deal MBE**, Medway Aircraft Preservation Society; **Oliver Deardon**, Bristol Aero Collection; **John Delaney**, Imperial War Museum, Duxford; **Doncaster Museum and Art Gallery**; **Dover Museum**; **Wayne Drurey**, Bomber County Aviation Museum, **Duxford Aviation Society**; **Eden Camp Modern History Theme Museum**; **Bryn Elliott**, North Weald Airfield Museum; **Mark Evans**, Midland Warplane Museum; **Huby Fairhead**, Norfolk and Suffolk Aviation Museum; **Aldon P Ferguson**, Burtonwood Heritage Centre; **Nick Forder**, Museum of Science and Industry, Manchester; **Ken Foteskew**, Museum of Berkshire Aviation; **Martin Garland**, Avro Heritage Group; **Sid Farmer**, Spitfire and Hurricane Memorial Museum; **Ken Fern**, for updates on his many projects; **Hack Green Secret Nuclear Bunker**; **Greta Foulkes-Halbard**, former Foulkes-Halbard collection; **John Francis**, RAF Museum Cosford; **Bruce Gordon**, de Havilland Aircraft Heritage Centre; **Derek G Griffiths**, International Cockpit Club; **Neil Hallett**, Farnborough Air Sciences; **Ian Hancock**, Norfolk and Suffolk Aviation Museum; **Raymond W Hansed**; **Roger Hargreaves**, Britannia Aircraft Preservation Trust; **Paul Hartley**, Vulcan XH558 Club and *three* Vulcan cockpits; **Howard Heeley**, Newark Air Museum; **Mike Hodgson**, Thorpe Camp Visitor Centre; **John Holder**, Historic Aircraft Restorations; **Stewart Holder**, Jet Aviation Preservation Group; **Daniel Hunt**, East Surrey Aviatio Group; **Stan Hurry**, 100th Bomb Group Memorial Museum; **George Inglis**, Glasgow Cultural and Leisure Services; **Roy Jerman**, Military Aircraft Cockpit Collection,; **Mark Jones**, Meteor Flight; **Mark A Jones**, Phantom Preservation Group and much gen on other fast-jets; **Tim Jones**, cockpit collector; **Paula Keene**, Shoreham Airport Historical Association; **Ricky Kelley**, Buccaneer Preservation Society; **Bob Kent**, Balloon Preservation Group; **Mike Killaspy**, Bassingbourn Tower Museum; **Andy King**, Bristol Industrial Museum; **David Kirkpatrick**, Solway Aviation Museum; **Andrew Lee**, Trident G-AWZI; **John Lewer**, Jet Age Museum; **Mark Lindsey**, Wessex XT604; **Steve McGovern**, Hooton Park Trust; **Trevor Matthews**, Lashenden Air Warfare Museum; **Vaughan K Meers**, Air Training Heritage Collection; **Midland Air Museum**; **Steve Milnthorpe**; **Naylan Moore**, AeroVenture; **John S Morgan**, cockpit collector; **Alex Murison**, North East Aircraft Museum; **Geoff** and **Lesley Nutkins**, Shoreham Aircraft Museum; **Dick Nutt**, Douglas Boston-Havoc UK Preservation Trust; **Chris Page**, Northern Aeroplane Workshops; **Martin Painter**, Nimrod XV148; **Norman Parker**, Boscombe Down Aviation Collection; **Terry Parker**, Venom J-1712; **Tom Perkins**, Parham Airfield Museum; **Derek Piggott**, Rolls-Royce Heritage Trust; **Tina Pittock**, Airborne Forces Museum; **Cyril Plimmer**, Boulton Paul Association; **Tony Podmore**, Shuttleworth Collection; **Nigel Ponsford** and **Anne Lindsay**, Real Aeroplane Museum and their own 'air force'; **Derek Powell**, Wellesbourne Wartime Museum and XM655 Maintenance and Preservation Society; **Simon Pulford**, Air Pulford; **RAF Manston History Museum**; **Ivor Ramsden**, Manx Aviation Preservation Society; **David Reid**, Dumfries and Galloway Aviation Museum; **Elfan ap Rees**, The Helicopter Museum; **Ridgewell Airfield Commemorative Museum**; **Charles Ross**, Lightning Association; **Colin Sharp**, The Flambards Experience; **Andy Simpson**,

RAF Museum; **Paul Singleton**, Wellesbourne Aviation Group; **Kelvin Sloper**, City of Norwich Aviation Museum; **Mike Smith**, Newark Air Museum; **Paul Spann**, Canberra WD954 and 'Cold War' Jets Collection; **Graham Sparkes**, The Aeroplane Collection; **Mike Sparrow**, Second World War Aircraft Preservation Society; **Dave Stubley**, Lincolnshire Aircraft Recovery Group; **Ralph Steiner**, de Havilland Aircraft Heritage Centre; **John Stelling**, Auster 'NJ719'; The **Stirling Project**; Stondon **Transport Museum**; **Philip Studfast**, Beech Restorations; **Christine Swettenham**, Muckleburgh Collection; **Bill Taylor**, Aerial Application Collection; **Hal Taylor**, Meteor Flight; **Roy Tebbutt**, 'Carpetbagger' Aviation Museum; **Robert Thomas**, Stanford Hall; **Steve Thompson**, Cotswold Aircraft Restoration Group; **Hugh Trevor**, Lightning Preservation Group and Lightnings in general; **Bob Trickett**, restorer/collector; **Bob Turner**, Fleet Air Arm Museum; **Jim Turner**, Station 146 Seething Tower; **Tim Turner**, British Balloon Museum and Library; **Gerry Tyack**, Wellington Aviation Museum; **Graham Vale**, East Midlands Airport Aeropark Volunteers Association; **Peter Vallance**, Gatwick Aviation Museum; **Sylvia Walker**, Cranwell Aviation Heritage Centre; **John Wilkins**, Yorkshire Air Museum; **John Williams**, Macclesfield College; **Keith Williams**, Bristol Scout 'A1742'; **Windermere Steamboat Centre**; **Colin Wingrave**, Thameside Aviation Museum; **Allan Wright**, BN Historians and specially to **Elly Sallingboe**, B-17 Preservation.

Many readers who take the time and trouble to send in reports of sightings, snippets and reports – large and small. Without their help this book would not be as topical or authoritative. Also listed here, as ever, are people who have supplied *other* services vital to the production of *W&R!* Thanks to each and every one of you!

Barry Abraham, Alan Addison, Martin Addison, Gerry Allen, Phil Ansell, Greg Baddeley, Malcolm Baldock, Alan G L Barclay, Allan Barley, Martin Barsley, Dave Bartillo, Mike Beatley, Dave Benfield, Steve Bond, Alan Brown, Mike Cain, Paul Carr, Ian Carroll, Graeme Carrott, Richard Cawsey, Alan Chalkley, H D Clark, Ricky Clarkson, John D Coleman, Glyn Coney, Paul Crellin, Howard J Curtis, Terry Dann, Nick Deakin, Stephen Dobson, Mike Dodd, Paul A Doyle, Michael Drake, Andy Durrant, David Ellis, Don Ellis, Martin Fenner, Peter Flitcroft, Paul Foden, Daniel Ford, B L Fox, Mike Freshney, Paul Fry, Gilmar Green, John V W Gregory, Phil Grimes, Jim Groom, James Halliday, Alan Hardcastle, Warren Hardcastle, Dave Harmsworth, Mark Harris, Ian Haskell, Michael Haslam, Jimmy Haslip, Joseph Heller, Phil Hewitt, Bruce Hornsby, Jonathan S Horswell, Nigel Howarth, Ian Howell, Jim Hughes, Alan Hutchings, Mike Illien, Gary Jacobs, Jim Jobe, Gareth Jones, Tim Jones, Paul J Kelsey, Dave King, Stewart Lanham, S Lapper, Kenny Lauder, David Legg, Neil Lomax, Jonathan Longbottom, Chris Mabbott, Stuart Maconie, Rob Martin, Rodney Martins, Wojtek Matusiak, David McNally, Andrew Messer, Alfred Milliken, Anthony Mills, Helen Mirren, John Molo, Martyn Morgan, Gary Morris, Ken Murray, Jan Nelson, Don Nind, Ann O'Raque, Graham Owers, Kevin Palmer, Bob Parnell, Tony Patten, Stephen Pearson, Dave Peel, Darren J Pitcher, Martin Pole, Brian Print, Doug Pritchard, Mark Ray, Hertz van Rental, Norman Roberson, Mark Roberts, Es Robinson, Stephen Robson, Robin Ruddock, Royston (Herts) Aviation Group, Chris Salter, Mike Screech, Daphne and Harry Seddon, Keith Sharp, Martin Sidwells, Sam Singer, Nick Skinner, Heather Small, Paul Snelling, Peter Spooner, Stacey's Mom; 'Stan' Stannard, Jonathan Steel, Andrew Stevens, Nick Stone, John Stride, Bas Stubert, Gareth Symington, Graham Tanner, Dave Thompson, Ian Thompson, Jurgen van Toor, Sergeant Towser, Tim Trethewey, Richard Tregear, David Underwood, Bob Uppendaun, Bob Vandereyt, Mark Vellenoweth, Hans van der Vlist, Howard H Walker, Johnnie Walker, Les Warrey, Michael Westwood, Jon Wickenden, Dr Mark Whitnall, Michael Wilcock, Pete Wild, Jerry Wilkinson, David Williams, David Willis, Nick Wilson, Tony Wood, Dave Woods, John Yossarian

Further Reading

Many references are made while assembling *W&R*, although the over-riding quest is for first-hand information and comment. The following enthusiast-published magazines have proved to be particularly conscientious in their coverage, sticking as much as possible to first-hand reportage and not the ever-increasing recirculation and 'massaging' of other journals, or acknowledging other sources when brought in. The first four offer specific 'leanings' for the *W&R* reader, the second batch offer regional coverage. I've noted how I find each particularly helpful, as a guide. All offer a variety of other features and articles. Addresses are given for further information.

Air-Britain News, monthly journal of Air-Britain (Historians) Ltd. Good coverage of the civil scene via the *Around and About* section. Barry Collman, 1 Rose Cottages, 179 Penn Road, Hazlemere, Bucks, HP15 7NE e-mail Barry.Collman@air-britain.co.uk www.air-britain.co.uk

Hawkeye, monthly journal of the Gatwick Aviation Society. Excellent, mostly primary, coverage of the UK civil scene in *Around the Dromes*. Mike Green, 144 The Crescent, Horley, RH6 7PA. fax / voice-mail 08701 327814 e-mail membership@gatwickaviationsociety.org.uk www.gatwickaviationsociety.org.uk

Military Aviation Review, monthly journal published by Military Aircraft Photographs. In-depth UK military and Andy Marden's absolutely excellent column *Out of Service* – perhaps I should have phrased that better! Brian Pickering, MAP, Westfield Lodge, Aslackby, near Sleaford, Lincs, NG34 0HG 01778 440760 fax 01778 440060 e-mail brianmap@btinternet.com

Osprey monthly journal of the Solent Aviation Society. Comprehensive coverage of civilian airfields in the *Focus* section, particularly the south of England, using almost exclusively first-hand information. Paul Chandler, 20 Goring Field, TG Down, Winchester, Hants, SO22 5NH. e-mail paulchand@hants.gov.uk www.solent-aviation-society.co.uk

Air North, monthly journal of the North-East Branch of Air-Britain. Detailed civil and military for the north-east of England, and Carlisle. Graeme Carrott, 47 Park Avenue, Grange Park, Gosforth, Newcastle-upon-Tyne, NE3 2HL. e-mail graeme@airnorth1.demon.co.uk www.airnorth.demon.co.uk

Humberside Air Review* monthly journal of the Humberside Aviation Society. Civil and military, from Yorkshire to the Wash. Also published is an excellent additional *Residents Review* annually. Pete Wild, 4 Bleach Yard, New Walk, Beverley, HU17 7HG e-mail pgwild117@aol.com www.focalplane.karoo.net/HAR/has/htm

Irish Air Letter monthly journal published by Paul Cunniffe, Karl Hayes and Eamon Power. Detailed coverage, civil and military, current and historic. 20 Kempton Way, Navan Road, Dublin 7, Ireland. fax 00 353 1 838 0629

Scottish Air News, monthly journal of the Central Scotland Aviation Group. In-depth coverage of Scotland, civil and military, plus Cumbrian aviation. Also publishes a comprehensive residents run-down, *The Scottish Register*, in the form of a supplement. Steve Martin, 3 Pittrichie View, Hattoncrook, Aberdeen, AB21 0UX. e-mail scan.members @btopenworld.com www.scottishairnews.co.uk

SWAG-Mag*, monthly journal of the South West Aviation Group. Detailed reporting of military happenings in the south-west and on other military concerns. Mike Screech, 4 West Meadow Road, Braunton, EX33 1EB. e-mail michael.screech@virgin.net www http://beehive.thisisnorthdevon.co.uk/swagmag

Ulster Air Mail, monthly journal of the Ulster Aviation Society, civil and military, modern and historic for Northern Ireland. Kevin Johnston, 16 Ravelston Avenue, Newtownabbey, BT36 6PF. www.ulsteraviationsociety.co.uk

Winged Words monthly journal of The Aviation Society. Increasingly good coverage of residents and happenings in the north-west of England. PO Box 36, Manchester M46 9YW 01942 795060 e-mail alanbirtles@tiscali.co.uk www.tasmanchester.com/

Several of the journal's above (marked *) include the *ELAS Newsletter*, edited and compiled by Graham Gaff of the East London Aviation Society. This covers UK current military by type and is an exceptional piece of work, with painstaking attention to original coverage. 2 Taveners Green Close, Wick Meadows, Wickford, SS12 9RQ. e-mail graham.gaff@ horwath.co.uk

Plus the following:
Propliner, superb, fully-illustrated quarterly published by Tony Eastwood and devoted to world coverage of piston- and turbo-powered airliners past and present. 'New Roots', Sutton Green Road, Sutton Green, Guildford, GU4 7QD

And of course (!):
FlyPast , monthly magazine published by Key Publishing Ltd. PO Box 300, Stamford, Lincs, PE9 1NA. 01780 480404 fax 01780 757812 e-mail subs@keypublishing.com www.flypast.com

A huge array of books have been dipped into, far too many to list completely. The following have been on and off the shelf with great speed and are regarded as trusted friends:

American Air Museum Duxford – A Tribute to American Air Power, Roger A Freeman, Midland Publishing, 2001
Aviation Museums of Britain, Ken Ellis, Midland Publishing, 1998
British Civil Aircraft Register 1919-1999, Michael Austin, Air-Britain, 1999
British Military Aircraft Directory, Bob Dunn and Mick Boulanger, Wolverhampton Aviation Group, 2002 and their wonderful monthly updates for WAG members
Combat Codes, Vic Flintham and Andrew Thomas, Airlife, 2003
Jet Airliner Production List, Tony Eastwood and John Roach, The Aviation Hobby Shop, Volume One, Boeing 1997, Volume Two, the rest, 1995
Military Airfields of the British Isles 1939-1945 (Omnibus Edition), Steve Willis and Barry Holliss, self-published, 1987
Piston Airliner Production List, Tony Eastwood and John Roach, The Aviation Hobby Shop, 2002
Pooleys Flight Guide, Robert Pooley and Roy Patel, Pooleys Flight Equipment, 2004
Royal Air Force Aircraft XA100 to XZ999, Jim Halley, Air-Britain, 2001 – and others in the series
Royal Air Force Flying Training and Support Units, Ray Sturtivant, John Hamlin and James J Halley, Air-Britain, 1997
Royal Navy Instructional Airframes, Ray Sturtivant and Rod Burden, British Aviation Research Group/Air-Britain, 1997
Squadrons of the Fleet Air Arm, Ray Sturtivant, Air-Britain, 1984
Squadrons of the Royal Air Force 1918-1988, Jim Halley, Air-Britain, 1988
Survivors 2002, Roy Blewett, Gatwick Aviation Society / Aviation Classics, 2002
Turbo-Prop Airliner Production List, Tony Eastwood and John Roach, The Aviation Hobby Shop, 2003
United Kingdom and Eire Civil Registers, Barry Womersley, Air-Britain, 2003
Warbirds Directory, 4th Edition, Geoff Goodall, published by Derek Macphail, 2003
70 Years of the Irish Civil Register, Peter J Hornfeck, Britten-Norman Historians, 1999

About *Wrecks & Relics*

Scope: *Wrecks & Relics* serves to outline, in as much detail as possible, the status and whereabouts of all known PRESERVED (ie in museum or other collections, under restoration etc); INSTRUCTIONAL (ie static airframes in use for training); and DERELICT (ie out of use for a long period of time, fire dump aircraft, scrapped or damaged etc) aircraft in the United Kingdom and Ireland and HM Forces aircraft based on Crown Territory. Where information permits, all aircraft that fall into these categories are included, with the following exceptions:–

• Airworthy aircraft not part of a specific collection.
• Aircraft that fall into any of the above categories for only a short period of time - generally less than a year.
• Aircraft without provision for a human pilot, below the size of the GAF Jindivik or Fieseler Fi 103.
• In general, aircraft will only be considered if they are at least a cockpit/nose section.

Locations: Are listed by county/province and then alphabetically. County Boundaries are as given by the Ordnance Survey and as defined by the Local Government Act and include the changes confirmed up to April 2001.

The entries for both Scotland and Wales are purely an alphabetic listing, primarily to help the English! From 1st April 1996 all of Scotland and all of Wales were wholly divided into 'Single Tier' Unitary Authorities, with their previously-held 'Counties' now having little meaning.

Directions are given after each place name. Readers should note that these are to the town or village mentioned and *not* necessarily to the actual site of the aircraft in question. Directions are *not* given in the following instances:

• Where the location is a large city or town.
• Where specific directions to the site are not fully known.
• At the request of several aircraft owners, who have every right to preserve their peace and quiet as well as their aircraft, some locations have been 'generalised'.

A form of notation relating to the status of an 'aerodrome' is given. Bearing in mind that in the Air Navigation Order *all* places where flying is conducted are known as aerodromes, a wider interpretation has been employed: 'Aerodrome' signifies a civilian flying ground used by aircraft up to King Air, 'biz-jet' etc size. 'Airfield' is used to signify a flying ground used by the forces, test establishments or manufacturers. 'Airport' is used to denote a flying ground that takes 'serious' sized airliners on a regular basis. For privacy and security purposes, private strips etc are frequently not denoted as such.

Access: Unless otherwise stated, all locations in this work are PRIVATE and access to them is strictly by prior permission, *if at all*. Museum opening times etc are given as a *guide only* and readers are advised to contact the museum in question *before* setting out on a journey. A couple of symbols have been adopted:

◆ Used to highlight access. Details beyond this explain times of admission or who to apply to if prior permission is needed. Occasionally used to draw attention to locations that particularly *do not* allow access or where prior permission is required.

▣ Contact details, starting with the postal address for enquiries, a stamped addressed envelope would be most helpful. Then, if applicable, come: ☎ Daytime telephone number for enquiries. This section also includes such new-fangled gizmos as **faxes**, recorded information lines, **c-mail** addresses and even **web-sites**, where applicable. Note that with web-sites, these are given for information only, no recommendation of content is meant, or to be implied.

Entries and Aircraft Listings: Generally, entries are all dealt with in a standard manner. As *W&R* covers a two year period, in this case 2002 to 2004, beyond the location header there is a narrative explaining the current status of the entry and outlining any airframes that have moved since the last edition. This narrative frequently includes discourses on life, the universe and everything! Airframes moving on are given underlined forwarding references, including the county, or province, that reference can be found in. This allows the reader to follow the more energetic examples around the book!

'Ownership' or 'custodianship' of airframes within this work is not to be inferred as definitive.

Any aircraft which fall out of any of the four categories above, or are exported, will not have forwarding references and their entry should be considered closed. The LOST! section acts as a 'safety net' for aircraft that have no determined fate. Where notes are made to further explain the listed entries, footnotes are used – see the HS.125 reference in the mock-up example given overleaf.

A few sample entries from the main text may help to familiarise readers with the data presented:

Col 1	Col 2	Column 3	Column 4	Column 5	Col 6
❑ G-AFIR*		Luton Minor	ex Cobham, Rearsby. CoA 30-7-71.		1-04
❑ –	DNB	Grunau Baby IIb	BGA.2238, ex Bicester, RAFGSA380, D-8039.		12-99
❑ 5N-AWD		HS.125-1	ex G-ASSI. Fire crews.	[1]	10-97
❑ XV140	'K'	Scout AH.1	✈ G-KAXL, ex Fleetlands.	®	7-03
❑ XV748	'3D'	Harrier GR.3	ex Bedford, 233 OCU, 1, 233 OCU, 1. Sectioned.		3-04
❑ –*		Typhoon I	ex Chippenham. Forward fuselage.		4-04
❑ –*	TAD.001	Gazelle CIM	ex Middle Wallop. First noted 5-96.		12-03
❑ 153008		F-4N-MC	ex VF-154 - USS *Coral Sea*. ABDR.		11-01
❑ –	BAPC.237	Fi 103 (V-1)	ex St Athan.		2-04
❑ –	BAPC.295	Da Vinci 'REP'	built by Skysport, 2003. Stored.	[1]	3-04

Columns 1 and 2: Aircraft are listed alpha-numerically, using the following rubric. British civil first (except in Ireland where EI- comes first), followed by British Gliding Association (BGA) and 'B Condition' (or 'trade plate') markings, then overseas civil registrations in alpha-numeric order. British military serials follow (with reversal again in Ireland) followed by overseas military listed by country – ie France before Netherlands before USA. Finally, come British Aviation Preservation Council (BAPC) identities as these can take in both civil or military airframes. Anonymous airframes are inserted where it is thought most logical! Incorrect or fictitious registrations and serials are marked in quotes, eg 'VZ999' or 'G-BKEN'. Codes worn by aircraft are given in column two, eg 'AF-V' or '825'. Entries new to a heading in this edition are marked *. A dash (–) is used to denote an airframe that has no confirmed primary identity.

Registrations or serials, where applicable, are given in Column 1 gives the *primary* identifier (if applicable). The primary identifier is most often the one *worn* on the airframe. The *secondary* identifier is a way of helping further identification of the airframe, most likely a code letter or number, or another form of identity that will help the reader 'place' the entry. Where space, permits, identities known not to be worn are given in Column 2, frequently leaving Column 1 empty. Note that other identities, present or previous, appear in Column 4.

Column 3: Aircraft type/designation, frequently abbreviated. To acquaint readers with the nature of some of the types listed, some abbreviations are used:
- ✈   Believed airworthy, at time of going to press.
- CIM   Purpose-built instructional airframe, not intended for flight – Classroom Instruction Model, or even Module.
- EMU   Purpose-built test and evaluation airframe, not intended for flight, in most cases using prototype or production jigs and tooling – Engineering Mock-up.
- FSM   Full-scale model. Faithful external reproduction of an aircraft, but using construction techniques completely unrelated to the original – frequently fibreglass.
- PAX   Cockpit section used for crew emergency egress training, mostly (now retired) Chipmunk T.10s – Passenger (= PAX) Trainer.
- REP   Reproduction, ie a faithful, or near-faithful copy or a facsimile of an aircraft type. Occasionally built to a different scale, but using construction techniques and proportions in keeping with the original. In the past, the author has used the word 'replica' but in strict usage the only people who can make a replica is the design company involved and in the aviation world, very few such instances exist. (The Yak-3UAs that came out of Orenburg, Russia, from the direct lineage of the Yakovlev OKB, are examples of 'true' replicas.)

Column 4: Where possible, brief historical details of the aircraft listed are given, in a necessarily abbreviated form. In each case, units, operators, previous identities etc are listed in *reverse* order, ie the last user (or identity) is given first. Readers should have little trouble with these potted histories, especially with reference to the 'Abbreviations' section. Also given here are other registrations, or maintenance serials applicable to the airframe. Note that Royal Navy maintenance serials, 'A' numbers were reallocated, creating a somewhat confusing vista. Second, third or even fourth allocations are known and are noted in square brackets after the 'A' serial [3]. Readers should refer to the masterful BARG/Air-Britain *Royal Navy Instructional Airframes* for the 'Full Monty'. Where a date is given prefixed 'CoA' (Certificate of Airworthiness), this is the date at which it lapsed and is given as an *indication* of how long the airframe has been flightless. The term 'CoA' is used for all levels of certification, eg Permit to Fly, Ferry Permit etc.

Column 5: Used to denote an aircraft known to be undergoing a restoration or conservation programme at time of going to press, with the symbol ®. Also used as footnotes – eg [7] – to refer readers back up to the narrative section for specific details on that airframe.

Column 6: 'Last noted' dates are given primarily to help historians to trace the history (or demise) of an airframe and perhaps to alert readers intending to visit the airframe involved as to the 'currency' of the information given. The listing of these dates, it is hoped, will persuade some readers and some of the less enlightened enthusiast and professional magazines to actually note the dates of sightings/reports in future jottings – the *date* of an observation can be a crucial form of evidence in many cases. Physical, first-hand reports – instead of assumptions and handed-on information – are vital for the monitoring of our aviation heritage.

Wrecks & Relics is put together using the best information available to the Author.
Every effort is made to be as accurate as possible. However, neither the Author nor
Midland Publishing can be held responsible for any errors or changes that may occur
in the location or status of aircraft or places listed.

PART ONE
ENGLAND

BEDFORDSHIRE

BEDFORD
Bedford College: Located adjacent to Cauldwell Street. Cessna F.172H G-AVCC was replaced by the Scout. No 'forwarding' address for it.

❏ [XM473]	Jet Provost T.3A	ex Norwich Airport 'G-TINY', Halton 8974M, 7 FTS, 1 FTS, 7 FTS, 1 FTS, CFS, 3 FTS, 1 FTS.	4-03
❏ XP854*	Scout AH.1	ex Ipswich, Wattisham, Middle Wallop TAD.043 / 7898M. Crashed 15-5-65. Arrived 17-10-02.	4-03

Others: By December 2002 J/1 Autocrat G-AJDY had moved to Spanhoe Lodge, Northants. Chipmunk T.20 1360 (G-BYYU) had moved to Little Staughton, Cambs, by April 2002.

❏ G-AGTT	J/1 Autocrat	CoA 11-2-93. Stored.	12-97
❏ G-AJUD	J/1 Autocrat	ex Camberley, Tongham. CoA 18-5-74.	12-97
❏ 1367	Chipmunk T.20	G-BYYW, ex Spanhoe, Viseu, Port AF. Stored.	2-00

BEDFORD AIRFIELD or Thurleigh, north of Bedford, east of the A6
Thurleigh is remembered at the **306th Bomb Group Museum** established in the wartime Small Arms and Ammunition Store and very much worth a visit.
◆ Follow 'Bedford Autodrome' signs from A6. Open alternative weekends or by prior arrangement.
✉ Ralph Franklin, National School Cottage, Mill Hill, Keysoe, MK44 2HP ☎ 01234 708715.

Defence Science and Technology Laboratory (DS&TL): The nose of Tornado F.2 ZD936 moved initially to the Manchester area and then settled upon Boscombe Down, Wilts, in 2002.

CRANFIELD AERODROME east of Newport Pagnell
Cranfield Institute of Technology (CIT) / **College of Aeronautics / Cranfield Aerospace Ltd:** The HS.125 is on a low-loader so it can move around has had its registration doctored to read G-DHEA. One possible 'translation' of this could be De Havilland Executive Aircraft! [1]

❏ G-AWBT	Twin Com' 160B	ex N8508Y. Damaged 10-3-88. Inst airframe.		7-02
❏ G-AZXG	Aztec 250D	ex Little Snoring, N6963Y. Crashed 25-10-91. Inst.		7-00
❏ 'G-DHEA'	HS.125-3B/RA	G-OHEA, ex Hatfield, G-AVRG, G-5-12. Dump.	[1]	7-02
❏ G-RAVL	Jetstream 200	ex G-AWVK, N1035S, G-AWVK. CoA 26-2-94.		7-00

Kennet Aviation: In late 2002 and early January 2003 Kennet relocated to North Weald, Essex, as follows: Seafire XVII SX336 7-11-02; Venom FB.50 'WK436' (G-VENM) via a brief stop-over at Yeovilton, Somerset, 1-03; Jet Provost T.1 'XD693' (G-AOBU) 19-12-02; Hunter F.6A XF515 (G-KAXF) 5-12-02; Provost T.1 XF690 (G-MOOS) via a brief stop-over at Yeovilton, Somerset, 1-03; Gnat T.1 'XM693' (G-TIMM) 9-11-02; Gnat T.1 'XR993' (G-BVPP) 9-11-02; Scout AH.1 XV140 (G-KAXL) 13-10-02; Jet Provost T.5A XW289 (G-JPVA) via a brief stop-over at Yeovilton, Somerset, 1-03; Wasp HAS.1 NZ3905 (G-KAXT) 7-11-02; Wasp HAS.1 NZ3909 5-11-02. Other than the Seafire and Wasp NZ3909, all flew to their new home.

Others: Gnat T.1 XS101 (G-GNAT) flew off to North Weald, Essex, on 18th December 2002 to co-locate with Kennet. It was followed, earthbound, by fellow G-FRCE on 8th January 2003. Several references here are now long-in-the-tooth and bound for LOST! [1]

❏ G-BAEW	Cessna F.172M	ex N12798. Crashed 12-11-93. Fuselage.	[1]	3-96
❏ G-BALI	DR.400 2+2	ex Meppershall. CoA 3-9-88.	[1]	3-96
❏ G-BAUJ	Aztec 250E	ex N14390. CoA 25-7-94. Stored.		6-02
❏ G-BDUX	Motor Cadet	CoA 23-2-84. Stored in trailer.	[1]	7-90
❏ G-BMSG	SAAB Lansen	ex VAT area, Swedish AF, Malmslatt, Fv32028. Stored.		2-04
❏ G-NITA*	Cherokee 180C	ex G-AVVG, N7517W. CoA 17-11-97. F/n 6-02.		6-02
❏ G-SADE*	Cessna F.150L	ex G-AZJW. CoA 21-9-97. First noted 7-02.		7-02
❏ G-SHIV*	Cougar	ex N713G. CoA 18-1-98. First noted 7-02.		7-02
❏ –	BXR L 13 Blanik	BGA.1321, ex G-ATPX. Stored, on trailer.	[1]	7-97
❏ –	CYR L 13 Blanik	BGA.1917, crashed 8-7-90. Original fuselage.	[1]	7-97
❏ XS458	'T' Lightning T.5	ex Binbrook, LTF, 11, LTF, 5-11 pool, LTF, 5, 226 OCU. 226 OCU c/s port, 111 Sqn, stb. Taxiable.		11-03

DUNSTABLE AERODROME on the B489 south-east of Dunstable

The nose of Canberra B.2T WJ731 moved to Hendon, Gtr Lon, by mid-2002.

❑ G-BLGS	Rallye 180T	ex Lasham. CoA 21-5-99. Stripped out.		7-03
❑ PH-MSB	Rallye Club	G-OIAN. Canx 2-9-91.	off-site	5-01

EATON BRAY west of Dunstable

Peter Underwood:

❑ –	ACH T.6 Kite I	BGA.400, ex Brooklands, VD165, BGA.400. Stored.		1-00
❑ –	ALZ Dagling	BGA.493 / BAPC.81, Dunstable, Duxford, Warton.	®	11-02
❑ –	BCF T.21B	BGA.856, ex Haddenham. Damaged 1980. Stored.		1-00
❑ –	DNB Grunau Baby IIb	BGA.2238, ex Bicester, RAFGSA380, D-8039.		11-02

Others: Evans VP-1 G-BEKM and VP-2 G-BFFB moved by November 2003 to Thirsk, N Yorks.

HATCH off the B658, south-west of Sandy

Skysport Engineering: Tim Moore and team have a DH.2 REP in its early stages. Skysport built a version of a Leonardo da Vinci hang-glider for the Channel 4 TV documentary *Leonardo's Dream Machines* and this is stored on site [1]. Humming Bird G-EBQP moved to London Colney, Herts, on 25th March 2003. By mid-2002 the fuselage of Mohawk G-AEKW had moved to Cosford, Shrop. Gemini 3A G-AKEK was put up for sale in February 2003. It was exported to Iceland in August 2003. SNCAN SV-4A G-AXRP flew again on 4th September 2003. DH.9 D5649 moved to St Leonards-on-Sea, E Sussex during 2002. The Wallace frame moved to Old Warden, Beds, by March 2004 for display.

Notes: Tigers G-ACDA and N6720 are being worked on for Bryn Hughes [2]. The Demon is for Demon Displays Ltd. It is reported to be a composite with the front end of a former Irish Air Corps Hector. This would almost certainly be the one that was at Cloughjordan, Ireland [3].

♦ Access *strictly* by prior permission only.

❑ G-ACDA	Tiger Moth	ex Chilbolton, BB724, G-ACDA. Cr 27-6-79.	[2]	10-99
❑ G-DINT	Beaufighter I	ex Halton, 3858M, X7688, 29, 153.		8-00
❑ F-BGNR	Viscount 708	ex Perth, Air Inter. Stored.	off-site	7-01
❑ N5595T	C-47A-85-DL	ex Thruxton, Blackbushe, G-BGCG, Spanish AF T3-27, N49V, N50322, 43-15536. Stored.		8-00
❑ K8203	Demon I	G-BTVE, ex Cardington, 2292M, 9 BGS, 9 AOS, 64.	® [3]	2-01
❑ N6720	Tiger Moth	G-BYTN, ex Levenshulme, 'G-ABEE' Kings Heath, West Bromwich, 7014M, 9 AFTS, 2 GS, Lon UAS, Queens UAS, 11 RFS, 11 EFTS, 4 CPF, 206.	® [2]	11-03
❑ –	Stampe SV-4	ex Spanhoe Lodge, Les Mureaux. Forward fuselage.		11-97
❑ – BAPC.295	Da Vinci 'REP'	built by Skysport, 2003. Stored.	[1]	3-04

HENLOW AIRFIELD on the A6007 south-west of Biggleswade

RAF Henlow: The Hunter guards the station. It was refurbished at Wittering, Cambs, in late 2003.

❑ WT612	Hunter F.1	ex Halton, Credenhill 7496M, Hawker, A&AEE. Gate.	11-03

Others: Dick Horsfield and Rod Robinson, trading as HCR and Sons, are rebuilding a Vampire.

♦ Visits not possible, but check progress on **www.project-vampire.org.uk**

❑ XE856	Vampire T.11	G-DUSK, ex Catfoss, Long Marston, Lasham, Welwyn GC, Woodford, Chester, St Athan, 219, North Weald SF, 226 OCU.	®	6-02

LOWER STONDON west of the A600/Henlow aerodrome, north of Hitchin

Stondon Transport Museum: A superb collection of 400-plus motor vehicles and other transport artefacts, including a full-scale replica of HMS *Endeavour* and a coffee shop and gift shop.

♦ Open daily, 10am to 5pm. ✉ Station Road, Lower Stondon, Henlow, SG16 6JN ☎ 01462 850339
e-mail info@transportmuseum.co.uk **www**.transportmuseum.co.uk

❏ 'G-ADRG'	HM.14 'Flea'	BAPC.77, ex Cheltenham, Long Marston, Innsworth, Ross-on-Wye, Staverton.	2-04
❏ G-AXOM	Penn-Smith gyro	wfu 11-10-74.	2-04
❏ XN341	Skeeter AOP.12	8002M, ex Luton, St Athan, 4 SoTT, 3 RTR, 651.	2-04

LUTON AIRPORT off the A505 east of Luton
The fire training area borders Wigmore Valley Park.

❏ G-AOVS	Britannia 312	ex Redcoat, 'G-BRAC', Lloyd, BOAC.	
		CoA 31-7-79. Fuselage. Fire crews.	8-02
❏ 5N-AWD	HS.125-1	ex G-ASSI. Fire crews.	10-00

OLD WARDEN AERODROME west of Biggleswade, signposted from the A1
Shuttleworth Collection: The ANEC II made its first flight since the mid-1930s on 9th March 2004. DH.88 Comet G-ACSS was air tested again on 28th October 2002. It made a faultless 50-minute test flight, but on landing the starboard undercarriage collapsed. Repairs were immediately put underway. During 2002 Desmond Penrose decided to give up his Arrow Active G-ABVE and Mew Gull reproduction G-AEXF. They were offered to the collection, but the decision was made not to purchase them as the price was considered "unrealistic". This compiler finds very regrettable as they were, and are, perfect for the operating policy of the collection. This is not to detract from the superb home that they have found, at Breighton. On 20th September 2003 the LVG C.VI made its last official flight at Old Warden. In the care of the collection since 1959, it had always been an Air Historic Branch airframe and was long earmarked for the RAF Museum's World War One collection at Hendon.

Notes: EE Wren G-EBNV is mostly the unregistered No.4 with parts from G-EBNV [1]. The Aero Vintage Bristol F.2b [2] is resident in readiness for flight. Provost XF603 carries the markings of an example on delivery to the Sultan of Oman's Air Force [3]. The Me 163B Komet full-scale model includes an original Walter HWK 509A-2 rocket motor [4]. Several aircraft based at Old Warden are on loan to the Shuttleworth Collection: Dove G-EAGA Andrew Wood; Moth G-EBLV and Avro XIX G-AHKX BAE Systems (Operations); Messenger G-AKBO Bravo-Oscar Syndicate; Cygnet repro G-CAMM Don Cashmore; Falcon Major G-AEEG and Hawk Trainer V1075 Peter Holloway; the Po-2, Pat Donovan; and the Wallace frame, Skysport. All are marked ‡. Some Shuttleworth aircraft can be found elsewhere: Archaeopteryx G-ABXL at Radcliffe on Trent, Notts and Northern Aeroplane Workshops – see under Batley, W Yorks. See under Hatfield, Herts, for 'another' G-ACSS. The Old Warden Airfield Volunteer Fire Service have acquired a Piper Tomahawk fuselage for rescue training [5].

Departures: Arrow Active G-ABVE and Mew Gull G-AEXF to Breighton, E Yorks, on 15th June 2002. As noted above, LVG C.VI 7198 left by road for Cosford, Shropshire, on 12th November 2003. Following completion of its flight tests, the Belgian-owned Hawker Fury REP 'K1930' (G-BKBB) departed for Belgium on 11th June 2003.

◆ Open daily throughout the year, but is closed for up to 14 days covering Xmas Eve, and up to and including New Year's Day. Open April to October 10am to 5pm, November to March 10am to 4pm, the hangar displays are closed one hour after the last admission time. Supporting the collection in many ways is the **Shuttleworth Veteran Aeroplane Society** (SVAS) which has an extensive series of activities during the year, a regular journal – the excellent *Prop-Swing* – and welcomes new members. They also fund-raise, eg the Jungmann arrived courtesy of fund-raising by SVAS. It will appear in Luftwaffe colours and will to some extent replace the LVG as the 'bad guy' on the flight line! [6] Address as the main collection. ⊠ Old Warden Aerodrome, Biggleswade, Beds, SG18 9EP
☎ 01767 627288 **fax** 01767 627053 **e-mail** collection@shuttleworth.com **www**.shuttleworth.org

❏ G-EAGA	Sopwith Dove	↦ ex Hatch, G-BLOO ntu, Australia, G-EAGA, K-157.	‡	3-04
❏ G-EBHX	Humming Bird	↦ ex Lympne No 8. *L'Oiseau Mouche*.		3-04
❏ G-EBIR	DH.51	↦ ex VP-KAA, G-KAA, G-EBIR. *Miss Kenya*.		3-04
❏ G-EBJO	ANEC II	↦ ex Radcliffe on Trent, Old Warden, Lympne No 7.		
		First flown 9-3-04.		3-04
❏ G-EBLV	DH.60 Moth	↦ ex Hatfield.	‡	3-04
❏ [G-EBNV] '4'	EE Wren	BAPC.11. CoA 23-6-87.	[1]	3-04
❏ G-EBWD	DH.60X Moth	↦ Bought by Richard Shuttleworth in 1932.		3-04
❏ G-AAIN	Parnall Elf II	↦ ex Southend, Fairoaks, Badminton.		3-04
❏ G-AANG	Blériot XI	↦ No.14, BAPC.3, ex Ampthill, Hendon.		3-04
❏ G-AANH	Deperdussin	↦ No.43, BAPC.4, ex Ampthill. CoA 14-5-83.		3-04

❑	G-AANI		Blackburn Mon✈	No.9, BAPC.5, ex Wittering.		3-04
❑	G-AAPZ		Desoutter I ✈	ex Higher Blagdon, Old Warden.		3-04
❑	G-AAYX		Southern Martlet ✈	ex Woodford.		3-04
❑	G-ABAG		DH.60 Moth ✈	ex Perth.		3-04
❑	G-ACSS	'34'	DH.88 Comet ✈	ex Hatfield, Farnborough, Old Warden, Leavesden,		
				K5084, G-ACSS. *Grosvenor House*. Dam 28-10-02.	®	3-04
❑	G-ACTF		Comper Swift ✈	ex Rhos, VT-ADO. *The Scarlet Angel*. CoA 6-10-90.		3-04
❑	G-AEBB		HM.14 'Flea'	ex Southampton. CoA 31-5-39. Taxies.		3-04
❑	G-AEEG		Falcon Major ✈	ex Turweston, SE-AFN, RSwAF Fv913,		
				SE-AFN, G-AEEG, U-20.	‡	3-04
❑	G-AHKX*		Avro XIX Srs 2	ex Woodford, Strathallan, Kemps, Treffield,		
			✈	Meridian, Smiths. Arrived 29-6-02.	‡	3-04
❑	G-AKBO		Messenger 2A ✈	–	‡	3-04
❑	[G-ARSG]		Triplane REP ✈	BAPC.1, ex *Those Magnificent Men...* Hants A/C built.		3-04
❑	[G-ASPP]		Boxkite REP ✈	BAPC.2, ex *Those Magnificent Men...* Miles-built.		3-04
❑	G-CAMM	'6'	Cygnet REP ✈	ex Hucknall, G-ERDB ntu.	‡	3-04
❑	G-RETA*		Jungmann 2000	ex North Weald, Spanish AF E3B-305. CoA 21-4-02.		
			✈	Arrived 23-10-03.	[6]	3-04
❑	D-EGLW*		Tomahawk 112	fuselage, fire crews.	[5]	3-04
❑	[ZK-POZ]*		Po-2 (CSS-13) ✈	ex New Zealand. Arrived 31-7-03.	‡	3-04
❑	'C4918'		Bristol M.1C REP ✈	G-BWJM. 72 Sqn c/s.		3-04
❑	D7889		Bristol F.2b	G-AANM / BAPC.166, ex St Leonards-on-Sea,		
				Sandown, St Leonards-on-Sea, Old Warden,		
				Weston-on-the-Green.	[2]	3-04
❑	D8096		Bristol F.2b ✈	G-AEPH, ex Filton, Watford, D8096, 208.		3-04
❑	F904	'H'	SE.5A ✈	G-EBIA, ex 'D7000', Farnborough, Whitley,		
				G-EBIA, F904 84 Sqn. 56 Sqn colours.		3-04
❑	H5199		Avro 504K ✈	G-ADEV, ex G-ACNB, 'E3404' and Avro 504N.		3-04
❑	K1786		Tomtit ✈	G-AFTA, ex 5 GCF, 23 GCF, 3 FTS.		3-04
❑	'K3241'		Tutor ✈	G-AHSA, ex K3215, HSA, RAFC. CFS colours.	®	3-04
❑	'K5414'		Hind (Afghan) ✈	G-AENP, BAPC.78. ex 'K5457', Kabul.		3-04
❑	'N6181'		Pup ✈	G-EBKY, ex N5180. *Happy*. 3 (Naval) Sqn c/s.		3-04
❑	'N6290'		Triplane ✈	G-BOCK, ex Dewsbury. 8 Sqn RNAS c/s, *Dixie II*.		3-04
❑	P6382		Magister I ✈	G-AJRS, ex 'G-AJDR', P6382, 3 EFTS, 16 EFTS.		3-04
❑	T6818	'19'	Tiger Moth II ✈	G-ANKT, ex Aston Down, 21 EFTS.		3-04
❑	V1075		Magister ✈	G-AKPF, ex Shoreham, Sandown, Shoreham,		
				V1075, 16 EFTS.		3-04
❑	'V9367'		Lysander III ✈	G-AZWT, ex 'V9441', Duxford, Strathallan,		
	'MA-B'			RCAF 2355. 161 Squadron colours.		3-04
❑	W9385		Hornet Moth ✈	G-ADND, ex Chester, W9385, St Athan SF,		
	'YG-L' '3'			3 CPF, G-ADND. 502 Sqn colours.		3-04
❑	Z7015	'7-L'	Sea Hurricane I	G-BKTH, ex Duxford, Staverton, Old Warden,		
			✈	Loughborough, Yeovilton, 759, 880. 880 Sqn c/s.		3-04
❑	AR501		Spitfire V ✈	G-AWII, ex Duxford, Henlow, Loughborough, CGS, 61		
	'NN-A'			OTU, 1 TEU, 58 OTU, 422, 312, 504, 310. 310 c/s.		3-04
❑	VS610	'K-L'	Prentice T.1	G-AOKL, ex Bassingbourn, VS610, 1 FTS,		
				22 FTS, RAFC, 22 FTS. CoA 20-9-96.	®	3-04
❑	XA241		G'hopper TX.1	ex Cambridge.		3-04
❑	XF603		Provost T.1 ✈	G-KAPW, ex Cranfield, Filton, Bristol, 27 MU,		
				CAW, RAFC. RAF grey / green camo.	[3]	3-04
❑	'18671'		Chipmunk 22	G-BNZC, ex G-ROYS, 7438M, WP905 CFS,		
			✈	664, RAFC. RCAF colours.		3-04
❑	'191454'		Me 163B FSM	BAPC.271. Wingless.	[4]	3-04
❑	'423'		Gladiator I ✈	G-AMRK, ex L8032, 'N2308', L8032, 'K8032',		
	and '427'			Gloster, Hamble, 8 MU, 61 OTU, 1624F, 2 AACU.		
				Norwegian AF c/s. '423' port, '427' stb.		3-04
❑	–	BAPC.8	Dixon Orni'	–		3-04
❑	–*		Wallace REP	ex Hatch. Fuselage frame.	‡	3-04

SANDY on the A1 north of Biggleswade
The Pitts was reported to be for sale during mid-2003.

❑ G-AXNZ	Pitts S-1S	ex Little Gransden. CoA 30-8-91. Stored.	12-97

BERKSHIRE

ARBORFIELD on the A327 south of Reading
Princess Marina College / School of Electrical and Aeronautical Engineering (SEAE) (See under Cosford, Shrop, for a glimpse of the future.) Within Hazebrouck Barracks, SEAE maintain a detachment at Middle Wallop, Hants, which see. Note that TAD stands for Technical Aid and Demonstrator – but there are other interpretations! Purpose-built instructional airframes and teaching aids are also known as 'CIMs' – Classroom Instructional Models.
   Departures: Scout AH.1 XP884 to Middle Wallop, Hants, by 7-02; Lynx AH.7 XZ613 to Fleetlands, Hants, mid-02 for return to service.

❑ XP848		Scout AH.1	ex Middle Wallop, Wroughton, 659, 669. Gate	9-03
❑ XP855		Scout AH.1	ex Wroughton, 652, 651, 655.	9-02
❑ XP899		Scout AH.1	ex Middle Wallop, ARWF. Crashed 1-11-79.	9-02
❑ XR601		Scout AH.1	ex BATUS, 657, 665, 666. Damaged 26-8-79.	9-02
❑ XT623		Scout AH.1	ex Wroughton, 655, 659, 655.	9-02
❑ XT633		Scout AH.1	ex Wroughton, 659, 653, 661, 660, Wroughton.	9-02
❑ XV124	'W'	Scout AH.1	ex Middle Wallop, Arborfield, Middle Wallop, Wroughton, 656, 653, 654.	9-02
❑ XV141		Scout AH.1	ex Wroughton, 657, 659, 654, 661. REME museum.	2-01
❑ [XW838]		Lynx 1-03	TAD.009, ex Middle Wallop, Yeovil.	9-02
❑ XW860		Gazelle HT.2	TAD.021, ex Middle Wallop, Fleetlands, Wroughton, 705. ABDR	9-02
❑ XW863		Gazelle HT.2	TAD.022, ex Middle Wallop, Wroughton, 705.	9-02
❑ XW888		Gazelle AH.1	TAD.017, ex Middle Wallop, ARWF, GCF.	9-02
❑ XW889		Gazelle AH.1	TAD.018, ex Middle Wallop, ARWF, GCF.	9-02
❑ XW900		Gazelle AH.1	TAD.900, ex Middle Wallop SEAE, 660. Cr 25-5-76.	9-02
❑ XW912		Gazelle AH.1	TAD.019, ex Fleetlands, 655, 3 CBAS, 656, 655, 3 CBAS.	9-02
❑ XX387		Gazelle AH.1	TAD.014, ex Fleetlands, 651, 661, 657, 16/5 Lancers. Crashed 15-12-95. Avionics and Systems trainer.	9-02
❑ XX454		Gazelle AH.1	TAD.023, ex Waddington, Middle Wallop, 663, 1 Rgt, 662, 656, 657, 4 Rgt, 3 Rgt, 4 Rgt, 659, 669, 664, 654, 4 Rgt, 669, 659.	9-02
❑ XZ188		Lynx AH.7	ex Fleetlands, 4 Rgt, 654, 662, 655, 665, 655, LCF, 651.	9-02
❑ XZ305		Gazelle AH.1	TAD.020, ex 3 Regt, 665, 662, 654, GCF.	9-02
❑ XZ325	'T'	Gazelle AH.1	ex Middle Wallop, 670, 655, 3 Regt.	9-02
❑ XZ332		Gazelle AH.1	ex Middle Wallop, 670, ARWF, 656, 664.	9-02
❑ XZ333		Gazelle AH.1	ex Middle Wallop, 670, ARWF.	9-02
❑ XZ666		Lynx AH.7	ex 669, 655, 665, 655, LCF, 651.	2-01
❑ ZA769	'K'	Gazelle AH.1	ex Middle Wallop, 670, ARWF.	9-02
❑ ZB668		Gazelle AH.1	TAD.015, ex Middle Wallop, Arborfield, Fleetlands, UNFICYP. Crashed 30-11-92.	2-01
❑ ZB678		Gazelle AH.1	ex 16 Flt.	9-02
❑ QP30		Lynx HC.28	TAD.013, ex Fleetlands, Almondbank, Wroughton, Qatar Police, G-BFDV.	9-02
❑	TAD.001	Gazelle CIM	ex Middle Wallop.	9-02
❑	TAD.002	Gazelle CIM	ex Middle Wallop.	8-99
❑	TAD.007	Lynx CIM	ex Middle Wallop. Fuselage number TO.42.	9-02
❑	TAD.008	Gazelle CIM	ex Middle Wallop. 'Engine/Control Systems' sim.	2-01
❑	TAD.010	Lynx CIM	Cockpit. 'Engine/Control Systems' sim.	2-01
❑	TAD.011	Lynx CIM	ex Middle Wallop.	9-02
❑	TAD.012	Lynx CIM	ex Middle Wallop.	9-02

BARKHAM south of the B3349, south-west of Wokingham
Barkham Antiques:

❑ G-KENN	Robinson R-22B	ex Stamford, Sandtoft. Damaged 31-10-94.	7-01

BINFIELD north of the B3034, north-west of Bracknell
Amen Corner:

❑ G-ASXF	Brantly 305	ex Thruxton, Biggin Hill, CoA 16-2-79.	12-03
❑ G-BJOD	HA-2M Sportster	ex Bracknell. Unflown?	7-01
❑ G-BPCJ	Cessna 150J	ex Solihull, Tattershall Thorpe, N61096. Damaged 25-1-90. *Charlie*.	12-03

GREENHAM COMMON north of the A339, south-east of Newbury
The former USAF base is now an extensive industrial estate. Within this, the aircraft associated with **Flying 'A' Services / Wizzard Investments Ltd** (that's double 'z') gravitated from North Weald by February 2004 and inhabit one of the famed cruise-missile bunkers. See under Norwich, Norfolk, for their Seafire III restoration project and Martham, Norfolk, for Spitfire XVIII SM969 (G-BRAF). The Lancaster nose section is a long-seated 'chestnut'. See under Sandtoft, Lincs, in *W&R18* (pp142/143) for the bulk of the rationale behind this. It is now thought that the extreme nose (ie from the windscreen forward) comes from Lancaster I TW911. See under Sandtoft, Lincs, for the bulk of G-29-1. [1]
◆ *Not* available for public inspection.

❑ N9950*	P-40N Warhawk	ex North Weald, ?, Biggin Hill, USA, USAAF 44-7983.Stored. Arrived by 2-04.		2-04
❑ N33870*	PT-19 Cornell	ex North Weald, G-BTNY, N33870, USAAF. Arrived 21-1-04. Stored.		1-04
❑ N7098V*	TF-51D Mustang	ex North Weald, Biggin Hill, Chino, Israel AF/DF, RCAF 9245, USAAF 44-73871. Stored.		2-04
❑ G-29-1	Lancaster B.10	ex North Weald etc, RF342. Nose. Arrived 21-1-04.	[1]	1-04
❑ NH238*	Spitfire IX	G-MKIX, ex North Weald, ?, Bournemouth, Biggin Hill, Bitteswell, N238V, Harlingen, Hemswell, Winthorpe, Southampton, Andover, COGEA OO-ARE, Coxyde, Belg AF SM-36, Dutch AF H-60, Sealand, 76 MU, 9 MU, 49 MU, 84 GSU. Stored. Arrived by 2-04.		2-04
❑ RW386* G-BXVI	Spitfire XVI	ex North Weald, ?, Audley End, Biggin Hill, Bitteswell, Blackbushe, St Athan, Halton 6944M, 58 MU, 604. Stored, dismantled. Arrived by 2-04.		2-04

HUNGERFORD on the A4 east of Marlborough
Newbury Aeroplane Company: Jan Cooper and team continue the standards of excellence that NAC is famed for. The Tiger Moth is being restored to static condition for the Brooklands Museum [1].

❑ G-AAUP	Klemm L.25	*Clementine*. CoA 21-11-84. Stored.			2-98
❑ G-ADWT	Hawk Trainer	ex CF-NXT, G-ADWT, NF750, 26 OTU, G-ADWT.	®		1-01
❑ G-AFGH	Chilton DW.1	ex Billingshurst. CoA 7-7-83.	®		2-98
❑ F-BGEQ	Tiger Moth	ex Brooklands, Chessington, Brooklands, Le Mans, French mil, NL846.	®	[1]	3-02

Others: The stored Bf 109E is more reasonably located at <u>Lambourn</u>, Berks.

LAMBOURN on the B4000 north of Hungerford
In the general area is a *private* strip with several out-of-use or under restoration airframes.

❑ G-BMJY*'07'	Yak C-18M (SPP)	ex North Weald, La Ferté Alais, Egyptian AF 627. CoA 27-11-01. Stored.	6-03
❑ G-TAFI*	Jungmeister	ex North Weald, Breighton, N2210, HB-MIF, Swiss AF U-77. CoA 5-7-01. Stored.	6-03

❑	KZ191*	Hurricane IV	ex North Weald, Fowlmere, Israel, 351, 1695F, AFDU. Arrived 6-03.	®	6-03
❑	XW893*	Gazelle AH.1	ex Poole (?), Shawbury, Fleetlands, Middle Wallop, 665, 657, 658, 660. Pod, spares.		6-03
❑	XX388*	Gazelle AH.1	ex Poole (?), Shawbury, Fleetlands, 652, 661, 652, 661, 657. Pod, spares.		6-03
❑	XX393* 'W'	Gazelle AH.1	ex Shawbury, Fleetlands, 664, 669, 654, 2F, 6F, GCF, 3 CBAS. Pod, spares.		6-03
❑	XX413*	Gazelle AH.1	ex Poole (?), Shawbury, Fleetlands, 847, 3 CBAS. Pod, spares.		6-03
❑	XX418*	Gazelle AH.1	ex Poole (?), Shawbury, Fleetlands, 651, 4 Regt, 669, 664, 658. Pod, spares.		6-03
❑	XX433*	Gazelle AH.1	ex Shawbury, Fleetlands, 685, 3 Regt, 663, 660. Pod, spares.		6-03
❑	152/17*	Fokker Dr.I REP	G-ATJM, ex North Weald, Duxford, Rendcomb, North Weald, Duxford, N78001, EI-APY, G-ATJM. CoA 10-9-93. Stored.		6-03
❑	C4E-88*	Bf 109E	ex Tangmere, Stubbington, Spain, SpanAF '6-88'.		6-03

Others: Work is being carried out in the general area on the Gannet to get it to ground-running status.

❑	XA459	Gannet AS.4	ex Cirencester, Cardiff, Culdrose SAH-7 / A2608, Lee-on-Solent, 831.	10-01

MEMBURY close to the Membury services, east of Swindon on the M4
Southern Sailplanes: The fuselage of Super Cub G-APZJ is the original one [1].

❑	G-AHAG	Dragon Rapide	ex Blandford, Ford, Whitney, RL944. CoA 15-7-73.		1-00
❑	G-APZJ	Super Cub 150	crashed 12-6-83. Original fuselage frame, stored.	[1]	9-89
❑	G-AWHX	Beta B.2	ex G-ATEE ntu. *Vertigo*. CoA 14-6-87.		1-00
❑	G-BAMT	DR.400 Knight	crashed 8-1-78. Wreck.		9-89
❑	G-BAVA	Super Cub 150	ex D-EFKC, ALAT 18-5391. Cr 20-11-77. Frame.		1-92
❑	G-BAZC	DR.400 Knight	crashed 21-5-88. Fuselage.		7-98
❑	G-BEHS	Pawnee 260C	ex Lancing, OE-AFX, N8755L. CoA 25-6-93.		2-95
❑	G-RBIN	DR.400 2+2	crashed 21-5-93. Wreck.		7-98
❑	'Z7258'	Dragon Rapide	G-AHGD, ex Old Warden, NR786. *Women of the Empire*. Crashed 30-6-91. Wreck.		8-97

NEWBURY on the A34 west of Reading
British Balloon Museum and Library (BBM&L): Envelopes are to be seen during events such as the Icicle Meet and the occasional inflation day. BBM&L maintains strong links with The Airship Heritage Trust (see below) and looks after the display in the West Berkshire Museum, also see below. Colt 56 G-BLKU moved to Manchester, Gtr Man, on loan. Thunder AX3 G-BHUR has been deleted.
✉ Tim Turner, Secretary, 19 Rother Close, West End, Southampton, Hants, SO18 3NJ e-mail tjthafb@aol.com www.britishballoonmuseum.org.uk

❑	G-ATGN	Thorn Coal Gas	2-04	❑	G-AZUV	Cameron O-56	2-04
❑	G-ATXR	Abingdon Gas	2-04	❑	G-AZYL	Portslade School	2-04
❑	G-AVTL	HAG Free	2-04	❑	G-BAMK	Cameron D-96	2-04
❑	G-AWCR	Piccard Ax6	2-04	❑	G-BAVU	Cameron A-105	2-04
❑	G-AWOK	Sussex Free Gas	2-04	❑	G-BAXF	Cameron O-77	2-04
❑	G-AXVU	Omega 84	2-04	❑	G-BAXK	Thunder Ax7-77	2-04
❑	G-AXXP	Bradshaw Free	2-04	❑	G-BBFS	Van Bemden Gas	2-04
❑	G-AYAJ	Cameron O-84	2-04	❑	G-BBGZ	Cambridge	¶ 2-04
❑	G-AYAL	Omega 56	2-04	❑	G-BBLL	Cameron O-84	2-04
❑	G-AZBH	Cameron O-84	2-04	❑	G-BBOD	Cameron O-5	2-04
❑	G-AZER	Cameron O-42	2-04	❑	G-BBOX	Thunder Ax7-77	2-04
❑	G-AZJI	Western O-65	2-04	❑	G-BBYU	Cameron O-65	2-04
❑	G-AZOO	Western O-65	2-04	❑	G-BCAR	Thunder Ax7-77	2-04
❑	G-AZSP	Cameron O-84	2-04	❑	G-BCFD	West	2-04

❏	G-BCFE	Portslade School	2-04	❏	G-BVBX	Cameron N-90M -	2-04
❏	G-BCGP	Gazebo Ax-65	2-04	❏	G-CHUB	Colt N-51 SS	2-04
❏	G-BDVG	Thunder Ax6-56A	2-04	❏	G-ERMS	Thunder AS-33	2-04
❏	G-BEEE	Thunder Ax6-56A	2-04	❏	G-FTFT	Colt 90SS	2-04
❏	G-BEFE*	Cameron N-77	2-04	❏	G-FZZZ	Colt 56A	2-04
❏	G-BEPO	Cameron N-77	2-04	❏	G-HOME	Colt 77A	2-04
❏	G-BEPZ	Cameron D-96	2-04	❏	G-HOUS	Colt 31A	2-04
❏	G-BETF	Cameron SS	2-04	❏	G-ICES	Thunder Ax6-56	2-04
❏	G-BETH	Thunder Ax6-56	2-04	❏	G-JONO*	Colt 77A	2-04
❏	G-BEVI	Thunder Ax7-77A	2-04	❏	G-LCIO	Colt 240A	2-04
❏	G-BFAB	Cameron N-56	2-04	❏	G-LOAG	Cameron N-77	2-04
❏	G-BGAS	Colt 105A	2-04	❏	G-NUTS	Cameron 35SS	2-04
❏	G-BGHS	Cameron N-31	2-04	❏	G-OBUD	Colt 69A	2-04
❏	G-BGOO	Colt 56	2-04	❏	G-ODAY*	Cameron N-56	2-04
❏	G-BGPF	Thunder Ax6-56Z	2-04	❏	G-OFIZ	Colt 80SS	2-04
❏	G-BHKN	Colt 14A	2-04	❏	G-OLLI*	Cameron O-31	2-04
❏	G-BHKR	Colt 14A	¶ 2-04	❏	G-PARR	Colt 90SS	2-04
❏	G-BIAZ	Cameron AT-165	2-04	❏	G-PERR	Cameron SS 60	2-04
❏	G-BIDV	Colt 17A	2-04	❏	G-PLUG	Colt 105A	2-04
❏	G-BIGT	Colt 77A	2-04	❏	G-PUBS	Colt SS	2-04
❏	G-BIUL	Cameron 60	2-04	❏	G-ZUMP	Cameron N-77	2-04
❏	G-BKES	Cameron SS 57	2-04	❏	EI-BAY	Cameron O-84	2-04
❏	G-BKMR	Thunder Ax3	2-04	❏	F-WGGM	T & Colt AS-261	2-04
❏	G-BKRZ	Dragon 77	2-04	❏	HB-BOU	Brighton HAB	2-04
❏	G-BLIO	Cameron R-42	2-04	❏	N4990T	Thunder Ax7-65B	2-04
❏	G-BLWB*	Thunder Ax6-56	2-04	❏	N12006	Raven S.50	2-04
❏	G-BMEZ	Cameron DP-50	2-04	❏	OY-BOB	Omega 80	2-04
❏	G-BMYA	Colt 56A	2-04	❏	OY-BOW	Colting 77A	2-04
❏	G-BNHN	Colt SS	2-04	❏	5Y-SIL	Cameron A-140	2-04
❏	G-BOGR	Colt 180A	2-04	❏	–	Gas balloon	2-04
❏	G-BOTL	Colt 42R	2-04	❏	–	Cam' DG28 Gas	2-04
❏	G-BPKN	Colt AS-80	2-04	❏	–	Military Gas	2-04
❏	G-BRZC	Cameron N-90	2-04	❏	– BAPC.258	GQ 5,000ft^3	2-04
❏	G-BUBL	Thunder Ax8-105	2-04				
❏	G-BUUU	Cameron 77SS	2-04				

West Berkshire Museum: BBM&L artefacts on show are marked ¶ above.
◆ At The Wharf in Newbury. Note, *closed* every Wed – except school holidays Open Apr to Sep 10am to 5pm Mon to Sat and 1pm to 5pm Sun and Bank Hols. Oct to March 10am to 4pm Mon to Sat and closed Sun and Bank Hols ✉ The Wharf, Newbury, RG14 5AS ☎ 01635 30511 **fax** 01635 519562

Airship Heritage Trust (AHT): Work closely with the BBML and their collection, although dispersed for now, is listed here for convenience.
◆ Not available for viewing at present. ✉ G/C Peter A Garth, 5 Orchard Lane, Brampton, PE1 8TF.

❏	G-BECE	AD-500 Skyship	ex Old Warden, Cardington, Kirkbymoorside. Gondola, damaged 9-3-79. Stored.	3-02
❏	G-BIHN	Skyship 500	ex Old Warden, Cardington. Dam 27-4-87. Gondola.	3-02
❏	–	K88 Airship	ex St Athan, Pensacola, USN. Gondola.	3-02

READING
Ben Borsberry: No news on the biplanes believed held in the area.

❏	G-AGNJ	Tiger Moth	ex VP-YOJ, ZS-BGF, SAAF 2366.	®	6-95
❏	G-AZGC	SNCAN SV-4C	ex Hungerford, Booker, F-BCGE, French mil No.120. Damaged 28-5-90. Stored.		6-95
❏	G-BRHW	Tiger Moth	ex 7Q-YMY, VP-YMY, ZS-DLB, SAAF 4606, DE671.	®	6-95

Kelvin Petty: Kelvin also has the MiG-21MF at Boscombe Down, Wilts - qv.

❏	ZF582	Lightning F.53	ex Llantrisant, Luton, Desborough, Portsmouth, Stretton, Warton, RSAF 207, 53-676, G-27-46. Nose.	12-01

Others:

❑ WW447   Provost T.1   ex Exeter, CATCS, CNCS, RAFC. Stored.   6-00

THATCHAM or Brimpton, north of the A4, west of Newbury
Sylmar Aviation / Provost Team: Alan House and team operate from a strip in the area. Two of the Provosts attended the '100 Years of Flight Experience' at Fairford, Glos, July 2003 ➡.

❑ G-HRLK	Safir	✈	ex G-BRZY, PH-RLK.	10-03
❑ G-SAFR	Safir		ex Cranfield, Coventry, Rugby, Bruntingthorpe,	
			PH-RLR RLS. .	® 1-02
❑ N16403	C34 Airmaster	✈	–	10-03
❑ WV486 'N-D'	Provost T.1		ex Reading, Halton 7694M, 6 FTS. Spares.	1-02
❑ XF545 'O-K'	Provost T.1		ex Linton-on-Ouse, Swinderby, Finningley 7957M,	
			Shawbury, 6 FTS, 2 FTS. Fuselage, stored.	1-02
❑ XF597 'AH'	Provost T.1	✈	G-BKFW, ex CAW, RAFC.	➡ 10-03
❑ XF836	Provost T.1		G-AWRY, ex Popham, Old Warden, 8043M, 27 MU,	
			CATCS, CNCS, RAFC, Man UAS. Dam 28-7-87.	® 7-03
❑ XF877* 'J-X'	Provost; T.1	✈	G-AWVF, ex Sandown, CATCS, CNCS, RAFC.	➡ 10-03
❑ 181	Provost T.51		ex Casement, IAAC. Spares.	1-02

WHITE WALTHAM AERODROME south of the A4 south-west of Maidenhead
The Automobile Association base a travelling composite Enstrom here. It wears their colours and is believed to be based upon the former Somersham, Cambs, hybrid, with the cabin of G-BATU with the tail from G-JDHI and other parts from other machines, including G-BACH [1]. They are also believed to have a Bö 105 pod - confirmation?

❑ G-AFLW	Miles Monarch	CoA 30-7-<u>98</u>. Stored.	6-01
❑ G-BBNY	Cessna FRA.150L	ex Lasham, Blackbushe. Crashed 8-6-86. Wreck.	9-96
❑ 'N-NAAS'	Enstrom F-28	composite. Travelling airframe.	[1] 6-03

WOODLEY east of Reading
Museum of Berkshire Aviation (MBA): Work continues on the major reconstruction of the Martinet – bringing an otherwise 'extinct' type back to the public gaze. Great to see the Elliotts of Newbury gliders coming into the fold. They arrived by December 2002, donated by Pat Pottinger [1]. The Gannet is on loan from the Fleet Air Arm Museum [2] and the Gyrodyne from the RAF Museum [3].

    Co-operating within the site are several other bodies: the **Royal Berkshire Aviation Society**, **The Herald Society** undertaking the restoration of *Whisky-Alpha* (contact for both K Freeman, 269 Wykeham Road, Reading, Berkshire RG6 1PL, e-mail keith_freeman@uk2.net) and **The Miles Aircraft Collection**. Items on show at MBA from MAC include the Bristol Mercury and propeller from the second prototype M.37 JN668 and a 'slice' of upper fuselage of Marathon G-AMEW. The bulk of the MAC collection is widely dispersed, their main 'reference' is under Pulborough, West Sussex.
◆ Sat, Sun and Bank Hols Mar to Oct, 10.30am to 5pm. May, Jun and Jul also open Wed 11.30am to 4pm. Sun only 12 noon to 4pm Nov to Mar. ⊠ Mohawk Way (off Bader Way), Woodley, near Reading, Berkshire RG5 4UF ☎/answerline 0118 9448089 e-mail museumofberkshireaviation @fly.to www.fly.to/museumofberkshireaviation

❑ G-APLK	Miles Student 2	ex North Weald, Bruntingthorpe, G-APLK,		
		Cranfield, G-MIOO, Duxford, G-APLK, Glasgow,		
		Shoreham, XS941, G-35-4. Crashed 24-8-85.	®	3-04
❑ G-APWA	Herald 100	ex Southend, BAF, PP-SDM, PP-ASV,		
		G-APWA. CoA 6-4-82.		3-04
❑ –* [A]	EoN Olympia 1	BGA.562, ex G-ALJZ, BGA.562. Crashed 20-7-<u>58</u>.	[1]	3-04
❑ –* [AQZ]	EoN Primary	BGA.589, ex Farnborough, G-ALMN, BGA.589.	[1]	3-04
❑ –* [ANL]	EoN Olympia 1	BGA.529, ex RAFGSA.103. Crashed 31-10-<u>57</u>.	[1]	3-04
❑ TF-SHC	Martinet TT.1	ex Reykjavik, Akureyri, MS902, Reykjavik SF,		
		251. Crashed 18-7-51. Major reconstruction.	®	3-04
❑ 'L6906'	Magister I	BAPC.44, ex Brooklands, Woodley, Wroughton,		
		Frenchay, G-AKKY, T9841, 11 EFTS, 16 EFTS.		3-04

❏	XG883	'773'	Gannet T.5	ex Cardiff, Yeovilton, 849. FAAM loan.	[2]	3-04
❏	XJ389		Jet Gyrodyne	ex Cosford, Southampton, G-AJJP, XD759, makers.	[3]	3-04
❏	–	BAPC.233	Wanderlust	ex Farnborough.		3-04
❏	–	BAPC.248	McBroom h-g	built 1974.		3-04

BUCKINGHAMSHIRE

AYLESBURY
No.1365 Squadron Air Cadets: Hunter F.6 nose XF522 moved to <u>Milton Keynes</u>, Bucks. **Others**: Stored in the area is a Luton Minor. **Stewart Thornley**'s Chipmunk is to become a full-blown motion simulator.

❏	G-AFIR		Luton Minor	ex Cobham, Rearsby. CoA 30-7-71.	1-96
❏	WB626		Chipmunk T.10 PAX	ex South Molton, Fownhope, Firbeck, Houghton-on-the-Hill, Southampton, Swanton Morley, Bicester, Kemble, Hendon SF, 5 FTS, 18 RFS.	6-01

BLETCHLEY PARK south of the A5, near Milton Keynes
Bletchley Park Museum: The mansion and its surroundings are embedded in military history as the home of the 'code breakers' and, as well as many other exhibits, there is a fascinating Cryptology Museum among many other 'themes'. Within the site can be found the **Buckinghamshire Aircraft Recovery Group** (c/o The Mansion as above, **www.bargbp.com**) who have a large collection of aviation memorabilia on display. BARG's collection includes uniforms, flying equipment, engines and other items from 'digs'.
◆ Off the B4034. Open weekends 10.30am to 5pm (last admission 3.30pm). ✉ The Mansion, Bletchley Park, MK3 6EB ☎ 01908 640404 **www.bletchleypark.org.uk**

HALTON AIRFIELD on the A4011 (camp) and east of the B4544 (airfield), north of Wendover
RAF Halton: Established as part of the station's 80th anniversary, the **Trenchard Museum** now includes a Cadet glider within. [1]. (The museum is available for inspection on a prior permission only basis, contact 01296 623535, ext 6300.) 'JP' XS215 is used by the Airman's Command School and is fitted with the wings of XS218 [2]. The Bulldogs are with **2409 Squadron ATC** (Herts and Bucks Wing ATC) with the plan to create one airframe [3]. Phantom FGR.2 XV408 attended the '100 Years of Flight Experience' static display at the International Air Tattoo, Fairford, Glos, in July 2003. It was only during its move that it was revealed that it was not to return and instructions to scrap it had been issued. It was replaced by a Tornado.

❏	–		ETE Fauvel AV.36C	BGA.2932, ex RAFGSA.53, D-5353, D-8259. CoA 6-98. Stored.		1-04
❏	'RA905'*		Cadet TX.1	BQE - BGA.1143, ex Aston Down, RAFGSA.273, RA905. CoA 14-3-00. First noted 7-03.	[1]	2-04
❏	XF527		Hunter F.6	8680M, ex 1 SoTT, Laarbruch SF, 4 FTS, CFE, 19, Church Fenton SF, Linton SF. Gate.		7-03
❏	XR672	'50'	Jet Provost T.4	8495M, ex SoRF, 6 FTS, CAW, CATCS, 3 FTS, 1 FTS. Fuselage in use as horse jump.		7-03
❏	[XS215]	'17'	Jet Provost T.4	8507M, ex CAW. Fuselage. GIA.	[2]	3-02
❏	XX665		Bulldog T.1	9289M, ex Newton, E Lowlands UAS, Abn UAS, E Lowlands UAS. Cr 20-9-97. Fuselage.	[3]	2-04
❏	XX669*	'F'	Bulldog T.1	ex Andover, Llantrisant, Bruntingthorpe, Cosford 8997M, 2 FTS, Birm UAS, Man UAS. Damaged 6-9-88. Hulk. Arrived by 8-03.	[3]	2-04
❏	XZ630*		Tornado GR.1	ex St Athan 8986M, Brüggen, BAe Warton, A&AEE. 'Gate'. Arrived 3-2-04.		2-04

HIGH WYCOMBE

❏ RM694	Spitfire XIV	ex USA, Southend, Henlow, Charnock Richard, Hoylake, Dishforth, Bicester, Hornchurch, Locking 6640M, CFE, 402, 91. Stored.	3-04
❏ RM927	Spitfire XIV	ex USA, Southend, Charnock Richard, Ostend, Belg AF SG-25, RAF, 29 MU, 403. Stored.	3-04

IVER HEATH on the A412 west of Uxbridge

Pinewood Film Studios: A couple of tours of the studio lots during 2003 found only a JetRanger tied securely to a clump of ISO containers of aviation interest. During March 2003 the forward fuselage of a former Bournemouth BAC 1-11 arrived for use in the TV series *Ultimate Force* starring someone who used to be in *East Enders* - probably Dot Cotton, going by the title. The cockpit of TriStar TF-ABP moved to North Weald, Essex, by mid-2002.

❏ G-AVMP*	BAC 111-510ED	ex Bournemouth, EAL, BA, BEA. Forward fuselage Arrived 263-03.	3-03
❏ –*	JetRanger	once had Alaskoil titles. First noted 4-03	1-04

LAVENDON on the A428 west of Bedford

Tony and **Nick Collins**: The collection continues to flourish with the arrival of a whole airframe.

❏ WT319	Canberra B(I).6	ex Castle Carey, ?, Filton, Samlesbury, 213, Laarbruch SF, 213. Nose.	10-03
❏ WT684	Hunter F.1	ex Doncaster, Firbeck, Long Marston, Brize Norton, Halton 7422M, 229 OCU, DFLS. Nose.	6-03
❏ XK627*	Vampire T.11	ex Barton, Bacup, Hazel Grove, Woodford, Chester, St Athan, 8 FTS, CFS.	12-02
❏ XN651	Sea Vixen FAW.2	ex Bletchley Park, Bristol, Culdrose A2616, SAH, 766, FAW.1, 893. Nose.	3-03
❏ XP642	Jet Provost T.4	ex Luton, Bruntingthorpe, Nottingham, Finchampstead Ridges, Lasham, Shawbury, 2 FTS, CFS. Nose.	3-03
❏ XS898	'BD' Lightning F.6	ex Bruntingthorpe, Cranfield, Binbrook, 11, 5. Nose.	3-03

MILTON KEYNES

No.2532 Squadron, Air Cadets: Have taken on the former Aylesbury Hunter nose.

❏ XF522*	Hunter F.6	ex Aylesbury, Halton, 92, 66, 92. Nose.	5-03

Others: By 1996 a collector in this area had acquired Grasshopper TX.1 XA226 from an unknown location in the Midlands. It had previously been at Turweston, Bucks, and with Ipswich Grammar School before that. By late 2000, the collector was offering XA226 for disposal/sale. No other details.

NEWPORT PAGNELL on the B526 north of Milton Keynes

Peter R Arnold:

❏ EN224	Spitfire XII	G-FXII, ex Cranfield, 595, 41.	3-02
❏ LA564	Seafire F.46	ex Redbourn, Newark, Southend, Charnock Richard, Carlisle, Anthorn, 738, 767, A&AEE.	3-02

TWYFORD east of Bicester

Peter Wood: Chipmunk T.10 WB763 (G-BBMR) moved to Nottingham, Notts, by December 2002.

❏ AD540	Spitfire V	ex Dumfries, Carsphairn, 242, 122. *Blue Peter*. Crashed 23-5-42.	® 3-04
❏ WK620	'T' Chipmunk T.10	ex Tattershall Thorpe, Middle Wallop, BFWF, Hull UAS, Mcr UAS, QUAS, Bri UAS, 22 RFS. Damaged 19-5-93. Stored.	6-01

WOBURN SANDS on the A5130 east of Milton Keynes

David Underwood: Still has the oldest surviving Slingsby Kite I AAF.

❏   AAF T.6 Kite I   ex Dunstable, G-ALUD, BGA.236, BGA.222. Stored.   6-01

WYCOMBE AIR PARK or Booker, on the B482 south-west of High Wycombe

Personal Plane Services (PPS) / **Antique Aero Engines**: An exodus of 'film-stars' occurred in the spring of 2003 to Compton Abbas, Dorset: Manning-Flanders G-BAAF; Blériot XI G-BPVE; Sopwith Camel 'B2458' (G-BPOB); Morane Saulnier Type 'N' 'MS824' (G-AWBU); Fokker E.III 422/15 (G-AVJO); Ornithopter BAPC.238. Several airframes are being restored or stored for US collector Kermit Weeks (KW). In line with other entries, only long-term non-flyers are now listed, SV-4C G-AWXZ has been deleted. The Travelair 2000 is bedecked as a Fokker D.VIII [1].

◆ Visits possible *only* by prior arrangement.

❏ G-AZTR	SNCAN SV-4C	ex F-BDEQ. CoA 15-7-94. Dismantled.		6-01
❏ [G-BTZE]	Yak C-11	ex OK-JIK. Last flown 12-6-76. Stored.		6-03
❏ I-CABI*	Jungmann	ex Italy, HB-UTZ, Swiss AF A-12. First noted 9-03.		9-03
❏ [OK-JIY]	Yak C-11	ex La Ferté Alais, Egypt AF. c/n 172673.	off-site	3-96
❏ AR213	Spitfire Ia	G-AIST, ex Patrick Lindsay, Old Warden, *Battle of Britain*, 8 MU, 53 OTU, 57 OTU. CoA 6-9-00.	®	3-04
❏ EJ693	Tempest V	N7027E, ex Norfolk (?), USA, Chichester, Henlow, Delft, 486. Crashed 1-10-44.	KW®	6-03
❏ MV262	Spitfire XIV	G-CCVV, ex Winchester, Bitteswell, Blackbushe, Calcutta, Ind AF, ACSEA, 9 MU. Stored.	KW	3-04
❏ TE517	Spitfire IX	G-CCIX, ex Winchester, Nailsworth, G-BIXP ntu, Duxford, Israel, Israel DF/AF 2046, Czech AF, RAF TE517, 313. Stored.	KW	3-04
❏ '626/8'	Travel Air 2000	N6268, ex USA, NC6268. Crash scene.	[2]	7-96
❏ –	Pilatus P.2	fuselage. Film mock-up. Luftwaffe colours.		2-04
❏ – BAPC.103	Hulton hang-glider	built 1969.		3-96

Parkhouse Aviation: MiG-21SPS cockpit 764 moved to Northampton, Northants, by June 2002. The nose of Lightning F.1 XM144 moved to Pershore, Worcs, on 28th November 2003.

❏ G-WGHB*	T-33A/N	ex Gainsborough, Sandtoft, Portsmouth, Southampton, Coventry, Duxford, Southend, CF-EHB, CAF 21640, 133640. CoA 13-6-77. Arrived 13-3-04.		3-04
❏ 'XF314' 'N'	Hunter F.51	ex Sandown, Tangmere, Dunsfold, G-9-439, Danish AF E-412, Esk.724. 43 Sqn c/s.		2-04
❏ XM172 'B'	Lightning F.1A	ex Coltishall 8427M, 226 OCU, 56.		2-04

Others: Tiger Moth T7230 (G-AFVE) was flying again by mid-2002 and likewise Musketeer G-AWFZ by the following year..

❏ G-BSVF	Warrior II	ex C-GVSJ, N9575N. Wreck. Stored.	7-03
❏ G-DYOU	Tomahawk 112	fuselage. Crashed 23-7-92.	7-03
❏ G-EORG	Tomahawk 112	original fuselage, trailer-mounted.	7-03
❏ G-KUTU	Quickie Q.2	damaged 18-5-85. Stored.	7-03
❏ [G-RPEZ]	Rutan LongEz	incomplete, stored up hangar wall.	8-00
❏ T7404 '04'	Tiger Moth	G-ANMV, ex F-BHAZ, G-ANMV, T7404, 2 RFS, 2 RFS, 8 RFS, 8 EFTS, 10 FIS, 26 EFTS. Stored.	6-01

CAMBRIDGESHIRE

ALCONBURY AIRFIELD north-west of Huntingdon at the A1/A14 junction

USAF Alconbury: A USAF enclave is still here. The A-10 guards the 'inner' gate [1].

❏ '01532'	F-5E Tiger II	mock up, on 'outer' gate, 527 TFTAS c/s.	12-03
❏ 80-0219	A-10A	ex 509th TFS, Bentwaters. Accident 4-4-89.	
	Thunderbolt II	10th TFW, 509th TFS-511th TFS c/s. *Phoenix*.	[1] 12-03

BASSINGBOURN on the A1198 north of Royston
Tower Museum and 91st Bomb Group (H) Museum: Run and maintained by the **East Anglian Aviation Society** (EAAS), the original tower is the basis for the long-established, but recently upgraded, museum dedicated to the history of the once resident 91st BG(H), 11 OTU, 231 OCU, the Army and others. EAAS share joint maintenance of the static 'Army' Canberra preserved within the camp – see below.
◆ Visits by prior appointment *only*, contact Steve Pena on ☎ / fax 01359 221151 e-mail AN6530 @aol.com, or Peter Roberts ☎ 01223 356314 e-mail prtrnmga@aol.com or Ray Jude ☎ / fax 01799 527932 e-mail margaretjude@hotmail.com ✉ (Society details) Mike Killaspy, 3 Sainfoin Close, Sawston, Cambs, CB2 4JY

Army Training Regiment, Bassingbourn: WJ821 is kept inside the camp, EAAS (see above) help maintain it. **No.2484 Squadron Air Cadets** have a Canberra nose. 'Parent' is Wyton, Cambs.
❏ WJ821		Canberra PR.7	8668M, ex RAE Bedford, 13, 58, 82. Displayed.	2-04
❏ WK127	'FO'	Canberra TT.18	8985M, ex Wyton, 100, 7, 10. Dam 13-12-88. Nose.	6-03

BOURN AERODROME on the A428 west of Cambridge
❏ G-AZLO	Cessna F.337F	ex Land's End. CoA 22-4-82. Poor state.	2-02
❏ G-BEKN	Cessna FRA.150M	ex Peterborough Sport. CoA 8-10-89. Stored.	11-03
❏ G-BEZS	Cessna FR.172J	ex Cranfield, Stapleford, I-CCAJ. Cr 15-6-79. Stored.	2-02
❏ G-BCJH	Mooney M.20F	ex N9549M. CoA 30-6-91. Engineless.	11-03
❏ G-BPIL*	Cessna 310B	ex N620GS, OO-SEF, N5420A. *Fast Lady*. CoA 28-4-00. Stored.	11-03

BRAMPTON on the A14/A141 south-west of Huntingdon
RAF Brampton / Defence Logistics Organisation: Is 'guarded' by a pristine Phantom.
❏ XT914	'Z' Phantom FGR.2	ex Leeming, 74, 56, 228 OCU, 92, 228 OCU, 56, 228 OCU, 14. 74 Sqn c/s. Gate.	2-04

CAMBRIDGE
Arbour College / Cambridge Regional College: In King Hedges Road. Gnat T.1 XP540 moved to North Weald, Essex, on 2nd October 2003. The Cessna 310 was up for auction in January 2004 [1].
❏ G-XITD	Cessna 310G	ex Tattershall Thorpe, Leavesden, Denham, G-ASYV, HB-LBY, N8948Z. Accident 14-7-88.	[1]	1-04
❏ XN582	'95' Jet Provost T.3A	ex Cambridge Airport, Cosford 8957M, 7 FTS, 1 FTS, 3 FTS, RAFC.		3-97

Others: Volunteers from the Cambridge Strut of the PFA should still be working on a 'Flea' in the area.
❏ G-ADXS	HM.14 'Flea'	ex East Tilbury, Andrewsfield, Southend, Staverton, Southend. CoA 1-12-36.	®	7-96

CAMBRIDGE AIRPORT or Teversham, on the A1303 east of Cambridge
Hercules C.1K XV296 was scrapped during July 2003. Hercules C.3 XV302 was first noted in October 2002 as a fuselage only. It has been modified for trials work, with a shortened tail, and was placed into a purpose-built shed in September 2003 [1].
❏ [N913PM]	TriStar 200	ex A40-TT Gulf Air. Arrived 15-5-98. Spares.		4-01
❏ WJ863	Canberra T.4	ex 231 OCU, 360, Akrotiri SF, 231 OCU, Honington SF, Cottesmore SF. Nose.		12-99
❏ XV201	Hercules C.1K	ex 1312F, LTW. Fuselage by 5-02, spares.		1-04
❏ XV302*	Hercules C.3	ex LTW, Fairford Wing, 30/47 Sqns. Arr 4-7-02.	[1]	1-04

COMBERTON on the B1046 west of J12 of the M11
The Moth continues to be registered to a local, but no physical sighting this century!
❏ G-AANO	DH.60GMW	ex Southampton, N590N, NC590N.	®	11-91

DUXFORD AERODROME south of Cambridge, Junction 10 M11

Imperial War Museum (IWM): On November 26, 2003, the IWM staged an open morning to show off the plans to regenerate the 'Superhangar' into what will be called 'AirSpace' dedicated to UK and Commonwealth aviation heritage. The £21 million project already has the backing of the Heritage Lottery Fund (£9 million to date), the East of England Development Agency and BAE Systems. Some aircraft (14 in present planning) will be hung from the ceiling of the extended building. Also within will be an education centre and a conservation workshop. Aircraft ear-marked at this stage for 'AirSpace' are marked ⇨. (Included are several Duxford Aviation Society airframes and the Bolingbroke being restored by the Aircraft Restoration Company - see further below in each case.)

Notes: The 'Superhangar' is home to the 'British Aircraft Collection'; while Hangar 4 contains the 'Air Defence Collection' of fighter types; Hangar 5 is the main restoration hangar; Hangars 2 and 3 continue their traditional role of housing the 'flyers' – see below. Because the aircraft inside the **American Air Museum** (AAM) are there on a long-term basis, they are listed separately from this edition – see below. Hurricane II 'Z2315' could well be BE146 if its upper cowling is anything to go by. BE146 was despatched to Russia on 2nd October 1941 [1]. (The F-105 originally intended for the AAM is still being restored and is listed below [2].)

♦ Open daily 10am to 6pm Apr to Oct and 10am to 4pm the remainder of the year. Last admission 45 minutes before closing. Closed New Year's Day and Dec 24-26. On days other than special events two of the civil airliners are open to inspection free of charge, one of which is normally Concorde. A large SAE will bring a leaflet on special events, airshows etc. ⊡ Imperial War Museum, Duxford Airfield, Cambs, CB2 4QR ☎ 01223 835000 **fax** 01223 837267 **www**.iwm.org.uk

❑ G-AFBS	Magister I	ex Staverton, G-AKKU ntu, BB661,			
		G-AFBS. CoA 25-2-63.		®⇨	3-04
❑ G-USUK	Colt 2500A	gondola. *Virgin Atlantic Flyer.*			3-04
❑ – G-9-185	Hunter F.6	ex Wroughton, South Kensington,			
		Kingston, Dutch AF N-250. Nose. Stored.			3-04
❑ E2581 '13'	Bristol F.2b	ex South Lambeth, Cardington (?), Crystal Palace,			
		Eastchurch, 2 GCF, 30 TDS, HQ Flt SE Area, 39.			3-04
❑ F3556	RE.8	ex South Lambeth, Cardington, Crystal Palace,			
		Tadcaster, no service. *[A Paddy Bird from Ceylon]*		®⇨	3-04
❑ N4877	Anson I	G-AMDA, ex Staverton, Derby AW, Watchfield			
'MK-V'		SF, 3 FP, ATA, 3 FPP. CoA 14-12-62.			
		500 Sqn colours, rolled-out 15-8-03.		⇨	3-04
❑ 'R4115'	Hurricane FSM	BAPC.267, ex South Lambeth. 242 Sqn colours.			
'LE-X'		'Gate'.			3-04
❑ V3388	Oxford I	G-AHTW, ex Staverton, Elstree, Boulton Paul,			
		V3388. CoA 15-12-60.		⇨	3-04
❑ 'V9673' 'MA-J'	Lysander III	G-LIZY, ex RCAF 1558, V9300. 161 Sqn c/s.		⇨	3-04
❑ 'Z2315' 'JU-E'	Hurricane IIb	ex TFC, Russia. 111 Sqn colours.		[1]	3-04
❑ 'DE998'*	Tiger Moth	ex ARCo, Stamford, Hooton, Warmingham, 'K2572',			
'RCU-T'		Hereford, Lutterworth, Holme-on-Spalding Moor.			
		Cam UAS colours. Handed over 5-3-02.		⇨	3-04
❑ HM580	Cierva C.30A	G-ACUU, ex Staverton, HM580, 529,			
		1448 Flt, G-ACUU. CoA 30-4-60.			3-04
❑ KB889 'NA-I'	Lancaster X	G-LANC, ex Bitteswell, Blackbushe, RCAF			
		107 MRU, 428. 428 Sqn colours.		⇨	3-04
❑ LZ766	Proctor III	G-ALCK, ex Staverton, Tamworth,			
		HQBC, 21 EFTS. CoA 19-6-63.			3-04
❑ ML796	Sunderland	ex La Baule, Maisden-le-Riviere, Aéronavale,			
	MR.5	27F, 7FE, RAF 230, 4 OTU, 228.		⇨	3-04
❑ NF370	Swordfish III	ex South Lambeth, Stretton, RAF.		®⇨	3-04
❑ TA719	Mosquito TT.35	ex Staverton, G-ASKC, Shawbury, 3/4 CAACU,			
		4 CAACU, Shawbury. Crashed 27-7-64.		⇨	3-04
❑ TG528	Hastings C.1A	ex Staverton, 24, 24-36, 242 OCU,			
		53-99 pool, 47. 24 Sqn colours.		⇨	3-04
❑ VN485	Spitfire F.24	ex Kai Tak 7326M, RHK Aux AF, 80.		®⇨	3-04
❑ WH725	Canberra B.2	ex Wroughton, 50, 44. 50 Sqn colours.		⇨	3-04

❑ WJ945	'21'	Varsity T.1	G-BEDV, ex CFS, 5 FTS, AE&AEOS, CFS, 115, 116, 527. CoA 15-10-87.		3-04
❑ WK991		Meteor F.8	ex Kemble, 7825M, 56, 46, 13 GCF, NSF.		3-04
❑ WM969	'10'	Sea Hawk FB.5	ex Culdrose, A2530, FRU, 806, 811, 898.	⇨	3-04
❑ WZ590	'19'	Vampire T.11	ex Woodford, Chester, St Athan, 8 FTS, 5 FTS, 228 OCU.		3-04
❑ XE627	'T'	Hunter F.6A	ex Brawdy, 1 TWU, TWU, 229 OCU, 1, 229 OCU, 54, 1, 54, Horsham St Faith SF, 54, 229 OCU, 92, 65. 65 colours.		3-04
❑ XF708	'C'	Shack' MR.3/3	ex Kemble, 203, 120, 201. 203 Sqn colours.		3-04
❑ XG613		Sea Ven FAW.21	ex Old Warden, RAE, A&AEE, RAE.		3-04
❑ XG743*	'597'	Sea Vampire T.22	ex Wymondham, Duxford, Brawdy SF, 736, 764. Returned in 2000. Stored.		3-04
❑ XG797	'277'	Gannet ECM.6	ex Arbroath, 831, 700, 810. 849 Sqn c/s. 831 Sqn colours and 'Flook' logo.		3-04
❑ XH648		Victor B.1A (K2P)	ex 57, 55, Honington Wing, 15, 57. 57 Sqn c/s.		3-04
❑ XH897		Javelin FAW.9	ex A&AEE, 5, 33, 25.		3-04
❑ XJ824		Vulcan B.2	ex 101, 9-35, 9, 230 OCU, 27.	⇨	3-04
❑ XK936	'62'	W'wind HAS.7	ex Wroughton, 705, 847, 848, 701, 820, 845.	⇨	3-04
❑ XM135	'B'	Lightning F.1	ex Leconfield, Leuchars TFF, 226 OCU, 74, AFDS. 74 Squadron colours.	⇨	3-04
❑ XN239	'G'	Cadet TX.3	ex CGS 8889M.		3-04
❑ XP281		Auster AOP.9	ex AFWF, Middle Wallop. MoAF loan. Stored.		3-04
❑ XR222		TSR-2 XO-4	ex Cranfield, Weybridge. Unflown.	⇨	3-04
❑ XS567	'434'	Wasp HAS.1	ex Lee-o-S, 829 *Endurance* Flt.		3-04
❑ XS576	'125'	Sea Vixen FAW.2	ex Sydenham, 899, Brawdy. 899 Sqn colours.		3-04
❑ XS863	'304'	Wessex HAS.1	ex A&AEE. Royal Navy colours.	⇨	3-04
❑ XV865		Buccaneer S.2B	ex Coningsby 9226M, Lossiemouth, 208, 12, 237 OCU, 208, 12, 208, 237 OCU, FAA, 809, 736.	® ⇨	3-04
❑ XX108*		Jaguar GR.1A	ex St Athan, BAe Warton, G-27-313 ntu, DERA, A&AEE. Arrived 29-10-03.	⇨	3-04
❑ XZ133	'10'	Harrier GR.3	ex South Lambeth, St Athan, 4, 1, 1417F, 233 OCU.	⇨ ®	3-04
❑ ZA465	'FF'	Tornado GR.1B	ex Lossiemouth, 12, 617, 17, 16.	⇨	3-04
❑		Hunter	play area. Cockpit, likely ex-procedure trainer.		3-04
❑		Typhoon	ex South Lambeth. Cockpit.		3-04
❑ A-549		FMA Pucará	ex ZD487 ntu, ex Boscombe Down, Yeovilton, Stanley, FAA.		3-04
❑ 18393		CF-100 Mk.4B	G-BCYK, ex Cranfield, RCAF, 440, 419, 409.	® ⇨	3-04
❑ 3794		MiG-15 (S-102)	ex Czech AF. Stored.		3-04
❑ 57	'8-MT'	Mystère IVA	ex Sculthorpe, FAF 8 Esc, 321 GI, 5 Esc.		3-04
❑ 1190		Bf 109E-3	ex Bournemouth, Buckfastleigh, Canada, USA, Canada, *White-4* of II/JG.26. Crashed 30-9-40.		3-04
❑ 100143		Fa 330A-1	ex Farnborough.		3-04
❑ 191660	'3'	Me 163B-1	ex South Lambeth, Cranwell, 6 MU, RAE, AM.214. Stored.		3-04
❑ –	'CF+HF'	MS.502	EI-AUY, ex USA, F-BCDG, ALAT.		3-04
❑ –	'4V+GH'	Ju 523mge	ex Port AF 6316. Luftwaffe c/s. (Amiot AAC.1)		3-04
❑ –	BAPC.93	Fi 103 (V-1)	ex Cosford. Inside.		3-04
❑ 96+21		Mi-24D *Hind*	ex Basepohl, WGAF HFS-80, LSK KHG-5 406.		3-04
❑ 501		MiG-21PF	ex St Athan, Farnborough, Hungarian AF.		3-04
❑ 3685		A6M3 Model 22	ex Boise, USA, Taroa, Marshall Islands.		3-04
	'Y2-176'	*Zeke*	Stored.		3-04
❑ B2I-27		CASA 2-111	ex OFMC, Seville, Spanish AF. Stored.		3-04
❑ 1133		Strikemaster 80	ex Warton, RSaudiAF, G-BESY, G-27-299.	⇨	3-04
❑ Fv 35075	'40'	J35A Draken	ex RSwAF F16.		3-04
❑ 252983		Schweizer TG-3A	ex AAM, N66630. Stored.		3-04
❑ 59-1822		F-105D-6-RE	ex AMARC Virg ANG 192nd TFG, 23rd, 355th, 388th, 18th, 23rd, 355th,TFWs, 4520 CCTW.	® [2]	3-04

American Air Museum (AAM): Former US President George Bush was a guest at the rededication of the AAM on 27th September 2002 along with a large number of US veterans. The B-24 and SR-71 have been squeezed in to the impressive building. Sadly, and I'm not alone in this opinion, this splendid museum-within-a-museum has been ruined by the 'black hole' cramming in of exhibits. The F-105, intended to go inside, remains under restoration on the main site and has been listed there. Schweizer TG-3A 252983 has gone into store - see above.

Notes: P-47 *Oregon's Britannia* was a major reconstruction based upon large elements of P-47D 45-49192 that were not used in the composite that created The Fighter Collection's machine *No Guts, No Glory* – see below [1]. The B-24D nose section will return to the USA eventually [2].

❑ 'S4513'		SPAD XIII REP	G-BFYO, ex 'S3398', Yeovilton, Land's End,	
	'1'		Chertsey, D-EOWM. CoA 21-6-82.	3-04
❑ 14286		T-33A-1-LO	ex Sculthorpe, FAF CIFAS 328. USAF c/s.	3-04
❑ 31171		B-25J-30-NC	N7614C, ex Shoreham, Dublin, Prestwick,	
		Mitchell	Luton, 44-31171. USMC PBJ-1J colours.	3-04
❑ 42165	'VM'	F-100D-11-NA	ex Sculthorpe, FAF *Esc* 2/11, *Esc* 1/3,	
		Super Sabre	USAF. 352nd TFS, 35th TFW colours.	3-04
❑ '46214'	'X-3'	TBM-3E	ex CF-KCG, RCN 326, USN 69327.	
		Avenger	'Lt George Bush' titling. *Ginny*.	3-04
❑ 60689		B-52D-40-BW	ex 7 BW Carswell and others, USAF.	3-04
❑ 66692		U-2CT-LO	ex Alconbury, 5 SRTS/9 SRW, Beale.	3-04
❑ 155529	'114'	F-4J(UK)	ZE359, ex Wattisham, 74, USN 155529.	
		Phantom II	USN VF-74, *America* colours.	3-04
❑ '217786'	'25'	PT-17 Kaydet	ex Swanton Morley, Duxford, CF-EQS,	
			Evergreen, New Brunswick, Canada, 41-8169.	3-04
❑ '226413'		P-47D-30-RA	N47DD, ex USA, Peru AF FAP 119 and 545,	
	'UN-Z'	Thunderbolt	USAAF 45-49192. Cr 9-2-80. 56th FG colours,	
			Zemke's a/c. *Oregon's Britannia*.	[1] 3-04
❑ '231983'		B-17G-95-DL	ex IGN F-BDRS, N68269, 44-83735.	
	'IY-G'	Flying Fortress	401st BG colours. *Mary Alice*.	3-04
❑ 251457		B-24D-5-FO	ex NASM. *Fightin' Sam*. Nose section. Stored.	[2] 3-04
❑ 315509		C-47A-85-DL	G-BHUB, ex Aces High G-BHUB, *Airline* :	
	'W7-S'	Skytrain	'G-AGIV', 'FD988' and 'KG418', Spanish AF	
			T3-29, N51V, N9985F, SAS SE-BBH, 315 TCG,	
			316 TCG, 43-15509. 37 TCS / 316 TCG colours.	3-04
❑ '450493'		B-24M-25-FO	44-51228, ex Lackland, EZB-24M.	
		Liberator	*Dugan*.	3-04
❑ 461748	'Y'	TB-29A-45-BN	G-BHDK, ex China Lake, 307th BG, Okinawa.	
		Superfortress	*It's Hawg Wild* (stb). 307th BG colours.	3-04
❑ '463209'	'WZ-S'	P-51D FSM	BAPC.255, ex OFMC, London. 78th FG colours.	3-04
❑ –		Harvard IIB	ex North Weald, Amsterdam, Dutch AF B-168,	
			FE984, RCAF, 2 FIS, 42-12471.	3-04
❑ 0242	'242'	F-86A-5-NA	N196B, ex Chino, 48-0242.	3-04
❑ 64-17962		SR-71A	ex Palmdale, 9th SRW.	3-04
❑ 67-0120		F-111E-CF	ex Upper Heyford, 20th TFW. *The Chief*.	3-04
❑ 72-1447		F-111F-CF	escape module.	3-04
❑ 72-21605		UH-1H 'Huey'	ex Coleman Barracks, ATCOM.	3-04
❑ 76-0020		F-15A-15-MC	ex AMARC Davis-Monthan, Mass ANG	
			102nd FIW,5th FIS, 33rd TFW, 36th TFW. 'Gate'.	3-04
❑ 77-0259	'AR'	A-10A	ex Alconbury, 10th TFW, 11th TASG,	
		Thunderbolt II	128th TFW.	3-04

Duxford Aviation Society (DAS) / **Friends of Duxford**: While the airliner collection is the most 'high profile' presence of these two organisations, without the many, many efforts put in by DAS crews on restoration projects, special events, vehicle displays, airshow days etc, the entire Duxford site would not function. DAS airframes destined for 'AirSpace' (aka the 'Superhangar Plus') are marked ⇨.
⊡ Duxford Airfield, Duxford, Cambridge, CB2 4QR ☎ 01223 836593 **www.das.org.uk**

❑ G-AGTO		J/1 Autocrat	✈ on loan.	2-04
❑ G-ALDG		Hermes 4	ex Gatwick, Silver City, Britavia, Airwork,	
			BOAC. CoA 9-1-63. BOAC c/s, *Horsa*. Fuselage.	⇨ 2-04

☐ G-ALFU	Dove 6	ex CAFU Stansted. CoA 4-6-71.	⇨ 2-04
☐ G-ALWF	Viscount 701	ex Liverpool, Cambrian, BEIA, Channel, BEA.	
		CoA 16-4-72. BEA colours, *Sir John Franklin*.	⇨ 2-04
☐ G-ALZO	Ambassador 2	ex Lasham, Dan-Air, Handley Page, Jordan AF	
		108, BEA. CoA 14-5-72. Dan-Air colours.	® 2-04
☐ G-ANTK	York C.1	ex Lasham, Dan-Air, MW232, Fairey, 511,	
		242. CoA 29-10-64. Dan-Air colours.	® ⇨ 2-04
☐ G-AOVT	Britannia 312	ex Monarch, British Eagle, BOAC. CoA 11-3-75.	
		Monarch colours.	2-04
☐ G-APDB	Comet 4	ex Dan-Air, MSA 9M-AOB, BOAC	
		G-APDB. CoA7-10-74. Dan-Air colours.	⇨ 2-04
☐ G-APWJ	Herald 201	ex Norwich, Air UK, BIA, BUIA.	
		CoA 21-12-85. Air UK colours.	2-04
☐ G-ASGC	Super VC-10	ex BA, BOAC. CoA 20-4-80. BOAC-Cunard c/s.	2-04
☐ G-AVFB	Trident 2E	ex BA, Cyprus 5B-DAC, BEA.	
		CoA 30-9-82. BEA colours.	2-04
☐ G-AVMU	BAC 111-510ED	ex Bournemouth, BA, BEA. CoA 8-1-95.	
		BA colours. *County of Dorset*.	2-04
☐ G-AXDN	Concorde 101	ex BAC/SNIAS. CoA 30-9-77.	⇨ 2-04
☐ G-OPAS	Viscount 806	ex Southend, Parcelforce/BWA, BAF, BA,	
		BEA G-AOYN. CoA 26-3-97. Nose.	2-04
☐ XB261	Beverley C.1	ex Southend, HAM, A&AEE. Cockpit.	2-04

Aircraft Restoration Company (ARC) / **PropShop Ltd**: ARC shares the 'M11-end' hangar in a co-operative arrangement with Historic Flying Ltd (HFL – see below). Long term restoration projects are located in – and listed – under the new facility. See under HFL for ARC's Spitfire Tr.IX project. The arrival of the Lysander in June 2003 was a surprise to many. Its restoration to flying condition will be on an 'as and when' basis. The two Fireflies were also eye-openers – SE-BRG will be rebuilt to flying condition and operated by ARC, SE-CAU will be restored to static condition [1].

Very sadly 'Blenheim' G-BPIV suffered engine problems upon return to Duxford on 18th August 2003. On final approach, the starboard engine failed completely and the aircraft hit the embankment short of the threshold, whipping away the main gear, resulting in a crash-landing on the grass just inside the airfield. Following the accident, Graham Warner passed on ownership of the aircraft to a new limited company, **Blenheim (Duxford) Ltd**, which has been set up to restore G-BPIV. Once flying again, it may be that it is operated by a trust fund. Initial thinking puts the rebuild at three years minimum [2].

Notes: The nose of Bolingbroke 9893 and other parts are being used in the static 'Blenheim' being built by ARC for the IWM. Accordingly, 9893 has been moved from a listing with the IWM above to under this heading. When complete it will 'fly' inside the 'AirSpace' hangar [3]. Spitfire IX TA805 is for fitting out and completion for its owners [4]. Aircraft marked ➥ attended the '100 Years of Flight Experience' static display at the International Air Tattoo, Fairford, Glos, July 2003. ARCo maintains and operates a series of aircraft on behalf of their owners: Golden Apple Trust (GA); Invicta Aviation (RA); Radial Revelations (RR – ie Martin Willing).

Departures: Avro 504K rep 'D8781' (G-ECKE) was exported to New Zealand 30-8-02. Tiger Moth R5136 (G-APAP) to Henlow, Beds, 28-5-03. Static Tiger Moth 'DE998' for IWM was completed by 5-02 and it moved to the 'Superhangar' for display 5-3-02 – see above. Radial Revelations sold Pembroke C.1 WV740 (G-BNPH) to the wonderfully-named Percy Airlines at Bournemouth, Dorset, on 19-9-03. Pilatus P.2-05 A-125 (G-BLKZ) to Elstree, Herts, 8-03. The former Paul Morgan FG-1D 92399 (G-CCMV) flew out to Southampton 2-9-02 where it was exported to the USA. Former Intrepid Aviation's P-51D 474008 (G-SIRR) was exported to the USA 28-2-03. Strikemaster OJ4 (G-UNNY) was sold within the UK and then to the Ivory Coast, departing in the spring of 2003. Strikemaster Mk.88 1108 became G-CBPB and then G-UPPI. It was restored in Ecuadorian colours as 'FAE259' and reflown 14-4-03. It was operated by Transair until 1-04 when it moved to Swansea, Wales.

From this edition Historic Aircraft Collection have been given its own section - see below. 'Moving' down are the following: Hurricane XII 'Z7381', Spitfire Vb BM597 and Chipmunk T.10 WZ879. MS.505'TA+RC' reflew following overhaul 19-3-03 and was sold to Aero Vintage - see below.
♦ Please note that the ARC/HFL building is *not* open to public inspection. ARCo aircraft can be viewed in other hangars during normal opening hours and during airshows.

| ☐ G-ASTG | Nord 1002 | ex Sutton Bridge, F-BGKI, FAF No.183. | |
| | | CoA 26-10-73. Stored. | 2-04 |

☐	G-BZGK		OV-10B	✈ ex Luftwaffe 99+32, D-9561, 158308.		IA	2-04
☐	G-BZGL		OV-10B	✈ ex Luftwaffe 99+26, D-9555, 158302.		IA	2-04
☐	SE-BRG*		Firefly TT.1	ex Sweden, 766, DT989. Arrived 10-2-04.		[1]	2-04
☐	SE-CAU*		Firefly TT.1	ex Sweden, 827, PP469. Arrived 10-2-04.		[1]	2-04
☐	'R3821'		Bolingbroke	G-BPIV, ex 'L8841', 'Z5722', Strathallan,			
	'UX-N'		IVT	Canada, RCAF 10201. *Spirit of Britain First.*			
				82 Sqn colours. Crashed 18-8-03.		➡ [2]	3-04
☐	'V6028'		Bolingbroke IVTG-MKIV, ex G-BLHM ntu, RCAF 10038.			
	'GB-D'			Crashed 21-6-87. Spares for rebuild of 9893.			1-02
☐	V9312*		Lysander TT.IIIAG-CCOM, ex N9309K. Florida, Canada, RCAF,			
				RAF, 4, 613, 225. Arrived 4-6-03. Stored.		®	2-04
☐	'MH415'*		Spitfire FSM	BAPC.209, ex 'MJ751' Shoreham, *Piece of Cake.*			
	'FU-N'			Arrived 14-6-03.			2-04
☐	TA805*		Spitfire IX	G-PMNF, ex Sandown, Battle, South Africa,			
				SAAF, 234, 183. Arrived 17-3-03.		® [4]	3-04
☐	WD373	'12'	Chipmunk T.10	G-BXDI, ex 2 AEF, S'ton UAS, Leeds UAS,			
				63 GCF, HCCS, 2 BFTS. Arrived by 9-03.			3-04
☐	WP929	'F'	Chipmunk T.10	G-BXCV, ex Shawbury, 8 AEF, Lpl UAS, Cam UAS,			
				✈ Wittering SF, RAFTTC, Coningsby SF, 61 GCF, 661.			3-04
☐	XP772		Beaver AL.1	G-BUCJ, ex Middle Wallop, Beverley, Leconfield,			
				Middle Wallop, 15 Flt, 667, 132 Flt, AFWF. Stored.			3-04
☐	XX543		Bulldog T.1	G-CBAB, ex Shawbury, York UAS, 6 FTS,			
				York UAS, RNEFTS, CFS. *Donna.*			2-04
☐	3349		NA-64 Yale	G-BYNF, N55904, ex N55904, Canada, RCAF.			
				First engine runs 2-03.		®	3-04
☐	9893		Bolingbroke IVTex Canada. RCAF 'TT' stripes.		[3]	3-04
☐	'42161'		Silver Star	G-TBRD, ex N33VC, Switzerland, G-JETT,			
			Mk.3	✈ G-OAHB, CF-IHB, CAF 133261, RCAF 21261.			
				'Official' first flight post restoration 4-4-01.		➡ GA	3-04
☐	119		T-28B Fennec	N14113, ex USA, Haiti AF 1236, N14113, FAF			
				✈ (No.119), USAF 51-7545. *Little Rascal.*		RR	3-04
☐	1747		Harvard IV	✈ G-BGPB, ex '20385' North Weald, Port AF			
				1747, WGAF BF+050, AA+050, 53-4619.			
				PortAF colours. *Taz.*		➡	3-04
☐	8178		F-86A-5-NA	✈ G-SABR, ex Bournemouth, N178, N68388,			
	'FU-178'		Sabre	48-0178. 4th FW colours. Reflew 13 6-02.		➡ GA	3-04
☐	'1164'		Beech 18 3TM	G-BKGL, ex Prestwick, CF-QPD, RCAF 5193,			
				✈ RCAF 1564. USAAC colours.		➡	2-04

B-17 Preservation Ltd / B-17 Charitable Trust: Lifeblood of the operation of this flying memorial and icon is the *Sally B Supporters' Club* – membership details from the contacts below. The club holds a variety of exclusive events and publishes the excellent *Sally B News*.
✉ PO Box 92, Bury St Edmunds, IP28 8RR ☎ 01638 721304 fax 01638 720506 e-mail sallyb@B-17preservation.demon.co.uk www.deltaweb.co.uk/sallyb

☐	'124485'		B-17G-105-VE ✈	G-BEDF, ex N17TE, IGN F-BGSR, 44-85784.			
	'DF-A'		Flying Fortress	*Sally B* (port), *Memphis Belle* (stb).			3-04

The Fighter Collection (TFC): Pete Kynsey was at the controls of Hurricane IV G-HURY at Earls Colne, Essex, on 8th July 2003 when it took to the air for the first time. Restored for TFC by Hawker Restorations (see under Sudbury, Suffolk), the Hurricane was ferried to Duxford the following day.
Notes: P-47 *No Guts, No Glory* is a composite airframe. It is based upon elements of P-47D N47DD (45-49192), a P-47N fuselage and other components. The original N47DD is also the basis for the static P-47D to be found in the American Air Museum, see above [1]. The 'P-51B' is a heavily-modified former Israeli AF/DF P-51D fuselage, fitted with the wings of a P-51B, also found in Israel [2]. Aircraft marked ➡ attended the '100 Years of Flight Experience' static display at the International Air Tattoo, Fairford, Glos, July 2003.
Departures: Mosquito T.3 TV959 departed by road 12-6-03 for preparation in a Norfolk workshop before export to the USA. Spitfire XIV SM832 (G-WWII) returned from France 19-3-02 where it had been operated as F-AZJS and was operated by TFC on behalf of the Friedkin Family Chino Warbirds Collection. It was crated for dispatch to the USA 1-04. AD-4NA Skyraider 126922 (G-RAID) was acquired by Kennet Aviation and flew to North Weald, Essex, as G-RADR on 27-1-04.

◆ Hangar open to the public during normal museum hours. TFC stages the annual 'Flying Legends' airshow and operates **Friends of the Fighter Collection** as a support group. ✉ c/o IWM, Duxford Airfield, Duxford, Cambs, CB2 4QR

❑	G-AKAZ'57-H'	L-4A-PI Cub	↣	ex F-BFYL, ALAT, 42-36375. USAAF c/s.	3-04
❑	G-AWAH	Baron D55	↣	'hack'.	3-04
❑	G-AYGE	SNCAN SV-4C	↣	ex F-BCGM.	3-04
❑	'D8084' 'S'	Bristol F.2b	↣	G-ACAA, ex Hatch, Weston-o-t-Green. 139 Sqn c/s.	3-04
❑	N5903	Gladiator II		G-GLAD, ex Yeovilton, 'N2276', 'N5226', Old Warden, 61 OTU.	® 3-04
❑	S1581 '573'	Nimrod I	↣	G-BWWK, ex St Leonards-on-Sea, St Just, Henlow, ?, 802. 802 Sqn colours.	3-02
❑	EP120 'AE-A'	Spitfire V	↣	G-LFVB, ex Audley End, Duxford, St Athan 8070M, Wattisham, Boulmer, Wilmslow, St Athan, 5377M, 53 OTU, 402, 501. *City of Winnipeg* , 402 Sqn c/s.	3-04
❑	FE695 '94'	Harvard IIB	↣	G-BTXI, ex Vasteras, RSwAF Fv16105, RCAF, 6 SFTS, RAF FE695, 42-892.	3-04
❑	'KD345' 'A-130'	FG-1D Corsair	↣	G-FGID, ex N8297, N9154Z, USN 88297. 1850 Sqn, SEAC colours.	3-04
❑	KZ321 'JV-N'	Hurricane IV	↣	G-HURY, ex Earls Colne, Biggin Hill, Bitteswell, Blackbushe, Israel, Yugoslav AF, RAF. 6 Sqn c/s. First flown 8-7-03, arrived 9-7-03.	3-04
❑	'MV268' 'JE-J'	Spitfire XIV	↣	G-SPIT, ex Sleaford, Blackbushe, G-BGHB ntu, Bangalore, Indian inst T20, Indian AF, MV293 ACSEA. 'Johnnie' Johnson colours by 4-01.	3-04
❑	PK624	Spitfire F.22		ex St Athan, Abingdon 8072M, Northolt, Uxbridge, North Weald, 'WP916', 9 MU, 614. Stored.	3-04
❑	RK858	Spitfire IX		ex CIS, USSR, RK858 no RAF service. Stored.	3-04
❑	VX653	Sea Fury FB.11		G-BUCM, ex Hendon, Yeovilton, Lee-on-Solent, Lossiemouth, FRU, 811, 738, 736.	® 3-04
❑	– 'F'	FM-2 Wildcat	↣	G-RUMW, ex USA N4845V, 86711. FAA colours.	➡ 3-04
❑	– 'VO-B'	B-25D-30-ND	↣	G-BYDR, N88972, ex CF-OGQ, KL161 5 OTU (RCAF), 43-3318. *Grumpy* (port). 98 Sqn c/s.	3-04
❑	'A19-144'	Beaufighter Mk.21		ex Melbourne, Sydney, RAAF A8-324.	® 3-04
❑	– 'LG+01'	Bü 133C Jungmeister	↣	G-AYSJ, ex D-EHVP, G-AYSJ, HB-MIW, Swiss AF U-91. Luftwaffe colours.	3-04
❑		Ki-43 Hyabusa		ex Australia. Stored.	1-02
❑	'20'	Lavochkin La-11		ex Monino, CIS, USSR. Stored	1-02
❑	'69'	Yak-50	↣	G-BTZB, ex USSR.	9-03
❑	–	P-40		ex USSR. Substantial remains. Stored.	1-02
❑	–	Yak-3U		G-BTHD, ex Russia, Duxford, LET-built C-11 La Ferté Alais, Egyptian AF 533.	3-04
❑	'40467' '19'	F6F-5K Hellcat	↣	G-BTCC, ex N10CN ntu, N100TF, Yankee Air Corps, N80142, USMC Museum, 80141.	3-04
❑	80425 'WT-4'	F7F-3P Tigercat	↣	G-RUMT, N7235C, ex Chino, Butler, USN 80425. VMP-254 colours.	3-04
❑	21714 '201'	F8F-2P Bearcat	↣	G-RUMM, ex NX700HL, N1YY, N4995V, 121714. VF-20 c/s, Lt/Cdr 'Whiff' Caldwell's a/c.	3-04
❑	219993	P-39Q-5-BE		N139DP, ex Santa Monica, Australia, New Zealand, New Guinea, 82nd TRS'71st TRG. *Brooklyn Bum.*	due
❑	'226671' 'MX-X'	P-47D/N	↣	G-THUN, ex N47DD, 45-49192. Composite. *No Guts, No Glory.* 78th FG colours.	[1] 3-04
❑	'2106449'	P-51C		G-PSIC, ex N51PR, Chino. Composite. *Princess Elizabeth*, 352nd FG colours.	[2] 3-04
❑	463864*	P-51D-20-NA	↣	G-CBNM, ex Sweden SE-BKG, N42805, N251L, IDF/AF3506, RSwAF Fv26158, USAAF 44-63864, 78th FG. *Twilight Tear*. Arrived 5-4-02.	➡ 3-04
❑	– '49'	P-40M-10-CU	↣	G-KITT, ex 'P8196', F-AZPJ, Duxford, N1009N, 'FR870', N1233N, RCAF 840, 43-5802. 343rd FG c/s.	➡ 3-04

Historic Aircraft Collection of Jersey (HAC): From this edition gets its own entry, having been previously listed under ARCo. The Hurricane was re-fabriced during the winter of 2003/2004 and both it and the Spitfire were due to take on new markings for 2004 [1]. The Chipmunk attended the '100 Years of Flight Experience' static at Fairford, Glos, July 2003 [2]. (See under Sudbury, Suffolk, for HAC's Yak-1 project and St Leonards-on-Sea, East Sussex, for details of HAC's closely-related Aero Vintage.)

❑ 'Z5140'		Hurricane XII	✈ G-HURI, ex 'Z7381', TFC, Coningsby, Coventry,		
			Canada. 71	[1]	3-04
❑ BM597		Spitfire Vb	✈ G-MKVB, ex Audley End, Fulbourne,		
'JH-C'			Church Fenton, Linton-on-Ouse, Church		
			Fenton, St Athan, 5713M, 58 OTU, 317.	[1]	3-04
❑ WZ879	'73'	Chipmunk T.10	ex Newton, CFS, RAFC, CFS, 3 FTS, RAFC, CFS,		
G-BWUT		✈	2 FTS, Benson SF, PFTS, AOTS, Wales UAS, AOTS,		
			PFS, AOTS, 1 ITS, Leeds UAS, Nott UAS, RAFC,		
			Marham SF, BCCF, Marham SF, BCCF.	[2]	3-04
❑ 'TA+RC'		MS.505	✈ G-BPHZ, ex F-BJQC, French mil. Luftwaffe c/s.		3-04

Historic Flying Ltd: HFL's hangar and much of their operational flying is shared with ARCo (see above). Only aircraft operated, or being restored by, HFL are given here. Spitfire XIV RN201 made its first post-restoration flight on 24th April 2002 in the hands of ARCo's John Romain.
    Notes: Tr.IX PV202 is being restored for ARCo and wears Irish Army Air Corps colours. It was engine running in late February 2004 [1]. Mk.XVI TD248 and Chipmunk WB569 are the personal mounts of HFL's owner, Karel Bos [2]. (See also under Flixton, Suffolk for 'another' TD248.) The former Burmese Spitfire is also theirs and is very likely ex-MH750 [3]. Aircraft marked ➠ attended the '100 Years of Flight Experience' display at Fairford, Glos, July 2003.
    Departures: Canadian Ed Russell acquired Harvard IIB FE992 (G-BDAM) and Spitfire IX MK912 (G-BRRA) during 2003 and on 11th September both were shipped to Niagara South, Ontario.
◆ *Not* available to public inspection, although the flyers regularly make appearances at airshows.

❑ JG891*		Spitfire Vc	ZK-MKV, ex Audley End, Auckland, RAAF A58-178,		
			79, RAF JG891. Accident 1-44.	®	3-04
❑ RN201		Spitfire XIV	✈ G-BSKP, ex Audley End, Sandown, Audley End,		
			Duxford, Paddock Wood, Audley End, Ludham,		
			Beauvechain 'SG-3', Belg AF SG-31, RAF, 350,		
			83 GSU, RN201. First flew 24-4-02.		
			41 Sqn 'racing' colours.	➠	3-04
❑ TD248	'D'	Spitfire XVI	✈ G-OXVI, ex Audley End, Braintree, Earls Colne,		
			Sealand, Hooton Park 7246M, 610, 2 CAACU,		
			695. 41 Sqn 'racing' colours.	[2]	3-04
❑ SM845		Spitfire XVIII	✈ G-BUOS, ex Audley End, Witney, USA,		
'GZ-J'			Ind AF HS687, SM845. 32 Squadron colours.	➠	3-04
❑ WB569		Chipmunk T.10	G-BYSJ, ex SE-BON, WB569, 1 AEF, Camb UAS,		
		✈	Ox UAS, South Cerney SF, RAFTC CF, 4 SoTT,		
			22 GCF, 2 SoTT, 22 RFS, Cam UAS, 22 RFS.	[2]	3-04
❑ WK522		Chipmunk T.10	G-BCOU, ex Audley End, Abn AUS, Lpl UAS,		
			Man UAS, Gla UAS, Bri UAS, 3 RFS,		
			5 BFTS. *Thunderbird 5*. CoA 30-3-95.	®	3-04
❑ 'UB424'*		Spitfire IX	ex USA, Myanmar, Burma AF UB425, Israel DF/AF,		
			RAF. Arrived 14-6-02. Stored.	[3]	3-04
❑ 161		Spitfire Tr.IX	G-CCCA, ex G-TRIX, Goodwood, G-BHGH ntu,		
			IAAC 161, G-15-174, PV202, 412, 33. IAAC c/s.	® [1]	3-04

Old Flying Machine Company (OFMC) / **Classic Aviation** (CA): In early May 2003, it was announced that the season would be the last for the Breitling Fighters Team. Restoration of OFMC's Lavochkin La-9 ZK-LIX (previously G-BWUD) was finished in early 2003 and it first flew at Papakura, New Zealand, on 1st March. Arriving at Duxford on 8th June, it made its public debut at the Paris Airshow at Le Bourget and its UK debut at 'Flying Legends' in July. Sadly, its stay in the UK was not long, it was crated in January 2004 and exported to New Zealand. Corsair NZ5648 attended the '100 Years of Flight Experience' static display at the International Air Tattoo, Fairford, Glos, July 2003. Alain de Cadenet's Spitfire XVI became a resident, under the 'wing' of OFMC, during March 2004. Like TE184, several aircraft 'lodge' with OFMC, these are marked ≠.

Departures: PT-17 G-BTGA sold in New Zealand in January 2003. Yak-50 G-BWFM no longer resident by June 2002. Hunter F.6A XF375 moved to Spanhoe Lodge, Northants, 18-11-2002. Hunter T.8C 'XJ615' (G-BWGL) moved to Exeter, Devon, in late 2002. In mid-December 2003 three aircraft were crated for export to New Zealand: P-40E NZ3009 (ZK-RMH, briefly allocated G-CCBE); long-stored Yak-3U G-BWOE; FG-1D Corsair NZ5648 (G-BXUL). L.39ZO '111' (G-OTAF) was sold to a private owner, but continued to be based at Duxford. It suffered a forced-landing nearby on 2nd August 2003 and was written off. The pilot was OK. Broussard No.316 (F-GGKR) returned to France in 2000.
◆ Aircraft on show to the public during normal museum hours. OFMC run **The Tiger Squadron**, a support group for their activities which includes a newsletter *Tiger Tales*. ✉ Tiger Squadron, The Old Flying Machine Co, Duxford Airfield, Duxford, CB2 4QR www.ofmc.co.uk

❑ LN-AMY		AT-6D Texan	ex Norway, LN-LCS ntu, LN-LCN ntu, N10595, ✈ 42-85068. .	3-04
❑ MH434		Spitfire IX	✈ G-ASJV, ex Booker, COGEA Nouvelle OO-ARA, Belgian AF SM-41, Fokker B-13, Netherlands H-68, H-105 322, MH434, 349, 84 GSU, 222, 350, 222.	3-04
❑ TE184*	'C'	Spitfire XVI	✈ G-MXVI, ex Halton, North Weald, St Merryn, Holywood, Aldergrove, Finningley, Cranwell, Henlow, Bicester, Royton. Arrived 16-3-04.	≠ 3-04
❑ XV474	'T'	Phantom FGR.2	ex Wattisham, 74, 56, 23, 56, 23, 19, 2, 31, 17. 74 Sqn colours.	3-04
❑ 517692		T-28A Fennec	✈ G-TROY, ex F-AZFR, AdA Fennec No.142, 51-7692. EALA 09/72 c/s.	≠ 3-04
❑		A6M *Zeke*	ex Russia (?), USA, Pacific. Stored.	3-04
❑ E3B-153		Jungmann	✈ G-BPTS, ex Spanish AF.	≠ 3-04
❑ '463221' 'B7-H'		P-51D-25-NA	✈ G-BTCD, ex TFC, N51JJ, N6340T, RCAF 9568, USAAF 44-73149. *Ferocious Frankie*.	3-04

Plane Sailing Ltd: After a long search, Paul Warren Wilson and team settled upon another Catalina for operation in the UK. It will fly in 'waterbomber' colours for the 2004 season.
✉ Duxford Airfield, Duxford, CB2 4QR. ☎ / fax 01223 837011 e-mail 106324.64 @compuserve.com

❑ C-FNJF*	Canso A	✈ G-PBYA, ex CF-NJF, F-ZBBD, CF-NJF, F-ZBAY, CF-NJF,RCAF 11005. Arrived 30-3-04.	4-04

Others: A series of aircraft are also resident. Owner/operator decodes are follows: Carolyn Grace (CG); Classic Wings (CW); Mark Miller and friends (MM). The Rapide emerged from its workshop on 23rd February 2003 and moved to Hangar 5. HG691 attended the '100 Years of Flight Experience' static display at the International Air Tattoo, Fairford, Glos, July 2003 ➡. The Meteor T.7 may only be transiting, as it is reported to have been sold in California, USA [1]. The pod of Vampire T.11 XH328 moved to London Colney, Herts, in June 2003. Gary Numan's Harvard II G-AZSC returned to North Weald, Essex, by 2002.

❑ G-ACMN		Leopard Moth	ex X9381, 9GCF, Netheravon SF, 297, ✈ 7 AACU, 6 AACU, 24, G-ACMN.	CG	3-04
❑ G-AGJG		Dragon Rapide	ex X7344, 1 Cam Flt. CoA 15-5-74.	® MM	3-04
❑ G-APAO		Tiger Moth	✈ ex R4922, 6 FTS, 7 EFTS.	CW	3-04
❑ G-AVGG		Cherokee 140	ex Leeds-Bradford. Crashed 10-8-70. Hulk.		2-00
❑ HG691		Dragon Rapide	✈ G-AIYR, ex HG691, Yatesbury SF. *Classic Lady*.	➡ CW	3-04
❑ ML407	'OU-V'	Spitfire Tr IX	✈ G-LFIX, ex Audley End, Goodwood, St Merryn, Strathallan, IAAC 162, G-15-175, ML407, 29 MU, 332, 485, 349, 341, 485. *Aon*. 485 Sqn colours.	CG	3-04
❑ WF877* G-BPOA		Meteor T.7 (mod)	ex Washington, Kemble, North Weald, Higher Blagdon, Tarrant Rushton, Chilbolton, Folland, Gloster, 96, Meteor Flight Wunstorf, 11. Arrived 18-9-03.	[1]	9-03

ELY on the A10 north-east of Cambridge
William Collins:

❑ XS791	Andover CC.2	ex Bruntingthorpe, Northolt, 32, 60, FEAF VIP Flt, 48, FECS, MECS, Abingdon SF. Cockpit.	1-04

No.1094 Squadron, ATC: Located at the former RAF Hospital. Work to restore the PAX continues apace with a full set of cowlings and bearers allowing for the refit of a more or less complete front end.
e-mail adj@1094sqnatc.org

❏ WG362	Chipmunk T.10 PAX	8630M/8437M, ex Newton, Swinderby, Filton, Bir UAS, Wales UAS, Ox UAS, Swanton Morley SF, Carlisle SF, Mildenhall CF, 100, Edn UAS, 3 BFTS, 16 RFS, 3 BFTS, 7 RFS.	® 1-04

EVERSDEN on the A603 west of Cambridge
At this *private* location, by June 2003, Tiger Moth G-ADJJ had moved to Chilbolton, Hants. Some of the references here are decidedly long-in-the-tooth.

❏ G-AYBV	Tourbillon	unfinished homebuild project. Stored.	11-99
❏ G-AZDY*	Tiger Moth	ex F-BGDJ, French AF, PG650. CoA 18-8-97.	2-01
❏ G-BAXV	Cessna F.150L	ex Bredhurst, Eversden, Sandtoft. Crashed 25-7-82.	4-95
❏ G-BKKS	Mercury Dart	unfinished homebuild project. Stored.	4-95
❏ G-GREG*	CEA DR.220	ex F-BOKR. CoA 19-2-91. Stored.	2-01

GAMLINGAY on the B1040 south-east of St Neots
By 2001 UH-12E-4 G-ASAZ was flying again. It is not known if its 'spares ship' has followed it north to its new base at Sherburn, Yorks.

❏ G-BBAZ	Hiller UH-12E	ex EC-DOR, G-BBAZ, N31707, CAF CH-112 112276, RCAF 10276. CoA 23-5-91. Stored.	2-00

GLATTON on the B660 south of Peterborough
Unaccounted for in *W&R18*, Piranha G-BKOT was to be found at Little Gransden, Cambs, by September 2002 at the latest.

❏ G-MJBN	Rainbow Eagle	stored.	7-95

GRANSDEN LODGE AERODROME north of the B1046 north-east of Gamlingay

❏ XA243	Grasshopper TX.1	ex St Athan 8886M, Bournemouth. Stored, poor.	4-03

HOUGHTON on the A1123 east of Huntingdon
Jon Wilson: Keeps his Canberra nose in the area.

❏ WJ567	Canberra B.2	ex Wyton, 100, 85, MinTech, 45, RNZAF, 45, 59, 149. Nose.	9-04

LITTLE GRANSDEN AERODROME south of the B1046, south of Great Gransden
Yak UK Ltd: Nipper 2 G-ASZV, last noted September 1997, has moved on, possibly to Cheshire. EKW C-3605 C-558 moved briefly to 'Norwich' and by September 2002 to Spanhoe Lodge, Northants.
♦ Visits are *strictly* by prior arrangement only.

❏ G-AIRI	Tiger Moth	ex N5488, 29 EFTS, 14 EFTS, 20 ERFTS. CoA 9-11-81. Stored.	10-03
❏ G-BIRI	Jungmann	ex E3B-113. CoA 20-10-94. Stored.	10-03
❏ G-BKOT*	WA.81 Piranha	ex Glatton, Eversden, F-GAIP. First noted 9-02.	9-03
❏ G-KEAC	Queen Air A80	ex G-REXY, G-AVNG, D-ILBO. CoA 18-8-89. Dismantled, stored.	10-03
❏ G-TINY*	Zlin Z.526F	ex OK-CMD, G-TINY, YR-ZAD. CoA 17-8-98.	9-03
❏ LY-ALJ	Yak-52	ex DOSAAF 132. Wreck, first noted 5-01.	9-03

LITTLE STAUGHTON AERODROME south of the A45, west of Eaton Socon

❏ G-ARAU	Cessna 150	ex Willingham, Sibson, Land's End, N6494T. Damaged 23-5-82.	9-96

❏ G-ARRG	Cessna 175B	ex Kimbolton, Great Yarmouth, N8299T. Dam 3-11-70.	2-00
❏ G-ARSB	Cessna 150A	ex Willingham, N7237X. CoA 10-6-88. Fuselage.	2-00
❏ G-BBVG	Aztec 250C	ex ET-AEB, 5Y-AAT. CoA 10-9-88. Derelict.	2-00
❏ SE-GVH	Tomahawk 112	ex Chessington. Stored.	2-00
❏ 1360*	Chipmunk T.20	G-BYYU, ex Bedford, Spanhoe, CS-DAP ntu, Cascais, Port AF. Stored.	4-02

MARCH on the A141 south of Wisbech
No.1220 Squadron Air Cadets: Have their HQ in Gas Road. 'Parent' is Wittering. The unit have an anonymous Cadet TX.3. No sign of the Harrier however...

❏ XZ990	Harrier GR.3	ex Wittering, 233 OCU, 3, 4, 3. Cr 14-5-92. Nose.	8-95
❏ –*	Cadet TX.3	dismantled. First noted 5-03.	5-03

PETERBOROUGH BUSINESS AERODROME or Conington, E of the A1, S of Wansford
❏ G-AVBP	Cherokee 140	Crashed 14-8-96. Stored.	4-97

PETERBOROUGH SPORT AERODROME or Sibson, west of the A1, south of Wansford
❏ G-ARBN	Apache 160	ex EI-AKI, N3421P ntu. Damaged 8-86. Stored.	8-03
❏ G-ARMA	Apache 160G	ex Oxford, N4448P. CoA 22-7-77.	® 10-02
❏ G-ATMU	Apache 160G	ex Beccles, Southend, N4478P. CoA 14-4-90. Fuselage, sectioned.	8-03
❏ G-ATNV	Comanche 260	ex N8896P. CoA 3-7-93.	® 9-01
❏ G-AWSD	Cessna F.150J	Damaged 16-10-87. Stored.	3-98
❏ G-AYRP	Cessna FA.150L	Crashed 1-8-87. Stored.	3-98
❏ G-BIHE	Cessna FA.152	Damaged 10-3-99. Stored.	10-01
❏ G-BDNR	Cessna FRA.150M	Damaged 22-1-92. Rebuild, wings of G-AYRP above.	10-01
❏ G-HUNY	Cessna F.150G	ex G-AVGL. Damaged 16-10-87. Stored.	10-97

ST IVES on the A1123 east of Huntingdon
The Stirling Project: Former Stirling pilot Brian Harris, project leader Giuseppe Lombardi, and others have established themselves to recreate the forward fuselage of a Short Stirling. They have gained a new workshop in the general area with extra facilities and comforts! An FN.5 nose turret is already on hand. Work is underway on the instrument panel presently.
◆ Visits by prior arrangement *only*. ✉ 9 Taylors Lane, Swavesey, Cambs, CB4 5QN ☎ 01954 200326 e-mail enquiries@stirlingproject.co.uk www.stirlingproject.co.uk

Others: David Collings *should* still have the B-2. Airedale G-ASBY has moved on, to Ashford, Kent.

❏ G-ADFV	Blackburn B-2	ex Breighton, E' Kirkby, Tattershall, Wigan, Caterham, 2893M, 4 EFTS, Hanworth. CoA 26-6-41. off site ®	7-01

WATERBEACH on the A10 north of Cambridge
No.39 Engineers Regiment: The Hunter reminds one and all of a different era at this location.

❏ WN904	Hunter F.2	ex Duxford, Newton 7544M, 257. Gate. 1 Sqn c/s.	10-02

WHITTLESEY on the A605 east of Peterborough
The Auster remains in long term store as a 'retirement project'.

❏ G-AOGV	J/5R Alpine	CoA 17-7-72. Stored.	12-97

WITCHFORD south of the A142 south west of Ely
RAF Witchford Museum: The former bomber airfield is now the Lancaster Way Business Park, with access off the A142. An excellent museum dedicated to RAF Witchford and nearby RAF Mepal and the units that served from them has been established within the foyer of the Grovemere Building within the

estate. Included in the displays is a Bristol Hercules engine from a 115 Squadron Lancaster II that was recovered in 1995. Also within the business park is a memorial to 115 Squadron.
◆ Open weekdays and Sundays 10am to 4.30pm May to September, by kind permission of Grovemere Holdings Ltd. ☎ 01353 666666

WITTERING AIRFIELD on the A1 south of Stamford
RAF Wittering: The Harrier Maintenance Training School (HMTS) cherishes the GR.1. The T.4 will go on display outside 20 Squadron's HQ [1].

❏ XV279	Harrier GR.1	8566M, ex Farnborough, Culdrose, A&AEE. HMTS		3-01
❏ XV779	Harrier GR.3	8931M, ex 233 OCU, 3, Wittering SF, 3, 20,		
		GR.1, 20, 4, 1. 20 Sqn colours. Gate.		3-04
❏ XW923	Harrier GR.3	8724M, ex 1417 Flt, 233 OCU, 1, GR.1, 1.		
		Nose. Crashed 26-5-81.		5-00
❏ XZ146	'S' Harrier T.4	9281M, ex North Luffenham, Shawbury, 20,		
		233 OCU, Gutersloh SF, 233 OCU, 4. 20 Sqn c/s.	[1]	3-02

Locally: Four Bulldogs, gifted by Prince Feisal of Jordan arrived air freight through Wittering and have been placed in store for the **British Disabled Flying Club** who plan to operate them in due course.

❏ 408*	JY-BAI	Bulldog 125	ex RJAF. Arrived 11-03. Stored.	1-04
❏ 417*		Bulldog 125A	ex RJAF. Arrived 11-03. Stored.	1-04
❏ 418*		Bulldog 125A	ex RJAF. Arrived 11-03. Stored.	1-04
❏ 420*		Bulldog 125A	ex RJAF. Arrived 11-03. Stored.	1-04

WOODHURST north of St Ives, west of the B1040
Chris Cannon: Still has the Canberra nose.

❏ WE113	Canberra B.2	ex Wyton, 231 OCU, 100, 85, 98, 231 OCU. Nose.	6-00

WYTON AIRFIELD on the B1090 north-west of St Ives
RAF Wyton: The forward fuselage of Canberra T.17 WJ633 is now on the dump. It is a composite with parts of PR.7 [1]. AV-8B 162730 returned to <u>St Athan</u>, Wales, by January 2004.

❏ WJ633	'EF'	Canberra T.17	ex St Athan, Wyton, 360, 231 OCU, 100. Dump.	[1] 12-03
❏ WT519	'CH'	Canberra PR.7	ex 100, 13, A&AEE, 31. Dump.	12-03
❏ XH170		Canberra PR.9	8739M, ex 39, RAE, 58. Gate guardian.	12-03

CHESHIRE

BURTONWOOD south of the M62, west of Warrington
RAF Burtonwood Heritage Centre: Very little of the once huge USAF Burtonwood air base remains, though cars that hurtle down the M62 are following the course of the main runway. Hangars to the north of the motorway are the most obvious survivors. The heritage centre serves to set this to rights and has amassed an incredible amount of artefacts and images to tell the tale of this great airfield. To further tempt, there is a cafe, shop and a cinema.
◆ Open every Sunday 2pm to 5pm or by prior arrangement. Access off the M62, Junction 8 and singed. Or from Warrington, turn north off the A57 up Whittle Avenue and follow the signs. ✉ RAF Burtonwood Heritage Centre, Door 5, RAF Burtonwood, Whittle Avenue, Chapelford, Warrington WA5 3AW ☎ 01925 850130 or 01925 725469

CHELFORD on the A537 west of Macclesfield
Fuji FA-200 G-BCNZ was flying again – from Barton, Gtr Man – by February 2002.

CHESTER

Ian Starnes: The 'JP' and trailer-mounted Vampire pod are both are kept in the vicinity.

❏ XD452	'66' Vampire T.11	ex Whixhall, Whitchurch, London Colney, Shawbury, 7990M, 3 FTS, 7 FTS, 1 FTS, 8 FTS, 5 FTS. Pod.	2-04
❏ XR654	Jet Provost T.4	ex Barton, Chelford, Macclesfield, Bournemouth, Coventry, Puckeridge, Hatfield, Shawbury, CAW, 3 FTS, 6 FTS. Nose.	2-04

A Vampire is stored, pod in one location and 'metal bits' in another, in this general area.

❏ XH312	'18' Vampire T.11	ex Knutsford, Woodford, Hawarden, St Athan, 8 FTS.	2-04

HOOTON PARK south of Junction 6 of the M53, near Eastham Locks

Hooton Park Trust (HPT): The trust manages the site, with other bodies basing themselves. These include the **Griffin Trust** (GT), **The Aeroplane Collection** (TAC - see separate entry) and the newly-formed **Friends of Hooton Park** (previously the Northwest Aviation Heritage Museum). During 2002, TAC donated their Avro XIX to HPT and it has moved in the listing accordingly [1].

    Notes: The Tutor is on loan from Peter Storrar [2]. Canberra B.2 WJ676 nose was acquired by Simon Pulford of Air Pulford and was the top winner at *CockpitFest* 2003 at the Newark Air Museum in June 2003. Simon also owns the Tornado F.3 nose FSM [3]. The Hunter is on loan from Mike Davey and Graham Sparkes [4]. Mike also owns the Phantom SIM [5]. Griffin Trust have an Easy-Rider stored for them at Manchester, Gtr Man.

    Departures: An An-2 CCCP-19731 returned to <u>Chester Airport</u>, Wales, during 2002. F-4J(UK) nose ZE352 moved to <u>Preston</u>, Lancs, during 2002. The Gannet CIM from Tangmere, W Sussex, arrived here on 23rd May 2002, but moved on 20th September 2003 to 'North Wales'.

◆ By prior arrangement, plus regular special events. Access off M53, Junction 6 marked 'Eastham Oil Terminal'. Go north to a roundabout then turn right into South Road. ⊠ Hooton Park Trust, The Hangars, South Road, Hooton Park Airfield, Ellesmere Port, CH65 1BQ ☎ 0151 327 3565 **fax** 0151 327 3564 **e-mail** info@hootonparktrust.co.uk **www**.hootonparktrust.co.uk

❏ G-AGPG	Avro XIX Srs 2	ex TAC, Woodford, Brenzett, Southend, Pye, Ekco, Avro. CoA 13-12-71.		[1]	3-04
❏ –	T.8 Tutor	BGA.791, ex VM684. CoA 2-71.		[2]	8-03
❏ WF911	Canberra B.2	ex Charnock Richard, Bacup, Preston, Samlesbury, G-27-161, 231 OCU. Nose.	GT		3-04
❏ WJ676	Canberra B.2	ex Heswall, Stock, Wroughton, Colerne, Melksham, 7796M, 245, 35, 50. Nose.		[3]	3-04
❏ XE584	Hunter FGA.9	ex Woodford, Barton, Chelford, Macclesfield, Bitteswell, G-9-450, 208, 8, 1. Nose.		[4]	3-04
❏ –	BAPC.68 Hurricane FSM	ex 'H3426', Coventry, Great Bridge, Wembley, Lincoln, *Battle of Britain* 'P3975'.	GT ®		3-04
❏ –*	Phantom SIM	ex Norway, Leuchars.		[5]	3-04
❏ –*	Tornado F.3 FSM	ex Elvington, BBC *Fighter Pilot*. Nose.	off-site [3]		3-04

The Aeroplane Collection (TAC): TAC is now based at Hooton, although it still has a strong presence at the Air and Space Gallery at Manchester, Gtr Man. In August 2002 The Miles Aircraft Collection's considerable cache of Gemini and Messenger components and airframes arrived here for assessment and restoration. The aim is to create a static Gemini (to be 'labelled' G-AKHZ) and a static Messenger (likewise, G-AHUI) in a long term project. Both will be complex composites, so the occasion has been taken to 'de-identify' the pieces as they have long led to many a headache for the 'number crunchers'! Gemini components are centred on: Mk.1A G-AKHZ plus Mk.1 G-AKGD [1] and the Messenger project is centred upon Mk.2A G-AHUI, plus Mk.2 G-AILL, Mk.2A G-AJFF, Mk.2A G-AKDF, Mk.1A G-ALUG, Mk.2A EI-AGB (G-AHFP) and Mk.4A VP-KJL (G-ALAR) [2]. Anyone interested in helping, or who has leads to parts: ⊠ Keith Cooper, 12 Warren Hey, Wirral, CH63 9LF.

    Apart from the machines noted below, TAC aircraft can be found under the following headings: Barton, Gtr Man (Parker CA-4 G-AFIU), Selby, N Yorks (Fa 330A-1); Manchester, Gtr Man, (Avian, Dragon Rapide, Bensen, Roe Triplane). TAC donated Avro XIX G-AGPG to HPT during 2002 – see above. Sioux AH.1 XT242 at Doncaster, S Yorks, was sold to YHPG during January 2004.

    ⊠ Graham Sparkes, 7 Mayfield Avenue, Stretford, Manchester M32 9HL ☎ 07711 407468 **e-mail** aeroplanecol@aol.com

❏	G-AJEB	J/1N Alpha	ex Manchester, Hooton, Warmingham, Brize Norton,		
			Wigan, Cosford. CoA 27-3-69.		8-03
❏	–*	Gemini	ex Pulborough. Arrived 22-8-02. Composite.	® [1]	8-03
❏	–*	Messenger	ex Pulborough. Arrived 22-8-02. Composite.	® [2]	8-03
❏	–*	BAPC.204 McBroom hang-g	ex Winthorpe, Hooton Park, Warmingham.		8-03

MACCLESFIELD on the A523 south of Manchester
Macclesfield College: Vampire T.11 XD624 moved to Manchester Airport, Gtr Man, on 13th August 2003 ready for a starring role at the visitor centre.

MALPAS west of the A41, north-west of Whitchurch
No.617 Squadron Air Cadets: Inside Bishop Heber County High, 617 keep their Whirlwind.
❏	[XK944]	Whirlwind	ex Bristol, Lee-on-Solent, Fleetlands, Arbroath,	
		HAS.7	Fleetlands, A2607, Lossiemouth SF, Fleetlands,	
			Yeovilton, 824, *Ark Royal* .	4-02

NANTWICH west of Crewe
Hack Green Secret Nuclear Bunker: Initially a World War Two radar station, it became a labyrinthine bunker for regional government officials to run to if the 'balloon' went up and is now a three-level visitor centre. Appropriate 'Cold War' exhibit here is the **Phantom Preservation Group**'s FGR.2 nose. A restoration programme is underway. Details of PRG can be found under Ruthin, Wales.
◆ 'Brown signed' off the A530 Nantwich to Whitchurch road. Open daily mid-March to end of October. Open weekends Nov, Jan, Feb, Mar. Closed all Dec. ✉ PO Box 127, Nantwich, Cheshire, CW5 8AQ ☎ 01270 629219 **fax** 01270 629218 **e-mail** coldwar@hackgreen.co.uk
| ❏ | XV490 | Phantom FGR.2 | ex Bruntingthorpe, Wattisham, 74, 228 OCU, | | |
| | | | 92, 56, 22, 92, 56, 23. Nose. | ® | 2-04 |

STRETTON on the A49 south of Warrington
John Sykes: Jungmann G-BZJV was flying by 2002. No recent news on the Jungmeister.
| ❏ | ES1-16 | Jungmeister | ex Spanish AF. | ® | 3-94 |

CORNWALL

BODMIN AERODROME east of the A30, north of Bodmin
By March 2003 the hulks of C.150M G-BFLM, A.152 G-BHJA and M.20C N7133J had all moved on.

CALLINGTON on the A390 south-west of Tavistock
Complete with over-wing tanks, a Lightning is kept at this *private* location.
| ❏ | XR755 | 'BA' Lightning F.6 | ex Binbrook, 5, 5-11 pool. | 8-03 |

CULDROSE AIRFIELD on the A3083 south of Helston
HMS *Sea Hawk* : The **School of Flight Deck Operations** (SFDO) is the main 'user' of *W&R* airframes on the base. Also here is the **Engineering Training School** (ETS). Airframes marked ➡ attended the '100 Years of Flight Experience' static display at the International Air Tattoo, Fairford, Glos, July 2003. Wessex HAS.1 XS876 was put up for tender in February 2004 [1].
    Departures: After appearing at Fairford (see above), Harrier GR.3 XZ969 moved on to Predannack, Cornwall, by October 2003. Wessex HAS.3 XM328 attended the Fairford 'bash' as noted above, and was put up for tender in February 2004 and moved to Weston-super-Mare, Som, in late March.

◆ There is a public viewing area with shop and cafe on the B3293 to the south of the base on the way to the village of Gweek. Viewing area open Monday to Friday late March to the end of October, 9.15am to 5pm. In association with the Fleet Air Arm Museum there are regular tours of RNAS *Sea Hawk* staged from the viewing area. Tours do not run during leave periods. Enquiries ☎ 01326 565085.

❑ WF225		Sea Hawk F.1	A2623 [2], ex A2645, FRU, 738, 802. Gate	10-03
❑ XP137	'711'	Wessex HAS.3	A2634 [2], ex A2712, Culdrose,	
			Lee-on-Solent, Wroughton, 737. Stored.	10-03
❑ XR528		Wessex HC.2	ex Predannack, St Mawgan, 60, 28, 240 OCU.	10-03
❑ XS876	'523'	Wessex HAS.1	A2626 [3], ex Lee-on-Solent, A2695,	
			Wroughton, 771. Stored.	➡ [1] 10-03
❑ XS885	'512'	Wessex HAS.1	A2631 [2], ex A2668, 772.	SFDO 10-03
❑ XV359	'035'	Buccaneer S.2B	A2693 [2], ex Predannack, Lossiemouth, 208,	
			237 OCU, 12, 208, 12. 809 Sqn c/s. Displayed	10-03
❑ XV371*	'261'	Sea King HAS.1	ex Gosport, A2699 [2], Boscombe Down, A&AEE.	
			Arrived 22-7-03.	SFDO 10-03
❑ XV372		SH-3D Sea King	ex Predannack, St Mawgan, Trowbridge,	
			Yeovil, Lee-on-Solent, RAE, Westlands. Hulk.	8-02
❑ XV654*	'705'	Sea King HAS.6	ex Gosport, A2698 [2], Fleetlands, 819.	
			Crashed 21-7-93. Arrived 21-1-03.	SFDO 10-03
❑ XV657	'132'	Sea King HAS.5	A2600 [4], ex ETS, Fleetlands, Wroughton, 826.	
			Tail of ZA135.	SFDO 10-03
❑ XV741	'5'	Harrier GR.3	A2608 [3], ex A2607, Cosford, 233 OCU,	
			3, 233 OCU, 3.	SFDO 10-03
❑ XV753	'4'	Harrier GR.3	A2691 [2], ex Halton, Abingdon, 9075M,	
			St Athan, 233 OCU, 1, 3, 233 OCU.	SFDO 10-03
❑ XV783		Harrier GR.3	A2609 [3], ex Lee-on-Solent, Culdrose SAH,	
			Cosford, 233 OCU, 4, 3, 233 OCU, 1, 233 OCU,	
			1, 233 OCU, 1417 Flt, 233 OCU, 4, 20, 4.	SFDO 10-03
❑ XV808		Harrier GR.3	A2687 [2], ex 9076M, 233 OCU, 3, 20.	SFDO 10-03
❑ XW271		Harrier T.4	A2692 [2], ex Cosford, 4, 1, 233 OCU.	SFDO 10-03
❑ XX492*	'A'	Jetstream T.1	ex Cranwell, 45, 3 FTS, 45, 6 FTS, METS.	
			Arrived 22-3-04. Spares.	3-04
❑ XX500*	'H'	Jetstream T.1	ex Cranwell, 45, 3 FTS, 45, 6 FTS, METS.	
			Arrived 22-3-04. Spares.	3-04
❑ XX510	'69'	Lynx HAS.2	A2683 [2], ex Gosport, A2601, A2772,	
			Lee-on-Solent, Foulness, Boscombe Down.	SFDO 10-03
❑ XZ145		Harrier T.4	A2610 [4], ex Shawbury, 20, 233 OCU, 3.	SFDO 10-03
❑ XZ243	'635'	Lynx HAS.3	A2613 [3], ex Gosport, Portland, Lee.	
			Crashed 10-3-88.Cabin. Spares recovery.	9-01
❑ XZ996	'3'	Harrier GR.3	A2685 [2], ex 1417 Flt, 4, 1417 Flt,	
			233 OCU, 1417 Flt, 233 OCU.	SFDO 10-03
❑ ZD667		Harrier GR.3	A2684 [2], 9201M, ex 1417 Flt, 233 OCU.	SFDO 10-03
❑ ZF641		EH-101 PP1	ex Fleetlands, Westland.	SFDO 10-03
❑ –		EH-101 EMU	ex Yeovil, avionics test.	SFDO 9-03

HELSTON on the A3083 north of Culdrose
The Flambards Experience: (Note change of name.) The diaspora of exhibits here has continued. Three moved to Bruntingthorpe, Leics, on 18th December 2002: Sea Prince T.1 WF122; Sea Hawk FGA.6 XE368; Whirlwind HAR.10 XP350. Whirlwind HAS.1 XA870 was dismantled and taken out through an incredibly challenging door, moving to Doncaster, S Yorks, in November 2002. Whittaker MW.2B G-BDDX moved to Newton Abbot, Devon, during the summer of 2003. With Concorde-mania breaking out all over the UK, the Concorde items here are reported to be up for auction [1].
◆ Open most days Easter to end of Oct 10am to 5pm. Signed off the A3083 south of Helston, next to RNAS Culdrose. ⌧ Clodgey Lane, Helston, TR13 0QA ☎ 01326 573404 **fax** 01326 573344 **e-mail** info@flambards.co.uk **www**.flambards.co.uk

❑ WG511		Shackleton T.4	ex Colerne, St Mawgan, MOTU, Kinloss Wing,
			MOTU, 120, 42. Nose. 1-04

❏ XG831 '396'	Gannet ECM.6	ex Culdrose SAH-8, A2539, 831.	1-04
❏ XS887 '403'	Wessex HAS.1	ex Culdrose A2690, Wroughton, 771.	1-04
❏ –	Concorde EMU	ex Filton, instrument layout trials.	[1] 1-04

LAND'S END on the A30 south-west of Penzance

Land's End: Suspended at a dramatic angle within the complex is a Bölkow 105. It has been given a new 'identity' to tie in with the *real* G-CDBS which belongs to the Cornwall Air Ambulance and is based at St Mawgan. G-BCXO was rebuilt with a new pod and flies on as G-THLS [1]. The identity of the 'Sopwith' on display here is now confirmed [2].

◆ From 10am daily, closing times vary. ✉ Land's End, Sennen, Penzance, TR19 7AA ☎ 0870 4580044
fax 01736 871812 **e-mail** info@landsend-landmark.co.uk **www**.landsend-landmark.co.uk

❏ 'G-CDBS'	MBB Bö 105D	G-BCXO, ex 'G-BOND', D-HDCE. wfu 4-3-92.	[1] 8-03
❏ –	BAPC.137	Sopwith Baby REP ex Land's End, Chertsey.	[2] 3-02

LAND'S END AERODROME or St Just, on the B3306 south of St Just

❏ G-BFNU	BN-2B-21	CoA 18-8-89. Fuselage, stored.	10-03
❏ G-PEAL*	Pitts S-2A	ex Plymouth, N81LF, N48KA. Damaged 28-6-91.	® 10-03
❏ '124'	Fokker D.VIII REP	G-BHCA. Crashed 21-8-81. Fuselage	10-03

LELANT on the A3074 south of St Ives

The Comper is *thought* to still be in store.

❏ G-ABTC	Comper Swift	CoA 18-7-84. *Spirit of Butler*. Stored.	11-93

LISKEARD on the A38 north-west of Plymouth

Castle Motors / Helicopters: The dramatically-posed Lightning graces the car park.

❏ G-USTA	A.109A	ex G-MEAN, G-BRYL, G-ROPE, G-OAMH.	
		Damaged 27-3-99. Spares recovery.	6-01
❏ SX-HCF	A.109A Mk.II	ex Greece. Spares recovery.	6-01
❏ XS936	Lightning F.6	ex Binbrook, 5, 11, LTF, 5/11, LTF, 5, 11, 23.	10-03

PREDANNACK AIRFIELD off the A3083 south of Helston

Fleet Air Arm Fire School:

❏ WT308	Canberra B(I).6	A2601, ex Culdrose, DRA Farnborough, A&AEE.	10-03
❏ XE668 '832'	Hunter GA.11	A2647 [2], Ex A2733, Culdrose SAH,	
		Yeovilton, FRADU, 738, 26, 4.	2-02
❏ XM868 '517'	Wessex HAS.1	A2630 [2], ex A2706, Lee-on-Solent, Wroughton, 737.	2-01
❏ XM870	Wessex HAS.1	A2634 [2], ex A2712, Gosport, Lee-o-Solent, 772.	10-03
❏ XM874 '521'	Wessex HAS.1	A2629 [2], ex A2689, Lee, Culdrose, Wroughton, 771.	2-01
❏ [XP160] '521'	Wessex HAS.1	A2628 [2], ex A2650, Lee-on-Solent, Culdrose, SAH-24.	2-02
❏ XS516 'YQ'	Wessex HU.5	A2652 [2], ex Gosport, A2739, Lee-on-Solent, 845.	10-03
❏ XS522 'ZL'	Wessex HU.5	A2663 [2], ex Gosport, A2753, Lee-on-Solent,	
		Wroughton, 848.	2-02
❏ XS529 '461'	Wasp HAS.1	A2696 [2], ex A2743, Culdrose, Manadon,	
		Lee-on-Solent, 829,*Galatea* Flt. Poor state.	10-03
❏ XS866 '520'	Wessex HAS.1	A2627 [2], ex Culdrose, Lee-on-Solent A2705	
		Wroughton, 771.	10-03
❏ XS868	Wessex HAS.1	A2686 [2], ex Culdrose, Gosport, A2791,	
		Lee-on-Solent, Fleetlands, A2691, Wroughton.	10-03
❏ XS881 '046'	Wessex HAS.1	A2688 [2], ex A2675, Yeovilton, Wroughton,	
		FAAM, Yeovilton, Culdrose.	2-01
❏ XT468 '628'	Wessex HU.5	A2667 [2], ex A2744, ex Culdrose, Gosport,	
		Lee-on-Solent, Wroughton, 772.	10-03
❏ XT762	Wessex HU.5	A2661 [2], ex Culdrose A2751, Lee-on-Solent,	
		Wroughton, RAE.	10-03

❏	XV786	'S'	Harrier GR.3	A2611 [3], ex Culdrose, A2615, St Athan, 3, 4, 1, 4.	10-03
❏	XX479	'563'	Jetstream T.2	A2611 [4], ex St Athan, 750, CFS, 5 FTS,	10-03
				Sywell, Radlett, G-AXXT.	
❏	XZ969*	'D'	Harrier GR.3	A2612 [3], ex Culdrose, A2610, Manadon, St Athan,	
				4, 1, 3. First noted 10-03.	10-03
❏	ZD631	'66'	Sea King HAS.6	A2621 [2], ex Gosport, Lee-on-Solent.	10-03
❏	ZH807*		Sea Harrier FA/2	ex St Athan, Yeovilton, 809. Arrived 9-10-03.	10-03

ST AUSTELL on the A390 north-east of Truro
The Shackleton is for sale. Nimrod MR.2 XV237 forward fuselage is believed to have been processed.

❏	WL756		Shackleton AEW.2	ex St Mawgan 9101M, 8, 204, 205, 37, 38. Nose.	6-02

ST MAWGAN AIRFIELD off the A3059, north-east of Newquay
RAF St Mawgan: There is a sensational 'synthetic' fire trainer here that would appear to be a cross between a Harrier and a Sea King! The Sea King HAS.6 is plinth-mounted for training with the **School of Combat Survival and Rescue** [1].

❏	WL795	'T'	Shackleton AEW.2	8753M, ex 8, 205, 38, 204, 210, 269, 204.	8-03
❏	XV709	'263'	Sea King HAS.6	ex Gosport, 810, 706, 820, 826, 820, 814, 706.	[1] 1-04

Barry Wallond: Aviation artist Barry displays a Spitfire FSM in his garden.

❏	N3317	'AI-A'	Spitfire IX FSM	BAPC.268, ex Duxford, *Dark Blue World*.	9-03

ST MERRYN AERODROME on the B3276 west of Padstow
Mosquito gyroplane G-AWIF was flying again by mid-2003. The McCandless G-ARTZ is the second user of the 'reggie'. See photo in Holywood, N Ireland for the other [1].

❏	G-ARTZ {2}	McCandless M4	Stored. CoA 13-10-69.	[1] 10-00
❏	'G-ATCX'	Cessna 182A	G-OLSC, ex G-ATNU, EI-ANC, N6078B.	
			Crashed 6-6-93. Fuselage.	10-00
❏	G-AXVN	McCandless M4	Stored.	10-00
❏	G-MLAS	Cessna 182E	ex Bodmin, OO-HPE, D-EGPE, N2826Y.	
			Damaged 14-12-80. Para-trainer.	4-99

TORPOINT on the A374, west of Plymouth, across the Tamar
HMS Releigh: Took delivery of a Wessex during 2002.

❏	XR523*	'M'	Wessex HC.2	ex Fleetlands, Gosport, Shawbury, Fleetlands, 72.	
				Arrived 6-02.	6-02

TREMAR north of the B3254, north of Liskeard
Roy Flood: The Lightning is kept in *private* grounds here. Sycamore XG544 has moved to LOST!

❏	XR751		Lightning F.3	ex Binbrook, 11, LTF, 29, 226 OCU, EE.	8-03

CUMBRIA

BARROW-IN-FURNESS
Martinis: The BD-5 (and the club!) was put up for sale in October 2003.

❏	G-BDTT	Bede BD-5	ex Tattershall Thorpe, Bourne.	10-03

CARK AERODROME south-west of Grange-over-Sands

❏	G-AWMZ	Cessna F.172H	ex Blackpool. Cr 18-1-76. Para-trainer, dumped.	9-03

CARLISLE or Kingstown, on the A7 north of the City

❑ G-AKTT	Silvaire 8A	ex N71852, NC71852. Crashed 6-7-91.	1-96

CARLISLE AIRPORT or Crosby-on-Eden, off the A689 east of Carlisle

Solway Aviation Museum / Edward Haughey Aviation Heritage Centre: Considerable work continues to be achieved within the impressive heritage centre with the displays being continually updated and refined. Improvements have also been made the workshop and storage areas.

Notes: SAM have a close relationship with Tom Stoddart, who owns Vulcan XJ823, and a share in the Sea Prince [1]. Meteor WS832 has been 'adopted' by **1862 Squadron ATC** and the unit is restoring the aircraft [2]. The Grasshopper is composite, with parts of WZ824 – see Strathaven, Scotland [3]. The Nimrod cockpit is owned by David Price [4]. The nose section of Twin Pioneer G-AYFA moved to Mold, Wales, during mid-2002.

♦ Open Apr to Oct Sundays Jun to Sep Saturdays also and July-Aug Fridays, same times. Open all Bank Hols. All days 10.30am to 5pm. ✉ 'Aviation House', Carlisle Airport, Crosby-on-Eden, Carlisle, CA6 4NW ☎/ fax / info-line 01228 573823 (the 'last three' honouring the Vulcan!) e-mail info@solway-aviation-museum.org.uk www.solway-aviation-museum.org.uk

❑ G-APLG		J/5L Aiglet Trainer	ex Maryport, Bletchley, Romsey, Southend, Rettendon, Corringham, Felthorpe. CoA 26-10-68.	®	1-04
❑ WE188		Canberra T.4	ex Samlesbury, 231 OCU, 360, 231 OCU, 360, 100,56, 231 OCU, Upwood SF, 231 OCU, Upwood SF, Waddington SF, Hemswell SF.		1-04
❑ WP314	'573'	Sea Prince T.1	ex Preston, Hull, Syerston, Halton, 8634M, Kemble, 750, Sydenham SF, 750, Lossiemouth SF, Shorts FU, Brawdy SF, Lossie SF, 750.	[1]	1-04
❑ WS832	'W'	Meteor NF.14	ex RRE Pershore, Llanbedr, 12 MU, 8 MU.	® [2]	1-04
❑ WV198	'K'	Whirlwind HAR.21	G-BJWY ex Firbeck, Warmingham, Chorley, Blackpool, Heysham, Carnforth, Gosport, Lee-on-Solent A2576, Arbroath, 781, 848, USN 130191.		1-04
❑ WZ515		Vampire T.11	ex Duxford, Staverton, Woodford, Chester, St Athan, 4 FTS, 8 FTS, 56, 253, 16.		1-04
❑ [WZ784]		G'hopper TX.1	ex Thurrock. Displayed indoors.	[3]	1-04
❑ XJ823		Vulcan B.2	ex 50, Wadd Wing, 35, 27, 9/35, Wadd Wing, 230 OCU, MoA.	[1]	1-04
❑ XV259		Nimrod AEW.3	ex Stock, Chattenden, Abingdon, Waddington, Woodford, Kin Wing, St Mawgan Wing. Nose.	[4]	1-04
❑ XV406	'CK'	Phantom FGR.2	ex Longtown, Carlisle, 9098M, St Athan, 29, 23, 111, HSA, A&AEE, HSA. On loan.		1-04
❑ ZF583		Lightning F.53	ex Warton, RSaudi AF 53-681, G-27-51. RAF c/s.		1-04

Others: Tomahawk 112 G-BRLO was flying again by early 2002.

HAVERIGG south of Millom

RAF Millom Museum: Run by the **South Copeland Aviation Group**.
The rear end of Chipmunk WD377 can also be found in a composite at Dumfries [1]. The wings of Vampire XD425 are on XD547 at Dumfries, Scotland [1].
♦ On the Bankhead Estate, North Lane, adjacent to HMP Haverigg. Open Sat, Sun, Mon, Wed and Fri 10am to 5pm during the summer. Winter Sun only. Other times by appointment. ✉ G Griffiths, 21 Holbrow Hill, Millom, LA18 5BH

❑ 'G-ADRX'		HM.14 'Flea'	BAPC.231, ex Torver, Ulverston.		3-04
❑ WD377		Chipmunk T.10	ex Dumfries, 12 AEF, Glas UAS, HCEU, 11 RFS, 2 BFTS. Cr 29-7-66. Cockpit.	® [1]	3-04
❑ XD425	'M'	Vampire T.11	ex Dumfries, West Freugh, Stranraer, Woodford, Chester, St Athan, 8 FTS, 5 FTS, 7 FTS, 202 AFS. Pod. 6 Sqn c/s.	[1]	3-04
❑ XK637	'56'	Vampire T.11	ex Royton, Woodford, Chester, St Athan, 4 FTS, 7 FTS.	®	3-04

❏ XM660		Whirlwind HAS.7	ex Sunderland, Almondbank, Fleetlands, Lee-on-Solent, Lossiemouth SAR Flt, 737, 700H, 824.	3-04
❏ XN597	'X'	Jet Provost T.3	7984M, ex Firbeck, Levenshulme, Stamford, Firbeck, Sunderland, Stoke-on-Trent, Bournemouth, Faygate, 2 FTS. Damaged 28-6-67. Nose.	3-04
❏ –	BAPC.260	HM.280	FAF colours. Touring exhibit.	3-04

KENDAL on the A685 south of Brough
Wrongly listed under 'Lancashire' in *W&R18*. A boomless Whirlwind came to a scrapyard here and is offered for sale. A collector here should still have a 'JP' procedure trainer.

| ❏ XN387* | | Whirlwind HAR.9 | – ex Spadeadam 8564M, Wroughton, Lee-on-Solent SAR Flt, Lossiemouth SF, 846, 719. | 1-04 |
| ❏ – | | Jet Provost T.3 | ex Welshpool, Elvington, Linton-on-Ouse. | 7-01 |

SPADEADAM FOREST north of the B6318, north-east of Carlisle
RAF Spadeadam / Electronic Warfare Tactics Range: A painstaking (and muddy!) visit in June 2002 succeeded in an accurate 'count' for the Mystères. The ranges are a complex series of sites centred around the former ballistic missile test/launch facility. Location codes are as follows: Prior Lancey PL; the mock airfield (also known as 'Collinski!) AF; the mock runway RW; revetment R7 RV; Wiley Sike bombing site and used as smoke bomb targets WS. The ranges have issued inventory numbers to most of the targets (and that includes armoured fighting vehicles etc). For completeness, column four gives these. They are prefixed 'SPA117', eg T-33 FT-06 is SPA117-7. Note that both FT-11 and No.180 appear to share the same inventory number! Whirlwind HAR.9 XN387 had gone by September 2003, moving to a yard at Kirkby Stephen, Cumbria.

❏ FT-01		T-33A-1-LO	–	ex Prestwick, Belgian AF, 51-4041.		6-03
❏ FT-02	'12'	T-33A-1-LO	–	ex Prestwick, Belgian AF, 51-4043.	WS	6-02
❏ FT-06	'10'	T-33A-1-LO	-7	ex Prestwick, Belgian AF, Neth AF M-44, 51-4231.	AF	6-02
❏ FT-07	'70'	T-33A-1-LO	-4	ex Prestwick, Belgian AF, Neth AF M-45, 51-4233.	AF	6-02
❏ FT-10		T-33A-1-LO	-6	ex Prestwick, Belgian AF, 51-6664.	AF	6-02
❏ FT-11		T-33A-1-LO	-8	ex Prestwick, Belgian AF, Neth AF M-47, 51-6661.	AF	6-02
❏ FT-29		T-33A-1-LO	–	ex Prestwick, Belgian AF, 53-5753.	WS	6-03
❏ 61	'38'	Mystère IVA	-2	ex Sculthorpe, FAF. Also coded '8-MI'.	RW	6-02
❏ 64 '36' + '60'		Mystère IVA	-3	ex Sculthorpe, FAF. Also coded '8-NO'.	RW	6-02
❏ 81	'8-NU'	Mystère IVA	-9	ex Sculthorpe, FAF.	AF	6-02
❏ 139	'8-MR'	Mystère IVA	-11	ex Sculthorpe, FAF.	AF	6-02
❏ 180	'MB'	Mystère IVA	-8	ex Sculthorpe, FAF.	AF	6-02
❏ 184	'87'	Mystère IVA	-10	ex Sculthorpe, FAF.	AF	6-02
❏ 207		Mystère IVA	–	ex Sculthorpe, FAF.	AF	6-02
❏ 282	'8-NW'	Mystère IVA	–	ex Sculthorpe, FAF.	AF	6-02
❏ 98+10		Su-22M-4	–	ex Farnborough, Boscombe Down, LSK-LV 820.	PL	6-03

WINDERMERE on the A592 north of Bowness on Windermere
Windermere Steamboat Centre: As well as the waterglider, two other aeronautical items are within this superb collection; a Sunderland wing float, modified into a 'canoe'; and the MV *Canfly* a 1920s speedboat powered by a Rolls-Royce Hawk from the RNAS airship SST.3.
◆ Open daily mid-March to late October 10am to 5pm. Special events and exhibitions staged. Shop and tea room, good car parking. Steamboat cruises available. ✉ Rayrigg Road, Windermere, Cumbria, LA23 1BN ☎ 015394 45565 fax 015394 48769. www.steamboat.co.uk

| ❏ – | BGA.266 | T.1 Falcon | Modified by Capt T C Pattinson DFC. f/f 3-2-43. | 1-04 |

DERBYSHIRE

CHESTERFIELD on the A61 south of Sheffield
4x4 Car Centre: On the Dronfield Road, have a former Finningley 'JP' as an attraction.
❑ XM480   '02' Jet Provost T.3   ex Finningley, Halton 8080M, 6 FTS, 1 FTS.   2-04

CLAY CROSS on the A61 south of Chesterfield
Cronifer Metals: The yard here has been very active in the processing of large amounts of scrap from St Athan, Wales, and some from Shawbury, Shropshire. The bulk of this has been Tornado GR.1s and F.2s plus some Jaguars. 'Processing' is just what happens here, with the hulks hardly languishing. A visit to the site in March 2003 found it completely clear. Refer to St Athan for details of the airframes that ended their days here.

DERBY
Derby Industrial Museum: Presents a staggering array of aero engines, nearly all of the home-spun Rolls-Royce variety, going from the Eagle to the RB.211 and is a must to visit. The rest of the museum – which is set in one of the world's first 'modern' factories, originally built in 1717 – has excellent displays on Derbyshire's industrial past. There are regular exhibitions and special events. The **Derbyshire Historical Aviation Society** works in support of the museum, on many other projects and stages regular meetings. (✉ Bill Harrison, 71 Mill Hill Lane, Derby, DE3 6SB **e-mail** williamharrison@tiscali.co.uk) The Rolls-Royce Heritage Trust, Derby and Hucknall Branch has many of its engines on show at the museum – see also below.
◆ Mon 11am to 5pm, Tue to Sat 10am to 5pm. Sun/Bank Hols 2pm to 5pm. ✉ Silk Mill Lane, off Full Street, Derby, DE1 3AR ☎ 01332 255308 **fax** 01332 716670 **e-mail** contact@derbymuseum. freeserve **www**.derby.gov.uk/museums

Rolls-Royce Heritage Trust: Located within the Rolls-Royce Learning and Development Centre in Willmore Road, the trust has established an incredible heritage exhibition of aero engines and other memorabilia during the autumn of 2001 using engines, artefacts and input from all of the branches. As well as the engines etc, a Canberra B.15 nose is on show. This flew 'ops' during the Suez crisis, 1956.
◆ Open to groups by prior arrangement *only*. ✉ PO Box 31, Derby DE24 8BJ, ☎ 01332 249118 **fax** 01332 249727, **e-mail** richard.haigh@rolls-royce.com **www**.rolls-royce.com
❑ WH960   Canberra B.15   ex Nottingham, Bruntingthorpe, Cosford 8344M,
                               Akrotiri Wing, 32, 9, 12. Nose.   2-04

Rolls-Royce Heritage Trust, Derby and Hucknall Branch and **Coventry Branch** (previously at Mickleover, Derbyshire) are busy establishing shared workshops and storage facilities in the Light Alloy Foundry within a part of the extensive Rolls-Royce complex.
◆ By prior arrangement *only*, and occasional open days. ✉ D J Piggott, ML-71, Rolls-Royce plc, PO Box 31, Derby DE24 8BJ
❑ 0767   MB.339AA   ex Mickleover, Filton, Yeovilton, Stanley, Argentine
                          Navy. FAAM loan. Stored.   2-04

Adrian Marshall: The frame of Auster J/1 G-AIJZ had moved to Northampton Airport, Northants, by late 2002. Either the Auster 6A frame or the AOP.6 frame has moved to Bruntingthorpe, Leics [1]. See also Bruntingthorpe, Leics, for the Beech 18 project.
❑ G-ASYN   Terrier 2   ex Southend, Sibson, Auster AOP.6 VF519, 661.
                             Damaged 2-1-76.   1-96
❑ –   Auster 6A   ex Hedge End, Warmingham, Wigan, Handforth. [1]   3-96
❑ –   Auster AOP.6   ex Shoreham, Hedge End, Warmingham,
                             East Kirkby, Sibson, Wigan, Handforth. c/n 1908   [1] 11-95

DERBY AERODROME or Egginton, south of the A5132 between Egginton and Hilton
Comet Racer Project Group: are making good progress with G-ACSP.
◆ Visits are possible *only* by prior arrangement. ✉ Derby Airfield, Hilton Road, Egginton, Derby, DE65 6GU ☎ 01283 733803 fax 01283 734829 **www**.cometracer.co.uk

❑ [G-ACSP]	DH.88 Comet	ex Stoke-on-Trent, Coventry / Staverton, Bodmin, Chirk, Portugal, CS-AAJ, E-1. *Black Magic*.	® 3-04

Others:

❑ G-AVLM	Pup 160	ex Shenstone, Tatenhill, Nottingham Airport, Chippenham. CoA 24-4-69. Stored.	1-02
❑ G-BHZS	Bulldog 120	ex Botswana DF 0D5, G-BHZS. CoA 8-2-99.	4-03
❑ G-SACF	Cessna 152 II	ex G-BHSZ, N47125. Crashed 21-3-97. Wreck.	5-03

RIPLEY on the A610 north-west of Nottingham
Anchor Supplies: Vampire T.11 XD382 moved to East Midlands, Leics, by October 2003.

SHARDLOW on the A6 south-east of Derby
Griffiths GH.4 G-ATGZ was last physically sighted here in July 1991. It has moved to LOST!

DEVON

BABCARY east of the A37, east of Somerton
Two Gazelle AH.1s arrived at a location in the area by April 2003. ZA730 was registered as G-FUKM (no comment) in August for a Reading Co. But ZA767 is thought to have lingered.

❑ ZA767*	Gazelle AH.1	ex Ipswich, Middle Wallop, 25F. Cr 11-9-99. Pod	4-03

BARNSTAPLE
Tim Jones: Added Tornado and Buccaneer cockpits to his collection in 2002. As Tim Andrew Jones and his 'JP' having been allocated G-ATAJ, Tim has the equivalent of a personalised number plate!
◆ By prior appointment only via e-mail timjones007@hotmail.com

❑ XS231	Jet Provost T.5	ex Ipswich, Bruntingthorpe, Bournemouth, Scampton, Shawbury, A&AEE, G-ATAJ ntu. Fuse.	9-03
❑ XX888*	Buccaneer S.2B	ex Dundonald, Ottershaw, Shawbury, St Athan, 16, 15. Nose. Sand colours. Arrived 11-02.	9-03
❑ ZD710*	Tornado GR.1	ex Welshpool, Robertsbridge, Stock, St Athan, 14. Crashed 14-9-89. Cockpit. Arrived 12-10-02.	9-03

DUNKESWELL AERODROME north of Honiton
Dunkeswell Memorial Museum: Dedicated to the history of the airfield and its resident units, including the US Navy's PB4Y-1-equipped FAW-7. Core is a collection of local artefacts, amassed since the early 1980s by founders, David Sharland, Darren Lillywhite and Rupert Fairclough. Spitfire FSM 'BR600' was not part of the collection and had gone from the site by early 2000 at the latest.
◆ Mar to Oct, Tue to Sun 10am to 6pm. Nov to Feb, Sat and Sun 10am to 6pm. ✉ Dunkeswell Aerodrome, Honiton, Devon, EX14 0RA ☎ 01404 891943

❑ XE982	Vampire T.11	ex Hereford, St Athan 7564M, RAFC.	8-03
❑ –	Gannet AS.x	cockpit section.	7-99

Aerodrome: An organisation called **Flightaid** bases itself here, raising funds through a travelling 'roadshow' that includes a Wasp [1]. They have a Cessna 'based' at Croydon, Gtr Lon - qv. J/1N Alpha had moved to Okehampton, Devon, by May 2002.

❑ G-ASSY	Turbulent	ex Redhill. Damaged 8-5-83.	® 5-93
❑ G-BJNG*	Slingsby T.67AM	CoA 23-7-01. Fuselage, stored.	7-02
❑ G-BPRV	Warrior II	ex N4292G. Crashed 29-3-97. Cockpit.	7-99
❑ XT788	'316' Wasp HAS.1	G-BMIR, ex Faygate, Tattershall Thorpe, Wroughton. [1]	7-03

EAGLESCOTT AERODROME west of the A377, north of Ashreigney

Aerodrome: The Currie Wot will re-appear in the guise of a scaled-down Pfalz D.VII! In a not unexpected move, the nose of Hunter T.7 PH-NLH was exported to the Netherlands in 2001.

❑ G-ARZW		Currie Wot	Crashed 12-2-88.	®	7-03
❑ G-BOLD		Tomahawk	ex N9740T. CoA 21-1-96. Stored.	®	3-04
❑ N24730		Tomahawk	G-BTIL. Stored, dismantled.		11-03
❑ WT744	'868'	Hunter GA.11	ex Yeovilton, FRADU, 738, 247, AFDS.		3-04
❑ WT867		Cadet TX.3	ex Syerston, 626 VGS. Stored.		3-04
❑ XA289		Cadet TX.3	ex Syerston, 636 VGS. Stored.		3-04

EXETER

Arden Family Trust: The late Bertram Arden's airframes are held in careful store in the general area.

❑ G-AALP	Surrey AL.1	CoA 17-5-40.	12-97
❑ G-AFGC	BA Swallow II	ex BK893, GTS, CLE, RAE, G-AFGC. CoA 20-3-51.	12-97
❑ G-AFHC	BA Swallow II	CoA 20-3-51.	12-97
❑ G-AJHJ	Auster V	ex NJ676, 83 GCS, 440. CoA 27-6-49.	12-97

Others: Spitfire IX RR232 (G-BRSF) moved to <u>Sandown</u>, IoW, on 11th July 2002.

❑ RX168	Seafire III	G-BWEM, ex Andover, Norwich, Battle, Dublin, IAAC 157, RX168.	12-01

EXETER AIRPORT on the A30, east of the city at Clyst Honiton

Classic Jet Aircraft Company (CJAC) / **Hunter Flying Club**: For a variety of reasons, the red colour-schemed Hunter 'WB188' (G-BZPC) did not fly as such during 2003, thereby missing the 50th anniversary of Neville Duke's world air speed record. (The *real* WB188 can be found at Tangmere, West Sussex.) Peter Hellier's Hunter F.6A XF516 (G-BVVC) encountered problems over Wales while returning from a display in Northern Ireland on 1st June 2003. The pilot, Craig Penrice, wisely elected to eject and the aircraft crashed in mid-Wales.

   Notes: CJAC operate several Hunters for other owners as well as their own. Gnat XM697 is owned by Derek Johnson and is for static restoration [1]. CJAC occasionally uses St Mawgan, Cornwall, for winter storage, but for the purposes of this entry all aircraft are noted under this heading.

◆ Visits possible *only* by prior arrangement. **www.classicjets.co.uk**

❑ 'WB188'		Hunter GA.11	G-BZPB, ex WV256, Shawbury, Yeovilton,	
		✈	FRADU, 738, 229 OCU, 26. Prototype colours.	9-02
❑ 'WB188'		Hunter GA.11	G-BZPC, ex Shawbury XF300, Yeovilton,	
			FRADU, 130, 234, 71. Record-breaker red colours.	3-02
❑ WT722	'878'	Hunter T.8C	G-BWGN, ex Shawbury, Yeovilton,	
			FRADU, 764, 703, 26, 54.	9-02
❑ WT723	'866'	Hunter PR.11	✈G-PRII, ex N723WT, A2616 [3], Culdrose,	
			FRADU, Lossiemouth SF, 14.	3-02
❑ WT799	'879'	Hunter T.8C	ex North Weald, Ipswich, Shawbury, FRADU,	
			FRU, 759, RAE, 4, 11. Stored.	11-03
❑ XE665	'876'	Hunter T.8C	✈ G-BWGM, ex Shawbury, Yeovilton,	
			FRADU, 764, Jever SF, 118.	9-02
❑ XE685	'861'	Hunter GA.11	G-GAII, ex Yeovilton, FRADU, 738, 98, 93.	
			CoA 24-6-98.	3-02
❑ XE689	'864'	Hunter GA.11	✈G-BWGK, ex North Weald, Exeter, Shawbury,	
			Yeovilton, FRADU, 234, 130, 67.	11-03
❑ XF321		Hunter T.7	A2734, ex Yeovilton A2734, Manadon A2648, RAE,	
			56, 130. Spares.	9-02
❑ 'XJ615'*		Hunter T.8C	✈ G-BWGL, ex Duxford, Exeter, XF357, Shawbury,	
			Yeovilton, FRADU, 130. Prototype T.7 colours.	1-03
❑ XJ639	'H'	Hunter F.6A	ex Ipswich, Ipswich aerodrome, Cranwell 8687M,	
			1 TWU, TWU, 229 OCU, 4. Stored.	11-03
❑ XL573		Hunter T.7	✈ G-BVGH, ex North Weald, Exeter, Shawbury, 237	
			OCU, Laarbruch SF, 237 OCU, 4 FTS, 229 OCU, FCS.	3-02

❑ XL592	'Y' Hunter T.7		ex Scampton 8836M, 1 TWU, TWU, 229 OCU. Stored.	9-02
❑ XL602	Hunter T.8M	✈	G-BWFT, ex Shawbury, Yeovilton, FRADU, 759, 764.	3-02
❑ XM697*	'S' Gnat T.1		G-NAAT, ex Bournemouth, Dunsfold, Bournemouth,	
			Woking, HSA, A&AEE, HSA. Arr 19-10-02.	® [1] 11-02
❑ XX467*	Hunter T.7		ex Kemble, Perth, 1 TWU, Jordan AF 836, Saudi AF	
	G-TVII		70-617, G-9-214, XL605, 66, 92. Arrived 7-2-03.	2-03

Airport: Like many airfields, Exeter has become a storage centre for airliners, in this case largely HS/BAe 146s and ATRs, most of which are not long-termers. By late 2002, Autocar G-AOIY had moved to Okehampton, Devon.

❑ G-AVXJ	HS.748-2A	ex Emerald, CAAFU. CoA 22-8-98. Spares.	11-03
❑ G-BAUR	F.27-200	ex JEA, PH-FEP, 9V-BAP, 9M-AMI, VR-RCZ ntu,	
		PH-FEP. CoA 5-4-96. Fuselage.	11-03
❑ [G-BORM]	HS.748-2B	ex RP-C1043, V2-LAA, VP-LAA, 9Y-TDH. Dump.	11-03

IVYBRIDGE on the A38 east of Plymouth
Tony Thorne: Keeps his airframes in the general area. They include the Stampe previously listed under this heading on its own. Skeeters XL738 and XL763 moved to Leeds, W Yorks, circa October 2003.

❑ G-ATWT	Napier-Bensen	ex Narborough, G-29-3. wfu 31-1-77.	2-04
❑ G-BIVL	Bensen B.8M	ex St Merryn. CoA 29-4-87.	8-01
❑ G-MBUZ*	Skycraft Scout II	–	2-04
❑ G-STMP	SNCAN SV-4A	ex St Merryn, F-BCKB.	® 2-04
❑ –	Hobbycopter	ex 'Leicestershire'.	2-04

KINGSBRIDGE on the A381 north of Salcombe

❑ G-AVXB	Bensen B-8	ex Swansea, G-ARTN. CoA 23-6-87.	10-98

NEWTON ABBOT on the A380 south of Exeter
'Flying' within the **Trago Mills** supermarket in the town is the one-off MW.2B [1]. A collector keeps a Sea Vixen cockpit in the general area [2].

❑ G-BDDX*	Excalibur	ex Helston. Only flight 1-7-76, built at Bodmin.	[1]	9-03
❑ XN650*	Sea Vixen	ex Welshpool, Bruntingthorpe, Cardiff, A2639,		
	'456' FAW.2	A2620,A2612, Culdrose, RAE, 892. Nose.	[2]	12-02

OKEHAMPTON on the A30 west of Exeter
A farm strip in the general area is home to a large number of 'resting' and recovering Austers and other types. Two AOP.9s have long been out of circulation, having been 'spares ships' for the late Mike Somerton-Rayner [1].

❑ G-AIGD*	J/1 Autocrat	CoA 6-7-00. Stored. First noted 5-02.		3-04
❑ G-AJAJ*	J/1 Autocrat	ex Dunkeswell. CoA 18-4-94. Stored. First noted 5-02.		3-04
❑ G-AMMS*	J/5K Aiglet Tnr	CoA 19-10-98. Stored. First noted 5-02.		7-03
❑ G-ANXC*	J/5R Alpine	ex 5Y-UBD, VP-UBD, G-ANXC, AP-AHG ntu,		
		G-ANXC. CoA 2-8-98. Stored. First noted 5-02.		3-04
❑ G-AOIY*	J/5G Autocar	ex Exeter. CoA 26-8-90. First noted 11-02.	®	3-04
❑ G-ARNO	Terrier 1	ex Northampton, Stamford, Nympsfield, Auster		
		AOP.6 VX113, 651, 662. CoA 19-6-81.	®	3-04
❑ G-AVYK*	Terrier 3	ex Aboyne, Auster AOP.6 WJ357, 651, 657,		
		1903 Flt. CoA 28-8-93.		7-01
❑ G-AXCZ*	SNCAN SV-4C	ex ZS-VFW, G-AXCZ, F-BCFG. CoA 10-7-83.		
		Stored. First noted 7-03.		3-04
❑ [G-BGKO]*	GY-20 Minicab	unfinished project. Stored. First noted 5-02.		3-04
❑ G-BGKZ*	J/5K Aiglet Tnr	ex Liverpool, Stretton, F-BGKZ. Crashed 30-1-93.		
		Stored. First noted 5-02.		7-03
❑ WZ662*	Auster AOP.9	G-BKVK, ex Middle Wallop. CoA 29-9-00.		3-04

❏ XK421*	Auster AOP.9	ex Doncaster, Firbeck, Thurcroft, Firbeck, Hedge End, Fownhope, Long Marston, Innsworth, Bristol, Caldicote, 8365M, St Athan, Detmold, Middle Wallop. Frame. First noted 11-03.		3-04
❏ XP241*	Auster AOP.9	ex Middle Wallop, Andrewsfield, Rabley Heath, St Athan, 653, Aden. Frame, stored. F/n 9-02.	[1]	3-04
❏ XP286*	Auster AOP.9	ex ?, Middle Wallop, Hull, 60 MU, 38 GCF, AAC Centre. Frame, stored. F/n 9-02.	[1]	3-04

Locally: In the general area are several airframes.

❏ G-ASBH*	Airedale	CoA 19-2-99. Stored.		5-02
❏ G-BKSX*	SNCAN SV-4C	ex F-BBAF, Fr mil. CoA 15-6-89.	®	9-02
❏ N6191K*	Seabee	(identity believed confirmed). Damaged, stored.		5-02

PLYMOUTH
Alan Thompson: Has acquired a Scout to turn into a travelling exhibit, to be based in the area.

❏ –*	Agusta A109	fuselage. First noted 2-04.	2-04
❏ XW281*	Scout AH.1	G-BYNZ, ex Thruxton. With boom of XP883. Crashed 24-9-00. Arrived 31-3-02.	2-04

PLYMOUTH AIRPORT
To clear up*W&R18*, p47, Pitts G-PEAL moved to Land's End, Cornwall.

❏ G-BAII*	Cessna FRA.150L	ex Bodmin. Cr 9-9-01. Fire crews. First noted 8-02.	8-02

TAVISTOCK AERODROME or Brent Nor, north of the town
Dartmoor Gliding Society:

❏ –*	BFP	Schleicher Ka-7	BGA.936. CoA 28-4-96. Stored.		1-04
❏ –*	FGZ	Schleicher Ka-7	BGA.3262, ex D-5376. CoA 9-10-99. Stored.		1-04
❏ –*	FTU	Schleicher Ka-7	BGA.3262, ex HB-599. *Fondue*. Cr 21-9-02.	off-site ®	1-04
❏ –*	HWE	Schleicher K-8B	BGA.4255, ex HB-700. Wreck.		1-04

YARNSCOMBE north of the B3227, west of Atherington

❏ G-BBAK	MS.894A Rallye	ex D-ENMK ntu. CoA 8-8-98.	7-03

DORSET

BOURNEMOUTH
Streetwise Safety Centre: Among the 'attractions' at the awareness training centre in Bournemouth is a Twin Squirrel about to 'land' on a Police helicopter pad.

❏ 'S-WISE'	AS.355 Squirrel	ex PAS Gloucestershire, N354E, F-GIRL.	2-04

BOURNEMOUTH AIRPORT or Hurn, west of the A338, north of the city
Bournemouth Aviation Museum (BAM) Operated by the Bournemouth Aviation Charitable Foundation. Note that other light aircraft 'lodge' within, but only 'long-termers' are noted here. De Havilland Aviation (DHA, see below) operates within the hangar complex, looking after its own, and other jets. There is a viewing gallery allowing a grandstand view of aircraft within the DHA but access to the engineering 'floor' is not permitted. From this edition DHA-owned aircraft or aircraft under restoration by DHA for other owners are given under their own heading, see below.

Notes: BAM owns Hunter XG160 and Grasshopper WZ798, all others are on loan from individuals or organisations. Some of these are as follows: The Dragon Rapide and 'JP5' G-BWOF are owned and operated by Phil Meeson (PM); the BAC 111 is on loan from European Aviation (EAL); Hunter T.68 G-HVIP is owned by German national Dr Karl Theurer, trading as Golden Europe Jet Ltd (GEJ). The nose of Vulcan XH537 is on loan from Paul Hartley (PH). Paul just so happens to own *two* other Vulcan noses (as you do!), at Bruntingthorpe, Leics, and Wellesbourne Mountford, Warks. It attended the '100 Years of Flight Experience' static display at the International Air Tattoo, Fairford, Glos, July 2003. After two years of restoration work, including the fabrication of a purpose-built tower, the Vulcan was opened to the public on 16th February 2004 [1].

Departures: Venom FB.50 G-GONE flew to Swansea, Wales, 15-5-03 for maintenance before settling on Coventry, Warks, 23-9-03; Bell UH-1H G-HUEY to North Weald, Essex, 12-11-03; Meteor TT.20 WM167 (G-LOSM) attended the '100 Years of Flight Experience' static display at the International Air Tattoo, Fairford, Glos, July 2003 and flew to a new home at Coventry, Warks, in March 2004; Hunter F.51 E-402 to Farnborough, Hants, 25-11-02; Gnat T.1 XM697 (G-NAAT) moved to Exeter, Devon, by 19-10-02; MiG-21PF 503 (G-BRAM) left the museum in 2-02. It was stored on the airfield site until moving to Farnborough, Hants, on 3rd March 2004.

◆ Daily Apr to Sep 10am to 5pm, Oct to Mar, 10am to 4pm ✉ BAM, Hangar 600, Bournemouth International Airport, Christchurch, BH23 6SE ☎ 01202 580858 **www**.aviation-museum.co.uk

❑	G-AGSH	Rapide 6	✈ ex Lower Upham, EI-AJO, G-AGSH, NR808. BEA colours, *Gemma Meeson*.	PM	2-04
❑	G-AVMN	BAC 111-510EDex AB Airlines, European, BA, BEA. CoA 21-6-00.		EAL	2-04
❑	G-BEYF	Herald 401	ex Channel Express, RMAF FM1022. On loan.		2-04
❑	G-BWOF	Jet Provost T.5 ✈	ex North Weald, XW291, Shawbury, 6 FTS, RAFC, CFS.	PM	2-04
❑	G-BRNM*	CMC Leopard	ex Old Sarum.		2-04
❑	G-HVIP	Hunter T.68 ✈	ex Swiss AF J-4208, G-9-415, RSweAF Fv34080.	GEJ	2-04
❑	N7SY	Sea Prince T.1	ex G-BRFC, North Weald, Bourn, WP321, Kemble, 750, 744.		2-04
❑	'K5673'	Isaacs Fury III ✈ G-BZAS. *Spirit of Dunsfold*.			2-04
❑	KF488	Harvard IIb	ex Bournemouth, Wimborne, Sandhurst, Avex. Composite.	®	2-04
❑	RT486 'PF-A'	Auster 5	✈ G-AJGJ, ex RT486, 43 OTU.		2-04
❑	WT532	Canberra PR.7	ex Airport, Lovaux, Cosford, 8890M / 8728M, RAE Bedford, 13, Wyton SF, 58, 31, 13, 80. Nose.		2-04
❑	WZ798	G'hopper TX.1	ex Bournemouth School.		2-04
❑	XG160	'U' Hunter F.6A	G-BWAF, ex 'RJAF', Scampton 8831M, 1 TWU, 229 OCU, 111, 43. 111 Sqn colours, black.		2-04
❑	XH537	Vulcan B.2MRR	ex Bruntingthorpe, Ottershaw, Camberley, Abingdon 8749M, 27, 230 OCU, MoA. Nose.	PH [1]	2-04
❑	XR537	'T' Gnat T.1	G-NATY, ex Cosford 8642M, Reds, 4 FTS.	®	2-04
❑	XX897	Buccaneer S.2B(mod)	ex airfield, DRA Bedford, RAE, RRE. Tornado nose. European Airlines colours.		2-04
❑	C-552	EKW C-3605 ✈	G-DORN, ex HB-RBJ, SwissAF C-552.		2-04
❑	[J-4083]*	Hunter F.58	G-EGHH, ex JHL, Swiss AF. Arrived 7-02.		2-04
❑	–	Hunter T.7	ex Biggin Hill, 'G-ERIC', Bournemouth, Leavesden, Elstree, Hatfield. Nose of XJ690.		2-04
❑	–	Vanguard SIM	ex South Kesington?		2-04

De Havilland Aviation (DHA) / **De Havilland Engineering**: Are the A8-20 approved maintenance organisation for their own and other resident jets. The operation a Swansea, Wales, was wound down by mid-2003. (See also under Bridgend, Wales.) The magnificent Sea Vixen remains their flagship, it performed 28 displays in the 2003 season. The MiG-17 is a major restoration project and should be the first afterburner equipped jet to fly on a permit in the UK. Airframes marked ➠ attended the '100 Years of Flight Experience' static display at the International Air Tattoo, Fairford, Glos, July 2003. Vampire T.55 'XJ771' (G-HELV) moved to Coventry, Warks, in March 2004.

◆ Aircraft viewable during normal museum opening hours from the gallery – see above.

❑	G-CVIX	Sea Vixen D.3 ✈	ex XP924, Swansea, Llanbedr, RAE, FRL, RAE, 899. 'Red Bull' colours.	➠	2-04

❏ WZ507*	'74' Vampire T.11	⤙ G-VTII, ex Swansea, Bruntingthorpe, Cranfield, Carlisle, CATCS, 3/4 CAACU, 5 FTS, 8 FTS, 229 OCU. Arrived 6-02.	2-04
❏ XE920	'A' Vampire T.11	⤙ G-VMPR, ex Swansea, Chester, Sealand, 8196M Scampton, Henlow, Shawbury, CATCS, 8 FTS, 5 FTS, 1 FTS. 603 Sqn c/s.	2-04
❏ 1211	SBLim-5 (MiG-17)	G-MIGG, ex G-BWUF Duxford, Polish AF. Korean colours.	® 2-04

Source Classic Jet Flight / Lindsay Wood Promotions Ltd: Four of the jet fleet have moved on: Venom FB.54 'WR410' (G-BLKA) to temporary storage in Norfolk on 17th June 2002 before settling upon <u>London Colney</u>, Herts, 23rd October 2003; Vampire T.11 WZ553 (G-DHYY) and Venom FB.50s J-1629 and J-1649 all to <u>Coventry</u>, Warks, 17th November 2003.

❏ –	[FLV] L-13 Blanik	BGA.3354, ex Eaglescott, D-1355. *Jenny.* Fuselage.	2-04
❏ 'VT871'	Vampire FB.6	⤙ G-DHXX, ex 'LZ551/G', Southampton, Swiss AF J-1173. 54 Squadron colours by 6-98.	2-04
❏ 'VV612'	Venom FB.50	G-VENI, ex 'WE402'. Swiss AF J-1523. CoA 25-7-01. Prototype colours.	2-04
❏ 'WR360'	Venom FB.50	⤙ G-DHSS, ex Swiss AF J-1<u>626</u>. White 60 Sqn c/s.	2-04
❏ 'WR410'	Venom FB.50	G-DHUU, G-BMOD ntu, ex Swiss AF J-1539. CoA 24-5-02. 6 Sqn colours, Suez stripes.	2-04
❏ 'WR421'	Venom FB.50	G-DHTT, G-BMOC ntu, ex Swiss AF J-1611. CoA 17-7-99. Red c/s.	2-04
❏ 'WZ589'	Vampire T.55	⤙ G-DHZZ, ex Southampton, Swiss AF U-1230. 20 Sqn colours by mid-2001.	2-04
❏ 'XE897'	Vampire T.55	⤙ G-DHVV, ex Southampton, Swiss AF U-1214. 54 Sqn colours.	2-04
❏ 'XG775'	Vampire T.55	⤙ G-DHWW, ex Southampton, Swiss AF U-1219. Navy FOFT c/s, as Sea Vampire T.22.	2-04
❏ XR954	'30' Gnat T.1	ex Ipswich, Halton 8570M, 4 FTS, CFS, 4 FTS.	2-04
❏ J-1573	Venom FB.50	G-VICI, ex HB-RVB, G-BMOB ntu, Swiss AF. CoA 24-11-99.	2-04

Airliners: Many scrappings to report: **Airbus A300B2s** G-CEAA 7-03; G-CEAB 6-03; ZS-SDA by 9-02 with the cockpit leaving on a truck 26-9-02 - bulk of fusclage reported to have gone to a Watford company for cabin air quality tests; ZS-SDD 4-02 with major parts to Germany by road 5-4-02; **BAC 111-510EDs** G-AVMH 10-02; G-AVMP 9-02 with the forward fuselage reported to have moved to <u>Iver Heath</u>, Bucks, 26-3-03; G-AVMS 7-03; G-AVMY 5-02 with the forward fuselage leaving by road 2-5-03 for display in Geneva, Switzerland; G-AVMZ 5/6-03; **Boeing 737-2H6** XA-PBA by 9-02; **Electra** G-CHNX 9-03, the cockpit to <u>Pershore</u>, Worcs, 1-10-03.

❏ G-AVMJ	BAC 111-510ED	ex Filton, BA, BEA. CoA 17-11-94. Cabin trainer.	2-04
❏ G-AVMT*	BAC 111-510ED	ex European, BA, BEA. CoA 5-12-03. Stored by 11-02.	2-04
❏ G-AWYV	BAC 111-501EX	ex 5N-OSA ntu, European, BA, BEA. Stored.	2-04
❏ G-AZMF*	BAC 111-530FX	ex European, 7Q-YKJ, G-AZMF, PT-TYY, G-AZMF. Stored by 6-02.	2-04
❏ G-CEXA*	F.27-500RF	ex ChannEx, N703A, PH-EXK. Stored by 5-03.	2-04
❏ G-CEXG*	F.27-500	ex ChannEx, G-JEAP, 9Q CBI, OY-APF, 9Q-CBI, PH-RUA, VH-EWR, F-BYAH, OY-APF, PH-EXD. Stored by 5-03.	2-04
❏ EC-CFI*	Boeing 727-256	ex Iberia. Arrived 10-02, stored.	2-04
❏ EC-DDX*	Boeing 727-256	ex Iberia. Arrived 10-02, stored.	2-04
❏ OO-SDK*	Boeing 727-256	ex Sabena, G-BYYK ntu. Arrived 30-11-<u>99</u>, stored.	2-04
❏ XA-TLJ	Boeing 737-2H6	ex TAESA, PK-IJE, 9M-MBH, 9M-ASR. Spares.	2-04

Others: The hulks of Cessna F.172H G-BDCE and FA.150K G-BUTT have moved on. Hunter F.58 J-4083 (G-EGHH) moved to the BAM (above) in July 2002. Hawk T.53 LL-5313 moved to <u>Brough</u>, E Yorks, in 2003.

❏ G-ASOX	Cessna 205A	ex ?, Newcastle, N4856U. CoA 1-8-92.	2-04
❏ G-ATPD	HS.125-1B/522	ex 5N-AGU, G-ATPD. CoA 14-10-98. To dump 8-02.	2-04

❏ G-AXAU	T Comanche 160C	ex N8613Y. CoA 8-3-86. Stored.		2-04
❏ G-BAVS	AA-5 Traveler	fuselage. CoA 8-11-94.		2-04
❏ G-BBFC	AA-1B Trainer	fuselage. Damaged 9-6-96.	®	2-04
❏ EI-BAS*	Cessna F.172M	stored, dismantled. First noted 7-03.		2-04
❏ N44DN	Malibu 350P	crashed 8-7-00. Stored.		2-04
❏ [SX-BFM]	Navajo	ex Southampton, N4504J. Cr 23-6-99. Fuselage.		2-04
❏ VR-BEB	BAC 111-527FK	ex airliner store, RP-C1181, PI-C1181. Fire crews.		2-04
❏ WJ992	Canberra T.4	ex DRA Bedford, RAE, 76. Fire dump.		2-04

BOVINGTON off the A352 near Wool, west of Wareham
Tank Museum: Houses the world's finest international collection of armoured fighting vehicles.
◆ Open daily (except Xmas) 10am to 5pm. Special events held throughout the year. ⊡ Bovington, Dorset, BH20 6JG ☎ 01929 405096 **fax** 01929 405360 **e-mail** admin@tankmuseum.co.uk **www.tankmuseum.co.uk** or **www.tiger-tank.com**

❏ TK718	GAL Hamilcar I	ex Beverley, Christian Malford.	4-03
❏ XM564	Skeeter AOP.12	ex 652, CFS, 12 Flt, 652.	9-03

COMPTON ABBAS AERODROME south-east of Shaftesbury
Flying Aces Museum: Opened on 7th June 2003, the museum is centred around the airframes and artefacts previously a part of the 'Blue Max' museum at Wycombe Air Park, Bucks. Also on show is the tail and top wing from a film mock-up Gotha G.IV ('983/16) used in *Mr Chips' War* in 2002.
◆ Open daily other than Xmas week. ⊡ Compton Abbas Airfield, Ashmore, near Shaftesbury, SP5 5AP ☎ 01747 811767 **www.abbasair.com**

❏ –*		MF.1 REP	G-BAAF, ex Wycombe AP. Blériot-like. CoA 6-8-96.	1-04
❏ –*	'10'	Blériot XI REP	G-BPVE, ex Wycombe AP, N1197.	1-04
❏ 'B2458'*	'R'	Camel REP	G-BPOB, ex Wycombe AP, N8997, Tallmantz Av. Arrived 19-3-03.	1-04
❏ 'B5539'*		Stampe SV-4 FSM	ex Wycombe AP, The Mummy, *Indiana Jones and the Lost Crusade*. Gun turret, crash scene.	1-04
❏ 'MS824'*		MS 'N' REP	G-AWBU, ex Wycombe APS. CoA 29-6-01.	1-04
❏ '422/15'*		Fokker E.III REP	G-AVJO, ex Wycombe AP.	1-04
❏ '8'*	BAPC.238	Ornithopter	ex Wycombe AP, Young *Sherlock Holmes*. PPS-built.	1-04

Elsewhere:

❏ G-AZRV	Arrow 200	ex N2309T. Crashed 30-12-00. Dump.	3-04

DORCHESTER
Wessex Aviation and Transport: Further disposals to note: DH.60G G-ABEV flying in Somerset by mid-2003; Moth Minor G-AFOB moved on, thought into Herts; Tiger Moth T5672 (G-ALRI) thought with an owner in Wales. The other two are thought to be still in situ.

❏ G-BMNV	SNCAN SV-4L	ex Booker, F-BBNI. CoA 8-6-94.	7-01
❏ N4712V	PT-13D Kaydet	ex 42-16931.	7-01

GALLOWS HILL on a minor road between Bere Regis and Wool, north of Bovington Camp
Dorset Gliding Club: Sedbergh TX.1 WB922 (JAT) moved to Hullavington, Wilts, during 2003 and became airworthy. Grasshopper TX.1 WZ755 moved to <u>Wolverhampton</u>, W Mids.

❏ XP492	FSB Grasshopper TX.1	BGA.3480. Ex 2 MGSP, Locking, Taunton, Greater Malvern. Stored.	5-03

POOLE on the A35 west of Bournemouth
The fuselage of G-DASI is in use as a shed (how appropriate!) on the Nuffield Industrial Estate.

❏ G-BGNG	Short 330-200	ex Bournemouth, Gill, N330FL, G-BGNG. Fuselage.	1-02
❏ G-DASI	Short 360	ex Guernsey, Gill, G-14-3606. Fuselage.	1-03

SOMERFORD on the A35 north east of Christchurch
The Lobster - The World's Biggest Maize Maze: Located at Stewarts Gardenlands, on the A35 next to Sainsbury's is an 8.8 mile maze pathway spread over 16.9 acres. Sadly, if you want to go and see the ST-10, you'll have to take the plunge! (Note that the maze's life seems quite short - in this case mid-July to mid-September - and it may well be that *Kilo-Golf* 'does the rounds' of mazes! See under Turners Hill, West Sussex.)
♦ Check first for opening times. ☎ 01425 272244 www.dorsetmaze.com
❑ G-AYKG*   ST-10 Diplomate   ex Turners Hill. Crashed 4-3-75. First noted 9-03.   9-03

STALBRIDGE on the A357 south-west of Shaftesbury
The Moth Minor Coupe is *thought* under restoration to open top format.
❑ G-AFNI   Moth Minor   ex Woodley, W7972, 100 GCF, Foulsham SF,
                            241, G-AFNI. CoA 26-5-67.   ® 12-99

DURHAM and CLEVELAND

☛ The unitary authorities of Hartlepool, Middlesbrough, Redcar and Cleveland and Stockton-on-Tees, and Darlington form the region.

TEES-SIDE AIRPORT or Middleton St George, south of the A67, east of Darlington
International Fire Training Centre: As well as the real airframes at the Serco-operated school, there is a convincing mock-up of a Tornado, complete with 9 Squadron badge, used for burning practice along with a 747 front fuselage, a 'Boeing 737', a light aircraft and a 'helicopter' mock-up.

❑ G-ARPO	Trident 1C	ex BA, BEA. CoA 12-1-86. Whole.	2-04
❑ G-AVFJ	Trident 2E	ex BA, BEA. CoA 18-9-83. Poor state.	11-03
❑ G-AWZR	Trident 3B-101	cx BA, BEA. CoA 9-4-86. Poor state.	11-03
❑ G-AWZS	Trident 3B-101	ex BA, BEA. CoA 9-9-86. Whole.	11-03
❑ G-AZLP	Viscount 813	ex BMA, SAA ZS-CDT. CoA 3-4-82. Fuselage.	3-02
❑ G-AZLS	Viscount 813	ex BMA, SAA ZS-CDV. CoA 9-6-83.	3-02
❑ 'G-JON'	Short 330-100	G-BKIE, ex Newcastle, G-SLUG, G-METP, G-METO,	
		G-BKIE, C-GTAS, G-14-3005. CoA 22-8-93.	3-00
❑ XP330	W'wind HAR.10	ex Stansted, 21, 32, 230, 110, 225. Poor state.	11-03

Others: G-AZNC is used by the fire services for non-destructive training [1]. Lightning F.3 XR749 was acquired by Score Energy Ltd and was due to move to Peterhead, Scotland, by May 2004 [1].
❑ G-AZNC	Viscount 813	ex BMA, G-AZLW ntu, SAA, ZS-SBZ, ZS-CDZ.	[1]	3-02
❑ G-BNGS	Tomahawk 112	ex Carlisle, Tees-side, Carlisle, N2463A.		
		Damaged 5-87. Spares.		3-02

YEARBY on the B1269 south of Redcar
Acro Engines and Airframes Ltd:
❑ G-APYB	Nipper III	CoA 12-6-96.	®	3-02
❑ G-ASFR	Bö 208A-1	ex D-EGMO. CoA 29-3-90.		3-02
❑ G-BAMG	Ganagobie	unfinished project. Stored.		3-02
❑ G-BHUO	Evans VP-2	unfinished project. Stored.		3-02
❑ G-OOSE	Rutan VariEze	unflown project. Damaged, stored.		3-02
❑ D-EFNO	Bö 208A-1	–	off-site ®	3-02

ESSEX

ANDREWSFIELD AERODROME or Great Saling, north of the A120, west of Braintree
On 4th June 2003 a lorry from a scrap dealer in Felsted, Essex, took away the remains of Piper Lance II G-BOON (and Warrior II G-BPAU – how long had that been here?). SIPA 903 G-ASXC was flying again by 2001 and Seneca 200 G-AZOT by the following year.

❑ G-AYUI	Cherokee 180F	ex N8557, G-AYUI. CoA 5-11-93. Stored.	6-03
❑ G-OWET*	TSC-1A2 Teal	ex C-FNOR, N1342W ntu. CoA 10-5-02.	10-03
❑ 319	'8-ND' Mystère IVA	ex Sculthorpe, French Air Force.	1-04

AUDLEY END off the B1383, west of Saffron Walden
Spitfire Vc JG891 had moved to Duxford, Cambs, by March 2004. Spitfire XVI TB252 (G-XVIE) was sold in the USA and moved to New Zealand for restoration.

❑ F-BGCJ	Tiger Moth	G-BTOG, ex France, French AF, NM192. Stored.	4-99

BRAINTREE on the A120 east of Colchester
In the general area are salvaged Spitfires - shot down within 72 hours of one another – plus a Seafire from Malta. All three are substantial remains and one day will form restoration projects.

❑ N3200	Spitfire Ia	ex Calais, 19. Shot down 27-5-40. Stored.	3-04
❑ P9374	Spitfire Ia	ex Calais, 92. Shot down 24-5-40. Stored.	3-04
❑ MB293	Seafire IIc	ex Malta, 879, 887, A&AEE. Stored.	3-04

Others:

❑ G-MJSP*	Tiger Cub 440	ex North Coates, Boston. CoA 31-1-86. Arr 21-3-03.	3-03

CHELMSFORD

De Havilland Hornet Project: David Collins has started work in this area on a long-term project that he calls a 'new-build' DH Hornet, using many original components. David is co-operating with Mark Reeder (see under Fyvie, Scotland) and would like to hear from others who may be able to help. Both Mark and David are using parts gleaned from the de Havilland Heritage Museum (see under London Colney, Herts) including tail sections salvaged by Tony Agar from St Davids, Wales. David estimates that he has one third of a Hornet at present and has several 'irons in the fire' for other airframe parts.
◆ Visits *not* possible to the project. Enquiries, offers of parts etc: **e-mail** dcollins103@hotmail.com

No.276 Squadron Air Cadets: In Meteor Way, off the Chelmsford-Harlow road, keep their T.7.

❑ WH132	'J' Meteor T.7	7906M, ex Kemble, CAW, CFS, CAW,	
		8 FTS, 207 AFS.	2-04

Others: The Hunter nose may well have moved on, perhaps in June 2000.

❑ XG209	'66' Hunter F.6	ex Stock, Halton, Cranwell, Halton 8709M,	
		12 DFLS, 111, 14. Nose.	2-96

CHIPPING ONGAR north of the A414, west of the town

Blake Hall 'Ops' Room and Airscene Museum: The hall is well known for its gardens, but also has within it a splendid array of artefacts centred around the hall's history as being the Operations Centre for Sector E when the 'ops' room at North Weald was dispersed from the airfield.
◆ Easter to October Sundays and Bank Holidays 11am to 5pm. ☎ 01277 362502 **fax** 01277 366947 **e-mail** austin@blakehall.net

CLACTON ON SEA

East Essex Aviation Museum (EEAM) **and Museum of the 1940s**: Located within one of the fine Martello towers that dot the coastline, EEAM includes a fine array of recovery items and other memorabilia. Dominating the contents is the fuselage of P-51D *Little Zippie*. Recovered during 1999 and on show is the substantial wreckage of 339th FG P-51D 44-15560 which crashed at Frinton-on-Sea.

◆ Within Point Clear caravan park. Open Mon 7pm to 10pm and Sun 10am to 2pm all year. Jun to Sep Wed 10am to 2pm, plus Sun 10am to 4pm and Bank Hols. ✉ Roger Barrell, 37 Brookland Road, Brantham, Essex, CO11 1RP

❏ 44-14574   P-51D-10-NA   ex 479th FG *Little Zippie*. Crashed off-shore 13-1-45.   2-04

Locally: Jet Provost T.4 XR670 moved to Ipswich, Suffolk by December 2002.

❏ G-AHTE*   Proctor V   ex Nayland, Llanelli, Cardiff, Swansea, Llanelli, ?, Hereford, Walsall. CoA 10-8-61.   ® 7-02

CLACTON AERODROME between Clacton on Sea and Jaywick

❏ G-ARAN*   Super Cub 150   ex N10F. Damaged 5-02. Dismantled, stored.   11-02

❏ G-BGWH*   Super Cub 150   ex ST-ABR, G-ARSR, N10F. Crashed 7-7-92.   ® 11-02

CLAVERING on the B1038 south-west of Saffron Walden

Still no news on the scrapyard at Starling's Green and its Cessna fuselage - on finals for LOST!

❏ G-AXWF   Cessna F.172H   ex Clacton, Andrewsfield. Dbr 26/27-11-83. Fuselage.   7-95

COLCHESTER

Charleston Aviation Services: Craig Charleston's workshop in the area specialises in Bf 109s.

❏ –	Sea Fury FB.11	composite.	3-94
❏ LA546	Seafire F.46	ex Newport Pagnell, Newark. Substantial parts.	3-02
❏ 7485	Bf 109F-4	ex Russia.	® 3-02
❏ 8147	Bf 109F-4	ex Lancing, Russia, 6/JG54.	® 3-02
❏ 15458	Bf 109G-2	ex Russia.	® 11-03

Others: The nose section of Canberra PR.3 WE168 moved to Flixton, Suffolk, during 2002.

EARLS COLNE AERODROME on the B1024 south of Earls Colne, east of Halstead

By September 2002 a Rotorway Scorpion was in use as a plaything at a house close to the aerodrome. By late 2003, it had moved on to the aerodrome [1].

❏ G-AOZL   J/5Q Alpine   ex Southend. CoA 28-5-88.   ® 11-03

❏ SE-HXF*   Scorpion   ex nearby. First noted 11-03.   [1] 11-03

EAST TILBURY on a minor road east of Tilbury

Thameside Aviation Museum (TAM): Located within the Coalhouse Fort 1860s Victorian Casemate Fortress, TAM is dedicated to aviation archaeology excavations carried out from the early 1970s, including a huge amount on the Battle of Britain over Essex. None of the noses are on public show.

◆ At Coalhouse Fort, 'brown signed' from A13. TAM open last Sun of the month and Bank Hols, Mar to Oct 11am to 4.30pm. Other times by arrangement. (Details of Coalhouse Fort ☎ 01375 844203) ✉ Coalhouse Fort, East Tilbury, Essex ☎ 07860 134946 e-mail museum@aviationmuseum.co.uk www.aviationmuseum.co.uk

❏ WG471	Chipmunk T.10 PAX	ex Bury St Edmunds, 8210M, Stowmarket, Leeming, Abn UAS, 1 FTS, 6 FTS, 220 OCU, Aston Down CF, MCCS, 4 SoTT, Nott UAS, Leeds UAS, 19 RFS, 24 RFS, 3 BFTS, 16 RFS, 4 BFTS.	3-04
❏ XM692	Gnat T.1	ex Boscombe Down, Robertsbridge, Salisbury, Southampton, Fareham, Folland. Nose.	3-04
❏ 0446	MiG-21UM	ex Salisbury, Farnborough, Egyptian AF. Nose.	3-04

FOULNESS ISLAND on a minor road north-east of Great Wakering

Defence Science and Technology Laboratory, Shoeburyness: The range functions in a small enclave, in the north-east of the 'island', beyond Courtsend. By late November 2003 Buccaneer S.2 XT272 had moved to Stock, Essex. No news on the F-4 cockpit, but its identity has been confirmed.

| ☐ XT895 | Phantom FGR.2 | ex Valley 9171M, 74, 228 OCU, 92, 228 OCU, 111, 6, 228 OCU. Cockpit. | 3-00 |
| ☐ '50' b* | MiG-23MF | ex Chester, Latvia, USSR. (023003508). F/n 11-03. | 3-04 |

FYFIELD on the B184 north of Chipping Ongar
The forward cockpit (ie the student's seat) of Gnat XS100 moved to London, Gtr Lon, during 2002.
| ☐ XK482 | Skeeter AOP.10 | G-BJWC, ex Northampton, Blackpool, Heysham, Horsham, Ottershaw, Middle Wallop 7840M, HTF, HS, MoS. | 6-01 |

GREAT DUNMOW on the A120 west of Braintree
Paul and **Andy Wood**: The Hunter was reported to be for sale during December 2002.
| ☐ WP185 | Hunter F.5 | ex Abingdon, Hendon, Henlow 7583M, 34, 1. Stored. | 12-02 |

GREAT WALTHAM on the A130 north of Chelmsford
Peter Lee: The Messenger restoration continues.
| ☐ G-AKEZ | Messenger 2A | ex 'RG333', Higher Blagdon, Bristol. CoA 15-11-68. ® | 10-01 |

HALSTEAD north-east of Braintree
Rebuild of the Auster and Tiger is *thought* to continue. A Navion B is under restoration in the area. It has consumed parts from Rangemaster D-ECDL [1].
☐ G-AJUL	J/1N Alpha	CoA 11-9-81.	® 12-90
☐ G-APBI	Tiger Moth	ex Audley End, EM903, 2 FIS, 26. Crashed 7-7-80.	® 12-90
☐ N3864*	Navion B	ex Norwich.	[1] ® 11-03

INGATESTONE on the A12 south west of Chelmsford
Stuart Gowans: Vampire XE864 is fitted with the wings of XD435 [1].
☐ WF145	Sea Hawk F.1	ex Welshpool, South Molton, Salisbury, Torbay, Brawdy, Abbotsinch, RAE, A&AEE.	9-02
☐ XD235	Scimitar F.1	ex Welshpool, Southampton, Ottershaw, Foulness, FRU, 803. Nose.	9-02
☐ XD599	'A' Vampire T.11	ex Welshpool, Shobdon, Caernarfon, Bournemouth, Blackbushe, Staverton, Stroud, CATCS, RAFC, 1.	6-03
☐ XE864	Vampire T.11	ex Welshpool, Shobdon, Stretton, Kibworth, Firbeck, Studley, Chester, Woodford, St Athan, 8 FTS, 7 FTS, 1 ANS, CFS, 4 FTS.	[1] 9-02

LAINDON north of the A127, near Basildon
☐ G-AFGE	Swallow II	ex BK894, CLE, RAE, G-AFGE. CoA 27-7-98.	1-04
☐ G-ARXP	Luton Minor	CoA 17-10-95. Stored.	1-04
☐ G-BAGF*	Jodel D.92	ex F-PHFC. Stored, off-site.	1-04

NORTH WEALD AERODROME off the A414, junction 7, M11 east of Harlow
Aces High Flying Museum: The DC-4 and the C-54 both arrived in September 2002 for a film on the Berlin Airlift. This has yet to transpire and the pair are in open store [1]. As with other elements of this superb aerodrome, the Aces High area hosts a series of airworthy 'modern' light aircraft. These are not given here. Catalina N285RA is registered to the Randsberg Corporation of the USA and was previously listed under Flying 'A' Services [2]. The real Aztec 250D G-ESKY is airworthy [2].
  Departures: CASA 2-111 G-AWHB left by road in late 2002, initially for a workshop in Norfolk, prior to export to the USA. The Dakota Trust's C-47A N47FK moved to Lee-on-Solent, Hants, by September 2002 for storage and sale. Dakota N147DC moved to Dunsfold, Surrey on 2nd September 2002. Optica G-BMPL was also stored here, but by November 2003 had moved to Dunsfold, Surrey and was airworthy. Beech D.18S N96240 moved to a new home in 'Area 39' by mid-2003 - see below.

◆ Visits strictly by prior appointment *only*. ✉ Aces High Flying Museum (NW) Ltd, North Weald Aerodrome, Epping, CM16 6AA.

❑ G-BMPF	OA.7 Optica	ex Bournemouth. CoA 14-1-9<u>3</u>. Stored.		2-04
❑ G-BOPR	OA.7 Optica	ex Bournemouth (?). Stored.		2-04
❑ 'G-ESKY'	Aztec 250D	G-BADI ex N6885Y. CoA 29-10-92. Hulk.	[3]	2-04
❑ G-CSFT	Aztec 250D	ex G-AYKU, N13885. CoA 3-12-94. Hulk.		2-04
❑ G-FLSI	Sprint 160	ex Stansted, Bournemouth. Stored.		2-04
❑ G-SAHI	Sprint 160	ex Stansted, Bournemouth. CoA 30-4-94. Stored.		2-04
❑ G-70-503	Sprint 160	G-BXWU, ex Stansted, Bournemouth. Stored.		2-04
❑ G-70-505	Sprint 160	G-BXWV, ex Stansted, Bournemouth. Stored.		2-04
❑ [D-HGBX]	Enstrom F-280	hulk. First noted (again!) 12-00.		2-04
❑ EC-FVM	OA.7 Optica	ex Farnborough, Bournemouth, G-BOPO. Stored.		2-04
❑ N47FL	C-47A-20-DK	ex Elstree, EC-FIN, EC-659, N7164E, C-GCTE,		
	✈	C-GXAV, N92A ntu, C-GXAV, CAF 12952,		
		RCAF 968, 42-93203.		2-04
❑ N285RA	PBY-6A Catalina	ex G-BPFY, Biggin Hill, North Weald, N212DM, G-BPFY, N212DM, G-BPFY, C-FHNH, F-ZBAV, N5555H, N2846D, BuNo 64017.	[2]	2-04
❑ N2700	C-119G-FA	ex Manston, 3C-ABA, Belg AF CP-9, 12700. Nose.		2-04
❑ [N3455]	C-47B-35-DK	ex North Weald, Sandtoft, North Weald, Exeter, G-AMSN, EI-BSI, N3455, SU-BFZ, N3455, G-AMSN, KN673, 240 OCU, 1382 TCU, 45 GCF, 44-77047.		10-03
❑ N70457*'511'	MD.600N	ex *Tomorrow Never Dies*. First noted 10-02.		2-04
❑ TF-ABP*	TriStar	ex Iver Heath, Bruntingthorpe, Air Atlanta Icelandic, VR-HOG Cathay Pacific, LTU, Eastern N323EA. Cockpit. First noted 9-02.		2-04
❑ [6W-SAF]	C-47A-65-DL	ex North Weald, Woodley, Kew, Cranfield, F-GEFU, Le Bourget, Senegalese AF, USAF MAAG Brussels, USAAF 42-100611. Nose.		2-04
❑ 'FL586' 'AI-N'	C-47B-10-DK	ex Pinewood, *Sword of Honour*, OO-SMA, N99346 ntu, Belg AF K-1 OT-CWA, 43-49240. Fuselage.		10-03
❑ XN437	Auster AOP.9	G-AXWA, ex ?, Lashenden, Welling, Biggin Hill, Luton, Odiham, Maghull, Hoylake, St Athan, Kenya.	®	9-03
❑ 56498*	C-54D-1-DC	N44914, ex BuNo 56498, 42-72525. Arrived 9-02. Stored	[1]	3-04
❑ '44-42914'*	DC-4-1009	N31356, C-FTAW, EL-ADR, N6404. Arrived 9-02. Stored.	[1]	3-04
❑ 430861	<u>V</u>B-25<u>N</u>-NC	N9089Z, ex Duxford, 'HD368', G-BKXW ntu, Southend, Biggin Hill, N9089Z, 44-30861. *Bedsheet Bomber*.		3-04

Flying 'A' Services / Wizzard Investments Ltd: By the end of February 2004 the hangar was empty, with only the PBY-6A left, on what is known as the Aces High ramp. Accordingly, it has been moved to that entry - see above. As has been the case with this entry since its inception, there is a certain uncertainty about the aircraft listed here. Most of the airframes stored here were held in dismantled state in ISO containers, hence the lack of confirmation regarding what-went-where. A persistent rumour has been that a 'razorback' P-47 Thunderbolt be amongst this cache!

Departures: The new storage facility is at <u>Greenham Common</u>, Berks, and the following made the move: P-40N Warhawk N9950; TF-51 N7098V*; Spitfire IX NH238 (G-MKIX); Spitfire RW386 (G-BXVI); PT-19 Cornell '02538' by road 21-1-04 along with the famed Lancaster nose - notes on that, and others, can be found under the new heading. **Other departures**: Spitfire XVIII SM969 (G-BRAF) to <u>Martham</u>, Norfolk, by 9-03; P-51D Mustang NL314BG and FM-2 Wildcat N909WJ both to the USA *at the very latest* by August 2003. * The identity of this machine is confirmed, N513PA having been in Mexico for many years.

Intrepid Aviation: The collection had completely dispersed by late 2002: Beech D.17S G-BRVE to a locally-based operator; SNJ-7 G-BRVG based at Goodwood, Sussex along with PT-13D N4596N; Yak-52 G-BVOK flying from Shoreham, Sussex.

Kennet Aviation: Relocated from Cranfield, Beds, during late 2003 and early 2004. Aircraft marked ➥ attended the '100 Years of Flight Experience' static display at the International Air Tattoo, Fairford, Glos, July 2003. Gnat T.1 XS101 (G-GNAT) flew in from Cranfield, Beds, on 18th December 2002. It departed on 3rd October 2003 for the USA via Tilbury docks.
◆ Visits strictly by prior appointment *only*.

❏ G-FRCE*	Gnat T.1	ex North Weald, Halton 8604M, XS104, 4 FTS, CFS, 4 FTS. CoA 17-4-95. Arrived 8-1-03.	3-04
❏ G-HUEY*	UH-1H	ex Bournemouth, Cranfield, Argentine Army AE-413, 73-22077. CoA 12-11-03. Arrived 12-11-03.	3-04
❏ SX336*	Seafire XVII	G-KASX, ex G-BRMG, Cranfield, Twyford, Newark, Warrington, Stretton A2055, Bramcote. Arrived 7-11-02.	off-site ® 3-04
❏ 'WK436'*	Venom FB.50 ✈	G-VENM, ex Cranfield, J-1614, East Dereham, G-BLIE, Ipswich, Glasgow, Swiss AF. 11 Sqn c/s.	➥ 3-04
❏ 'XD693'* 'Z-Q'	Jet Provost T.1 ✈	G-AOBU, ex Cranfield, Winchester, Thatcham, Old Warden, Loughborough, Luton, XM129, G-42-1. 2 FTS colours. Arrived 19-12-02.	3-04
❏ XF515* 'R'	Hunter F.6A ✈	G-KAXF, ex Cranfield, Binbrook, Scampton 8830M, Kemble, 1 TWU, 229 OCU, 43, 247. 43 Sqn c/s. Arrived 5-12-02.	➥ 3-04
❏ XF690*	Provost T.1 ✈	G-MOOS, ex Cranfield, Thatcham, G-BGKA, 8041M, XF690, CATCS, CNCS, 64 GCF, Queens UAS.	➥ 3-04
❏ XL500*	Gannet AEW.3	G-KAEW, ex Chatham, Culdrose A2701, Lee-on-Solent, Culdrose, Dowty-Rotol, Culdrose, Lossiemouth, 849.	**due**
❏ 'XM693'*	Gnat T.1 ✈	G-TIMM, ex Cranfield, Leavesden, Halton 8618M, XP504, 4 FTS, CFS, 4 FTS. Arrived 9-11-02.	➥ 3-04
❏ XP540* '62'	Gnat T.1	ex Cambridge, Bruntingthorpe, Halton 8608M, 4 FTS. Arrived 2-10-03.	3-04
❏ 'XR993'*	Gnat T.1 ✈	G-BVPP, ex Cranfield, XP534, Halton 8620M, 4 FTS, CFS, 4 FTS, CFS, 4 FTS. Red Arrows c/s. Arr 9-11-02.	3-04
❏ XV140* 'K'	Scout AH.1 ✈	G-KAXL, ex Cranfield, Fleetlands. Arrived 13-10-02.	3-04
❏ XW289* '73'	Jet Provost T.5A	G-JPVA, ex Cranfield, G-BVXT, Binbrook, ✈ Shawbury, 1 FTS, RAFC, CFS.	➥ 3-04
❏ NZ3905*	Wasp HAS.1	G-KAXT ex Cranfield, Weston-super-Mare, RNZN, XT787. Arrived 7-11-02.	3-04
❏ NZ3909*	Wasp HAS.1	ex Cranfield, RNZN, XT782. Composite. Arr 5-11-02.	3-04
❏ 126922* 'AK-402'	AD-4NA Skyraider ✈	G-RADR, ex G-RAID, F-AZED, La Ferté Alais, Gabon AF, FAF No.42, USN 126922. VA-176, *Intrepid* c/s. Arrived 27-1-04.	3-04

Robs Lamplough / Fighter Wing Display Team: (See also Filton, Glos.) There has been a thinning out of the aircraft held in the hangar here. The following had moved on to Lambourn, Berks, by June 2003: Yak C.18M G-BMJY; Jungmeister G-TAFI; Hurricane IV KZ191 and Fokker Dr.I 152/17 (G-ATJM). Paris 2 N999PJ was crated for export to the USA during September 2003.
◆ Visits *strictly* by prior arrangement only.

❏ LV-RIE	Nord 1002	ex Duxford, Kersey, Argentina. Stored.	2-04
❏ 'EN398'	Spitfire IX FSM	BAPC.184, ex Duxford, Huntingdon.	9-00
❏ J-1758	Venom FB.54	G-BLSD, ex N203DM, Cranfield, G-BLSD, SwAF.	2-04
❏ 'DR628''PB1'	Beech D.17S	N18V, ex NC18, Bu32898, FT507, 44-67761. Stored.	2-04
❏ '14'	Noralpha	G-BSMD, ex F-GDPQ, F-YEEE, F-YCZK, CAN-11, Fr military No 139. *Luftwaffe* c/s. CoA 4-5-96.	2-04
❏ 472216 'HO-M'	P-51D-20-NA ✈	G-BIXL, ex Duxford, Ein-Gedi, Israeli AF/DF 43, RSweAF Fv26116, 44-72216. *Miss Helen,* 352nd FG colours by 5-01.	2-04

Area 51: The Jet Centre changed its name in 2003 as shown and probably inspired the naming of the new blister hangar - see below. As before, only aircraft under long-term maintenance or held in store here are listed. Strikemaster 84 G-SARK arrived by mid-2003 and made its first post-restoration flight in January 2004. Two Strikemasters have gone to the USA: Mk.80 1121 became G-CCAI and left in

December 2002; Mk.84 OJ9 (G-BXFR) became N604GV in mid-1999. T-33AN N36TH moved across to the Squadron area by July 2002 - see below.

North Weald Airfield Museum: Based at 'Ad Astra' House, located at the former main gate of the station, with a very impressive memorial dedicated to all those who served at 'Weald and another to the Norwegians who flew from there in the foreground. All of 'Ad Astra House' is now the museum's. The material on display is superb – an important place of pilgrimage.
◆ 'Ad Astra' House is off Hurricane Way, from North Weald *village* – ie the B181 – not via the aerodrome. Open Sun noon to 5pm. Other times by arrangement. Tours of the airfield can be arranged. ✉ 'Ad Astra House', Hurricane Way, North Weald Aerodrome, Epping, CM16 6AA. ☎ 07778 296650 e-mail bryn.elliott@btopenworld.com web http://fly.to/northweald

'The Squadron' / North Weald Flying Services (NWFS): As with other venues on this fantastic aerodrome, only airframes stored or under long-term work are listed under this heading.
◆ Visits by prior permission *only*. A series of fly-ins are staged during the season. ✉ North Weald Airfield, Epping, Essex, CM16, 6AA ☎ 01992 52 4510 fax 01992 52 2238

❏ 143	G-MSAL	MS.733 Alcyon	ex Wycombe AP, F-BLXV, Fr No.143.	® 3-04
❏ N36TH		T-33AN	G-BYOY, N333DV, N134AT, N10018,	
			N134AT,RCAF 21231. 'Thunderbird' c/s.	3-04

Others: This includes the newly-erected 'blister' hangar (known as '**Area 39**' close to the 13 threshold). Meteor TT.20 WM224 moved to East Midlands, Leics, on 12th January 2003. 'JP' T.4 XS181 moved during the summer of 2002 via Bruntingthorpe, to Market Harborough, Leics. The Opticas and Sprints are stored within the Aces High hangar - see above.

❏ G-AKUP*	Silvaire 8E	ex N2774K, NC2774K. Stored.		2-04
❏ G-AVLH*	Cherokee 140	ex N11C. CoA 18-8-00. Stored.		6-03
❏ G-BIVV*	AA-5A Cheetah	ex Elstree, N26979. Wreck, fire crews.		3-04
❏ N96240	Beech D.18S	ex Rochester, Spain, Wellesbourne Mountford,		
		Blackbushe, G-AYAH, N6123, RCAF 1559.		2-04
❏ SP-CHD*	PZL.101 Gawron	ex Sandown, Augsburg. In shed.	®	3-04

Locally: Two airframes are under restoration nearby.

❏ G-BDXX*	SNCAN NC.854	ex airfield, F-BEZQ. CoA 3-7-96.	®	2-04
❏ [G-BXIY]	Blake Bluetit	ex Old Warden, BAPC.37, Winchester.	®	2-04

PURFLEET on A1090 west of the Dartford Bridge
Purfleet Heritage and Military Centre: Incorporating the **Hornchurch Wing** and housed in the incredible Royal Gunpowder Magazine 18th century arsenal, the centre holds an incredible wealth of aviation artefacts. The section dedicated to Hornchurch is exceptional.
◆ Just off the A1090, in Centurion Way. Open the first weekend of each month and Saturdays March 31 to November 11, 10am to 4.30pm.

RAYLEIGH on the A1095 north-west of Southend-on-Sea
The Cockpit Collection: Nigel Towler's collection is located variously within the region. The wings of Vampire WZ608 can be found on WZ518 at Sunderland, N&T [1].
◆ The collection is scattered in various locations and, accordingly, visits are *not* possible.

❏ WZ608	Vampire T.11	ex Market Harborough, Lutterworth, Bitteswell,		
		Woodford, St Athan, 3 CAACU, 5 FTS, 266,		
		Fassberg SF, 11 Vampire Flt, 5, Wunstorf SF, 266.	[1]	4-00
❏ 'WZ826'	Valiant BK.1	XD826, ex Cardiff-Wales, Abingdon, Stratford,		
		Cosford, Feltwell 7872M, 543, 232 OCU, 138, 90, 7.		4-00
❏ XH560	Vulcan B.2	ex Marham, Waddington, 50, Wadd W, 27,		
		Akrotiri Wing, Cott W, Wadd W, Cott W,		
		230 OCU, 12, MoA, 230 OCU.		4-00
❏ XH669	Victor K.2	ex Waddington 9092M, 55, 57, Witt Wing, A&AEE.		4-00
❏ XH670	Victor B.2	ex East Kirkby, Tattershall, Woodford, Radlett, MoA.		4-00
❏ XN795	Lightning F.2A	ex Foulness, RAE Bedford, A&AEE, BAC.		4-00
❏ XS421	Lightning T.5	ex Foulness, RAE, 23, 111, 226 OCU.		4-00

No.1476 Squadron Air Cadets: In Connaught Road.

❑ '1476'	Cessna F.172H	G-BOVG, ex Southend, OO-ANN, D-ELTR.	
		Damaged 1991. Poor state.	2-04
❑ XG325	Lightning F.1	ex Southend, Wattisham, Foulness, A&AEE. Nose.	5-03

RETTENDON on the A1245 south-east of Chelmsford
'The Wheatsheaf': Locals call it 'The Pink Pub' – note that it is a distance outside the village.

❑ XP399	Whirlwind	ex Kettering, Glastonbury, Hadfield,	
	HAR.10	Pyrton Hill, 32, 1563 Flt, 230.	2-04

RIDGEWELL on the A1017 south-east of Haverhill
Ridgewell Airfield Commemorative Museum / 381st Bomb Group Memorial Museum:
Established in USAAF Station No.167's former hospital buildings. A series of displays - including the Tony Ince Collection – are dedicated to the 381st and to the RAF units that operated from the base.
◆ Second Sunday of each month, April to September, 11am to 5pm. Other times by arrangement.
✉ Ridgewell Airfield Commemorative Association, 'White Wings', Ashen Road, Ovington, Sudbury, CO10 8JX ☎ 01787 277310 or 07881 518572 e-mail jim@381st.com www.381st.com

SOUTHEND AIRPORT or Rochford, on the B1013 north of Southend-on-Sea
Vulcan Restoration Trust (VRT): The VRT has continued to develop the infrastructure needed to support a live airframe. This now includes a new apron, workshop, stores and office. Laid down in July 2002, the new apron was originally priced at £65,000 but use of 'in house' design and labour reduced this to a more affordable £16,000. VRT continues to play a major support role in the Vulcan to the Sky campaign for XH558 – see under Bruntingthorpe, Leics.
◆ Occasional open and 'up-and-running' days. Other times by appointment. VRT publish the excellent *Vulcan News*. ✉ Richard Clarkson, VRT, 39 Breakspears Drive, St Pauls Cray, Orpington, BR5 2RX. e-mail richard.clarkson@avrovulcan.com www.avrovulcan.com

❑ XL426	Vulcan B.2	ex Waddington, VDF , Waddington SF, 50, 617, 27,	
	G-VJET	617, 230 OCU, 617, 230 OCU, 617, 230 OCU,	
		617, 230 OCU, Scampton Wing, 83.	3-04

Airport: On the dump, Navajo T G-AYEI was reduced to wings and centre section by January 2004. Boeing 727-276 G-BNNI was gutted by June 2003 and it left on a series of trucks on 22nd September 2003 bound for Denmark where it was to be incorporated into an office development. Gazelle G-BXTH left by road to Blackpool, Lancs, 8th April 2003. Bandeirante G-OBPL and Short 330 G-DACS were stored by late 2001 and both were removed by summer 2003, going to Stock, Essex. Bandeirante G-OFLT was in open store by early 2002, it was dismantled in May 2003 and roaded out on the 23rd. It is reported to have destined for a gravel pit at Aveley, Essex, to be sunk for rescue training. Boeing 707-329C 9Q-CBW became TL-ALM by May 2002 before settling upon TL-ADJ in August and departing these shores on 31st December. Hitting the national headlines on 16th October 2001 was Boeing 707-373 3C-GIG which was impounded when 271 kilos of cocaine were discovered. It became a part of the Southend scenery until flying out on October 11, 2003. Boeing 727-251 OY-SES arrived 16th March 2002 for parting out, finally being removed in July 2003.

❑ G-OFLT*	Bandeirante	ex G-MOBL, G-BGCS ntu, PT-GMD. CoA 1-1-02.	1-03
❑ G-AOHL	Viscount 802	ex BAF, BA, BEA. CoA 11-4-80. Fuselage.	2-04
❑ G-ATAA	Cherokee 180C	Damaged 12-9-86. Wreck.	1-04
❑ G-ATRP	Cherokee 140	Damaged 16-10-81. Wreck.	1-04
❑ G-AVNP*	Cherokee 180C	ex N11C. Crashed 28-4-01. Wreck.	1-04
❑ G-BEPS	Belfast	ex G-27-13, XR368, 53. Last flight 30-3-01.	2-04
❑ G-BPEL	Warrior 151	ex C-FEYM. CoA 8-2-92. Wreck.	1-04
❑ G-BTYT	Cessna 152 II	ex N24931. CoA 20-3-99. Stored.	1-04
❑ G-BVFS*	Motor Cadet III	ex ?? Unflown. Arrived 30-6-00. Stored, dismantled.	1-04
❑ G-CHTT	Varga Kachina	ex Elstree. Crashed 27-4-86. Spares for G-BPVK.	1-04
❑ G-OBWD*	BAC 111-518FG	ex G-BDAE, G-AXMI. CoA 14-4-02. Stored.	2-04
❑ G-SSWP*	Short 330-100	ex CS-DBY, 5N-OJU ntu, G-BGNB, N330VM,	
		G-BGNB, G-14-3030. Arrived 6-02. Stored.	2-04

❑ EI-PAK*	Boeing 727-227F	ex TNT Express, OY-SET, N16762, N569PE, N444BN. Arrived 12-10-01. Stored.	2-04
❑ EL-AKJ	Boeing 707-321C	N2NF ntu, ex Omega, PP-BRR, EL-AKJ, 9Q-CSW, 5N-TAS, N864BX, OB-R1243, HK-2473X, N473RN, N473PA. Stored.	2-04
❑ F-GFLD	King Air C90	ex HB-GGW, I-AZIO. Stored.	1-04
❑ N150JC	Bonanza A35	ex Andover, Wick, N8674A. Dam 18-6-83. Stored.	1-03
❑ HZ-123*	Boeing 707-138B	ex N138M, N220M, N138TA, C-FPWV, VH-EBA, N31239. Stored.	2-04
❑ 3C-QSB*	F.27-200MAR	ex M-1 RNethAF, PH-EXC. Arrived 28-2-02. Stored.	2-04
❑ 3C-QSC*	F.27-200MAR	ex M-2 RNethAF, PH-FSI, PH-EXD. Arrived 28-2-02. Stored.	2-04
❑ 5N-HHH	BAC 111-401AK	ex HZ-NB2, N5024. Stored.	2-04

SOUTHEND-ON-SEA
Adventure Island: On Marine Parade is Lost City Adventure Golf, which has a novel putting hazard.

❑ G-AZRX	Horizon 160	ex Great Yarmouth, Tattershall Thorpe (?), F-BLIJ. Crashed 14-8-91. Wreck.	2-04

SOUTH WOODHAM FERRERS on the A132 north of Rayleigh
This reference is long-in-the-tooth and heading for LOST!

❑ WT525	'855' Canberra T.22	ex Stock, St Athan, FRADU, 17, 80. Nose.	2-94

STANSTED AIRPORT north of the A120 east of Bishop's Stortford M11, junction 8
Trident 3B-101 G-AWZU was scrapped by GJD Services in September 2003. The cockpit moved on to Basingstoke, Hants. The same company parted out HS.125-400B VR-BMB on 8th August, 2003. The fire crews have a realistic-looking, steel plate, BAe 146-ish fuselage to torch.

❑ G-IOIT	TriStar 100	ex Classic Airways, G-CEAP, SE-DPM, G-BEAL. Flew in 13-4-98. Stored.	9-03

STAPLEFORD TAWNEY AERODROME on the A113 south of the M11/M25 junction
Several of the long-term *W&R* items here are still to be found, if you know which shed to look in!

❑ G-AZTO	Seneca 200-2	ex Linley Hill, N4516T. Crashed 27-8-92. Spares.	6-01
❑ G-BHUP	Cessna F.152	ex Tattershall Thorpe. Crashed 17-5-89. Fuselage.	6-01
❑ G-BOIP	Cessna 152 II	ex Tattershall Thorpe, Staverton, N49264. Damaged 11-1-90.	6-01
❑ G-ORDN	Arrow II	ex G-BAJT. CoA 9-4-96. Fuselage. Dump.	6-01

STOCK on the B1007 south of Chelmsford
Hanningfield Metals / H&M Sales: Processing of airframes is but a shadow of what it once was. MoD scrap and airliners from Southend remain the staple 'diet' (including Bandeirante G-OBPL and Short 330 G-DACS in mid-2003). The hulk of Cessna A.152 G-BOPW had gone by April 2003. The Andover nose is held in a nearby yard [1]. The Phantom nose is believed to be held in the immediate area [2]. The HS.125 fuselage arrived in late 2002 but left again on January 7, 2003 for a film set in which it was destined to play a Learjet. It returned by August 2003 [2]. Buccaneer S.2 XT272 arrived from Foulness, Essex, by November 2003. It was suffering from fire damage within the cockpit and really beyond help, so parts were stripped for another project and it was scrapped.

❑ G-AVXI*	HS.748-2A/238	ex Southend, Emerald, CAFU. CoA 30-8-98. F/n 4-02.	2-04
❑ XH175	Canberra PR.9	ex St Athan, 1 PRU, 39, 58. Nose, travelling exhibit.	12-03
❑ XS643*	Andover E.3A	ex Manston 9278M, Boscombe Down, 32, A&AEE, 115, 84. Nose.	[1] 2-04
❑ XT677	Wessex HC.2	8016M, ex Brize Norton, Lyneham, Thorney Island, 18. Crashed 25-4-68.	2-04

❏ XV399	Phantom FGR.2	ex Wattisham, 56, 228 OCU, 29, 41, 2. Nose.	[2] 12-99
❏ ZF130*	HS.125-600B	ex Farnborough, St Athan, Cranfield, G-BLUW,	
		HZ-SJP, HZ-DAC, G-5-19.	[3] 2-04

WEST HANNINGFIELD west of the A130, south of Chelmsford

The fuselage hulk of Blackburn B-2 G-ACBH, last noted here in March 1998, had gone by May 2001. It is reported to have moved to Chelmsford.

WEST HORNDON west of Basildon, south of the A127

Buccaneer Preservation Society: Ricky Kelley still keeps his Buccaneer nose here.
◆ Viewing by prior arrangement *only*. ✉ Ricky Kelley, 47 Freshwell Gardens, West Horndon, CM13 3NE e-mail rickykelley@aol.com

| ❏ XW550 | Buccaneer S.2B | ex Stock, St Athan, 16, 15. Nose. | 2-04 |

WEST THURROCK near Purfleet, north of the Dartford Bridge

By May 2003, the hulk of Warrior 161 G-BTKT had moved to Biggin Hill, Gtr Lon.

| ❏ G-ASUE | Cessna 150D | ex N6018T. CoA 1-8-90. Stored. | 6-94 |
| ❏ G-AYFJ | Rallye Club | ex F-BKZR. CoA 18-5-92. Stored. | 6-94 |

GLOUCESTERSHIRE

ASTON DOWN AIRFIELD south of the A419 west of Cirencester

Cotswold Gliding Club: By July 2003 Ka 7 FMD had moved on - no other details.

❏ –	ASR EoN Baby	BGA.628, ex G-ALRU. Crashed 28-5-71. Stored.	1-04
❏ –	CVX Kestrel 19	BGA.1851. Stored.	7-99
❏ –	CWV Rhonlerche II	BGA.1873. Ex D-8226. CoA 5-94. Stored.	1-04
❏ –	'DVW ASW 20	BGA.2424. Stored.	7-99
❏ –	'EQP DG-202/17	BGA.2869. Crashed 12-7-92. Stored.	7-03
❏ XP493	Grasshopper TX.1	ex Syerston. Last flight 9-8-84.	1-04

BRISTOL

City Museum and Art Gallery: The Bristol Boxkite remains the main aeronautical attraction at the Museum, although there are other aviation artefacts. It 'flies' in the foyer.
◆ Daily 10am to 5pm. ✉ Queen's Road, Clifton, Bristol, BS8 1RL ☎ 0117 9223571 **fax** 0117 9222047 **e-mail** general_museums@bristol_city.gov.uk **www**.bristol-city.gov.uk/museums

| ❏ – | BAPC.40 Boxkite repro | ex Old Warden, *Those Magnificent Men...* | 3-02 |

Bristol Industrial Museum: As well as the Sycamore, there is a fabulous array of Bristol aero engines on show – many having been restored by the Rolls-Royce Heritage Trust, Bristol Branch – see below. Also here is a 'walk-through' engineering mock-up of Concorde.
◆ Sat to Wed 10am to 5pm all year,✉ Prince's Wharf, Bristol BS1 4RN ☎ 0117 9251470 **fax** 0117 9297318 **e-mail** andy_king@bristol-city.gov.uk **www**bristol-city.gov.uk /museums

| ❏ – | Concorde EMU | ex Filton. Forward fuselage. | 1-04 |
| ❏ XL829 | Sycamore HR.14 | ex 32, MCS, Khormaksar SAR Flight. | 1-04 |

Bristol Plane Preservation Unit (BPPU): Jim Buckingham and friends operate the well-known 'Miles Duo'. The Messenger and Gemini can be seen around and about at airshows and fly-ins. Both attended the '100 Years of Flight Experience' static display at Fairford, Glos, July 2003.
◆ Visits to the strip are *not* possible, but both aircraft can be seen in the air regularly.

| ❏ G-AKKB | Gemini 1A ✈ – | | 7-03 |
| ❏ 'RG333' | Messenger 2A ✈ G-AIEK, ex Miles 'B' condition U-9. | | 7-03 |

Brunel Technical College: The Beagle 206 is owned by the Midland Air Museum of Coventry, Warks, and is on temporary loan [1]. The College has airframes at Bristol Airport, Somerset – qv. Although somewhat dated, the entries are believed current.

❏	G-ASWJ	Beagle 206-1	ex Halton 8449M, Rolls-Royce. CoA 30-1-75.	[1]	2-04
❏	G-ATHA	Apache 235	ex Bristol Airport, N4326Y. CoA 7-6-86.		6-91
❏	G-AVDR	Queen Air B80	ex Bournemouth, Shobdon, Exeter, A40-CR, G-AVDR. CoA 30-6-86.		6-91
❏	G-AVVW	Cessna F.150H	ex Bristol Airport. CoA 31-5-82.		6-91
❏	G-AWBW	Cessna F.172H	ex Bristol Airport, Compton Abbas. Dam 20-5-73.		6-91

Others: Nearing completion as a long-term project by **Tim Cox** and team at their workshop in the general area – the Miles Sparrowjet for the Dunkerley family. All the 'metal' leavings from the M.77 conversion and salvaged metal parts from the fire hulk will be used to recreate G-ADNL and its days as an M.5. See under West Chiltington, W Sussex, for a *possible* airframe 'donor' for this project.

❏	G-ADNL*	Sparrowhawk	reconstruction - see above.	®	9-03
❏	G-AETG	Aeronca 100	ex Hanwell, Booker. Crashed 7-4-69.	®	9-01
❏	G-AEWV	Aeronca 100	ex Hanwell. Fuselage frame, other parts. Spares.		9-01
❏	–	'252' Cadet TX.1	BGA.427, ex Stoke-on-Trent, Firbeck, Bickmarsh, RAFGSA.258.		9-01
❏	EI-ALU	Avro Cadet	ex New Castle, Dublin, G-ACIH.		9-01

CHELTENHAM
Nick Parker: Cherishes his Scimitar nose.

❏	XD215	Scimitar F.1	ex Ottershaw, Foulness, Culdrose A2573, 764B, 800, 803, A&AEE. Nose.		3-04

CHIPPING CAMPDEN on the B4081 north of Stow on the Wold
The former Boscombe Down Comet nose is still kept in the area.

❏	XV814	Comet 4	ex Boscombe Down, RAE, BOAC, G-APDF. Nose.	6-01

CHIPPING SODBURY
In the general area an owner has two Whirlwinds. Both may be available for sale or exchange. The HAS.7 was last listed under Adlington, Lancs, in *W&R17* (p93). The HAR.10 was last noted in *W&R16* (p84) as being auctioned at Middle Wallop.

❏	XK911*	'519' Whirlwind HAS.7	ex Adlington, Derby, Colton, Ipswich, Wroughton, Lee-on-Solent, Arbroath A2603,771, 829, *Ark Royal* Flt, 824, 820, 845. First noted 3-00.	2-04
❏	XR458*	'H' Whirlwind HAR.10	ex Moreton Valence, Middle Wallop, Netheravon, Halton 8662M, 2 FTS, CFS, 28, 110, 103.	2-04

DURSLEY on the A4135 south-west of Stroud
Retro Track and Air Ltd: A specialist engine overhaul and airframe company which as the name implies is equally as at home with historic Grand Prix racing car restoration. The company, in association with the Jet Age Museum, built the fuselage of Sea Gladiator 'N5579' which was handed over to the Fleet Air Arm Museum at Yeovilton, Somerset, on 17th July 2002 – qv. Retro Track and Air have their own Gladiator project underway, although it is in the early stages - see under Gloucestershire Airport, Glos, for more on the background to this project. The Hurricane awaits its turn for restoration. JAM's Gamecock project was stored here once courtesy of Retro Track and Air, but moved back to Gloucestershire Airport, Glos, by January 2004.

❏	N5719*	Gladiator I	G-CBHO, ex Narvik, 263.	®	6-02
❏	Z5207*	Hurricane IIB	G-BYDL, ex Sudbury, Audley End, Russia, 151 Wing, 81. Stored.		6-02
❏	–*	Jurca Sirocco	unfinished project. Stored.		6-02

FAIRFORD AIRFIELD south of the A417 east of Cirencester

USAF Fairford: The former Halton Phantom arrived for the '100 Years of Flight Experience' exhibition (see the Appendix) and it was promptly announced that it would not return, but would be scrapped. It is not expected to see much of 2004 before the axe falls...

❑ XV408* Phantom FGR.2 9165M, ex Halton, Cranwell, Wattisham, 92, 29, 23, 228 OCU. Arrived 6-03. 3-04

FILTON AIRFIELD south of the M5 at Patchway, north of Bristol

Rolls-Royce Heritage Trust - Bristol Branch (RRHT): The Branch has an astounding collection of aero engines, centred on two former test-beds that were used for Proteus work within the R-R plant. As well as Bristol and Bristol Siddeley engines and Rolls-Royce (from 1966), de Havilland engines and archive from the former Leavesden Branch are also here.

◆ By prior permission *only*. ✉ Rolls-Royce Heritage Trust, Peter Pavey, 23 Morley Avenue, Mangotsfield, Bristol, BS16 9JE.

Rolls-Royce: AV-8B Harrier is believed to be as given, but may be 162071.
❑ 162074 AV-8B Harrier ex Wittering, AMARC, VMA-231. Stripped hulk. 2-00

Airfield: On 26th November 2003 Concorde 102 G-BOAF made the type's last-ever flight when it came 'home' on a flight from Heathrow. It will be kept courtesy of Airbus UK. An apron and a visitor centre were under construction during the spring of 2004, with a view to its first opening to the public in May 2004. The plot is that eventually it will come under the 'wing' of the Bristol Aero Collection should the proposed museum be established on the site. *Alpha-Fox* remains the property of British Airways [1].During February 2004 the first work started on the difficult job of moving Concorde 100 G-BBDG to Brooklands, Surrey [2] by road.

Rolls-Royce (RR) and Robs Lamplough (RL) base their Spitfires here. See also under North Weald, Essex, for the bulk of Robs' collection. The Canberra is a composite, with the starboard wing of Q497, see under Dumfries, Scotland [3]. The Sea Devon acts as a source of spares for Dove G-HBBC [4].

For reasons that evade the compiler, Airbus UK/Aviation Services announced they were to give up A300 freighter conversion work in May 2003. The last two undergoing conversion were N158GE (arrived 14th March 2002) and N161GE (arrived 20th April 2002) and both were scrapped, in April and March 2003 respectively. A300B4-2C S7-AAW was broken up during August/September 2003 with its cockpit noted leaving by road on 10th September.

◆ Access to Concorde will be via the Airbus UK site and for security and safety reasons *all* visits will need to be pre-booked. Finals details will be published widely, but check on the Bristol Aero Collection website: **www**.bristolaero.com

❑ G-AVDS	Queen Air B80	ex Bristol, Bournemouth, Exeter, A40-CS, G-AVDS. CoA 26-8-77. Dump		2-04
❑ G-BBDG	Concorde 100	CoA 1-3-82. BA spares, stored.	[2]	2-04
❑ G-BOAF*	Concorde 102	ex BA, G-N94AF, G-BFKX, BOAC. Arr 26-11-03.	[1]	3-04
❑ 'MT928' 'ZX-M'	Spitfire VIII ✈	G-BKMI, ex Huntingdon, Duxford, Australia, RAAF A58-671, MV154, 82 MU, 6MU. 145 Sqn c/s.	RL	2-04
❑ PS853 'C'	Spitfire PR.XIX ✈	G-RRGN, ex East Midlands, Filton, G-MXIX, North Weald, Coningsby, BBMF, West Raynham, CFE, North Weald SF, Biggin Hill SF, THUM Flt, 16, 268, 16.	RR	3-04
❑ WH665 'J'	Canberra T.17	ex Samlesbury, Cosford 8736M, 360, RNZAF, 45, 10. Dump	[3]	2-04
❑ XK896	Sea Devon C.20	G-RNAS, ex Gloucestershire, North Coates, Gloucestershire, 781, Hal Far SF, 781. CoA 3-7-84. Fuselage, dump.	[4]	2-04

GLOUCESTERSHIRE AIRPORT or Staverton, on the B4063 west of Cheltenham

Jet Age Museum (JAM) operated by the **Gloucestershire Aviation Collection**. Late in 2003, JAM had a major breakthrough in their plans to establish a permanent museum. Heritage Lottery Fund approved a Project Planning grant so that the museum could be planned along with other business elements of the case. The plan is now for a museum on the airport site and not at the previously hoped

for Brockworth (Hucclecote). Work has started on the construction of a Gloster E28/39 full-scale model, using the mouldings generated for the Farnborough and Lutterworth examples.
Many thanks to JAM's indefatigable John Lewer for a thorough explanation of the Gladiator project: "A few years ago JAM was successful, with the Fleet Air Arm Museum, in bidding for the wreckage stored at Cardington. This consisted of a fuselage with a few tail sections, but no wings. These had been sent to Malta for *Faith*. [N5520 at the Malta Aviation Museum.] About the same time a photo taken in recent times on the Norwegian/Swedish border, of what was obviously a Gladiator wreck. To cut a long story short the Cardington wreckage, in toto, was allocated to FAAM in return for their support in obtaining the 'Glad' wreck from Norway. This was approved by the Norwegians in return for a composite fuselage recreation which will be mated with a complete set of wings at Gardermoen. Delivery is estimated for summer 2004. A composite fuselage was completed for the FAAM ['N5579' handed over on 17th July 2002 and now in Cobham Hall - see under Yeovilton, Somerset.] N5914, the wreck in the photo, will be restored to full static condition for JAM. Other recovered wreckage, as part of the overall deal, and identified as N5719 will be rebuilt to flying condition in the ownership of Retro Track and Air [at Dursley, Glos]" [1]
   Notes: Meteor T.7 WL345 is owned by JAM (previously listed on the airport site) and, with modification, will be mated to the nose of F.3 EE425 to create a complete F.3 [2]. Vampire T.11 pod XD616 is stored for the de Havilland Aircraft Heritage Centre, London Colney, Herts [3]. The Sea Venom has a split-personality. The pod is in store off-site, the wings are with the rest of the externally stored airframes at the airport [4]. The Vulcan nose is on loan from Gary Spoors and David Price [5]. Airframes marked ➡ attended the '100 Years of Flight Experience' static display at the International Air Tattoo, Fairford, Glos, July 2003.
   Departures: Buccaneer S.2B nose XV165 to <u>Farnborough</u>, Hants, by 10-02 on loan.
◆ Aircraft in store at various locations. Access *not* possible at present. **e-mail** noel.griffiths@virgin.net
   www.jetagemuseum.org

❑	N5914	Gladiator II	ex Norway, 263. Crashed 2-6-40.	off-site [1]	2-04
❑	'V6799' 'SD-X'	Hurricane FSM	BAPC.72, ex 'V7767', Bournemouth, Sopley, Bournemouth, Brooklands, North Weald, Coventry, *Battle of Britain*. 501 Sqn c/s.	off-site	2-04
❑	EE425	Meteor F.3	ex Yatesbury, Earls Colne, Andrewsfield, Foulness, MoS, 206 AFS, 210 AFS, 206 AFS, 63, 266, 1, 222. Nose.	off-site [2]	2-04
❑	VM325	Anson C.19	ex Bentham, Staverton, Coventry, Halfpenny Green, WCS, NCS, WCS, TCCF, Upavon CF, 173, 4 FP.		2-04
❑	WF784	Meteor T.7	ex Bentham, Staverton, Quedgeley, Kemble 7895M, 5 CAACU, CAW, FTU, 130, 26.		2-04
❑	WH364*	Meteor F.8	ex Kemble 8169M, 601, Safi SF, Takali SF, Idris SF, Takali SF, Safi SF, 85. Arrived 10-9-03.	➡	2-04
❑	WK126 '843'	Canberra TT.18	ex Bentham, Staverton, Hucclecote, N2138J ntu, St Athan, FRADU, 100, 9.		2-04
❑	WL349 'Z'	Meteor T.7	ex Kemble, 1 ANS, 2 ANS, CFE, 229 OCU.	[2]	2-04
❑	WS807 'N'	Meteor NF.14	ex Bentham, Staverton, Yatesbury, Watton 7973M, Kemble, 1 ANS, 2 ANS. 46 Squadron c/s.		2-04
❑	XD506	Vampire T.11	ex Bentham, Staverton, Thrupp, Staverton, Swinderby, Finningley 7983M, CATCS, CNCS, 5 FTS, 206 AFS.		2-04
❑	XD616	Vampire T.11	ex Bentham, Staverton, London Colney, Hoddesdon, Old Warden, Woodford, Chester, St Athan, 8 FTS, 1 FTS, 8 FTS, 65. Pod. Stored.	[3]	2-04
❑	XE664	Hunter F.4	ex Marlborough, ?, HSA, 26. Nose.	off-site	2-04
❑	XG331	Lightning F.1	ex Hucclecote, Barton, Chelford, Long Marston, Innsworth, Staverton, Foulness, A&AEE, makers. Nose.	off-site	2-04
❑	XG691	Sea Venom FAW.22	ex Hucclecote; Helston, Chilton Cantello, Yeovilton, FRU, 891, 894.	off-site [4]	2-04
❑	XH903 'G'	Javelin FAW.9	ex Bentham, Staverton, Hucclecote, Innsworth 7938M, Shawbury, 5, 33, 29, 33, 23. 33 SQN c/s.	➡	2-04
❑	XM569	Vulcan B.2	ex Bentham, Staverton, Enstone, Cardiff, 44, Wadd Wing, 27, Cott Wing, 27. Nose.	➡ [5]	2-04

❑ XW264	Harrier T.2	ex Hucclecote, Innsworth, Dowty, Boscombe Down, HSA. Damaged 11-7-70. Nose.	off-site	2-04
❑ XX889	Buccaneer S.2B	ex Bentham, Staverton, Enstone, St Athan, 12, 208, 12, 16. 208 Sqn c/s.	➟	2-04
❑ –	McBroom Arion	ex Hucclecote. Hang-glider. Stored.		2-04
❑ –	Typhoon I	ex Twyford, Chippenham. Cockpit.	off-site	2-04
❑ –* BAPC.259	Gamecock REP	ex Dursley, Staverton. Under construction.	off-site ®	2-04

Airport: LongEZ G-WILY was flying again by 2000. Meteor T.7 WL349 is owned by JAM and has 'moved': see above. A company called Pennants works on simulators and acquired at least three Lynx AH.7 cabins early in 2003 (XZ662, XZ664 and XZ665 identified). Likewise, the cabin (actually the second fuselage) of Danish Lynx 80 S-191 was also noted by April 2002. None lingered long enough to merit a formal listing.

❑ G-AVVF	Dove 8	CoA 11-2-88. Dump. Changed location 3-98.		12-03
❑ G-AXPA	Pup 100	ex Bidford, D-EATL, G-AXPA, G-35-116. CoA 4-11-87.		1-00
❑ G-WACO	Waco UPF-7	ex N29903, NC29903. Crashed 15-4-89.	®	1-98
❑ N309LJ*	Learjet 25	ex N309AJ, N19FN, N17AR, N3UC, N6GC, N242WT, N954FA, N954GA. Arr 20-8-03. Inst afm.		8-03
❑ –	BN-2	nose for trials work.		4-99
❑ XR442	Sea Heron C.1	G-HRON, ex Yeovilton, 781, G-AORH. Stored.		12-03

INNSWORTH west of the B4063, near Parton, north-east of Gloucester
Cotswold Aircraft Restoration Group (CARG): Are still based within the RAF camp. The Fairey Ultra-Light for The Helicopter Museum, Weston-super-Mare [1] and the Monospar for the Newark Air Museum, Winthorpe, Notts [2].
◆ Visits to the workshop are possible by prior application *only*. ✉ Steve Thompson, CARG, Kia-Ora, Risbury, Leominster, Herefordshire, HR6 0NQ e-mail stevet@heli-bull.fsnet.co.uk

❑ G-AOUJ	Fairey ULH	ex Weston-super-Mare, Harlow, White Waltham, XJ928. CoA 29-3-59.	® [1]	2-04
❑ VH-UTH	Monospar ST-12	ex Winthorpe, Booker, Biggin Hill, Australia.	® [2]	2-04
❑ R9371	Halifax II	ex local, 10. Crashed 9-3-42. Cockpit.		2-04

RAF Innsworth: Personnel and Training Command HQ, the Meteor graces the main entrance.

❑ VW453	'Z' Meteor T.7	8703M, ex Salisbury Plain, Hullavington, Takali, 604, 226 OCU, 203 AFS. Gate.		2-04

KEMBLE AIRFIELD on the A429 south-west of Cirencester
Bristol Aero Collection (BAC): See under Filton, Glos, for a co-operative agreement with Airbus UK and the last-to-fly Concorde.
Notes: BAC work closely with the Britannia Aircraft Preservation Trust (BAPT – see below) and host their Series 101 nose and all of *Charlie-Fox*. The latter will become a 'walk-through' exhibit. The Beagle 206 started life as the Bristol 220 and the nose is on loan from the Science Museum [1]. The Brigand is highly appropriate and on loan from Unimetal Industries via the North East Aircraft Museum [2]. The Bristol 173 is on loan from the RAF Museum [3]. The Harrier used the BSE Pegasus [4], while the Jindivik represents the first application for the BSE (*née* Armstrong Siddeley) Viper [5].
◆ Open Easter and every Sun mid-Apr to Oct 10am to 4pm. Parties at other times by arrangement.
✉ A1 Hangar, Kemble Airfield, Cirencester, GL7 6BA ☎ 01285 771204, or ☎ / fax 0117 950 0908
www.bristolaero.com

❑ 'G-EASQ'	Babe III REP	BAPC.87, ex Banwell, Stoke, Hemswell, Cleethorpes, Selby.		3-04
❑ G-ALRX	Britannia 101	ex Banwell, Boscombe Down, WB473 ntu, VX447 ntu. Crashed 4-2-54. Nose.	BAPT	3-04
❑ G-ANCF	Britannia 308F	ex Banwell, Brooklands, Manston, 5Y-AZP, G-ANCF, LV-GJB, LV-PPJ, G-ANCF ntu, G-14-1, G-18-4, N6597C ntu, G-ANCF. CoA 12-1-81. Dism.	BAPT	3-04

❑	G-ARRM	Beagle 206-1X	ex Banwell, Brooklands, Shoreham, Duxford, Shoreham. CoA 28-12-64.	[1]	3-04
❑	G-ATDD	Beagle 206-1	ex Filton, Wroughton, South Kensington, Leeds. Damaged 6-73. Nose.	[1]	3-04
❑		Concorde EMU	ex Brooklands. Test shell, nose. Plus cabin mock-up.		3-04
❑	RH746	Brigand TF.1	ex Sunderland, Failsworth, CS(A), ATDU Gosport, Bristol, ATDU, A&AEE, Bristol. Fuselage.	[2]	3-04
❑	XF785	Bristol 173 Srs 1	ex Cosford, Henlow 7648M, G-ALBN. Arr 3-1-02.	[3]	3-04
❑	XJ917 'S-H'	Sycamore HR.14	ex Banwell, Helston, Wroughton, CFS, 275.		3-04
❑	XV798	Harrier GR.1	ex Banwell, Foulness, PCB rig, Dunsfold, 20, 233 OCU. Cr 23-4-71. Wing from T.2 XW264.	[4]	3-04
❑	A92-708	Jindivik 3	ex Llanbedr.	[5]	3-04

Britannia Aircraft Preservation Trust: See above for two of the Trust's airframes. Those who know of Roger's prowess in helping preserve Britannias and other propliners will see his e-mail address as an understatement!
✉ Roger Hargreaves, 8 Mill Park, Park Road, Burgess Hill, Sussex, RH15 8ET ☎ 014446 244613
e-mail britboss1@aol.com www.bristol-britannia.co.uk

❑	XM496	Britannia 253	ex Lanseria, EL-WXA, Transair Cargo 9Q-CJH, Aerocaribbean CU-T120, Afrek, G-BDUP, Kemble, XM496 99/511. *Jack / Regulus.*	2-04

Buccaneer Supporters Club / Buccaneer Engineering: Under the name Buccaneer Restorations, have acquired on long-term loan XW544 – see under Shawbury, Shropshire – which is due to travel to Bruntingthorpe, Leics. S.2B XX894 moved to Farnborough, Hants, by July 2002.

Delta Jets: A thriving selection of jets, restored and maintained from this super airfield. As with several other locations within this work, the bulk of the jets here are owner-operated and not part of a collection as such. The listing is restricted to aircraft on long-term restoration or storage. A composite Hunter, mostly XL578 with the tail of XG290, is in use by the fire crews [1].
Departures: Going back to *W&R18* (p66), Buccaneer S.2B XW986 was acquired by Nina and Ian Pringle and appropriately registered ZU-NIP. It was ferried to its new home at Cape Town, South Africa, arriving there on 7th August 2002. Jet Provost T.4 XS209 to Bruntingthorpe, Leics, by 1-03. Hunter T.7 XX467 moved to Exeter, Devon, on 7th February 2003.
♦ Visits by prior arrangement *only*. Occasional open days/airshows staged. **www.deltajets.com**

❑	XF995 'K'	Hunter T.8B	G-BZSF, ex Cranwell, 9237M, ex 208, 12, Laarbruch SF, 237 OCU, Honington SF, 237 OCU, FAA, 229 OCU, 245, 247.		10-03
❑	XL577 'W'	Hunter T.7	G-BXKF, ex Navenby, Cranwell 8676M, 2 TWU, 237 OCU, 1 TWU, TWU, 229 OCU.	®	9-03
❑	XL578 '77'	Hunter T.7	ex Norwich, Bruntingthorpe, Cranfield, St Athan, 1 TWU, TWU, 229 OCU. Dump, composite.	[1]	1-04
❑	XL586	Hunter T.7	ex Ipswich, Colsterworth, Shawbury, BAe Warton, 1 TWU, 2 TWU, 1 TWU, 229 OCU.		5-02
❑	XP502	Gnat T.1	ex Ipswich, St Athan 8576M, 4 FTS. Red Arrows c/s.		10-03

Others: The Boeing 727 is for spares reclamation and then destined for fire training [1]. The airfield is used for the scrapping of jetliners, but few last long enough to merit a formal inclusion in these pages. Recent examples: Canada 3000 A310s, an Air India A300 and My Travel DC-10s. Inside the Devonair Aviation Services hangar can be found a DH Mosquito-ish nose. This is part of a long-term project by David Hall to created a completely equipped, full-scale model *taxiable* Mosquito [1]. By April 2002, the hulk of Airtourer G-AZMN had moved to Oaksey Park, Wilts. Meteor F.8 WH364 moved to Fairford, Glos, for the July 2003 shindig and then took up residence at Gloucestershire Airport, Glos.

❑	G-AJOE	Messenger 2A	ex Gloucestershire, Innsworth, 'RH378'. Stored.	4-03
❑	G-AKUE	Tiger Moth	ex Chilbolton, ZS-FZL, CR-AGM, Port AF. Crashed 2-1-89. Stored.	2-00
❑	[G-APSO]	Dove 5	ex Coventry, Cumbernauld, Carlisle, Shobdon, N1046T ntu. CoA 8-7-78. Engine test rig.	4-03

❏	G-ARJB	Dove 8	ex Cumbernauld, Carlisle, Rocester, East Midlands.		
			CoΛ 10-12-73. *Exporter.*		4-03
❏	G-ASIP	Auster 6A	ex Oaksey Park, Innsworth, Staverton, Nympsfield,		
			Heathrow, VF608, 12 Flt, 652, 1904 Flt, Hague Air		
			Attaché. Damaged 7-5-73. Frame.		8-98
❏	G-ATKI	J3C-75 Cub	ex N70536, NC70536. Crashed 14-11-93.	⑧	8-98
❏	G-AXCN	Rallye Club	ex Thruxton. Wrecked 16-10-87.		7-99
❏	G-AXRU	Cessna FA.150K	ex Withybush. CoA 10-12-87.	⑧	7-97
❏	G-BDFX	Auster 5	ex Oaksey Park, F-BGXG, TW517, 661. Cr 10-10-93.		8-01
❏	G-BFEH	SAN D.117A	ex F-BITG. CoA 30-9-94.	⑧	7-99
❏	G-BMSC*	Evans VP-2	CoA 8-10-99. Stored.		10-03
❏	G-BPNL*	Quickie Q2	CoA 16-1-96. Stored.		5-03
❏	G-BSVZ*	Aircamper	ex N3265. CoA 6-9-93. Stored.		10-03
❏	G-LUST*	Silvaire 8E	ex N2065B, NC2065B. CoA 9-7-98. Stored.		10-03
❏	G-OEWA	Dove 8	ex Staverton, Biggin Hill, G-DDCD, G-ARUM.		
			CoA 7-10-91. Stored.		4-03
❏	EI-HCB*	Boeing 727-223F	ex Air Contractors, N6817, EI-HCB, N6817.		
			Arrived 8-1-03. Scrapping 3-03. Fuselage.	[1]	4-03
❏	N73410	PT-17 Kaydet	ex G-BSGR, Bristol, EC-ATY, N55050, 42-16558.		4-02
❏	VP955	Devon C.2/2	G-DVON, ex Little Staughton, Cranfield, G-BLPD ntu,		
			VP955, 207, 21, C.1 WCS, MCS, 31, Upavon SF,		
			Hendon SF, MEAF, Malta CF. CoA 29-5-96. Stored.		9-03
❏	XA880	Devon C.2	G-BVXR, ex RAE, RRE, TRE.		9-03
❏	XK895*	Sea Devon C.20	G-SDEV, ex Swansea, ex Bruntingthorpe, Cambridge,		
			Culdrose SF, 781Sqn. CoA 17-9-01.		9-03
❏	–*	'Mosquito'	cockpit. *Anopheles de Havillandus.* First noted 4-03.		7-03

MORETON-IN-MARSH on the A44 north-east of Cheltenham

Wellington Aviation Museum: Gerry Tyack's superb collection of artefacts, together with aviation art and prints (many for sale), is always worth a visit. Among the impressive array is the tail section of Wellington L7775 of 20 OTU which crashed near Braemar 23rd October 1940.

◆ Tue to Sun 10am to 12.30am and 2pm to 5.30pm. On the A44 west of the town, signed. ▣ British School House, Moreton-in-Marsh, GL56 0BG ☎ 01608 650323 www.wellingtonaviation.org

Home Office Fire and Emergency Training Centre:

❏	G-AZDZ	Cessna 172K	ex Firbeck, Fownhope, Warmingham, Southend,	
			5N-AIH, N1647C, N84508. Crashed 19-9-81.	2-02
❏	G-BAPF	Viscount 814	ex Southend, SE-FOY, G-BAPF, D-ANUN.	
			CoA 13-6-90.	2-02
❏	G-BKRD	Cessna 320	ex Sandtoft, D-IACB, HB-LDN, N2201Q. Cr 5-11-90.	6-01
❏	G-BLHL	Emeraude	ex Hooton Park, Warmingham, Wigan, East Kirkby,	
			Tattershall, Chinnor, Booker, F-BLHL, F-OBLM.	
			Crashed 4-8-81. Fuselage frame.	8-98
❏	G-BNJJ	Cessna 152 II	ex Stamford area, Spanhoe, Nayland, Cranfield.	
			Damaged 18-5-88. Hulk.	6-01
❏	G-BPAD	Seneca 200T	ex N21208. Crashed 15-7-92. Crash scene.	6-01
❏	G-BPJT	Cadet 161	ex Oxford, N9156X. Crashed 12-7-92. Wreck.	4-03
❏	G-SULL	Saratoga SP	ex Stamford, Spanhoe, N82818. Crashed 1-2-95.	8-98
❏	WT804 '831'	Hunter GA.11	ex Culdrose A2646, A2732, , Shawbury, FRADU,	
			Lossiemouth, 247. Pole mounted, nose in ground.	4-03
❏	XM404	Jet Provost T.3	ex Halton, Newton, 8055BM, Shawbury, 3 FTS, 2 FTS.	4-03
❏	XP150	Wessex HAS.3	ex Lee-o-S A2764, Wroughton, 829, *Antrim* Flt.	4-03
❏	XP680	Jet Provost T.4	8460M, ex St Athan, CAW, 6 FTS. 'Crash' scene.	6-01

NYMPSFIELD AERODROME off the B4066, south-west of Stroud

| ❏ | – | T.8 Tutor | BGA.1745, ex XE760, VM539. Stored. | 7-03 |
| ❏ | WZ831 | Grasshopper TX.1 | ex Locking, Reading, Halton, Lightwater. Stored. | 7-03 |

QUEDGELEY east of the A38, south of Gloucester
Raymond and Meryl Hansed gifted their Hunter F.5 WP190 and Lightning F.53 'XR753' to the Tangmere Military Aviation Museum and they moved to Tangmere, W Sussex, in June 2002 and, with that, **Hunter Restoration Flight** was disbanded. (Sadly, Meryl died shortly afterwards.)
    Historic Aircraft Restorations: Formed to restore the Meteor, which will be finished in 2 ANS colours. The team are the owners John Holder, Sandy Mullen and Sid Griffiths, assisted by Alex Walsh.
◆ Access by prior permission *only*.

❏ WS774	Meteor NF.14	ex Fearn, Ely, Upwood 7959M, Kemble,	
		1 ANS, 2 ANS. Stored.	2-04

RENDCOMB AERODROME east of the A435 north of Cirencester
The Utterly Butterly Barnstormers'road-show' has a short-span PT-17 travelling airframe that *may* be based upon one of the frames noted below.
◆ Access on a *strictly* prior permission basis.

❏ [XB-RIY]	PT-17	ex Hatch, Sudbury. Stored.	7-01
❏ –	PT-17	fuselage frame, stored.	7-01

HAMPSHIRE

ALDERSHOT on the A325 south of Farnborough
Parachute Regiment and Airborne Forces Museum: Devoted to the exploits of paratroop and glider-borne forces, the museum stages regular special displays and events.
◆ Open Mon to Fri 10am to 4.30pm - last admission 3.45pm. Sat, Sun and Bank Hols 10am to 4pm. Closed Xmas period. Other times by prior arrangement. Note that photography is not permitted within the museum. ✉ Browning Barracks, Aldershot,. Hampshire, GU11 2BU ☎ 01252 349619 **fax** 01252 349203 **e-mail** airborneforcesmuseum@army.mod.uk.net

❏ KP208	'YS' Dakota IV	ex Kemble, AFNE, Air Adviser New Delhi,	
		AFNE, HCCF, 24, MEAF, USAAF 44-77087.	2-04
❏ –	Hotspur II	nose section.	2-04
❏ –	Horsa II	nose section.	2-04

Keogh Barracks: Have two exit trainers.

❏ XR501	Wessex HC.2	ex Gosport, Shawbury, 22, 72, 18, 1 FTU, A&AEE.	4-01
❏ XS515	'N' Wessex HU.5	ex Gosport, A2658 [2], A2747, Lee-on-Solent, 845.	4-01

ALTON on the A31 south-west of Farnham
Air Salvage International: The yard here specialises in airliner salvage. Note that some, or even all, of the aircraft listed here may have only a brief existence before being 'parted out'. ASI also have a 'Shed' at nearby Lasham, Hants – qv. ASI were tasked with moving Concorde G-BOAA to East Fortune, Scotland. In late 2002 the cockpit and fuselage sections of Trident 3B-101 G-AWZI arrived from Reigate. The cockpit was acquired by Andrew Lee and in August 2003 moved to Lasham, Hants.

❏ G-ARAY	HS.748-1/100	ex Lasham, Dan-Air, OY-DFV, PI-C784, G-ARAY,	
		PP-VJQ, YV-C-AMC, G-ARAY. Nose.	1-02
❏ G-BITW	Short 330-100	ex Coventry, G-EASI, G-BITW ntu, G-14-3070.	
		CoA 9-6-98. Fuselage.	1-02
❏ G-ODUB*	Bandeirante	ex Leeds-Bradford, PH-FVC, G-BNIX, N8536J.	
		CoA 6-2-01. Fuselage. First noted 11-03.	1-04
❏ G-OHIG	Bandeirante	ex G-OPPP, XC-DAI, PT-SAB. CoA 30-4-96. Fuse.	4-02
❏ G-OJEM	HS.748-2B/378	ex Stansted, Emerald, ZK-MCH, G-BKAL,	
		9N-ADF,G-BKAL,V2-LDK, D-AHSD, G-BKAL.	
		Tashy's Kite. Nose. Crashed 31-3-98.	1-00

❑ A6-SHK	BAe 146-100	ex UAE Gov, G-BOMA, G-5-091. Fuse, scrapping.	4-02
❑ EI-EXP	Short 330-100	ex G-BKMU, SE-IYO, G-BKMU, G-14-3092,	
		EI-BEH, EI-BEG, G-BKMU, G-14-3092. Fuselage.	1-00
❑ HB-IZY*	SAAB 2000	ex Swiss, SE-047. Crashed 10-7-02. Fuselage.	11-03
❑ OY-BNM	Bandeirante	ex Bournemouth, N5071N, G-BFZK. F/n 7-00.	7-00
❑ OY-MUB	Short 330-200	ex Bournemouth, Muk Air, G-BITX, G-14-3069.	
		Fuselage. First noted 7-01.	4-02
❑ –	BAC 111	ex Nigerian. Cockpit.	1-02

ANDOVER
Aerofab Restorations: Cessna 180 G-AXZO was flying again by late 2002. To Bulldogs have moved on: XX657 to Colerne, Wilts, by July 2002 and XX669 to Halton, Bucks, by August 2003.

❑ G-AVDF	Pup 200	ex St Ives, Brooklands, Shoreham, Duxford,	
		Shoreham. CoA 22-5-68. Stored for owner.	4-02
❑ G-AWKM	Pup 100	ex Swansea. CoA 29-6-84. Stored.	2-03
❑ G-BGZJ	Tomahawk 112	ex Halfpenny Green. Damaged 5-8-90. Stored.	2-03
❑ G-BOPX	Cessna A.152	ex N761BK. CoA 24-1-98.	2-03
❑ XX623 'M'	Bulldog T.1	ex Newton, CFS, York UAS. EM UAS. Cr 26-7-95.	5-03
❑ G-102	Bulldog 122	ex Ghana AF. Stored.	5-03
❑ G-108	Bulldog 122	ex Ghana AF, G-BCUP.	5-03

Durney Collection:

❑ G-ALAX	Dragon Rapide	ex Old Warden, Luton, RL948, ERS, 27 GCF.	
		CoA 8-3-67. Composite. Stored, poor state.	2-99

AWBRIDGE on the B3084 north of Romsey
A fascinating find is the nose section of long-lost Pembroke, last recorded being scrapped in 1984.

❑ WV705*	Pembroke C.1	ex Wimborne, Bournemouth, BAC, 60, Wildenrath CS,	
		2 TAF CS, 152, 78, Khormaksar SF, 1417F,	
		Levant CF, Eastleigh SF, APSF, MECS. Nose	10-02

BASINGSTOKE on the M3 north-east of Winchester
The nose of the former Stansted Trident gravitated here. Previously noted under this heading, the Automobile Association's travelling F-28 is actually based at White Waltham, Berks - qv.

❑ G-AWZU*	Trident 3B-101	ex Stansted, Heathrow, BA, BEA. CoA 3-7-85.	
		Tina. Nose. Arrived 8-03.	8-03

BLACKBUSHE AERODROME on the A30 west of Yateley.

❑ [G-XIIX]	Robinson R-22	CoA 21-3-97. Pole-mounted.	9-03

BRAMLEY south-east of Tadley, east of the A340
Army Training Estate (ATE) Home Counties:

❑ XP856	Scout AH.1	ex Middle Wallop, AETW.	7-00
❑ XZ300 'L'	Gazelle AH.1	ex Middle Wallop, 670, 664, 662. Crashed 14-2-97.	7-00

CHILBOLTON AERODROME east of the A3057, south of Andover
Hampshire Light Plane Services: Dragon I G-ECAN was flying by 2002.

❑ G-ADJJ*	Tiger Moth	ex Eversden, BB819, 25 RFS, 28 EFTS, 1 EFTS,		
		9 EFTS, G-ADJJ. CoA 20-3-75. First noted 6-03.		8-03
❑ G-ANFV*	Tiger Moth	ex DF155, 25 RFS, 28 EFTS. CoA 4-2-01.	®	8-03
❑ G-BEPF	SNCAN SV-4A	ex Warminster, Raveningham, F-BCVD. Stored.		4-02
❑ G-FORD	SNCAN SV-4C	ex F-BBNS. Crashed 16-7-96. Stored.		4-02
❑ N1134K	Silvaire 8AE	ex NC1134K. Crashed 28-8-96. Spares.		5-01

Others:
❑ G-PRIM*	Tomahawk 112	ex N2398A. CoA 25-12-01. Stored.	8-03
❑ G-REPM	Tomahawk 112	ex N2528D. CoA 9-10-95. Cockpit.	8-03

COVE on the B3014 north west of Farnborough

Gary Spoors: Acquired the 707 cockpit from Bruntingthorpe and is restoring it.

❑ G-APFG*	Boeing 707-436	ex Bruntingthorpe, Cardington, Stansted, British Airtours, BOAC. CoA 24-5-81. Nose.	®	5-03

FARNBOROUGH

Whittle Memorial: Dramatically displayed on the Ively roundabout to the north of the airfield, close to the Southwood Golf Course, is a superb full-scale model of the Gloster E28/39 as a tribute to Sir Frank Whittle. This and the similar monument at Lutterworth, Leics, (qv) were financed and built by the Sir Frank Whittle Commemorative Trust. The FSM attended the '100 Years of Flight Experience' static at the International Air Tattoo, Fairford, Glos, in July 2003 prior to arriving here on 8th August 2003.

❑ –*	Gloster E28/39 FSM	BAPC.285, displayed. Unveiled 28-8-03	3-04

Prince's Mead Shopping Centre: The SE.5A still provides 'top cover' for the shoppers.

❑ 'D276'	'A' SE.5A REP	BAPC.208, built by AJD Engineering.	7-02

FARNBOROUGH AIRFIELD east of the A325, north of Aldershot

Farnborough Air Sciences Trust (FAST): On 31st October 2002, FAST moved out of Building R52 within the wind tunnel complex and into Building G1 on the A325. Much of FAST's huge collection of artefacts has moved into deep store at nearby Pyestock. G1 is also known as the Old Balloon School and was built in 1907 and is a very appropriate place to open up to the public. (FAST hope that they will be able to return to the historic and listed wind tunnel buildings in due course.) After the move, work commenced at a pace within G1 to bring it up to standard and to ready it for the public. On 28th June 2003, FAST opened its doors to the public.

Tragically, the following day, leading light in FAST's development, **John Hallett,** died during a family day out. John worked with BAE Systems and its predecessors for over 40 years. After retirement, he was instrumental in the setting up of the Bournemouth Aviation Museum and he acquired a small collection of classic jets. (See below and Southampton, Hants.) John then became chairman of the trading arm of FAST, Farnborough Air Sciences Ltd and set to developing the Old Balloon School with gusto. With John's passing, the planned high-profile ceremony was delayed until 1st October .

Notes: Several airframes are on loan: Trident 3B nose from Andrew Lee [1]; the balloons from BPG [2]; Hunter T.7 from DERA [3]; Lightning T.5 XS420 from Murray Flint [4]; the Lightning nose from Hugh Trevor [5]; the Hunter F.51, MiG-21 and Vampire T.11 from the Hallett family [6]. See under QinetiQ, below, for two more additions, on loan, for the FAST 'fleet'.

Departures: Cameron DG-19 G-BKIK and Cameron Zero 25 OO-JAT returned to the BPG at Lancing, E Sussex. Buccaneer S.2B XX894 arrived from Kemble, Glos, by July 2002, but on 27th September 2003 it departed for Bruntingthorpe, Leics.

♦ Sat and Sun 10am to 4pm, other times by arrangement. ✉ The Old Balloon School, 85 Farnborough Road, Farnborough GU14 6TF. ☎ 01252 375050. e-mail info@fasta.co.uk www.fasta.co.uk

❑ G-AWZI*	Trident 3B-101	ex Lasham, Alton, Reigate, Heathrow, BA, BEA. CoA 5-8-85. Cockpit. BEA c/s. Arrived 15-12-03.	[1]	3-04
❑ G-BKIK	Cameron DG-19	ex Lancing. CoA 4-9-88. (Helium Airship).	[2]	3-04
❑ OO-JAT	Cameron Zero 25	ex Lancing. Stored.	[2]	3-04
❑ WT309	Canberra B(I).6	ex Wycombe Air Park, Boscombe Down, Farnborough, Boscombe Down, A&AEE, HS. Nose.		3-04
❑ WV383	Hunter T.7	ex Boscombe Down, DERA, RAE, 28, Jever SF, Gutersloh SF, F.4 RAFFC. *Hecate–Lady of the Night.*	[3]	3-04
❑ XS420*	Lightning T.5	ex Walpole St Andrew, West Walton Highway, Narborough, Binbrook, LTF, 5, LTF, 226 OCU. Arrived 3-9-03.	[4]	3-04
❑ XS932	Lightning F.6	ex Shoreham, Bruntingthorpe, Rossington, Binbrook, 5, 11, 56, 11. Nose.	[5]	3-04

❏ XV165*	Buccaneer S.2B	ex Staverton, Bentham, Staverton, Hucclecote, Heathrow, Stock, Shawbury, 12. Nose. 12 Sqn c/s. First noted 10-02.		3-04
❏ E-402*	Hunter F.51	ex Bournemouth, Kemble, Bournemouth, Macclesfield, Dunsfold, G-9-433, RDanAF Esk.724. Esk 724 c/s. Arrived 25-11-02.	[6]	3-04
❏ 503*	MiG-21PF	G-BRAM, ex Bournemouth, North Weald, Hungarian AF. Arrived 3-3-04.	[6]	3-04
❏ 'U-1215'	Vampire T.11	XE998, ex Wisbech, Huntingdon, Horley, Charlwood, Biggin Hill, Warmingham, Wigan, Woodford, Chester, St Athan, 8 FTS, 4 FTS, 8 FTS. Stored, off-site.	[6]	3-04

Defence Science and Technology Laboratory / QinetiQ (DS&TL): Lynx AH.1 XX907 moved to Yeovil, Somerset, by March 2003. Lynx XZ649 is fitted with the boom of XZ646 [1]. The Gnat and the Jaguar were due to move to FAST (see above) in late March 2004 [2].

❏ XP516	Gnat T.1	ex 8580M, 4 FTS. Static tests.	[2]	3-04
❏ XV344	Buccaneer S.2C	ex Boscombe Down, Farnborough, RAE. *Nightbird*. Gate.		3-03
❏ XW241	Puma (SA.330E)	ex RAE Bedford, F-ZJUX. Stored.		3-03
❏ XW566	Jaguar T.2	ex RAE, A&AEE. Stored.	[2]	3-03
❏ XW934 'Y'	Harrier T.4	ex 20, 233 OCU, 1. Stored.		3-03
❏ XZ649*	Lynx AH.7	ex Boscombe Down, 657. Static tests. F/n 10-02.	[1]	3-03
❏	Mil Mi-24	ex ? Stored.		2-02
❏	MiG-23 / -27	ex ? Stored.		2-02

Others: An HS.125 has arrived for spares recovery.

❏ G-AXDM*	HS.125-400B	ex Edinburgh, BAE Systems/GEC-Marconi. CoA 7-6-03. Arrived by road 24-9-03.		9-03

FLEET on the A323 north-west of Aldershot

The themed restaurant 'Dakotas' closed down during 2002 and the chunks of C-47A N9050T moved initially to Cosford, Shropshire, for preparation before settling upon Hendon, Gtr Lon, in early 2003.

FLEETLANDS on the B3334 south of Fareham

RNAY Fleetlands Museum: Clearing up this entry, the nose of Sea Hawk FGA.6 WV838 moved to Bruntingthorpe, Leics, and then out to Liverpool, Merseyside, 3rd December 2002. Going back to *W&R18* (p71), it was noted that the nose of Buccaneer S.2B XK527 moved in April 2001 for 'Scotland', it is now known in 2002 it relocated again, this time to 'North Wales'.

Defence Aviation Repair Agency (DARA) **Training Centre**:

❏ XS539 '435'	Wasp HAS.1	A2640 [2], ex A2718, Lee, 829 *Endurance* Flt.		8-02
❏ XS569	Wasp HAS.1	A2639 [2], ex A2717, Wroughton, NATIU, 703.		8-02
❏ XT434 '455'	Wasp HAS.1	A2643 [2], ex A2723, Lee-on-Solent, 829.		8-02
❏ XT780 '636'	Wasp HAS.1	A2638 [2], ex A2716, Wroughton, 703.		8-02
❏ XW844	Gazelle AH.1	ex Wroughton. 659.		8-02
❏ XX440	Gazelle AH.1	A2702 [2], ex 665, 3 Regt, 12F, 669.		8-02
❏ XZ213	Lynx AH.1	TAD.213, ex Wroughton, Middle Wallop, Wroughton, 659.		8-02
❏ XZ307	Gazelle AH.1	A2703 [2], ex 665, 662, 663, 654, GCF.		8-02
❏ XZ318	Gazelle AH.1	ex Yeovil, Fleetlands. DBR 2-1-97.		1-02
❏ ZA733	Gazelle AH.1	A2704 [2], ex 665, 664, BATUS.		8-02
❏ QP31	Lynx HC.28	ex Almondbank, Wroughton, Qatar Police.	TC	8-02

Others: Wessex HU.5 XT480 moved via Hixon, Staffs, to Inverness, Scotland, in January 2004.

❏ ZH257	CH-47C Chinook	ex Wattisham 9217M, Fleetlands, Wroughton, Fleetlands, Brize Norton, Fleetlands, Portsmouth, St Athan, Stanley, Arg Army AE-520. Tail of ZA704.	®	8-02

GOSPORT on the B3333 south of Fareham
HMS *Sultan:* **Air Engineering and Survival School**: (See under Cosford, Shrop, for a glimpse of the future.) The wholly fictitious unit, 760 Training Squadron, 'operates' the airframes here and has given some airframes codes in the '2xx' series. Wessex HAS.3 XS122 is used by the medical school at **Fort Grange** (FG). Airframes marked ➥ attended the '100 Years of Flight Experience' static display at the International Air Tattoo, Fairford, Glos, July 2003. Some Sea Kings were offered for tender during February 2004 [1].

    Departures: Sea King HAS.1 XV371 to Culdrose, Cornwall, 22-7-03; HAS.6, XV643 to St Athan, Wales, by 9-02; XV654 to Culdrose, Cornwall, 1-03; XV659 and XV710 arrived at Cosford, Shropshire, 7-10-02; ZA129 to Westlands (presumed at Yeovil) for spares recovery 13-1-03; **Wessex HC.2** XR499 to Hitchin, Herts 1-4-04; HC.2 XR516 to Shawbury, Shrop, 5-02; HC.2 XR520 to Hitchin, Herts 1-4-04; HC.2 XR523 moved on to Fleetlands, Hants, and then to Torpoint, Cornwall; HC.2 XT602 scrapped 10-02; HU.5s XS485, XS517 and XT764 all scrapped 10-02; XS513 to Yeovilton, Som, 3-2-04; HU.5 XT474 to Hitchin, Herts 1-4-04.

❑ XP110	'55'	Wessex HAS.1	A2636 [2], ex A2714 [2], A2728,	
			Lee-on-Solent, Fleetlands. ABDRT	4-03
❑ XR508	'B'	Wessex HC.2	'XR499', ex Shawbury, 72, 18, 28.	4-03
❑ XR518*	'J'	Wessex HC.2	ex Shawbury, 60, 72, 22, 18, 72, 18. F/n 3-02.	4-03
❑ XS122	'655'	Wessex HAS.3	A2632 [2], ex A2707, Lee-on-Solent,	
			Manadon, Wroughton, 737. FG	4-03
❑ XS488	'XK'	Wessex HU.5	ex Wattisham, Halton, Wroughton, 846.	4-03
❑ XS489	'R"	Wessex HU.5C	ex Ballymena, Odiham, Wroughton,	
			845, 707, 846, 848. ABDRT	1-04
❑ XS496		Wessex HU.5	A2675 [2], ex A2763, Lee-on-Solent, 772.	4-03
❑ XS507	'627'	Wessex HU.5	A2674 [2], ex A2762, Lee-on-Solent, 772.	4-03
❑ XS510	'626'	Wessex HU.5	A2676 [2], ex A2765, Lee-on-Solent, 772.	4-03
❑ XS511	'YM'	Wessex HU.5	A2660 [2], ex A2750, Lee-on-Solent, 845.	4-03
❑ XS514	'YL'	Wessex HU.5	A2653 [2], ex A2740, Lee-on-Solent, 845.	4-03
❑ XS520	'YF'	Wessex HU.5	A2659 [2], ex A2749, Lee-on-Solent, 845.	1-04
❑ XS568	'441'	Wasp HAS.1	A2637 [2], ex A2715, Fleetlands, 829.	4-03
❑ XT453	'A/B'	Wessex HU.5	A2666 [2], ex A2756, Yeovilton, Lee-on-Solent, 845. ➥	7-03
❑ XT455	'U'	Wessex HU.5	A2654 [2], ex A2741, Lee-on-Solent. 845.	1-04
❑ XT458	'622'	Wessex HU.5	A2679 [2], ex A2768, Lee-on-Solent, 772.	4-03
❑ XT466	'XV'	Wessex HU.5	A2617 [4], ex Weeton 8921M, Cosford,	
			Wroughton, 847.	4-03
❑ XT484	'H'	Wessex HU.5	A2655 [2], ex A2742, Lee-on-Solent, 845.	1-04
❑ XT485	'621'	Wessex HU.5	A2680 [2], ex A2769, Lee-on-Solent, 772.	4-03
❑ XT607*	'P'	Wessex HC.2	ex Shawbury, Fleetlands, 72. First noted 3-02.	4-03
❑ XT761		Wessex HU.5	A2678 [2], ex A2767, Lee-on-Solent, Wroughton.	4-03
❑ XT765	'J'	Wessex HU.5	A2665 [2], ex A2755, Lee-on-Solent, 845.	4-03
❑ XT771	'620'	Wessex HU.5	A2673 [2], ex A2761, Lee-on-Solent, 772.	4-03
❑ XV370	'260'	SH-3D Sea King	A2682 [2], ex A2771, Lee-on-Solent, Yeovil, G-ATYU.	1-04
❑ XV625	'471'	Wasp HAS.1	A2649 [2], ex A2735, Lee-on-Solent,	
			Culdrose, Manadon, 815. ➥	8-03
❑ XV642	'259'	Sea King	A2614 [3], ex A2613, Lee-on-Solent, Yeovil,	
		HAS.2A	A&AEE, Yeovil, A&AEE, Yeovil.	4-03
❑ XV655	'270'	Sea King HAS.6	ex 814, 819, 826, 845, 826, 814, 826, 819, 737, 824.	4-03
❑ XV660	'269'	Sea King HAS.6	ex Culdrose, 819, 810, 706, 810, 819, 810,	
			826, 810, 824, 706.	4-03
❑ XV663		Sea King HAS.6	ex Fleetlands, 819, 810, 820, 819, 737, 706, 826.	4-03
❑ XV665	'507'	Sea King HAS.6	ex 810, 820, 810, 824, 826.	4-03
❑ XV669	'410'	Sea King HAS.1	A2602 [4], ex Culdrose, Fleetlands 820. *Mr Walter*.	4-03
❑ XV674*	'015'	Sea King HAS.6	ex 820, 819, 826, 814, 819. Arrived 21-1-03. [1]	2-04
❑ XV675	'701'	Sea King HAS.6	ex 819, 706, 824, 814, 706, 819, 814, 737, 819.	4-03
❑ XV677	'269'	Sea King HAS.6	ex Fleetlands, 814, 820, 810, 819, 814, 820, 819.	4-03
❑ XV696	'269'	Sea King HAS.6	ex Culdrose, 814, 819, 826, 825, 814, 820.	4-03
❑ XV701	'268'	Sea King HAS.6	ex 814, 820, 706, 810, 819, 706, 814, 824.	4-03
❑ XV705	'821'	Sea King HU.5	ex Fleetlands, 771, 819, 706, 819, 814, 824.	4-03
❑ XV708	'501'	Sea King HAS.6	ex 810, 819, 706, 819, 706, 820, 737.	4-03

❑ XV711*	'515'	Sea King HAS.6	ex 810, 819, 814, 706, 820, 706, 824, 706, 819,		
			814, 819. Arrived by 3-03.		4-03
❑ XV712	'266'	Sea King HAS.6	ex 814, 820, 814, 820, 810, 820, 706, 826, 706, 814.		4-03
❑ XV713	'018'	Sea King HAS.6	ex Fleetlands, 820, 810, 706, 826, 810, 814, 820.		4-03
❑ XV720		Wessex HC.2	A2701 [2], ex Fleetlands, SARTU, 22, 18.		1-04
❑ XV724		Wessex HC.2	ex Shawbury, Fleetlands, 22, SARTS, 18.		4-03
❑ XV725	'C'	Wessex HC.2	A2707 [2], ex Shawbury, 72, 18.		1-04
❑ XZ570*		Sea King HAS.5	ex QinetiQ, Yeovil, A&AEE. Arrived by 10-01.		4-03
❑ XZ576*		Sea King HAS.6	ex A&AEE, Yeovil, 820. Arrived by 4-02.		4-03
❑ XZ579	'707'	Sea King HAS.6	ex 819, 820, 814, 820, 819, 824, 826, 824.	[1]	4-03
❑ XZ581	'269'	Sea King HAS.6	ex Fleetlands, 810, 826, 819, 814, 824, 826, 706, 814.		4-03
❑ XZ930	'Q'	Gazelle HT.3	ex Shawbury, 2 FTS, CFS.		4-03
❑ ZA126	'504'	Sea King HAS.6	ex 810, 706, 820, 810, 820.		4-03
❑ ZA127	'509'	Sea King HAS.6	ex 810, 706, 810, 826, 810, 706, 820.	[1]	2-04
❑ ZA128*	'010'	Sea King HAS.6	ex 820, 706, 820,nArrived by 11-02.	[1]	2-04
❑ ZA131	'271'	Sea King HAS.6	ex 814, 820, 826, 810, 826.		1-04
❑ ZA136	'18'	Sea King HAS.6	ex 820, 706, 820, 819, 706, 824, 814, 826.		
			Ditched 4-9-98.		4-03
❑ ZA170*		Sea King HAS.5	ex Fleetlands, 706, 810. Arrived by 10-00. Black c/s.		4-03
❑ ZF649		EH-101 PP5	ex Yeovil.		4-03
❑ ZD630*	'012'	Sea King HAS.6	ex Culdrose, 820. Arrived 22-1-04.		1-04
❑ ZD633	'014'	Sea King HAS.6	ex 820, 810, 814, 810, 820, 706.	[1]	2-04
❑ ZD637*	'700'	Sea King HAS.6	ex 819. 814. 810. 819. Arrived 11-10-01.		4-03
❑ ZG817	'702'	Sea King HAS.6	ex 819, 810.		4-03
❑ ZG818	'707'	Sea King HAS.6	ex Fleetlands, 819, 814.	[1]	2-04
❑ ZG819	'265'	Sea King HAS.6	ex 814, 820.		4-03
❑ ZG875	'013'	Sea King HAS.6	ex Yeovilton, 820, 819, 814. Cr 12-6-99. Wreck.		4-03

Bernie Salter: Kept in the general area is Bernie's superb mock-up Lancaster nose section, used in many film sequences. The Lancaster nose that was listed here in the past (B.10 FM118 from Shilo, Canada) is indeed Bernie's, but still awaits shipment to the UK. The nose here is none other than the top section of the former Charles Church B.10AR KB976. The story of the unfortunate KB976 can be found under Sandtoft, Lincs, in *W&R18*. Suffice it to say that the bulk can be found in the USA, small elements at Sandtoft and the extreme rear fuselage is at AeroVenture, Doncaster, S Yorks.

❑ KB976	Lancaster	G-BCOH, ex North Weald, Bournemouth, Biggin		
		Hill, Cranfield, Bedford, Woodford, Strathallan,		
		CF-TQC, CF-AMD, KB976, 405. Nose.		4-03
❑ –	Lancaster REP	mock-up forward fuselage.		4-03

Gosport Aviation Society / Gosport Aviation Museum Trust: The society maintains a collection of photographs, artefacts and display boards largely devoted to the history of aviation in the Gosport area at the **Royal Naval Armaments Museum**.
✉ GAS, c/o Royal Naval Armaments Museum, Priddy's Hard, Gosport, PO12 4LE ☎ 02392 422115

HAMBLE south-east of Southampton
Hamble Aerostructures: On the B3397 into Hamble, opposite 'The Harrier' public house, can be found the Gnat, still guarding the former Folland plant.
❑ XM693   Gnat T.1   ex Abingdon, Bicester 7891M, A&AEE.   5-03

HEDGE END on the A334 east of Southampton
Auster 5 G-AKXP moved to Keevil, Wilts, by March 2003.

HOOK north of the M3, near Junction 5
❑ G-AJXC   Auster 5   ex TJ343, 652, 655. CoA 2-8-82. Dam 16-10-87.   6-02

LASHAM AERODROME west of Golden Pot, north-west of Alton

Second World War Aircraft Preservation Society (SWWAPS): As well as the aircraft and artefact collection, SWWAPS offers great views of the intensive gliding activity on the airfield. The Meteor NF.13 is a complex composite, with the centre section, wings and tailplane from Israel, the nose from TT.20 WM234, latterly at Arborfield, and rear fuselage of F.8 VZ462 from Biggin Hill [1].
♦ Located to the east of the gliding headquarters, on the north side of the airfield. Open Sun and Bank Hols 10.30am to 5pm (or dusk if first) and other times by arrangement. ✉ Bob Coles, 8 Barracane Drive, Crowthorne, Berks, RG45 7NU.

❑ 'VH-FDT'	DHA Drover II	G-APXX, ex Blackbushe, Southend, G-APXX, VH-EAS.		2-04
❑ 4X-FNA	Meteor NF.13	ex Israel, IDF-AF, WM366, A&AEE, RRE.	[1]	2-04
❑ VR192	Prentice 1	G-APIT, ex Biggin Hill, Southend, VR192, 1 ASS, 6 FTS, CFS, 2 FTS, Blackburn's. CoA 7-9-67.		2-04
❑ WF137	Sea Prince C.1	ex Yeovilton, Culdrose SF, Shorts FU, Arbroath SF, 781. 'Admiral's Barge' c/s.		2-04
❑ WH291	Meteor F.8	ex Kemble, 229 OCU, 85, CAW, 257. 79 Sqn c/s.		2-04
❑ WV798 '026'	Sea Hawk FGA.6	ex Chertsey, Culdrose A2557, FRU, 801, 803, 787.		2-04
❑ XK418	Auster AOP.9	ex Basingstoke, Thruxton, Middle Wallop 7876M, 654.		2-04
❑ XM833	Wessex HAS.3	ex Lasham, Wroughton.		2-04
❑ E-423	Hunter F.51	ex Elstree, Bitteswell, Dunsfold G-9-444, Dan AF, Esk 724 and in their colours.		2-04
❑ 22+35	F-104G	ex Manching, JbG34, KE+413, DD+105.		2-04

Others: Andrew Lee acquired the cockpit of a Trident during June 2003 and it moved here in August. With great help from the resident ATC Engineering and the Trident Preservation Society (see under London Airport, Gtr Lon) a restoration programme was set up and the whole thing was mounted on a purpose-built trailer. On 15th December 2003, it moved to Farnborough, Hants, on loan to FAST. The Shorts 360 is held by ASI of Alton, Hants [1].

❑ G-BLGB	Short 360-100	ex BRA / Loganair, G-14-3641. Damaged 9-2-98.	[1]	7-01
❑ OO-DHN*	Boeing 727-31	ex DHL, N260NE, N97891. Stored. First noted 11-02.		1-04

LEE-ON-SOLENT AIRFIELD east of the B3385, south of Fareham

Super Catalina Restoration:
♦ Visits possible *only* by prior permission. www.supercatalina.com

❑ N423RS	PBY-5A Catalina	ex Duxford, Greenpeace, C-FJJG, CF-JJG, ⤲ N4002A, USN 48423.		3-04
❑ VR-BPS	PBY-5A Catalina	ex Lasham, Hamble, Duxford, '9754', G-BLSC, 'JV928', Barkston Heath, South Africa, C-FMIR, N608FF, CF-MIR, N10023, Bu46633. Crashed 27-7-98.	®	3-04

Others: By September 2002 a pair of Dakotas were in open store.

❑ G-BNJM*	Warrior II	ex Biggin Hill, Carlisle, N8015V. Damaged 18-5-89.	®	9-03
❑ 'G-DAKK*	C-47A-35-DL ⤲	ex South Coast Airlines, G-OFON ntu, F-GEOM, Fr Navy 36, OK-WZB, OK-WDU, 42-23936. CoA 23-5-03. First noted 9-02. Stored.		9-03
❑ '292912'* 'NF-L'	C-47A-35-DL ⟩	N47FK, ex North Weald, Elstree, EC-FNS, EC-187, N2669A, C-FEEX, CF-EEX, N308FN, N3PG, N3W, N7V, NC49538, 42-23838. RAF c/s by 9-03. First noted 9-02. Stored.		10-03

MIDDLE WALLOP AIRFIELD on the A343 south-west of Andover

Museum of Army Flying (MoAF): The acquisition of the prototype utility Lynx, XX153, is quite a coup for the museum. The restoration was carried out at Yeovil by AgustaWestland apprentices [1].
Notes: The AFEE 10/42 is centred upon an original Jeep and is on loan from the Wessex Aviation Society [2]. Largest Horsa airframe on show is 'KJ351' which is an amalgam of LH208, TL659 and 8569M [3]. Another nose section and other large Horsa sections can be found on display within Hayward

Hall. Several other sections are held in store. The battered centre fuselage of TL659 is currently at Shawbury, Shropshire, along with other parts, to act as a reference for a project there. [4]. The GAL Hotspur re-creation has adopted the identity and colours of an example that flew with the Shobdon-based 5 Glider Training School [5]. The Hamilcar (made up of parts from NX836 and TK718) is a 'walk-through' exhibit, currently under restoration. Mannequins and workbenches inside the capacious fuselage cheerfully 'hide' this work-in-progress! [6] The ML Utility inflatable aircraft had three wing options, 'Clouy', 'Delta' and 'Gadfly', all three are in store [7]. The Prospector is a composite [8]. MoAF aircraft out on loan are as follows: Gazelle XW276 at Winthorpe, Notts, Pucará A-528 at Sunderland, T&W; and Skeeter AOP.12 XL770 at Southampton.

Departures: UH-1H AE-406 moved to Valley, Wales, 17-9-02. The Scout CIM moved to Boscombe Down, Wilts.

◆ 10am to 4.30pm every day - last entry 4pm. Also within is 'Choppers' cafe (renamed and now with an AH-64 Apache 'pub' sign on the A343) offering commanding views of the activity on the airfield. ▣ Middle Wallop, Stockbridge, SO20 8DY ☎ 01980 674421 fax 01264 781694 e-mail daa@flying-museum.org.uk www.flying-museum.org.uk

❏	G-AXKS		W-Bell 47G-4A	ex Bristow, ARWF, G-17-8. CoA 21-9-82.		1-02
❏	'B-415'		AFEE 10/42 REP	BAPC.163, ex Wimborne.	[2]	10-01
❏	P-5		Rotachute III	8381M, ex Henlow. On loan from RAF Museum, built F. Hills & Son, Barton to Spec 11/42.		1-02
❏	'N5195'		Sopwith Pup	G-ABOX, ex Redhill. On loan. CoA 18-6-90.		1-02
❏	'T9707'		Magister I	ex Cardington, Manchester, Hendon 8378M, Gaydon, Henlow, G-AKKR, 'T9967', T9708, 51 MU, 16 EFTS, 239. CoA 10-4-65.		1-02
❏	'KJ351'		Horsa II	BAPC.80, fuselage.	[3]	1-02
❏	'HH268'		Hotspur II REP	BAPC.261. Unveiled 13-12-01.	[5]	1-02
❏	TJ569		Auster 5	G-AKOW, ex PH-NAD, PH-NEG, TJ569, 652, 660, 659. CoA 26-6-82.		1-02
❏	TK777		Hamilcar I	ex Christian Malford. Forward fuselage.	[6]	1-02
❏	WG432	'L'	Chipmunk T.10	ex AFWF, LAS, Bri UAS, 19 RFS, Cam UAS, 4 BFTS.		10-01
❏	WJ358		Auster AOP.6	G-ARYD, ex Perth, WJ358, 651, 657, 1913 Flt.		1-02
❏	WZ721		Auster AOP.9	ex 4 RTR, 656, 6 Flt. Dragon.		1-02
❏	WZ772		G'hopper TX.1	ex Halton, 1 MGSP, Brentwood. Stored.		11-03
❏	XG502		Sycamore HR.14	ex gate, Wroughton, Bristol, JEHU.		1-02
❏	XK776		ML Utility Mk 1	ex Cardington, Middle Wallop, A&AEE. On loan.	[7]	1-02
❏	XL813		Skeeter AOP.12	ex ARWF, 4 Regt, 9 Flt.		1-02
❏	'XM819'		Prospector	ex Durrington. Composite.	[8]	1-02
❏	XP821		Beaver AL.1	ex Shawbury, Kemble, St Athan, Defence Attaché,		
	'MCO'			Laos, 130 Flt, 30 Flt RASC, 656. White/grey c/s.		1-02
❏	XP822		Beaver AL.1	ex Duxford, 'Wallop, Shawbury, Kemble, 132 Flt, 667, 18 Flt. 'Gate'.		10-01
❏	XP847		Scout AH.1	ex AETW, Wroughton, Yeovil.		1-02
❏	XP910	'D'	Scout AH.1	ex SEAE. Crashed 13-9-89.	®	1-02
❏	XR232		Alouette AH.2	ex Historic Flight, Wroughton, A&AEE, Middle Wallop, EW&AU, 656, A&AEE, 16 Flt, 6 Flt.		1-02
❏	XT108	'U'	Sioux AH.1	ex Duxford, Yeovilton, 'Wallop, D&T Flt, 'Wallop.		1-02
❏	XV127		Scout AH.1	ex Fleetlands, Chelsea, Wroughton, 655.		1-02
❏	XX153*		Lynx AH.1	ex Yeovil, Wattisham 9320M, Foulness, Westlands. Arrived 28-10-03.	[1]	11-03
❏	ZA737		Gazelle AH.1	ex 1 Rgt, 847, Fleetlands 'hack', 670, ARWS.		1-02
❏	AE-409	'656'	UH-1H 'Huey'	ex Duxford, Middle Wallop, 656, Stanley, Argentine Army, 72-21506.		1-02
❏	111989		L-19A Bird Dog	N33600, ex Fort Rucker, Alabama.		1-02
❏	'243809'		CG-4A Hadrian	BAPC.185, ex Burtonwood, Shrewsbury. Fuselage.		1-02
❏	70-15990*		AH-1F Cobra	ex US Army. Arrived by 2-03.		11-03
❏	–		Horsa II	Fuselage.	[4]	10-01
❏	–		Horsa II	Cockpit.	[4]	10-01

Army Air Corps Historic Aircraft Flight / Army Air Corps Reserve Collection Trust (RCT): The Trust was formed to support the Flight. Some aircraft within the Trust are on loan, including Tiger Moth G-AOHY. The Trust's Beaver XP772 (G-BUCJ) is at Duxford, Cambs. A Chipmunk has joined the flight. Aircraft marked ➥ attended the '100 Years of Flight Experience' static display at the International Air Tattoo, Fairford, Glos, July 2003. Two Skeeters from the estate of the late Francis Chamberlain are held in store [1]. Last recorded in *W&R16*, Auster AOP.9 WZ706 was noted in the museum workshop in November 2003. It was cancelled by the CAA 18th March 1999 [2].
◆ *Not* available for public inspection, but does 'do the rounds' of the airshow circuit.

❑ G-AOHY		Tiger Moth	ex Shobdon, Land's End, Elmdon, N6537, Dyce SF, Ringway SF, 11 RFS, 11 EFTS, 35 ERFTS. CoA 20-8-60.	RCT ®	3-97
❑ G-APOI*		Skeeter Mk.8	ex Ipswich. CoA 2-8-00.	[1]	2-04
❑ N6985		Tiger Moth ➥	G-AHMN, ex 2 EFTS, 22 EFTS, Andover SF. Loan.		3-98
❑ NX534*		Auster III	G-BUDL, ex PH-POL, RNeth AF 8A-2, R-17, NX534, 84 GCS, 4, 130 AF, 658. F/n 11-03.	®	11-03
❑ WD325*	'N'	Chipmunk T.10 ➥	ex BFWF, LAS, 12 GCF, 17 RFS.	➥	2-04
❑ WZ706*		Auster AOP.9	G-BURR, ex 656. First noted 11-03.	[2]	11-03
❑ XL812*		Skeeter AOP.12	G-SARO, ex Ipswich. CoA 1-8-01.	[1]	2-04
❑ XL814		Skeeter AOP.12	ex 1 Wing, 2 Wing, 651.	®	7-03
❑ XP242		Auster AOP.9 ➥	G-BUCI. Ex AFWF. CoA 19-5-00.	RCT	3-98
❑ XP820		Beaver AL.1 ➥	ex 7 Regt, 667, 132 Flt RCT, 130 Flt RCT, 30 Flt RASC, 11 Flt, 656.	➥	2-04
❑ XP884*		Scout AH.1	ex Arborfield, Middle Wallop. Spares.		2-04
❑ XR244		Auster AOP.9 ➥	ex AFWF.	➥	7-03
❑ XR379		Alouette AH.2 ➥	ex Almondbank, 667, 16F, 6(A) Flt.	➥	2-04
❑ XT131	'B'	Sioux AH.1 ➥	ex D&T Flight. Stored.	➥	2-04
❑ XT151		Sioux AH.1	ex ARWF. Spares.		2-04
❑ XT626	'Q'	Scout AH.1	ex 666, Wroughton, 656, BATUS, 656, 663.	➥	2-04

No.2 Training Regiment, Aircrew Technical Training Detachment / No.70 Aircraft Workshops (ACW): Technical training here is a detachment of SEAE at Arborfield, Berks, qv. Three airframes serve in this role, within Stockwell Hall. The Sioux on the gate has its complex side. The plate in the cockpit gives it as WA-S-179, which makes it XT827, latterly a 'spares ship' with the Historic Flight [1]. Sioux AH.1 XT151 is used by the Historic Flight as a spares source - see above.

❑ WZ724		Auster AOP.9	7432M, ex 'WZ670', 656, FEAF. Tan/brown colours. Gate.		2-04
❑ XP893		Scout AH.1	ex Wroughton, Garrison Air Sqn, 3 CBAS, 655, 666, 656. ABDR.	70 ACW	3-00
❑ XR436		SARO P.531-2	ex MoAF, A&AEE. ABDR.		7-90
❑ XR630		Scout AH.1	ex 658, 664, 666, 664. Hulk.		6-98
❑ 'XT123'	'D'	Sioux AH.1	XT827, ex Wroughton, Yeovilton, Coypool, 3 CBAS. Composite. Gate.	[1]	8-03
❑ XT638	'N'	Scout AH.1	ex Fleetlands, 666. Gate.		2-04
❑ XV131	'Y'	Scout AH.1	ex Wroughton, 660, 665,.653, D&TS. ABDR.	70 ACW	3-00
❑ XV629		Wasp HAS.1	ex Wroughton, 703. ABDR.		5-94
❑ XX443	'Y'	Gazelle AH.1	ex 658, 662, 663, 3 Regt, 669, 659. Cr 28-9-97.	SEAE	4-98
❑ QP32		Lynx HC.28	TAD.016, ex Middle Wallop, Almondbank, Wroughton, Qatar Police.	SEAE	4-98

ODIHAM AIRFIELD on the A32 south of Odiham
RAF Odiham: The Wessex on the dump has the tail of HC.2 XT601 [1].

❑ XR453	'A'	Whirlwind HAR.10	8883M, ex Foulness, 2 FTS, CFS, 230, 1563 Flt, CFS. Gate		4-03
❑ XS498	'WK'	Wessex HU.5C	9277M, ex Predannack, Gosport A2641 [3], Shawbury, Akrotiri, 84, FAA. 'Joker'. Dump.	[1]	5-01
❑ ZA678	'EZ'	Chinook HC.1	9229M, ex Fleetlands, 7, N37023. Crashed 24-7-89.		6-01

Steve Markham: A SIPA is stored locally.

| ❏ G-AWLG | SIPA 903 | ex F-BGHG. CoA 22-8-79. Stored. | 12-97 |

POPHAM AERODROME on the A303 west of North Waltham
Not noted since August 1996, Cessna 150B G-ARTY has moved to LOST! Mini Coupe G-BPDJ had moved on by July 2003.

❏ G-ATKU	Cessna F.172G	ex Hinton-in-the-Hedges. Damaged 20-7-91. Fuselage.	1-97
❏ G-BSTV	Cherokee Six	ex N4069R. Stored.	9-03
❏ G-MTBC	Gemini Flash 2	CoA 11-5-92. Stored.	5-98

PORTSMOUTH
Marine Salvage Ltd: Correcting *W&R18* (p77) Lightning F.53 ZF581 moved to Rochester, Kent.

| ❏ XM369 | 'C' Jet Provost T.3 | 8084M, ex Harry Pounds, East Wretham, Halton, Shawbury, 2 FTS. | 5-01 |

Royal Navy Diving School: The Wessex is still kept in a deep lake off Horsea Island.

| ❏ XT760 | Wessex HU.5 | A2669 [2], ex Fleetlands. | 1-00 |

ROMSEY or Farley, on the A27 north-west of Southampton
A farm strip in this general area has a number of *W&R* inmates. F.150H G-AWUH and Fuji FA.200 G-BAPM had gone by May 2003.

❏ G-AXCX	Pup 150	ex G-35-046. CoA 10-7-94. Stored.	5-00
❏ G-BFJJ	Evans VP-1	CoA 23-6-96. Stored.	2-01
❏ G-BHDO	Cessna F.182Q	Forward fuselage. Crashed 7-5-89.	1-96
❏ G-BNHE	ARV Super 2	CoA 7-8-99. Stored.	2-01
❏ EC-AOZ	PA-20-150 Pacer	G-BXBB, ex N1133C.	10-02
❏ N5052P	Comanche 180	ex Nuthampstead, Panshanger, G-ATFS, N5052P.	10-02
❏ OO-VPC	Cessna 185A	Stored.	1-96

SOPLEY on the B3347 north of Christchurch
The Kraguj from Shoreham came here. There *may* be others of the breed in the area.

| ❏ 30151* | P-2 Kraguj | ex Shoreham, Fordingbridge, Bournemouth, Yugoslav AF. Fuselage. | 2-04 |

SOUTHAMPTON
Hall of Aviation: There has been no progress to report of on a potential move.
   Notes: The Tiger Moth is a composite, with parts from G-AOAC and G-AOJJ [1]. Several airframes are on loan, the Sandringham from the Science Museum [2], the SR.A.1 from the Imperial War Museum [3], the Sea Vixen from the late John Hallett. On 7th December 2003 Neville Duke presided at a ceremony dedicating the Sea Vixen in John's memory. (For details of John, see under Farnborough, Hants.) [4]. The museum has an excellent relationship with **424 Squadron, Air Cadets** (424). The unit have their headquarters within the museum complex, although not open to the public. All but one of 424's airframes are their own, ie not MoD property. Within their HQ are several impressive procedure trainers and simulators, including a three-axis 'JP' cockpit which may be wholly 'synthetic' but may also owe its origins to a Mk.3 or Mk.4, although it is emblazoned 'T Mk 5-A' (*sic*). Airframes marked ➥ attended the '100 Years of Flight Experience' static Fairford, Glos, July 2003.
◆ Open daily *except* Mondays and over Christmas, 10am to 5pm (Tue to Sat) and 2pm to 5pm (Sun)
   ✉ Albert Road South, Southampton, Hants, SO1 1FR ☎ 023 80635830 **fax** 023 80223383 **e-mail** aviation@spitfireclub.com **www**.spitfireonline.co.uk

❏ 'G-ADZW'	HM.14 'Flea'	BAPC.253, ex Sandown, Lake, Isle of Wight.	10-03
❏ G-ALZE	BN-1F	ex Cosford, Kemble, Bembridge.	10-03
❏ VH-BRC	Sandringham 4	ex Lee-on-Solent, VP-LVE *Southern Cross*, N158C, VH-BRC, ZK-AMH, JM715.	[2] 10-03

❏	'C4451'		Avro 504J REP	BAPC.210, built by AJD Engineering.		10-03
❏	N248		Supermarine	ex Cowes, Southampton, Henlow, Southampton		
			S.6A	Pier, 'S1596', Eastleigh, Calshot, RAFHSF.		10-03
❏	'N546'		Wight Quad'plane	BAPC.164, ex Wimborne. Repro.		10-03
❏	'K5054'		Spitfire REP	G-BRDV, ex Sandown, Keevil. CoA 18-2-95. off-site	➧	10-03
❏	BB807		Tiger Moth	G-ADWO, ex Wimborne.	[1]	10-03
❏	PK683		Spitfire F.24	ex Kingsbridge Lane, Kemble, Colerne, Changi		
				7150M, Singapore Aux AF.		10-03
❏	TG263		SARO SR.A.1	ex Duxford, Staverton, Cranfield, G-12-1, TG263.	[3]	10-03
❏	WK570		Chipmunk T.10	8211M, ex Bournemouth Airport, Hamble,		
			PAX	663, Hull UAS, 663, RAFC.	424	10-03
❏	WM571		Sea Ven FAW.22	ex Wimborne, Staverton, ADS, 831B, HS. Stored.		3-02
❏	WZ753		Grasshopper TX.1	ex Halton, Emanuel School, London.		10-03
❏	XD332		Scimitar F.1	ex Helston, Culdrose SAH-19, Lee-on-Solent		
		'194'		A2574, 764B, 736, 807, 804. Stored, outside.	➧	10-03
❏	XD596		Vampire T.11	ex Calmore, St Athan 7939M, CATCS,		
				CNCS, 5 FTS, 4 FTS.	424	10-03
❏	XJ476		Sea Vixen FAW.1	ex Boscombe Down, A&AEE. Nose. Stored.	424	3-04
❏	XJ571*	'242'	Sea Vixen FAW.2	ex Brooklands, Dunsfold, Southampton, Cosford 8140M,		
				Halton, Sydenham, 893, 892, 899. Arrived 5-2-03.	[4]	12-03
❏	XK740		Gnat F.1	ex Hamble, Cosford 8396M, Bicester,		
				Church Fenton, MoS, Filton.		10-03
❏	XL770		Skeeter AOP.12	ex Middle Wallop, Shrivenham 8046M,		
				Wroughton, 15/19 Hussars, 652, 654.		10-03
❏	XN246		Cadet TX.3	ex Syerston, 617 GS.		10-03
❏	–		Swift CIM	–		10-03
❏	–		Jet Provost CIM	marked 'CRAN 22/2'.	424	3-02
❏	–	BAPC.7	SUMPAC	ex Old Warden, Southampton. Man-powered aircraft.		10-03
❏	–	BAPC.215	Airwave HG	prototype.		10-03
❏	–		HM.14 'Flea'	ex Rayleigh.		3-04

Aero Antiques and AeroTech Ltd: The DH.71 Tiger Moth (monoplane) project has been abandoned. The DH.34 project is based on original wings, all else is new [1]. The provenance of Tiger Moth G-ASPV is unknown. The original went to Norway in 1974 [2]. Tiger Moth G-DHTM is effectively a 'from new' project [3].
◆ Visits possible strictly by prior application *only*.

❏	G-ABDX*	DH.60G Moth	ex HB-UAS, G-ABDX. CoA 28-7-99. Stored.		11-03
❏	G-ACET	DH.84 Dragon	ex Bishop's Stortford, AW171, Ringway SF,		
			6 AACU, G-ACET.	® [1]	11-03
❏	G-AERV*	Whitney Straight	ex Upper Ballinderry, Newtownards, EM999,		
			Kemble, Abingdon SF, Halton SF, G-AERV.		
			CoA 9-4-66. Arrived 4-02. Stored.		11-03
❏	G-AFSW	Chilton DW.2	ex Chilton Manor. Unflown. Stored.		1-00
❏	G-AHMM	Tiger Moth	ex EM870, 25 ETFS. Crashed 10-7-54.	®	1-00
❏	G-ALJL	Tiger Moth	ex T6311, Fairford SF, 38 GCF, Tarrant Rushton		
			SF, 11 OTU, 25 PEFTS. CoA 28-9-50.	®	1-00
❏	G-AMIU	Tiger Moth	ex Membury, Wycombe Air Park, T5495, 16 EFTS,		
			54 OTU, Church Fenton SF. Crashed 15-10-69. Stored.	11-03
❏	G-ANFP	Tiger Moth	ex Fownhope, London Colney, Denham, Rush Green,		
			N9503, 2 RFS, 7 RFS, 2 RFS, 4 RFS, 4 EFTS.		
			CoA 1-7-63. Frame.	®	1-00
❏	G-ARTH	Super Cruiser	ex EI-ADO. CoA 21-4-95. Stored.	®	11-03
❏	G-ASPV*	Tiger Moth	ex Laindon, T7794. CoA 31-8-97. Arrived 2-7-03.	[2]	7-03
❏	G-DHTM	Tiger Moth	Under construction.	[3]	1-00
❏	DR613	GM.1 Wicko	G-AFJB, ex Berkswell, Coventry, ATA, G-AFJB.		
			CoA 12-7-63.	®	11-03

Frank Lund: Keeps his Canberra nose in the area. Frank has restored not only the airframe but sourced and renovated to working condition all of the photo-recce gear.

❏	WT536	Canberra PR.7	ex Bruntingthorpe, Cosford 8063M 80, 31, 13, 17. Nose.	6-03

The World's End: A large pub-cum-night-club– among other things – has/had an 'Avro 504' hanging from the ceiling in the main bar area. The fuselage looks relatively convincing – while the lettering ICE PATROL does not, but the wings are truncated and poorly prepared.

❏ –	'Avro 504' FSM	–	12-99

Others: A collector in the general area has two Vampires and a Gannet.

❏ WN411	Gannet AS.1	ex Abbotsinch, 820. Fuselage.	5-03
❏ 'XD614' '65'	Vampire T.11	WZ572, ex Southampton museum, Leeming, 8 FTS, 7 FTS, 202 AFS. Pod.	5-03
❏ XH318 '64'	Vampire T.11	ex Calmore, Southampton, Ferndown, 7761M, Shawbury, RAFC.	5-03

SOUTHAMPTON AIRPORT or Eastleigh, at the A335/M27 junction north of the City
The hulk of HS.125-600B G-BKBH had gone from the dump by May 2003 (last noted February 2002). The JetStar serves on in a non-destructive role.

❏ N6NE	JetStar 731	ex VR-CCC ntu, N222Y, N731JS, N227K, N12R, N280R. Damaged 27-11-92. Non-destructive.	2-03

THRUXTON AERODROME north of the A303 west of Andover
Classic Aero Engineering have established a workshop here and are working on all of the airframes listed. Scout AH.1 XV123 moved to Shawbury, Shropshire, by July 2003.

❏ G-AOAA	Tiger Moth	ex Chilbolton, DF159, 24 GCF, 1 RS, 1 GTS, 20 PAFU, 5 GTS. Crashed 4-6-89.	®	5-03
❏ G-BKXP	Auster AOP.6	ex Little Gransden, Royston, Oakington, Belgian AF A-14, VT987.	®	5-03
❏ 'KF729'	Harvard IV	G-BJST, ex Little Gransden, Coventry, *Empire of the Sun*, ItAF MM53795.	®	6-03
❏ –	Tiger Moth	ex Little Gransden, Cranfield, VAT et al.	®	5-03
❏ –*	Hurricane XII	G-CBOE, ex RCAF 5487. First noted 5-02.	®	5-03

TITCHFIELD on the A27 west of Fareham
Melvyn Hiscock: The climax of the restoration approacheth – sort of!

❏ G-BVLK	Cloudster	ex Thruxton, Sudbury, N25403, NC25403.	®	3-04

YATELEY on the B3272 west of Camberley
Mick Long: Keeps three cockpits in the general area.

❏ WP977	Chipmunk T.10	G-BHRD, ex Crowland, Doncaster, Stamford, Burford, 9M-ANA, VR-SEK, WP977, Malayan Aux AF, Rufforth SF, Man UAS, Lpl UAS, 63 GCF, QUAS, Man UAS. Crashed 21-1-97.	6-01
❏ WZ876	Chipmunk T.10	G-BBWN, ex Twyford, Tattershall Thorpe, Lon UAS, 1 AEF, Lon UAS, Biggin Hill SF, Lon UAS, Ox UAS, Birm UAS, MCS, 31. Forward cockpit.	6-01
❏ XN657	Sea Vixen D.3	ex Stock, Llanbedr, RAE, FRL, RAE, ADS, 899, 893. Cockpit.	6-01

HEREFORDSHIRE

☛ From this edition, Worcestershire receives its own heading again, with the following locations from *W&R18* relocating: Birlingham, Bromsgrove, Defford, Evesham.

EWYAS HAROLD on the A465 south west of Hereford
No.22 Regiment, Special Air Service: *W&R16*, p90, spoke of the arrival on site of "a purpose-built, and larger, airliner mock-up" to replace Trident 1E G-AVYB. Aerial reconnaissance of the area in July 2003 showed that this mock-up very much has the look of a Boeing 747 about it. (The 'about it' being say, 70ft of fuselage from the nose backwards, married to a tiny tail section and small, swept, wings.) *W&R16*, this time p140, also mentioned the destruction of 747-100 F-BPVE at Bruntingthorpe, Leics, in anti-terrorist trials. It was reported that much of the forward fuselage was removed for use by the SAS, so this is a *likely* candidate for the fuselage here. A *possible* candidate is 747-136 G-AWNA which was 'parted out' at Bruntingthorpe in late 1998.

❏ –*	Boeing 747	forward fuselage in 'airliner' mock-up. F/n 7-03	7-03

HEREFORD on the A49 south of Leominster
A enthusiast in the general area has a pair of Hunters.

❏ XG252	'U' Hunter FGA.9	8840M, ex Cosford, 1 TWU, 2 TWU, 1 TWU, TWU, 45, 8, Wittering SF, MoA, 54, 66.	7-00
❏ XL563	Hunter T.7	9218M, ex Kempston, Farnborough, IAM, MoA, mkrs.	8-99

KINGTON west of Leominster, on the A44
Martin Albery: (Note the more correct location for this private collection.) The Edwards is owned by Computair Consultants [1]. The glider was designed in Gloucestershire and is similar in design to the SG.38, Dagling etc but with a metal frame and is owned by CARG, see under Innsworth, Glos [2].

❏ G-ARIF*	OH-7 Coupe	ex Breighton, Wigan. Arrived 22-11-03.		11-03
❏ G-ASDF	Edwards Helic	ex Innsworth, Woking, Coulsdon.	® [1]	3-02
❏ G-MBWI*	Lafayette 1	ex Selby, Leeds, Leigh. Arrived 22-11-03.		11-03
❏ –	Primary glider	ex Innsworth, 'Glos'.	® [2]	3-02

MADLEY on the B4352 west of Hereford

❏ G-ADWJ	Tiger Moth	ex Shobdon, Defford, BB803, 9 EFTS, 20 EFTS, 12 EFTS, G-ADWJ.	®	6-97

SHOBDON AERODROME north of the A44 west of Leominster

❏ G-BEPN	Pawnee 235D	ex N54877. Crashed 11-2-78. Fuselage frame. Dump.	5-01
❏ –	Cessna F.150	cockpit. Dump.	5-01

UPPER HILL between the A4110 and the A49 south of Leominster
Sheppards Surplus and Garden Centre: The Swift still guards the entrance to this amazing emporium while the Whirlwind moulders in a yard at the rear.

❏ WK275	Swift F.4	ex Hatfield, Filton, C(A). Displayed.	11-03
❏ XP360	'V' W'wind HAR.10	ex Sunderland, Warmingham, Lasham, Fawkham Green, CFS, 225. Stored.	11-03

HERTFORDSHIRE

BENINGTON on minor road east of Stevenage
❑ G-AXDU*   Pup 150   ex G-35-048. Crashed 22-10-<u>96</u>. Fuselage.   1-04

BERKHAMSTED on the A4251 west of Hemel Hempstead
Stuart McKay: Is the driving force of the **de Havilland Moth Club** uniting all who restore, own, operate or just love DH biplanes. As well as the annual Woburn fly-in, they produce by far and away the best magazine of any 'type' organisation anywhere in the UK – *The Moth*.
✉ De Havilland Moth Club, 23 Hall Park Hill, Berkhamsted, Herts, HP4 2NH.
❑ G-AVPD   Jodel D.9 Bebe   ex Langley. CoA 6-6-75.   3-04

CHESHUNT on the A10 north of Junction 25 of the M25
❑ G-AOBV   J/5P Autocar   ex Laindon, Stapleford Tawney, Benington. CoA 7-4-71.   10-97

CHIPPERFIELD south of Hemel Hempstead
A private owner in this area has taken delivery of a Canberra nose as a plaything for his children.
❑ WK122*   Canberra TT.18   ex Bruntingthorpe, Helston, Samlesbury, 7, 15, 61.
                                        Nose. Arrived 21-2-04.   2-04

CLOTHALL COMMON on the A507 south-east of Baldock
❑ G-APYU   Tri-Traveler   ex Moreton-in-Marsh. Crashed 23-4-72. Stored.   10-99

ELSTREE AERODROME north of Junction 4, M1
In early November 2002 Fokker S.11-1 'KM.174' (G-BEPV) was ferried through to Spanhoe Lodge, Northants, for full restoration. Note that the 'accepted' state of things for AA-5s G-OBSF and G-ODAE are that the latter was a rebuild of the former! [1]

❑ G-ASON	Twin Comanche	ex N7273Y ntu. CoA 30-11-91. Stored.	1-00
❑ G-AXGC	MS.880B Rallye	CoA 12-5-88. Stored.	9-95
❑ G-BSCR	Cessna 172M	ex N12693. Crashed 19-6-99. Dump.	6-00
❑ G-GCNZ*	Cessna 150M	ex C-GCNZ. CoA 27-3-98. Fuselage. First noted 5-02.	2-04
❑ G-NGBI	AA-5B Tiger	ex G-JAKK, G-BHWI, N3752E.	
		Crashed 12-7-90. Fuselage. Dump.	6-00
❑ G-OBSF	AA-5A Cheetah	ex G-ODSF, G-BEUW, N6158A.	
		Damaged 8-2-97. Fuselage. Dump.	[1] 6-00
❑ G-ODAE	AA-5A Cheetah	ex G-OBSF, G-ODSF, G-BEUW, N6158A.	
		Fuselage. Dump.	[1] 6-00
❑ C-FQIP	Lake LA-4-200	ex N1068L. Stored, first noted 5-02.	2-04
❑ N320MR*	Twin Comanche	ex G-CALV, G-AZFO, N8761Y. Stored. F/n 7-02.	10-03
❑ ST-AHZ	Navajo 310	ex G-AXMR, N6558L. Fire dump.	6-00
❑ 30146*	Soko Kraguj	G-BSXD, ex Yugoslavia. CoA 22-4-99. Stored.	2-04
❑ –	Cherokee	fuselage, dump. Last letter 'H'.	10-03
❑ –	AA-5	fuselage, dump. Last letter 'X'.	6-00

HATFIELD
Galleria: The Comet 'flies' inside the mall. (The 'real' – ie hugely reconstructed – G-ACSS can be found at Old Warden, Beds, and see under London Colney, Herts.)
❑ 'G-ACSS'   DH.88 FSM   BAPC.257. *Grosvenor House.*   3-04

Gerry Atwell and **Frank Telling**: No news on the HM.21 – inbound for LOST!?
❑ –   Mignet HM.21   ex Agonac, France. Stored.   10-94

University of Hertfordshire: The Jetstream test-shell is used as a teaching aid within the campus. It is described as the third example built which would *probably* make it the whole static airframe laid down in early 1967 between G-ATXI (c/n 199/02) and G-ATXJ (c/n 200/03).

| ❏ | – | Jetstream 1 EMU | ex Radlett. Fuselage. | 1-97 |

HATFIELD AIRFIELD west of the A1 at Hatfield

W&R18 (p82) noted that the fuselage of Trident 1E-140 G-AVYE was "thought to have been scrapped in 2000". The hulk actually lingered on the former airfield site until at least September 2002 when it was removed. A Waco Hadrian mock-up used in *Saving Private Ryan* and/or *Band of Brothers* was also noted dumped on the airfield in early 2002. This was *not* the one at Doncaster, S Yorks. On 6th August 2002, the de Havilland Heritage Museum's Trident 3B-101 G-AWZO was scrapped. It was the last aircraft resident at the once great airfield, and of course it was born there. Game over...

HEMEL HEMPSTEAD on the A414 west of St Albans

The Vampire Collection: Alan Allen took delivery of a former SAAF Vampire for another UK collector. Also arriving was a complete Wasp.

◆ Visits by prior arrangement *only*. ✉ Alan Allen, 201 High Street Green, Hemel Hempstead, HP2 7AA. e-mail alan.allen@lineone.net

❏	WZ581	'77' Vampire T.11	ex Ruislip, Bushey, Keevil, Exeter, 3/4 CAACU, 229 OCU, 233 OCU, 25. Pod.	3-04
❏	XT439*	Wasp HAS.1	ex King's Lynn, Bruntingthorpe, Cranfield, Wroughton, 829. Cr 25-3-86. Arrived 10-5-02.	3-04
❏	221*	Vampire T.55	ex Liss, SAAF. Arrived 10-8-02.	3-04

HITCHIN on the A505 north-east of Luton

Philip Leaver: The GR.1 is thought to have been a 'spare' with the cockpit number FL/R 41H 725624, and – contrary to previous thinking – not a damaged 'flyer'.

| ❏ | – | Harrier GR.1 | ex Llantrisant, Welshpool, Stafford, Abingdon, Hamble. Nose. | 3-02 |
| ❏ | XV759 | 'O' Harrier GR.3 | ex Bruntingthorpe, Barnstaple (?), Welshpool, Llantrisant, Pendine, St Athan, 233 OCU, 1417F, 233 OCU, 1, 233 OCU, 1, 233 OCU. Nose. | 3-02 |

Others: The Martin Monoplane project is *thought* still to be underway here. The wings are being used on the Humming Bird project, to be found at Hatch, Beds. The yard of **H Williams and Sons** took three Wessex (HC.2s XR499, XR520 and HU.5 XT474) from Gosport, Hants, on 1st April 2004. The yard has a rapid processing policy. More disposals are very likely via this venue.

| ❏ | G-AEYY | Martin Monoplane ex Bishop's Stortford, Meir. | ® | 4-92 |

KINGS LANGLEY on the A41 north of Watford

Gnat T.1 XM708 moved initially to Bruntingthorpe, Leics, by November 2002.

LEAVESDEN south of Abbots Langley, north of the A41

Studios: Eon Productions have a travelling 'roadshow' dedicated to James Bond. Part of the display is the Bede 'Acrostar' (BD-5J) used in *Octopussy*.

| ❏ | – | Bede BD-5J | ex *Octopussy*. | 1-98 |

LONDON COLNEY off the A6 between London Colney and South Mimms

De Havilland Aircraft Heritage Centre (note name change) incorporating the **Mosquito Aircraft Museum** and administered by the De Havilland Aircraft Museum Trust. Restoration of the Mosquito prototype continues with work on the tailplane having been carried out by Skysport (of Hatch, Beds) during 2003. BAE Systems continue to support the project, with work on the cowlings taking place at Filton and Chester. Marshall Aerospace at Cambridge have assisted with the elevators and the

ailerons and Deltair Airmotive, the propellers. Rolls-Royce Heritage Trust at Derby have made good progress with the engines, one of which will be test run before returning to London Colney [1]. Trident 3B G-AWZO was scrapped at Hatfield, Herts, in August 2002.
Notes: The de Havilland-built Cierva C.24 is on loan from the Science Museum [2]. The Humming Bird uses the wings of the Martin Monoplane G-AEYY – see under Hitchin, Herts – and is on loan from Mike Russell. [3]. Mosquito FB.6 TA122 is being rebuilt using the wing of TR.33 TW233 acquired in Israel [4]. The Chipmunk PAX will be turned into an educational exhibit and fitted with a sectioned Gipsy Major 10 Mk.2 and the rear fuselage of fellow WG418. The cockpit of WG418 is to be found at Levenshulme, Gtr Man [5]. The DH.88 Comet FSM was built for use in the film *The Great Air Race*. It will re-appear in the colours of G-ACSP *Black Magic*. The 'real' G-ACSS can be found at Old Warden, Beds. See also Hatfield, Herts, for 'another' G-ACSS [6]. The Comet SIM is a nose section that was built at the same time as the noses for the first two prototypes and was used for structural tests. It then went to the DH Servicing School and was later converted into a simulator. It is now fitted with Mk.4 instrumentation [7]. See under Fyvie, Scotland, for an ambitious and long term project; and under Gloucestershire Airport, Glos, for the pod of Vampire T.11 XD616.

♦ Open from first Sun of Mar to last Sun of Oct, Tue, Thu and Sat 2pm to 5.30pm, Sun and Bank Hols 10.30am to 5.30pm. Last admission 4.30pm ✉ PO Box 107, Salisbury Hall, London Colney, St Albans, AL2 1BU ☎ 01727 822051 **fax** 01727 826400 **e-mail** w4050@dhamt.freeserve.co.uk **www.dehavillandmuseum.co.uk**

❏ G-ABLM	Cierva C.24	ex Hatfield. CoA 16-1-35.		[2]	1-04
❏ G-ADOT	Hornet Moth	ex Hatfield, Old Warden, Stoke Ferry, Stapleford, Houghton-on-the-Hill, X9326, 5 GCF, 23 OTU, 24 GCF, 6 AONS, Halton SF, 2 CPF, G-ADOT. CoA 5-10-59.			1-04
❏ G-AFOJ	Moth Minor	ex Navestock, E-1, E-0236, G-AFOJ. CoA 27-8-69. *Bugs 2.*		®	1-04
❏ G-AKDW	Dragon Rapide	ex Aviodome, Amsterdam store, F-BCDB, G-AKDW,YI-ABD, NR833. *City of Winchester.*		®	1-04
❏ G-ANRX	Tiger Moth	ex Belchamp Walter, N6550, SLAW, 25 EFTS, 18 EFTS, 241, 14 EFTS, 56 ERFTS. CoA 20-6-61. Crop duster. *Border City*			1-04
❏ G-AOTI	Heron 2D	ex Biggin Hill, Exeter, G-5-19. CoA 24-6-87.		®	1-04
❏ G-AREA	Dove 8	ex Hatfield. CoA 8-9-87.			1-04
❏ G-ARYA*	HS.125-1	ex Wrexham, Connah's Quay, Hawarden, Connah's Quay, Chester, Hatfield. Nose. Arrived 13-2-04.			3-04
❏ G-ARYC	HS.125 Srs 1	ex Hatfield, Filton, R-R. CoA 1-8-73. Rolls-Royce (stbd), BSE (pt) colours.		®	1-04
❏ G-AVFH	Trident 2	ex Heathrow, BA, BEA. Forward fuselage.			1-04
❏ D-IFSB	Dove 6	ex Hatfield, BFS, D-CFSB, Panshanger, G-AMXR, N4280V.			1-04
❏ F-BGNX	Comet 1XB	G-AOJT, ex Farnborough, F-BGNX. Fuselage.			1-04
❏ J-7326*	Humming Bird	G-EBQP, ex Hatch, Audley End, Bishop's Stortford. Fuselage. Arrived 25-3-03.		[3]	1-04
❏ W4050 (pt) E-0234 (stb)	Mosquito I prototype	ex Hatfield, Chester, Hatfield, Panshanger, Hatfield, Rolls-Royce, DH, A&AEE, E-0234.		® [1]	1-04
❏ LF789 'R2-K'	Queen Bee	BAPC.186, ex 'K3584', Hadfield, Droylesden, Redhill, St Athan, Pilotless A/c Unit, Manorbier, St Athan.		®	1-04
❏ TA122 'UP-G'	Mosquito FB.6	ex Soesterberg, 4, 2 GCS, 48, 4, 605, 417 ARF. 605 Sqn colours.		® [4]	1-04
❏ TA634 '8K-K'	Mosquito TT.35	ex Liverpool, G-AWJV, Aldergrove, 3 CAACU, APS Schleswigland, APS Ahlorn, APS Sylt, 4 CAACU. 571 Sqn colours.			1-04
❏ TJ118	Mosquito TT.35	ex Elstree, Exeter, 3/4 CAACU, 3 CAACU. Fuselage.			1-04
❏ WP790 'T'	Chipmunk T.10	G-BBNC, ex Rush Green, WP790, Bir UAS, Wales UAS, PFTS, AOTS, 1 ITS, RAFC, Man UAS, G&S UAS, Stn UAS, 24 GCF, 5 RFS, 17 RFS.		®	1-04
❏ WP927	Chipmunk T.10 PAX	8216M, ex Ashton-under-Lyne, Woodvale, Ashton-under-Lyne, Crosby, Hamble G-ATJK, MCS, Oxf UAS, Lon UAS, Detling SF, Lon UAS.		[5]	1-04

❏	WM729		Vampire NF.10	ex Gloucestershire, London Colney, Ruislip, Bingley, Bradford, Church Fenton, CNCS, 2 ANS, 25, 151. Nose. Stored.	®	1-04
❏	'WR410'*'N'		Venom FB.54	G-BLKA, ex 'Norfolk', Bournemouth, Bruntingthorpe, Cranfield, G-VENM ntu, Swiss AF J-1790. Arrived 23-10-03.		1-04
❏	WR539		Venom FB.4	ex Gloucestershire, London Colney, Fownhope, Cardiff, 'Midlands', Cosford, 8399M, Kai Tak, 28, 60. Dismantled, stored.	®	1-04
❏	WX853		Venom NF.3	ex Debden 7443M, Shawbury, 23. Dismantled.	®	1-04
❏	XG730	'499'	Sea Ven FAW.22	ex Southwick, Portsmouth, Lee-on-Solent, ADS, Sydenham, 893, 894, 891. 894 Sqn colours.		1-04
❏	XH328*		Vampire T.11	ex Duxford, Bournemouth, Cranfield, Hemel Hempstead, Croxley Green, Bushey, Keevil, Exeter, 3 CAACU, 60. Arrived 6-03.		1-04
❏	XJ565		Sea Vixen FAW.2	ex RAE, 899, 893, 766B. '127-E', 899 Sqn c/s.		1-04
❏	XJ772	'H'	Vampire T.11	ex Brooklands, Wisley, Shawbury, CATCS, 1 FTS, 8 FTS, RAFC, RNorAF 15018 'XP-G'.	®	1-04
❏	XK695		Comet C.2(R)	ex Stock, Newton 9164M, Duxford, Wyton, 51, 216, G-AMXH. Nose.		1-04
❏	J-1008		Vampire FB.6	ex Hatfield, Swiss AF.		1-04
❏	J-1632		Venom FB.50	G-VNOM, ex Cranfield, Bridgend, Bruntingthorpe, Cranfield, Swiss AF. Dismantled.		1-04
❏	–		DH.88 FSM	BAPC.216, ex 'G-ACSS', St Albans, Kings Langley, Wroughton, Australia.	® [6]	1-04
❏	–		Comet 2 SIM	ex Wroughton, Crawley.	[7]	1-04
❏	–	BAPC.232	Horsa I / II	composite fuselage.		1-04

PANSHANGER AERODROME east of Welwyn Garden City, south of the B1000

❏	G-BSKC	Tomahawk 112	ex OY-PJB, N748RM, C-GRQI. Crashed 2-6-96.	6-97
❏	G-DTOO	Tomahawk 112	ex Seething. Crashed 9-7-94.	9-02
❏	N93938*	Ercoupe 415C	Stored. First noted 4-01.	12-03

RUSH GREEN AERODROME east of the B656 west of Stevenage

W&R16 recorded - under Firbeck, S Yorks - the removal of Chipmunk T.10 WP869 in December 1996 to 'Hertfordshire' prior to moving on as a 'static' to Poland. It came here, but did not go further.

| ❏ | WP869* | Chipmunk T.10 | ex Firbeck, Stamford, Brierley Hill, Castle Bromwich, 8215M, 8207M, Shawbury, Spitalgate CF, RAFTC, 664 RAFC. Arrived 12-96. | 3-04 |

ST ALBANS

Eric Littledike: Has the former Science Museum Pilcher REP and is working on it.

| ❏ | – | BAPC.57 | Pilcher Hawk REP | ex Wroughton, Hayes, South Lambeth. Built 1930. | ® 11-01 |

Microlight strip:

❏	G-AZZX	Cessna FRA.150L	damaged 28-2-87. Stored, spares use.	1-02
❏	N7263S	Cessna 150H	Stored.	1-02
❏	N13253	Cessna 172M	Stored, spares use.	1-02
❏	–	Cessna F.150K	ex N5927G. Stored, spares use.	6-99

ISLE OF MAN

ISLE OF MAN AIRPORT or Ronaldsway, north-east of Castletown

Aeroservice (IoM) Ltd:

❏ G-AJEE	J/1 Autocrat	ex Compton Abbas. CoA 10-7-89.	®	8-92
❏ G-APSZ	Cessna 172	ex Barton, N6372E. Damaged 2-3-84. Stored.		6-96
❏ G-BCGA	Seneca 200-2	ex Panshanger, N41975. Crashed 18-12-77. Fuselage.		6-96

Airport:

❏ G-AZRG	Aztec 250D	ex Aldergrove, N6536Y. CoA 8-7-93. Dump.	7-96
❏ –	BAPC.282 Eider Duck	Single-seat pusher, unflown.	7-01

Manx Aviation and Military Museum: Opened in November 2000, and run by the Manx Aviation Preservation Society, the museum charts the island's varied aviation history and occupies wartime buildings on the airport site. A 56ft Nissen hut has been newly erected and will open in 2004. The nose section of Bolingbroke IVT 9041 is to be delivered from Canada during 2004 for restoration.
◆ Open 10am to 4.30pm weekends, Bank Holidays and during the TT Race period, or by appointment.
✉ Ronaldsway Airport, Ballasalla, Isle of Man, IM9 2AT ☎ 01624 829294 e-mail iramsden@talk21.com www.maps.iofm.net

---

JURBY AERODROME west of Andreas

The Spitfire fsm is owned by A Saunders and was built by Feggans Brown as a taxiable 'extra' for the series *Piece of Cake* [1].

❏ G-ACLL	Leopard Moth	ex AW165, AFEE, 7 AACU, 6 AACU, Ringway SF. CoA 6-12-95. Stored.		2-04
❏ –	CEV Bergfalke II	BGA.1492. CoA 12-93. Stored.		10-96
❏ –*	BAPC.283 Spitfire FSM	ex Farnsfield, Newtown, Kettering, *Piece of Cake*.	[1]	2-04

ISLE OF WIGHT

BEMBRIDGE AERODROME on the B3395 south-west of Bembridge

Britten Norman Aircraft Preservation Society: During the spring of 2003, BNAPS signed an agreement with the B-N Group to restore G-AVCN – the oldest surviving BN-2 – to flying condition.
◆ Visits *strictly* by prior permission: ✉ 32 Budesbury Road, Staines, TW18 2AX e-mail savecn@ bnaps.co.uk www.bnaps.co.uk

❏ G-AVCN	BN-2A	ex Puerto Rico, N290VL, F-OGHG, G-AVCN.	®	1-04

B-N Group: The Trislander is a pattern airframe for the re-opened Trislander 'line' for China [1]. It has replaced G-BEVV which had returned to Cumbernauld, Scotland, by May 2003. Correcting *W&R18* (p86), Islander AL.1 ZG994 is still to be found here [2]. (Refer to St Athan, Wales, for the rest of the plot!) BN-2B-20 fuselage G-BVYE moved to London, Gtr London. BN-2T fuselage A40-CT is still to be found in the bushes, but it lacks a cockpit and can be deleted.

❏ G-BEVR*	Trislander	ex Cumbernauld, JY-JQE, G-BEVR, XA-THE[2], G-BEVR. CoA 6-7-82. Fuselage. Arrived 4-03.	[1]	1-04
❏ G-BVHX	BN-2T-4R	Radar-nosed, fuselage. Tests.		1-04
❏ G-BVHY*	BN-2T-4R	complete, unflown.		11-02
❏ G-BWPM*	BN-2T-4R	fuselage. Unbuilt kit, stored.		11-02
❏ G-RAPA*	BN-2T-4R	prototype. Fuselage, first noted 4-02.		1-04
❏ ZG994*	Islander AL.1	ex 1 Flt AAC. Crashed 30-6-99. Test rig.	[2]	5-03

COWES on the A3020, north of the island

Cliftongrade Ltd: The scrap dealers still use the cockpit to advertise their business.

❏ XT863	'AS' Phantom FG.1	ex Abingdon, 43, 111, 892, 767. Nose.	12-03

NEWPORT on the A3054, middle of the island
Stored in the area in two separate places are two homebuilds, their status *believed* unchanged.

❏ G-AZJE	Minicab	ex Sandown. CoA 7-7-82. Stored.	12-01
❏ G-BCMF	Levi Go-Plane	one and only flight 16-11-74. Stored.	1-98

SANDOWN on the A3055 south of Ryde, east coast
Airframe Assemblies: The company moved premises within Sandown during early 2001 and by late 2003 relocated yet again to Sandown Aerodrome, IoW - see below. **Locally**: The Tipsy is stored.

❏ G-AMVP*	Tipsy Junior	ex OO-ULA. CoA 22-6-94. Stored.	10-03

SANDOWN AERODROME north of the A3056, west of Sandown
Airframe Assemblies: Relocated to the former Desmond Norman hangar on the aerodrome during late 2003. They continue to produce fine and detailed work, specialising in wings for several Spitfire projects and some Messerschmitt Bf 109 projects. Spitfire SM520 will be completed as a two-seater [1]. Spitfire IX TA805 (G-PMNF) moved to a location in Sussex on 28th June 2002 and then Duxford, Cambs, on 17th March 2003 for completion.
◆ *Private* premises - visits *strictly* by prior permission.

❏ BH238	Hurricane IIb	ex Front Line Sandown, Russia, Soviet AF. Wreck.		1-04
❏ RM689*	Spitfire XIV	G-ALGT, ex Filton, Hucknall, East Midlands, 'RM619', Hucknall, 443, 350. Crashed 27-6-92. Arr 25-9-02.	®	1-04
❏ RR232* G-BRSF	Spitfire IX	ex Exeter, Lancing, Winchester, Nowra, Bankstown, Point Cook, Cape Town, Ysterplaat, SAAF 5632, RR232, 47 MU, ECFS. Arrived 11-7-02.	®	1-04
❏ RW382	Spitfire XVI	N382RW, ex USA, Audley End, Braintree, Uxbridge 8075M, Leconfield, Church Fenton 7245M, C&RS, 3 CAACU, 604. Wreck, stored.		1-04
❏ SM520*	Spitfire IX	G-ILDA, ex Ramsbottom, G-BXHZ, Oxford, Pretoria, SAAF. Arrived 17-6-02.	® [1]	3-04
❏ 2100 'V7+1H'	Fw 189A-1	G-BZKY, ex Sandtoft, Lancing, USSR, Luftwaffe. Crashed 4-5-43. Stored.	off-site	1-04

Elsewhere: Describing the dispersal of the Front Line Aviation Museum, *W&R18* (p86) said that PZL Gawron SP-CHD had returned to Germany or 'moved on to Essex'. The latter was spot on, see under North Weald, Essex. Tipsy Junior G-AMVP is stored locally, not on the aerodrome - see above.

❏ G-BHMR	Stinson 108-3	ex F-BABO, F-DABO, NC6352M. CoA 23-11-90.	1-04
❏ G-NRDC	Fieldmaster	ex Old Sarum. CoA 17-10-87. Fuselage.	1-04
❏ –	Fieldmaster EMU	ex Old Sarum. Stored.	1-04

SHANKLIN
An amusement arcade on the seafront has a Rallye – complete with skeletal pilot! -as an attraction.

❏ G-BIRB	MS.880B Rallye	ex Manston, Firbeck, Carlisle, Hooton Park, Moston, Carlisle, F-BVAQ. CoA 16-6-90.	12-03

YARMOUTH on the A3054 west of Newport
A private collector has a Vampire T.11 pod.

❏ XE921	'64' Vampire T.11	ex Welshpool, Stoke-on-Trent, Barton, Firbeck, Retford, Firbeck, Keevil, Exeter, 3/4 CAACU, 1 FTS, CFS. Pod.	1-04

KENT

ASHFORD on the M20 west of Folkestone
The Jackaroo is *thought* unchanged. An Airedale has moved into the general area.

❏ G-ANFY	Jackaroo	ex NL906, 9 RFS, 23 EFTS, 9 FTS. CoA 25-5-68.	1-96
❏ G-ASBY*	Airedale	ex St Ives, 'Eversden', Royston. CoA 22-3-80.	6-00

BREDHURST or Farthing Corner, south of Junction 4 of the M2, south of Gillingham

❏ G-ARWH	Cessna 172C	ex Golders Green, Fenland, N1466Y.	
		CoA 28-4-86. Spares.	5-99

BRENCHLEY east of the B2160, east of Royal Tunbridge Wells

❏ G-ATKH	Luton Minor	ex Rochester. CoA 24-6-92. Stored.	1-96
❏ G-AYXO	Luton Major	ex Beeston Rylands. Stored.	1-96

BRENZETT on the A2070 north-west of New Romney
Brenzett Aeronautical Museum Trust: Occupying buildings to the west of the Brenzett (or Ivychurch) Advanced Landing Ground.
◆ Open weekends from Easter to end of Oct, also Bank Holidays, 11am to 5.30pm. Also open Jul, Aug, Sep Fridays 11am to 5.30pm. ✉ Ivychurch Road, Brenzett, Romney Marsh, TN29 0EE ☎ 01797 344747 or 01233 627911 **www**.kent2do.com/brenzettaeronautical

❏ G-AMSM	Dakota 4	ex Booker, Brenzett, Duxford, Brenzett, Lydd, Skyways, Eagle, Starways, KN274, TCDU, 77, St Eval SF, Azores SF, 43-49948. Damaged 17-8-78. Nose. Silver City colours.	2-04
❏ V7350	Hurricane I	ex Robertsbridge, 85. Crashed 29-8-40. Cockpit.	2-04
❏ WH657	Canberra B.2	ex Godalming, RAE, 231 OCU.	2-04
❏ XK625	Vampire T.11	ex Firbeck, North Weald, Southend, Woodford, St Athan, 8 FTS, 7 FTS.	2-04

CANTERBURY
BB Aviation: Bill Baker and friends have two airframes. *Likely* identity for the Canberra is WJ581 [1].
✉ Bur Oak, Bossingham, near Canterbury, Kent, CT4 6DX.

❏ –	BAPC.17 Woodhams Sprite	ex Manchester, Hooton Park, Wigan, Irlam, Wigan, Liverpool, Leamington Spa. Incomplete.	®	2-04
❏ –	Canberra PR.7	ex Cardiff-Wales, WAM, CTTS St Athan. Nose.	® [1]	2-04

Maypole Air: Brian Mayo is at work on a Stampe locally. It will be fitted with a DH Gipsy Major 10.

❏ N33528*	SNCAN SV-4C	G-BRXP, ex Barton, F-BGGU, Fr mil 678, F-BDNX ntu.	®	6-02

CAPEL LE FERNE on the B2011 north east of Folkestone
National Battle of Britain Memorial: The deeply-moving statue of a pilot sitting, contemplating the English Channel, set against a huge three-bladed propeller akin to the ancient chalk figures found on the South Downs, is well known and a place of pilgrimage for many. There is an excellent visitor centre and small shop. After considerable fund-raising, two 'gate guardians' have joined the centre. The Hurricane is in the colours of the aircraft flown by P/O Geoffrey Page when he was shot down on 12th August 1940, while the Spitfire is the one flown by P/O Herbert Case who was shot down within sight of the memorial on 12th October 1940.
◆ **www**.spitfire-museum.com

❏ 'P2970'*	Hurricane I FSM	BAPC.291. 56 Squadron colours. *Little Willie*.	
'US-X'		Built by GB Replicas. Unveiled 6-03.	3-04
❏ 'P9338'*	Spitfire I FSM	72 Sqn c/s. Built by GB Replicas.	**due**

CHATHAM east of Rochester

Chatham Historic Dockyard Trust: In January 2004 the Gannet was registered as G-KAEW for Kennet Aviation at North Weald, Essex. It was due to make the move in the spring of 2004 [1].
◆ North of the A231, signed. Open mid-Feb to late Oct daily 10am to 6pm. ⊠ Chatham ME4 4TZ
☎ 01634 823800 **fax** 01634 823801 **e-mail** info@chdt.org.uk **www**.chdt.org.uk

❑ WG751	Dragonfly HR.3	ex Gosport, Condover, Ramsgreave, Ancoats,	
	'710'	*The Last Caravan*, Wisbech, Blackbushe,	
		Fleetlands, 705. 705 Squadron colours.	10-03
❑ XL500	Gannet AEW.3	G-KAEW, ex Culdrose A2701, Lee-on-Solent, Culdrose,	
		Dowty-Rotol, Culdrose, Lossiemouth, 849.	[1] 1-04

Royal Engineers Museum: There is much to interest the aviation enthusiast here including the medals etc of James McCudden VC DSO* MC* MM and many other artefacts. The history of military aviation in the UK from 1880 with balloons, through to man-lifting kites and airships to the Air Battalion of the Royal Engineers of 1912 is all well charted. The wing of a Cody monoplane, on loan from the RAeS, is also on display. Sioux AH.1 XT133 is at Chattenden, Kent, possibly on behalf of the museum.
◆ On the B2004 to the north of Chatham. Mon to Thu 10am to 5pm, Sat, Sun and Bank Hols 11.30am to 5pm. *Not* open on Fridays. ⊠ Prince Arthur Road, Gillingham, Chatham, ME4 4UG ☎ 01634 406397 **fax** 01634 822371 **e-mail** remuseum.rhqre@gtnet.gov.uk **www**.royalengineers.org.uk

❑ –		Vulcan hang-glider –	3-02
❑ XZ964	'D' Harrier GR.3	ex St Athan, 1417F, 233 OCU, 3, 233 OCU, 1.	
		Ninja One. 1417 Flight colours.	3-02
❑ –		Military balloon	basket only. RAFM loan.	3-02

No.1404 Squadron Air Cadets: In Boundary Road, still have their Chipmunk.

❑ WZ846	Chipmunk T.10	8439M, ex G-BCSC, Bicester, Manston, Wales UAS,	
		AOTS, 202, 228, CFE, W Raynham SF, G&S UAS,	
		Bri UAS, 1 AEF, St Athan, Nott UAS, 63 GCF,	
		Edn UAS, S'tn UAS.	10-03

CHATTENDEN on the A228 north of Rochester

Defence Explosives Ordnance Disposal School: The 'JP' is in the Lodge Hill Camp site. The Sioux was intended for display at Chatham and may be held here for that eventuality [1].

❑ XM410	Jet Provost T.3	8054AM, ex North Luffenham, Halton, Shawbury,	
		RAFC, 7 FTS, 2 FTS.	5-03
❑ XT133*	Sioux AH.1	ex Chatham, Arborfield, Middle Wallop 7923M.	
		Stored.	[1] 5-03
❑ XT907	'W' Phantom FGR.2	9151M, ex 74, 228 OCU. EOD.	5-03
❑ –	BAPC.158 Fieseler Fi 103	held inside the camp.	5-00
❑ –	BAPC.159 Ohka 11	held inside the camp.	5-03

CHISLET north of the A28 south-east of Herne Bay

By June 2003 Ercoupe 415C N3188H moved to Doncaster, S Yorks.

❑ G-ASMT*	Linnet 2	CoA 25-9-01. Stored.	9-03

DOVER

Dover Museum: Among a wide sweep of exhibits is a full-size model V-1. Other items of interest include a small piece of Blériot's cross-Channel Type XI and a piece from the first bomb ever to drop on the UK - Dover, Christmas 1914.
◆ Open daily 10am to 5.30pm. Closed Sun, Oct to Apr. ⊠ Market Square, Dover, CT16 1PB ☎ 01304 201066 **fax** 01304 241186 **e-mail** museumenquiries@dover.gov.uk **www**.dovermuseum.co.uk

❑ –	BAPC.290 Fieseler Fi 103 REP —		3-04

Others: An unknown ATC unit have the former Manston Pup on loan.

❑ HB-NAV	'A' Pup 150	ex Stock, Henley-on-Thames, Henlow, Redhill,	
		G-AZCM. Blue/white c/s. Forward fuselage.	3-04

FAVERSHAM on the A2 east of Sittingbourne
No.1242 Squadron Air Cadets: By March 2003, Hunter nose XG226 moved to Manston, Kent.

GRAVESEND on the A226 east of Dartford
A Buccaneer S.1 nose is with a local collector.

❑ XN928   Buccaneer S.1   ex Manston, Bruntingthorpe, Cardiff, St Athan 8179M,
                                      736, 809, 801. Desert pink, *Glenfiddich*, *Jaws* and *Liz*.10-01

Gravesend Police College:
❑ G-AVMK   BAC 111-510ED ex Bournemouth, BA, BEA. Sections.   1-02

HAWKINGE on the A260 north of Folkestone
Kent Battle of Britain Museum: The depth and intensity of the displays is exceptional, especially when remembering that the museum occupies buildings used during the Battle of Britain by the famous RAF station. The Miles Aircraft Collection (see under Pulborough, W Sussex) have passed on a large amount of Miles Master material to the museum for their project to build a Kestrel-engined reproduction.
    The Spitfire IX FSM has a real counterpart, at Coningsby, Lincs, and there is yet another MK356 at Cosford, Shrop! [1]. The Tiger Moth should be a complete airframe by mid-2004 [1]. Note that the full-size models are occasionally repainted with new identities and it is not easy to keep track of them! One of the 'Bf 109s' (marked '7') attended the '100 Years of Flight Experience' static display at the International Air Tattoo, Fairford, Glos, July 2003.
◆ Daily Easter to end Sept 10am to 5pm and October 11am to 4pm. Signed off the A260. (Note that photography is *not* permitted within the museum.) ◪ Aerodrome Road, Hawkinge Airfield, Folkestone, CT18 7AG ☎ 01303 89340 www.kbobm.org

❑ 'D-3-340'	Grunau Baby	ex Ramsgate. True identity unknown.	8-01
❑ 'K5054'	Spitfire proto REP	ex Luton, Lowestoft, Luton.	6-00
❑ 'N2532''GZ-H'	Hurricane FSM	BAPC.272, new build, arr by 4-00. 32 Sqn colours.	8-01
❑ 'N3289'* 'DW-K'	Spitfire FSM	BAPC.65, ex Chilham Castle, *Battle of Britain*. 610 Sqn colours.	8-01
❑ 'N3313' 'KL-B'	Spitfire FSM	BAPC.69, ex Higher Blagdon, Stoneleigh, *Battle of Britain*. 54 Sqn colours.	8-01
❑ 'N7033'	Harvard IIb	ex FX442, Bournemouth, Fordingbridge, Bournemouth, Sandhurst, Hullavington, 501, 226 OCU, 203 AFS, 61 OTU.	9-02
❑ 'P2921' 'GZ-L'	Hurricane FSM	BAPC.273, new build, arr by 4-00. 32 Sqn colours.	8-01
❑ 'P3059' 'SD-N'	Hurricane FSM	BAPC.64, ex Chilham Castle, *Battle of Britain*, 501 Sqn colours.	4-98
❑ 'P3208' 'SD-T' '	Hurricane FSM	BAPC.63, ex 'L1592', Higher Blagdon, *Battle of Britain*. 501 Sqn colours.	8-01
❑ 'P3679''GZ-K'	Hurricane FSM	BAPC.278, new build, arr by 4-00. 32 Sqn colours.	8-01
❑ 'MK356''2I-V'	Spitfire IX FSM	–	[1] 8-01
❑ –	Hurricane FSM	ex Lowestoft. 'RF-U' 303 Squadron colours.	4-98
❑ –*	Tiger Moth	ex Bedford area. Fuselage, arrived by 12-03.	[1] 12-03
❑ '425/17'	Fokker Dr I FSM	BAPC.133, ex Winthorpe, Higher Blagdon.	8-01
❑ – BAPC.36	Fi 103 (V-1) FSM	ex Old Warden, Duxford, Old Warden.	8-01
❑ – BAPC.66	'Bf 109' FSM	ex '1480', Chilham Castle, *Battle of Britain*.	8-01
❑ '14' BAPC.67	'Bf 109' FSM	ex Coventry, North Weald, Newark, *Battle of Britain*. JG52 colours.	8-01
❑ BAPC.74	'Bf 109' FSM	ex '6357', '6', Higher Blagdon, *Battle of Britain*.	8-01

Peter Smith: The Typhoon projects continue to progress. EJ922 will include the rear fuselage of a Sea Fury FB.11 [1]. The **Hawkinge Airfield Youth Club** are working on the former Manston BE.2 [1]. Peter has a Chipmunk PAX on loan at Brooklands, Surrey - qv.
◆ Airframes are stored in a variety of places and visits are not possible. ◪ Peter Smith, 1 Daniels Terrace, St Luke's Walk, Hawkinge, CT18 7EF e-mail peter-tiffy9.freeserve.co.uk

❑ G-AAXK   Klemm L 25   ex Sevenoaks, CoA 29-11-60. Damaged 3-62. Fuse.   3-02

❑	EJ922	Typhoon Ib	ex Manston, Brooklands, Sevenoaks, Biggin Hill, Southend, Brooklands, Brownhills, 3. Cockpit.	[1]	3-02
❑	–	'SE.5A' FSM	ex Sevenoaks, Coventry. Poor state.		3-02
❑	–	Typhoon I	ex Manston, Brooklands, Sevenoaks, Innsworth, Leeds, Cheltenham, Kemble. Cockpit.		3-02
❑	–	BAPC.117 BE.2c FSM	ex Manston, Sevenoaks, Brooklands, North Weald, BBC *Wings*. Stored.	[1]	3-02
❑	–	BAPC.190 Spitfire FSM	ex Barton, Chelford, 'K5054', Sevenoaks. Poor state.		3-02

IVYCHURCH north of the A259, east of New Romney
| ❑ | G-BEOD | Cessna 180 | ex Errol, OO-SPZ, D-EDAH, SL-AAT, N3294D. Crashed 29-6-89. | | 3-97 |

LASHENDEN AERODROME or Headcorn, on the A247 south of Headcorn
Lashenden Air Warfare Museum (LAWM): Great strides have been made with expansion plans. Planning permission has been obtained for a new museum building which will allow the aircraft to be displayed under cover and the majority of stored wartime exhibits to be displayed. It is hoped to open the new museum in 2007/2008. The V-1 is due to go to Munich, Germany, for restoration by a small workshop who specialise in such work. Fund raising is underway (donations welcome) to achieve this. The Lightning nose was split vertically for use in the sci-fi film *Wing Commander*. It is on loan from Mike Coleman [1]. The Reichenberg V-1 carries a manually-operated fuel pump. The museum have the remains of the rudder pedals, control column and their cockpit mountings plus the aileron controls and mountings. All of this adds up to physical evidence that this was one of 175 built at either Dannenberg or Pulverhof. See also above [2].
Departures: Vampire T.11 WZ589 was exchanged for a large cache of remains of crashed World War Two relics and moved to Rochester, Kent, in September 2002. The pod of Vampire T.11 WZ450 was acquired by a local restorer in an exchange that brought a Jumo 211 to the museum. The pod left in September 2003 for the local area (see below).
◆ Sun and Bank Hols 10.30am to 6pm, Easter until end of Oct. Sun 10.30am to 3.30pm Nov to Easter. Other times by prior arrangement. ⌧ Lashenden Aerodrome, Ashford, TN27 9HX ☎ 01622 890226 or '206783 **fax** 01622 206783 **e-mail** lashairwar@aol.com

❑	ZF587	Lightning F.53	ex Reading, Portsmouth, *Wing Commander*, Portsmouth, Stretton, Warton, RSAF 215, 53-691, G-27-61. Nose.	[1]	3-04
❑	84	'8-NF' Mystère IVA	ex Sculthorpe, French AF.		3-04
❑	63938	'11-MU' F-100F-16-NA	ex Sculthorpe, French AF.		3-04
❑	100549	Fa 330A-1	ex Manchester, Liverpool, Blackpool, Lavenham, Hullavington, Biggin Hill, Farnborough.		3-04
❑	–	BAPC.91 Fi 103R-IV	ex Horsham, Farnborough.	[2]	3-04

Aerodrome: *W&R18* (p91) recorded the breaking up of Cherokee Arrow G-TOBE. The forward fuselage moved to Eckington, Worcs.
❑	G-AHAV	J/1 Autocrat	ex HB-EOM ntu. CoA 21-6-75. Stored.	off-site	3-02
❑	G-ARBZ	Turbulent	Damaged 17-7-99. Stored.		7-00
❑	G-ARHL	Aztec 250	CoA 23-11-79. Stored.		3-02
❑	G-ARZM	Turbulent	ex Chessington, Headcorn. Crashed 23-6-91.		3-02
❑	G-ASAM	Turbulent	ex Chessington, Headcorn. Crashed 23-6-91.		6-03
❑	G-AZZP	Cessna F.172H	ex LN-RTA. Crashed 8-6-97. Stored.		3-02
❑	G-BMCS	Tri-Pacer 135	ex 5Y-KMH, VP-KMH, ZS-DJI. CoA 15-7-01. Stored.		3-02
❑	G-BSPC	SAN D.140C	ex F-BMFN. CoA 31-10-85. Stored.		6-03
❑	A-806	Pilatus P.3-03	G-BTLL, ex Swiss AF. CoA 23-6-94. Stored.		7-03

Locally: The former LAWM (see above) Vampire pod arrived here during September 2003. It will be restored and mated with wings, tail etc and eventually returned to the museum for display.
| ❑ | WZ450* | Vampire T.11 | ex LAWM, North Weald, Birmingham, Sealand, Wrexham, Woodford, Chester, Shawbury, RAFC, 233 OCU, 202 AFS. Pod. Arrived 9-03. | ® | 9-03 |

LYDD AIRPORT south of New Romney, at the end of the B2075, beyond Lydd itself

❑ G-ASER	Aztec 250B	ex Smeeth, Biggin Hill. Crashed 14-9-72. Dumped.	3-01
❑ G-AZLJ*	Trislander	ex Coventry, Highland, G-OREG, SX-CBN, G-OREG, G-OAVW, G-AZLJ, G-51-319. CoA 2-2-00. Spares, dismantled.	3-03

MANSTON AIRPORT or London (Manston) Airport, on the A253 west of Ramsgate

Hurricane and Spitfire Memorial Museum: The superb Hurricane and Spitfire dominate the exhibition – both examples of the workmanship of Medway APS, Rochester. 'BN230' is a composite, with parts from Mk.II Z3687 (SOC with RAE 9th April 1951) and Mk.IIc PG593 (crashed 21st February 1945) [1]. There is a wealth of other material to see and the superb 'Merlin Cafeteria' to sample.
◆ Open daily, Apr to Sep 10am to 5pm, Oct to Mar 10am to 4pm. Closed 25th-27th Dec and 1st Jan. Signed off the A253 Ramsgate road. ⌥ Manston Road, Ramsgate, Kent, CT12 5DF ☎ / fax 08143 821940 e-mail TheTrust@spitfire752.freeserve.co.uk www.spitfire-museum.com

❑ 'BN230' 'FT-A'	Hurricane II	LF751, ex Rochester, Bentley Priory, Waterbeach 5466M, 27 OTU, 1681 BDTF. 43 Sqn colours.	[1] 2-04
❑ TB752 'KH-Z'	Spitfire XVI	8086M, ex Rochester, Manston 7256M / 7279M, Lyneham, 5 CAACU, 103, 102 FRSs, 403, 66. *Val* (port). 403 Sqn colours.	2-04

RAF Manston History Museum: In the old MT building, the museum is run by the RAF Manston History Society and concentrates on the 80-plus year history of Manston, both military and civil.
Departures: Pup 150 HB-NAV is on loan to an ATC unit in Dover, Kent; Chipmunk T.10 WK638 left for Stamford, Lincs, in late 2002.
◆ Daily Mar to Oct 10am to 4pm. Nov to Mar Sat and Sun 10am to 4pm.⌥ Manston Road, Manston, Ramsgate, CT12 5DF ☎ 01843 825224 e-mail info@rafmanson.co.uk www.rafmanston.co.uk

❑ 'VM791'		Cadet TX.3	XA312/8876M. Ex Kenley.	3-02
❑ 'WD615'		Meteor TT.20	WD646, ex North Weald, Birmingham, Cosford 8189M, 5 CAACU, 3/4 CAACU, AWA, CSE. 85 Sqn, NF.11 colours.	2-04
❑ WP772		Chipmunk T.10	ex Lyneham, Colerne, Abingdon, St Athan, Middle Wallop, BFWF, QUAS, Hull UAS, 17 RFS.	® 2-04
❑ WT205		Canberra B.15	ex Eastwood, Foulness, MoA, 9. Nose. On loan.	2-04
❑ XA231		Grasshopper TX.1	8888M, ex Stockport, 'Sealand', Cosford, Warwick, Kimbolton, Petersfield.	2-04
❑ XD857		Valiant BK.1	ex Rayleigh, Foulness, 49. Nose.	2-04
❑ XG226*		Hunter F.6A	ex Faversham, Manston, Faygate, Catterick 8800M, 1 TWU, TWU, 229 OCU, 92, 66, 92. Nose.	2-04
❑ XJ727	'L'	Whirlwind HAR.10	ex Dishforth, Halton 8661M, 2 FTS, CFS, 1310 Flt, 228, 22.	® 2-04
❑ XL190		Victor K.2	9216M, ex St Mawgan, 55, 232 OCU, Witt Wing, 139. Nose.	2-04
❑ XN380	'67'	Whirlwind HAS.7	ex Lashenden, Wroughton, 705, 771, 829, 824, 825. SAR c/s. Spares.	2-04
❑ XS482	'A-D'	Wessex HU.5	ex DSFCTE, Farnborough, A&AEE.	2-04
❑ XV352*		Buccaneer S.2B	ex Gravesend, Manston, Stock, St Athan, Lossiemouth, 237 OCU, 208. Nose.	2-04
❑ –*		Auster V	ex Perth. Frame, marked 'TAY614B'. F/n 3-03.	2-04
❑ –*		Huntair Pathfinder	ex ?. F/n 12-03.	2-04

Defence Fire Services Central Training Establishment (DFSCTE): Operates as an RAF Enclave, 'parented' by Odiham. Back to *W&R18* (p92) Andover E.3A XS643 moved to Stock, Essex.

❑ WK124	'CR'	Canberra TT.18	9093M, ex Wyton, 100, 7, 213, 59, 103.	2-03
❑ XR503		Wessex HC.2	ex Boscombe Down, Gosport A2705 [2], RAE, A&AEE, MoA. Tail of XT463.	3-03
❑ XS714	'P'	Dominie T.1	9246M, ex Finningley, 6 FTS, RAFC, CAW.	3-03
❑ XV411	'L'	Phantom FGR.2	9103M, ex 56, 92, 19, 92, 14. Scorched.	2-03

❏	XV864		Buccaneer S.2B	9234M, ex 12, 237 OCU, 16.	3-03
❏	XW870	'F'	Gazelle HT.3	ex Shawbury, 2 FTS, CFS.	3-03
❏	XW922		Harrier GR.3	8885M, ex Laarbruch, Brüggen, Foulness, Enfield,	
				233 OCU, 1, 233 OCU, 1. Crashed 19-11-85.	3-03
❏	XX655	'V'	Bulldog T.1	ex Colerne, Bri UAS, 2 FTS. Poor state.	9-03
❏	XZ966	'G'	Harrier GR.3	9221M, ex Cottesmore, St Athan, 1417 Flt,	
				4, 1417 Flt, 233 OCU, 1, 1417, 1.	2-03
❏	ZE353	'E'	F-4J(UK)	9083M, ex 74, USN 153785.	2-02
❏	ZE360	'O'	F-4J(UK)	9059M, ex 74, USN 155529.	5-02

Airport: Boeing 707-347C EL-AKU was scrapped in June 2001.

❏	N812TC*	DC-8-55F	ex ST-AJD, N907R, JA8016. Arr 21-10-02. Stored.		1-04
❏	TF-ABW	Boeing 747-128	ex Iberia, C-GCIS, TF-ABW, F-BPVF. Cockpit.		6-03
❏	SP-DOF*	Iskra	G-BXVZ. ex Shoreham. First noted 5-02.	®	5-02

ROCHESTER AERODROME on the A229 south of Rochester

Medway Aircraft Preservation Society Ltd (MAPS): On 22nd July 2002, a 230 Squadron Puma HC.1 delivered the original Turboméca Palas turbojets fitted to the Sherpa and passed on by the Ulster Aviation Society. MAPS completed its latest restoration for the RAF Museum in early 2003. Complete with CFS colours, Sycamore HR.12 WV783 was completed in the usual immaculate fashion and moved to Hendon, Gtr Lon, in September 2003. The cockpit of the C-47A is the latest restoration project for the RAF Museum. Sections of this airframe are already at Hendon, Gtr Lon. When finished, the cockpit will join them [1]. The Harvard is being restored for its owner to 1941/1942 RAF configuration [2].

◆ The workshop is open to the public on Sun, Mon and Wed 9am to 1pm. Airport rules must be observed – the threshold of Runway 34 needs negotiating ✉ AFIS Unit, Rochester Airport, Maidstone Road, Chatham, ME5 9SD ☎ / **fax** 01634 204492

❏	G-36-1	SB.4 Sherpa	ex Duxford, Staverton, Bristol, Cranfield, G-14-1.		
			Fuselage, stored, pending construction of wings.		2-04
❏	[N9050T]*	C-47A-10-DK	ex Cosford, Fleet, Thruxton, Hal Safi, 5N-ATA, PH-MAG,		
			G-AGYX, KG437, 42-92656. Cockpit. Arr 4-03.	[1] ®	2-04
❏	'54137'*	Harvard IIB	ex North Weald, G-BKWZ ntu, ItAF MM54137,		
			RCAF 3064.	[2] ®	2-04

BAE Systems: The former Saudi Lightning has been restored by Robin Sleight's team and will become a 'gate guardian'. The *Hind* is a marketing tool of the various upgrades that BAE are offering.

❏	ZF581*	Lightning F.53	ex Portsmouth, Wing Commander, Portsmouth,	
			Warton, RSAF 206, 53-675, G-27-45.	2-04
❏	–*	Mi-24 *Hind-D*	ex Chester, Latvia, USSR, '06' red. (353246405029).	
			Arrived 25-6-03.	2-04

Others: Spitfire IX UB441 moved to Sedlescombe, E Sussex. A Vampire is with a private owner.

❏	WZ589*	'19'	Vampire T.11	ex Lashenden, Woodford, Chester, St Athan, 56.	
				Arrived 9-02.	9-02

SEVENOAKS

❏	G-APJZ	J/1N Alpha	ex St Albans, 5N-ACY, VR-NDR ntu, G-APJZ.		
			Crashed 10-11-75.	®	12-97

SHOREHAM west of the A225 north of Sevenoaks

Shoreham Aircraft Museum (SAM): A superb museum based upon SAM's extensive number of 'digs', all beautifully researched and presented. Included in the incredible selection of artefacts, is the rear fuselage skin from Bf 109 *Black 6*. Also on show are some of the paintings of SAM's leading light, Geoff Nutkins. The cockpit of Spitfire XVI TB885 is *not* available for inspection.

◆ Open May to Sep Sun only 10am to 5pm, or by prior arrangement. ✉ High Street, Shoreham Village, Sevenoaks, Kent, TN14 7TB ☎ 01959 524416 **www.shoreham-aircraft-museum.co.uk**

❏	TB885	Spitfire XVI	ex Kenley, *Reach for the Sky* as 'R1247',		
			Cosford.	off-site	3-04

LANCASHIRE

BACUP on the A671 north of Rochdale
Neil Dykes:

❏ –		Flexiform h-glider ex local area.	4-96
❏ –	BAPC.192	Weedhopper ex Hooton Park, Warmingham.	4-96
❏ –	BAPC.193	Whing Ding ex Hooton Park, Warmingham.	4-96

BLACKPOOL AIRPORT or Squires Gate, off the A584 south of Blackpool
Airport: Chipmunk 21 G-ANWB was flying by 2002; MS.880B Rallye G-ARTT (last noted 7-97) long
since gone; Cherokee 140 G-AVWG extant only as wings; Aztec 250C G-BBTL (last noted 9-01) left by
road; Aztec 250C G-BCBM flying by 1999; BN-2B-26-cum-van 'G-FOXY' last noted in late 1997.

❏ G-ARCI	Cessna 310D	ex N6966T. Damaged 22-8-86. Stored.		1-04
❏ G-ATMI	HS.748-2A/225	ex Emerald, VP-LIU, G-ATMI, VP-LIU, G-ATMI,		
		VP-LIU, G-ATMI. *Old Ben.* CoA 18-5-00. Dump.		1-04
❏ G-ATOO	Cherokee 140	ex Carlisle, Stanley. CoA 24-9-84.	®	8-02
❏ G-AVWE	Cherokee 140	ex Stanley, Biggin Hill. CoA 24-4-82.		8-00
❏ G-AWKP	CEA DR.253	Damaged 8-6-98. Fuselage, stored.		8-02
❏ G-AWUA	Cessna P.206D	ex Thruxton, N8750Z. Damaged 16-10-87.		8-02
❏ G-BCEO*	AA-5 Traveler	Crashed 28-4-02. Wreck. First noted 7-02.		1-04
❏ G-BJZX	Grob G-109	ex D-KGRO ntu. Stored.		10-00
❏ G-BMIY	Great Lakes	ex G-NOME. CoA 27-8-87. Stored.		8-02
❏ G-BMJG	Arrow 200	ex ZS-TNS, ZS-FYC, N9345N. Cr 11-10-98. Fuselage.		8-02
❏ G-BSPF	T.303 Crusader	ex OY-SVH, N3116C. Wreck.		8-02
❏ G-BTEF	Pitts S-1	ex N88PR. CoA 6-6-92. Stored.		8-02
❏ G-BXTH*	Gazelle HT.3	ex Southend, XW866, Shawbury, 2 FTS, CFS.		
		Arrived 8-4-03.	®	4-03
❏ G-LYDD	Navajo 300	ex Lydd, G-BBDU, N6796L. Dam 17-7-91. Fuselage.		
		Fire dump by 8-02.		1-04
❏ G-PLAH*	Jetstream 31	ex Platinum Air, G-LOVA, G-OAKA, G-BUFM,		
		G-LAKH, G-BUFM, N410MX, G-31-640.		
		CoA 26-7-02. Stored. First noted 9-01.		1-04
❏ G-SFHR*	Aztec 250F	ex G-BHSO, N2527Z. CoA 22-11-01. Stored.		1-04
❏ G-TAIL	Cessna 150J	ex N60220. Crashed 1-9-98. Stored.		10-00
❏ ZS-ODJ*	HS.748-2A	ex South Africa, F-GHKA, G-BPNJ, 9J-ABW,		
		G-11-4. Withdrawn and near dump by 11-03.		1-04
❏ –	ATP	ex Chadderton. c/n 2073. Dump.		1-04
❏ XL391	Vulcan B.2	ex 44, 101, 44, 9/35, BCDU, MoA.		1-04

CAPENWRAY on the A6 north of Carnforth
Capenwray Diving Centre: Joining Dragonfly HR.3 WP503 and Wessex HU.5 XS491 in the depths
of the lake during September 2002 was Cessna F.150L G-BFWL from Barton, Lancs.

CHARNOCK RICHARD on the A49, south-west of Chorley
Dave Stansfield: Artefacts from the former Pennine Aviation Museum are kept in the area. The
Albemarle is best described as '1¹/₂ nose sections' plus some other pieces. Dave is hard at work on these
with the long-term aim of making a fitted out cockpit. Also here is the 'tilting' nose of the CG-4A
Hadrian at Elvington, N Yorks (qv), the latter wearing a mock-up nose section.
◆ Not available for public inspection. ✉ 54 Hillcrest Avenue, Cliviger, Burnley, BB10 4JA.

❏ –	Albemarle	ex Bacup, Carlisle, Westnewton. Frames.	8-01

CHORLEY on the A6 south of Preston
Botany Bay Village: By September 2003, 'Sopwith 1¹/₂ Strutter' 'N5177' (last noted March 2000),
Whirlwind HAS.7 XN385 (December 2002) and Jet Provost T.4 XP688 (likewise) had all moved to

Bolton, Gtr Man. The pod of Venom FB.54 J-1712 moved briefly to Charnock Richard, Lancs, and then to Connah's Quay, Wales, 15th August 2003.

◆ Open 9am to 5.30pm daily. North of Hartwood, access off the B6228. ✉ Canal Mill, Botany Brow, Chorley, PR6 9AF ☎ 01257 261220

❑	G-OBAY	JetRanger	ex Blackpool, G-BVWR, C-GNXQ, N4714R. Crashed 5-1-01.	9-02
❑		Pegasus Q	'trike', no wings.	1-99
❑	'A4850'	SE.5A scale	BAPC.176, ex Barton, Firbeck, Pontefract.	8-99

International Fire Training Centre: At Washington Hall. *W&R16* (p169) noted under Chadderton, Gtr Man, the possible departure of unfinished ATP fuselage c/no 2070 to either Chorley or another destination by late 1997. With no sightings under this heading to confirm, the ATP was never listed. It now can be, but it needs be said it cannot be confirmed as c/no 2070, but this is its very likely identity.

❑	–*	ATP	ex Chadderton. Dump. See above.	11-02
❑	XN298 '10'	Whirlwind HAR.9	ex Warmingham, Stoke, Bournemouth, Yeovilton, Wroughton, Lee SAR Flt, Fleetlands, Lee, 846, 848.	11-02

Others: An Auster is under restoration in the general area.

❑	G-AKSZ*	Auster 5C	ex F-BGPQ, G-AKSZ, TJ457, 2 GCF, 666. CoA 9-5-02.	® 12-03

COCKERHAM on the A588 between Lancaster and Fleetwood

❑	G-ARZE	Cessna 172C	ex Blackpool. Damaged 11-9-76. Para-trainer.	8-01
❑	G-MWWE	Team Minimax	CoA 23-7-97. Stored.	7-99

ECCLESTON on the B5250 south of Leyland

Bygone Times Antique Warehouse:

◆ Open 9am to 5.30pm daily. ✉ Grove Mill, The Green, Eccleston, PR7 5PD ☎ 01257 451889 **fax** 01257 451090.

❑	'F-OTAN-6'	Noralpha	G-BAYV, ex Barton, Chelford, Sevenoaks, Booker, Hawkinge, Maidstone, Ford, F-BLTN, French AF. Crashed 23-2-74. Fuselage.	1-99

KENDAL on the A6 east of Windermere

Is in Cumbria! - qv.

LUMB on the B6238 north west of Bacup

Paul Spann: Acquired a Canberra B.2 nose in November 2002 and is restoring it.

◆ Viewing by prior arrangement only. **e-mail** paul@wd954.co.uk **www**.wd954.co.uk

❑	WD954*	Canberra B.2	ex Hendon area, Rayleigh, East Kirkby, Tattershall, Bicester, 76, Upwood, Hemswell. Cockpit. Arrived 7-11-02.	® 11-02

LYTHAM ST ANNE'S south of Blackpool.

Donald Campbell Exhibition: A Gnat arrived here during 2002.

❑	XM708*	Gnat T.1	ex Bruntingthorpe, Kings Langley, Locking, Halton 8573M, 4 FTS, CFS, HS.	11-02

PRESTON

Marsh Lane Technical School: Have a complex composite Harrier for instruction. It has the nose section of XV281, the centre fuselage of XW272 and the rear of a P.1127 test-rig.

| ❏ XV281 | Harrier GR.1 | ex Samlesbury, Dunsfold, Boscombe Down, A&AEE, BSE, Dunsfold. | | 4-02 |

Others: Mike Davey's and Graham Sparkes' Phantom is held in store in this general area.

| ❏ ZE352* | 'G' F-4J(UK) | ex Hooton Park area, Stock, Foulness, Pendine, Laarbruch 9086M, 74, USN 153783. Nose, stored. | | 8-03 |

RAMSBOTTOM on the A56 north of Bury
Spitfire IX SM520 (G-BXHZ) was sold in late 2002 and moved to Sandown, Isle of Wight.

SAMLESBURY AIRFIELD on the A59 east of Preston
BAE Systems:

❏ WH914	Canberra B.92	G-27-373, ex frustrated Argentine AF B.62, 231 OCU, 35, 76, 50, 61, 100. Dismantled and stored.		9-91
❏ WT537	Canberra PR.7	ex 13, 31, 17. Displayed.		8-03
❏ ZF580	Lightning F.53	ex RSAF 53-672, G-27-42. Displayed.		8-03

THORNTON-CLEVELEYS north of the A585, north of Blackpool

| ❏ WP839 | Chipmunk T.10 | G-BZXE, ex Newton, 8 AEF, 2 FTS, PFTS, Liv UAS, St A UAS, CUAS, 231 OCU, Birm UAS, 10 AFTS. | ® | 4-97 |

WARTON AIRFIELD on the A584 west of Preston
BAE Systems: The Blackburn B-2 is now based but it is believed that it will eventually operate from Old Warden, Beds. It attended the '100 Years of Flight Experience' static display at the International Air Tattoo, Fairford, Glos, July 2003 [1]. Nimrod second prototype XV147 was scrapped on 17th March 2003. Some parts were saved for Martin Painter's project – see under Guildford, Surrey.

The Strikemaster composite uses the nose of a 'spare' BAC.167, centre-section from an engineering mock-up, the rear end from 'JP' Mk 3 XN634, a wing from a 'JP3' and a wing from a 'JP5' [2]. A Tornado serves with the Overseas Customer Training Unit (OCTU) as an instructional airframe, the Hawk 200 having moved to the Apprentices School in October 2002.

Also on site are the **BAE Systems North West Heritage Group** (NWHG): The group now have three airframes on site. Please note that inspection is *not* possible without prior permission. The former Saudi T.55 nose is a mobile exhibit. General enquires: ✉ 3 Kingsway Avenue, Broughton, near Preston, PR3 5JN .

❏ G-AEBJ*		Blackburn B-2 ✈	ex Brough. Flew in 16-8-02. Operated by BAE.	[1]	7-03
❏ XS928	'AD'	Lightning F.6	ex BAe, Binbrook, 5-11, 56, 11, 56, 74, 5, 11. 5 Squadron colours, displayed.	NWHG	9-02
❏ XV263		Nimrod AEW.3	ex Bournemouth, Finningley 8967M, Waddington, JTU, Woodford, St M Wing, 203. Nose		9-01
❏ XW363	'36'	Jet Provost T.5A	ex Samlesbury, Preston, Warton, RAFC, 6 FTS, 1 FTS.	NWHG	3-03
❏ ZA359	'B-55'	Tornado GR.1	ex TTTE.	OCTU	9-01
❏ [ZF596]		Lightning T.55	ex Portsmouth, Stretton, Warton, RSAF 233, 55-715, G-27-71. Nose	NWHG	9-02
❏ ZH200		Hawk 200	ex BAe. Apprentice School.		10-02
❏	c/n 06402	Comet 4	ex Woodford. Fuselage.		4-97
❏		Strikemaster	ex SSU. Dump	[2]	9-01

No.967 Squadron Air Cadets: On the Bank Lane site.

| ❏ WT520 | Canberra PR.7 | ex Lytham St Annes, Eaglescott, Burntwood, Swinderby, 8184M, 8094M, CAW, 31, 17, 1, 17, 31, 80. Nose. | | 9-01 |

LEICESTERSHIRE and RUTLAND

☞ Bowing a little bit to pressure, within the administrative county boundaries of Leicestershire is the unitary authority - and far from a county - of the People's Republic of Rutland!

BRUNTINGTHORPE AERODROME between the M1 and the A50 south of Leicester
☞ The Bruntingthorpe site is large and aircraft are listed below under their nominal 'keepers'. It is possible to find aircraft 'owned' by one heading parked in an area 'operated' by another. Please note also that admission on the regular Sunday openings need not necessarily provide access to *all* areas.

Cold War Jets Collection / Vulcan Operating Company (VOC) / **C Walton (Aviation Division) Ltd:** The 'Vulcan to the Sky' appeal suffered a blow on 15th November 2002 when the Heritage Lottery Fund turned down their application for a grant. Undaunted, the team had another go! On 11th December 2003 it was announced that HLF had granted a 'Stage One Pass' for the project with £2.5 million being set aside. At the time of going to press, there are still hurdles to be cleared, but they are of smaller stature! The matched funding was still to be completed and there is still plenty of time for YOU to make your contribution. The programme aims for test flying in the summer of 2005 with the first appearance at flying displays in 2006. A flying life of 400 hours in anticipated - that could be up to 15 years if continuing funding can be found. To meet this, engineering work will have to start in the late summer of 2004 - start salivating!
Supporting XH558 in many important ways is the **Vulcan 558 Club** which also unites lovers of Vulcans every where. They publish a superb journal, The *Vulcan*, and stage meetings and events.
✉ Vulcan XH558 Club, c/o 79 Attfield Drive, Whetstone, Leics LE8 6ND **info hotline:** 07626 965302 www.vulcan558club.com
Notes: The Boeing 747 is intended to become a conference centre [1]. The Vulcan nose is owned by Paul Hartley, who also has one at Bournemouth, Dorset, and Wellesbourne Mountford, Warks! [2] The Jaguar is on loan from a US owner. It may eventually travel to Florida [3].
Departures: Valiant B.1 nose XD875 moved to Winthorpe, Notts, on 14-6-02.
◆ Open every Sunday 10am to 4pm. Other times by prior arrangement – ☎ Caroline Richmond 0116 2478030. Please note that there are *no* catering facilities on the airfield. 'Rolling Thunder' days staged when several aircraft are fired up and taxied, in association with other airfield operators. Details published in the aviation press. ✉ C Walton (Aviation Division) Ltd / Vulcan Operating Co, Bruntingthorpe Airfield, Lutterworth, LE17 5QS ☎ 0116 2478030 **fax** 0116 2478031 www.tvoc.co.uk www.coldwarjets.co.uk

❏	G-CPDA		Comet 4C	ex XS235, Boscombe Down, DTEO, A&AEE, BLEU. *Canopus.* Taxiable.		3-04
❏	F-BTGV	'1'	Super Guppy 201	ex Airbus Skylink, N211AS.		3-04
❏	SX-OAD*		Boeing 747-212B	ex Olympic, 9V-SQH. *Olympic Flame.* Flew in 12-6-02. Stored.	[1]	3-04
❏	XH558 G-VLCN		Vulcan B.2(MRR)	ex Waddington, VDF, Marham, Waddington, 50, Wadd Wing, A&AEE, Wadd Wing, 27, 230 OCU, 27, Wadd Wing, 230 OCU.	®	3-04
❏	XH563*		Vulcan B.2MRR	ex Banchory, Rotherham, Scampton 8744M, 27, 230 OCU, MoA, 230 OCU, Wadd W, 230 OCU, 12, 83. Nose. Arrived 21-5-03.	[2]	5-03
❏	XM715		Victor K.2	ex 55, 232 OCU, 543, 232 OCU, 100, 139. *Teasin' Tina.* Taxiable.		3-04
❏	XX900		Buccaneer S.2B	ex St Athan, 208, 12, 208, 216, 12, 208. Taxiable.		3-04
❏	XZ382	''AE'	Jaguar GR.1	8908M, ex Coltishall, Halton, Shawbury, 14, 17. Grey scheme by 10-03. 'Gate'.	[3]	3-04
❏	85	'8-MV'	Mystère IVA	ex East Midlands, Sculthorpe, Fr AF.		3-04
❏	1018		Iskra 100	G-ISKA, ex Polish AF. Taxiable.		3-04

Beech Restorations and **Tomcat T6 Restorations:** Adrian Marshall, Philip Turland and friends are restoring G-BKRN. (See also under Derby, Derbyshire.) The project received a major boost during the summer of 2003 when the Beech was allowed to move into the 'Vulcan Hangar'. Its job done, spares-ship C-45G G-BKRG left on 9th October 2003 bound for the Aviodrome, Netherlands. Next project is the former French Air Force T-6G. In Algeria, the French knew such armed Texans as

'Tomcats' because of their growl – hence the registration. As well as the J/1, an Auster 6 frame is stored here - it is one of two possibilities - see under Derby, Derbyshire.
◆ Exhibited at open days, otherwise by prior arrangement *only*. ✉ 14 Hallam Close, Moulton, Northampton, NN3 7LB ☎ 01604 790901 **fax** 01604 492946 **e-mail** philipstudfast@btconnect.com www.beechrestorations.com

❑	G-AJPZ*	J/1 Autocrat	ex Stoke, Sopley, Bournemouth, Wimborne, New Milton, Thruxton, F-BFPE, G-AJPZ. Dam 2-3-84. Frame.		3-04
❑	G-BKRN	Beech D.18S	ex Cranfield, Perth, Prestwick, CF-DTN, RCAF inst A675, RCAF 1500. CoA 26-6-83. US Navy c/s. *Naval Encounter.*		3-04
❑	114700	T-6G-NT Texan	ex Stoke-on-Trent, Eccleshall, North Weald, Coventry,		
	G-TOMC,	*Empire of the Sun,*	La Ferté Alais, FAF.	off-site	3-04
❑	–*	Auster 6	ex Derby. Frame. Stored.		3-04

Blackburn Buccaneer Society: Having taken delivery of Guy Hulme's XX894, wasted no time and on 4th January 2004 got the port side Spey spooled up and on the 10th got both running.
◆ Plan to exhibit at open days, otherwise by prior arrangement only. ✉ Nigel J Goodall, 32 The Haven, Inkpen Road, Kintbury, Hungerford, RG17 9TY **e-mail** nigel@buccsociety.freeserve.co.uk www.buccsociety.com

| ❑ | XX894* | '020' | Buccaneer S.2B | ex Farnborough, Kemble, Bruntingthorpe, St Athan, 208, 16, 12, 208, 12. 809 Sqn c/s. Arr 28-9-03. | ® | 1-04 |

Lightning Preservation Group (LPG): Work continues on keeping their two machines 'live' and LPG undertakes regular 'running' days. While planning permission for the erection of the QRA shed has been approved by Harborough District Council, fund-raising still needs a boost. Dig deep and help out!
◆ Regular open days, otherwise by prior appointment *only*. ✉ 66 Stoneage Close, Bognor Regis, PO22 9QW **e-mail** htrevorh@tesco.net www.lightnings.org.uk

| ❑ | XR728 | 'JS' | Lightning F.6 | ex Binbrook, 11, LTF, 5, 56, 23, 11, 23. Taxiable. | 3-04 |
| ❑ | XS904 | 'BQ' | Lightning F.6 | ex BAe Warton, Binbrook, 5-11 pool. Taxiable. | 3-04 |

Phoenix Aviation: Continue a lively trade, particularly in nose sections. The nose of Sea Vixen XN647 is being held for collector Robin Phipps [1] – see under Coventry, Warks, for his Buccaneer nose. Hunter T.7 XL565 was purchased by Geoffrey Pool on 13th April 2002 and is now to be found under 'Others' below. Airframes marked ➨ attended the '100 Years of Flight Experience' static display at the International Air Tattoo, Fairford, Glos, July 2003. Now, go back to *W&R16* (p142) where the departure of Canberra E.15 nose WH964 was noted as going to "a collector in the Southampton area". That wasn't bad, it can be found at Lewes, E Sussex. **Departures**: Boeing 707-436 nose G-APFG moved to Cove, Hants, by 4-03; Sea Prince T.1 WF122 arrived from Helston, Cornwall, 18-12-02, but moved on to Doncaster, S Yorks, 20-8-03; Canberra TT.18 nose WK122 moved to Chipperfield, Herts, 21-2-04; Sea Hawk FGA.6 XE327 left for Sinsheim, Germany on 23-10-02; Harrier T.4 XW270 to Ipswich, Suffolk, 10-9-03. Gnat T.1 XM708 arrived from Kings Langley, Herts, by 11-02 but quickly moved on to Lytham St Annes, Lancs; Whirlwind HAR.10 XP350 arrived from Helston, Cornwall 18-12-02 but moved on quickly to a paintball park, reportedly in the West Bromwich area; Harrier GR.3 XV751 to Charlwood, Surrey, by late 2002. Gnat T.1 XP540 was on loan to Arbury College, Cambridge, Cambs, but moved on to North Weald, Essex, on 2-10-03 - qv.

❑	[G-AYKA]	Baron 55A	ex Shoreham, Elstree, HB-GEW, G-AYKA,		
	'AY'		D-IKUN, N8683M. Crashed 18-6-89.		
			Converted to a car at Shoreham and in 2 Sqn marks!		3-04
❑	G-KEAB	Queen Air B80	ex Shoreham, Manston, G-BSSL, G-BFEP, F-BRNR, OO-VDE. Fuselage.		3-04
❑	WV795	Sea Hawk FGA.6	ex Cranfield, Bruntingthorpe, Bournemouth, Bath, Cardiff-Wales, Culdrose A2661, Halton 8151M, Sydenham, 738, 806, 700.	➨	3-04
❑	XE368*	Sea Hawk FGA.6	ex Helston, Culdrose SAH-3, Shotley A2534,		
	'200'		738, 806, 803, Ware. Arrived 14-12-02.		3-04
❑	XE624*	'G' Hunter FGA.9	ex Brawdy, 88775M, 1 TWU, 2 TWU, TWU, 229 OCU, West Raynham SF, 1. Arrived 18-4-02.		3-04

❑	'XF324'		Hunter F.51	E-427, ex Brough, Holme-on-Spalding Moor, Brough, Dunsfold, G-9-447, Danish AF, Esk.724. RAF 92 Sqn 'Blue Diamonds' colours.		3-04
❑	XF844	'70'	Provost T.1	ex Farnborough, RAE, 6 FTS.		3-04
❑	XH136	'W'	Canberra PR.9	ex Cosford 8782M, 1 PRU, A&AEE, 39, 13, 58, MoA. Nose.		3-04
❑	XH592	'L'	Victor B.1A	ex Cosford 8429M St Athan, 232 OCU, TTF, 232 OCU, Honington Wing, 15. Nose.	➥	3-04
❑	XJ494		Sea Vixen FAW.2	ex Kings Langley, Farnborough, FRL, A&AEE, HSA, Sydenham, 899, Sydenham, 892.		3-04
❑	XN647	'707'	Sea Vixen FAW.2	ex Helston, Culdrose SAH-10, A2610, 766, 899. Cockpit.	[1]	3-04
❑	XS217	'O'	Jet Provost T.4	ex Halton 9029M, Shawbury, CATCS, CFS, RAFC. Taxiable.		3-04
❑	XT630*	'X'	Scout AH.1	G-BXRL, ex Burbage. Cr 16-10-99. Arrived 10-02.		3-04
❑	XV328	'BZ'	Lightning T.5	ex Cranfield, Binbrook, LTF, 5, LTF, 5, 29. Nose.	➥	3-04
❑	XZ431*		Buccaneer S.2B	ex Marham 9233M, 12, 208, 12, 208. Nose. Arrived 15-5-02.		3-04
❑	J-4091		Hunter F.58	ex FSt7/FSt9, Swiss AF. Taxiable.		3-04

Others: A series of machines are held on the aerodrome by private individuals or organisations: Dale Featherby [1]; Ken Fern [2]; Roger Wintle and Arthur Perks [3]; Geoffrey Pool, with Jon Nuttall owning a share [4]; Alan Witt (See also under Barton, Gtr Man.) [5]; Malcolm and Sarah Bent (wings of XN584 are fitted to T.4 XP627 at Sunderland, N&T) [6]; Graham Smith (See also Wigston, Leics.) [7]; John and Mark Wood [8]. Canberra WT333 was built as a B(I).8 but was later fitted with the cockpit from B.2 WK135 [1]. Canberra B.2/6 G-BVIC (= Great Britain, Mk VI Canberra) was built as a B.6 and was then fitted with the cockpit from B.2 WG788. It has been acquired for spares by Air Atlantique and may well be on the move [9]. LET 410 9L-LCI became 3D-ACL and departed on 17th September 2003.

❑	G-HRVD*		Harvard IV	ex Swanton Morley, Wellesbourne, Thruxton G-BSBC, Mozambique, Port AF 1741, WGAF BF+055, AA+055, 53-4629. Arrived 4-03.	® [1]	3-04
❑	FX322*		Harvard II	ex Stoke, ?, French AF? Arrived 31-12-03	® [2]	3-04
❑	WT333		Canberra B(I).8	G-BVXC, ex Farnborough, Bedford, RAE, C(A).	[3]	3-04
❑	XH568		Canberra B.2/6	G-BVIC, ex Bedford, RAE, MoA. CoA 30-1-97.	[9]	3-04
❑	XL565		Hunter T.7	ex Kemble, Ipswich, Colsterworth, Shawbury, Lossiemouth, FRADU, 237 OCU, 4 FTS, 208, 8, West Raynham SF, 8, 1417F, 8, mkrs.	[4]	3-04
❑	XM355	'D'	Jet Provost T.3	ex Shobdon, Cambridge, Bruntingthorpe, Halton 8229M, Shawbury, 1 FTS, 7 FTS, CFS. Taxiable.	[5]	3-04
❑	XN584	'E' and '88'	Jet Provost T.3A	ex Halton 9014M, 1 FTS, CFS, RAFC, CFS, RAFC, TWU, RAFC. Taxiable.	® [6]	3-04
❑	XS209*	'29'	Jet Provost T.4	ex Kemble, Staverton, Halton 8409M, St Athan, Kemble, Shawbury, CAW. '5 MU' tail marking. Arrived 10-5-02.	[5]	3-04
❑	XV810	'K'	Harrier GR.3	9038M, ex 233 OCU, 4, 20. Nose.	[7]	3-04
❑	–		Auster	frame.	® [8]	3-04

Off-site: At a nearby Business Park is a workshop that specialises in Comanche spares.

❑	G-ARIN*	Comanche 250	ex N6084P. Crashed 20-5-90. First noted 11-02.		5-03
❑	G-ARUO*	Comanche 180	ex N7251P. CoA 22-8-00. First noted 11-02.		2-04
❑	G-ASCJ*	Comanche 250	ex 5N-AEB, N7197P. Crashed 10-9-86. F/n 11-02.		2-04
❑	G-ASYK*	Twin Com' 160	ex N7543Y. Crashed 11-5-96. First noted 2-04.		2-04
❑	G-ATFK*	Twin Com' 160	ex Romsey, N7642Y. Crashed 12-6-89. F/n 2-04.		3-04
❑	G-ATWR*	Twin Com' 160B	ex N8025Y. Crashed 14-9-93. First noted 2-04.		2-04
❑	G-AVCY*	Twin Com' 160B	ex N8241Y. Crashed 9-3-91. First noted 11-02.		2-04
❑	G-AVVI*	Twin Com' 160B	ex Shipdham, EI-AVD, G-AVVI, N8241Y. Crashed 6-4-91. First noted 2-04.		2-04
❑	G-AWBN*	Twin Com' 160B	ex N8517Y. First noted 2-04.		2-04
❑	G-BAWN*	Twin Com' 160C	ex N8790Y. CoA 3-5-98. First noted 11-02.		8-03
❑	N8911Y*	Twin Com' C/R	ex G-AYFT, N8911Y.	®	2-04

BURBAGE on the B578 south-east of Hinckley
Midland Helicopters: By January 2003, Scout AH.1 XT630 had moved to Bruntingthorpe, Leics.

COALVILLE on the A511 north-west of Leicester
Snibston Discovery Park: Within can be found a host of fascinating material on the industrial and transport heritage of the county. Items acknowledging aviation in Leicestershire are the Auster AOP.9 and a sectioned Whittle turbojet. Other airframes are in store and listed under this heading as a 'port of convenience'. They are not available for inspection. See under Winthorpe, Notts, for Auster G-AGOH.
◆ Daily 10am to 5pm, except Xmas and a week in January for maintenance. Signed off the A511.
🖃 Ashby Road, Coalville, Leicestershire, LE67 3LN ☎ 01530 278444 **fax** 01530 813301 **info-line** 01530 813256 **e-mail** snibston@leics.gov.uk

❏ G-AFTN	Taylorcraft Plus C2	ex Heavitree, HL535, 43 OTU, 652, 651, G-AFTN. CoA 1-11-57.	®	3-02
❏ G-AIJK	Auster J/4	ex Leicester, Stratford. CoA 24-8-68. off-site		3-02
❏ VZ728	Desford Trainer	G-AGOS, ex Perth, Strathallan, Thruxton, RAE. CoA 28-11-80. Stored.		3-02
❏ XP280	Auster AOP.9	ex Leicester, St Athan, 2 Wing, Queen's Dragoon Guards, 2 RTR, 651. On display.		3-02

COTTESMORE AIRFIELD north of the B668, north-east of Oakham
RAF Cottesmore: The Spitfire F.21 is owned by the 1 Squadron Association and kept in a hangar [1]. The Hunter is kept in the 4 Squadron hangar [2]. Both appear outside when needed. Harrier XW917 adorns the 'inner' gate and is painted in joint 3 (port) and 4 (starboard) Squadron colours [3], while XW924 is displayed outside the 3 Squadron hangar (the most westerly) in their markings [4]. Cottesmore is another base to take on a 'synthetic' fire crash rescue rig. In this case it is of the combined 'Harricopter' sort .

❏ LA255	Spitfire F.21	6490M, ex Wittering West Raynham, Cardington, Tangmere, 1.	[1]	7-01
❏ 'XJ673'	Hunter F.6A	XE606, ex Laarbruch 8841M, 1 TWU, TWU, 229 OCU, 92, 74, 65, 54, CFE. 8737M ntu.	[2]	7-01
❏ XW917	Harrier GR.3	8975M, ex Laarbruch, 3, 4, 3. SOC 3-4-88. 'Gate'	[3]	7-01
❏ XW924	Harrier GR.3	9073M, ex Laarbruch, Halton, 3, 4, 1, 233 OCU, 4.	[4]	7-01
❏ 162068	AV-8B Harrier	9250M, ex Wittering, AMARC, VMAT-203. Fuse.		6-00

DISEWORTH on the B5401 south of East Midlands Airport
Joe Goy: The Buccaneer is thought to still be resident.

❏ XV337	Buccaneer S.2C	ex Stock, St Athan, Abingdon 8852M, A&AEE, 208, A&AEE, 809, 800. Nose.	11-99

DONINGTON CIRCUIT or Donington Park, near to East Midlands Airport
A Spitfire FSM is mounted on a dramatic 'wishbone' plinth over-looking the Craner Curves.

❏ –	'K-W'	Spitfire FSM	–	4-01

EAST MIDLANDS AIRPORT or Castle Donington junction 24 M1, on the A453
On January 20, 2004, it was announced that the airport had changed its name to **NOTTINGHAM EAST MIDLANDS AIRPORT** while moving not one inch nearer to the city of that name! Accordingly, this reference has moved 'south' in the book - see below. (Derby, which is stone's throw away was not well known enough apparently and potential passengers are far less confused with 'Nottingham' as a major departure point. Other possible names were Robin Hood International and the compiler's preferred one - Nott's Landing!)

Tread boldy through the photo-spread for more Leicestershire (and Rutland!) on page 129

BEDFORDSHIRE

Avro XIX G-AHKX
Old Warden, July 2002
Roger Richards

CSS-13 (Po-2) ZK-POZ
Old Warden, October 2003
Tim R Badham

Fury REP 'K1930'
Old Warden, July 2002
Roger Richards

BUCKINGHAMSHIRE

JetRanger
Iver Heath, April 2003
Anthony Mills

Hunter F.1 'XF314'
Wycombe Air Park, October 2003
Anthony Mills

CAMBRIDGESHIRE

Mooney M.20F G-BCJH
Bourn, June 2003
Alf Jenks

CAMBRIDGESHIRE

Anson I N4877
Duxford, September 2003
Tim R Badham

B-24M Liberator '450493'
Duxford, October 2002
Tim R Badham

OV-10B Bronco G-BZGK
Duxford, September 2003
Col Pope

CAMBRIDGESHIRE

Bolingbroke IVT 'R3821'
Duxford, August 2003
Col Pope

Lysander TT.IIIA G-CCOM
Duxford, July 2003
Col Pope

Mosquito T.3 TV959
Duxford, June 2003
Col Pope

CAMBRIDGESHIRE

Lavochkin La-9 ZK-LIX
Duxford, June 2003
(here at Le Bourget)
David Willis

Queen Air A80 G-KEAC
Little Gransden, September 2002
Tony McCarthy

CORNWALL

Buccaneer S.2B XV359
Culdrose, August 2002
Tim Trethewey

CORNWALL
Harrier T.4 XZ145
Culdrose, August 2002
Tim Trethewey

CUMBRIA
Grasshopper TX.1 WZ784
Carlisle, July 2003
Ken Ellis

DERBYSHIRE
DH Comet G-ACSP
Derby, September 2002
Alf Jenks

DEVON

Hunter F.6A XJ639
Exeter, February 2002
David S Johnstone

Hobbycopter
Ivybridge, July 2002
John Phillips

HS.748-2A G-AVXJ
Exeter, August 2002
Tony McCarthy

DEVON

Minicab G-BGKO
Okehampton, July 2003
Tony McCarthy

Aiglet Trainer G-AMMS
Okehampton, July 2003
Tony McCarthy

Aiglet Trainer G-BGKZ
Okehampton, July 2003
Tony McCarthy

DORSET

Sea Prince T.1 N7SY
Bournemouth, August 2003
Mike Cain

Canberra PR.7 WT532 and
Vulcan B.2MRR XH537
Bournemouth, August 2003
Ian Haskell

Hunter F.51 E-402 and
Airbus A300B2 ZS-SDA
Bournemouth, May 2002
Tim Trethewey

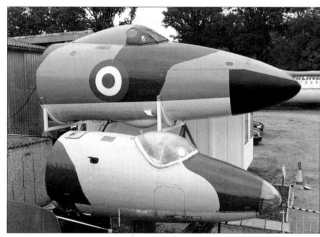

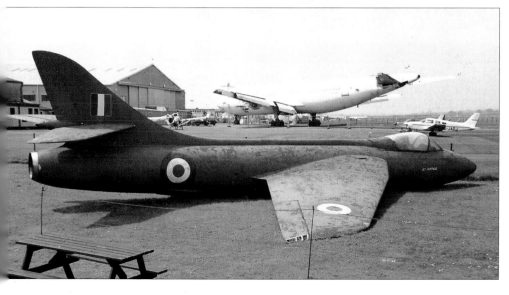

DORSET

SBLim-5 1211 (G-BWUF)
Bournemouth, January 2004
Ken Ellis

Navajo SX-BFM
Bournemouth, November 2003
Mark Roberts

Morane-Saulnier 'N' REP G-AWBU
Compton Abbas, January 2004
Ken Ellis

DORSET

Stampe SV-4 FSM 'B5539'
Compton Abbas, January 2004
Ken Ellis

Waxflatter Ornithopter BAPC.238
Compton Abbas, January 2004
Ken Ellis

ESSEX

Mystère IVA 319
Andrewsfield, June 2003
Alf Jenks

ESSEX

Vampire T.11 XD599
Ingatestone (here at Winthorpe)
June 2003
Ken Ellis

Gnat T.1 XM692
East Tilbury, July 2002
Mike Cain

CASA 2-111 G-AWHB
North Weald, September 2002
Tim R Badham

ESSEX

Douglas DC-4 '44-42914'
North Weald, September 2003
Ian Howell

Optica
North Weald, September 2002
Tony McCarthy

Belfast G-BEPS
and Boeing 707 EL-AKJ
Southend, July 2001
Phil Whalley

ESSEX

Short 330 G-DACS
Southend, July 2003
Phil Whalley

HS.125-600B ZF130
Stock, May 2002
Mark A Jones

GLOUCESTERSHIRE

Airbus A310 N440XS
Kemble, July 2003
Roger Richards

GLOUCESTERSHIRE

Boeing 727 EI-HCB
Kemble, April 2003
Tony McCarthy

Dove 5 G-APSO
Kemble, April 2003
Tony McCarthy

Douglas DC-10 N571RY
Kemble, July 2003
Roger Richards

HAMPSHIRE

Bulldog 122 G-102
Andover, May 2003
Tony Wood

Trident 3B G-AWZI
Farnborough, January 2004
Mark Roberts

Lightning T.5 XS420
Farnborough, September 2003
Tony McCarthy

HAMPSHIRE

Hunter F.51 E-402
Farnborough, October 2003
Ian Howell

Buccaneer S.2B XV165
Farnborough, October 2002
Ken Ellis

Wasp HAS.1 XV625
Gosport, August 2003
Mark Harris

HAMPSHIRE

Sea King HAS.6 ZG875
Gosport, August 2002
Tony Wood

F-104G Starfighter 22+35
Lasham, October 2003
Ian Howell

Auster AOP.9 WZ724
Middle Wallop, May 2002
Tim R Badham

HAMPSHIRE

Lynx AH.1 XX153
Middle Wallop, November 2003
Museum of Army Flying

HS.125-600B G-BKBH
Southampton, February 2002
Ian Haskell

JetStar 731 N6NE
Southampton, February 2002
Ian Haskell

HERTFORDSHIRE

Kraguj 30146
Elstree, November 2003
Anthony Mills

Trident 1E G-AVYE
(and Hadrian mock-up)
Hatfield, September 2002
Martin Pole

Twin Comanche N320MR
Elstree, September 2003
Brian Roffee

HERTFORDSHIRE

HS.125-1 G-ARYC
London Colney, May 2003
Ian Haskell

Humming Bird J-7326
and Hornet Moth G-ADOT
London Colney, October 2003
Tim R Badham

Ercoupe 415C N93938
Panshanger, October 2003
Brian Roffee

KENT

Hurricane I FSM 'P2970'
Capel le Ferne, April 2003
Mike Cain

LANCASHIRE

ATP
Chorley, October 2003
Tim R Badham

Whirlwind HAR.9 XN298
Chorley, October 2003
Tim R Badham

LEICESTERSHIRE

Boeing 747 SX-OAD
Bruntingthorpe, June 2002
Geoffrey Pool

Lightning F.6 XR728
Bruntingthorpe, June 2002
Hugh Trevor

Hunter T.7 XL565
Bruntingthorpe, March 2002
Geoffrey Pool

LEICESTERSHIRE

LET 410 9L-LCI
Bruntingthorpe, April 2002
Ken Ellis

Queen Air B80 G-KEAB
and Sea Vixen FAW.2 XN647
Bruntingthorpe, June 2003
David J Burke

Buccaneer S.2B XX894
Bruntingthorpe, September 2003
Geoffrey Pool

LEICESTERSHIRE

Twin Comanche G-ATWR
Bruntingthorpe, March 2003
Tim R Badham

Comanche G-ARUO
Bruntingthorpe, March 2003
Tim R Badham

Argosy 101 G-BEOZ
Nottingham East Midlands,
September 2002
Roger Richards

LEICESTERSHIRE

Canberra T.17 WH740
Nottingham East Midlands,
September 2002
Roger Richards

LINCOLNSHIRE

Phantom FGR.2 XT891
Coningsby, October 2003
Mark A Jones

Tornado F.3 ZE760
Coningsby, October 2003
Mark A Jones

Comet 1 'XV238'
Cranwell (here at East Fortune),
July 2003
Ken Ellis

Hawk T.1 'XX253'
Cranwell (here at East Fortune),
July 2003
Ken Ellis

'Hercules' '035'
Cranwell (here at Plymouth),
July 2002
Alan G L Barclay

LINCOLNSHIRE

Vampire T.11 XE946
Cranwell, May 2003
Tony Wood

Jet Provost T.4 XP556
Cranwell, May 2003
Tony Wood

Hampden I AE436
East Kirkby, April 2003
Brian Roffee

LINCOLNSHIRE

Dornier Do 28D-2 G-BWCO
Hibaldstow, February 2003
Jon Wickenden

Provost T.1 WW421
Sandtoft, December 2002
Tony Wood

Gannet AEW.3 XL502
Sandtoft, August 2003
Ian Haskell

LINCOLNSHIRE

Argus BAPC.294
Woodhall Spa, January 2003
David J Burke

GREATER LONDON

Hunter FR.10 853
Hendon, November 2003
David Willis
SE.5A F938 and Vimy REP 'F8614'
Hendon, March 2003
Ken Ellis

GREATER LONDON

BE.2c 2699
South Lambeth, May 2003
Mike Cain

Lockheed 10 NC5171N
South Kensington, August 2002
Andy Wood

Cessna F.150H G-AWAW
South Kensington, August 2002
Andy Wood

GREATER LONDON
He 162A-1 120235
South Lambeth, May 2003
Mike Cain

GREATER MANCHESTER
DC-10 G-DMCA
Manchester, February 2004
Ken Ellis

RJX 100 G-IRJX
Manchester, August 2003
Roger Richards

HINCKLEY south-west of Leicester

Douglas Boston-Havoc UK Preservation Trust: The Trust holds artefacts amounting to 50% of a Boston IIIA that served last with 418 Squadron RCAF at Bradwell Bay in long-term store. The main item is a skeleton 'birdcage' nose, a 13ft section of forward fuselage, port inner mainplane, main and nose landing gear, Boston-fit Wright Cyclone and rear fuselage and tailplane parts. Also held are the instrument panels, A-20G Havoc 'attack' nose and Martin gun turret.

◆ Please note that visits are *only* possible by prior arrangement. ✉ Dick Nutt, 17 Hinckley Road, Barwell, Leics, LE9 8DL ☎ 01455 845517

❑ Z2186	Boston IIA	ex Bethesda, 418, 85, 605, 23. Cr 17-10-42. Stored.	3-04
❑ 43-9628	A-20G-30-DO	ex RAAF Museum, Papua New Guinea, USAAF. Forward fuselage.	® 3-04

Others: Hurricane I P3717 that was under restoration in the area, moved to Sudbury, Suffolk, in 2002.

HUSBANDS BOSWORTH AERODROME south of the A427, south of the village

❑ G-BDCC	Chipmunk 22	ex WD321, DH. Damaged.	3-03
❑ G-MNGO	Hiway Skytrike	CoA 3-89. Stored.	6-98
❑ –*	EPR Hutter H-17	BGA.2847. Ex Keevil, PH-269. CoA 6-97. Arr 14-2-04.	2-02
❑ XK790	Grasshopper TX.1	ex Halton. Stored.	3-03

LEICESTER

John Poyser: John has built a full-size Spitfire IX and keeps it at his home in the city.

❑ –	'JE-J' Spitfire FSM	fuselage.	1-02

LEICESTER AERODROME or Leicester East, or Stoughton, south-east of Leicester

Apha 5 G-APTU moved to Northampton, Northants.

❑ G-AEXZ	J-2 Cub	CoA 2-11-78.	off-site ®	8-92
❑ G-AHLK	Auster III	ex NJ889, 43 OTU. CoA 21-9-97.	®	6-01
❑ G-AMTD	J/5F Aiglet Tnr	ex EI-AVL, G-AMTD. Crashed 7-8-93. Frame.		8-02
❑ G-ARDJ	Auster D.6/180	crashed 30-5-86. Stored.		9-03
❑ G-BSNN*	Rans S-10	CoA 27-6-00. Stored.		5-03

LOUGHBOROUGH on the A6 north of Leicester

Charnwood Museum: Within the museum the 1956 King's Cup-winning Auster J/1N 'flies' as a memorial to the wonders worked at nearby Rearsby.

◆ Mon to Sat 10am to 4.30pm, Sun 2pm to 5pm. Exhibitions and special events ✉ Granby Street, Loughborough, LE11 3QU ☎ 01509 233754, **fax** 01509 268140 **e-mail** charnwood@leics.gov.uk

❑ G-AJRH	'7' J/1N Alpha	ex Leicester area, Harrogate, Wigan. CoA 5-6-69.	3-04

University: Department of Aeronautical, Automotive Engineering and Transport Studies.

❑ ZF534	BAe EAP	ex Warton.	11-03

LUTTERWORTH

Lutterworth Museum: Moved into new premises at Wycliffe House and was officially re-opened on 1st March 2003. The museum includes a huge amount of Sir Frank Whittle/Power Jets material and an incredible archive.

◆ In Gilmorton Road, close to the monument, see below. Open March to November 10am to 4pm daily. ☎ 01455 555585.

Whittle Memorial: Dramatically displayed to the south of the town on the A426 roundabout is a superb full-scale model of the Gloster E28/39 as a tribute to Sir Frank Whittle. This and the similar monument at Farnborough, Hants (qv) were financed and built by the Sir Frank Whittle Commemorative Trust. The memorial was unveiled on 18th May 2003.

❑ –*	Gloster E28/39 FSM BAPC.284, displayed.		3-04

MARKET HARBOROUGH on the A6 south-east of Leicester

No.1084 Squadron, Air Training Corps: Took delivery of a Jet Provost nose during mid-2002. It spends a lot of its time at Bruntingthorpe, Leics, but is 'based' here.

❑ XS181*	'F' Jet Provost T.4	ex North Weald, Bletchley, Desborough, Bruntingthorpe, Halton 9033M, Shawbury, CATCS, RAFC, 3 FTS. Nose, trailer-mounted.	12-03

MELTON MOWBRAY on the A607 north-east of Leicester

Auster Nine Group: Have workshops in the general area. Contrary to p133 of *W&R18*, AOP.9 XN412 did *not* leave here.

❑ G-AYUA	Auster AOP.9	ex Bruntingthorpe, Cranfield, Bushey, Luton, Sibson, XK416, Middle Wallop, 7855M, 651, 19 MU.	12-96
❑ XN412	Auster AOP.9	ex Innsworth, Swindon, Dorchester, Middle Wallop, 6 Flt, C(A). Stored.	1-01
❑ XR267	Auster AOP.9	G-BJXR, ex Innsworth, Staverton, Congresbury, St Athan, 655, 652.	1-01
❑ XP282	Auster AOP.9	G-BGTC, ex XP282. Damaged 2-10-96. Stored.	7-97

David Hall: Is working on an Auster 4 in the general area.

❑ G-AJXY	Auster 4	ex Ipswich, MT243.	®	3-04

NORTH LUFFENHAM north of the A6121 south-west of Stamford

St George's Barracks: Within is an enclave on the eastern side of the former airfield for the **RAF Explosive Ordnance Disposal** unit, a sub-site from EOD at Wittering, Cambs. The Hunter is mostly hangar-bound and has had the nose cone removed to render it more MiG-looking, aided considerably by the red stars it carries! It is used by EOD to simulate a fully-armed 'defector' complete with 'strange' weaponry to assess and then disarm [1]. The Jet Provosts were all put up for disposal during 2002. All – T.3 XN554, T.3A XN579, T.4s XP629 and XP686 - moved to Ipswich, Suffolk.

❑ [XG194]	'69' Hunter FGA.9	8839M, ex Cosford, 1 TWU, TWU, 229 OCU, 1, 92, 111, 43. Soviet red stars.	[1]	1-04
❑ XP344	Whirlwind 'H723' HAR.10	8764M, ex Cranwell, Finningley, Chivenor, 22, SAR Wing, CFS. French roundel, olive drab.		9-03
❑ [XT905]	'P' Phantom FGR.2	9286M, ex Coningsby, 74, 228 OCU, 29, 228 OCU, 31, 17.		1-04
❑ XV804	'O' Harrier GR.3	9280M, ex Winterbourne Gunner, 4, 3, 1, 3, 4, 233 OCU, 1417F, 233 OCU.		9-03

NOTTINGHAM EAST MIDLANDS AIRPORT or Castle Donington

on junction 24 M1, on the A453 (See under East Midlands Airport, above for details of the name change... And see under Coventry Airport, Warks, for a venue going the other way!)

Aeropark: The Viscount nose was last recorded in *W&R17* (p59) when we reported the scrapping of all of it at Southend, Essex. It was acquired from a private house in Coleorton, Leics and is owned by AVA member C Jacobs [1]. Varsity WL626 is owned by Graham Vale [2] and Wessex XT604 by Mark Lindsey [3]. Vampire T.11 XD459 moved to Doncaster, S Yorks, in February 2003. The pod of recently-arrived XD534 will be used in a composite restoration of XD459. Following this the pod of XD534 will be restored in its own right.

Supporting the Aeropark is the **East Midlands Airport Volunteers Association** (AVA) (✉ Graham Vale, 76 Springfield Road, Midway, Derbyshire ☎ 01283 552397 e-mail graham. vale4@btinternet.com) who are now staging regular events, including open cockpit days, an aerojumble and a fund-raising air ambulance day. Details in the aviation press and via the number below.

◆ Open Thu (10.30am to 5pm), Sat (noon to 5pm) and Sun (10.30am to 7pm) 1st May to 30th Sep, and Sun 10.30am to 5pm or dusk in the winter. Also Bank Holidays other than Christmas. 'Open cockpit' and special event days staged. ☎ 07741 937310 - during opening hours.

EAST DEREHAM on the A47 west of Norwich
Russell Dagless: Scout XP849 (G-CBUH) was flying by late 2003.

❏ 5X-UUX		Scout Srs 1	G-BKLJ, ex Tattershall Thorpe, Heysham, Panshanger, Uganda Police Air Wing.	7-02
❏ XP166		Scout AH.1	G-APVL, ex Farnborough, RAE, G-APVL.	7-02
❏ XT420		Wasp HAS.1	G-CBUI, ex Fleetlands, Wroughton.	7-02
❏ XV134	'P'	Scout AH.1	G-BWLX, ex Ipswich, Fleetlands, Middle Wallop.	7-02
❏ XV138		Scout AH.1	ex Almondbank, Wroughton, 658. Arrived by 12-97.	7-02

EAST WINCH AERODROME on the A47 east of King's Lynn

❏ G-BEXK	Pawnee 235D	ex N82424 ntu. Crashed 4-10-92.Frame.	8-97

EAST WRETHAM east of the A1075 north of Thetford
Thorpe Camp: See also the 'northern' end of this area, listed under Bodney Camp, Norfolk.

❏ XM386	'08'	Jet Provost T.3	ex St Athan 8076M, Halton, Shawbury, 2 FTS, CFS	11-03
❏ [XT643]		Scout AH.1	ex Waterbeach, Wroughton, 660, 661. Poor state.	11-03

FELTHORPE AERODROME south of the B1149, north-west of Norwich
Another long-in-the-tooth sighting, preparing for the realms of LOST!

❏ G-ARBG	Nipper II	crashed 16-5-84.	®	5-91

GREAT YARMOUTH
Dick Melton Aviation (DMA): During early 2003 Dick put this exceptional project up for sale. It is located at a *private* address in this general area.

❏ W2718	Walrus I	G-RNLI, ex Winchester, Southampton, 276, 751, 764.	4-03

Sea-Front Crazee Golf: The hulk of a Cessna Centurion adorns part of the course.

❏ G-MANT	Cessna 210L II	ex Oxford, G-MAXY, N550SV. Crashed 16-2-92.	9-02

HARDWICK or Shelton Common, east of the A140, west of Bungay
93rd Bomb Group Museum: An incredible museum set in three Nissen huts on the former Station 104's Communal Site A with superb displays.
◆ Open the third Sunday of each month, May to October. 10am to 5pm. Refreshments available. Other times by appointment. ✉ Paul Thrower, 12 St David's Close, Long Stratton, Norfolk, NR15 2PP ☎ 01508 531405 www.93rd-bg-museum.org.uk

Maurice Hammond: Well-known warbird operator, Maurice, has had a second P-51 under restoration since 1999. (He operates G-MSTG from a strip nearby.)

❏ 44-13521	P-51D-20-NT	ex Etampes, Tech college, USAAF.	®	3-04

KING'S LYNN
Bob Trickett: The mindless element has reared its head again. One of the buildings that forms Bob's workshop and store in this general area was burned down in an arson attack early in 2004. The following items were totally destroyed: the BAC Drone project, based around an original centre-section and other parts plus all the newly-made parts and the drawings; an Isaacs Fury; a Currie Wot; the new 'tail feathers' and other newly-made parts for the ANEC Missel Thrush REP - the fuselage of which is at Wolverhampton, W Mids (qv); all newly-made parts and drawings for an Avro 504 REP and a Sopwith Snipe REP; several original parts for the Bristol F.2b project; and large amounts of Hurricane parts plus large numbers of misc World War One parts, instruments etc. Referring to *W&R18* (p162) the 'Salmson' FSM did *not* come here from Doncaster, it was sold on to another owner in South Yorkshire.
    One of the Hurricanes is said to be a salvage from a Scottish loch and a Mk.I [1]. The other is a former Soviet Union Hurricane project . This *may* be Mk.IIb BD713 [2].

❑ –	Bristol F.2b	ex Weston-on-the-Green. Fuselage.	off-site ®	3-04
❑ –*	Hurricane	ex UK crash site.	[1]	3-04
❑ –*	Hurricane	ex Russia.	[2]	3-04

Others: A Terrier is under restoration in the area. *W&R17*, p160, noted that Wasp HAS.1 XT439 was unaccounted for when a small collection was wound up in the area. See under Hemel Hempstead, Herts.

❑ G-AYDW	Terrier 2	ex Little Gransden, King's Lynn, Camberley, Cranfield, Bushey, G-ARLM, AOP.6 TW568, LAS, AOPS, 227 OCU, 43 OTU. CoA 1-7-73.	®	10-01

LITTLE SNORING AERODROME north of the A148, north of the village

❑ G-BPMU	Nord 3202B	ex High Ham, N22546, G-BIZJ ntu, Liverpool, USA, ALAT No.70 'AIX'. CoA 19-10-90.	7-96
❑ G-FISK*	Pazmany PL-4A	CoA 11-4-96. Stored.	9-03

MARHAM AIRFIELD south of the A47 west of Swaffham
RAF Marham: As related in *W&R18* (p163), Buccaneer S.2B XZ431 needed to be moved and it was scrapped, the nose going to Bruntingthorpe, Leics, on 15th May 2002. **Tornado Training School** (TTS) has at least two airframes. Tornados are beginning to be withdrawn, 'lying out' prior to disposal.

❑ WT509	'BR' Canberra PR.7	ex 100, 13, MoS, 58, 80, 17, 31. Dump by 11-03.		3-04
❑ XH673	Victor K.2	8911M, ex 57, Witt Wing, 139, MoA. Outside SHQ. Joint 55 and 57 Sqn colours. Hemp scheme.		6-00
❑ ZA267	Tornado F.2	9284M, ex Boscombe Down. Inst..	TTS	10-02
❑ ZA322*'TAC'	Tornado GR.1	9334M, ex 15. Gutted and derelict by 11-03. Spares.		3-04
❑ ZA356*	Tornado GR.1	ex St Athan, 15. Cockpit.	TTS	3-03
❑ ZA375*'AJW'	Tornado GR.1	9335M, ex 13, 617. Derelict by 11-03. Spares.		3-04
❑ ZA407*	Tornado GR.1	9336M. ex 617, TWCU. Last flew 22-11-01. For gate.		3-04

MARTHAM on the B1152 north of Great Yarmouth
JME Aviation: Jeremy Moore's workshop has expanded the number of projects in hand. The bulk of these are *believed* to be under way for the Flying Heritage Collection (also known as Vulcan Warbirds Inc) which is being assembled in Seattle, USA by the Microsoft mogul Bill Allen. Seafire III PP972 (G-BUAR) moved to Norwich, Norfolk [1]. It *may* be that the Spitfire is also destined for this collection.

❑ –*	Mystery Ship	ex USA.	[1]	1-04
❑ SM969*'D-A' G-BRAF	Spitfire XVIII	ex North Weald, ?, Bournemouth, Biggin Hill, Bitteswell, Blackbushe, New Delhi, Indian AF HS877, RAF SM969, 47 MU, India, ACSEA, 76 MU. CoA 23-9-93. Arrived by 9-03. Stored, dismantled.		1-04
❑ 1227	Fw 190A-5	N19027, ex North Weald, G-FOKW, Biggin Hill, Wycombe Air Park, Russia, 'DG+HO'. Cr 19-7-43. ®	[1]	1-04
❑ '111617'*	Me 262A-1a/U3	N94503, ex Chino, Glendale, Hughes, USAAF, FE-4012 / T2-4012, Lechfeld.	[1]	1-04
❑ –*	Yakovlev Yak-3	ex Sudbury, (?), Russia.		1-04

NARBOROUGH south of the A47, north west of Swaffham
Wellesley Aviation: Took delivery of a Canberra nose in October 2002.

❑ WH850*	Canberra T.4	ex Winthorpe, Barton, Chelford, Samlesbury, St Athan, Laarbruch SF, Wildenrath SF, 14, 88, Marham SF. Nose. Arrived 10-02.	10-02

NEATISHEAD east of the A1151, north of Hoveton, near Horning
Air Defence Radar Museum: The museum is dedicated to every aspect of the history of radar, air defence and battle management. Housed in the original 1942 Operations Building, exhibits include a Battle of Britain 'Ops' Filter Room, a 'Cold War' era 'Ops' Room, ROC Field Post and much more.
♦ Open 10am to 5pm (last entry 3pm) on the second Saturday of each month, Bank Holiday Mondays and every Tuesday and Thursday, early April to end of October. Group visits by prior arrangement. 'Brown signed' off the A1062. ✉ Museum Manager, RAF Air Defence Radar Museum, RAF Neatishead, Norwich, NR12 8YB. ☎ 01692 633309 **www**.radarmuseum.co.uk

RAF Neatishead: The Phantom guards the gate. The base awaits closure.
❑ XV420   'BT' Phantom FGR.2   9247M, ex Wattisham, 92, 23, 29, 23, 19, 56, 29.   2-04

NORWICH
Hull Aero: Ralph Hull is working on variety of projects. The Seafire is registered to Wizzard Investments, see under Greenham Common, Berks [1]. The Spitfire XVI is for storage and sale [2], the Mk.IX will return to Canada when completed [3]. Work is also reported underway on the former OFMC Sea Fury, for Kermit Weeks.

❑ D-CACY	Sea Fury FB.11	G-BWOL, ex Wycombe (!), Duxford, Uetersen, DLB ES3617, G-9-66, WG599.	®	8-02
❑ N4806E*	B-26C Invader	ex Manston and area, Southend Airport, Rockford (Illinois), 44-34172, Davis-Monthan, 3 BW, 17 BW, 7 ADW. Stored. First noted 8-02.		8-02
❑ PP972*	Seafire III	G-BUAR, ex Martham, Earls Colne, Audley End, East Midlands, Biggin Hill, Thruxton, Biggin Hill, Vannes-Meucon, Gavres, Aéronavale 12F, Bien Hoa, 1F, PP972, FAA, 767, 809. Arr by 1-04.	® [1]	1-04
❑ TD135*	Spitfire XVI	ex Geneseo, USA, Dishforth, Newcastle, 609, 611, 226 OCU, 202 AFS, 61 OTU, 345, 485, 74. Stored. Arrived 2-04.	[2]	2-04
❑ TD314	Spitfire IX	ex Canada, 'N601DA', South Africa, SAAF, 234, 183.	® [3]	1-04
❑ 417657	B-26K Invader	N99218, ex Ludham, Booker, Canterbury, Southend, Chino, USAF. Nose. Stored.		8-02

Ted Sinclair: Has two Tempest cockpits. The former Ludham example is the most complete and has been used as a pattern for the Tempest Too project – see under Gainsborough, Lincs.

❑	Tempest V	ex Spanhoe. Cockpit.	®	2-02
❑	Tempest V	ex Ludham, Norwich. Cockpit.	®	4-95

Others: A former Russian Spitfire IX is believed stored in the area, awaiting restoration.

❑ SM639	Spitfire IX	ex Russia, USSR. Stored.	3-96

NORWICH AIRPORT or Horsham St Faith, east of the A140, north of the city
City of Norwich Aviation Museum (CNAM): The museum has recently expanded the area of the museum site, allowing for more room around some of the aircraft. Relocation of the workshop has allowed for increased area within the indoor exhibitions. The RAF 100 Group Association collection is in a special section devoted to Bomber Command. Other displays show the history of RAF Horsham St Faith, the 8th Air Force, the role of women in aviation and local aviation pioneers. Hunter F.6A XG172 is on loan from Mick Jennings (he of Coltishall, Norfolk, fame) [1].
♦ Access from the A140, north of the airport, follow 'brown signs'. Apr to Oct: Tue to Sat and Bank Hols, 10am to 5pm; Sun noon to 5pm. Nov to Mar: Wed and Sat 10am to 4pm, Sun noon to 4pm. Closed 21st Dec to 5th Jan. Evening on Tue and Thu by prior arrangement. ✉ Old Norwich Road, Horsham St Faith, Norwich, NR10 3JF ☎/ fax 01603 893080 **e-mail** norwichairmuseum @hotmail.com **www**.cnam.co.uk

❑ G-ASKK	Herald 211	ex Air UK, PP-ASU, G-ASKK, PI-C910, CF-MCK. CoA 19-5-85.	3-04

❑	G-BHMY		Friendship 200	ex KLM uk, Air UK, F-GBDK, F-GBRV ntu,		
				PK-PFS, JA8606, PH-FDL.		3-04
❑	WK654		Meteor F.8	ex Neatishead 8092M, Kemble, 85, CFE,		
				Odiham SF, AWFCS, 247.		3-04
❑	'XF383'	'G'	Hunter F.51	E-409, ex 'XF383' Cardiff-Wales, 'WV309', 'XF383',		
				Dunsfold, G-9-437, DanAF Esk.724. 74 Sqn c/s.		3-04
❑	'XG168'	'10'	Hunter F.6A	XG172, ex North Weald, Ipswich, Scampton 8832M,		
				1 TWU, 229 OCU, 263, 19. 229 OCU c/s by 9-03.	[1]	3-04
❑	XM612		Vulcan B.2	ex 44, Wadd Wing, Scampton Wing, 9.		3-04
❑	XP355	'A'	W'wind HAR.10	ex G-BEBC, Faygate, 8463M, 38 GCF, 21, CFS.		3-04
❑	XP458		Grasshopper TX.1	ex Fakenham area. On loan. Stored.		3-04
❑	ZF592		Lightning F.53	ex Portsmouth, Luxembourg, *Wing Commander*,		
				Stretton, Warton, RSAF 223, 53-686, G-AWON,		
				G-27-56. On loan.		3-04
❑	–		Scimitar CIM	–		3-04
❑	121		Mystère IVA	ex Sculthorpe, FAF. '8-MY'. *Patrouille de France* c/s.		3-04
❑	16718'TR-999'		T-33A-5-LO	ex Sculthorpe, Turkish AF ntu, FAF. USAF colours.		3-04

Airport: The hulk of Herald 201 G-APWH was scrapped during 2002.

❑	G-ATIG	Herald 214	ex BAC Express, PP-SDI, G-ATIG. Towing trainer.	2-04
❑	G-AVEZ	Herald 210	ex Museum, Air UK, BIA, BUA, PP-ASW,	
			G-AVEZ, HB-AAH. CoA 5-1-81. Fire.	2-04
❑	G-BCDN	Friendship 200	ex Air UK, PH-OGA, JA8615, LV-PMR ntu,	
			PH-FDP. CoA 19-7-96. Training airframe, fuselage.	3-01
❑	G-BCDO	Friendship 200	ex Air UK, PH-OGB, JA8621, PH-FEZ. *Lord Butler*.	
			Fuselage. Damaged 19-7-90. Air UK Tech College.	9-99
❑	G-BTOM	Tomahawk 112	ex Tattershall Thorpe. Crashed 26-9-92.	6-99
❑	EI-CAZ	FH.227D	ex Iona, SE-KBR, EI-CAZ, SE-KBR, C-FNAK,	
			CF-NAK, N2735R. Dump by 9-95.	2-04

Offshore Fire and Survival Training Centre: Helicopter rig 'G-DRNT' had moved on to Stansted, Essex, by October 2003 and then quickly disappeared.

| ❑ | [N5880T] | WG.30-100 | ex Weston-super-Mare, Yeovil, Air Spur, G-17-31. | 9-03 |

REYMERSTON near East Dereham

Wallis Autogiros: See under London, Gtr Lon, for another 'G-ARZB'. (And there's another in 'Planet Hollywood' in Times Square, New York!)

◆ *Not* open to public inspection.

❑	G-ARRT	WA-116/McC	CoA 26-5-83.	8-03
❑	G-ARZB	WA-116 Srs 1	ex XR943, G-ARZB. CoA 29-6-93. *Little Nellie*.	8-03
❑	G-ASDY	WA-116/F	CoA 30-4-90.	8-03
❑	G-ATHM	WA-116/F	ex 4R-ACK, G-ATHM. CoA 23-5-93.	8-03
❑	G-AVDG	WA-116 Srs 1	CoA 23-5-92.	8-03
❑	G-AVJV	WA-117	CoA 21-4-89.	8-03
❑	G-AVJW	WA-118/M	CoA 21-4-83.	8-03
❑	G-AXAS	WA-116-T/Mc	CoA 23-5-92.	8-03
❑	G-AYVO	WA-120 Srs 1	ex South Kensington. CoA 31-12-78.	8-03
❑	G-BAHH	WA-121/Mc	CoA 26-10-93.	8-03
❑	G-BGGU	WA-116	—	8-03
❑	G-BGGW	WA-122/RR	CoA 26-10-93.	8-03
❑	G-BLIK	WA-116/F-S	CoA 24-4-98.	8-03
❑	G-BMJX	WA-116/X	CoA 1-4-89.	8-03
❑	G-BNDG	WA-201/R	CoA 3-3-88.	8-03
❑	G-SCAN	WA-116-100	CoA 10-7-91.	8-03
❑	G-VIEW	WA-116/L	CoA 6-10-85.	8-03
❑	[G-VTEN]	WA-117	CoA 3-12-85.	8-03
❑	XR944	WA-116/F	G-ATTB, ex XR944, G-ARZC. CoA 23-5-92.	8-03

SEETHING AERODROME east of the B1332, north of Bungay

Station 146 Control Tower Museum: The original control tower has been restored and contains a museum dedicated to the history of the aerodrome and the surrounding area. The tower is a living memorial to the Liberator-equipped 448th BG. There is a shop and refreshments are available.
◆ Access from the Thwaite St Mary road to the south. First Sun May to Oct, 10am to 5pm. Other times by appointment. ▣ 'The Beeches', Brooke Road, Seething, Norwich, NR15 1DJ ☎ 01508 550288

SHIPDHAM AERODROME off the A1075 south-west of East Dereham

❏ G-AYAF	Twin Com' 160C	ex N8842Y. CoA 8-5-77. Stored.		4-96
❏ G-AYUM*	Slingsby T.61A	ex Swanton Morley. CoA 10-6-02.	®	9-03
❏ G-JDIX	Mooney M.20B	ex G-ARTB. CoA 16-1-00. Stored.		9-03
❏ G-MJUC	Tiger Cub 440	CoA 20-1-92. Stored.		9-03
❏ D-5829*	Blanik	Stored.		9-03

SWANTON MORLEY AERODROME east of the B1110, north of East Dereham

With the closure, a mass clear-out: Cherokee 140 G-ATTG and Tomahawk N39132, no 'forwarding address'; Harvard IV G-HRVD to Norwich, Norfolk; Tiger Cub G-MJSU to Flixton, Suffolk, 8-8-02; PT-17 N53091, N2S-3 N73410 and PT-17 40-1766, no details. A75N1 N65200 flying by June 2002.

❏ G-ARHF	Aircoupe	ex Shipdham. CoA 10-5-94. Stored.	5-02
❏ G-BBXZ	Evans VP-1	CoA 8-3-96. Stored.	5-02
❏ G-BGRC	Cherokee 140B	ex SE-FHF. CoA 26-10-97. Stored.	5-02
❏ G-BTOA*	Mong Sport	ex N1067Z. CoA 16-9-94. Stored. First noted 5-02.	5-02

TERRINGTON ST CLEMENT north of the A17, west of King's Lynn

Terrington Aviation Collection: Jet Provost XM468 is located at West Walton Highway, Norfolk.

THORPE ABBOTTS off the A140 at Dickleburgh, north of Scole

100th Bomb Group Memorial Museum: Contents of the tower museum are exceptional, offering poignant insights into the life and times of the men and machines of the 'Bloody Hundredth'.
◆ 'Brown signed'. Open 10am to 5pm weekends and Bank Hols. Also Wed 10am to 5pm May to Sep. *Closed* November to end of January. Other times by appointment. Regular special events are staged.
▣ 100th BG Memorial Museum, Common Road, Dickleburgh, Diss, IP21 4PH ☎ 01379 740708, or Sam Hurry on 01553 766089

TIBENHAM north of the B1134, north of Diss

Black Barn Aviation: Fairchild 24 N16676 moved to Flixton, Suffolk, on 18th March 2003.

❏ G-AYPP	Super Cub 95	ex ALAT 18-1626, 51-15626. Frame.		6-96
❏ G-FANC*	Fairchild 24R-46	ex Felthorpe, N77647, NC77647. Arson attack 18-2-03. Stored.		5-03
❏ N1325M	N2S-5 Kaydet	ex USA, BuNo 43390. Stored.		4-03
❏ N1328	Fairchild 24KS	ex USA, NC1328.	®	4-03
❏ N62842	PT-17D	ex USA. Stored.		9-03
❏ N68427	N2S-4 Kaydet	ex USA, BuNo 55771. Stored.		9-03

TUNSTEAD east of the B1150, north of Hoveton

❏ G-BARD	Cessna 337C	ex North Coates, SE-FBU, N2557S. Cr 12-6-94.	9-99

WALPOLE ST ANDREW south of the A17, south-east of Sutton Bridge

Murray Flint: Lightning T.5 XS420 attended the '100 Years of Flight Experience' static display at Fairford, Glos, during July 2003. It left here on 28th May 2003 for refurbishment at Cranwell, Lincs, before moving to RIAT. After the show, it moved to Farnborough, Hants, on 3rd September 2003.

WATTON on the A1075, south of East Dereham
Wartime Watton Exhibition: No news on this collection, but the former Officers' Mess has been demolished. **No.611 Volunteer Gliding School**: still have their Grasshopper.
❑ XP490   Grasshopper TX.1 ex Swanton Morley, Ipswich, Syerston, Grantham.   1-04

WEST WALTON HIGHWAY on the A47 north-east of Wisbech
Fenland and West Norfolk Aviation Museum: Run by the Fenland and West Norfolk Aircraft Preservation Society. The museum has a close association with the Terrington Aviation Collection (TAC) and among the latter's artefacts on loan are the Buccaneer and MiG-29 cockpit sections. Airframes not available for public inspection are marked §.
◆ At Bamber's Garden Centre, Old Lynn Road – signed off the A47/B198 junction. Weekends, Bank Hols, Mar and Oct 9.30am to 5pm. (Other times by appointment.) Old Lynn Road, West Walton, Wisbech, PE14 7DA ☎ 01945 584440 e-mail petewinning@btinternet.com

❑ G-ARNH		Colt 108	ex Chatteris, Elstree. Damaged 1-9-72. Off-site.	§ ®	3-02
❑ WR971	'Q'	Shackleton MR.3/3	ex Narborough, Cosford 8119M, 120, Kinloss Wing, 201, 120, Kinloss Wing, CA. Fuselage.		3-02
❑ XD434	'25'	Vampire T.11	ex Marham, Barton, Woodford, Chester, St Athan, 5 FTS, 7 FTS.		3-02
❑ XM402	'J'	Jet Provost T.3	ex Narborough, West Raynham, Halton, Newton 8055AM, Shawbury, 6 FTS, 2 FTS.		3-02
❑ XM468*		Jet Provost T.3	ex Terrington, St Clement, King's Lynn, Stock, St Athan, Halton 8081M, Shawbury, 6 FTS, RAFC. Stored.	TAC §	2-04
❑ XN983		Buccaneer S.2B	ex Terrington St Clement, 12, 208, 15, 12. Nose.	TAC	3-02
❑ XP488		Grasshopper TX.1	ex Long Sutton, Halton, West Malling. Stored.	§	3-02
❑ XS459	'AW'	Lightning T.5	ex Narborough, Binbrook, 5, LTF, 56, 29, 226 OCU.		3-02
❑ –		Jet Provost	Procedure trainer. On loan from March Air Cadets.		3-02
❑ 526		MiG-29 *Fulcrum*	25887, ex Fairford. Crashed 21-7-93. Cockpit.	TAC	3-02

WEYBOURNE on the A149 west of Cromer
Muckleburgh Collection: Bannered as Britain's largest working military collection, there is much to fascinate here, including 'live' tank demonstrations during school holidays - check in advance for details.
◆ Open mid-Feb to Oct 10am to 5pm daily. ✉ Weybourne Military Camp, Weybourne, NR25 7EG ☎ 01263 588210 fax 01263 588425 e-mail info@muckleburgh.co.uk www.muckleburgh.co.uk

❑ WD686	'S'	Meteor NF.11	ex Duxford, RAE Bedford, Wroughton, TRE Defford. 141 Sqn colours.	3-04
❑ XN967	'103'	Buccaneer S.1	ex Fleckney, Helston, Culdrose A2627 / SAH-20, Lossiemouth. Cockpit, stored.	3-04
❑ XZ968	'3G'	Harrier GR.3	ex Marham 9222M, St Athan, 233 OCU, 1417F, 1, 4.	3-04
❑ –		Fi 103 V-1 REP	on ramp	3-04

WYMONDHAM on the A11 south-west of Norwich
Catching up on this entry, Sea Vampire T.22 XG743 returned to Duxford, Cambs, during 2001.

NORTHAMPTONSHIRE

CORBY
Frank and **Lee Millar**: Took on a complete Vampire T.11 during 2002. See under Winthorpe, Notts, for their Canberra PR.9 nose.
❑ XE849* 'V3' Vampire T.11   ex Barton, Shobdon, Mildenhall, Long Marston, Yatesbury, Monkton Farleigh, Conington, Ware, St Athan, 7928M, CNCS, 5 FTS, 7 FTS, 1 FTS, 4 FTS. Arr by 5-02.   5-02

'**The Works**': The 112A should still 'fly' from the ceiling.

❏ G-TCSL   Commander 112A ex Spanhoe, N506CA, N1322J. Crashed 5-12-94.   12-95

CROUGHTON on the B4031 south-west of Brackley
USAF Croughton:

❏ 24428 'WW'	F-105G-RE	ex Upper Heyford, Davis-Monthan 'FK095', 128 TFS, Georgia ANG. 561 TFS, Korat, colours.	7-03
❏ '63000' '000'	F-100D-11-NA	42212, ex Upper Heyford, Sculthorpe, FAF.	7-03

HARRINGTON south-east of Market Harborough
'**Carpetbagger**' **Aviation Museum**: The museum is centred upon the hardened group operations building of what was once USAAF Station 179, home of the clandestine 492nd and 801st BGs. This building, restored to its wartime state, houses exhibitions describing the covert operations carried out by the US from Harrington and by the RAF from Tempsford, Beds.

Notes: Working in support of the museum is the **Harrington Aviation Museum Society** (Ron Clarke, 43 Greenhill Road, Kettering, NN15 7LP). In the former Paymaster's building, is the **Northants Aviation Museum** run by the Northamptonshire Aviation Society. This benefits from the NAS's extensive 'dig' activity in the county. (✉ Membership enquiries for NAS to 53 Palmerston Road, Northampton, NN1 5EU.) The Harvard is on loan from Gordon King [1]. The Widgeon's identity is now confirmed [2]. The cockpit of former Coventry Canberra T.17 WJ565 arrived here from North Coates, Lincs, by September 2002. It moved on to <u>Doncaster</u>, S Yorks, on 22nd March 2003.

◆ Take the minor road south out of Harrington village, towards Lamport, and turn right after the A14 underpass – follow the signs. Open from Easter to October weekends and Bank Holidays, 10am to 5pm. Other times by prior appointment – minimum 15 people – to the address and number below.
✉ Sunny Vale Farm Nursery, off Lamport Road, Harrington, Northampton, NN6 9PF. ☎ 01604 686608 e-mail cbaggermuseum@aol.com www.harringtonmuseum.org.uk

❏ 42-12417	Harvard IIB	ex East Tilbury, Windsor, North Weald, Amsterdam, Dutch AF B-163, RCAF FE930, 42-12417. US Navy SNJ-2 colours.	[1]	2-04
❏ [G-APWK]	Widgeon	ex Corby (?), Sywell, *Eye of the Needle*, Yeovil. Forward fuselage.	[2]	2-04

HINTON-IN-THE-HEDGES just west of Brackley
Returning to *W&R18* (p168) the T.42 Eagle wreck is confirmed as BGA.847. The colour scheme of the wreck noted dumped out in July 2001 matches BGA.847 so it would seem its fate is sewed up.

❏ G-AZKN	Robin HR.100	ex East Midlands. Crashed 1-9-95. Wreck.	10-01
❏ G-AZLL	Cessna FRA.150L	crashed 4-2-99.	10-01
❏ G-BONU*	T.67B Firefly	CoA 29-6-00. Stored. First noted 3-03.	10-03

KING'S CLIFFE south of the A47, west of Peterborough
John Tempest: About 90% of the parts from the *original* Cosmic Wind G-ARUL are held plus other components. (G-ARUL, as *Ballerina II* is airworthy.)

❏ G-ARUL	Cosmic Wind	ex Halfpenny Green, N22C. Crashed 29-8-66.	®	7-02

NORTHAMPTON
Murray Jacobsen: Took delivery of a MiG-21 cockpit during 2002. It has been offered for sale.

❏ 764*	MiG-21SPS	ex Wycombe Air Park, Bonn-Hangelar, East GermAF. Cockpit.	6-02

NORTHAMPTON AERODROME or Sywell, north-east of Northampton, off the A43
Sywell Aviation Museum: Situated adjacent to the lovely art-deco 'terminal' building – now 'The Aviator Hotel' – the museum had expanded to the extent that for 2004 a wartime blister hangar will be erected. The hangar will be used as the base of operations for Messenger G-AKIN - see below.

On 6th September 2002, Norman Spiller gifted Miles Messenger G-AKIN to the **Sywell Messenger Trust**. Owned by the Spiller family since August 1949, *India-November* has been resident at Sywell for over 50 years. The aim of the trust is to keep the aircraft in airworthy condition and to show it off to the public on regular occasions [1]. The Grasshopper is on permanent loan from the Visitor Centre and Archive, Shoreham, W Sussex [2].

◆ Open weekends and Bank Hols 10am to 4.30pm, Easter to end of Oct. Other times by appointment.

⊠ Sywell Aerodrome, Sywell, Northants, NN6 0BN ☎ 01604 890925, or '811582 e-mail bbrown@sherwooddunham.com www.sywellaerodrome.co.uk/aviation

❑ G-AIJZ*	J/1 Autocrat	ex Derby, Hooton Park, Warmingham, Southend, Shobdon. Crashed 25-10-70. Cockpit. Stored.		2-04
❑ G-AKIN*	Messenger 2A ✈	handed over 6-9-02.	[1]	2-04
❑ WZ820	Grasshopper TX.1	ex Shoreham, Lancing College.	® [2]	2-04

Aerodrome: Sloane Helicopters have a travelling R-22 airframe, used at fetes and other events [1]. The Aero C-104 is a Czech-built Bücker Jungmann acquired from the USA is being used as a source of spares for 'flyer' G-CCOB at Spanhoe Lodge, but may well be restored in its own right [2]. As predicted, Widgeon G-ANLW moved to Flixton, Suffolk, on 1st May 2002. Cessna F.150G G-AVGU was flying again by 2003 and Emeraude G-BIVF likewise by 2001. The Enstrom F-28A shell on the dump was last noted in November 1997 and is considered long to have given up this mortal coil.

❑ G-AFFD	Percival Q.6	ex Isle of Man, Sutton Coldfield, Duxford, Redhill, G-AIEY ntu, X9407, MCS, 510, Old Sarum SF, Halton SF, Heston SF, Northolt SF, 6 AACU, G-AFFD. CoA 31-8-56.	® off-site	9-01
❑ G-APTU*	Alpha 5	ex Leicester. CoA 8-6-98. Stored, dismantled.		12-03
❑ G-AYIA	Hughes 369HS	damaged 1-6-88. Spares.		2-98
❑ G-BAUK	Hughes 269C	CoA 20-9-93. Stored.		2-98
❑ 'G-BEAR'	Robinson R-22	G-HOVR, ex N2647M. Crashed 9-1-89.	[1]	7-97
❑ G-BWEC	Colson Cassutt	ex Little Gransden. CoA 11-9-91.	®	10-98
❑ G-MNUL	SX130/Firefly	Cancelled 12-9-94. Stored.		4-02
❑ –*	Aero C-104	ex USA. Badly damaged - spares use.	[2]	1-04
❑ NL985	Tiger Moth	G-BWIK, ex Cranfield, Leighton Buzzard, Bushey, Leamington Spa, Hendon, Finningley, Colerne, Cwmfelinfach 7015M, 9 AFTS, 2 GS, Lon UAS, Queens UAS, 11 RFS, 5 RFS, Birm UAS, 16 EFTS, 14 EFTS. Destroyed by fire 23-5-73. Frame.		3-03
❑ 472773* 'AJ-C'	P-51D-25-NA	G-SUSY, ex N12066, Nicaragua AF GN120, USAAF 44-72773. *Susy*. 354th FG c/s. CoA 20-501. Stored.		2-04

SPANHOE LODGE AERODROME south-east of Harringworth

Windmill Aviation: The C-3605 is being restored and it may be fitted with a Hispano HS 12Y-51. This was just the first taste of a Swiss flavour at Spanhoe. In September three EKW D-3801 fuselages arrived having been discovered in a Swiss scrapyard. (The D-3801 was a development of the MS.406 single-seat fighter.) These frames are being assessed for restoration. SV-4C G-AYZI flew again in November 2003 and moved to Sheffield. The former instructional airframe Cherokee is being assessed for restoration to flying condition. The Hunter was owned by Paul Smith and is kept as a 'static' but has since changed hands [2].

❑ G-AHCN*	Auster J/1	ex OY-RCH, OY-AVM, G-AHCN, OY-AVM, G-AHCN. First noted 11-02.	®	4-03
❑ G-AOFJ*	Auster 5	ex Perth. CoA 20-9-79. Arrived by 9-03.	®	9-03
❑ G-AVLC*	Cherokee 140	ex Wrexham. CoA 25-9-98. Arrived 14-3-04.	[1]	3-04
❑ EI-AYL	Airedale	ex Abbeyshrule, G-ARRO, EI-AVP ntu, G-ARRO. CoA 1-2-86.		4-03
❑ EI-BAL	Airedale	ex Abbeyshrule, G-ARZS. Cancelled 29-6-79.		9-01
❑ EI-BBK	Airedale	ex Abbeyshrule, G-ARXB, EI-ATE ntu, G-ARXB. CoA 11-11-83.		4-03
❑ XF375* '05'	Hunter F.6A	G-BUEZ, ex Duxford, Cranwell, 8736M, ETPS, Warton, AWA, C(A). Arrived 18-11-02.	[1]	8-03

❏ C-558*	EKW C-3605	ex Norwich, Little Gransden, Wycombe AP,		
		Lodrino, Swiss AF. Arrived 9-02.	®	4-03
❏ J-95*	EKW D-3801	ex Switzerland, Swiss AF. Fuselage frame.		10-03
❏ J-146*	EKW D-3801	ex Switzerland, Swiss AF. Fuselage frame.		10-03
❏ –*	EKW D-3801	ex Switzerland, Swiss AF. Fuselage frame.		10-03

Locally: Geoff Brown is working on another Auster project and has had the Turner for several years. See also Woodhall Spa, Lincs.

❏ G-AJDY*	J/1 Autocrat	ex Bedford, Cranfield, Northampton, Spanhoe,		
		Cossall, Sherburn. CoA 9-7-71.	®	3-04
❏ G-BRIO*	Turner T-40A	ex Liverpool. CoA 15-8-00.		3-04

WELLINGBOROUGH
Wellingborough School: The Grasshopper is kept by the school.

❏ XP454	G'hopper TX.1	ex Kimbolton, Holt.	2-02

NORTHUMBERLAND and TYNESIDE

☛ The five unitary authorities of Gateshead, Newcastle-upon-Tyne, Sunderland, North Tyneside and South Tyneside comprise the 'counties'.

BAMBURGH on the B4130 east of Belford and north-west of Seahouses
Bamburgh Castle Aviation Artefacts Museum: As the name might imply, this small museum is located within the castle. Run by Derek Walton, the two rooms cover a wide sweep of local aviation history, including wreckage from local 'digs'.
◆ 'Brown signed' off the A1. Open daily Mar to Oct 11am to 5pm – last entry 4.30pm. ✉ Bamburgh Castle, Bamburgh, NE69 7DF ☎ 01668 214515 **fax** 01668 214060 **www**.bamburghcastle.com/

BOULMER AIRFIELD east of Alnwick
RAF Boulmer: The Phantom which is looked after by NEAM - see Sunderland, below.

❏ XV415	'E' Phantom FGR.2	9163M, ex 56, 74, 228 OCU, 23, 56, 92, 29, 228 OCU,	
		56, 228 OCU, 31, 228 OCU, 41, 228 OCU, 41, 54,	
		A&AEE. Gate	3-04

ESHOTT south of the B6345 north of Morpeth
A Taylorcraft is under restoration off-site. Contrary to *W&R18* (p170), the Hiller lives on.

❏ G-ATKG	Hiller UH-12B	ex Thai AF 103. CoA 28-11-69. Dumped.		5-03
❏ 42-58687*'IY'	T'craft DF-65	G-BRIY, ex N59687, NC59687, TG-6 42-58678.		
		CoA 10-7-98.	®	8-02

MORPETH
A Turbulent has moved into the area for restoration.

❏ G-APOL*	Turbulent	ex Charterhall. Damaged 24-7-93.	®	2-03

NEWCASTLE AIRPORT or Woolsington, on the A696 north-west of Newcastle
Newcastle Aviation Academy: A compound holds two airframes for this newly-founded institution.

❏ C-GWJO*	Boeing 737-2A3	ex Westjet, HR-SHO, CX-BHM, N1797B, N1787B.	
		Arrived 13-2-03.	11-03
❏ 5N-AAN*	HS.125-3B/RA	ex Biggin Hill, F-GFMP, G-AVAI, LN-NPA,	
		G-AVAI. Arrived 16-10-03.	11-03

NEWCASTLE UPON TYNE
Military Vehicle Museum: Created by the North East Military Vehicle Club, a wide array of vehicles and other exhibits are on show. John Stelling's Auster composite is stored here, for eventual display. It comprises G-ANFU's forward fuselage, attached to a 'spare' AOP.6 frame, the starboard wing of G-AKPH and the port from an AOP.6 [1]. Please note the Auster is not available for public viewing.
◆ Off the A167(M) at the junction with the B1318. Open summer 10am to 4pm daily, Nov to March 10am to dusk on weekends and school holidays only. Other times by appointment. ⊠ Military Vehicle Museum, Exhibition Park Pavilion, Newcastle upon Tyne, NE2 4PZ ☎ 0191 281 7222 **www.military-museum.org.uk/**

❏ 'NJ719'	Auster 5	G-ANFU, ex NEAM, Bristol, TW385, 663, 227 OCU, 13 OTU. Stored.	[1]	3-04

SOUTH SHIELDS on the A1018 north of Sunderland.
Karl Edmondson: Continues to restore his Vampire in the general area.
◆ Visits are possible *only* by prior arrangement. **e-mail** karl.edmondson@btopenworld.com **www.karl.edmundson@btinternet.co.uk**

❏ XD602	Vampire T.11	ex Dundonald, Firbeck, Crowland, ?, Brands Hatch, Birmingham, 7737M, Sutton Coldfield, Smethwick, RAFC, 125.	®	8-02

SUNDERLAND site of the former Usworth aerodrome, west of Sunderland
North East Aircraft Museum (NEAM): The Officer Commanding RAF Boulmer (see above) has invited NEAM to maintain the Phantom gate guardian. A nice pat on the back for the team at NEAM!
Not a NEAM matter as such, but the demolition of the nearby Junkers Lamella hangar during 2003 was a major disappointment to the museum and to local, if not national, heritage. It was the last remaining reminder of Usworth Aerodrome and a rare - if not unique - example of its type.
Notes: Flea 'G-ADVU' (BAPC.207) incorporates parts from an original, built in Congleton, Ches [1]. Work is underway to turn the Short 330 into a 'hands-on' exhibit, including access for wheelchair-users [2]. The exotically-registered Bö 105 pod (c/n S.863) was donated by Rotortech and is being converted into a 'hands-on' cockpit and travelling exhibit by a NEAM member in Surrey [3]. Chipmunk T.10 WB685 is a composite, including the rear fuselage of WP969 (G-ATHC) [4]. The rear fuselage of Firefly AS.5 VT409 is stored, ready for fitment to WD889 in due course [5]. Vampire T.11 WZ518 is fitted with the wings of WZ608, the 'pod' of which can be found at Rayleigh, Essex [6]. 'JP4' XP627 is fitted with the wings of Mk.3 XN584, the fuselage of which can be found at Bruntingthorpe, Leics [7].
◆ East of Washington on the Old Washington Road between the A1290 and A1231. Signed off the A1290 and the A19. Daily 10am to 5pm (or dusk in winter). ⊠ Old Washington Road, Sunderland, SR5 3HZ ☎ 0191 519 0662 **e-mail** neam_uk@yahoo.com **www.neam.org.uk**

❏ 'G-ADVU'	HM.14 'Flea'	BAPC.211, ex Stoke-on-Trent.	[1]	3-04
❏ 'G-AFUG'	Luton Minor	BAPC.97, ex Stoke-on-Trent, Sunderland,		
		Sibson, Sywell, Sunderland, Stanley.		3-04
❏ G-APTW	Widgeon	ex Helston, Southend, Westlands. CoA 26-9-75.		3-04
❏ G-ARAD	Luton Major	ex local, Borgue. Unflown, started 1959.		3-04
❏ G-ASOL	Bell 47D-1	ex Weston-s-Mare, Panshanger, N146B. CoA 6-9-71.		3-04
❏ G-AWRS	Anson C.19	ex Strathallan, Kemps, Junex, Hewitts, TX213,		
		WCS, 22 GCF, OCTU, 18 GCF, 2 TAF CS,		
		527, CSE, RCCF. CoA 10-8-73. On loan.	®	3-04
❏ G-BEEX	Comet 4C	ex East Kirkby, Tattershall, Woodford,		
		Lasham, Dan-Air, SU-ALM. Nose.		3-04
❏ G-MBDL	Lone Ranger	microlight. Stored.		3-04
❏ G-OGIL	Short 330-100	ex Gill, G-BITV, G-14-3068. Damaged 1-7-92.	[2]	3-04
❏ 'G-BAGJ'	Gazelle 1	ex Carlisle, G-SFTA, HB-XIL, G-BAGJ,		
		XW858 ntu. Crashed 7-3-84.	®	3-04
❏ LQ-BLT	MBB Bö 105CBS	ex Bourn, Brazil. Cr 8-6-96. Original pod.	off-site ® [3]	3-04
❏ VV217	Vampire FB.5	ex Barnham, Bury St Edmunds, 'VV271',		
		7323M, Oakington, DH. Stored.		3-04
❏ WA577	Sycamore 3	ex King's Heath, Shirley, St Athan 7718M,		
		A&AEE, G-ALST ntu.		3-04

❑	WB685		Chipmunk T.10	ex Leeds, Irlam, Edn UAS, Lyneham SF,		
				8 RFS, 1 RFS.	[4]	3-04
❑	WD790		Meteor NF.11	ex Darlington, Leeming, 8743M, RAE Llanbedr,		
				RS&RE, RRE, TRE. Nose, travelling exhibit.		3-04
❑	WD889		Firefly AS.5	ex Failsworth. Cockpit section.	[5]	3-04
❑	WG724		Dragonfly HR.5	ex Chester-le-Street, Moor Monkton,		
				Blackbushe, Lossiemouth SF, Ford SF.	®	3-04
❑	WJ639		Canberra TT.18	ex Samlesbury, 7, 57.		3-04
❑	WK198		Swift F.4	ex Failsworth, Kirkham, 7428M,		
				Aldergrove, MoS. Fuselage.	®	3-04
❑	WL181	'X'	Meteor F.8	ex Chester-le-Street, Acklington, Kemble,		
				CAW, Tangmere SF, 34.		3-04
❑	WN516		Balliol T.2	ex Failsworth, RAFC. Cockpit, stored.		3-02
❑	WZ518		Vampire T.11	ex Chester-le-Street, Handforth, Pomona Dock,		
				5 FTS, Oldenburg SF, 2 TAF CF, 14.	[6]	3-04
❑	WZ767		Grasshopper TX.1	ex Halton. On loan. Stored.		3-04
❑	XG680	'438'	S' Venom '22	ex Sydenham, ADS, 891, Yeovilton SF.		3-04
❑	XL319		Vulcan B.2	ex 44, Wadd Wing, 35, 230 OCU, 617, 230		
				OCU, Scampton Wing, 617.		3-04
❑	XN258	'589'	Whirlwind	ex Helston, Culdrose SF, *Endurance* Flt,		
			HAR.9	Culdrose SF, *Hermes* Flt.		3-04
❑	XP627		Jet Provost T.4	ex London Colney, Hatfield, Shawbury,		
				6 FTS, 3 FTS, 1 FTS.	[7]	3-04
❑	XT236		Sioux AH.1	ex Middle Wallop, MoAF, Sek Kong.	®	3-04
❑	ZF594		Lightning F.53	ex Warton, RSAF 53-696, G-27-66.		3-04
❑	A-522		FMA Pucará	ex Yeovilton, St Athan 8768M, Stanley,		
				Argentine AF. FAA Museum loan.		3-04
❑	E-419		Hunter F.51	ex Dunsfold, G-9-441, Dan AF Esk.724.		3-04
❑	146	'8-MG'	Mystère IVA	ex Sculthorpe, French AF.		3-04
❑	42157	'11-ML'	F-100D-16-NA	ex Sculthorpe, French AF.		3-04
❑	54439	'WI'	T-33A-1-LO	ex Sculthorpe, French AF.		3-04
❑	6171		F-86D-35-NA	ex Hellenikon, Greek AF, USAF 51-6171.	®	3-04
❑	26541		F-84F-40-RE	ex Hellenikon, Greek AF, USAF 52-6541.		3-04
❑	BAPC.96		Brown Helicopter	ex Stanley.		3-04
❑	BAPC.119		Bensen B.7	ex Stanley.		3-04
❑	–	BAPC.228	Olympus	hang glider. Stored, in its bag!		3-04

No.2214 Squadron Air Cadets: 'Parented' by Leeming.

❑	XD622		Vampire T.11	ex Leeming, Barkston Ash 8160M, Shawbury,	
				118, RAFC.	3-04
❑	XV460	'R'	Phantom FGR.2	ex Coningsby, 74, 92, 228 OCU, 29, 228 OCU,	
				92, 19, 56, 31. Nose.	3-04

NOTTINGHAMSHIRE

BALDERTON on the A1 south-east of Newark-on-Trent
The only relic on the site of the former A1 Commercials yard is the increasingly distressed Lightning.
❑ XN728 'V' Lightning F.2A ex Coningsby, 8546M, 92. Poor state. 4-04

FARNSFIELD south of the A617, east of Mansfield
Wonderland Pleasure Park: On the A614, 'brown signed'. Returning to *W&R18* (p172), the Spitfire
FSM did indeed go to the Isle of Man, to Jurby, in November 2000. The Hurricane up the pole here is not
to be confused with the one in similar stance at Coltishall, Norfolk!
❑ 'V7467'*'LE-D' Hurricane FSM BAPC.288, 242 Sqn colours. 9-02
❑ XS919 Lightning F.6 ex Devonport, Lower Tremar, Binbrook, 11, 5,
         11, 5, 56, 11. 9-02

HUCKNALL AERODROME south of the town

The Drone is a composite with the wings of G-AEJH and tail of G-AEEN. By mid-2002 at the latest, the wreck of Spitfire XIV RM689 (G-ALGT) had moved to Sandown, Isle of Wight, via Filton, Glos.

❏ G-AEDB	BAC Drone 2	ex Tadlow, Bishop's Stortford, Duxford, BGA 2731.CoA 26-5-87.	®	8-01
❏ G-ARXN	Nipper 2	CoA 19-8-80. Stored.		8-01

LANGAR AERODROME east of the A46, south of Whatton

The para-club *should* still have its exit-trainer.

❏ G-BATD	Cessna U.206F	ex Isle of Man, Sibson, Shobdon, N60204. Cr 5-4-80.	4-98

MANSFIELD on the A60 north of Nottingham

No.384 Squadron Air Cadets: Have a Canberra nose. 'Parent' is Newton.

❏ WT507	Canberra PR.7	8548M, ex Halton 8131M, St Athan, 31, 17, 58, A&AEE, 58, 527, 58. Nose.	12-02

NEWARK-ON-TRENT

Cliff Baker: The Agricola and its 'spares ship' duly arrived and is being worked on. By late 2002 another interesting Auster 'shape' was taking place using a so far unknown airframe. This is 'rear'-loading' ambulance one-off, the B.4 which will wear the original's identity, 'G-AMKL' [1]. J/1 G-AJPZ was briefly here for assessment and moved on.

♦ The workshop/store is *not* open to the public and visits are *strictly* by prior permission.

❏ G-AIGR	J/1N Alpha	ex Northampton Airport, fuselage frame.		1-03
❏ G-AIJI	J/1N Alpha	ex East Midlands, Elsham Hall, Goxhill, Kirmington. Damaged 12-1-75. Frame, spares.		1-03
❏ G-AIKE	Auster 5	ex Portsmouth, NJ728, 661. Crashed 1-9-65.		1-03
❏ G-AJAS	J/1N Alpha	CoA 11-4-90.		1-03
❏ G-AKWT	Auster 5	ex East Midlands, Elsham Hall, Goxhill, Stroxton Lodge, Tollerton, MT360, 26, 175, 121 Wing, 181, 80, 486, 56, 19. Crashed 7-8-48. Frame.		1-03
❏ G-ALNV	Auster 5	ex Nottingham, Leicester, RT578, 341, 329. CoA 4-7-50.		1-03
❏ 'G-AMKL'*	Auster 'B.4'	under way by 11-02.	[1]	1-03
❏ G-ANHU	Auster 4	ex Shoreham, EC-AXR, G-ANHU, MT255, 659.	®	1-03
❏ G-ANHW	Auster 5D	ex Shipdham, TJ320, 664. CoA 9-3-70.	®	1-03
❏ G-ANHX	Auster 5D	ex Leicester, TW519, 661, A&AEE. Cr 28-3-70.		1-03
❏ G-AOCP	Auster 5	ex TW462, 666. Damaged 4-70. Composite.		1-03
❏ G-APKM	J/1N Alpha	CoA 9-1-89.		1-03
❏ G-APTR	J/1N Alpha	CoA 11-4-87.		1-03
❏ G-ARGB	Auster 6A	ex Waddington, VF635, 662, 1901F. CoA 21-6-74.		1-03
❏ G-AROJ	Airedale	ex Leicester, Thorney, HB-EUC, G-AROJ. CoA 8-1-76.		1-03
❏ G-ARTM	Terrier 1	ex Chirk, Auster T.7 WE536, 651, 657, Schwechat SF. Crashed 28-5-70.	®	1-03
❏ G-ARXC	Airedale	ex Kirton-in-Linsey, EI-ATD, G-ARXC. CoA 27-6-76.	®	1-03
❏ G-ASWF	Airedale	ex Leicester. CoA 27-4-83.		1-03
❏ EI-AMF	Taylorcraft Plus D	ex Abbeyshrule, G-ARRK, G-AHUM, LB286, Coltishall SF, 309, 70 GCF, 84 GCF, 22 EFTS, 43 OTU, 653.		1-03
❏ F-BBSO	Auster 5	ex Taunton, G-AMJM, TW452, 62 GCF. Frame.		1-03
❏ ZK-BBI*	Agricola	ex New Zealand. Fuselage and other parts.. Arr 5-02.		1-03
❏ ZK-BXO*	Agricola	G-CBOA, ex New Zealand, ZK-BMN. Arr 5-02.	®	1-03
❏ –	Auster D.6-180	ex White Waltham, Rearsby. Frame. c/no 3705		1-03
❏ –	Terrier 3	ex White Waltham, Rearsby. Frame.		1-03
❏ WZ729	Auster AOP.9	G-BXON, ex Singapore. c/no 648	®	1-03

NOTTINGHAM AERODROME or Tollerton, south of the A52, east of the city

Contrary to *W&R18*, p173, the Seabee continues its restoration, but under its US identity. J/1N Alpha G-AJIW and Tomahawk 112 G-BGGF were flying again by mid-2003.

❑ G-GRAY	Cessna 172N	ex N4859D. Ditched 2-4-93. Stored.	9-01
❑ N6210K*	RC-3 Seabee	ex G-SEAB, Glasgow, N6210K, NC6210K.	® 3-04
❑ WB763*	Chipmunk T.10	ex Twyford, Camberley, Feltham, Southall, 2 FTS,	
G-BBMR		4 FTS, AOTS, 1 ITS, 1 AEF, Bri UAS, 3 AEF,	
		AAC, 652, Odiham SF, 24 RFS, 14 RFS.	® 12-02

RADCLIFFE ON TRENT on the A52, east of Nottingham

Don Cashmore: Don Cashmore is working on the restoration of Shuttleworth's Archaeopteryx.

❑ G-ABXL	Archaeopteryx	ex Old Warden, Chilwell. CoA 22-9-82.	® 12-00

RETFORD AERODROME or Gamston, off the B6387 south of East Retford

❑ G-AYGD*	CEA DR.1050	ex F-BLRE. Crashed 24-6-99. Stored.	off-site 5-03

SOUTH SCARLE in between the A46 and the A1133 south-west of Lincoln

South Scarle Aviation: Fournier RF-3 G-AYJD was flying again by mid-2003.

SYERSTON AIRFIELD off the A46 south-west of Newark-on-Trent

RAF Syerston / Air Cadets Central Gliding School: Sedbergh TX.1 XN185 was airworthy and flying from Hullavington, Wilts, during much of 2003. However, it was back here in store by late 2003 and possible to be donated to the RAF Museum [1]. Several Viking TX.1s have gathered here, possible withdrawn from use, possibly for rebuild - we will wait and see!

❑ XA302	Cadet TX.3	HAK/BGA.3786. CoA 5-96.	® 3-97
❑ XE799	Cadet TX.3	ex 8943M, CGS.	® 2-96
❑ XN185	Sedbergh TX.1	HNS/BGA.4077, ex 8942M, CGS, 643 VGS,	
		4 MGSP, 633 VGS, 635 VGS. Stored.	[1] 3-04

TOTON on the A6005 south-west of Nottingham

No.350 Field Squadron Headquarters, Chetwynd Barracks: In Swiney Way, which links the B6003 and the A6005.

❑ XW267	'SA' Harrier T.4	ex 'Chilwell', Boscombe Down, SAOEU, RAE,	
		A&AEE, RAE, 233 OCU.	1-02

WINTHORPE SHOWGROUND on the A46 north east of Newark-on-Trent

Newark Air Museum (NAM): In April 2003 the museum proudly announced that it had been granted £453,000 from the Heritage Lottery Fund for a second exhibition hall to be erected on the south side. This will put at least 11 airframes under cover, including Varsity T.1 WF369, the first of its type to go indoors. Construction started in late 2003. The Avro Ashton forward fuselage is a major coup. It was donated by BAE Systems [1]. NAM is host to the annual *CockpitFest* gathering -see page 305.

Notes: Several airframes are on loan from outside bodies: the Autocrat from Leicestershire Museum, Arts and Records Service; the Canberra PR.7 from the 81 Squadron Associates; the Canberra T.17 from Aaron Braid; the Gazelle from the Museum of Army Flying, Middle Wallop, Hants; the Canberra PR.9 nose from Frank Millar; and the *Floggers* from Hawarden Aviation Services. These are marked ±. Chipmunk T.10 WB624 was acquired from The Aeroplane Collection by NAM during 2002 [2].

The recently-arrived Powerchute Kestrel must be one of the fastest from-birth-to-museum careers! Registered on 5th November 2003, it was deregistered 34 days later as permanently withdrawn from use! [3] Tiger Moth 'G-MAZY' is very likely BAPC.21 [4]. Canberra T.19 WH904 was built by Shorts Brothers and Harland as a B.2 and therefore the forward fuselage *should* have a plate reading SHB-0-2388. Inspection found the nose to have the plate EEP71123, which would make it WH651. The logic works out like this... WH651 was issued to English Electric for conversion from a B.2 to a T.4 on 5th July 1956 and in this process it would have been fitted with a new-build T.4 cockpit. It looks as though the old cockpit passed on to Boulton Paul for use in the B.2 to T.11 conversions. WH904 was issued to BP on 17th October 1957 for T.11 fit. It received the cockpit of WH651. (And, later was further converted to T.19 status.) [5] Correcting *W&R18* (p176) the Auster AOP.9 is the long-lost TA200 and therefore very probably XR268 or perhaps XS238 [6]. XN412 has been re-consigned to Melton Mowbray, Leics! Previously listed as a Hiway Demon, this machine is now thought to be a Hiway Skytrike, but thought never to have been registered [7]. Monospar VH-UTH is at Innsworth, Glos.

The **Shackleton Association**'s trailer-mounted nose 'lodges' care of the museum. They serve to unite air and ground crew and all interested in the 'Shack', producing a house magazine, *The Growler*. (Peter Dunn, *Meadow View*, Parks Lane, Prestwood, Great Missenden, Bucks HP16 0JH.) [8]

Departures: Valiant B.1 XD875 arrived from Bruntingthorpe, Leics, 14-6-02 on loan. It continued its migrations in 10-03 moving to Inverness, Scotland. Antonov An-2 RA-02974 flew in 15-2-03, on loan from John Dunnett. It was sold in the USA early in 12-03 and was dismantled ready for removal. (It was still on site in late 2-04.) TAC's McBroom hang-glider BAPC.204 returned to them at Hooton Park, Cheshire. *Lenny the Lynx*, the Lynx mock-up was assessed as suffering from too much wood rot and used on the fire dump during the 'Rescue 2002' event and was burnt.

♦ Signposted from the A1, on Newark Showground, access off the A46, or A17. Open daily Mar to Oct 10am to 5pm, Nov to Feb daily 10am to 4pm. Closed Dec 24, 25, 26 and Jan 1. Buildings suitable for the disabled. Special events are also staged – SAE for details. Membership brings many benefits, including the journal *The Dispersal*. ✉ The Airfield, Winthorpe, Newark, Notts, NG24 2NY ☎ / fax 01636 707170 e-mail newarkair@lineone.net www.newarkairmuseum.co.uk

❏	G-AGOH	J/1 Autocrat	ex Leicester. CoA 24-8-95. On loan.	±	2-04
❏	G-AHRI	Dove 1	ex Long Marston, East Kirkby, Tattershall, Little Staughton, 4X-ARI, G-AHRI. 'Newark Air Museum'.		2-04
❏	G-ANXB	Heron 1	ex Biggin Hill, Fairflight, BEA, G-5-14. CoA 25-3-79. BEA Scottish colours. *Sir James Young Simpson*.		2-04
❏	G-APNJ*	Cessna 310	ex Shoreham, EI-AJY, N3635D. CoA 28-11-74. Arrived 4-3-04.		3-04
❏	G-APVV	Mooney M.20A	ex Skelmersdale, Barton, N8164E. Cr 11-1-81. Stored.		2-04
❏	[G-AXMB]*	Motor Cadet Mk.2	ex Ringmer, BGA.805, VM590. CoA 9-7-82. Arrived 10-02. Dismantled.		2-04
❏	G-BFTZ	Rallye Club	ex Firbeck, Hooton Park, Warmingham, Fownhope, Cardiff-Wales, F-BPAX. CoA 19-9-81.		2-04
❏	G-BJAD	FRED Srs 2	ex Retford. Uncompleted project.		2-04
❏	G-BKPG	Rattler Strike	ex Egginton, Tatenhill. Stored.		2-04
❏	G-CCLT*	Powerchute	ex Nantwich. Canx 9-12-03. Arrived 11-03.	[3]	2-04
❏	'G-MAZY'	Tiger Moth	ex Innsworth, Staverton, Newark area. Composite, mostly G-AMBB/T6801, ex Scampton SF, 6 FTS, 18 EFTS. Partially uncovered.	[4]	2-04
❏	G-MBBZ	Volmer VJ-24W	ex Old Sarum. CoA 3-9-93.		2-04
❏	G-MBUE	Tiger Cub 440	ex Retford, Worksop. *The Dormouse Zeitgeist*.		2-04
❏	KF532	Harvard IIB	ex 781, 799, 727, 799, 758. Cockpit section.		2-04
❏	RA897	Cadet TX.1	Stored.		2-04
❏	TG517	Hastings T.5	ex 230 OCU, SCBS, BCBS, 202, 53, 47.		2-04
❏	VL348	Anson C.19	G-AVVO, ex Southend, Shawbury, 22 GCF, 24 GCF, Colerne SF, 62 GCF, HCMSU, RCCF.		2-04
❏	VP293* 'A'	Shackleton T.4	ex Coventry, Woodford, Coventry, East Kirkby, Strathallan, RAE, MOTU, 206, 224. Trailer-mounted nose. Arrived by 7-03.	[8]	2-04
❏	VR249 'FA-EL'	Prentice T.1	G-APIY, ex 1 ASS, RAFC. CoA 18-3-67.		2-04
❏	VZ608	Meteor FR.9	ex Hucknall, Shoreham, MoS, RR. RB.108 test-bed.		2-04
❏	VZ634	Meteor T.7	ex Wattisham 8657M, 5 MU, MoA, Leeming SF, Stradishall SF, 41, 141, 609, 247.		2-04
❏	WB624	Chipmunk T.10	ex Hooton Park, Firbeck, Long Marston, Warmingham, East Midlands, Wigan, Dur UAS, Abn UAS, Henlow, St Athan, 22 GCF, Debden, Jurby SF, 8 FTS, 18 RFS.	® [2]	2-04
❏	WB491*	Ashton 2	ex Woodford, Cardiff-Wales, Dunsfold, Farnborough, RAE. Forward fuselage. Arrived 26-2-03.	[1]	2-04

❏	WF369	'F'	Varsity T.1	ex 6 FTS, AE&AEOS, AES, 2 ANS, 201 AFS.	2-04
❏	WH791		Canberra PR.7	8187M, ex Cottesmore, St Athan 8165M,	
				8176M, 81, 58, 82, 542.	± 2-04
❏	WH863		Canberra T.17	ex Marham 8693M, 360, RAE, IAM. Nose.	± 2-04
❏	WH904	'04'	Canberra T.19	ex Cambridge, 7, 85, West Raynham TFF,	
				228 OCU, 35, 207.	[5] 2-04
❏	WK277	'N'	Swift FR.5	ex Cosford, Leconfield 7719M, 2. 2 Sqn colours.	2-04
❏	WM913	'456'	Sea Hawk FB.3	ex Fleetwood, Sealand 8162M, Culdrose	
				A2510, Abbotsinch, 736.	2-04
❏	WR977	'B'	Shackleton	ex Finningley, 8186M 203, 42, 206, 203, 42,	
			MR.3/3	201, 206, 201, 220.	2-04
❏	WS692	'C'	Meteor NF.12	ex Cranwell, Henlow 7605M, 72, 46.	2-04
❏	WS739		Meteor NF.14	ex Misson, Church Fenton 7961M, Kemble,	
				1 ANS, 2 ANS, 25.	2-04
❏	WT651	'C'	Hunter F.1	ex Lawford Heath, Halton, Credenhill 7532M,	
				229 OCU, 233 OCU, 229 OCU, 222.	2-04
❏	WT933		Sycamore 3	ex Sutton, Strensall, Halton 7709M, G-ALSW ntu.	2-04
❏	WV606	'P-B'	Provost T.1	ex Halton 7622M, 1 FTS.	2-04
❏	WV787		Canberra B.2/8	ex Abingdon 8799M, A&AEE. Hefner 'bunny' logo.	2-04
❏	WW217	'351'	Sea Ven FAW.21	ex Cardiff, Ottershaw, Culdrose, Yeovilton,	
				ADS, 891, 890.	2-04
❏	WX905		Venom NF.3	ex Henlow, Hendon, Yatesbury 7458M, 27 MU, 23.	2-04
❏	XD593	'50'	Vampire T.11	ex Woodford, Chester, St Athan, 8 FTS, CFS,	
				FWS, 5 FTS, 4 FTS. CFS colours.	2-04
❏	XH177		Canberra PR.9	ex Corby, Stock, Cardiff-Wales, Boscombe, 13,	
				58. Nose.	± 2-04
❏	XH992	'P'	Javelin FAW.8	ex Cosford 7829M, Shawbury, 85. 85 Sqn colours.	2-04
❏	XJ560	'243'	Sea Vixen FAW.2	ex RAE Bedford, Farnborough, Halton 8142M,	
				893, 899, 892, 890.	2-04
❏	XL149		Beverley C.1	ex Finningley 7988M, 84, 30, 84, 242 OCU. Cockpit.	2-04
❏	XL764	'J'	Skeeter AOP.12	ex Nostell Priory, Rotherham, Middle Wallop,	
				Arborfield 7940M, Hayes, A&AEE, MoA, AAC,	
				Saro, AAC.	2-04
❏	XM383	'90'	Jet Provost T.3A	ex Crowland, Scampton, 7 FTS, 1 FTS, RAFC,	
				6 FTS, BSE, 2 FTS, A&AEE, 2 FTS.	2-04
❏	XM594		Vulcan B.2	ex 44, Scampton Wing, 617, 27.	2-04
❏	XM685	'513'	Whirlwind	ex Panshanger area, Elstree, Luton, G-AYZJ ntu,	
			HAS.7	Fleetlands, Lee-o-S, 771, *Ark* Ship's Flt, 847, 848.	2-04
❏	XN573		Jet Provost T.3	ex Blackpool Airport, Kemble, 1 FTS, CFS. Nose.	2-04
❏	XN819		Argosy C.1	ex Finningley 8205M, Shawbury, Benson Wing,	
				105, MoA. Cockpit section, in small display hall.	2-04
❏	XN964	'613'	Buccaneer S.1	ex Bruntingthorpe, East Midlands, Brough,	
				Pershore, 807.	2-04
❏	XP226	'073'	Gannet AEW.3	ex Lee-on-Solent, Southwick, Lee-on-Solent,	
				A2667, Lossiemouth, Ilchester, 849.	2-04
❏	XR534	'65'	Gnat T.1	ex Dunholme Bridge, Valley 8578M, 4 FTS, CFS.	® 2-04
❏	XS417	'DZ'	Lightning T.5	ex Binbrook, LTF, 5, 11, 5, 11, LTF, 56,	
				23, 11, 23, 226 OCU.	2-04
❏	XT200	'F'	Sioux AH.1	ex Middle Wallop.	2-04
❏	XV728	'A'	Wessex HC.2	ex Fleetlands, 72, 2 FTS, CFS, 18. *Argonaut.*	2-04
❏	XW276		Gazelle 03	ex Sunderland, Wroughton, Southampton, Middle	
				Wallop, Farnborough, Leatherhead, F-ZWRI.	± 2-04
❏	–	TA200	Auster AOP.9	ex Middle Wallop. Stored.	[6] 2-04
❏	AR-107		S.35XD Draken	ex Scampton, Esk.729, RDanAF.	2-04
❏	83	'8-MS'	Mystère IVA	ex Sculthorpe, French AF.	2-04
❏	56321		SAAB Safir	G-BKPY, ex Norwegian AF.	2-04
❏	'04'*		MiG-23ML	ex Chester, Latvia, USSR. (024003607).	
				Arrived 22-5-02.	± 2-04
❏	'71'*		MiG-27K	ex Chester, Latvia, USSR. (61912507006).	
				Arrived 22-5-02.	± 2-04
❏	42223		F-100D-16-NA	ex Sculthorpe, French AF.	2-04

❏	51-9036	T-33A-1-LO	19036, ex '5547', Sculthorpe, Fr AF. 48th FIS c/s.		2-04
❏	–	BAPC.43	HM.14 'Flea'	ex East Kirkby, Tattershall, Wellingore.		2-04
❏	–	BAPC.101	HM.14 'Flea'	ex Tumby Woodside, East Kirkby, Tattershall, Sleaford. Fuselage. (Also G-AFUL's rudder.)		2-04
❏	–	BAPC.183	Zurowski ZP.1	ex Burton-on-Trent. Homebuilt helicopter, unflown.		2-04
❏	–		Hiway Skytrike	–	[7]	2-04
❏	–*		Grasshopper TX.1	ex 'Northampton'. Arrived 10-02.		2-04
❏	–		Jet Provost CIM	Procedures trainer.		2-04
❏	–		Gnat T.1 CIM	ex Melton Mowbray. Procedures trainer.		2-04
❏	–		Phantom CIM	ex Wattisham. Full-axis simulator.		2-04

Newark Gliding Club: An SF-27MB is under slow restoration in the hangar.

❏	G-BSUM	Scheibe SF-27MB	ex D-KIBE.	®	9-97

OXFORDSHIRE

ABINGDON
A collector in the general area has a Vampire pod.

❏	XH330*	'76' Vampire T.11	ex Camberley, Bridgnorth, Bushey, London Colney, Chester, Woodford, Chester, Shawbury, RAFC. Pod.	3-04

ARNCOTT south of the A41 south-east of Bicester
Auster 6A G-ASEF moved to Eccleshall, Staffs, in December 2003.

BANBURY
John Horton: At this *private* location, there is a Cessna plaything.

❏	G-ARRF	Cessna 150A	ex Perranporth, N7197X. Cr 11-3-88. Fuselage.	3-00

BENSON AIRFIELD east of the A4074, east of Wallingford
RAF Benson:

❏	'EN343'	Spitfire FSM	BAPC.226, gate.	3-02
❏	[XT681]	'U' Wessex HC.2	9279M, ex Shawbury, 72, WTF, 18. ABDR	7-01

BICESTER
Defence and Distribution Centre: This is *not* the aerodrome, but it is well signed and can be found close to the 'Plough' public house.

❏	ZA319*'TAV'	Tornado GR.1	ex St Athan, 15, TTTE. Arrived 5-12-02.	1-04

BICESTER AERODROME on the A421 north-east of Bicester
RAF Gliding and Soaring Association Centre: Primary CLJ moved to France by March 2004.

❏	G-AYUP		T.61A Falke	ex XW983, G-AYUP. CoA 15-7-96. Stored.	8-99
❏	–*	BPT	T.49 Capstan	BGA.1132. CoA 11-12-95. Stored. First noted 3-03.	3-04
❏	–	EVU	Doppleraab	BGA.2944. Stored.	1-02
❏	WB556		Chipmunk T.10	ex Oxf UAS. SOC 12-9-73. Fuselage.	8-99
❏	WB645		Chipmunk T.10	8218M, ex Little Rissington, Cottesmore SF, Edn UAS, 8 FTS, 1 CAACU, 17 RFS, 1 RFS. Fuselage. Spares	8-99
❏	WG303		Chipmunk T.10	8208M, ex Shawbury, Kemble, Ox UAS, Gatow SF, Wittering SF, Marham SF, Bir UAS, 5 RFS, 2 BFTS.	8-99
❏	ZE589		Viking T.1	EXT/BGA.3045, ex 634 VGS, Shawbury, Syerston. Crashed 9-7-92. Stored.	11-99
❏	–		Chipmunk T.10	cockpit section. Hulk.	3-95

Locally: The Swift was offered for sale in October 2002. It attended the '100 Years of Flight Experience' static display at the International Air Tattoo, Fairford, Glos, July 2003.

❑ XF114	Swift F.7	G-SWIF, ex Scampton, Bournemouth, Connah's Quay, Aston Down, CS(A), Cranfield. Stored.	7-03

BRIZE NORTON AIRFIELD on the A4095 south-west of Witney
RAF Brize Norton: The nose of VC-10 ZD234 *should* still serve as a procedures simulator [1].

❑ XR806	VC-10 C.1K	9285M, ex 10. Dam 18-12-97. Fuselage. ABDR		1-00
❑ ZD234	Super VC-10	8700M, ex Heathrow, G-ASGF, BA, BOAC. Nose.	[1]	4-92

Air Movements School: Scout AH.1 XV118 was put up for tender in February 2004 [1].

❑ XV118	'T' Scout AH.1	9141M, ex Wroughton, 657, 658, 652, 651, 660.	[1]	2-04
❑ XX914*	VC-10	8777M, ex RAE, G-ATDJ, BUA. Fuselage.		9-02
❑ XZ994	'O' Harrier GR.3	9170M, ex St A', 1417F, 233 OCU, 1417F, 233'.		9-02
❑ ZB684*	Gazelle AH.1	ex Fleetlands, 667, 665, 655. Arrived 8-7-02.		9-02

CHALGROVE AIRFIELD on the B480 north-west of Watlington
Martin Baker: Meteor T.7 WL419 *Asterix* and T.7(mod) WA638 act as flying test-beds for MB.

❑ EE416	Meteor III	ex Wroughton, South Kensington, MB. Nose.	3-03
❑ –	Northrop F-5A	ex Greek AF, 63-8418. Nose. Dump.	3-03
❑ –	MiG-19 *Farmer*	ex Pakistan? Nose. Dump.	7-02
❑ –*	IAI Lavi EMU	Nose. Dump.	7-02

CULHAM on the A415 south-east of Abingdon
UKAEA, Lightning Studies Unit: Still have their Hunter in an upstairs lab.

❑ WV381	'732' Hunter GA.11	ex Kemble, FRADU, FRU, FWS, 222. Fuselage.	7-02

ENSTONE AERODROME on the B4030 east of Chipping Norton

❑ G-AVGJ	SAN DR.1050	ex F-BJYJ. CoA 22-4-85.	® off-site	10-01
❑ G-AWSP	Condor	CoA 23-1-95. Stored.		6-03
❑ G-AZTD	Cherokee Six 300	ex N8611N. CoA 16-8-98. Stored.		6-03
❑ G-BBRY	Cessna 210	ex Cranfield, Blackbushe, Chessington, 5Y-KRZ, VP-KRZ, N7391E. Crashed 2-4-78. Stored.		7-02
❑ G-BSGJ*	Sonerai II	ex N34WH. CoA 6-9-91. Stored.		6-03
❑ G-DKGF*	Dragonfly 1	unflown project. Dumped by 7-02.		10-03

HENLEY-ON-THAMES on the A4155 north of Reading
No.447 Squadron Air Cadets: 'Parented' by Benson.

❑ XS218	Jet Provost T.4	ex Woodley, Halton 8508M, Shawbury, 3 FTS. Nose.	10-02

KIDLINGTON on the A423 north of Oxford
Julian Mitchell: Should still have his Hunter nose.

❑ XF383	Hunter F.6	ex North Scarle, Wittering 8706M, Kemble, 12, 216, 237 OCU, 4 FTS, 229 OCU, 65, 111, 263. Nose.	12-00

NORTH MORETON south of the A4130, west of Wallingford

❑ G-ARET	Tri-Pacer 160	CoA 20-5-83.	®	5-96

OXFORD AIRPORT or Kidlington, on the A4260, north of Oxford
Oxford Air Training School: *W&R16* (p196) wrote 'out' Sioux AH.1 XT175 from this heading. The thinking was that it had been reported sold to a local collector, or that it had gone to Cambridgeshire. Not so, it is still to be found in a classroom here [1].

❑ G-ARJR	Apache 160G	ex N4447P. CoA 24-10-78.	6-97
❑ G-RING	FR.182RG	ex D-EFGP. Crashed 23-2-91. Dump.	7-98
❑ [XN500]	Jet Provost T.3A	ex 1 FTS, 7 FTS, RAFC, 3 FTS, RAFC.	2-04
❑ XT175	Sioux AH.1	ex TAD175, Middle Wallop.	[1] 5-03

SHENINGTON AERODROME west of the A422, west of Banbury
A Grasshopper is stored at the glider strip and has been for many years.

❑ –*	G'hopper TX.1	stored on trailer. First noted 4-03.	4-03

SHRIVENHAM east of Swindon, south of the A420
Royal Military College of Science: The Gnat is painted in Red Arrows colours on one side and air defence grey on the other! [1] A Harrier and Scout are displayed within the grounds [2] all others are within the Aviation Hall.

❑ XP542	'42'	Gnat T.1	8575M, ex St Athan, 4 FTS.	[1] 7-02
❑ XT621		Scout AH.1	ex Wroughton, 655, 656, 666, 664, 666.	7-02
❑ XV122	'A'	Scout AH.1	ex Almondbank, Wroughton.	[2] 7-02
❑ XV744	'3K'	Harrier GR.3	9167M, ex St Athan, 233 OCU, 1, 233 OCU.	[2] 7-02
❑ XW919	'W'	Harrier GR.3	A2610 [3], ex A2609, Culdrose, Cosford,	
			4, 1, 233 OCU.	7-02
❑ 69-16445		AH-1F Cobra	ex US Army, 1/1CAV, Budingen. 'IFOR' markings.	
			Last flight 2-7-96.	7-02
❑ 70-15154		OH-58CR Kiowa	ex Lyneham (transit), US Army.	7-02

WITNEY north of the A40 west of Oxford
Witney Technical College: No news on this airframe.

❑ 'G-IRIS'	Aztec / Apache	ex Faringdon?	6-00

SHROPSHIRE

ASTLEY east of the A49 north of Shrewsbury

❑ G-AWGM	Kittiwake II	ex Hanworth, Halton. Damaged 18-1-86.	® 9-95

BRIDGNORTH on the A442 south of Telford
Canberra B.2 nose WD935 (last noted here in May 1995) moved to Doncaster, S Yorks, by May 2003.

CHETWYND AERODROME on the A41 north-west of Newport
Staffordshire Sports Skydiving Club: *Should* still have the Cessna hulk.

❑ G-ATIE	Cessna 150F	ex Market Drayton, N6291R. Crashed 28-7-79.	5-97

COSFORD AIRFIELD south of Junction 3 of the M54
Royal Air Force Museum: As Hendon was getting ready to unveil the 'Milestones' building, early in December 2003, Cosford announced its ambitious plans. These will centre around the building of a huge new display hall, £12 million-worth, with a 'Cold War' theme that should open in the autumn of 2006. The new display hall will go under the title of 'Divided World : Connected World'. Heritage Lottery

Fund awarded £4.9 million to the project in March 2004. The scale is perhaps best taken in when it is considered that it will house the Belfast and *three* V-bombers plus much more! Three? Yes, the plan is to move the Valiant from Hendon (and the Sabre will also relocate from there). Aircraft slated for the new display hall are marked ➩. This should see all of the military airframes other than the Neptune indoors – some taking up the space left by moving the Hastings and York from what is now the main exhibition hangar. There are no plans at present for the airliner collection.

Notes: The Michael Beetham Conservation Centre is treated separately, see below. Airframes on site, but in 'deep store' and not available for inspection have been given a separate entry, see below. These are: Vampire FB.5 WA346; Valetta C.2 VX573; Canberra B.2 nose WD931; Prefect TX.1 WE982; Jet Provost T.1 XD674; the P.1121; Ventura II 6130; F-84F '6771'. As the RAF Museum's airframes are theirs and no longer owned by the Ministry of Defence, the opportunity has been taken to 'downgrade' the maintenance serial status to the appropriate place in the aircraft's 'movement' history. The T-tail rear fuselage of the Short SB.5 is displayed alongside WG768 [1]. Airframes marked ➥ attended the '100 Years of Flight Experience' static at Fairford, Glos, July 2003.

Departures: The following to Hendon, Gtr Lon: Moth G-AAMX 30-7-03; Blériot XI '164' 4-03; Camel F6314 4-03; Hart Trainer K4972 by 1-03; Thunderbolt 'KL216' 20-5-03; Skeeter AOP.12 XM555 3-02; Whirlwind HAR.10 XP299; Buccaneer S.2B XW547 8/9-02-03; Me 262 112372 14-7-03; Ki 100-1b '24' by 12-03. Sopwith Camel REP 'B5577' donated to Museum of Flight and moved to East Fortune, Scotland, 26-11-02. Spitfire XVI RW393 moved to Stafford, Staffs. Me 163B-1a 191614 moved to the comforts of the Michael Beetham Centre (see below) to continue its restoration. By 2-04 Meteor NF.14 WS843 had also moved to the centre.

◆ Open daily 10am to 6pm (last admission 4pm) with the exception of Xmas and New Year. Annual airshow in which several museum aircraft (and others from the SoTT) that are not normally outside are displayed - extra charges apply. Near to Junction 3 of the M54 and well signposted. The **Aerospace Museum Society** provides a vital link in both the restoration of exhibits and the running of the museum and special events. ✉ Cosford, Shifnal, Shropshire, TF11 8UP ☎ 01902 376200 **fax** 01902 376211 **e-mail** cosford@rafmuseum.org **www**.rafmuseum.org

❏ G-EBMB	Hawker Cygnet	ex Hendon, Cardington, Henlow, Lympne No.14. CoA 30-11-61.	➥	2-04
❏ G-AEEH	HM.14 'Flea'	ex St Athan, Colerne, Bath, Whitchurch.		2-04
❏ 'G-AFAP'	CASA 352L	ex Spanish AF T2B-272. British Airways c/s.		2-04
❏ 'G-AJOV'	Dragonfly HR.3	WP495, ex Biggin Hill, Banstead, Warnham, Wimbledon. BEA colours.		2-04
❏ G-AMOG	Viscount 701	ex Cardiff-Wales, BOAC, Cambrian, BEA *Robert Falcon Scott*, G-AMNZ ntu. CoA 14-6-77. BEA c/s.		2-04
❏ G-AOVF	Britannia 312F	ex Southend, 9Q-CAZ, G-AOVF, Stansted, Donaldson, British Eagle, BOAC. BOAC c/s.		2-04
❏ G-APAS	Comet 1XB	ex Shawbury 8351M, XM823, G-APAS, G-5-23, Air France, F-BGNZ. BOAC c/s.		2-04
❏ G-APFJ	Boeing 707-436	ex British Airtours, BOAC. CoA 16-2-82. Airtours c/s.		2-04
❏ G-ARPH	Trident 1C	ex BA, BEA. CoA 8-9-82. BA colours.		2-04
❏ G-ARVM	VC-10 Srs 1101	ex BA, BOAC. CoA 5-8-80. BA colours.		2-04
❏ G-AVMO	BAC 111-510ED	ex Bournemouth, BA, BEA. *Lothian Region*.		2-04
❏ G-BBYM	Jetstream 200	ex Cranfield, BAe, G-AYWR, G-8-13. CoA 20-9-98.		2-04
❏ K9942*	Spitfire I	ex Hendon 8383M, Rochester, Hendon, 71 MU Bicester, Fulbeck, Wroughton, Newark, Cardiff, 53 OTU, 57 OTU, 72. 72 Sqn c/s. Arrived 15-11-02.		2-04
	'SD-D'			
❏ DG202/G	F.9/40 Meteor	ex Yatesbury, Locking 5758M, Moreton Valance.	➥	2-04
❏ 'FS628'	Argus II	ex Rochester, G-AIZE, Cosford, Henlow, Hanwell, N9996F, 43-14601. CoA 6-8-66. SEAC colours.		2-04
❏ 'KG374' 'YS'	Dakota IV	KN645, 8355M, ex Colerne, AFN CF, MinTech, AFN CF, MinTech, AFN HQ, SHAPE CF, Malta CF, BAFO CS, 2nd TAF CS, 44-77003.	➩	2-04
❏ KN751	Liberator VI	ex Colerne, Ind AF 6 Sqn HE807, RAF KN751, 99.		2-04
❏ LF738	Hurricane II	ex Rochester, Biggin Hill, Wellesbourne Mountford, 5405M, 22 OTU, 1682 BDTF. 1682 BDTF colours.		2-04
	'UH-A'			
❏ RF398	Lincoln B.2/4A	ex 8376M, Henlow, Abingdon, CSE, BCBS.		2-04
❏ TA639 'AZ-E'	Mosquito TT.35	ex 7806M, CFS, 3 CAACU, Aldergrove TT Flt.		2-04

❑	TG511		Hastings T.5	ex 8554M, 230 OCU, SCBS, BCBS, 202, 47.	⇨ 2-04
❑	[TS798]		York C.1	ex 'MW100', Shawbury, Brize Norton, Staverton, 'LV633', G-AGNV, Skyways, BOAC, TS798. CoA 6-3-65.	⇨ 2-04
❑	TX214		Anson C.19	ex Henlow 7817M, HCCS, MCS, RCCF, Staff College CF, 1 FU, 16 FU.	2-04
❑	VP952		Devon C.2/2	ex St Athan 8820M, 207, 21, WCS, SCS, Upavon SF, TCCF, MCS, BCCS, HCCS, A&AEE, MCCF, AAFCE, TCCF, Hendon SF, HS.	2-04
❑	WA634		Meteor T.7(mod)	ex St Athan, Martin Baker.	2-04
❑	WE600		Auster C4 (T.7 mod)	ex St Athan, Swinderby, Finningley 7602M, Trans-Antarctic Expedition, 663. Skis.	2-04
❑	WG760		EE P.1A	ex Binbrook, Henlow, Bicester 7755M, St Athan, Warton, A&AEE.	2-04
❑	WG768		Short SB.5	ex Topcliffe, Finningley 8005M, ETPS, RAE Bedford, RAE Farnborough, A&AEE, RAE Bedford, A&AEE. [1]	2-04
❑	WG777		Fairey FD-2	ex Topcliffe, Finningley 7986M, RAE Bedford.	2-04
❑	WK935		Meteor F.8(mod)	ex St Athan, Colerne 7869M, RAE. Prone-pilot.	2-04
❑	WL679		Varsity T.1	ex 9155M, Farnborough, RAE, BLEU.	2-04
❑	WL732		Sea Balliol T.21	ex Henlow, A&AEE, Lossiemouth, Anthorn.	2-04
❑	WP912		Chipmunk T.10	ex Hendon 8467M, Man UAS, RAFC, ITS, Cam UAS, CFS, 2 FTS, Lon UAS, FTCCS, HCCS, 8 FTS.	2-04
❑	WV562	'P-C'	Provost T.1	ex Cranwell 7606M, Henlow, 22 FTS.	2-04
❑	WV746		Pembroke C.1	ex 8938M, 60, 207, 21, WCS, TCCF, FTCCS, BCCS, HS, 2 TAF CF.	2-04
❑	WZ744		Avro 707C	ex Topcliffe, Finningley 7932M, RAE, Avro.	2-04
❑	XA564		Javelin FAW.1	ex 2 SoTT, Locking 7464M, Filton.	⇨ 2-04
❑	XA893		Vulcan B.1	ex Abingdon, Bicester 8591M, A&AEE, Avro. Nose.	⇨ 2-04
❑	XD145		SARO SR.53	ex Brize Norton, Henlow, Westcott, A&AEE.	➡ 2-04
❑	XE670		Hunter F.4	ex St Athan 8585M / 7762M, Abingdon, Bicester, 93, 26. Nose. Stored.	⇨ 2-04
❑	XF926		Bristol 188	ex 8368M, Foulness Island, RAE.	2-04
❑	XG337		Lightning F.1	ex 2 SoTT 8056M, Warton, A&AEE, Warton.	2-04
❑	XH171	'U'	Canberra PR.9	ex 2 SoTT 8746M, 39, 13, 39 MoA, 58.	⇨ 2-04
❑	XH672		Victor K.2	ex 9242M, Shawbury, 55, 57, 543, MoA. *Maid Marion.*	⇨ 2-04
❑	XJ918		Sycamore HR.14	ex 2 SoTT 8190M, 32, MCS, Kemble, Wroughton, 110, Seletar, A&AEE, 275.	2-04
❑	XK724		Gnat F.1	ex Cranwell, Bicester, Henlow 7715M, Folland.	2-04
❑	XL568	'C'	Hunter T.7A	ex 9224M, Cranwell, Lossie', 12, 74, MoA, 74, HS.	2-04
❑	XL703		Pioneer CC.1	ex Manchester, Henlow 8034M, 209, 230. Stored.	2-04
❑	XL993		T' Pioneer CC.1	ex 8388M, Henlow, Shawbury, 21, 78. Stored.	2-04
❑	XM351	'Y'	Jet Provost T.3	ex 1 SoTT 8078M, Halton, Shawbury, 3 FTS, 7 FTS, 2 FTS.	2-04
❑	XM598		Vulcan B.2	ex 8778M, 44, Wadd Wing, Cott Wing, 12.	⇨ 2-04
❑	XN714		Hunting 126/50	ex RAE Bedford, NASA Ames and Moffett, Holme-on-Spalding Moor, RAE.	2-04
❑	XP411		Argosy C.1	ex 2 SoTT 8442M, 6 FTS, Kemble, 70. Stored.	2-04
❑	XR220		TSR-2 XO-2	ex Henlow 7933M, A&AEE. Never flown.	2-04
❑	XR371		Belfast C.1	ex Hucknall, Kemble, 53. *Enceladus.*	⇨ 2-04
❑	XR977		Gnat T.1	ex 2 SoTT 8640M, Red Arrows, 4 FTS. 'Reds' c/s.	2-04
❑	XS639		Andover E.3A	ex 9241M, Northolt, 32, 115, 32, 46.	2-04
❑	XV591		Phantom FG.1	ex St Athan, 111, 43, 892. Trans-Atlantic c/s. Nose. Stored.	2-04
❑	XX496*	'D'	Jetstream T.1	ex Cranwell, 45, 6 FTS, 3 FTS. Arrived 22-3-04.	3-04
❑	XX654*	'3'	Bulldog T.1	ex Shawbury Newton, CFS, 3 FTS, CFS, 3 FTS, Bri UAS, 2 FTS. Arrived 14-1-04.	2-04
❑	XX765		Jaguar GR.1 (mod)	ex Loughborough, Warton, BAe, RAE, A&AEE, 226 OCU, 14. ACT 'fly-by-wire' test-bed.	2-04

❏	XX946* 'WT'	Tornado P.02	ex Hendon, Honington 8883M, Laarbruch, Honington, Warton. Arrived 3-03.		2-04
❏	–* BAPC.82	Afghan Hind	ex Hendon, Kabul, RAfghan AF, RAF. Ex storage.		2-04
❏	A-515	FMA Pucará	ex 9245M, ZD485, A&AEE, Yeovilton, Stanley, Arg AF A-515.		2-04
❏	L-866	PBY-6A Catalina	ex 8466M, Colerne, Danish AF Esk.721, 82-866, BuNo 63993.		2-04
❏	420430 '3U+CC'	Me 410A-1-U2	ex St Athan 8483M, Cosford, Fulbeck, Wroughton, Stanmore Park, Brize Norton, Farnborough, AM.72, Vaerlose.		2-04
❏	475081	Fi 156C-7	ex St Athan, Coltishall, Bircham Newton, Finningley 7362M, Fulbeck, VP546, AM.101, Farnborough.		2-04
❏	–	Fa 330A-1	ex 8469M, Henlow, Farnborough.		2-04
❏	–	Fi 103 (V-1)	BAPC.94, ex 8583M.		2-04
❏	5439	Ki 46 *Dinah*	BAPC.84, ex St Athan 8484M, Biggin Hill, Fulbeck, Wroughton, Stanmore Park, Sealand, ATAIU-SEA.		2-04
❏	–	Ohka 11	BAPC.99, ex St Athan 8486M, Cosford, Westcott.		2-04
❏	204	SP-2H Neptune	ex Dutch Navy, 320 Sqn, Valkenburg, 5 Sqn, 321 Sqn.		2-04
❏	01120	MiG-15*bis* (Lim-2)	ex Hendon, Cardington, South Lambeth, Hendon, Middlesborough, Polish AF.	⇨	2-04
❏	J-1704	Venom FB.54	ex Greenham Common and Swiss Air Force.	⇨	2-04
❏	'413573'* 'B6-K'	P-51D-25-NA	ex Hendon 9133M, Halton, N6526D, RCAF 9289, 44-73415. Composite. 363rd FS c/s, *Little Friend*. Arrived 15-7-03.		2-04

Michael Beetham Conservation Centre: MRAF Sir Michael Beetham opened the £2.4 million centre on 13th May 2002. As well as the workshop and storage space, the centre includes component bays, a paint shop, offices, technical records library and is also the headquarters for Cosford's curatorial staff. There is a purpose-built viewing gallery that has been described as 'public'. Sadly, this is not the case. Parties of up to a maximum of 20 can be accommodated on a prior arrangement basis. This is certainly better than nothing, but to have had the gallery available to visitors within normal museum opening hours would have been a major plus point. The Meteor NF.14 is destined for the new 'Cold War' building [1]. The Kestrel's wings are to be found on P.1127 XP984 at Brooklands, Surrey [2].

Departures: Hawker Cygnet G-EBMB to display in Hangar 3 – see above; The following to <u>Hendon</u>, Gtr Lon: Kittyhawk IV 'FX760', 3-03; Tempest TT.5 NV778 by 12-03; Vampire F.3 VT812 2-6-03; And the following to 'deep store' at <u>Stafford</u>, Staffs: Dragon Rapide G-AHED by 9-02; Hawk Major DG590 by 9-02; Swordfish IV HS503 by 9-02; Spitfire F.21 LA226 by 9-02; Spitfire F.22 PK664 by 9-02; Spitfire PR.XIX PM651 by 9-02; Spitfire XVI SL674 by 2-03; Sedbergh TX.1 VX275 by 9-02; Cornell 15195 by 9-02; Vampire FB.6 J-1172 by 9-02; Blériot XXVII 433 by 9-02. Hind BAPC.82 went on show at the museum 9-03 - see above. Auster I LB264 (G-AIXA) flew in from Spanhoe, Northants, 23-10-02 but moved to Hendon, Gtr Lon, by 10-03.
◆ Viewing on Fridays by prior arrangement only to groups, max 20 persons. ☎ 01902 376208.

❏	[G-AEKW]*	Mohawk	ex Hatch, Wyton, USA, Tablada, Spain, HM503, MCCS, Turnhouse SF, G-AEKW. Arr by 6-02.	®	2-04
❏	F-HMFI	Farman F.<u>41</u>	ex 9204M, Wyton, Cardington, Henlow, Benson, Nash, Henri Farman.		2-04
❏	D5329	5F1 Dolphin REP	ex Wyton, Cardington. Using original parts.	®	2-04
❏	P1344 'PL-K'	Hampden I	ex 9175M, Wyton, Cardington, Hatch, Petsamo, USSR, 144, 14 OTU. Forced down 6-9-42.	®	2-04
❏	WS843* 'Y'	Meteor NF.14	ex museum, Hendon, St Athan, Henlow 7937M, St Athan, Kemble, 1 ANS, MoA, 228 OCU.	® [1]	2-04
❏	XS695	Kestrel FGA.1	ex Wyton, Cardington, Yeovilton, Culdrose A2619, Manadon, Tri-Partite Eval Sqn, A&AEE, RAE.	[2]	2-04
❏	XT903 'X'	Phantom FGR.2	ex Wyton, Leuchars, 56, 92, 228 OCU, 23, 228 OCU. Nose. Stored.		11-01
❏	7198/18*	LVG C.VI	ex Old Warden, 9239M, G-AANJ, ex Stanmore, Colerne, Fulbeck. Last flight 20-9-03. Arr 12-11-03.		2-04
❏	191614*	Me 163B-1a	ex museum 8481M, Biggin Hill, Westcott, Brize Norton, Farnborough, Hussum, II/JG400.	®	2-04

Stored: As related above, museum airframes on site but in 'deep store' are now listed separately. They are not available for inspection. The Canberra B.2 nose carries the c/n EEP.71038 which should make it WD956 (which had no service life, undertaking 'Red Dean' missile trials), comments? [1].

❑ VX573	Valetta C.2	ex 8389M, Henlow, Wildenrath CF, Buckeburg CF. *Lorelei*. Stored.		2-04
❑ WA346	Vampire FB.5	ex Cardington, Cosford, Henlow, Hendon, 3/4 CAACU, 1 FTS, 7 FTS, 130, 98, 102 FRS. Booms of VX461. Identity confirmed.		2-04
❑ WD931	Canberra B.2	ex Aldridge, Pershore, RRE, RAE. Nose.	[1]	2-04
❑ WE982	Prefect TX.1	ex 8781M, Cardington, Henlow, Syerston, Manston, ACCGS, CGS, 1 GC, 621 GS, 612 GS, 644 GS, 643 GS, 166 GS, 143 GS.		2-04
❑ XD674	Jet Provost T.1	ex St Athan, Swinderby, Finningley 7570M, 71 MU, Hunting.		2-04
❑ XG225*	'S' Hunter F.6A	ex gate 8713M, Weapons School, 2 SoTT, Kemble, 229 OCU, 92, 74, 20. Parade ground.		3-04
❑ —	P.1121	ex Henlow, Cranfield. Fuselage sections.		2-04
❑ 6130	Ventura II	ex SAAF Museum, SAAF, RAF AJ469.		2-04
❑ '6771'	F-84F-51-RE	ex Rochester, Southend, Belgian AF FU-6, 52-7133.		2-04

Defence College of Aeronautical Engineering: From 1st April 2004, Cosford and **1 School of Technical Training** (SoTT) became the centre of a new tri-service structure of Defence Training Establishments: Eventually coming under the 'fold' will be St Athan, Wales, Cranwell, Lincs, and the Navy at Gosport, Hants, and the Army at Arborfield, Berks. Full structure will be in place by 2008. The School is split into a series of squadrons and flights, each teaching specialist elements: Airframe Training Squadron; Electrical Trade Training Flight; Engineering Standards Training Squadron; Hangar Training Flight; Propulsion and Weapons Training Squadron; and the Line Training Flight.

The SoTT has taken delivery of four very sophisticated Eurofighter Typhoon purpose-built training rigs, called Genflies. These have the capacity to generate over 100 different faults, to really annoy the trainees. They have been allocated serials not because they are intended to fly, but because they have a maintenance schedule and cost a considerable amount of money... just like any modern-day warplane! [1]

Departures: Harrier T.4 XW265 to St Athan, Wales, 6-1-03; Tornado P.03 XX947 was up for disposal 5-03, to Ipswich, Suffolk; Harrier GR.7 ZD462 to St Athan, Wales, 30-1-04.

❑ XM362		Jet Provost T.3	8230M, ex Halton, Kemble, Shawbury, 3 FTS, 2 FTS. 'Cutaway' and camouflaged.	10-03
❑ XR498*	'X'	Wessex HC.2	9342M, ex Shawbury, 72, 60, 72, A&AEE. Arr 3-6-03.	10-03
❑ XR506*	'V'	Wessex HC.2	9343M, ex Shawbury, 72, 60, 72, 18. Arrived 3-6-03.	10-03
❑ XR574	'72'	Gnat T.1	8631M, ex Halton, Cosford, Kemble, 4 FTS.	10-03
❑ XS177*	'N'	Jet Provost T.4	9044M, ex Valley, Shawbury, CATCS, 3 FTS, 2 FTS. Arrived by 4-02.	10-03
❑ XS641	'Z'	Andover C.1(PR)	9198M, ex Shawbury, 60, 115, 46, 84, SAR Flt, 84.	10-03
❑ XS710	'O'	Dominie T.1	9259M, ex Cranwell, 3 FTS, 6 FTS, CAW.	10-03
❑ XS726	'T'	Dominie T.1	9273M, ex Cranwell, 3 FTS, 6 FTS, CAW.	10-03
❑ XS729	'G'	Dominie T.1	9275M, ex Cranwell, 3 FTS, 6 FTS.	10-03
❑ XS733	'Q'	Dominie T.1	9276M, ex Cranwell, 3 FTS, 6 FTS, RAFC, CAW.	10-03
❑ XS734	'N'	Dominie T.1	9260M, ex Cranwell, 3 FTS, 6 FTS.	10-03
❑ XS738	'U'	Dominie T.1	9274M, ex Cranwell, 3 FTS, 6 FTS.	10-03
❑ XT773*		Wessex HU.5	9123M, ex St Athan, Abingdon, Wroughton, 771, 845, 847, 772, 845, 707. Arrived 8-9-03.	10-03
❑ XV653*	'63'	Sea King HAS.6	9326M, ex Gosport, 810, 706. Arrived 15-10-02.	10-03
❑ XV659*	'62'	Sea King HAS.6	9324M, ex Gosport, Fleetlands, 810, 814, 819, 706, 826, 824, 819, 814, FTU, 824. Arrived 7-10-02.	10-03
❑ XV710*	'64'	Sea King HAS.6	9325M, ex Gosport, 814, 820, 814, 819, 824. Arrived 7-10-02.	10-03
❑ XV752	'B'	Harrier GR.3	9078M, ex 4, 3, 1, 233 OCU, 1, 233 OCU.	10-03
❑ XW290	'MA'	Jet Provost T.5A	9199M, ex Shawbury, 3 FTS, RAFC, CFS.	10-03
❑ XW292	'32'	Jet Provost T.5A	9128M, ex Halton, Shawbury, 3 FTS, RAFC, CFS.	10-03
❑ XW294	'45'	Jet Provost T.5A	9129M, ex Halton, Shawbury, 3 FTS, RAFC, Leeming SF, 1 FTS, CFS.	10-03

❏	XW299	'MB'	Jet Provost T.5A	9146M, ex Halton, 1 FTS, RAFC, 1 FTS.	10-03
❏	XW301	'MC'	Jet Provost T.5A	9147M, ex Halton, 1 FTS.	10-03
❏	XW303	'127'	Jet Provost T.5A	9119M, ex Halton, 7 FTS, 1 FTS.	10-03
❏	XW304	'MD'	Jet Provost T.5	9172M, ex 6 FTS, CFS, 1 FTS.	10-03
❏	XW309	'ME'	Jet Provost T.5	9179M, ex Shawbury, 6 FTS, 1 FTS.	10-03
❏	XW311	'MF'	Jet Provost T.5	9180M, ex Shawbury 6 FTS.	10-03
❏	XW312	'64'	Jet Provost T.5A	9109M, ex Halton, 1 FTS.	10-03
❏	XW318	'MG'	Jet Provost T.5A	9190M, ex 1 FTS, RAFC, CFS, RAFC, CFS, 3 FTS.	10-03
❏	XW320	'71'	Jet Provost T.5A	'9015M', ex Halton, 1 FTS, Leeming 'hack', 3 FTS, RAFC. Really 9016M.	10-03
❏	XW321	'MH'	Jet Provost T.5A	9154M, ex Shawbury, 1 FTS, 7 FTS, RAFC, 3 FTS.	10-03
❏	XW327	'62'	Jet Provost T.5A	9130M, ex Halton, CFS, 7 FTS, 6 FTS, 7 FTS, 1 FTS, CFS, RAFC.	10-03
❏	XW328	'MI'	Jet Provost T.5A	9177M, ex 1 FTS, RAFC, CFS, RAFC.	10-03
❏	XW330	'MJ'	Jet Provost T.5A	9195M, ex 1 FTS, 7 FTS, 3 FTS, Leeming SF, CFS, RAFC, 3 FTS.	10-03
❏	XW335	'74'	Jet Provost T.5A	9061M, ex Halton, Kemble, 3 FTS, RAFC, CFS, RAFC.	10-03
❏	XW351	'31'	Jet Provost T.5A	9062M, ex Halton, Kemble, 3 FTS, RAFC, 1 FTS, RAFC.	10-03
❏	XW358	'MK'	Jet Provost T.5A	9181M, ex Shawbury, 1 FTS, RAFC.	10-03
❏	XW360	'ML'	Jet Provost T.5A	9153M, ex Shawbury, 1 FTS, RAFC, 7 FTS.	10-03
❏	XW361	'MM'	Jet Provost T.5A	9192M, ex 1 FTS, RAFC, 7 FTS, RAFC.	10-03
❏	XW364	'MO'	Jet Provost T.5A	9188M, ex Shawbury, 3 FTS, RAFC, CFS, 1 FTS.	10-03
❏	XW365	'73'	Jet Provost T.5A	'9015M', ex Halton, 1 FTS, RAFC. Really 9018M.	10-03
❏	XW366	'75'	Jet Provost T.5A	9097M, ex Halton, 1 FTS, 3 FTS, RAFC.	10-03
❏	XW367	'MO'	Jet Provost T.5A	9193M, ex 1 FTS, RAFC.	10-03
❏	XW370	'MP'	Jet Provost T.5A	9196M, ex 1 FTS, 3 FTS.	10-03
❏	XW375	'52'	Jet Provost T.5A	9149M, ex Halton, CFS, 6 FTS, RAFC.	10-03
❏	XW405	'MQ'	Jet Provost T.5A	9187M, ex Shawbury, 6 FTS, 1 FTS, 7 FTS, 6 FTS, 1 FTS, RAFC.	10-03
❏	XW410	'MR'	Jet Provost T.5A	9125M, ex Shawbury, 1 FTS, RAFC, 3 FTS.	10-03
❏	XW413	'69'	Jet Provost T.5A	9126M, ex Halton, 1 FTS, RAFC.	10-03
❏	XW416	'MS'	Jet Provost T.5A	9191M, ex 1 FTS, RAFC.	10-03
❏	XW418	'MT'	Jet Provost T.5A	9173M, ex Shawbury, 1 FTS, 7 FTS, CFS, 3 FTS, Leeming SF, 3 FTS.	10-03
❏	XW419	'125'	Jet Provost T.5A	9120M, ex Halton, 7 FTS, 1 FTS, RAFC.	10-03
❏	XW420	'MU'	Jet Provost T.5A	9194M, ex 1 FTS, RAFC.	10-03
❏	XW421	'60'	Jet Provost T.5A	9111M, ex PWTS, Halton, Shawbury, CFS, 3 FTS, Leeming SF, 3 FTS.	5-03
❏	XW425	'MV'	Jet Provost T.5A	9200M, ex CFS, 6 FTS, CFS, 3 FTS, Leeming SF, CFS.	10-03
❏	XW427	'67'	Jet Provost T.5A	9124M, ex Halton, 1 FTS, CFS, 3 FTS, CFS, 3 FTS.	10-03
❏	XW430	'MW'	Jet Provost T.5A	9176M, ex 1 FTS, CFS, 3 FTS, Leeming SF, 3 FTS.	10-03
❏	XW432	'MX'	Jet Provost T.5A	9127M, ex Shawbury, 1 FTS, Leeming SF, 3 FTS.	10-03
❏	XW434	'MY'	Jet Provost T.5A	9091M, ex Halton, 1 FTS, 7 FTS, 3 FTS, CFS.	10-03
❏	XW436	'68'	Jet Provost T.5A	9148M, ex Halton, 1 FTS, CFS, 3 FTS, Leeming SF, 3 FTS, RAFC.	10-03
❏	XW768	'N'	Harrier GR.3	9072M, ex Halton, 4, 1, 4, 20.	10-03
❏	XW852*		Gazelle HT.3	9331M, ex St Athan, Fleetlands, 32. Arrived 26-6-02.	10-03
❏	XX110	'EP'	Jaguar GR.1	8955M, ex Shawbury, 6, A&AEE, BAC.	10-03
❏	'XX110'		Jaguar GR.1 rig	BAPC.169, ex Halton. Engine systems rig.	7-99
❏	XX726	'EB'	Jaguar GR.1	8947M, ex Halton, Shawbury, 6, 54, 14, 54, 6, JOCU.	10-03
❏	XX727	'ER'	Jaguar GR.1	8951M, ex PWTS, Shawbury, 6, 54, 6, JOCU.	10-03
❏	XX730	'EC'	Jaguar GR.1	8952M, ex Shawbury, 6, JOCU.	10-03
❏	XX739	'I'	Jaguar GR.1	8902M, ex Halton, Shawbury, Gibraltar Det, 6.	10-03
❏	XX743	'EG'	Jaguar GR.1	8949M, ex Halton, Shawbury, 6.	10-03
❏	XX746	'09'	Jaguar GR.1A	8895M, ex Halton, 226 OCU, 14, 17, 6, 31, 226 OCU.	10-03
❏	XX751	'10'	Jaguar GR.1	8937M, ex 226 OCU, 14.	10-03
❏	XX756	'AM'	Jaguar GR.1	8899M, ex 14, 41, 14, 20, 226 OCU, 14.	10-03
❏	XX757	'CU'	Jaguar GR.1	8948M, ex Halton, Shawbury, 20, 226 OCU, 14.	10-03
❏	XX818	'DE'	Jaguar GR.1	8945M, ex Halton, Shawbury, 31, 20, 17.	10-03

❏	XX819	'CE'	Jaguar GR.1	8923M, ex Shawbury, 20, 17.	10-03
❏	XX824	'AD'	Jaguar GR.1	9019M, ex Halton, Shawbury, 14, 17, 14.	10-03
❏	XX825	'BN'	Jaguar GR.1	9020M, ex Halton, Shawbury, 17, 31, 14.	10-03
❏	XX826	'JH'	Jaguar GR.1	9021M, ex Shawbury, 2, 20, 14.	10-03
❏	XX837	'Z'	Jaguar T.2	8978M, ex Halton, Shawbury, 226 OCU.	10-03
❏	XX948	'P'	Tornado P.06	8879M, ex Warton. 617 Sqn colours.	10-03
❏	XX956	'BE'	Jaguar GR.1	8950M, ex Halton, Shawbury, 17, 31, 14, 17.	10-03
❏	XX958	'BK'	Jaguar GR.1	9022M, ex Shawbury, 17, 14.	10-03
❏	XX959	'CJ'	Jaguar GR.1	8953M, ex Shawbury, 20, 14.	10-03
❏	XX962*	'e'	Jaguar GR.1B	9257M. ex Cranwell, Coltishall, 6, 17, 20, 17.	
				Arrived by 7-02.	10-03
❏	XX966	'JJ'	Jaguar GR.1A	8904M, ex Halton, Shawbury, 6, 54, 20,	
				A&AEE, 20, 17.	10-03
❏	XX967	'AC'	Jaguar GR.1	9006M, ex Shawbury, 14, 31.	10-03
❏	XX968	'AJ'	Jaguar GR.1	9007M, ex Shawbury, 14, 31.	10-03
❏	XX969	'01'	Jaguar GR.1	8897M, ex 226 OCU, 3, 17, 31, 14, 31.	10-03
❏	XX975	'07'	Jaguar GR.1A	8905M, ex Halton, 226 OCU, 31, 17, 226 OCU.	10-03
❏	XX976	'BD'	Jaguar GR.1	8906M, ex Halton, Shawbury, 17, 31.	10-03
❏	XZ130	'A'	Harrier GR.3	9079M, ex 4, 3, 233 OCU, 3, 1453F, 1, 4, 20.	10-03
❏	XZ368	'AG'	Jaguar GR.1	8900M, ex Coltishall, 14, 41, 14, 6, 14.	10-03
❏	XZ370	'JB'	Jaguar GR.1	9004M, ex Shawbury, 17.	10-03
❏	XZ371	'AP'	Jaguar GR.1	8907M, ex Shawbury, 14, 17.	10-03
❏	XZ374	'JC'	Jaguar GR.1	9005M, ex Shawbury, 14, 20.	10-03
❏	XZ383	'AF'	Jaguar GR.1	8901M, ex Colt', 14, 41, 54, 14, 226 OCU, 14, 17.	10-03
❏	XZ384	'BC'	Jaguar GR.1	8954M, ex Shawbury, 17, 31, 20.	10-03
❏	XZ389	'BL'	Jaguar GR.1	8946M, ex Halton, Shawbury, 17, 31, 20.	10-03
❏	XZ390	'DM'	Jaguar GR.1	9003M, ex Shawbury, 2, 20, 31.	10-03
❏	XZ935*		Gazelle HT.3	9332M, ex St Athan, Fleetlands, 32, CFS.	10-03
❏	ZA320*	'TAW'	Tornado GR.1	9314M, ex St Athan, 15, TTTE. Arrived 8-4-02.	10-03
❏	ZA323*	'TAZ'	Tornado GR.1	ex St Athan, 15, TTTE. Arrived 18-8-03.	10-03
❏	ZA325*	'TAX'	Tornado GR.1	ex St Athan, 15, TTTE. Arrived 13-8-03.	10-03
❏	ZA357*	'TTV'	Tornado GR.1	ex St Athan, 15, TTTE. Arrived 18-8-03.	10-03
❏	ZA450*	'TH'	Tornado GR.1	9317M, ex St Athan, 15, 12, 617, 12, 27, 20, 15.	10-03
❏	ZD939	'AS'	Tornado F.2	ex St Athan, Warton, St Athan, 229 OCU.	
				Forward fuselage.	10-03
❏	ZE340	'GO'	Tornado F.3	9298M, ex Coningsby, 56. Rear fuselage of ZE758.	10-03
❏	ZJ695*	001	GenFly Mk.2	Typhoon training rig. First noted 4-02	[1] 10-03
❏	ZJ696*	002	GenFly Mk.2	Typhoon training rig. First noted 4-02	[1] 10-03
❏	ZJ697*	003	GenFly Mk.2	Typhoon training rig. First noted 4-02	[1] 10-03
❏	ZJ698*	004	GenFly Mk.2	Typhoon training rig. First noted 4-02	[1] 10-03

PT Flight: Care of the CO of RAF Cosford, Bob Mitchell's PT Flight and other airframes are kept here. All are *not* available for inspection.

❏	G-AEUJ*		Whitney Straight	ex Sutton Coldfield, Marple, East Midlands,	
				Bournemouth. CoA 4-6-70. Stored.	5-02
❏	G-AFRZ*		Monarch	ex Sutton Coldfield, Shipdham, G-AIDE, W6463,	
				Kemble, 10 GCF, FTCCF, 13 EFTS, G-AFRZ.	
				CoA 29-6-70. Stored.	5-02
❏	G-AWIW		SNCAN SV-4B	ex museum, F-BDCC. CoA 6-5-73.	5-02
❏	G-AYKZ		SAI KZ-VIII	ex Coventry, HB-EPB, OY-ACB. CoA 17-7-81. Stored.	5-02
❏	G-BADW		Pitts S-2A	ex museum. CoA 6-9-95.	5-02
❏	G-RIDE		Stephens Akro	ex N81AC, N55NM. CoA 13-8-92.	5-02
❏	N1344		PT-22 Recruit	ex 41-20877.	5-02
❏	N49272	'23'	PT-23-HO	ex USAAF.	5-02
❏	N56421	'855'	PT-22 Recruit	ex 41-15510.	5-02
❏	N58566		BT-15 Valiant	ex USAAF.	5-02

Others: By October 2003 Hunter F.6A XG225 was removed from its place on the parade ground and moved to the RAF Museum, see above. It was replaced by a full-scale model Spitfire. Note that the decidedly *real* MK356 can be found at Coningsby, Lincs, while another 'MK356' is at Hawkinge, Kent.

| ❏ | 'MK356' | | Spitfire IX FSM | arrived 10-03. Unveiled on parade ground 3-04. | 3-04 |

Locally: In a field near Junction 3 of the M54 is a Vampire, used by a paintball group.
❑ XE993   Vampire T.11   ex Cosford 8161M, 8, 73. Poor state.   10-02

DONNINGTON south of the A518, north east of Telford
HQ Defence Storage and Disposition Centre: This huge logistics base has a gate guardian.
❑ XZ971*   'U' Harrier GR.3   9219M, ex Shawbury, Benson, HOCU, 1417F,
                                    233 OCU. Gate.   9-03

LONG MYND AERODROME west of Church Stretton
❑ XN157*   FGS Sedbergh TX.1   ex Sealand. CoA 30-7-95. Stored in trailer.   3-03

LUDLOW on the A49 north of Leominster
The two are *thought* still in store.
❑ G-ABUS   Comper Swift   ex Heathfield. CoA 19-6-79.   ®   2-91
❑ G-BADV   MB.50 Pipistrelle ex Dunkeswell, F-PBRJ. CoA 9-5-79.   ®   2-91

MARKET DRAYTON on the A53 north-east of Shrewsbury
Richard Parr: Has acquired two cockpits and keeps them in the general area. Hunter IF-68 was acquired
by HSA in December 1962 and was converted into a T.69 for the Iraqi Air Force, hence its nose became
'spare' [4].
❑ WP515* 'CD' Canberra B.2   ex Welshpool, Bridgend, Cardiff-Wales, St Athan,
                                    100, 85, CAW, RAFC, 231 OCU, 109, 12. Nose.
                                    Arrived 3-04.   3-04
❑ IF-68*   Hunter FGA.9   ex Welshpool, Firbeck, Kexborough, Macclesfield,
                                    Bitteswell, Dunsfold, G-9-83, Belgian AF IF-68.
                                    Nose. Arrived 2003.   [1] 1-04

SHAWBURY on the A53 north-east of Shrewsbury
Buccaneer Restorations: Was launched at the 4th May 2003 open day at Bruntingthorpe, Leics. They
plan to move XW544 there in due course. E-mail buccrestorations@blueyonder.co.uk
❑ XW544   'Y' Buccaneer S.2C   8857M, ex Cosford, Shawbury, 16, 15.   5-03

SHAWBURY AIRFIELD on the B5063 north of Shawbury
Assault Glider Association (AGA): Located within the base, AGA are making exceptional progress
with their complete Horsa reproduction. A fuselage section of TL659 and other parts have been loaned by
the Museum of Army Flying at Middle Wallop, Hants, to act as patterns. Many other organisations and
individuals have also helped this dynamic project. Not least of which is Air Atlantique... On 7th
November 2002, Stuart Powney announced that Dakota G-AMHJ would be gifted to the AGA to act as a
static tug. This would create an incredible scene. The aim is to display the finished product, and tug,
somewhere in the Midlands as a tribute to airborne forces.
◆ Available for inspection *strictly* by prior permission. ✉ Major Ray Conningham, The Manor,
   Streethay, Lichfield, WS13 8LU **fax** 01543 418191, **e-mail** ray@conningham.fsnet.co.uk
   www.assaultgliderproject.co.uk
❑ G-AMHJ*   C-47B-25-DK   ex Coventry, SU-AZI, G-AMHJ, ZS-BRW, KG651,
                                    1333 CU, 1383 CU, 24, 109 OTU,
                                    42-108962. CoA 5-12-00. Arrived 4-12-03.   3-04
❑ –   Horsa REP   BAPC.279. See above.   3-04

Defence Aviation Repair Agency (DARA): *W&R18* (p186) had Gazelle HT.3 ZA803 leaving on 4th
June 2001 for an unknown destination. By September 2002 it was to be found at <u>Angmering</u>, West
Sussex, but only briefly before becoming 9Q-CMF. Only long term inmates are listed here. While it may
not seem so, the Shorts Tucano store is in a state of 'rotation' and the McDD (or Boeing by adoption)
Apache AH.1s are technically in short term storage prior to service issue.

Harrier GR.3 XZ971 attended the '100 Years of Flight Experience' static display at the International Air Tattoo, Fairford, Glos, July 2003. After that it moved to Donnington, Shropshire. **Departures: Bulldog T.1** XX654 to Cosford, Shrop, 14-1-04; Canberra PR.7 WH779 should be deleted, airframe sections only ever here, the nose is as Boscombe Down, Wilts; **Gazelle HT.2** XW845 left 24-5-02, becoming G-CBSA; XW854 left 23-5-02, becoming G-CBSD; XW857 left 29-5-02, becoming G-CBSB; XW864 to Yeovilton, Somerset, 21-10-02; XW871 left 30-5-02, becoming G-CBSC; **Gazelle HT.3** XW852 to Cosford, Shropshire, 26-6-02; XZ935 to Cosford, Shropshire, 26-6-02; ZA802 left 6-6-02, becoming G-CBSJ; ZB627 left 27-5-02, becoming G-CBSK; **Gazelle HCC.4** XW855 to Hendon, Gtr Lon, 3-3-03; XX436 left 16-5-02, becoming G-CBSE; XZ934 left 28-5-02, becoming G-CBSI; ZB647 left 31-5-02, becoming G-CBSF; ZB649 left 17-5-02, becoming G-CBSG; **Tornado GR.1** ZD789 left 16-4-02 for Clay Cross, Derbys; **Jaguar GR.1A** XX724 moved to St Athan 22-2-00 for return to service; XZ114 moved to St Athan 10-4-03 for return to service; XZ392 moved to St Athan 1-12-02 for return to service; **Jaguar GR.3** XZ367 to Coltishall, Norfolk, 2-10-02; **Tornado F.2** hybrid ZD935 left 23-4-02 for Clay Cross, Derbys; **Wessex HC.2** XR506 to Cosford, Shropshire, 3-6-03; XR511 ex 72 arrived by 9-02, to Hixon, Staffs, 8-1-04; XR588 ex 72 arrived by 9-02, left 6-1-04 for New Zealand; XS675 ex 84 arrived by 9-02, left 8-1-04 for New Zealand; XT607 to Gosport, Hants, by 4-03; XT670 ex 84 arrived by 9-02, left 6-1-04 for New Zealand; XV730 ex 84 arrived by 9-03, left 6-1-04 for New Zealand.

❑	WH849*'AW'	Canberra T.4	ex 39 Sqn, 1 PRU, 231 OCU, 100, 360, 85, 231 OCU, 232 OCU, Gaydon SF, Binbrook SF, Marham SF. Arrived 20-8-02. Stored.	3-04
❑	WT480 'AT'	Canberra T.4	ex Marham, 1 PRU/39 Sqn, 231 OCU, 360, 7, 231 OCU, 13, 7, 231 OCU, CFS, 102.	3-04
❑	XH174	Canberra PR.9	ex 1 PRU, 39, 13, 39, MoS, 39, 58. Nose.	3-04
❑	XR516* 'WB'	Wessex HC.2	ex Gosport, 9319M, A2709 [2], Shawbury, 2 FTS, 18. Arrived 5-02.	3-04
❑	XR525* 'G'	Wessex HC.2	ex 72, 60, 72, Benson SF, SAR Wing, Benson SF, 72. First noted 9-02.	3-04
❑	XV726* 'J'	Wessex HC.2	ex 72, 60, 72, 60, 72, Queen's Flt. First noted 5-02.	3-04
❑	XW200	Puma HC.1	ex 33, 240 OCU, HOCF. Crashed 9-4-01.	3-04
❑	XW892	Gazelle AH.1	ex 666, 658, 662, 663, 662, 653, 663, 660.	9-03
❑	XX144 'U'	Jaguar T.2A	ex 16, 226 OCU, 6, 54, 226 OCU, JOCU.	3-04
❑	XX304	Hawk T.1A	ex Shawbury, St Athan, 'Reds'. Cat 4 24-6-88. Nose held as FRP spare.	3-04
❑	XX431 '43'	Gazelle HT.2	9300M, ex 705, FONA, 705. Inst airframe.	3-04
❑	XX482* 'J'	Jetstream T.1	ex Cranwell, 45, 3 FTS, 45, 6 FTS, 3 FTS, 5 FTS, CFS. Arrived 12-12-03.	12-03
❑	XX494* 'B'	Jetstream T.1	ex Cranwell, 45, 3 FTS, 45, 6 FTS, METS. Arrived 22-3-04.	3-04
❑	XX495* 'C'	Jetstream T.1	ex Cranwell, 45, 3 FTS, 45, 6 FTS, METS. Arrived 22-3-04.	3-04
❑	XX497* 'J'	Jetstream T.1	ex Cranwell, 45, 3 FTS, 45, 6 FTS, METS. Arrived 12-12-03.	12-03
❑	XX499* 'G'	Jetstream T.1	ex Cranwell, 45, 3 FTS, 45, 6 FTS, METS. Arrived 22-3-04.	3-04
❑	XX741 '04'	Jaguar GR.1A	ex 16, 6, 54.	3-04
❑	XX745 'GV'	Jaguar GR.1A	ex St Athan, 54, 16, 6, 16, 226 OCU, 6, 226 OCU, 6, 54, 6, 20, 226 OCU. Damaged 31-5-00.	9-03
❑	XX829 'GZ'	Jaguar T.2A	ex St Athan, 54, 16, 6, A&AEE, 226 OCU, 6, 54, 6, 54, 6, 54, 41, 54.	3-04
❑	XX832 'EZ'	Jaguar T.2A	ex 6, 16, 226 OCU, ETPS, 226 OCU.	3-04
❑	XX836 'ER'	Jaguar T.2A	ex 6, 17, 14, 226 OCU, 14. Spares.	3-04
❑	XX955 'GK'	Jaguar GR.1A	ex 54, 14, 17, 14.	3-04
❑	XZ378 'EP'	Jaguar GR.1A	ex 6, 41, 17, 41, 20.	3-04
❑	XZ942 '42'	Gazelle HT.2	ex 705, Fleetlands.	2-02
❑	ZD938 'AR'	Tornado F.2	ex St Athan, 229 OCU. Forward fuselage.	3-04

Others: By July 2003 a Scout was placed on display outside the Defence Helicopter Flying School building. Both the Scout and the displayed Wessex are believed to be privately owned. The Wessex is named *Aries*, shades of the famous Lancaster and Lincolns operated by the resident Central Navigation

School and the Empire Air Navigation School, 1943-1949 [1]. Having been replaced by the Wessex, former gate guardian Whirlwind HAR.10 XP351 moved to Charlwood, Surrey, on 15th October 2003. On 9th July 2003 the chopped up hulk of Wessex HAS.3 XM927 left by road, very likely for a local scrap merchant, perhaps at Wellington.

❑	XN549		Jet Provost T.3	'8235M' / 8225M, ex Halton, Shawbury, 1 FTS, CFS. Dump.		11-01
❑	XT672*	'WE'	Wessex HC.2	ex Hixon, Shawbury, 2 FTS, Benson SF, 72. *Aries*. Arrived 28-10-03.	[1]	3-04
❑	XV123*		Scout AH.1	ex Thruxton, Ipswich, Weston-super-Mare, Fleetlands. First noted 7-03. Displayed.		10-03

SLEAP AERODROME south-west of Wem

Wartime Aircraft Recovery Group Aviation Museum: As well as the airframes there are plenty of aero engines and artefacts recovered from 'digs' – including WAG's 'founder', 61 OTU Spitfire IIa P7304 involved in a mid-air collision near High Ercall on 22nd August 1943 and recovered in 1977. The Fury, Hunter and Typhoon are on loan from chairman Roger Marley. The Spitfire FSM with *original* instrumentation etc is on loan from Keith Jones.

◆ Open the second and fourth Sun in summer, also often open Sat afternoons. Please 'phone to check. Otherwise by prior arrangement. ☎ 01630 672969 www.wargroup.homestead.com

❑	'K7271'	Fury II REP	BAPC.148, ex Market Drayton, Cosford.		3-02
❑	'EN398' 'JE-J'	Spitfire IX FSM	ex Cannock.		3-02
❑	'GBH-7'	'Gunbus' REP	BAPC.234, ex High Halden, Hawkinge, Manston, Chelford, Coventry, Old Warden, White Waltham. Based on modified DH.2 frame.	℞	3-02
❑	–	Typhoon	ex Market Drayton. Cockpit.	off-site	3-02

Aerodrome:

| ❑ | G-BLLO | Super Cub 95 | ex D-EAUB, Belg AF OL-L25, 53-4699. CoA 12-10-96. Fuselage. | 8-03 |
| ❑ | G-BLWW* | Aerocar Mini-Imp | CoA 4-6-87. Stored. First noted 8-03. | 8-03 |

TILSTOCK AERODROME on the A41 south of Whitchurch

The para-trainer may well have moved on.

| ❑ | G-ASNN | Cessna 182F | ex N3612U. Crashed 5-1-85. Para-trainer. | 1-98 |

SOMERSET

AXBRIDGE on the A38 west of Cheddar

An anonymous Robin HR.100 is the fifth to be built, it is reported to have been the personal aircraft of Pierre Robin - that should tie an identity down!

| ❑ | – | HR.100-200B | ex Keynsham. Dismantled, spares. | 12-00 |

BATH

No.93 Squadron Air Cadets: By January 2003 Wessex HU.5 XS486 had appeared at Colerne, Wilts. It is possible that it had made the move in late 2000/early 2001.

BRISTOL AIRPORT or Lulsgate, on the A38 south-west of Bristol

In the fire pits is a convincing helicopter mock-up and a pseudo-Boeing 767. Brunel Technical College airframes are marked I – see also Bristol, Glos (!).

| ❑ | G-ANAP | Dove 6 | ex CAFU Stansted. CoA 6-9-73. Dump. | 2-02 |

❏ G-AVFM	Trident 2E	ex BA and BEA. CoA 2-6-84. Orange/yellow c/s.	I 12-03
❏ G-AVPK	Rallye Comm	CoA 10-1-92. Stored.	11-03
❏ G-BAUI	Aztec 250D	ex LN-RTS. CoA 15-12-88.	I 2-00
❏ G-BFRL	Cessna F.152 II	Crashed 24-8-92. Stored.	2-00
❏ G-BIUO	Commander 112A	ex Staverton, OY-PRH, N1281J. Cr 12-5-84.	12-03
❏ G-NERI	Archer II	ex G-BMKO, N31880. Wreck.	2-00
❏ WF410	'F' Varsity T.1	ex 6 FTS, 2 ANS, 5 FTS, 2 ANS, RAFC, CNCS, 201 AFS. Dump	1-04

Paintball Adventure West: On the edge of the airport. Still have their Wessex. S-55C S-882 did *not* come here. It went to a completely different battleground, at Portishead, Somerset.

| ❏ G-AWOX | Wessex 60 | ex Weston-super-Mare, Bournemouth, Weston, G-17-2, G-AWOX, 5N-AJO, G-AWOX, 9Y-TFB, G-AWOX, VH-BHE, G-AWOX, VR-BCV, G-AWOX, G-17-1. CoA 13-1-83. | 2-04 |

BURNHAM ON SEA south of Weston-super-Mare, on the B3140

There are always 'discoveries' to be made! Turn to *W&R9* (p38) which records the scrapping of Britannia 307F 5Y-AYR. The cockpit was known to have survived beyond this date at a nearby site. It was acquired by a private owner in this general area and has been resident since 1997!

| ❏ 5Y-AYR* | Britannia 307F | ex Bournemouth, African Cargo, G-ANCD, Gemini, Lloyd, BUA, Air Charter, 4X-AGE El Al, N6595C ntu, G-ANCD, G-18-3. | 2-04 |

CLEVEDON west of Junction 20, M5

A former Kennet Aviation Provost is under restoration in the area.

| ❏ WW453 | Provost T.1 | G-TMKI, ex Cranfield, Thatcham, Strathallan, Perth, Hunting, 1 FTS, 2 FTS. | ® 8-03 |

HENSTRIDGE AERODROME south of the A30, east of Henstridge Marsh

❏ G-ALYG	Auster 5D	ex Charlton Mackrell, Heathrow, Irby-on-Humber, MS968, 661, 653. CoA 19-1-70. Frame. Stored.	9-02
❏ G-ANEW	Tiger Moth	ex NM138, Oxf UAS, 8 RFS, 29 EFTS. CoA 18-6-62.	3-02
❏ G-ARJD	Colt 108	crashed 17-11-71. Frame. Stored.	4-97
❏ G-AWYX	Rallye Club	ex Compton Abbas. CoA 27-6-86. Stored.	8-97
❏ NC2612	Stinson Junior R	stored, dismantled.	9-02

KEW STOKE north of Weston-super-Mare
Mark Templeman:

| ❏ — | Hunter F.4 | ex Portishead, Boscombe Down, Salisbury, Cove, Farnborough. Nose. Red c/s. | 12-01 |

MARKSBURY on the A39 west of Bath
Hamburger Hill: The paintball wargaming park still has its S-55.

| ❏ S-887 | S-55C | ex Weston-super-Mare, Panshanger, Elstree, RDanAF | 2-04 |

POOLE on minor road north of Wellington
Military Aircraft Spares Ltd (MASL): Located in the Poole Industrial Estate. MASL very probably have another yard nearby (in Wellington itself?) in which it is believed spares reclamation takes place. Of the Gazelle AH.1s mentioned in *W&R18* (p190) XW893, XX388, XX413 and XX418 have 'appeared' at Lambourne, Berks, while ZA730 was noted at Ipswich, Suffolk, by October 2002. Hunter XG164 has the starboard wing of T.7 XL623. The port wing is at Beck Row, Suffolk. The fuselage – with *altogether different wings* – at Woking, Surrey!

❑ XG164   Hunter F.6   ex Shawbury, Halton 8681M, Kemble, West Raynham
SF, 74, 111. Composite.   9-03

PORTISHEAD west of the M5, Junction 19
1st Twilight Zone: A paintball battleground here for sweaty mid-management, took delivery of a S-55C in during early 2002. (This airframe was previously listed under 'Bristol', incorrectly.
❑ [S-882]   S-55C   ex Weston-super-Mare, Panshanger, Elstree,
Dan AF Esk.722. First noted 2-02.   2-04

ROOKS BRIDGE on the A38 south of Weston-super-Mare
Derelict at a location is this area is a long-forgotten modified Piper Pacer.
❑ G-BHMO*   PA-20M Pacer   ex Little Gransden, F-BDRO. Cr 20-8-89. Stored.   3-03

WESTON-SUPER-MARE AERODROME on the A371 east of Weston-super-Mare
The Helicopter Museum (THM): The museum has applied for Heritage Lottery Fund monies for its new venture, a Learning and Discovery Centre which will also house THM's extensive archives. In a separate venture, a new restoration facility is planned, along with the refurbishing of the original 1930s Weston Airfield control tower block on land adjacent to the existing museum site.
     Notes: The identity of Bö 105D G-PASA is confirmed. It was rebuilt in 1993, discarding the original pod (and much else) going on to become G-BUXS which is currently operational in Scotland [1]. The Frelon started life as SA.321 c/n 116. It is in Olympic Airways colours and the scheme it wore at the 1969 Paris Salon [2]. Airframes on loan from Elfan ap Rees are marked EAR. Widgeon G-AOZE and Belvedere XG452 are now owned by the museum [3]. For Fairey Ultra-Light G-AOUJ see Innsworth, Glos. In 'the pipeline' awaiting funding or sponsorship to cover transport costs are the following a Kaman HH-43F Huskie 62-4552 ex Pakistan Air Force and a Sikorsky CH-37C 145872 (N7393) ex US Marines. Airframes marked ➡ attended the '100 Years of Flight Experience' static display at the Fairford, Glos, July 2003. The following were listed under the main collection, but are now to be found in the 'Reserve Collection' below: Grasshopper 1 G-ARVN; Cranfield Vertigo BAPC.213.
◆   All year Wed to Sun 10am to 5pm (4.30pm Nov to Mar). Also Bank Hols, Easter fortnight and every day mid-Jul to end of Aug. 'Open Cockpit' days are held every second Sunday, Mar to Oct and the annual 'HeliDays' fly-in is held on the Weston Sea Front on the last weekend of July. Also regular 'Helicopter Experience Flight' days. SAE brings leaflet. THM run an excellent gift shop, and the 'Choppers' cafeteria. There is also a **Friends of the Helicopter Museum** – which produces their own quarterly bulletin - SAE for information. ✉ The Heliport, Locking Moor Road, Weston-super-Mare, BS24 8PP ☏ 01934 635227 **fax** 01934 645230 **e-mail** office@helimuseumfsnet.co.uk **www**.helicoptermuseum.co.uk

❑ [G-ACWM]	Cierva C.30A	ex Staverton, Tewkesbury, AP506, 529, 1448 Flt,		
		74 Wing, 5 RSS, G-ACWM. Frame.	EAR	3-04
❑ G-ALSX	Sycamore 3	ex Duxford, Staverton, G-48/1, G-ALSX,		
		VR-TBS ntu, G-ALSX. CoA 24-9-65.	EAR	3-04
❑ [G-ANFH]	Whirlwind Srs 1	ex Redhill, Gt Yarmouth, Bristow, BEAH.		
		CoA 17-7-71.	EAR	3-04
❑ G-AODA	Whirlwind Srs 3	ex Redhill, Bristow, 9Y-TDA, EP-HAC, G-AODA.		
		Dorado. CoA 23-8-91.		3-04
❑ G-AOZE	Widgeon 2	ex Cuckfield, Shoreham, 5N-ABW, G-AOZE.		
		Rolled-out 19-8-03.	➡ [3]	3-04
❑ G-ASTP	Hiller UH-12C	ex Biggin Hill, Thornicombe, 'Wales', Thornicombe,		
		Redhill, N9750C. CoA 3-7-82.		3-04
❑ G-ATFG*	Brantly B.2B	ex East Fortune, Newport Pagnell. CoA 25-3-85.		
		Arrived 21-1-04.	EAR	3-04
❑ G-AVKE	Gadfly HDW-1	ex Southend, Thruxton. Stored.	EAR	3-04
❑ G-AVNE and G-17-3	Wessex 60 Srs 1	ex Bournemouth, Weston-super-Mare, G-17-3, 5N-AJL, G-AVNE, 9M-ASS, VH-BHC, PK-HBQ, G-AVNE. CoA 7-2-83.		3-04
❑ G-AWRP	Grasshopper III	ex Blackpool, Heysham, Shoreham, Redhill.		
		CoA 12-5-72.		3-04

❏	G-BAPS		Campbell Cougar	ex Weston-super-Mare. CoA 20-5-74.		3-04
❏	G-BGHF		WG.30-100	ex Yeovil, Westlands. CoA 1-8-86.		3-04
❏	G-BKGD		WG.30-100	ex Yeovil, Penzance, G-BKBJ ntu. CoA 6-7-93.		3-04
❏	G-EHIL		EH-101 PP3	ex Yeovil, ZH647.		3-04
❏	G-ELEC		WG.30-200	ex Westland W-s-M, Yeovil, G-BKNV. CoA 28-6-85.		
				'Rescue' and 'Helicopter Museum' titles.		3-04
❏	G-HAUL		WG.30-TT300	ex G-17-22, Yeovil. CoA 27-10-86.		3-04
❏	G-LYNX		Lynx 800	ZB500 ex Yeovil, ZA500 ntu, G-LYNX.	➠	3-04
❏	G-OAPR		Brantly B.2B	⤳ ex G-BPST ntu, N2280U.	EAR	3-04
❏	G-OTED		Robinson R-22	⤳ ex Elstree, G-BMYR, ZS-HLG.		3-04
❏	G-PASA		MBB Bö 105D	ex Devon and Cornwall Police, G-BGWP, F-ODMZ,		
				G-BGWP, HB-XFD, N153BB and D-HDAS. Pod	[1]	3-04
❏	G-PASB		MBB Bö 105D	ex Bourn, VH-LSA, G-BDMC, D-HDEC.		3-04
❏	[D-HMQV]		Bö 102 Helitrainer	ground trainer. (c/n 6216)	EAR	3-04
❏	DDR-SPY		Ka-26 *Hoodlum*	ex D-HOAY, Germany, Interflug DDR-SPY.	®	3-04
❏	'F-OCMF'		SA.321F Frelon	ex Aérospatiale, Olympic, F-BTRP, F-WKQC,		
		'335'		F-OCZV, F-RAFR, F-OCMF, F-BMHC,		
				F-WMHC. Olympic c/s, *Hermes*.	[2]	3-04
❏	F-WQAP*		SA.365N Dauphin	ex Eurocopter, Marignane, F-WZJJ.		
				Handed over 19-3-03.		3-04
❏	OO-SHW		Bell 47H-1	ex Thruxton, G-AZYB, LN-OQG, SE-HBE,		
				OO-SHW. Crashed 21-4-84.	EAR	3-04
❏	SP-SAY		Mil Mi-2	ex PZL-Swidnik, Hiscso, ZEUS, PZL.		3-04
❏	N114WG		WG.30-160	ex Yeovil, Westland Inc, G-EFIS, G-17-8. Boomless.		3-04
❏	WG719		Dragonfly HR.5	G-BRMA, ex 'WG718', Shawbury, Weston,		
				Yeovilton, Yeovilton SF, 705.	EAR	3-04
❏	XD163	'X'	Whirlwind	ex Wroughton, 8645M, CFS, Akrotiri SAR Flt,		
			HAR.10	MoA, 228, 275, 155, MoA.	EAR	3-04
❏	—	XE521	Rotodyne Y	ex Cranfield, White Waltham. Large sections.	EAR	3-04
❏	XG452		Belvedere HC.1	G-BRMB, ex Ternhill, 2 SoTT 7997M, Westlands.		
					® [3]	3-04
❏	XG462		Belvedere HC.1	ex Henlow, Weston-super-Mare, 72, 66.		
				Crashed 5-10-63. Nose.		3-04
❏	XG547	'S-T'	Sycamore HR.14	G-HAPR, ex St Athan 8010M, Kemble, CFS.	➠ EAR	3-04
❏	XK940		Whirlwind	G-AYXT, ex Tibenham, Redhill, Northampton,		
		'911'	HAS.7	Heysham, Carnforth, Panshanger, Elstree, Luton,		
				Blackpool, Fleetlands, 771, Culdrose SF, 705,		
				825, 824, 845. CoA 4-2-99.		3-04
❏	XL811		Skeeter AOP.12	ex Stoke-on-Trent, Warmingham, Southend,		
				9/12 Lancers, 17F, 652, 651.	EAR	3-04
❏	XM328*	'650'	Wessex HAS.3	ex Culdrose, A2644 [2], A2727, Wroughton, 737.		
				The Sow. Arrived 3-04.		3-04
❏	XM330		Wessex HAS.1	ex Farnborough, RAE.		3-04
❏	XP165		Scout AH.1	ex Yeovilton, Weston, HAM Southend, RAE.		3-04
❏	XR486		Whirlwind	G-RWWW, ex Redhill, Tattershall Thorpe, 32, QF,		
			HCC.12	32, QF. CoA 25-8-96.	➠ EAR	3-04
❏	XT190		Sioux AH.1	ex Wattisham, Soest, Middle Wallop, UNFICYP.		3-04
❏	XT443	'422'	Wasp HAS.1	ex Oldmixon, Sherborne, *Aurora* Flt.		3-04
❏	[XT472]	'XC'	Wessex HU.5	ex Hullavington, Netheravon, Wroughton, 845.		3-04
❏	XV733		Wessex HCC.4	ex Shawbury, Queen's Flight.		3-04
❏	XW839		Lynx 00-05	ex Yeovilton, A2624 [2], A2657, A2710,		
				Manadon, BS Engines.		3-04
❏	XX910		Lynx HAS.2	ex DERA/RAE Farnborough, Aberporth, A&AEE.		
				Boomless.		3-04
❏	ZE477		Lynx 3	ex G-17-24, Yeovil, Westlands.		3-04
❏	622		HUP-3 Retriever	ex N6699D, RCN, 51-16622.		3-04
❏	09147		Mil Mi-4 *Hound*	ex Prague, Sechov, Tabor, Czech AF.		3-04
❏	[S-886]		S-55C	ex Panshanger, Elstree, Dan AF Esk.722.	EAR	3-04
❏	FR-108	'CDL'	Djinn	ex France, ALAT F-MCDL.		3-04
❏	96+26		Mi-24 *Hind-D*	ex Basepohl, Luftwaffe, E German 421.		3-04
❏	1005	'05'	WSK SM-2	ex Poland.		3-04

❏ 2007	Mil Mi-1 (SM-1)	ex Poland. Soviet colours.	3-04
❏ 16506	OH-6A Cayuse	ex US Army. (FY67)	3-04
❏ [66-16579]	UH-1H-BF	ex US Army.	3-04
❏ –	Lynx 3 EMU	ex Yeovil. Built 1984 using Lynx and WG.30 parts.	3-04
❏ –*	Husband Gyro	ex Sheffiled. Built 2003. Arrived 3-04.	3-04
❏ – BAPC.10	Hafner R-II	ex Middle Wallop, Locking, Weston-super-M, Old Warden, Yeovil.	3-04
❏ – BAPC.60	Murray Helicopter	ex Wigan, Salford.	3-04
❏ – BAPC.128	Watkinson CG-4	ex Horley, Bexhill. Man powered rotorcraft.	3-04
❏ – BAPC.153	WG.33 EMU	ex Yeovil. Ultra-light helicopter. Restored 2001.	3-04
❏ – BAPC.264	Bensen B.8M	ex Westbury-on-Trym. Built 1984. Unflown.	3-04
❏ –* BAPC.289	Gyro-Boat	ex Brooklands. Arrived 11-10-03.	3-04

THM 'Reserve Collection': Airframes in deep store, used for spares or held for potential exchange are not generally available for public inspection, and their listing above might well frustrate the visitor. (Depending on staffing levels, THM are happy to show visitors these airframes, with prior application.) Wessex HAS.3 XS149 is fitted with the rear fuselage of Srs 60 G-17-6 [1]. Belvedere HC.1 nose XG462 is now within the main museum - see above. Sioux AH.1 XT148 moved to Sunderland, N&T.

❏ XT148*	Sioux AH.1	ex Weston-super-Mare, Halton, Panshanger, Wroughton, ARWF.		3-04
❏ [G-ANJV]	Whirlwind Srs 3	ex Redhill, Bristow and VR-BET.		3-04
❏ G-ARVN	Grasshopper 1	ex Shoreham, Redhill. CoA 18-5-63. Dismantled.		3-04
❏ G-ASCT	Bensen B.8M	ex Hungerford. CoA 11-11-66.		3-04
❏ G-ASHD	Brantly B.2A	ex Oxford and area. Crashed 19-2-67. Spares.		3-04
❏ G-ATBZ	Wessex 60 Srs 1	ex Bournemouth, G-17-4, Weston. CoA 15-12-81.		3-04
❏ G-AXFM	Grasshopper III	ex Blackpool, Heysham, Shoreham, Redhill. Rig.		3-04
❏ G-AZAU	Grasshopper III	ex Blackpool, Heysham, Shoreham, Redhill. Rig.		3-04
❏ N112WG	WG.30-100	ex Yeovil, Midway.		3-04
❏ [N118WG]	WG.30-160	ex Yeovil, PanAm.		3-04
❏ [N5820T]	WG.30-100	ex Yeovil, Air Spur, G-BKFD.		3-04
❏ [N5840T]	WG.30-100	ex Yeovil, Air Spur, G-BKFF.		3-04
❏ [VR-BEU]	Whirlwind Srs 3	ex Redhill, VR-BEU, G-ATKV, EP-HAN, G-ATKV.		3-04
❏ VZ962	Dragonfly HR.1	ex Helston, BRNC Dartmouth.		3-04
❏ [XA862]	Whirlwind HAS.1	ex Coventry, Wroughton, Lee-on-Solent A2542, Seafield Park, Haslar, Lee-on-Solent, Fleetlands, 781, 771, 700, *Protector* Flt, 700, *Protector* Flt, 705, G-AMJT ntu.		3-04
❏ [XG596] '66'	Whirlwind HAS.7	ex Wroughton, A2651, 705, 829, 771, 705, 737. Returned from off-site 8-99.	EAR	3-04
❏ [XP404]	Whirlwind HAR.10	ex Finningley, Benson 8682M, 22, SAR Wing, 202, 228. Boomless.		3-04
❏ XR526	Wessex HC.2	ex Yeovil, Sherborne, Farnborough, Odiham 8147M, 72. Damaged 27-5-70. Hydraulics rig.		3-04
❏ XS149 '61'	Wessex HAS.3	ex Templecombe, Wroughton, 737.	[1]	3-04
❏	WG.30-300 EMU	ex Yeovil. Transmission rig, using parts from c/n 022.		3-04
❏ [S-881]	S-55C	ex Panshanger, Elstree, Dan AF Esk.722. Spares.		3-04
❏ – BAPC.212	Bensen B.6	gyroglider.		3-04
❏ – BAPC.213	Cranfield Vertigo	ex Yeovil, Cardington, Yeovil. Man-powered helo.		3-04

WESTON ZOYLAND AERODROME on the A372 east of Bridgwater

❏ G-MNSN	Pegasus Flash 2	CoA 19-4-97. Stored.	5-98
❏ G-MVMA	Pegasus XL-Q	CoA 28-2-98. Damaged. Stored.	5-98

YEOVIL AIRFIELD to the west of Yeovil

AgustaWestland: The apprentices restored Lynx XX153 - see Middle Wallop, Hants, for details.

❏ XX907*	Lynx AH.1	ex Farnborough, RAE, Rolls-Royce G-1-1. Arrived by 3-03. Dump.	2-04

❑	XZ181	Lynx AH.7	ex Arborfield, Fleetlands, 656, 663, 653, 654. Spares.	10-99
❑	XZ671	Lynx AH.7	ex Fleetlands, Yeovil, Wroughton, 652. Crashed 24-1-85.	
			With boom of ZE377. Systems trials.	10-99
❑	–	'961' EH.101 EMU	static test airframe. Stored.	3-02

Yeovil Technical College:

| ❑ | [XP886] | Scout AH.1 | ex Arborfield, Wroughton, 652, 660, 651. | 2-04 |
| ❑ | 'XV137' | Scout AH.1 | XV139, ex Arborfield, Wroughton, 657, 656, 662, 653. | 2-04 |

YEOVILTON AIRFIELD on the B5131, south of the A303, north of Yeovil
Fleet Air Arm Museum (FAAM): On 9th December 2002 the newly revamped 'Carrier' exhibition and the new 'Projecting Power' display were officially opened. During the revamp of 'Carrier', one of the aircraft on the 'deck' needed to be removed and this fell to Sea Venom FAW.22 WW138 which moved to Cobham Hall on 30th July 2002. Aircraft on view inside the 'Leading Edge' exhibition are marked ➤. The exceptional Cobham Hall storage facility is listed separately, below.
   Notes: Several aircraft are on loan and are marked as follows ±. These are: Concorde, Sea Vampire LZ551 and Ohka from the Science Museum; the Short 184 from the Imperial War Museum; the Bristol Scout D REP from Sir George White. Its 'serial' number is actually its US civil registration [1]. Sopwith Baby 'N2078' is a composite, using parts from the sequential 8214 and 8215. Both of these machines, ordered in 1915, were passed on to the Italian government to act as pattern aircraft in July 1916, for production by Macchi. This would go a long way to explaining the Italian tricolour on the rudder of the components acquired by R G J Nash [2]. The long-term restoration of Barracuda II DP872 will use the substantial wreckage of Mk.II LS931 from its crash site on the Scottish Isle of Jura [3]. Visitors to the incredible 'Carrier' exhibition travel to the flight deck 'on board' Wessex XT769 and disembark from XT482 [4]!
   FAAM aircraft can be found at the following: Coventry, Warks, Gannet XA508; East Fortune, Scotland, F-4S 155848; Mickleover, Derby, MB.339 0767; Montrose, Scotland, Sea Hawk XE340; Sunderland, Tyneside, Pucará A-522; Weston-super-Mare, Som, Dragonfly VZ962; Woodley, Berks, Gannet XG883. And, a little further away, Scimitar F.1 XD220 on the USS *Intrepid* in New York! Whirlwind HAR.3 XG574 moved over to Cobham Hall on 25th July 2002 and was followed by P.531 XN332 on 1st August 2002.
◆ Open every day (other than Xmas) Apr to Oct 10am to 5.30pm and Nov to Mar 10am to 4.30pm. There is a very active **Friends of the FAAM**. Membership enquiries via the museum.
✉ RNAS Yeovilton, Ilchester, BA22 8HT ☎ 01935 840565 **fax** 01935 842630 **e-mail** info@fleetairarm.co **www**.fleetairarm.com

❑	G-BSST	Concorde 002	UK prototype, ff 9-4-69. CoA 30-10-74.	± ➤	3-04
❑	8359	Short 184	ex Duxford, South Lambeth, Buncrana, Rosyth,		
			Dundee, Killingholme. Forward fuselage.	±	3-04
❑	'B6401'	Camel REP	G-AWYY, ex 'C1701', N1917H, G-AWYY.		
			CoA 1-9-85.		3-04
❑	L2301	Walrus I	ex Arbroath, Thame, G-AIZG, EI-ACC,		
			IAAC N18, Supermarine N18, L2301.		3-04
❑	L2940	Skua I	ex Lake Grotli, Norway, 800. Crashed 27-4-40.		3-04
❑	N1854	Fulmar II	ex Lossie', Fairey G-AIBE, A&AEE. CoA 6-7-59.		3-04
❑	'N2078'	Sopwith Baby	ex Fleetlands, Heathrow, Nash. *The Jabberwock.*	[2]	3-04
❑	'N4389' '4M'	Albacore	N4172, ex Land's End, Yeovilton.		3-04
❑	N5419	Bristol Scout REP	ex Kemble, Banwell, Cardington, USA.	± [1]	3-04
❑	'N5492'	Sopwith Triplane REP	BAPC.111, ex Chertsey. *Black Maria.*		
			10 (Naval) Sqn, 'B' Flight colours.		3-04
❑	'N6452'	Pup REP	G-BIAU, ex Whitehall. CoA 13-9-89.		3-04
❑	'P4139'	Swordfish II	HS618, ex 'W5984', Manadon A2001, Donibristle.		3-04
❑	'S1287'	Flycatcher REP	G-BEYB, ex Andover, Middle Wallop, Duxford,		
			Middle Wallop, Yeovilton. 405 Flt colours.		3-04
❑	Z2033 '275'	Firefly TT.1	G-ASTL, ex Duxford, Staverton, G-ASTL, SE-BRD,		
			Z2033, 731. 1771 Sqn c/s, *Evelyn Tentions.*		3-04
❑	AL246	Martlet I	ex Loughborough, 768, 802.		3-04
❑	DP872	Barracuda II	ex Andover area, Yeovilton, Enagh Lough, 769.		
			Cr 18-1-44. Forward fuselage. Remainder stored.	[3]	3-04

❏	EX976		Harvard IIA	ex Portuguese AF 1657, EX976, 41-33959.		3-04
❏	KD431	'E2-M'	Corsair IV	ex Cranfield, 768, 1835, BuNo 14862. 768 Sqn c/s.	®	3-04
❏	KE209		Hellcat II	ex Lossie, Stretton, Anthorn, BuNo 79779.		3-04
❏	LZ551/G		Sea Vampire I	ex CS(A), DH, A&AEE, RAE.	±	3-04
❏	SX137		Seafire F.17	ex Culdrose, 'W9132', Stretton, 759, 1831, Culham.		3-04
❏	VH127	'200'	Firefly TT.4	ex Wroughton, Y'ton, Culdrose, FRU, 700, 737, 812.		3-04
❏	VR137		Wyvern TF.1	ex Cranfield. Eagle-powered proto, not flown.	➤	3-04
❏	WA473	'102'	Attacker F.1	ex Abbotsinch, 736, 702, 800.		3-04
❏	WG774		BAC 221	ex East Fortune, RAE Bedford, Filton.	➤	3-04
❏	WJ231	'115'	Sea Fury FB.11	ex Wroughton, Yeovilton 'WE726', Y'ton SF, FRU.		3-04
❏	WN493		Dragonfly HR.5	ex Culdrose, 705, 701, A&AEE.		3-04
❏	WV856		Sea Hawk FGA.6	ex RAE, 781, 806.		3-04
❏	XA127		Sea Vampire T.22	ex CIFE, 736. Pod.	➤	3-04
❏	XB446		Avenger ECM.6B	ex Culdrose SF, 831, 751, 820, USN 69502.		
				D-Day stripes and camouflage.		3-04
❏	XD317	'112'	Scimitar F.1	ex FRU, RAE, 800, 736, 807.		3-04
❏	XL503	'070'	Gannet AEW.3	ex RRE, 849 'D', 'A' Flts, A&AEE, 849 HQ Flt,		
				C(A), 849 'A' Flt.		3-04
❏	XL580	'723'	Hunter T.8M	ex FRADU, FOFT, 764.	➤	3-04
❏	XN957	'630'	Buccaneer S.1	ex 736, 809.		3-04
❏	XP142		Wessex HAS.3	ex Cobham, Wroughton, Yeovilton, 737. *Humphrey.*		3-04
❏	XP841		HP.115	ex Cosford, Colerne, RAE Bedford.	➤	3-04
❏	XP980		P.1127	A2700, ex Culdrose, Tarrant Rushton,		
				RAE Bedford, Cranwell, A&AEE.	➤	3-04
❏	XS590	'131'	Sea Vixen FAW.2	ex 899, 892.		3-04
❏	XT482	'ZM'	Wessex HU.5	A2656 [2], ex A2745, Lee-on-Solent, Wroughton, 848.	[4]	3-04
❏	XT596		Phantom FG.1	ex BAe Scampton, Holme-on-Spalding Moor,		
				RAE Thurleigh, Holme, Filton, Hucknall,		
				Patuxent River, Edwards. Dbr 11-10-74.		3-04
❏	XT769	'823'	Wessex HU.5	ex Lee-on-Solent, Wroughton, Culdrose,		
				771, 846, 848.	[4]	3-04
❏	XV333	'234'	Buccaneer S.2B	ex 208, 12, 15, 16, FAA, 237 OCU, 12. 801 Sqn c/s.		3-04
❏	XZ493	'001'	Sea Harrier	ex Dunsfold, Yeovilton, Lee-on-Solent, 899, 801.		
			FRS.1	Ditched 15-12-94.	➤	3-04
❏			Fairey IIIF	fuselage frame.	®	3-04
❏	'D.5397'		Albatros D.Va	G-BFXL, ex Leisure Sport, Land's End,		
			REP	Chertsey, D-EGKO. CoA 5-11-91.		3-04
❏	'102 /17'		Fokker Dr.I REP	BAPC.88, scale REP, based on a Lawrence Parasol.		3-04
❏	15-1585		Ohka 11	BAPC.58, ex Hayes, South Kensington.	±	3-04
❏	01420		MiG-15*bis*	G-BMZF, ex North Weald, Gamston, Retford,		
			/ Lim-2	Polish AF. North Korean colours.		3-04

Fleet Air Arm Museum Cobham Hall: Home of the FAAM's reserve collection, workshop, archive and much more. The first of a regular season of open days will be staged in May 2004 - a great initiative that other large museums could well follow!

Notes: The Sea Gladiator frame was handed over by the Jet Age Museum [1]. See under Gloucestershire Airport, Glos, for the background to this complex project. Dragonfly HR.1 VX595 is on loan from the RAF Museum [2]. The Jet Provost might seem an odd choice. It was donated by a former RN pilot who earned his wings on this very aircraft while with 1 FTS – where a large number of Navy pilots received their training [3]. One of the two Sea Harrier FA.2s delivered for storage is a Falklands veteran. As an FRS.1, XZ499 shot down A-4C Skyhawk C-204 on 8th June 1982 and completed 38 operational sorties [4]. Being well on the edge (if not beyond) of the museum's collecting policy, the Bensen and the Super Eagle hang-glider were offered for disposal in March 2004 [5].

◆ *Not* open to the public on a regular basis. A series of special open days will be staged - 2004 dates are: 29th May, 25th July and 17th September. Enquiries to the contact points above.

❏	'G-ABUL'	Tiger Moth	XL717, ex G-AOXG, T7291, 24 EFTS, 19 EFTS.		2-04
❏	G-AZAZ	Bensen B.8M	ex Wroughton, Houndstone, Yeovilton, Manadon.	[5]	2-04
❏	[G-BGWZ]	Super Eagle h/g	ex Wroughton, Houndstone, Yeovilton.	[5]	2-04
❏	'N5579'*	Sea Gladiator II	ex Dursley, Cardington, Norway. Frame.		
			Handed over 17-7-02.	[1]	2-04

❑	VV106	Supermarine 510	ex Wroughton, Lee-on-Solent, Cosford, St Athan, Colerne, Cardington, Halton 7175M.	2-04
❑	VX272	Hawker P.1052	ex Wroughton, Lee-on-Solent, Cosford, St Athan, Colerne, Cardington, Halton 7174M.	2-04
❑	VX595	Dragonfly HR.1	ex Portland, Gosport, Fleetlands, Henlow, Fleetlands. [2]	2-04
❑	WM292 '841'	Meteor TT.20	ex B'thorpe, Cardiff, Yeovilton, FRU, Kemble, 527.	2-04
❑	WP313 '568'	Sea Prince T.1	ex Wroughton, Kemble, 750, Sydenham SF, 750, Lossiemouth SF, 750.	2-04
❑	WS103	Meteor T.7	ex Wroughton, Crawley, Wroughton, Lee-on-Solent, FRU, Kemble, Yeovilton Standards Sqn, Anthorn.	2-04
❑	WT121 '415'	Skyraider AEW.1	WT983, ex Culdrose, 849, USN 124121.	2-04
❑	WV106 '427'	Skyraider AEW.1	ex Culdrose, Helston, Culdrose, 849, Donibristle, Abbotsinch, 124086. 849 Sqn c/s.	2-04
❑	WW138*'227'	Sea Ven FAW.22	ex 'Carrier', AWS, 831, 809. Suez stripes. Arrived 30-7-02.	11-02
❑	XA129	Sea Vampire T.22	ex Wroughton, Yeovilton, CIFE, 736.	2-04
❑	XA466 '777'	Gannet COD.4	ex Wroughton, Yeovilton, Lee-on-Solent, Lossie', 849.	2-04
❑	XA864	Whirlwind HAR.1	ex Wroughton, Yeovilton, RAE, A&AEE, RAE, CA, G-17-1.	2-04
❑	XB480 '537'	Hiller HT.1	ex Wroughton, Yeovilton, Manadon, A2577, 705.	2-04
❑	XG574*	Whirlwind '752' HAR.3	ex FAAM, Portland, Wroughton, Yeovilton, Wroughton, Lee-on-Solent, A2575, 771, 705, 701, *Bulwark* Flt, *Ark Royal* Flt. Arrived 25-7-02.	2-04
❑	XG594* '517'	Whirlwind HAS.7	ex East Fortune, Strathallan, Wroughton, 71, A&AEE, 705, 846, 737, 701, RAE Bedford, 700. Arrived 11-12-03.	2-04
❑	XJ481	Sea Vixen FAW.1	ex Fleetlands, Southampton, Ilkeston, Yeovilton, Portland, Yeovilton, Boscombe Down, LRWE.	2-04
❑	XK488	Buccaneer S.1	ex museum, BSE Filton and Blackburns.	2-04
❑	XL853	Whirlwind HAS.7	ex Portland, Fleetlands, Southampton, Middle Wallop, Lee-on-Solent, A2630, Wroughton, Y'ton SF, 824.	2-04
❑	XN332* '759'	SARO P.531	ex FAAM, Portland, Wroughton, Yeovilton, Wroughton, Yeovilton, Manadon, A2579, G-APNV. Arr 1-8-02.	2-04
❑	XN334	SARO P.531	ex Wroughton, Crawley, Weston-super-Mare, Yeovilton, Arbroath, Lee-on-Solent A2525.	2-04
❑	XN462 '17'	Jet Provost T.3A	ex Wroughton, Sharnford, Shawbury, 1 FTS, 2 FTS, CFS, 3 FTS, 7 FTS, 1 FTS. [3]	2-04
❑	XS508	Wessex HU.5	A2677 [2], ex A2766, Lee-on-Solent, Wroughton.	2-04
❑	XS527	Wasp HAS.1	ex Wroughton, *Endurance* Flt.	2-04
❑	XT176 'U'	Sioux AH.1	ex Wroughton, 3 CBAS.	2-04
❑	XT427 '606'	Wasp HAS.1	ex Helston, Yeovilton, Wroughton.	2-04
❑	XT778 '430'	Wasp HAS.1	A2642 [2], ex A2722, ex Portland, West Moors, Lee-on-Solent. *Achilles* Flt c/s.	2-04
❑	XW864* '54'	Gazelle HT.2	ex Shawbury, 705, Wroughton. Arrived 21-10-02.	2-04
❑	XZ499*	Sea Harrier '003' FA.2	ex St Athan, 801, 800, 801, 899, 800, 801, 800, 809, 801. Tail fin of ZA195. Arr 13-11-02. [4]	2-04
❑	ZA195*	Sea Harrier FA.2	ex St Athan, Warton, BAE, 899 BAe. Spares recovered, stripped out airframe. Arr 24-9-02.	2-04
❑	—	BAPC.149 Short S.27 REP	ex Lee-on-Solent. Dismantled.	2-04
❑		Sea Vixen CIM	ex Wroughton, Yeovilton. Cockpit.	2-04
❑	AE-422	UH-1H Iroquois	ex Wroughton, Yeovilton, Stanley, Arg Army, 74-22520.	2-04
❑	0729 '411'	T-34C-1 Turbo Mentor	ex Wroughton, Yeovilton, Stanley, Pebble Island, Arg Navy. Dismantled.	2-04
❑	100545	Fa 330A-1	ex Wroughton, Yeovilton, Higher Blagdon, Cranfield, Farnborough.	2-04

Royal Navy Historic Flight (RNHF) / **The Swordfish Trust**: The Firefly made its first post-restoration flight on 14th May 2002. While displaying at the 'Flying Legends' Airshow at Duxford, Cambs, on 12th July 2003, Fairey Firefly TT.5 WB271 crashed, killing pilot Lt Cdr Bill Murton and crewman Neil Rix. Five days later, the remains of the aircraft were moved to the accident investigation unit at Yeovilton. The hulk will not be rebuilt.

The Trust is a charitable concern designed to support RNHF – and, by definition, particularly the 'Stringbags'. Swordfish NF389 is at Brough, E Yorks, under restoration to flying condition.
◆ Not available for public inspection, but the aircraft are frequently at airshows. ✉ RNHF Support Group, RNAS Yeovilton, Ilchester, BA22 8HT ☎ 01935 456279 www.flynavyheritage.org/uk

❏	W5856	'A2A'	Swordfish II	✈	G-BMGC, ex Brough, Strathallan, Alabama, RCN, Wroughton, Manston. 810 Sqn c/s. *City of Leeds.*		11-03
❏	LS326	'L2'	Swordfish II	✈	ex Westlands, White Waltham, G-AJVH, Worthy Down, 836. 836 Sqn colours. *City of Liverpool.*	®	11-03
❏	VR930		Sea Fury FB.11 '110'		ex Brough, Yeovilton, Boscombe Down, Lee-on-Solent, Wroughton, Yeovilton, 8382M, Colerne, Dunsfold, FRU, Lossiemouth, Anthorn, 801, Anthorn, 802. Grounded 21-8-01. Stored.		11-03
❏	VZ345		Sea Fury T.20S		ex Brough, Yeovilton, Boscombe Down, DLB D-CATA, D-FATA, ES.8503, G-9-30, Hawker, Dunsfold, VZ345, 1832. Accident 19-4-85. Stored.		11-03
❏	WB657	'908'	Chipmunk T.10	✈	ex BRNC, Leeds UAS, 16 RFS, 25 RFS, Leeds UAS, 25 RFS. 'Hack'.		11-03
❏	WK608	'906'	Chipmunk T.10	✈	ex BRNC, Bri UAS, 7 FTS, 3 FTS, Edin UAS,11 RFS. 'Hack'.		11-03
❏	WV908	'188'	Sea Hawk FGA.6		ex Dunsfold, Yeovilton, Dunsfold, Yeovilton, Culdrose SF, Halton 8154M, Sydenham A2660, 738, 806, 898, 807.		11-03
❏	WV911	'115'	Sea Hawk FGA.6		ex Dunsfold, Lee-on-Solent A2622 [2], A2626, Fleetlands, Lee-on-Solent A2526. Stored.		11-03

Others: Airframes dealt with by the **Flight Safety and Accident Investigation Unit** (FSAIU) tend to be too transitory to merit inclusion. Two airframes are used by the **Engineering Training School** (ETS). The **Heron Gliding Club** (HGC) also operate from here. Gazelle XW890 (with the boom of AH.1 ZB668) is displayed outside the DHSA building [1]. The Sea Harrier orientation trainer was made by Ogle Design Ltd of Letchworth, Herts [2].

❏	WV903	'128'	Sea Hawk FGA.4	ex Dunsfold, Lee-on-Solent, Culdrose A2632, Halton 8153M, Sydenham. Dump.		11-03
❏	XE339	'149'	Sea Hawk FGA.6	ex Dunsfold, Lee-on-Solent, Culdrose A2635, Halton 8156M. Dump.		11-03
❏	XS513*		Wessex HU.5	A2681 [2], ex Gosport, A2770, Lee-on-Solent, 772. Arrived 3-2-04. Dump.		2-04
❏	XT653		Swallow TX.1	FUW/BGA.3545, ex Halesland, Syerston, CGS. Stored.	HGC	5-98
❏	[XV280]		Harrier GR.1	A2700 [2], ex Foulness, Boscombe Down, A&AEE, HSA. Nose, Sea Harrier style, trailer-mounted.		11-03
❏	XV755	'M'	Harrier GR.3	A2606 [3], ex A2604, 233 OCU, 3, 233 OCU, 3, 233 OCU, 1, 233 OCU, 1, 233 OCU. Dump.		11-03
❏	XW630		Harrier GR.3	A2671 [2], ex Gosport, A2759 Lee-on-Solent, 3, 4, 3, 20. FAA colours. Dump.		11-03
❏	XW890		Gazelle HT.2	ex Fleetlands, Wroughton, 705. Displayed.	[1]	11-03
❏	XZ129	'ETS'	Harrier GR.3	A2604 [3], ex A2602, Cranfield, 233 OCU, 1, 233 OCU, 1, 233 OCU.	ETS	9-03
❏	XZ455*		Sea Harrier FA.2	ex FSAIU, 801, 899, 800, 899, 801, 899, 700A Crashed 14-2-96. To dump 16-9-03.		9-03
❏	ZB601		Harrier T.4	ex Dunsfold, St Athan, ETS Yeovilton, 899, 233 OCU. BDRT.		11-03
❏	ZD578*		Sea Harrier FA.2	ex St Athan, 899, 801, 899, 801, 800, 899, 801, 800, 899. Gate, mounted 4-12-02. 800 Sqn colours (port). 801 (stb)		11-03
❏	ZD612*	'731'	Sea Harrier FA.2	ex St Athan, 899, 800, 899, 800, 801, 899.	ETS	9-03
❏	–*		Sea Harrier FA.2	EMU, cockpit, orientation trainer.	ETS [2]	9-02
❏	–	RG-05	Lynx static rig	ex Weston-super-Mare, Blackpool, Coventry, Ycovil. Fire training, poor state.		11-03

STAFFORDSHIRE

BURSLEM on the A50 north-west of Stoke-on-Trent
Supermarine Aero Engineering: Work is undertaken on SL611 on a time available basis, in between work on purpose-built components for Spitfire projects worldwide. Ken Fern's Tiger Moth project is also being worked on.
- ❏ G-OOSY*   Tiger Moth   ex Stoke-on-Trent, Eccleshall, F-BGFI, FAF, DE971.   ®   1-03
- ❏ SL611   Spitfire XVI   ex Scafell, 603, 111 OTU. Crashed 20-11-47.   6-01

BURTON-UPON-TRENT
No.351 Squadron Air Cadets: Located on the northern edge of the town, near a railway yard. Examination of the EE cockpit number plate in the wheel bay has revealed this to be XP743.
- ❏ XP743   Lightning F.3   ex Stafford, Pendine, Leconfield, 29, 56, 29, 56, Wattisham TFF, 56. Nose.   2-04

ECCLESHALL on the A5013 north-west of Stafford
Malcolm Goosey: Tiger Moth G-ANNN moved to Spanhoe Lodge, Northants, in March 2004.
- ❏ G-ASEF*   Auster 6A   ex Arncott, Somerton, Bicester, RAFGSA, VW985, 664. CoA 19-12-66. Arrived 12-03.   ®   2-04
- ❏ WK638*   Chipmunk T.10   G-BWJZ, ex Stamford, Manston, 9 AEF, RAFC, 9 AEF, York UAS, 1 FTS, 1 AEF, Ox UAS, 1 RFS. Crashed 22-8-99. Stored.   2-04

HEDNESFORD on the A460 northeast of Cannock
Martyn Jones: *Should* still have his 'JP' nose.
- ❏ XM417   'D' Jet Provost T.3   ex Fownhope, Halton 8054BM, Shawbury, 6 FTS, 7 FTS, 2 FTS. Nose.   8-94

HIXON west of the A51, east of Stafford
Air and Ground Aviation: Located on the former airfield, have tendered for a series of helicopters in recent times. Wessex HC.2 XT604 came through here en route to East Midlands Airport, Leics, qv. Wessex HC.2 XT672 was first noted here in August 2002, having been previously at Shawbury, Shropshire. It was air-lifted by an 18 Squadron Chinook HC.2 ZA679 on 28th October 2003 to its new home, err... err... Shawbury, Shropshire!
- ❏ XR507*   Wessex HC.2   ex Shawbury, 22, SARTU, 22, SARTU, 22, SARTS, 18. First noted 8-02.   8-02
- ❏ XR511*   'L' Wessex HC.2   ex St Athan, 72, 60, 72, 18. Arrived 8-1-04.   1-04
- ❏ XT463   'D' Wessex HU.5C   ex Predannack, Gosport A2624 [3], Shawbury, Akrotiri, 84, FAA. Tail of XR503.   12-00
- ❏ XV722* 'WH' Wessex HC.2   ex Shawbury, 2 FTS, CATCS, 18, 72, 18. F/n 8-02.   10-03

LICHFIELD north-west of Tamworth
No.1206 Squadron Air Cadets: Cherry Orchard, near the city railway station. 'Parent' is Stafford.
- ❏ WK576   Chipmunk T.10   8357M, ex AOTS, 3/4 CAACU, Cam UAS, Oxf UAS,
  PAX   Lon UAS, Cam UAS, Lon UAS, Cam UAS, Hull UAS, Cam UAS, Bir UAS, Cam UAS, 22 RFS.   11-03

Others: This reference is getting long in the tooth. It could well be on finals for LOST!
- ❏ G-AXCI   Bensen B.8M   ex Lutterworth, East Midlands. Stored.   9-93

LONGTON on the A50 south of Stoke-on-Trent
Motor Clinic: On the Trentham Road, have a 'JP'.
- ❏ XM425 '88' Jet Provost T.3A ex King's Lynn, Bruntingthorpe, Halton 8995M,
7 FTS, 1 FTS, RAFC, 3 FTS, CFS. 3-04

RUGELEY on the A51 east of Stafford
Two airframes are under restoration in the general area.
- ❏ WW444 'D' Provost T.1 ex Sibson, Coventry, Bitteswell, Shawbury,
CAW, 5 AEF, 6 FTS, 3 FTS, 22 FTS. ® 2-96
- ❏ XD515 Vampire T.11 ex Winthorpe, Misson, Linton-on-Ouse 7998M,
3 FTS, 7 FTS, 1 FTS, 5 FTS, 206 AFS. ® 3-04

STAFFORD (Beaconside, west of the city)
Royal Air Force Museum Reserve Collection: This 60,000ft^2 (5,574m^2) facility was taken over by the RAF Museum as long ago as March 1999. In an incredibly hectic five month period no less than 160 lorry loads brought over 100,000 items from Spitfire to tunic button to this huge store. The work of cataloguing and placing still goes on.
    Departures: Blériot XXVII 433 arrived from Cosford, Shrop, by September 2002. It moved to Hendon, Gtr Lon, 17th November 2003.
◆ Viewing is possible *only* via prior arrangement.

- ❏ G-AHED* Dragon Rapide ex Cosford, Wyton, Cardington, Henlow, RL962,
Witney. CoA 17-4-68. 2-04
- ❏ A301 Morane BB ex Wyton, Cardington, Hendon. Fuselage. 2-04
- ❏ Z7197 Proctor III ex Hendon 8380M, St Athan, Swinderby, Finningley,
G-AKZN, AST, 18 EFTS, 1 RS, 2 SS. CoA 29-11-63. 2-04
- ❏ DG590* Hawk Major ex Cosford, Wyton, Cardington, Middle Wallop,
Henlow, Ternhill, G-ADMW, Swanton Morley SF,
Wyton SF, G-ADMW. CoA 4-6-83. 2-04
- ❏ HS503* Swordfish IV ex Cosford, Wyton, Cardington, Cosford, Henlow,
    BAPC.108 Canada, RCAF, 754, 745. 2-04
- ❏ LA226* Spitfire F.21 ex Cosford, Wyton, Cardington, St Athan, Shawbury,
Abingdon, Biggin Hill, South Marston, London, South
Marston, Little Rissington, 7119M, 3 CAACU, 122. 2-04
- ❏ PK664* Spitfire F.22 ex Cosford, Wyton, Cardington, St Athan, Binbrook,
    'V6-B' Waterbeach, 7759M, 615. 2-04
- ❏ PM651* 'X' Spitfire PR.XIX ex Cosford, Wyton, Cardington, St Athan, Hendon,
Benson, Bicester, Andover, Hucknall, Leconfield,
Church Fenton, 7758M, C&RS, 3 CAACU, 604. 2-04
- ❏ RW393* Spitfire XVI ex Cosford, St Athan, Turnhouse 7293M, 602, 3
    'XT-A' CAACU, 31, FCCS, 203 AFS. 603 Sqn c/s. 2-04
- ❏ SL674* Spitfire XVI ex Cosford, Wyton, Cardington, St Athan, 8392M,
    'RAS-H' Biggin Hill, Little Rissington, 501, 17 OTU. 2-04
- ❏ VX275* Sedbergh TX.1 ex Cosford, Wyton, Cardington, St Athan, BGA.572,
8884M, 612 GS, 613 GS, 623 GS, 123 GS. 2-04
- ❏ – FE.2b ex Wyton, Cardington. Cockpit nacelle. 2-04
- ❏ 15195* PT-19A Cornell ex Cosford, Wyton, Cardington, Henlow, Canada 2-04
- ❏ J-1172* Vampire FB.6 ex Cosford, Wyton, Cardington, Manchester,
Cosford, 8487M, Colerne, Swiss AF. 2-04
- ❏ – BAPC.194 Demoiselle REP ex Wyton, Cardington, Brooklands, Henlow, Gatow. 2-04
- ❏ – BAPC.237 Fi 103 (V-1) ex Wyton, Cardington, St Athan. 2-04

Defence Storage and Distribution Centre (DSDC) / Tactical Supply Wing (TSW).
- ❏ XT469 Wessex HU.5 8920M, ex Wroughton. TSW 3-03
- ❏ XZ287 Nimrod AEW.3 9140M, ex Abingdon, Waddington, JTU,
Woodford. Fuselage. *Fly Suki Airways*. TSW 9-02
- ❏ XZ987 'C' Harrier GR.3 9185M, ex St Athan, 1417 Flt, 3, 4. Gate. 2-04

STOKE-ON-TRENT
The Potteries Museum and Art Gallery: The Spitfire is being restored – with visitors able to watch progress – by volunteers from local company Supermarine Aero Engineering.
◆ Open Mar to Oct Mon to Sat 10am to 5pm, Sun 2pm to 5pm; Nov to Feb Mon to Sat 10am to 4pm, Sun 1pm to 4pm. ✉ Bethesda Street, Hanley, Stoke ST1 3DE ☎ 01782 232323 **fax** 01782 232500 **e-mail** museums@stoke.gov.uk **www**.stoke.gov.uk/museums
❑ RW388   Spitfire XVI   ex Kemble, 'AB917', 71 MU 6946M, 19 MU, 5 MU,
     'U4-U'   Andover, Benson, FC&RS, 612, 667. 667 Sqn c/s.   ®   3-04

Ken Fern: As predicted in *W&R18* (p199) Ken moved to Derbyshire. Tiger Moth G-OOSY moved to Burslem, Staffs. The DH.88 project is not far away at Derby Aerodrome, Derbys, - qv. Ken also has a Harvard project at Bruntingthorpe, Leics - qv.

STONE on the A34 north of Stafford
Alan Simpson:
❑ XG629   Sea Venom   ex Long Marston, Fleetlands, Higher Blagdon,
     '668'   FAW.22   Culdrose, ADS, 831, 893.   3-04

Watson's: The scrapyard here still holds a Jet Provost nose and a cockpit-less Lightning fuselage.
❑ XN550*   Jet Provost T.3   ex Truro, Kemble, CFS. Cockpit.   10-03

TAMWORTH
Martyn Morgan: Martyn, a member of the Wolverhampton Aviation Group, acquired a Cadet TX.3 from AeroVenture's Bill Fern and it is kept in this general area.
◆ Visits by prior arrangement *only*, e-mail martyn.morgan67@btopenworld.com
❑ XE793*   Cadet TX.3   ex Doncaster, Ringmer, St Athan, 8666M.   3-04

TATENHILL AERODROME south of the B5234, west of Burton-on-Trent
❑ G-ARNN   GC-1B Swift   ex Leicester, VP-YMJ, VP-RDA, ZS-BMX,
                             NC3279K. Crashed 1-9-73.   ®   7-91
❑ G-AZHE   Slingsby T.61B   ex N61TB, G-AZHE. Damaged 17-6-88.   ®   7-91
❑ G-BUPJ   Fournier RF-4D ex N7752.   ®   6-95
❑ G-BUXM   Quickie TriQ   ex N4435Y. CoA 10-8-95. Stored.   7-98
❑ G-BXGE   Cessna 152 II   ex N89283. CoA 16-7-00. Fuselage, stored.   7-03

WESTON-ON-TRENT on the A51 north-east of Stafford
Chell Air: In Salt Works Lane. Jetstream T.1 XX483 cockpit moved to Welshpool, Wales.

WOLVERHAMPTON AERODROME, or Halfpenny Green, south of the B4176, east of Bridgnorth
(NB the word 'Business' has been dropped from the title.) Mandark Aviation, who specialise in resprays, have acquired a retired WAR Fw 190 to act as an attraction for their business [1].
❑ G-BSYK   Tomahawk 112   ex N23449. Stored. First noted 9-97.   10-01
❑ G-BSYL   Tomahawk 112   ex N91333. Stored.   8-03
❑ G-BUJN   Cessna 172N II ex Wellesbourne, N6315D. Damaged 18-1-95.   ®   8-00
❑ G-OBEY   Aztec 250C   ex G-BAAJ, SE-EIU. CoA 4-8-86.   12-97
❑ G-WULF*   WAR Fw 190   CoA 22-6-01.   [1] 8-03
❑ –   T.31   BGA.1346, ex Bidford, RAFGSA.297. Air Scouts.   2-00

SUFFOLK

BECCLES AERODROME south of the A146 west of Lowestoft

❑ G-ASMY*	Apache 160H	ex N4309Y. CoA 25-11-<u>95</u>. Stored.	9-03
❑ G-ATHZ*	Cessna 150F	ex EI-AOP ntu, N6286R. CoA 27-3-98. Stored.	6-03
❑ G-AVPH	Cessna F.150G	ex Blackpool, Woodvale. CoA 9-4-86.	3-00
❑ G-BAOP*	Cessna FRA.150L	crashed 22-6-01. Stored. First noted 6-03.	9-03

BECK ROW on the A1101 north of Mildenhall

The Hunter (with the starboard wing of XL572 and XL623 to port) is kept on a farm in the area. (See under Poole, Somerset, for the saga of XL623.)

❑ XG210	Hunter F.6	ex DRA Bedford, BAe Hatfield, CFE, 19, 14.	9-03

BENTWATERS AIRFIELD south of the A1152, north-east of Woodbridge

The former USAF airfield is now a development park, known as Bentwaters Park. Since May 2003, the Bentwaters Aviation Society started work to establish the **Bentwaters 'Cold War' Museum** centred, initially at least on the Wing Command Post. Work is at early stages and it is not yet open to the public.

BURY ST EDMUNDS on the A14 east of Newmarket

Nigel Hamlin-Wright: Has the Chrislea FC.1 Airguard for restoration. Only original components are being used, the reproduction elements having been discarded.

❑ G-AFIN	Chrislea Airguard	ex Wigan, Stoke-on-Trent, Warmingham, Wigan, Finningley.	®	1-00

FELIXSTOWE at the end of the A14, south-east of Ipswich

Glenn Cattermole: Restoration of the Buccaneer cockpit is well in hand.

❑ XT284	'<u>H</u>' Buccaneer S.2A	ex Stock, St Athan, Abingdon 8855M, St Athan, 237 OCU, 15, 208, 809, 803, 736. Nose.	®	3-04

FLIXTON on the B1062 west of Bungay

Norfolk and Suffolk Aviation Museum (N&SAM): A grant of £77,000 from the Heritage Lottery Fund was given early in 2003 for moving, conservation and re-erection of a Boulton & Paul-built hangar previously at the former Ipswich aerodrome. The hangar was donated by Ipswich Borough Council in 2000. Erection work started in the summer of 2003 and it is due to be opened in April 2004.

Notes: The Widgeon is on loan from Sloane Helicopters [1]. The Taylor Titch was donated by Peter Hoffman [2]. The Rooster and Pegasus were donated by the widow of the late John M Lee, who built the wings of the museum's Colditz Cock. The Lightwing Rooster 1 Srs 4 biplane is in unpowered form. [3] The Penrose Pegasus 2 is a reproduction of the original Harald Penrose example [4]. The Striker microlight was the last aircraft to fly from Flixton before the runways were broken up [5]. The EoN Primary is on loan from the Norfolk Gliding Club [6]. Canberra nose WE168 will be prepared as a 'hands-on' exhibit [7]. Canberra nose WG789 is on loan from Steve Pickup [8]. The extreme nose section of a Felixstowe flying-boat, once used as a potting shed, amounts to some 10ft, and while not fitting our criteria totally, does represent a singular survivor. Another section of Felixstowe, about 8ft long, is on hand from the RAF Museum [9].

Ian Hancock owns several of the airframes - IH. An interesting exhibit of Ian's in the main hangar is a Spitfire XVI fuselage centred around the original skin of TD248 acquired from Historic Flying (HF). The skin, coupled with an original frame No.19, and a fibreglass tail section has created a fuselage that will, ultimately, contain as many original fittings as possible. The fuselage is due to be painted in the colours of 695 Squadron as '8Q-T'. (See under Duxford, Cambs, for the airworthy TD248.) [10]

♦ Open Apr to Oct, Sun to Thu 10am to 5pm (last admission 4pm); Nov to Mar, Tue, Wed and Sun 10am to 4pm (last admission 3pm). Important note from N&SAM Secretary Huby Fairhead, the adjoining 'Flixton Buck' pub is now so popular – rightly so – that it is advisable to reserve lunch, get them on ☎ 01986 892382! ✉ The Street, Flixton, near Bungay, NR35 1NZ. ☎ 01986 896644 during opening hours e-mail nsam.flixton@virgin.net www.aviationmuseum.net

❏ G-ANLW*	Widgeon 2	ex Northampton, Blackpool, 'MD497', Wellingborough, Little Staughton, Tattershall Thorpe, *Eye of the Needle*, S'end. CoA 27-5-81. Arr 1-5-02.	[1]	2-04
❏ G-AZLM	Cessna F.172L	ex Badminton. Cr 23-3-91. Hulk.		2-04
❏ G-BABY*	JT.2 Titch	CoA 10-10-91. Arrived 28-7-03.	[2]	2-04
❏ G-BDVS	Friendship 200	ex Norwich, Air UK, S2-ABK, PH-FEX, PH-EXC, 9M-AMM, PH-EXC, PH-FEX. *Eric Gander Dower*. Nose, on loan.		2-04
❏ [G-BFIP]	Wallbro Mono REP	ex Shipdham, Swanton Morley. CoA 22-4-82.		2-04
❏ G-MJSU*	Tiger Cub	ex Swanton Morley. CoA 31-1-86. Arrived 8-8-02		2-04
❏ G-MJVI*	Rooster 1	ex Littlehampton. Canx 13-6-90. Arrived 24-2-04.	[3]	2-04
❏ G-MTFK	Flexiform Striker	On loan.	[5]	2-04
❏ – CDN	EoN Primary	BGA.1461, ex Tibenham area. CoA 5-69.	[6]	2-04
❏ –* DUD	Grunau Baby III	BGA.2384, ex Bristol area, BGA.2074, RAFGSA.374, D-9142. Arrived by 7-02.		2-04
❏ –* HKJ	Pegasus 2 REP	BGA.4002, ex Littlehampton. CoA 15-9-98. Arrived 24-2-02	[4]	2-04
❏ –* JTA	Colditz Cock REP	BGA.4757, ex Duxford. *Spirit of Colditz*.		2-04
❏ N16676*	Fairchild 24C8F	ex Tibenham, USA, NC16676. Arrived 18-3-03.	®	2-04
❏ 'P8140' 'ZP-K'	Spitfire FSM	BAPC.71, ex Chilham Castle, 'P9390' and 'N3317', *Battle of Britain. Nuflier*. 74 Sqn c/s.		2-04
❏ 'TD248''8Q-T'	Spitfire XVI	see above. 695 Sqn colours.	[10]	2-04
❏ VL349 'V7-Q'	Anson C.19	ex Norwich, N5054, G-AWSA, SCS, NCS, North Coates SF, WSF, FCCS, HCCS, HCEU, 116, CSE, 1 FU.		2-04
❏ VX580	Valetta C.2	ex Norwich, MCS, MEAFCS, 114, HS. Loan.		2-04
❏ WE168*	Canberra PR.3	ex Colchester, Manston 8049M, 231 OCU, 39, 69, 540. Nose, minus skin. Arrived -02. off-site	[7]	2-04
❏ WF128 '676'	Sea Prince T.1	ex Honington 8611M, Kemble, Sydenham SF, A&AEE, 750.		2-04
❏ WF643 'P'	Meteor F(TT).8	ex Coltishall, Kemble, 29, Nicosia SF, 611, 1, 56. 56 Squadron colours.		2-04
❏ WG789	Canberra B.2/6	ex Mendlesham, Wycombe, Kew, Burgess Hill, Bedford, 231 OCU. Nose.	[8]	2-04
❏ WH840	Canberra T.4	ex Seighford, Locking 8350M, St Athan, Geilenkirchen SF, A&AEE, 97, 151, 245, 88, 231 OCU, CFS.	IH	2-04
❏ WV605 'T-B'	Provost T.1	ex Henlow, Higher Blagdon, 6 FTS, 3 FTS, 22 FTS.		2-04
❏ XG254 'A'	Hunter FGA.9	8881M, ex Clacton, Coltishall, Weybourne, Coltishall, St Athan, 1 TWU, 2 TWU, TWU, 229 OCU, 54, HS, 54. 54 Sqn colours.	IH	2-04
❏ XG329	Lightning F.1	ex Swinderby, Cranwell 8050M, A&AEE, Warton.	IH	2-04
❏ XG518	Sycamore HR.14	ex Sunderland, Balloch, Halton 8009M, Wroughton, Khormaksar SF, El Adem SF, Habbiniya SF, CFS, Amman SF.	IH	2-04
❏ XG523 'K'	Sycamore HR.14	ex Sunderland, Hayes, Middle Wallop, Ternhill 7793M, CFS, JEHU. Damaged 25-9-62. Nose.	IH	2-04
❏ XH892 'J'	Javelin FAW.9R	ex Duxford, Colerne 7982M, Shawbury, 29, 64, 23.		2-04
❏ XJ482 '713'	Sea Vixen FAW.1	ex Wimborne Minster, A2598, 766, 700Y.		2-04
❏ XK624 '32'	Vampire T.11	ex Lytham St Annes, Blackpool, CFS, 3 FTS, 7 FTS, 1 FTS, 23 GCF, CFS, 7 FTS.		2-04
❏ XM279	Canberra B(I).8	ex Firbeck, Nostell Priory, Cambridge, 16, 3. Nose.	IH	2-04
❏ XN304 'W'	Whirlwind HAS.7	ex Bedford, Henlow, Wroughton, Shrivenham, Wroughton, 705, Old Sarum, 848. 848 Sqn c/s.		2-04
❏ XR485 'Q'	W'wind HAR.10	ex Wroughton, 2 FTS, CFS.		2-04
❏ A-528	FMA Pucará	ex Sunderland, Middle Wallop, Cosford, Abingdon 8769M, Stanley, Argentine AF, 9th AB, 3rd AB.		2-04
❏ 79 '2-EG'	Mystère IVA	ex Sculthorpe, FAF, ET.2/8, 314 GE, EC.1/5.		2-04
❏ '694' B'.239	Fokker D.VIII	ex Lowestoft. 5/8th scale reproduction.		2-04
❏ 42196	F-100D-11-NA	ex Sculthorpe, French AF. EC.4/11, EC.2/11, USAF 48th FBW, 45th FS. 'Skyblazers' colours.		2-04

❏	54433	T-33A-5-LO	ex Sculthorpe, French AF, 328 CIFAS, 338		
		'TR-433'	CEVSV, USAF 803rd ABG. 20th FBG c/s.		2-04
❏	146289	T-28C Trojan	ex East Ham, France, N99153, Zaire AF FG-289,		
			Congolese FA-289, USN VT-3, VT-5, NABTC		
			146289. Crashed 14-12-77. Fuselage.		2-04
❏	–	Felixstowe F.5	ex Felixstowe. Nose section.	[9]	2-04
❏	–*	Wasp Falcon 4	hang-glider. First noted 4-03.		2-04
❏	–*	Antonov C.14	hang-glider. First noted 4-03.		2-04
❏	–	'LHS-1' Bensen B.7	BAPC.147, ex Loddon, Marham, Coltishall.		2-04
❏	–	BAPC.115 HM.14 'Flea'	ex Earls Colne, Andrewsfield, Balham, South Wales.	IH	V

FRAMLINGHAM AERODROME or Parham, on the B1116 north of Woodbridge
Parham Airfield Museum: During early 2003 the museum changed its name and it incorporates the **390th Bomb Group Memorial Air Museum** and the **Museum of British Resistance.** The tower here houses a superb museum dedicated to the 390th and Parham, USAAF Station No.153. Within can be found a wide array of engines and many other artefacts. The Resistance Museum is dedicated to the work of the Auxiliary Units - the so-called 'Stay Behind' cells should an invasion have become a reality. The plan is to continue with the construction of the blister hangar. DC-3 N4565L moved to <u>Doncaster</u>, S Yorks, on 6th August 2003.
◆ Open 11am to 6pm on Sun and Bank Hols Mar to Oct. Also Wed 11am to 4pm in Jun-Sep. Other times by arrangement. ✉ 37 Stubbs Lane, Braintree, Essex, CM7 3NR ☎ 01376 320848 e-mail parhamair@tesco.net

HALESWORTH on the A144 south of Bungay
No.56th Fighter Group Museum: Established on the former 8th Air Force airfield, this small museum includes a wide range of small exhibits, including items from crash sites.

John Flanagan: Keeps his Carvair cockpit section nearby.
| ❏ | CF-EPV | Carvair | ex Beccles, Thorpe Abbotts, Fritton Lake, Woodbridge, | |
| | | | Southend, EI-AMR, N88819, 42-72343. Cockpit. | 1-00 |

HONINGTON AIRFIELD on the A1088 south-east of Thetford
RAF Honington:
| ❏ | XK526 | Buccaneer S.2 | 8648M, ex RAE Bedford, RRE. Gate. | 12-03 |

HORHAM on the B1117 east of Eye
Horham Airfield Heritage Association: Is seeking to preserve, research and promote the heritage of the former USAAF Station 119, once home to the B-17s of the 95th Bomb Group. Main project is the restoration of the 'Red Feather' club on the former airfield site, in association with Friends of the 95th.
◆ Occasional open days. Otherwise, viewing *only* by prior application. ✉ Park Farm, Hoxne, Eye, IP21 5BS. ☎ 01379 678471 e-mail frank.sherman@bushinternet.com

IPSWICH
Everett Aero: (Located in this general area.) ICA IS.29D 'DEZ' is believed to have moved on. Scout AH.1 'XR625' was last noted in March 2000 and is also thought to have migrated.
 Departures: Jet Provost: T.3A G-TORE to <u>Islington</u>, Gtr Lon, 23-9-03; T.3A XM412 to <u>Balado Bridge</u>, Scotland; T.4 XR670 arrived from Clacton, Essex, by 12-02 and moved to Hermeskeil, Germany, during 4-03; **Scout AH.1** XP854 to <u>Bedford</u>, Beds, 17-10-02; Wasp HAS.1 XS463 to <u>Crawley</u>, W Sussex. Two stripped out Gazelle AH.1s had arrived by 10-02, ZA730 (from Poole, Somerset) and ZA767 (last noted at Middle Wallop), both moved to <u>Babcary</u>, Somerset, by 4-03. Tornado P.03 XX947 arrived from Cosford during the summer of 2003, but moved again on 9-12-03, this time to <u>Shoreham</u>, West Sussex. Jet Provost T.4 XS186 came in from North Luffenham, Leics, by early 2003, but moved to <u>Metheringham</u>, Lincs, on 5th March 2004.
◆ Visits *only* possible by prior appointment.

❏	WZ792		G'hopper TX.1	ex Falgunzeon, Dishforth, Barnard Castle.	2-04
❏	XK788		Grasshopper TX.1	ex Hamois (Belgium), Halton, West Malling, Sevenoaks, Godalming.	2-04
❏	XN510	'40'	Jet Provost T.3A	G-BXBI, ex Binbrook, Shawbury, Linton-on-Ouse, 1 FTS, 3 FTS, RAFC, 7 FTS, 1 FTS.	2-04
❏	[XN554]*		Jet Provost T.3	ex North Luffenham, Halton 8436M, St Athan, Shawbury, CFS. Arrived by 3-03.	2-04
❏	XN579*		Jet Provost T.3A	ex North Luffenham 9137M, ex Shawbury, 1 FTS, 7 FTS, 1 FTS, RAFC,TWU, RAFC. Arrived by 3-03.	2-04
❏	XN634	'53'	Jet Provost T.3	ex Scampton, 1 FTS, 7 FTS, RAFC, 6 FTS. Fuselage.	2-04
❏	XP558	'20'	Jet Provost T.4	ex Norwich, Honington 8648M, St Athan, Culdrose A2628, CAW, 3 CAACU, RAFC.	2-04
❏	XP563	'C'	Jet Provost T.4	ex Bicester, Witney, Bruntingthorpe, Halton 9028M, Shawbury, CATCS, SoRF, 6 FTS, CATCS, RAFC.	2-04
❏	XP629*		Jet Provost T.4	ex North Luffenham 9026M, ex Halton, Shawbury, CATCS, SoRF, CAW, 2 FTS. Arrived by 3-03.	2-04
❏	XP672*	'03'	Jet Provost T.4	G-RAFI, ex North Weald, Bournemouth, Jurby, Halton, 8458M, SoRF, CAW, CATCS, CAW, 2 FTS. CoA 11-3-00. Arrived 2-4-03.	1-04
❏	XP686*		Jet Provost T.4	ex North Luffenham, Halton 8502M, 8401M, CATCS, 6 FTS, CAW, CATCS, CAW, 3 FTS. Arr by 3-03.	2-04
❏	XP888		Scout AH.1	ex Arborfield, Middle Wallop, Wroughton, 651, 652, 14 Flt.	2-04
❏	XP905		Scout AH.1	ex Arborfield, Middle Wallop, Wroughton, 656, 655, 652, 654, 652.	2-04
❏	XR597		Scout AH.1	ex Wattisham, Arborfield, Middle Wallop, Wroughton, 654, 655, 653, 665, 653. Pod	2-04
❏	XR627	'X'	Scout AH.1	ex Wattisham, Arborfield, Dishforth, Middle Wallop, Wroughton, Garrison Air Sqn, 3 CBAS.	2-04
❏	XR635		Scout AH.1	ex Arborfield, Yeovilton, Middle Wallop, 653, 660.	2-04
❏	XS674	'R'	Wessex HC.2	ex Fleetlands, 60, 72, 18, 78, 72.	2-04
❏	XT467*	'BF'	Wessex HU.5	ex Bramley, Odiham 8922M, Brüggen, Gütersloh, 'XR504', Wroughton, 771, 707. First noted 10-02.	2-04
❏	XT640		Scout AH.1	ex Arborfield, Lee-on-Solent, Middle Wallop, 654, 666, 663.	2-04
❏	XW270*		Harrier T.4	ex Bruntingthorpe, Cranfield, Wittering, 4, 1, 233 OCU, 1, 233 OCU. Wing from XV748. Arr 9-03.	2-04
❏	XW796	'X'	Scout AH.1	ex Wattisham, Middle Wallop, Wroughton, 660, 659.	2-04
❏	XX744*	'DJ'	Jaguar GR.1	ex Coltishall 9251M, Cosford, Shawbury, 31, 17, A&AEE. Fuselage. First noted 10-02.	2-04
❏	XZ315*		Gazelle AH.1	ex Fleetlands, 665, ARWS. First noted 10-02.	2-04
❏	ZB666*		Gazelle AH.1	ex Middle Wallop, 9 Regt, 670, ARWS. Pod only. Crashed 24-2-00.	2-04
❏	ZB685*		Gazelle AH.1	ex Fleetlands, 665, 655. First noted 10-02.	2-04
❏	ZD580*	'002'	Sea Harrier FA.2	ex St Athan, Yeovilton, 899, 800, 899, 801. Collision 16-9-96. Arrived 27-9-02.	2-04
❏	ZD614*	'122'	Sea Harrier FA.2	ex St Athan, Yeovilton, 800, 801, 800, 801, 800, 801, 800. 801, 800. Crashed 8-10-01. Arrived 8-10-02.	2-04
❏	ZD991*	'722'	Harrier T.8	ex St Athan, Chadderton, St Athan, 899, RAF, 20, 230 OCU, 4. Crashed 24-6-97.	2-04
❏	ZE691*	'710'	Sea Harrier FA.2	ex St Athan, Yeovilton, 899, 801, 899, 800, 899, 801, 800. Crashed 4-2-98.	2-04
❏	ZE695*	'718'	Sea Harrier FA.2	ex St Athan, Yeovilton, 800, 899. Crashed 26-7-00. Arrived 24-9-02.	2-04

Others: The late Francis Chamberlain's Skeeters were in store in the area. Adding to p202 in *W&R18*, a large cache of spares was imported from Germany in mid-1999, but no airframes were included. By February 2004, G-APOI and XL812 (G-SARO) had moved to Middle Wallop, Hants. The Scout AH.1s (XP890m XR628, XR629, XT631, XT645, XW284) acquired by Bolenda Engineering in late 1997 are believed to have been 'parted out'.

❏ XN351   Skeeter AOP.12   G-BKSC, ex Lossiemouth, Inverness, Shobdon,
Cardiff, Higher Blagdon, Old Warden, Wroughton,
3 RTR, 652, 651. CoA 8-11-84.   4-03

KESGRAVE on the A12 east of Ipswich
The Super Cub is still to be found in Monument Farm Lane, near Foxhall.
❏ MM54-2372   Piper L-21B   ex Embry-Riddle, Woodbridge, Italian Army
'EI-184', I-EIXM, USAF 54-2372. Derelict.   2-03

LAKENHEATH AIRFIELD on the A1065 south of Brandon
USAF Lakenheath – Wings of Liberty Memorial Park (MEM).
◆ Visitor centre and memorial park are viewable *only* by prior permission.

❏ 'BM631' 'XR-C'	Spitfire V FSM	BAPC.269, 71 'Eagle' Sqn, Chesley Peterson colours.	MEM 7-99
❏ '65-777' 'SA'	F-4C-15-MC	37419, ex Alconbury, Texas ANG. 48th TFW c/s.	MEM 3-00
❏ 30091	F-15A-8-MC	ex Soesterberg. ABDR. 'ABDR'.	10-96
❏ '92-048' 'LN'	F-15A-12-MC	40131, ex 122 TFS / Louisiana ANG.	MEM 3-00
❏ 60029	F-15A-15-MC	ABDR.	10-96
❏ 60124	F-15B-15-MC	ABDR.	2-00
❏ '63319''FW-319'	F-100D-16-NA	42269, ex '54048', French AF. Main gate.	3-00
❏ '72-448' 'LN'	F-111E-CF	68011, ex U' Heyford, 20 TFW. *Miss Liberty*.	MEM 3-00

LOWESTOFT
Hannants Model Warehouse: In Harbour Road, Oulton Broad, holds two Harriers 'in limbo' pending export to the USA, though they are registered to a 'keeper' in Belgium.
◆ Open Mon to Sat 9am to 5.30pm www.hannants.co.uk
❏ XZ995* ' 3G' Harrier GR.3   G-CBGK, ex Shoreham, Ipswich, St Mawgan
9220M, Chivenor, 1417 Flt, 4, 3, 233 OCU, 3.
Arrived 30-10-01. Stored.   3-04
❏ ZD668* '3A' Harrier GR.3   G-CBCU, ex Bruntingthorpe, Wittering, 233 OCU.
Arrived 10-6-00. Stored.   3-04

MONEWDEN south of the A1120, north of Ipswich
❏ G-ARDZ	SAN D.140A	CoA 29-11-91. Stored.	7-03
❏ G-AVTT	Ercoupe 415D	ex SE-BFZ, NC3774H. CoA 20-1-86. Stored.	7-03
❏ G-BENF	Cessna T.210L	ex Ipswich, N732AE, D-EIPY, N732AE. Cr 29-5-81.	5-01

NAYLAND on the B1087 north-west of Colchester
Proctor V G-AHTE moved to <u>Clacton</u>, Essex, to continue its rebuild.
❏ G-BMWV   Putzer Elster B   ex D-EEKB, 97+14, D-EBGI. Stored.   9-02

NEWMARKET on the A1304 east of Cambridge
A private collector has a Hunter in the area.
❏ XG274 '71' Hunter F.6   ex Ipswich, Halton 8710M, 4 FTS, 229 OCU, 66, 14.   3-04

RATTLESDEN west of Stowmarket
❏ XP494   Grasshopper TX.1   ex Breighton, Stoke-on-Trent, Syerston, Stamford,
Cosford, Ratcliffe College, Syerston.   ® 4-03

STOWMARKET on the A14 east of Bury St Edmunds
Giles Howell: The EE P.1B is in this general area for restoration and eventual display.

❑ XA847	EE P.1B	ex Portsmouth, Southampton, Hendon 8371M, Farnborough, A&AEE, EE.	7-99

SUDBURY on the A134 north-west of Colchester

AJD Engineering / Hawker Restorations Ltd (HRL): See under Duxford, Cambs, for The Fighter Collection's Hurricane IV which was crafted by HRL. The JN4 'Jenny' is stored for Aero Vintage (see St Leonards-on-Sea, East Sussex) [1].

Departures: Avro 504L floatplane S-AHAA (G-EASD) had moved to Richmond, N Yorks, by mid-2000. BE.2e A1325 (G-BVGR) is thought to have gone to New Zealand in mid-2002. Yak-1 1342 (G-BTZD) moved to St Leonards-on-Sea, E Sussex. The anonymous Yak-3, last noted in 9-94 no less, is believed to have gone to Martham, Norfolk.

❑ –	JN4 'Jenny'	ex USA, *Great Waldo Pepper*. Stored.		[1]	4-94
❑ P2902	Hurricane I	G-ROBT, ex Dunkirk, P2902, 245. Crashed 3-5-40.		®	11-02
❑ P3717*	Hurricane I	ex Hinckley, Russia, Mk IIA DR348, 8 FTS, 55 OTU, 43, 257, 253, 238. Composite. For sale.			3-04
❑ V7497*	Hurricane I	G-HRLI, ex 501. Crashed 28-9-40.		®	4-02
❑ Z5053	Hurricane II	G-BWHA, ex Cam, Russia, 151 Wing, 402. Composite. Under restoration as 'Z5252'.		®	11-02
❑ BW853	Hurricane XIIA	ex G-BRKE, Canada, RCAF. Project.			7-99
❑ BW881	Hurricane XIIA	G-KAMM, ex Canada, RCAF.		®	11-02

WALPOLE on the B1117 south-east of Halesworth

Blyth Valley Aviation Collection: The trimming down of the collection continues. Vulcan B.2 nose XL388 moved to Doncaster, S Yorks, on 7th April 2003. The Victor nose, or Project XL160, is owned by the **HP Victor Association**, who are working to restore it [1]. The association serves to link all those who flew, worked on, or just love, the Victor and publishes a newsletter. (Ken McGill, 15 Burnside Flotta, Stromness, Orkney, KW16 3NP e-mail aldaniti@supanet.com.)
◆ By prior permission *only*. ✉ Cliff Aldred, 'Vulcan's End', Mells Road, Walpole, Halesworth, Suffolk, IP19 0PL ☎ 019867 84436

❑ WE122	'845'	Canberra TT.18	ex North Weald, Stock, St Athan, FRADU, 7, 98, 245, 231 OCU. Nose.		2-04
❑ WE192		Canberra T.4	ex Long Marston, Firbeck, Winsford, Samlesbury, St Athan, 231 OCU, 360, 231 OCU, 39, 231 OCU, 3, 231 OCU. Cockpit, in shed.		2-04
❑ WH953		Canberra B.6(M)	ex Lowestoft, Stock, Farnborough, RAE. Nose, in shed.		2-04
❑ WM267		Meteor NF.11	ex Firbeck, Hemswell, Misson, 151, 256, 11. Nose.		2-04
❑ XH165		Canberra PR.9	ex Stock, St Athan, 1 PRU, 39, 13, 58. Nose.		2-04
❑ XL160		Victor K.2	ex Marham 8910M, 57, 55, 57, 55, Witt Wing, 100, MoA. Nose.	[1]	2-04
❑ XL445		Vulcan K.2	ex Lyneham 8811M, 50, 44, 35, 230 OCU, Wadd Wing, Akrotiri Wing, Wadd Wing, 27. Nose.		2-04
❑ XN696	'751'	Sea Vixen FAW.2	ex Farnborough, Tarrant Rushton, ADS, 899. Nose, in shed.		2-04
❑ XP919	'706'	Sea Vixen FAW.2	ex Norwich, Chertsey, Halton 8163M, 766, 899, A&AEE.		2-04
❑ XR718	'DA'	Lightning F.3	ex Wattisham 8932M, ABDR, LTF, 11, LTF, 11, 5, LTF, 5, 11, LTF, 5, LTF, 5, 226 OCU, 29, 56.		2-04

WATTISHAM AIRFIELD north of the B1078, south of Stowmarket

No.3 Regiment, Army Air Corps / 24 Air Mobile Brigade / 7 Battalion, REME: The Chinook is for Air Mobility Training – AMT. During March 2003 the hulk of Lynx 1-03 XW835 was removed by a Suffolk scrappy. Lynx AH.1 XX153 moved to Yeovil, Somerset, for restoration by Westland before moving to Middle Wallop, Hants, on 28th October 2003.

❏	XL739		Skeeter AOP.12	ex Detmold, 15/19 Hussars, 1 Wing, 651, A&AEE,	
				BATUS, A&AEE. Displayed, pole-mounted	2-01
❏	XP852		Scout AH.1	ex Hildesheim, Wroughton, ARWF, 651. Cabin only.	2-98
❏	XT550	'D'	Sioux AH.1	ex Detmold, Middle Wallop, Wroughton, 651. Gate.	11-94
❏	XT617		Scout AH.1	ex Almondbank, Wroughton, 653, 660. Displayed	4-03
❏	ZA676	'FG'	Chinook HC.1	9230M, ex Odiham, Manston, Fleetlands, N37023.	
				Crashed 15-11-84.	AMT 6-00
❏	ZA729*		Gazelle AH.1	ex Gütersloh, Shawbury, Fleetlands, 658, 1 Regt.	
				4 Regt, 661, 652. ABDR. First noted 5-02	8-02

Locally: An Evans has moved into the general area.
| ❏ | G-BICT* | Evans VP-1 | ex Upavon. CoA 20-2-97. | 1-04 |

SURREY

BROOKLANDS or Weybridge, on the B374 south of Weybridge
Brooklands Museum: The former factory site was, of course, deeply part of the Concorde development and production programme and so the appeal of having an example of the supersonic white elephant here is strong. As with East Fortune, Scotland (qv), this museum is in the throes of moving an example by land to be reassembled and displayed. Once this huge - and very expensive - task is complete, it is imagined that fund-raising will go ahead to put a roof over pre-production Series 100 G-BBDG [1]. If this roof sees no other airframes ousted (a la Scotland) *and* the BAC 111, VC-10 and Viscount also under cover then all well and good. If, as is likely, the covered space is devoted solely to the hot-rod, then in the compiler's opinion, this will all have been another example of Concorde-mania. The supersonic tail wagging the dog...
　　Perhaps some stats will help the case... Twenty Concordes were built. One was scrapped - F-BVFD in December 1994. One crashed - F-BTSC on 25th July 2000. Eighteen survive, of which seven are in the UK – Brooklands (currently at Filton), Duxford, East Fortune, Filton, London-Heathrow, Manchester, Yeovilton. That's 38.8% of the survivors. Two of these - the iconic G-BSST at Yeovilton and the slightly less significant G-AXDN at Duxford already have had considerable assets and resources devoted to them. *(Sierra-Tango* is magnificently presented and interpreted by the Royal Navy on behalf of the Science Museum. *Delta-November* will be central to the 'AirSpace' gallery at Duxford in due course.) The other five face varying financial and infra-structure demands of their new keepers. Two of those five will incur huge surface transportation and re-erection costs. All of this for an audience who won't forget and within 12 months will not be straining to seek out their 'local', or any, Concorde. My conclusion? The financial drain to 'preserve' the latest fiver in near-, mid- and long-term will far outweigh any benefits they ultimately bring in. Unless cunning curators allow Concorde to 'sex-up' their demands to put other airframes – with far less than 38.8% survivor ratings – under cover at the same time.
　　Notes: Several airframes are on loan, as follows: the Ladybird from the estate of the late Bill Manuel; the Harrier and Hunter F.51 from BAE Systems; the Valiant nose from the RAF Museum; the Chipmunk PAX from Peter Smith (see under Hawkinge, Kent); the P.1127 from the RAF Museum and BAE Systems jointly; Hunter XL621 from the late John Hallett. These are marked ±. See also under Bournemouth, Dorset, for another K5673 [2]. The Hunter is marked as 'G-BCNX' on the starboard side [3]. The P.1127 is fitted with the wing of Kestrel XS695 which is at Cosford, Shrop [4]. The Demoiselle was built by Julian Aubert and friends and uses the original method of construction, employing bamboo and using wing-warping [5]. See under Kemble, Glos, for Beagle 206 G-ARRM which is on loan to BAC. Airframes marked ➡ attended the '100 Years of Flight Experience' at Fairford, Glos, July 2003.
　　Departures: Sea Vixen FAW.2 XJ571 moved to <u>Southampton</u>, Hants, on 5th February 2003.
◆　On the B374 south of Weybridge, access from Junctions 10 or 11 of the M25 - well signed. Open Tuesday to Sunday 10am to 5pm (last entry 4pm), Easter to October. Winter months, 10am to 4pm, last entry is 3pm. Note: *closed* on Mondays. Normally closed Good Friday, Xmas. Pre-arranged guided tours available Tuesdays to Fridays, contact 01932 857381. There is an **Association of Friends of Brooklands**, membership details from the address below. The **Brooklands Hurricane Fund** has been set up. Those who wish to support Z2389 – born and bred at Brooklands – can do so by donation; details from the address below.
　　✉ Brooklands Museum, Brooklands Road, Weybridge, KT13 OQN ☎ 01932 857381 **fax** 01932 855465 **e-mail** info@brooklandsmuseum.com **www**.brooklandsmuseum.com

❑	'G-EBED'	Viking REP	BAPC.114, ex 'R4', Chertsey, *The Land Time Forgot.*	10-03
❑	'G-AACA'	Avro 504K REP	BAPC.177, ex 'G1381', Henlow.	➡ 10-03
❑	'G-ADRY'	HM.14 'Flea'	BAPC.29, ex Aberdare, Swansea.	3-02
❑	G-AEKV	Kronfeld Drone	BGA.2510/DZQ. CoA 6-10-60.	3-02
❑	G-AGRU	Viking 1	ex Cosford, Soesterberg, Channel, Kuwait Oil, BWIA, VP-TAX, G-AGRU, BEA. *Vagrant.* CoA 9-1-64.	® 10-03
❑	G-APEJ	Merchantman	ex Hunting Cargo, ABC, BEA. *Ajax.* Nose.	10-03
❑	G-APEP	Merchantman	ex Hunting Cargo, ABC, BEA. *Superb.*	10-03
❑	G-APIM	Viscount 806	ex Southend, BAF, BA, BEA. Damaged 11-1-88. *Viscount Stephen Piercey.*	® 10-03
❑	G-ASYD	BAC 111-475AM	ex Filton, BAe, BAC. 'Fly By Light Technology'.	10-03
❑	G-BBDG*	Concorde 100	ex Filton. CoA 1-3-82.	[1] **due**
❑	[G-LOTI]	'2' Blériot XI REP	CoA 19-7-82.	➡ 10-03
❑	G-MJPB	Ladybird	microlight	± 3-02
❑	G-VTOL	Harrier T.52	ex ZA250, Dunsfold. CoA 2-11-86.	± 10-03
❑	–	ATH Slingsby Gull 3	BGA.643, (Hawkridge Kittiwake).	3-02
❑	–	HFZ Scud I REP	BGA.3922.	3-02
❑	–	Willow Wren	BGA.162, ex Bishop's Stortford. *Yellow Wren.*	3-02
❑	–	Voisin scale REP	G-BJHV, ex Old Warden.	3-02
❑	–	Vimy repro	cockpit section.	3-02
❑	–	VC-10 EMU	test shell, nose section. BOAC colours.	10-03
❑	–	Rogallo hang glider	*Aerial.* On loan.	3-02
❑	A4O-AB	VC-10 1103	ex Sultan of Oman, G-ASIX.	10-03
❑	'B7270'	Camel REP	G-BFCZ, ex Land's End, Duxford, Chertsey. CoA 23-2-89. Ground-runs.	➡ 10-03
❑	'F5475'	'A' SE.5A REP	BAPC.250, built on site. *1st Battalion Honourable Artillery Company.*	➡ 10-03
❑	'K5673'	Fury I FSM	BAPC.249, built on site. 1 Sqn 'A' Flt colours.	[2] 10-03
❑	N2980	'R' Wellington Ia	ex Loch Ness, 20 OTU, 37, 149. Ditched 31-12-40.	10-03
❑	Z2389	Hurricane II	ex St Petersburg, Siberia, Sov AF, RAF 253, 136, 247, 71, 249.	® 10-03
❑	WF372	'A' Varsity T.1	ex Sibson, 6 FTS, 1 ANS, RAFC, 201 AFS.	10-03
❑	[WP921]	Chipmunk T.10 PAX	ex Croydon, Henley-on-Thames, Benson, G-ATJJ, Colerne SF, Ox UAS, HCMSU, 10 RFS.	± 10-03
❑	XD816	Valiant BK.1	ex Henlow, Abingdon, BAC, 214, 148. Nose. 'Stratosphere' chamber.	± 10-03
❑	XL621	Hunter T.7	ex Bournemouth, G-BNCX, RAE Bedford, 238 OCU, RAE. ETPS colours.	± [3] 10-03
❑	XP984	Hawker P.1127	ex Dunsfold, Lee-on-S, Manadon A2658, RAE.	± [4] 3-02
❑	XT575	Viscount 837	ex Bruntingthorpe, DRA Bedford, OE-LAG. Nose.	10-03
❑	–	TSR-2 EMU	ex Farnborough. Nose.	10-03
❑	E-421	Hunter F.51	ex Brooklands Tech, Kingston, Dunsfold, G-9-443, Aalborg, Esk.724, RDanAF.	➡ ± 10-03
❑	–	BAPC.187 Roe I Biplane REP	displayed in reproduction of Roe's shed.	3-02
❑	–	BAPC.256 Demoiselle REP	Taxiable.	[5] 3-02

CAMBERLEY on the M3 south of Bracknell
Parkhouse Aviation: Vampire pod XH330 moved to Abingdon, Oxon. (See also Wycombe, Bucks.)

❑	XL449	'044' Gannet AEW.3	ex Wycombe Air Park, Camberley, Cardiff, Lossiemouth, 849. Cockpit.	3-04

Others: No news on Keith Attfield's and Paul Raymond's Eagle or 'JP'.

❑	G-MBTY	American Eagle	ex Ottershaw, Southall.	2-96
❑	'XN493'	Jet Provost T.3	XN137, ex Ottershaw, Camberley, Abingdon, 3 FTS, CFS, Hunting. Nose.	9-93

CATERHAM west of the A22, north-east of Redhill

A yard in the general area seems to deal in insurance write-off hulks. Some are in-and-out (or expired?) quickly, others - ie those listed here - of a longer term nature.

❏ G-ASSE	Colt 108	ex N5961Z. CoA 12-6-00.	2-04
❏ G-BADL	Seneca 200 II	ex N5307T. Crashed 21-10-95.	2-04
❏ G-BBEW	Aztec 250E	ex EI-BYK, G-BBEW, N40262. Crashed 20-4-99.	1-01
❏ G-BCCP	Robin HR.200	Crashed 9-4-89.	1-01
❏ G-BGTP	Robin HR.200	ex G-BGTN ntu, F-BVCP. Canx 25-1-00.	1-01
❏ G-BIAB	TB-9 Tampico	Crashed 6-8-93.	1-04
❏ G-BSIB	Warrior II	ex N8182C. Canx 22-11-99.	1-01
❏ G-WIGL	Robinson R-22	Damaged 21-11-97.	1-01

CHARLWOOD west of the A23/A217 Junction, north of Gatwick Airport

Gatwick Aviation Museum: From April 2004 the museum has adopted regular opening times - alternate Sundays with other times by appointment. Several airframes are capable of ground-running and visitors are often treated to a 'live' run during open days. The planning dispute with Mole Valley District Council is still in a period of grace. Gazelle 1 G-TURP pod was parted out and scrapped.

◆ Open Apr to Oct, alternative Sundays and holidays, 10a, to 4pm. (eg Jun 13 etc) – SAE for details. Otherwise by prior appointment. ✉ Lowfield Heath Road, Charlwood, RH6 0BT ☎ / fax 01293 862915 e-mail gpvgat@aol.com www.gatwick-aviation-museum.co.uk

❏ VZ638		Meteor T.7	G-JETM, ex North Weald, Bournemouth, Southampton, Southend, Kemble, CAW, RAFC, 237 OCU, 501, Biggin Hill SF, FCCS, 85, 54, 25, 500.
			2-04
❏ WF118	'569'	Sea Prince T.1	G-DACA, ex Gloucester-Cheltenham, Kemble, 750, A&AEE, 727, A&AEE, RAE.
			2-04
❏ WH773		Canberra PR.7	ex Wyton, 8696M, 13, 58, 80, 31, 82, 540.	2-04
❏ WK146		Canberra B.2	ex Hull, Wr'ton, Abingdon, Bicester, 59, 102. Nose.	2-04
❏ WP308	'572'	Sea Prince T.1	G-GACA, ex Staverton, Kemble, 750.	2-04
❏ WR974	'K'	Shackleton MR.3/3	ex Cosford 8117M, Kinloss Wing, 203, 42, 203, SWDU, MinTech, ASWDU, CA.	2-04
❏ WR982	'J'	Shack' MR.3/3	ex Cosford 8106M, 201, 206, MoA, 205, 203, 206.	2-04
❏ WW442	'N'	Provost T.1	ex Kings Langley, Leverstock Green, Cranfield, Booker, St Merryn, Houghton-on-the-Hill, Kidlington, Halton 7618M, CNCS, 3 FTS.	2-04
❏ [XE489]		Sea Hawk FB.5	G-JETH, ex Bournemouth, Southend, 'XE364', XE489, FRU, 899. 'Bournemouth Flying Club'	2-04
❏ XK885		Pembroke C.1	N46EA, ex Staverton, St Athan, 8452M, 60, 21, WCS, Seletar SF, B&TTF, Seletar SF, S&TFF, 209, 267.	2-04
❏ XL164		Victor K.2	ex Brize Norton 9215M, 55, 57, 55, 57, MoA. Nose.	2-04
❏ XL472	'044'	Gannet AEW.3	ex Boscombe Down, 849 'B', HQ, 'A' Flts.	2-04
❏ XL591*		Hunter T.7	ex Kemble, Ipswich, Colsterworth, Shawbury, 237 OCU, 208, 237 OCU, 208, 237 OCU, 4 FTS, RAE, 4 FTS, 229 OCU, FCS. Arrived by 4-02.	2-04
❏ XN923		Buccaneer S.1	ex Boscombe Down, West Freugh.	2-04
❏ XP351*	'Z'	Whirlwind HAR.10	ex Shawbury 8672M, 2 FTS, SAR Wing, 22. Arrived 15-10-03.	2-04
❏ XP398		Whirlwind HAR.10	ex Peckham Rye, Shawbury, 8794M, 22, 1563 Flt, 202, 103, 110, 225.	2-04
❏ XS587		Sea Vixen FAW.2	G-VIXN, ex Bournemouth, TT mod, FRL, RAE, 8828M, FRL, ADS, 899.	2-04
❏ XV751*		Harrier GR.3	ex Bruntingthorpe, Charlwood, Lee-on-Solent A2672, A2760, 3, 1, 3, 20, 233 OCU. Grey c/s, Royal Navy titles.	2-04
❏ XX734		Jaguar GR.1	ex Park Aviation, Coltishall, Abingdon, 8816M, Indian AF JI014, XX734, 6, JOCU. Damaged hulk.	2-04
❏ ZF579		Lightning F.53	ex Portsmouth, Luxembourg, *Wing Commander*, Stretton, Warton, RSAF 203, 53-671, G-27-40.	2-04

❑ [E-430]	Hunter F.51	ex Faygate, Chertsey, Dunsfold, G-9-448,	
		Esk.724, Dan AF. FAA colours, GA.11-style.	2-04
❑ J-1605	Venom FB.50	G-BLID, ex Duxford, Swiss AF.	2-04

Park Aviation Supply / Aerospace Logistics:

❑ XX121	'EQ' Jaguar GR.1	ex Cosford, Shawbury, 6, 54, 226 OCU, JOCU.	4-02
❑ XX140	Jaguar T.2	ex Faygate, 226 OCU, 54, JOCU, JCT. Cockpit.	4-02
❑ XX223	Hawk T.1	ex Henlow, 4 FTS. Crashed 7-7-86. Cockpit.	8-03
❑ XX257	Hawk T.1A	ex St Athan, Red Arrows. Crashed 17-11-98.	8-03

DUNSFOLD AIRFIELD (or Dunsfold Park) on the A281 south of Guildford
Now a *private* airstrip, the Aces High Dakota arrived in 2002. It attended the '100 Years of Flight Experience' static display at the International Air Tattoo, Fairford, Glos, July 2003.

❑ –*	Dakota 3	↦ N147DC, ex North Weald, G-DAKS, Duxford,	
'NF-A'		'10884', 'KG374', *Airline* 'G-AGHY', TS423,	
		RAE, Ferranti, Airwork, Gatow SF, 436, 1 HGSU,	
		42-100884. Arrived 2-9-02.	2-04

EGHAM on the A30 west of Staines
Jeremy Hall: Using as many original parts as possible, Jeremy has created the forward fuselage (all 21ft of it) of a Lancaster. It 'does the rounds' of shows and events.

| ❑ – | Lancaster REP | *Hi Ho!, Hi Ho!* Forward fuselage. | 6-98 |

FARNHAM on the A31 south-west of Aldershot
A collector in the general area has a Lightning nose.

| ❑ XS933 | Lightning F.6 | ex Langport, Terrington St Clement, Narborough, | |
| | | Binbrook, 5, 11, BAC, 5, 56, 11. Nose. | 3-02 |

GODALMING on the A3100 south of Guildford
No.1254 Squadron Air Cadets: By August 2003 the nose of Hunter F.4 WV332 had moved on loan to Tangmere, W Sussex.

GUILDFORD
Martin Painter: Moved himself and Nimrod XV148 nose to Malmesbury, Wilts, in mid-October 2003.

HASLEMERE on the A286 south-west of Godalming
Sea Vixen Preservation Group: Located in Weyhill, just off the B2131, this is the preservation 'arm' of **1268 Squadron Air Cadets**. A workshop has greatly helped in the restoration work.
◆ Visits by prior appointment *only*. ✉ Flt Lt Kevin Burchett, 43 Beech Road, Waterlooville, Hants, PO8 0LN, ☎ 02392 595408, e-mail kevin@seavixen.fsnet.co.uk.

| ❑ XP925 | Sea Vixen FAW.2 | ex Farnborough, Tarrant Rushton, ADS, 899. Nose. | ® | 3-04 |
| ❑ | Lightning CIM | ex Farnborough. Cockpit. | ® | 3-04 |

HORLEY on the A23 south of Reigate
Nothing concrete on these two, they may well be bound for LOST!

| ❑ G-AFZE | Heath Parasol | CoA 10-5-64. Stored. | 11-93 |
| ❑ | Bensen gyroplane | Stored. | 11-93 |

LINGFIELD on the B2028 north of East Grinstead
Gary Brown: Work should continue on the Bf 109.

| ❑ 'FM+BB' | Bf 109G FSM | ex Germany. | ® | 6-99 |

MYTCHETT on the B3411 south of Camberley

Defence Medical Services Training Centre: Is guarded by a Hunter. A fascinating observation in April 2002 was an olive drab Beech Baron fuselage in the trees close to the visitors car park - thoughts?

❑ XG196	'31' Hunter F.6A	8702M, ex Bracknell, Kemble, 1 TWU, TWU, 229 OCU, 19. Gate.	4-03

REDHILL on the A23 east of Reigate

Turbine World: Located on a *private* site in this general area. Wessex 60 9G-DAN is believed to have gone to the land of its registration. Wessex HC.2 G-HANA (XV729) was cancelled as sold in Ghana as 9G-BOB in September 2003 and is also thought to have moved on.

❑ G-AZBY	Wessex 60 Srs 1	ex Weston-super-Mare, Bournemouth, W-s-M, *Full Metal Jacket* 'EM-16', 5N-ALR, G-AZBY. CoA 14-12-82.	10-99
❑ 'VT-EKG'*	Westland WG.30	VT-EKK. Ex Biggin Hill. First noted 9-02.	9-02
❑ XT671	Wessex HC.2	G-BYRC, ex 72.	8-03
❑ XV731	Wessex HC.2	ex Fleetlands, 72, WTF, 240 OCU, 18, 78.	9-02

No.135 Squadron Air Training Corps: Sea Devon C.2/2 'G-DOVE' moved to Goodwood, West Sussex, for temporary store, before settling upon, Redhill Aerodrome, Surrey - see below.

REDHILL AERODROME south of South Nutfield, south-east of Redhill

Acebell Aviation: On 15th June 2002 John Pothecary delivered G-ABNX to be looked after by Acebell on behalf of the **Redwing Preservation Trust** which was officially launched on 16th August 2002. The trust will look after the operation and future of this under-rated survivor [1]. (Viewing by prior permission *only* from: Redwing Preservation Trust, c/o Hangar 8, Redhill Aerodrome, Kingsmill Lane, Surrey, RH1 5JY.) The Scion is owned by the Historic Aircraft Society of Southend, Essex [2].

❑ G-ABNX*	Redwing 2 ✈	ex Old Sarum, Shoreham. Arrived 15-6-02.	[1]	12-02
❑ G-AEZF	Scion II	ex East Tilbury, Southend. CoA 5-5-54. Frame.	® [2]	5-00
❑ –	G'hopper TX.1	'fuselage' frame. Stored.		7-00

East Surrey Aviation Group / Daniel and **Kevin Hunt**: The Sea Devon project is being worked on by the ESAG and the aim is to display it statically at the aerodrome. The brothers have also brought a large amount of material back from the former Soviet Union. They have acquired the tail section of HP Hampden I P1273, A-20 Havoc parts and others, also from Russia.

♦ Visits by prior application *only*. ✉ 28 Windmill Way, Reigate, Surrey RH2 0JA
  e-mail daniel@esag.demon.co.uk

❑ G-AIUA*	Hawk Trainer III	ex King's Lynn, West Chiltington, Benington, Bushey, Old Warden, Duxford, Felthorpe, T9768, 10 AGS, 7 FIS, 15 EFTS, Wyton SF. CoA 13-7-67. Fuselage.		3-04
❑ G-OJAS*	J/1U Workmaster	ex F-BJAS, F-WJAS, F-OBHT ntu. Frame.		3-04
❑ BD731*	Hurricane II	ex Murmansk, 605, 135. Remains, plus other parts.		3-04
❑ VP967*	Sea Devon C.2/2	G-KOOL, ex Goodwood, Redhill, East Surrey Tech 'G-DOVE', Biggin Hill, VP967, Kemble, 781, 21, 207, SCCS, SCS, WCS, SCS, NCS, SCS, MCS, MoA, MCS, CCCF, 38 GCF, TTCCF, FCCS, 2 TAF CS, MCCS, RAFG CS, 2 TAF CS, Wahn SF, RCCF. Arrived 3-11-02.	®	3-04
❑ –*	Jet Provost	cockpit. Arrived 2-04.		3-04
❑ –*	Nakajima B5N2	ex Kurile Island. Front fuselage.		3-04
❑ –*	Mitsubishi A6M2	ex Kurile Island. Front fuselage.		3-04
❑ 44-4315*	P-63C	ex Kurile Island. Remains. Arrived by 3-03.		3-04
❑ 44-4368*	P-63C	ex Kurile Island. Remains. Arrived to 3-03.		3-04
❑ –*	B-25 Mitchell	ex Kurile Island. Front fuselage.		3-04

Others:

❑ G-BOSC	Cessna U.206F	F-GHEN (ntu?). ex 5N-ASU, N7256N. Fuselage.	9-99
❑ G-BOVY	Hughes 269C	ex EI-CIL, G-BOVY, N1096K. Crashed 17-3-99.	5-00

❏	G-BXVC	Turbo Arrow IV	ex D-ELIV, N2152V. Crashed 22-8-98. Wreck.	9-99
❏	G-FISS	Robinson R-22	ex N40833. Crashed 31-3-96. Pod	9-99
❏	G-OROB	Robinson R-22	ex G-TBFC, N80287. CoA 25-6-95. Pod	9-99
❏	5N-ALQ	Bell 212	ex Nigeria. Crashed 11-9-95. Stored.	3-00
❏	5N-AQW	Bell 212	ex Nigeria. Crashed 14-1-93. Stored.	3-00

REIGATE on the A217 west of Redhill
Surrey Fire and Rescue Service Headquarters: Trident 3B-101 G-AWZI's fuselage was scrapped here during 2002 and moved to <u>Alton</u>, Hants.

Others: Inspection of the Vulcan nose here establishes it as an 'unplumbed' B.1 with a B.2 'hood'.

❏	–	Vulcan B.1 EMU	ex East Kirkby, Tattershall, Waddington. Nose.	®	6-01

SUNBURY-ON-THAMES south of J1 of the M3
J and C Motor Spares: In Fordbridge Road, the B375.

❏	—	Hobbycopter	—		7-03

WALTON ON THAMES
Adrian Windsor: Still has his Hunter cockpit.

❏	E-420	Hunter F.51	ex Marlow, Ascot, Dunsfold G-9-442, RDanAF. Cockpit.	3-02

WEYBRIDGE on the B374 south of the town
Brooklands Technical College: The airframes are believed unchanged.

❏	G-ASSB	Twin Comanche	ex Bournemouth. CoA 6-5-88.	10-03
❏	XN586	'91' Jet Provost T.3A	ex Cosford 9039M, 7 FTS, 1 FTS, CFS, 2 FTS, RAFC.	10-03

WOKING on the A320 north of Guildford
Big Apple: The Hunter-on-a-stick is still outside and the Hunter nose can still be found in the 'assault course' in the crèche! (See under Poole, Somerset, for the saga of XL623.) *W&R18* (p210) noted that the nose of Hunter FGA.78 QA-12 had moved in 2000 to 'Wales'. The location was <u>Cwmbran</u>, Wales.

❏	XL623	Hunter T.7	8770M, ex Newton, Cosford, 1 TWU, 74, 19, 1, 43, 92, 208, 65. Pole-mounted.	12-01

Glenn Lacey: Under this heading we will 'park' the exciting series of Luftwaffe projects being acquired and restored but with the proviso that the workshop (or workshops!) that constitute the base of this collection are *not* open to inspection and are not in this area – this is merely a 'port of convenience'! The Nord Noralpha should fly during 2004 and will have an Argus As 10 powerplant and the markings of the Bf 208 V1 prototype. Beyond this will come the 'A-1 Storch.

❏	G-MESS*	Noralpha	ex F-BEEV, F-WZBI, Fr Navy 87.	®	2-04
❏	OO-JKT*	Fw 44J Stieglitz	G-STIG, ex Belgium, D-EHDH, LV-YYX. F/n 1-04.	®	3-04
❏	6234*	Ju 87B/R-4	G-STUK, ex Germany, New Zealand, Lancing, Russia, 'L1+FW'. Shot down 24-4-42.	®	2-04
❏	1983*	Bf 109E-3	G-EMIL, ex 'Essex', Russia, JG5. Shot down 17-7-41.	®	2-04
❏	2008*	Fi 156A-1	G-STCH, ex Russia?	®	2-04
❏	110451*	Fi 156D-0	G-STOR, ex Russia?	®	2-04
❏	211028*	'8' Fw 190D-9	G-DORA, ex Germany, JG26, JG54.	®	2-04

BEXHILL on the A259 west of Hastings
❏ G-ACXE   L25cl Swallow   ex 'Hastings', Bagshot, Birmingham. CoA 7-4-40.   ® 10-98

BRIGHTON
No.225 Squadron Air Cadets: There are reports that this PAX trainer has been sold off.
❏ WD370   Chipmunk T.10   ex Hove, 3 AEF, 2 SoTT, 1 AEF, Hull UAS,
                   PAX   2 BTFS. SOC 12-3-75.   1-04

Others: A balloon, previously held by the BPG, is stored in the area.
❏ G-AZBT   Western O-65   ex Lancing. *Hermes*. CoA 9-4-76. Stored.   3-98

DEANLAND south of the B2124, west of Hailsham
❏ G-BRKY   Dragonfly II   CoA 8-6-94. Fuselage. Stored.   8-01

HAILSHAM on the A22 north of Eastbourne
Grenville Helicopters: The helipad at the Boship Manor Hotel still has its 'guardian' which carries the
tail stabiliser of G-AXKW – to confuse all and sundry! The main aim of this composite is to act as a
recognition aid for those who are rotor-bound and trying to find the 'pad'!
❏ 'G-AXKW'   Bell 47G   G-AYOE, ex F-OCBF, F-BKQZ, D-HEBO.
                                      Cr 16-7-77. Composite, including Sioux parts.   10-00

Others: A local strip has two long-term *W&R* inmates.
❏ G-BARN   Taylor Titch   CoA 2-10-92. Stored.   8-00
❏ 'K3731'   Isaacs Fury   G-RODI. CoA 17-8-95. Stored.   8-00

HOLLINGTON on the B2159 west of Hastings
St Leonard's Motors: In Church Wood Drive, is the pole-mounted former Hastings Meteor.
❏ WL345   Meteor T.7   ex Hastings, Kemble, CAW, 8 FTS,
                                      5 FTS, CFE, 229 OCU.   1-02

LEWES on the A27 north-east of Brighton
Wassmer D.120 G-BKCZ moved on by mid-2001. A collector has a Canberra and a Hunter locally [1].
❏ G-AMYL   PA-17 Vagabond   ex N4613H, NC4613H. CoA 20-6-89. *Yankee Lady*.   8-00
❏ G-APNS   Fairtravel Linnet ex Chessington. CoA 6-10-78.   8-00
❏ G-AYMU   Wassmer D.112   ex F-BJPB. Damaged 7-1-92.   8-00
❏ WH964*   Canberra E.15   ex Bruntingthorpe, Cosford 8870M, St Athan, 100,
                                      98, Akrotiri Wing, 32, 12. Nose.   [1] 1-04
❏ XG195   Hunter FGA.9   ex Sleap, Seighford, Macclesfield, Bitteswell,
                                      G-9-453, 208, 1, 19. Nose.   [1] 1-04

NEWHAVEN east of Brighton on the A259
Newhaven Fort: Robertsbridge Aviation Society (see below) have an on-going display here. Also within
the Fort (but not RAS originated) is a feature on the much-missed Royal Observer Corps.
◆ Apr to Oct, daily 10.30am to 6.00pm. Weekends in Mar and Oct and Half Terms. ✉ Newhaven Fort,
   Fort Road, Newhaven, BN9 9DL ☎ 01273 517622 **fax** 01273 512059

ROBERTSBRIDGE on the A21 north-west of Hastings
Robertsbridge Aviation Centre: Operated by the Robertsbridge Aviation Society (RAS), the museum
is a barrage of artefacts covering many aspects of aviation. Lottery funding has allowed a

considerable enhancement in the displays. RAS has a close relationship with Newhaven Fort, E Sussex, with a series of displays there. The Phantom FGR.2 cockpit previously at Welshpool, Wales, came here but was exported to the Netherlands in early 2003. The Sukhoi was put up for sale in March 2003 [1].
♦ Open by appointment *only*. Membership of the RAS includes meetings, trips and a newsletter, *Rob Air*. ✉ Philip Baldock, 53 Wannock Avenue, Willingdon, BN20 9RH ☎ 01323 483845 e-mail pbaldock@breathermail.net

❑ WA630	Meteor T.7	ex Newhaven, Robertsbridge, Oakington SF, 4 FTS, 205 AFS, RAFC. Nose.		2-04
❑ WE173	Canberra PR.3	ex Stock, Coltishall, Farnborough, 231 OCU, 39, RAE, 39, 69, 82. Nose.		2-04
❑ WN907	Hunter F.2	ex Walpole, Ascot, St Athan, Colerne 7416M, 257. Nose.		2-04
❑ XJ488	Sea Vixen FAW.1	ex Nottingham, New Milton, Portsmouth, Boscombe Down, 22 JSTU, A&AEE. Nose.		2-04
❑ XP701	Lightning F.3	ex High Halden, Hawkinge, Binbrook 8924M, LTF, 5, 11, 56, 29, 111, 29, A&AEE. Nose.		2-04
❑ XR681	Jet Provost T.4	ex Newhaven, Odiham, Abingdon 8588M, RAFEF, CATCS, 6 FTS, RAFC. Nose.		2-04
❑ 7907	Su-7 *Fitter*	ex Farnborough, Egyptian AF. Nose.	[1]	2-04

ST LEONARDS-ON-SEA west of Hastings

Aero Vintage: The former Afghan Hind was acquired by Aero Vintage in 1995 from Canada, but work only began on it early in 2002. Tiger Moth G-BUJY (VT-DPE) was cancelled as exported to Belgium in November 2002. The **Historic Aircraft Collection of Jersey** is closely associated – and see under Duxford, Cambs, for more details. For other AV/HAC aircraft see also: Bristol F.2b at Old Warden, Beds; JN4 'Jenny' at Sudbury, Suffolk.

❑ D5649*	Airco DH.9	ex Hatch, Bikaner, India, Imperial Gift 1920, RAF/RFC. Major components, long-term project.		12-03
❑ K3661	Nimrod II	G-BURZ, ex 802 Sqn. Other history obscure.	®	12-03
❑ K5600	Audax I	G-BVVI, ex 2015M, Kirkham, SAC, 226.	®	12-03
❑ L7181*	Hind I	G-CBLK, ex Rockliffe, Canada, Kabul, Afghanistan AF, RAF, 211.	®	12-03
❑ –*	Fury I	G-CBZP, ex SAAF.	®	12-03
❑ –	Fury REP	–	®	8-95
❑ 1342*	Yakovlev Yak-1	G-BTZD, ex Sudbury, Audley End, Paddock Wood, USSR.	®	3-04

SEDLESCOMBE AERODROME on the B2244 north of Hastings

❑ G-AXPG	Mignet HM.293	CoA 20-1-77. Stored.	11-01
❑ G-BLUL	CEA DR.1051M	ex F-BMPJ. CoA 24-10-91. Stored.	11-01
❑ G-BUNS	Cessna F.150K	ex F-BSIL. Stored.	11-01

Locally: A Spitfire is in storage.

❑ UB441*	Spitfire IX	ex Rochester, USA, Myanmar, Burmese AF, Israeli DF/AF 2020 Czech AF, RAF ML119, 1. Stored. First noted. 8-03.	8-03

WANNOCK east of the A22, north of Eastbourne

Foulkes-Halbard Collection: With the death of the owner of the transport collection in October 2003, the collection became a private one, no longer accessible to the public.

❑ G-BHNG	Aztec 250E	ex Seaford, Shoreham, N54125. Cr 19-12-81. Fuse.		2-00
❑ –	BAPC.127 Halton Jupiter	ex Old Warden, Cranwell, Halton. Stored.		2-00
❑ –	IAHC.2 Aldritt Mono REP	ex Portlaoise.	®	2-00

WEST SUSSEX

ASHINGTON west of the A24, at the junction of the A283, north of Worthing
Paul Whelland: The 'JP' is still kept at an antique shop.
❑ 'XN594' '19' Jet Provost T.3   XN458, ex WAM Cardiff, St Athan 8334M,
                                      Halton, Shawbury, 1 FTS.   1-04

BOSHAM north of the A259, south-west of Chichester
Mike Jelley: Keeps the Whirlwind in his garden in the area.
❑ XN263   'H'   Whirlwind   ex Wroughton, Shrivenham, Wroughton, Middle
                  HAS.7   Wallop, Wroughton, 771, Brawdy SF, 705, 848.   1-04

CRAWLEY
Crawley Technical College:
❑ XN494   '43' Jet Provost T.3A   ex Bruntingthorpe, Middle Wallop, Halton
                                      9012M, 1 FTS, RAFC.   12-03
❑ XS463*   Wasp HAS.1   XT431, ex Ipswich, Weston-super-Mare,
                                        Fleetlands, Lee-on-Solent. Boom of XT431.   12-03

EAST GRINSTEAD on the A264 east of Crawley
Sabrewatch: Lingfield Road. This location is *private* property. The Varsity is for disposal.
❑ WF408   Varsity T.1   ex Northolt, 8395M Cosford, 2 SoTT, 6 SS,
                                       2 ANS, 1 RS, 11 FTS, 201 AFS.   1-04
❑ XT257   Wessex HAS.3   ex Cosford 8719M, Halton, A&AEE. Yellow c/s.   1-04

No.1343 Squadron Air Cadets: Morton Road, close to Sunnyside Post Office. 'Parent' is Odiham.
❑ XP677   Jet Provost T.4   8587M, ex Headley, Abingdon, RAFEF,
                                      2 FTS. Nose.   8-01
❑ –   Jaguar GR.1   cockpit.   ®   9-96

Locally: Martin Cobb's Sea Vampire is under restoration in the general area.
❑ N6-766*   Sea Vampire T.22   G-SPDR, ex Swansea, VH-RAN ntu, RAN, XG766.   ®   10-03

FAYGATE on the A264 between Horsham and Crawley
Park Aviation Supply / Sheet Metal Products: The yard and the surrounding area are due to become
a housing estate. Note that there are several noseless Sea Harrier fuselages here as well. The smashed
remains of Hawk T.1 XX163 and the anonymous Jaguar GR.1 fuselage can be deleted.
❑ XW268 '720' Harrier T.4N   ex Yeovilton, 899, 233 OCU.   12-03
❑ XX733 'ER' Jaguar GR.1B   ex Coltishall, 6, 54, A&AEE, 6, JOCU.
                                       Crashed 23-1-95. Wreck.   12-03
❑ XZ492   Sea Harrier FA.2   ex 800, 801, 899, 800. Ditched 10-12-96.   12-03
❑ ZD400   Harrier GR.7   ex Wittering, 1, Dunsfold, Shawbury, 1. Cr 19-5-97.   12-03

FORD north of the A259 west of Littlehampton
Peter Hague: Perched atop a lofty plinth on the appropriately-named Hunterford site on the periphery of
the former entrance of what was HMS *Peregrine*, the famed FAA station, is Peter's Hunter.
❑ WW654 '834' Hunter GA.11   ex Oving, Portsmouth, Culdrose A2664, A2753,
                                       SAH, FRADU, 738, 229 OCU, 98, 4, 98.   2-04

GATWICK AIRPORT junction 9 of the M23 north of Crawley
Airport: The Comet and Trident are ground trainers. See under Skyview below for notes on the Herald.
As if we needed reminding to always keep our eyes open, during February 2004 while on a property

survey of buildings within the complex two long 'forgotten' Condor fuselages were found strapped to a wall. Negotiations are underway for their removal [1].

❏	G-APMB	Comet 4B	ex Dan-Air, Channel, BEA. CoA 18-5-79.		1-04
❏	G-ARWG*	Condor	uncompleted project. Fuselage, stored.	[1]	2-04
❏	G-AWZX	Trident 3B-101	ex Heathrow, BA, BEA. CoA 30-4-84.		1-04
❏	G-AXGU*	Condor	crashed 31-3-75. Fuselage, stored.	[1]	2-04
❏	G-CEXP*	Herald 209	ex Skyview, ChanEx, I-ZERC, G-BFRJ, 4X-AHO. Skyview colours. External stored from 11-03.		1-04

Skyview Visitors Centre: Located in the South Terminal, much of what is on offer is inter-active and 'virtual', but the Comet nose atop the northern corner of the terminal is well worth admiring and there is a spectators' gallery. Herald G-CEXP was removed from its lofty perch during November 2003 and moved to external store (see above), its fate uncertain.

◆ Daily, summer 7am to 7pm and winter 9am to 4pm. Parking in South Terminal ☎ 01293 502244

❏	'G-AMXA'	Comet C.2R	XK655, ex Hatch, Carlisle, Maryport, Lutterworth, Strathallan, 51, BOAC, G-AMXA ntu. Nose. BOAC c/s.	2-02

Gatwick Hilton: As predicted in *W&R18*, extensions to the hotel meant that DH.60G rep 'G-AAAH' had to check out. After a 21-year stay it moved briefly to Redhill, Surrey, in December 2002, before settling upon <u>Croydon</u>, Surrey.

GOODWOOD AERODROME or Westhampnett, north of Chichester

❏	[G-BGRN]	Tomahawk 112	ex N9684N. CoA 12-2-00. Dump.	5-03
❏	G-COUP	Ercoupe 415C	ex N99280, NC99280. CoA 17-7-99. *Jenny Lin.*	9-01
❏	N281Q	Enstrom 280C	Hulk. Spares recovery.	11-96

HAYWARD'S HEATH on the A272 north of Brighton
No.172 Squadron, Air Training Corps:

❏	XX520	Bulldog T.1	9288M, ex Newton, EM UAS, CFS, RNEFTS, 2 FTS.	1-04

KIRDFORD north of the A272, west of Billingshurst
Sailplane Preservation Group (SPG): The group has disbanded due to lack of support. Ka-4 CWU (BGA.1872) is stored by the SPG's sister-ground, the BPG, see <u>Lancing</u>, W Sussex.

LANCING on the A27 east of Worthing
Balloon Preservation Group (BPG): Formed in 1993 by Bob Kent, BPG is the world's largest balloon collection. The majority of the balloons are held in a storage facility in the county. Balloons are regularly displayed at venues across the country. The group are willing to attend events with balloons on request and have equipment available for long-term loan to museums etc. Contact the address below. See under Farnborough, Hants, for two BPG balloons out on loan. The Sailplane Preservation Group's Ka-4 is stored care of BPG [1]. The following have been deleted: Cameron N-90 G-BPZO, Cameron N-31 G-COOP and Barnes SS N9045C.

◆ Visits possible by prior permission *only*. ✉ 44 Shadwells Road, Lancing, BN15 9EW ☎ 01903 533835 e-mail bpg@ntlworld.com www.bpg.flyer.co.uk

☞ A two-column layout has been adopted. Some of the details previously given have been omitted, but for those with a specific interest in balloons and airships, this will be readily available elsewhere.

❏	–*	CWU	Schleicher Ka-4	BGA.1872, ex D-5427. Stored.			[1]	3-04
❏	G-AYVA	Cameron O-84		3-04	❏	G-BBDJ	Thunder Ax7-56	3-04
❏	G-BAKO	Cameron O-84		3-04	❏	G-BBYL*	Cameron O-77	3-04
❏	G-BAND	Cameron O-84		3-04	❏	G-BBYR	Cameron O-65	3-04
❏	G-BAOW	Cameron O-65		3-04	❏	G-BCAP*	Cameron O-56	3-04
❏	G-BAST	Cameron O-84		3-04	❏	G-BCAS	Thunder Ax7-77	3-04
❏	G-BAYC*	Cameron O-65		3-04	❏	G-BCCH	Thunder Ax6-56A	3-04

❏	G-BCNR*	Thunder Ax7-77A	3-04
❏	G-BCRE	Cameron O-77	3-04
❏	G-BDGO	Thunder Ax7-77	3-04
❏	G-BDMO	Thunder Ax7-77	3-04
❏	G-BEIF	Cameron O-65	3-04
❏	G-BEJB	Thunder Ax6-56	3-04
❏	G-BGST	Thunder Ax7-65	3-04
❏	G-BHAT	Thunder Ax7-77	3-04
❏	G-BHYO*	Cameron N-77	3-04
❏	G-BJZC	Thunder Ax7-65	3-04
❏	G-BKIY	Thunder Ax3	3-04
❏	G-BKOW	Colt 77A	3-04
❏	G-BKPN*	Cameron N-77	3-04
❏	G-BKZB*	Cameron 56SS	3-04
❏	G-BLDL	Cameron V-77	3-04
❏	G-BLGX*	Thunder Ax7-65	3-04
❏	G-BLIP	Cameron N-77	3-04
❏	G-BLKJ	Thunder Ax7-65	3-04
❏	G-BLSH	Cameron V-77	3-04
❏	G-BLZB	Cameron N-65	3-04
❏	G-BMKX	Cameron 77SS	3-04
❏	G-BMMU*	Thunder Ax7-77	3-04
❏	G-BMST	Cameron N-31	3-04
❏	G-BMUJ*	Colt SS	3-04
❏	G-BMUK*	Colt SS	3-04
❏	G-BMUL*	Colt SS	3-04
❏	G-BMWU	Cameron N-42	3-04
❏	G-BNCH*	Cameron V-77	3-04
❏	G-BNHL	Colt Beer Glass 90	3-04
❏	G-BNMI*	Colt SS	3-04
❏	G-BOCF*	Colt 77A	3-04
❏	G-BOGT	Colt 77A	3-04
❏	G-BONK	Colt 180A	3-04
❏	G-BONV	Colt 17A	3-04
❏	G-BOOP	Cameron N-90	3-04
❏	G-BORA	Colt 77A	3-04
❏	G-BOSF*	Colt 69A	3-04
❏	G-BOTE	Thunder Ax8-90	3-04
❏	G-BPAH	Colt 69A	3-04
❏	G-BPDF*	Cameron V-77	3-04
❏	G-BPFJ	Cameron 90SS	3-04
❏	G-BPFX	Colt 21A	3-04
❏	G-BPSZ	Cameron N-180	3-04
❏	G-BRDP*	Colt SS	3-04
❏	G-BRFR	Cameron N-105	3-04
❏	G-BRLX	Cameron N-77	3-04
❏	G-BSBM	Cameron N-77	3-04
❏	G-BSGB*	Gaertner AX-3	3-04
❏	G-BSWZ	Cameron A-180	3-04
❏	G-BTJF*	Thunder Ax10-180	3-04
❏	G-BTML	Cameron SS	3-04
❏	G-BTPV	Colt 90A	3-04
❏	G-BTXM*	Colt 21A	3-04
❏	G-BUET	Cameron SS	3-04
❏	G-BUEU	Colt 21A	3-04
❏	G-BUIZ	Cameron N-90	3-04
❏	G-BUKC	Cameron A-180	3-04
❏	G-BUNI*	Cameron SS Bunny	3-04
❏	G-BUUV*	Lindstrand LBL-77	3-04
❏	G-BUXA	Colt 210A	3-04

❏	G-BVBJ	Colt SS Coffee Jar	3-04
❏	G-BVBK	Colt SS Coffee Jar	3-04
❏	G-BVFY	Colt 210A	3-04
❏	G-BVIO	Colt SS Can	3-04
❏	G-BVWH	Cameron N-90 Bulb	3-04
❏	G-BVWI	Colt 65SS	3-04
❏	G-BWAN	Cameron N-77	3-04
❏	G-BWFK*	Lindstrand LBL-77A	3-04
❏	G-BWGA	Lindstrand LBL-105A	3-04
❏	G-BWLA*	Colt 69A	3-04
❏	G-BWUR	Thunder Ax10-210	3-04
❏	G-BWZP*	Cameron SS Home	3-04
❏	G-BXAL	Cameron SS	3-04
❏	G-BXAM*	Cameron N-90	3-04
❏	G-BXAX*	Cameron N-77	3-04
❏	G-BXHM	Lindstrand LBL-25A	3-04
❏	G-BXHN	Lindstrand SS Can	3-04
❏	G-BXIZ*	Lindstrand LBL-31A	3-04
❏	G-BXND*	Cameron SS Thomas	3-04
❏	G-BXUG*	Lindstrand SS Baby Bel	3-04
❏	G-BXUH*	Lindstrand LBL-31A	3-04
❏	G-BYFK*	Cameron SS Printer	3-04
❏	G-BZIH	Lindstrand 31A	3-04
❏	G-BZTS*	Cameron SS Bertie	3-04
❏	G-CBPG*	Barnes SS Condom	3-04
❏	G-CFBI*	Colt 56A	3-04
❏	G-COLR	Colt 69A	3-04
❏	G-COMP*	Cameron N-90	3-04
❏	G-CURE	Colt 77A	3-04
❏	G-DHLI	Colt 90SS	3-04
❏	G-DHLZ	Colt 31A	3-04
❏	G-ENRY*	Cameron N-105	3-04
❏	G-ETFT	Colt SS Fin Times	3-04
❏	G-FZZY	Colt 69A	3-04
❏	G-GEUP	Cameron N-77	3-04
❏	G-GOAL*	Lindstrand LBL-105A	3-04
❏	G-GURL	Cameron A-210	3-04
❏	G-HELP	Colt 17A	3-04
❏	G-HENS	Cameron N-65	3-04
❏	G-HLIX	Cameron SS	3-04
❏	G-IAMP	Cameron H-34	3-04
❏	G-IBBC*	Cameron SS Globe	3-04
❏	G-IGEL	Cameron N-90	3-04
❏	G-IMAG	Colt 77A	3-04
❏	G-JANB	Colt SS	3-04
❏	G-KNOB*	Lindstrand LBL-180A	3-04
❏	G-KORN	Cameron 70SS	3-04
❏	G-LBCS*	Colt 31A	3-04
❏	G-LBNK*	Cameron N-105	3-04
❏	G-LLAI	Colt 21A	3-04
❏	G-LLYD*	Cameron N-31	3-04
❏	G-MAAC*	ANR-1 Airship	3-04
❏	G-MAPS	Thunder Ax7-77	3-04
❏	G-MHBD*	Cameron O-105	3-04
❏	G-MOLI	Cameron A-250	3-04
❏	G-NPNP	Cameron N-105	3-04
❏	G-NPWR	Cameron RX-100	3-04
❏	G-NWPB	Thunder Ax7-77Z	3-04
❏	G-OAFC	Airtour AH-56	3-04
❏	G-OBUY*	Colt 69A	3-04

❑	G-OCAR*	Colt 77A	3-04	❑	G-SEUK	Cameron TV-80SS	3-04
❑	G-OCAW*	Lindstrand SS Bananas	3-04	❑	G-TTWO	Colt 56A	3-04
❑	G-OCND	Cameron O-77	3-04	❑	G-UMBO*	Colt SS Jumbo	3-04
❑	G-OEGG*	Cameron SS Egg	3-04	❑	G-UNIP	Cameron SS Oil Can	3-04
❑	G-OFLI*	Colt 105A	3-04	❑	G-UNRL*	Lindstrand RR-21	3-04
❑	G-OGGS*	Thunder Ax8-84	3-04	❑	G-USGB*	Colt 105A	3-04
❑	G-OHDC	Colt SS Film Can	3-04	❑	G-VOLT	Cameron N-77	3-04
❑	G-OLDV	Colt 90A	3-04	❑	G-WATT	Cameron SS	3-04
❑	G-OMXS*	Lindstrand LBL-105A	3-04	❑	G-WCAT	Colt SS	3-04
❑	G-OSVY	Sky 31-24	3-04	❑	G-WINE	Thunder Ax7-77	3-04
❑	G-OVAA*	Colt SS Jumbo	3-04	❑	G-WORK*	Thunder Ax10-180	3-04
❑	G-OXRG	Colt SS Film Can	3-04	❑	C-GYZI	Cameron O-77	3-04
❑	G-PHOT*	Colt SS Film Cassette	3-04	❑	D-OPHA	Fire Balloons 3000	3-04
❑	G-PNEU*	Colt SS Bibendum	3-04	❑	D-PAMGAS	Cameron N-90	3-04
❑	G-PONY	Colt 31A	3-04	❑	DQ-PBF	Thunder Ax10-180	3-04
❑	G-POPP	Colt 105A	3-04	❑	N413JB	Cameron O-84	3-04
❑	G-PSON	Colt SS	3-04	❑	N4519U	Head Ax-09-118	3-04
❑	G-PURE	Colt 70SS Can	3-04	❑	N5023U	Avian Magnum IX	3-04
❑	G-PYLN	Colt 80SS	3-04	❑	OO-ARK*	Cameron N-56	3-04
❑	G-RARE	Thunder Ax5-42	3-04	❑	OO-BDO	Cameron N-90	3-04
❑	G-RIPS	Colt 110SS	3-04	❑	OO-BRM*	Thunder Ax7-77	3-04
❑	G-SCAH	Cameron V-77	3-04	❑	OO-JAT*	Cameron Zero 25	3-04
❑	G-SCFO	Cameron O-77	3-04	❑	VH-AYY	Kavanagh D-77	3-04
❑	G-SEGA	Cameron SS	3-04				

Jim Pearce: In December 2003, the well-known salvage expert acquired another gem from Russia.
❑ 3523*   Bf 109E-7   ex Russia, 5/JG5 'CS+AJ'. Crashed 3-4-42.   12-03

LITTLEHAMPTON on the A259 west of Worthing
Frank Matthews: No update on the Islander project.
❑ VQ-SAC   BN-2A Islander   ex Shoreham. Crashed 4-9-76. Forward fuselage.   ®   3-94

PULBOROUGH on the A29 south-west of Horsham
The Miles Aircraft Collection (TMAC and note the addition of 'The'!): In late August 2002, MAC's cache of Gemini and Messenger parts and airframes (including Geminis G-AKGD and G-AKHZ and Messenger VP-KJL) stored in this general area moved to <u>Hooton Park</u>, Cheshire, for restoration. In a similar venture, MAC have supplied wings and other components to the Kent Battle of Britain Museum, Hawkinge, Kent, for their project to create a Kestrel-engined Master. Several MAC artefacts can be found under Woodley, Berks.
✉ Membership enquiries only - no airframes held: Peter Amos, 4 Castle Bungalows, Storrington, near Pulborough, RH20 4LB, **fax** 01903 893700 **e-mail** amos@milesaircraft.fsnet.co.uk

SHOREHAM AIRPORT west of the River Adur, south of the A27
Visitor Centre and **Shoreham Airport Historical Association**: Located near the entrance to the 1930s terminal building, a wide array of archives and artefacts are on show. The 'Flea' was built during 2001 by friends and is used as a travelling exhibit. (Grasshopper TX.1 WZ820 is on loan at Northampton, Northants.)
◆ Open daily 10am to 5pm. Guided tours on Tue, Thu and Sat from 1pm - booking *essential.*
✉ 14J Cecil Pashley Way, Shoreham Airport, Shoreham-by-Sea, BN43 5FF. ☎ 01273 441061
e-mail saha.archive@virgin.net **www**.thearchiveshoreham.co.uk
❑ –   BAPC.20 Lee-Richards   ex Winthorpe, *Those Magnificent Men...*
             Annular REP   350cc Douglas for ground-running.   2-04
❑ –   BAPC.277 HM.14 'Flea'   see above.   2-04

Museum of D-Day Aviation: A series of events in the spring of 2003 led founders Barry Field and Ken Rimmel to call it a day with this fascinating museum. Auctioneers Rupert Toovey and Company staged an auction of the contents on 17th May 2003. Spitfire FSM 'MJ751' moved to Duxford, Cambs, during June 2003. P-2 Kraguj 30151 moved to Sopley, Hants. That leaves the Typhoon cockpit section unaccounted for.

Elsewhere: Transair's 'gate guardian' Wessex was replaced in December 2003 with the Tornado [1]. The Wessex may well be travelling to Langford Lodge, N Ireland [2]. Colt 108 G-ARNG was flying again by 2001. Iskra SP-DOF (G-BXVZ) had moved to Manston, Kent, by May 2002.

❑ G-ASRB	Condor	CoA 1-11-98. Stored.		5-03
❑ G-ATRL	Cessna F.150F	CoA 21-2-98. Dump.		5-03
❑ G-BAXP*	Aztec 250E	ex N13990. CoA 5-3-<u>92</u>. Dump, first noted 5-03.		5-03
❑ G-BHEH	Cessna 310G	ex Bagby, N1720, N8916Z. CoA 9-12-96. Dump.		2-02
❑ G-BPRP	Cessna 150E	ex N3569J. CoA 23-5-98. Dump.		5-03
❑ G-BWDE	Navajo P	ex G-HWKN, HB-LIR, D-IAIR, N7304L. CoA 18-12-96. Stored.		2-04
❑ G-CKCK	Enstrom 280FX	ex OO-PVL. CoA 14-5-98. Original pod.		1-00
❑ G-MBTS	Whing Ding II	Cancelled 6-9-94. Stored in container.		2-02
❑ G-REBL	Hughes 269B	ex N9493F. CoA 9-10-95.	®	5-03
❑ N6819F	Cessna 150F	Dump.		5-03
❑ XR517 'N'	Wessex HC.2	ex Ipswich, Fleetlands, 60, 72, 18.	[2]	3-04
❑ XX947*	Tornado P.03	ex Ipswich, Cosford 8979M, St Athan, Marham, Warton. Arrived 9-12-03. Displayed.	[1]	3-04

Northbrook College: Queen Air G-AWKX is dismantled but still very much with the college [1]. (*W&R18*, p217 refers.) Cessna 310 G-APNJ departed on 2nd March 2004 for Winthorpe, Notts. Pembroke C.1 XL929 moved by road to Coventry, Warks, on 25th July 2002.

❑ G-AWKX	Queen Air A65	CoA 25-10-89.	[1]	5-03
❑ G-OBUS	Archer 181	ex G-BMTT, N3002K. Crashed 18-4-89. Fuselage.		3-00
❑ G-TOBY	Cessna 172B	ex Sandown, G-ARCM, N6952X. Dam 15-10-83.		5-03
❑ WT806	Hunter GA.11	ex Ipswich, Shawbury, Abingdon, Chivenor, FRADU, CFS, 14. Inst.		5-03
❑ '2807' '103'	T-6G Texan	G-BHTH, ex N2807G, 49-3072. Crashed 13-3-95.	®	5-03
❑ 51-14526	T-6G Texan	G-BRWB, ex Duxford, FAF, 51-14526.		
'RC'		*Thumper*. Crashed 5-7-01.	®	2-02

TANGMERE south of the A27, east of Chichester
Tangmere Military Aviation Museum: During the summer of 2003, the trustees launched an appeal to raise £300,000 to provide for a second display hall and other improvements to the site.
   The Swift, while an operational version, stands handsomely for the record breaking of Mike Lithgow. EE459, WB188 and WK281 are on loan from the RAF Museum – RAFM [1]. The Meteor F.8 is a complex composite, including items from VZ530, and includes a rare IFR probe [1]. The Hunter F.4 nose is on loan from 1254 Squadron ATC, Godalming. The rest of that Hunter became T.68 J-4201 of the Swiss Air Force and is still extant [2]. The Lightning is in the markings of F.6 XR753 'A', 23 Squadron. The *real* XR753 can be found at Leeming, N Yorks [3]. It and the Hunter F.5 were gifted by Raymond and Meryl Hansed. The Gannet cockpit mentioned in *W&R18* (p217) moved to Hooton Park, Cheshire, arriving there on 23rd May 2002.
◆ Signposted from the A27. Open daily 10am to 5.30pm from Mar to Oct and 10am to 4.30pm in February and November. *Closed* December and January. Parties at other times by arrangement.
   ✉ Tangmere Airfield, Chichester, West Sussex, PO20 6ES ☎ 01243 775223 **fax** 01243 789490
   e-mail admin@tangmere-museum.org.uk **www**.tangmere-museum.org.uk

❑ 'K5054'	Spitfire proto FSM	BAPC.214, ex Southampton, Hendon, Thruxton, Middle Wallop, Thruxton, Andover.	8-03
❑ 'L1679' 'JX-G'	Hurricane FSM	BAPC.241, ex Chilbolton, Middle Wallop, Thruxton. 1 Sqn colours. Built by AeroFab.	8-03
❑ P3179*	Hurricane I	ex Hove, 43. Shot down 30-8-40. Cockpit.	8-03
❑ 'BL924''AZ-G'	Spitfire FSM	BAPC.242, *Valdemar Atterdag*, 234 Sqn colours.	8-03

❑ EE549	Meteor IV Special	ex Cosford, St Athan, Abingdon, Hendon, St Athan, Innsworth 7008M, Fulbeck, Cranwell, CFE, FCCS, RAFHSF.		RAFM	8-03
❑ 'WA829' 'A'	Meteor F.8	WA984, ex Southampton, Wimborne, Tarrant Rushton, 211 AFS, 19. IFR probe. 245 Sqn c/s.		[1]	8-03
❑ WB188	Hawker P.1067 (Hunter F.3)	ex Cosford, St Athan, Colerne, Melksham, Halton 7154M, Hawkers. Hunter prototype.		RAFM	8-03
❑ WK281 'S'	Swift FR.5	ex Hendon, St Athan, Swinderby, Finningley, Colerne 7712M, Northolt, 79. 79 Sqn colours.		RAFM	8-03
❑ WP190* 'K'	Hunter F.5	ex Quedgeley, Hucclecote, Stanbridge 8473M, Upwood, Finningley, Bircham Newton 7582M, Nicosia, 1. 1 Sqn colours, Suez stripes. Arrived 2-6-02.		®	6-02
❑ WV332*	Hunter F.4	7673M, ex Godalming, Dunsfold G-9-406, Halton, 234, 112, 67. 234 Squadron colours. Nose.		[2]	8-03
❑ XJ580 '131'	Sea Vixen FAW.2	ex Christchurch, Bournemouth FRL, RAE Farnborough, 899. 899 Sqn c/s.		®	8-03
❑ XN299 '758'	Whirlwind HAR.7	ex Southsea, Higher Blagdon, Culdrose, JWE Old Sarum, Fleetlands, 847 'B' Flt, 847, Culdrose, 848. 848 Sqn c/s, *Bulwark. The Iron Chicken.*			8-03
❑ 'XR753'* 'A'	Lightning F.53	ZF578, ex Quedgeley, Cardiff-Wales, Warton, RSAF 53-670, G-27-40. 23 Squadron c/s. Arr 6-02.		[3]	8-03
❑ 19252	T-33A-1-LO	ex Hailsham, Sculthorpe, French AF. USAF c/s.			7-03

TURNERS HILL on the B2110 east of Crawley

Tulley's Farm Maize Maze: (Please note that there is no apostrophe in Turners, but there is in Tulley's!) Diplomate G-AYKG was first noted at this attraction in August 2002 and was last noted in May 2003, by September it had moved on to pastures new at Somerford, Dorset. (Note that the life of a maze seems quite short and it *may* well be that *Kilo-Golf* 'does the rounds' of mazes! See under Somerford for more thoughts.)

WASHINGTON east of the A24 north of Worthing

The hulk of EP.9 Prospector G-ARDG left by road in April 2002 believed bound for New Zealand. Meteor T.79mod) WF877 left by road on 18th September 2003 for Duxford, Cambs.

WEST CHILTINGTON on the B2139 south of Horsham

Adrian Brook: G-AGOY will fly in prototype colours when complete.

❑ G-AGOY	Messenger 3	ex Hatch, Southill, Castletown, EI-AGE, HB-EIP, G-AGOY, U-0247.	®	1-00

WARWICKSHIRE

BAXTERLEY AERODROME south of the A5 near Atherstone

Midland Warplane Museum (MWM): With the help of a series of friends of other organisations, MWM pulled off a complex and challenging recovery of the forward fuselage and other items from a Wellington IV that had force-landed on the beach at Uig Bay, Isle of Lewis in July 2002. The Oxford was fitted with Standard Beam Approach equipment and was DH built. It *may* be AT601 [1]. The Harvard has a plate giving the c/n as 14-2441, built in 1944. This *might* make it KF741. Comments? [2]

♦ Visits possible by prior appointment *only*. ✉ Mark J Evans, Spring View, Crackley Lane, Kenilworth, CV8 2JS.

❑ Z1206*	Wellington IV	ex Isle of Lewis, 104 OTU, 142. Crashed 26-1-44. Forward fuselage, arrived 7-02.		2-04
❑ –	Oxford	ex Canada. Off-site.	® [1]	2-04
❑ –	Harvard IIB	cockpit section. Stored, off site.	[2]	2-04

Others: Along with Tiger Moth G-APGL is an anonymous fuselage frame.

❏ G-APGL	Tiger Moth	ex Fairoaks, NM140, LAS, AOPS, 14 RFS, 8 RFS, 8 EFTS, 3 EFTS, 22 EFTS, 3 EFTS, ORTU, Tarrant Rushton SF.	®	3-00
❏ –	Tiger Moth	ex Cranfield, VAT et al.		7-02

BIDFORD AERODROME Or Bickmarsh, north-east of Evesham south of Bidford-on-Avon
Avon Soaring Centre: Glider references now long-ish-in-the-tooth...

❏ G-BGKC*	Rallye 110ST	CoA 8-9-99. Stored. First noted 6-02.	10-03
❏ G-BAOM*	Rallye	fuselage. First noted 10-03.	10-03
❏ – DKY	Ka7 Rhonadler	BGA.2187. Ex RAFGSA.342. CoA 4-98. Stored.	9-99
❏ – DYR	Ka7 Rhonadler	BGA.2489. Ex D-5220. CoA 8-99. Stored.	9-99
❏ –	L.13 Blanik	BGA.2121. CoA 4-85. Stored.	5-98

COVENTRY AIRPORT or Baginton, or even West Midlands Airport
at the A45/A423 junction, south of the city
Midland Air Museum (MAM), incorporating the **Sir Frank Whittle Jet Heritage Centre**.
Notes: See under Keevil, Wilts, for 'another' BGA.804 [1]. Prentice VS623 is fitted with the wings
from G-AONB (VR244) [2]. Meteor NF.14 WS838 is on loan from the RAF Museum [3]. The Gannet
T.2 is on loan from FAAM [4]. The Buccaneer nose section, a Gulf War veteran, is on loan from Robin
Phipps [5] - see also under Bruntingthorpe, Leics. The Beaufighter nose section is possibly Mk.VI
T5298. In which case it was previously 4552M and TFU Defford [6]. The HH-43B uses parts from
24538, including the fins [7]. See under Bristol, Glos, for MAM's Beagle 206.
Departures: Typhoon cockpit 'JR505' had left the site by 3-04; Shackleton T.4 VP293 nose moved
to Winthorpe, Notts, by 9-03.
♦ Well signed from the A45/A423 junction. Open Apr to Oct Mon to Sat 10am to 5pm, Sun and Bank
Hols 10am to 6pm. Nov to Mar daily 10am to 4.30pm. Closed Xmas and Boxing Day. Other times
by appointment. ✉ Coventry Airport, Rowley Road, Baginton, Coventry CV8 3AZ ☎ / fax 024 76
301033 e-mail midlandairmuseum@aol.com www.midlandairmuseum.org.uk

❏ G-EBJG	Pixie III	ex Coventry, Stratford. CoA 2-10-36. Remains.		2-04
❏ G-ABOI	Wheeler Slymph	ex Coventry, Old Warden. On loan. Stored.		2-04
❏ G-AEGV	HM.14 'Flea'	ex Coventry, Knowle, Northampton, Sywell.		2-04
❏ G-ALCU	Dove 2	ex airfield, VT-CEH. CoA 16-3-73.		2-04
❏ G-APJJ	Fairey Ultra Light	ex Heaton Chapel, Coventry, Hayes. CoA 1-4-59.		2-04
❏ G-APRL	Argosy 101	ex ABC/Elan, Sagittair, N890U, N602Z, N6507R, G-APRL. *Edna*. CoA 23-3-87.		2-04
❏ G-APWN	Whirlwind Srs 3	ex Cranfield, Redhill, VR-BER, G-APWN, 5N-AGI, G-APWN. CoA 17-5-78. Bristows c/s.		2-04
❏ G-ARYB	HS.125 Srs 1	ex Hatfield. CoA 22-1-68.		2-04
❏ G-MJWH	Vortex 120	hang glider, former microlight.		2-04
❏ – BGA.804	Cadet TX.1	ex VM589. Stored.	[1]	2-04
❏ 'A7317'	Pup REP	BAPC.179, ex Waltham Abbey, North Weald, *Wings*.		2-04
❏ EE531	Meteor F.4	ex Bentham, Coventry , Birmingham, Weston Park, Birmingham, RAE Lasham, 7090M, A&AEE, makers.		2-04
❏ VF301 'RAL-G'	Vampire F.1	ex Stoneleigh, Debden, 7060M, 208 AFS, 595, 226 OCU. 605 Sqn colours.		2-04
❏ VS623	Prentice T.1	G-AOKZ, ex Shoreham, Redhill, Southend, VS623, CFS, 2 FTS, 22 FTS.	® [2]	2-04
❏ VT935	BP P. 111A	ex Cranfield, RAE Bedford.		2-04
❏ VZ477	Meteor F.8	ex Kimbolton, 7741M, APS, 245. Nose.		2-04
❏ WF922	Canberra PR.3	ex Cambridge, 39, 69, 58, 82.		2-04
❏ WH646 'EG'	Canberra T.17A	ex Wyton, 360, 45, RNZAF, 45, 10, 50. Nose.		2-04
❏ WS838	Meteor NF.14	ex Cosford, Manchester, Cosford, Shawbury, Colerne, RAE Bedford, RRE, MoS, 64, 238 OCU.	[3]	2-04
❏ WV797 '491'	Sea Hawk FGA.6	ex Perth, Culdrose A2637, Halton 8155M, Sydenham, 738, 898, 899, Fleetlands, 787.		2-04

❑	XA508	'627'	Gannet T.2	ex Yeovilton, Manadon, A2472, 737. 737 Sqn c/s.	[4]	2-04
❑	XA699		Javelin FAW.5	ex Cosford, Locking, 7809M, Shawbury, Kemble,		
				Shawbury, 5, 151. 5 Squadron colours.		2-04
❑	XD626		Vampire T.11	ex Bitteswell, Shawbury, CATCS, CNCS,		
				5 FTS, RAFC, CFS. Stored.		2-04
❑	XE855		Vampire T.11	ex Upton-by-Chester, Woodford, Chester, 27 MU,		
				22 MU, 10 MU, AWOCU. Pod, spares.		2-04
❑	XF382	'15'	Hunter F.6A	ex Brawdy, 1 TWU, TWU, 229 OCU, FCS, 65, 63, 92.		2-04
❑	'XG190'		Hunter F.51	E-425, ex Dunsfold, G-9-446, DanAF Esk.724.		
				111 Sqn 'Black Arrows' colours by 6-00.		2-04
❑	XJ579		Sea Vixen FAW.2	ex Farnborough, A&AEE, Llanbedr, 899, 766. Nose.		2-04
❑	XK741		Gnat F.1	ex Leamington Spa, Fordhouses, Dunsfold,		
				Hamble, Boscombe Down, Dunsfold. Fuselage.		2-04
❑	XK789		Grasshopper TX.1	ex Warwick, Cosford, Stamford.		2-04
❑	XK907		Whirlwind	ex Bubbenhall, Panshanger, Elstree, Luton,		
			HAS.7	ETPS, RRE, Alvis. Cockpit. Stored.		2-04
❑	XL360		Vulcan B.2	ex 44, 101, 35, 617, 230 OCU, Wadd Wing, 230 OCU,		
				Scamp W, 617. *City of Coventry*. 617 Sqn c/s.		2-04
❑	XN685		Sea Vixen FAW.2	ex Chester, Cosford, Cranwell, 8173M,		
				890, 766, 893, HSA Hatfield.		2-04
❑	XR771	'BM'	Lightning F.6	ex Binbrook, 5, 11, 5, 56, 74.		2-04
❑	XX899		Buccaneer S.2B	ex Kidlington, Stock, St Athan, Lossiemouth,		
				208, 12, Gulf Det, 237 OCU, 12, 237 OCU,		
				12, 237 OCU, 16, 15, 12, 208. Nose.	® [5]	2-04
❑			Beaufighter	ex Birmingham, Coventry. Cockpit.	[6]	2-04
❑	R-756		F-104G	ex Aalborg, Danish AF, 64-17756.	®	2-04
❑	70		Mystère IVA	ex Sculthorpe, Fr AF. *Patrouille de France* colours.		2-04
❑	51-4419		T-33A-1-LO	ex Sculthorpe, French AF. Blue with shark's mouth.		2-04
❑	17473		T-33A-1-LO	ex Cosford, Sculthorpe, French AF.		2-04
❑	54-2174	'SM'	F-100D-16-NA	ex Sculthorpe, French AF.		2-04
❑	280020		Fl 282B V-20	ex Coventry, Cranfield, Brize Norton,		
				Travemünde 'CJ+SN'. Frame.		2-04
❑	959		MiG-21SPS	ex Duxford, Cottbus, LSK.		2-04
❑	55-713	'C'	Lightning T.55	ex Warton, ZF598, RSAF 55-713, G-27-72. Saudi c/s.		2-04
❑	29640	'08'	SAAB J29F	ex Southend, R Swedish AF.		2-04
❑	24535		HH-43B Huskie	ex Woodbridge, 40 ARRS, Det 2. Stored.	[7]	2-04
❑	37414		F-4C-15-MC	ex Woodbridge, New York ANG. Stored.		2-04
❑	37699	'CG'	F-4C-21-MC	ex Upper Heyford, Fairford, Illinois ANG, 557 TFS,		
				356 TFS, 480 TFS. 366th TFW c/s, MiG 'kill'.		2-04
❑	60312		F-101B-80-MC	ex Alconbury, Davis-Monthan, Kentucky ANG.		2-04
❑	58-2062		U-6A Beaver	ex Mannheim, US Army.		2-04
❑	—	BAPC.9	Humber Mono	ex Birmingham Airport, Yeovilton,		
			REP	Wroughton, Yeovilton, Coventry.		2-04
❑	—	BAPC.32	Tom Thumb	ex Coventry, Bewdley, Coventry, Banbury.		
				Unfinished 1930s homebuild. Stored.		2-04
❑	—	BAPC.126	Turbulent	ex Shoreham, Croydon. Static airframe.		2-04

Air Atlantique Classic Flight: (Note the correct name.) On 1st March 2004 it was announced that as
well as a significant expansion of the Flight's jet element, several aircraft from the Atlantic Air Transport
fleet had been transferred and would operate under the Classic Flight banner. These are marked Ω. Other
than the CV-440, all were previously part of the airline's active list, so well this entry considerably.
   Classic Aviation Projects operates in association with the Classic Flight under the title **Canberra
Display Team** [1].The **Shackleton Preservation Trust** (formerly known as the **963 Support Group**)
have made significant progress with WR963, which regularly ground runs. It has had the radome
removed and has been painted as an MR.2 [2]. (e-mail shack106.chalk@lineone.net) Aircraft marked ➥
attended the '100 Years of Flight Experience' static display at the International Air Tattoo, Fairford, Glos,
July 2003. Proctor V G-AKIU is being restored at <u>Seaton Ross,</u> E Yorks, for the Flight.
   ◆ All visits by prior arrangement.

❑	G-AGTM		Dragon Rapide ✈	ex JY-ACL, OD-ABP, G-AGTM, NF875.		2-04
❑	G-AIDL		Dragon Rapide ✈	ex Biggin Hill, Allied Airways, TX310.	➥	2-04

❑ G-AJRE*   J/1 Autocrat   ex 'Suffolk'. CoA 8-8-02. Arrived 10-03.   2-04
❑ G-AMPY*   C-47B-15-DK ✈ ex EI-BKJ ntu, G-AMPY, N15751, G-AMPY,
    TF-FIO, G-AMPY, JY-ABE, G-AMPY, KN442,
    44-76540. Stored.   Ω 3-04
❑ G-AMRA*   C-47B-15-DK ✈ ex XE280, G-AMRA, KK151, 43-49474.   Ω 3-04
❑ G-AMSV*   C-47B-25-DK ✈ ex F-BSGV ntu, G-AMSV, KN397, 44-76488.   Ω 3-04
❑ G-ANAF*   C-47B-35-DK ✈ ex Thales, N170GP, Duxford, G-ANAF, KP220,
    44-77104. Former radar test-bed.   Ω 3-04
❑ G-APRS   Twin Pioneer 3   ex Staverton, G-BCWF, XT610, G-APRS,
    ✈ PI-C430 ntu. *Primrose.* 'Raspberry Ripple' c/s. ➥ 2-04
❑ G-APSA*   DC-6A ✈ ex 4W-ABQ, HZ-ADA, G-APSA, CF-MCK,
    CF-CZY.   Ω 3-04
❑ G-AYWA   Avro XIX Srs 2   ex Bridge of Wier, Lochwinnoch, Strathallan,
    Thruxton, OO-VIT, OO-DFA. Spares. off-site 3-02
❑ G-AZHJ   Twin Pioneer 3   ex Prestwick, Staverton, Prestwick, G-31-16,
    XP295, Odiham SF, MoA, 1310F, Odiham SF,
    230. CoA 23-8-90. Spares. off-site 3-02
❑ G-CONV*   CV-440-54   ex Atlantic Group, CS-TML, N357SA, N28KE,
    N4402. Stored.   3-04
❑ G-DHDV   Devon C.2/2 ✈ ex BBMF VP981, Northolt, 207, 21, WCS,
    Wildenrath CF, AAFCE, MinTech, AAFCE, Paris
    Air Attaché, Hendon SF, AFWE. Gulf Aviation c/s. 2-04
❑ G-JAYI   J/1 Autocrat ✈ ex OY-ALU, D-EGYK, OO-ABF.   2-04
❑ G-SIXC*   DC-6A/B ✈ ex N93459, N90645, B-1006, XW-PFZ, B-1006. Ω 3-04
❑ TX226   Anson C.19   ex Duxford, Little Staughton, East Dereham, Colerne
    7865M, Shawbury, FTCCF, OCTU Jurby, 187,
    Hemswell SF, Coningsby CF, CBE. Spares. off-site 3-02
❑ TX235   Anson C.19/2   ex Caernarfon, Higher Blagdon, Andover, Shawbury,
    SCS, FCCS, CTFU, OCTU, 64 GCS, 2 GCS. off-site 3-02
❑ VP959 'L' Devon C.2   ex Wellesbourne, Biggin Hill, N959VP ntu,
  N959VP   G-BWFB, VP959, RAE. Stored. off-site 3-02
❑ VR259 'M' Prentice 1 ✈ G-APJB, ex VR259, 1 ASS, 2 ASS, RAFC.
    2 ASS colours. ➥ 2-04
❑ 'WD379' 'K' Chipmunk T.10   G-APLO, ex EI-AHU, WB696, 11 RFS,
    ✈ Ab UAS, 11 RFS. Cam UAS colours. 3-02
❑ WD413   Anson C.21 ✈ G-VROE, ex G-BFIR, Duxford, Lee-on-Solent,
    Enstone, Tees-side, Strathallan, Bournemouth,
    East Midlands, 7881M, Aldergrove, TCCS,
    BCCS, 1 ANS. Yellow 'T' bands colours. ➥ 2-04
❑ WK163   Canberra B.2/6 ✈ G-BVWC, ex DRA Farnborough, DRA Bedford,
    RAE, Napier, ASM, MoA. B.2 nose format.
    617 Squadron colours. ➥ [1] 2-04
❑ WM167*   Meteor TT.20 ✈ ex Bournemouth, Blackbushe, RAE Llanbedr,
  G-LOSM   228, Colerne CS, 228 OCU. Arrived 3-04. 3-04
❑ 'WR470'*   Venom FB.50   G-DHVM, ex G-GONE, Bournemouth, Chester,
    ✈ Bournemouth, Swiss AF J-1542. Arr 23-9-03. 2-04
❑ WT711 '833' Hunter GA.11   ex Culdrose A2645, A2731, Shawbury,
    FRADU, 14, 54. 2-04
❑ WR963 'X' Shackleton   ex SPT, Waddington, Lossiemouth, 8, 205,
    AEW.2   28, 210, 224. *Ermintrude.* 38 Sqn colours. [2] 2-04
❑ WZ553* '40' Vampire T.11   ex Bournemouth, Bruntingthorpe, Cranfield,
  G-DHYY   Lichfield, Winthorpe, South Wigston, Bruntingthorpe,
    Loughborough, East Midlands, Liverpool, Woodford,
    Chester, St Athan, 4 FTS, 7 FTS, 202 AFS.
    Spares. Arrived 17-11-03. off-site 11-03
❑ 'XJ771'*   Vampire T.55 ✈ ex Bournemouth, '215' Sion, Swiss AF U-1215.
  G-HELV   RAF colours. Arrived 3-04. 3-04
❑ XL929*   Pembroke C.1   G-BNPU, ex Shoreham, Sandown, Shawbury, 60, Kemble,
    207, SCCS, TCCS, FCCS, BCCS. Arr 25-7-02. off-site 8-02
❑ XL954   Pembroke C.1   G-BXES, ex N4234C, Tatenhill, White Waltham,
    ✈ 9042M, Northolt, 60, RAFG CS, 2 TAF CS. ➥ 2-04

❑	XM223	Dove 7	G-BWWC, ex Cumbernauld, West Freugh, DGTE, T&EE, RAE. Wings from Dove 5 G-APSO. Moved to off-site store 26-7-02.	off-site	8-02
❑	[J-1629]*	Venom FB.50	ex Bournemouth, Dubendorf, Swiss AF. Stored. Arrived 17-11-03.		2-04
❑	[J-1649]*	Venom FB.50	ex Bournemouth, Dubendorf, Swiss AF. Stored. Arrived 17-11-03.		2-04

The Atlantic Group / Air Atlantique / Atlantic Aeroengineering / CFS Aeroproducts: By March 2003 Trislander G-AZLJ had moved to Lydd, Kent. C-47B G-AMCA departed by road on 10th October 2003 bound for the Aviodrome at Lelystad, Netherlands. C-47B G-AMHJ left by road on 4th December 2003 for Shawbury, Shropshire. CV-440 G-CONV was transferred to the Classic Flight in March 2004 and will be restored to airworthiness - see above.

❑	G-AVDB	Cessna 310L	ex Popham, Perth, N2279F. CoA 8-7-79. Spares.	off-site	3-02
❑	G-BWPG	Robin HR.200	ex Inverness. Crashed 29-10-97. Stored.	off-site	3-02
❑	G-LOFA	L.188CF Electra	ex Atlantic, N359Q, F-OGST, N359AC, TI-LRM, N359AC, HC-AVX, N359AC, VH-ECA. CoA 9-2-00. To fire service 5-02 and sectioned.		11-02
❑	G-LOFF	L.188CF Electra	ex Fred Olsen LN-FON, N342HA, N417MA, OB-R-1138, HP-684, N417MA, CF-ZST, N7142C. Spares use.		2-04
❑	G-OFRT	L.188CF Electra	ex Bournemouth, N347HA, N423MA, N23AF, N64405, SE-FGC, N5537. CoA 28-10-01. Spares.		5-03
❑	LN-FOI	L.188CF Electra	ex Fred Olsen, N31231, ZK-TEA, N9724C, ZK-BMP ntu. Stored.		2-04
❑	LN-FOL	L.188CF Electra	G-LOFG, ex Fred Olsen, N669F, N404GN, N6126A. Fire compound.		2-04
❑	N2RK*	L.188C Electra	ex G-LOFH, Reeve Aleutian, CF-NAX, N851U, N33506, ZK-TEB, ZK-BMQ.N9744C. Arrived 5-9-02. Stored. Reeve *Illusion* titles!		2-04
❑	N4HG*	L.188C Electra	ex G-LOFH, Reeve Aleutian, N9744C. Arrived 22-8-02. Stored.		2-04

Others: Spitfire Tr.IX MJ627 (G-BMSB) reflew following repair on 14th February 2002, transiting that day to Coningsby, Lincs, before settling on its new base of East Kirkby, Lincs, on 7th May 2003. See under Coventry, West Mids, for its associated Hurricane project. Freelance G-NACA and the five unfinished Freelance fuselages had gone – destination unknown – by mid-2003. Firecracker G-NDNI was registered in mid-2003 as N182FR to a reported New Zealand owner and had left by July 2003.

❑	G-BBXU	Sierra 200	CoA 18-11-93. Wreck.		7-97
❑	G-BDCL	AA-5 Traveler	ex EI-CCI, G-BDCL, EI-BGV, G-BDCL, N1373R. CoA 29-11-93. Stored.		3-00
❑	G-BGTS	Cherokee 140F	ex Liverpool, OY-BGD. Crashed 17-6-89. Stored.		12-92
❑	G-BHFL	Cherokee 180	ex N15189. Crashed 1-11-89. Wreck.		12-92
❑	G-BMIU	Enstrom F.28A	ex OO-BAM, F-BVRE ntu. Cr 9-7-86. Cabin, stored.		2-98
❑	G-BPJF	Tomahawk 112	ex N9312T. Crashed 20-6-98. Dump.		3-02
❑	–	Enstrom F.28A	cabin, stored.		2-98
❑	408	Iskra 100	ex Scampton, Duxford, Polish AF.	®	8-02
❑	70270	F-101B-80-MC	ex MAM, Woodbridge, Davis-Monthan, Texas ANG. Nose. Dump		10-00

KING'S COUGHTON on the A435 north of Alcester

| ❑ | G-BBED | Rallye 220 | CoA 13-9-87. Stored. | 8-01 |

LONG MARSTON AERODROME on the B4632, south-west of Stratford-upon-Avon
Jet Aviation Preservation Group (JAPG): Several airframes are on loan, as follows: the Dove and Meteor T.7 from Gordon Yates and the Shackleton, Canberra and Whirlwind from the local land owner.

They are marked ±. Chipmunk T.10 WP784 continues to make excellent progress. It will be a composite rebuild when completed [1]. The single-seat composite Hunter is a complex beast; with an unused F.6 cockpit from Stafford, the centre section of F.6 XG226, the rear end of a Danish T.7 and the wings from PH-NLH (see under Eaglescott, Devon). All of this will be completed as an FR.10 [2]. The Gazelle will ultimately become a complete airframe, JAPG have at least 95% of the helicopter in store [3]. The nose of Supermarine 544 WT589 moved to Boscombe Down, Wilts, by October 2002.

◆ *Please note*: no longer open to the public. ✉ Stewart Holder, 62 Avon Street, Evesham, WR11 4LG

❏	G-ANUW	Dove 6	ex Welshpool, North Weald, Stansted, CAFU. CoA 22-7-81.	±	2-04
❏	WL332	Meteor T.7	ex SAC, Cardiff-Wales, Croston, Moston, FRU, Lossiemouth SF, Ford SF.	±	2-04
❏	WM367	Meteor NF.13	ex Firbeck, North Weald, Powick, Boscombe Down, AWA, MoA. Nose.		2-04
❏	WP784	Chipmunk T.10	ex Hemel Hempstead, Wycombe AP, Boston, Holbeach, Wellingborough, Reading, Benson, Abingdon, 6 AEF, Leeds UAS, Abn UAS, 8 FTS, Man UAS, QUAS, Air Att Paris, 5 RFS, 17 RFS.	® [1]	2-04
❏	WR985	'H' Shack' MR.3/3	ex SAC, Cosford, 8103M, 201, 120, 206, 203, 206, A&AEE, 206.	±	2-04
❏	WT483	'83' Canberra T.4	ex Filton, Samlesbury, 231 OCU, 39, 231 OCU, 16, Laarbruch SF, 68, Laarbruch SF, 69.	±	2-04
❏	WV382	Hunter GA.11	ex Smethwick, Lee-on-Solent, Shawbury, FRADU, 67.		2-04
❏	XD447	'50' Vampire T.11	ex SAC, E Kirkby, Tattershall, Woodford, Chester, St Athan, 8 FTS, RAFC, 5 FTS.	®	2-04
❏	XG737	Sea Ven FAW.22	ex Cardiff-Wales, Yeovilton, FRU, Sydenham, 894, 893, 891. Stored.		2-04
❏	'XJ714'	Hunter 'FR.10'	composite	® [2]	2-04
❏	XP346	W'wind HAR.10	ex Tattershall Thorpe, Shawbury, 8793M, Lee-on-Solent, Akrotiri, 84, 22, 225.	±	2-04
❏	XP568	Jet Provost T.4	ex Faygate, Hatfield, Shawbury, RAFC.	®	2-04
❏	XX457	'Z' Gazelle AH.1	ex Arborfield, 2 Flt, 662, 656, ARWF, GCF.	[3]	2-04
❏	N-315	Hunter T.7	ex Hucclecote, Batley, Amsterdam, NLS spares, RNethAF, XM121.		2-04

Others: The Sea Prince is 'gate guardian' for the aerodrome.

❏	G-MMIR	Mainair Gemini	original 'trike', c/n 051.		6-98
❏	G-RACA	'571' Sea Prince T.1	ex WM735, Staverton, Kemble, 750, BTU, A&AEE.		5-03

NUNEATON on the A444 north of Coventry

Ted Gautrey: Is *thought* to continue to restore his Fox Moth.

❏	G-ACCB	Fox Moth	ex Coventry, Redhill, Blackpool, Southport. Ditched 25-9-56.	®	10-95

RUGBY on the A426 east of Coventry

There are no fewer than three Auster AOP.9s in the general area. 'XR239' might also be XR237 or XR238 [1]! Also here, in poor condition, is the former Museum of Army Flying DH.2 reproduction.

❏	'5964'*	DH.2 repro	BAPC.112, ex Middle Wallop, Chertsey. Wreck.		9-03
❏	XR239	Auster AOP.9	ex Popham. Fuselage frame and wings.	® [1]	9-03
❏	XP244*	Auster AOP.9	ex Middle Wallop, Arborfield 7864M 'M7922'. Fuse.		9-03
❏	-*	Auster AOP.9	ex Kenya.		9-02

STONELEIGH on the B4113 south of Coventry

A strip in the general area is the home to a 'spares ship' Ryan PT-22.

❏	-	Ryan PT-22	spares for G-BTBH.	1-02

WARWICK on the A429 west of Royal Leamington Spa

The Fleet continues to make progress in the general area. No news on the gliders held by Paul Williams.

❏ G-FLCA		Fleet Canuck	ex Baxterley, Chilbolton, Coventry, Rochester, Blackbushe, CS-ACQ, CF-DQP.	®	3-01
❏ –		Hutter H.17a	ex Moreton-in-Marsh.	®	1-92
❏ –	BAPC.25	Nyborg TGN.III	ex Moreton-in-Marsh, Stratford. Stored.		1-92

WELLESBOURNE MOUNTFORD AERODROME south of the B4086, east of Stratford

Wellesbourne Wartime Museum: Operated by the **Wellesbourne Aviation Group**, the Museum charts the history of the airfield centred on the restored underground Battle Headquarters. The Vulcan nose is owned by Paul Hartley and will be restored to display condition [1]. The nose has been placed on a trestle to allow viewing of the cockpit via the crew entry door. Not content with owning this Vulcan nose, Paul owns the examples at Bournemouth, Dorset, and Bruntingthorpe, Leics!

◆ Open every Sunday 10am to 4pm and Bank Holidays, same times. ✉ Derek Powell, 167 Colebourne Road, Kingsheath, Birmingham, B13 0HB **e-mail** d.powell@iclway.co.uk

❏ –		McBroom Argus	hang-glider, built 1974. Stored.		3-04
❏ RA-01378		Yak-52	ex DOSAAF '14'.		3-04
❏ WV679	'O-J'	Provost T.1	ex Dunkeswell, Higher Blagdon, Halton 7615M, 2 FTS.	®	3-04
❏ XA903		Vulcan B.1	ex Sidcup, Cardiff, Farnborough, RB.199 and Olympus test-bed, Blue Steel trials, Avro. Nose.	[1]	3-04
❏ XJ575		Sea Vixen FAW.2	ex Long Marston, Helston, Culdrose, A2611, 766. Nose.		3-04
❏ XK590	'V'	Vampire T.11	ex Witney, Brize Norton, CATCS, 4 FTS, 7 FTS.		3-04

XM655 Maintenance and Preservation Society: Much tender, loving care continues to be lavished on XM655 and she returned to taxying fettle in fine style on 15th June 2003 following three years of major servicing. XM655 is owned by John Littler of Radarmoor, the airfield owners.

◆ Occasional ground-running days. Otherwise visits by prior arrangement. ✉ Derek Powell, see above. www.xm655.co.uk

| ❏ XM655 | | Vulcan B.2 | G-VULC, ex N655AV ntu, 44, 101, 50, 12, 35, 9. | 3-04 |

Others: Chipmunk T.10 'WZ868' (G-ARMF) moved by mid-2000 to Redditch, Worcs.

❏ G-APPA		Chipmunk 22	ex Carlisle, Glasgow, N5703E, G-APPA, WP917, Glas UAS, 11 RFS, 8 RFS. Stored, dismantled.	6-01
❏ G-BLLV		Slingsby T.67C	wreck.	1-02
❏ G-BSYM		Tomahawk II	ex N2507V. Damaged 27-7-94. Dump.	7-03
❏ –*		Robinson R-44	cabin. Dump. First noted 4-03.	4-03
❏ 'N3320'	'A'	Spitfire FSM	ex Winthorpe. Stored, off-site	1-04
❏ XX634	'T'	Bulldog T.1	ex Shawbury, Lpl UAS, Man UAS, EMUAS, CFS, 3 FTS, CFS, Cam UAS, 2 FTS.	2-04
❏ XX671	'D'	Bulldog T.1	ex Shawbury, Birm UAS, 2 FTS.	2-04

WILTSHIRE

BOSCOMBE DOWN AIRFIELD south of the A303 at Amesbury

Boscombe Down Aviation Collection (formerly the Boscombe Down Museum Project): A wide array of airframes and artefacts have been added to the collection – telling Boscombe's rich tale of aviation history and trials of technology. As well as the airframes, there are ground support vehicles, flight clothing, ejection seats, an Alpha Jet simulator etc. As a reminder that many of the airframes are not the property of the collection, Hunter F.6 XE601 was put up for tender during February 2004 [1]. The construction of a BE.2c reproduction has been started.

Notes: Many items from the Air Defence Collection are on loan to the project – marked ADC. The Lightning nose section is on loan from Hugh Trevor [2]. The MiG-21MF is on loan from Kelvin Petty, see also under Reading, Berks [3]. Airframes marked ➡ attended the '100 Years of Flight Experience' static display at the International Air Tattoo, Fairford, Glos, July 2003.

◆ By prior arrangement *only*. ✉ Museum Project, c/o RAF Unit, Boscombe Down, SP4 0JF.

❏	P3554*		Hurricane I	ex Salisbury, Swanage, 607, 213, 56, 32.		
				Shot down 5-10-40.	off-site ADC	6-03
❏	WH779*		Canberra PR.7	ex Farnborough, Marham, RAE, 100, 13, 31, 80,		
				13, 542. Nose.		3-04
❏	WH876		Canberra B.2	ex Aberporth, Boscombe Down, A&AEE, 73,		
			(mod)	207, 115. Nose.	➡	7-03
❏	WT534		Canberra PR.7	8549M, ex Solihull, Halton, St Athan, 17. Nose.		
				Spares for WH876.		4-02
❏	WT648		Hunter F.1	ex Salisbury, Kexborough, Stock, St Athan		
				7530M, DFLS. Nose.	ADC	4-02
❏	WT859*		Supermarine 544	ex Long Marston, Brooklands, Ruislip, Foulness,		
				Culdrose, Fleetlands, Culdrose, Lee-on-Solent A2499,		
				RAE Bedford. Nose. Arrived by 10-02.	±	10-02
❏	XF113		Swift F.7	ex Salisbury, Bath, Frome, Farnborough,		
				ETPS, A&AEE, HS. Nose.	ADC	4-02
❏	XE601		Hunter F.6	ex RAE, ETPS, Hawker.	[1]	3-04
❏	XF994	'873'	Hunter T.8C	ex Apprentices, Shawbury, Yeovilton, FRADU,		
				759, 229 OCU, AFDS, 66.		4-02
❏	XG290		Hunter F.6	ex Salisbury, Bournemouth, Bruntingthorpe,		
				Swanton Morley, Bentley Priory, Halton		
				8711M, Laarbruch SF, A&AEE. Nose.	ADC	4-02
❏	XL564		Hunter T.7	ex ETPS, HS, 229 OCU, Hawker. Nose.		
				Poor state. Crashed 6-8-98.		4-02
❏	XL609		Hunter T.7	ex Firbeck, Elgin, Lossiemouth 8866M, 12, 216,		
				237 OCU, 4 FTS, 56. Nose. 12 Sqn c/s.	ADC	3-02
❏	XN726		Lightning F.2A	ex Rayleigh, Foulness, Farnborough, 8545M,		
				Gütersloh, 92, 19. Nose.	[2]	4-02
❏	XR650	'28'	Jet Provost T.4	ex DERA, Halton 8459M, SoRF, CAW,		
				CATCS, 3 FTS, CAW, 7 FTS.		4-02
❏	XS790		Andover CC.2	ex DERA, Queen's Flight. Nose.		4-02
❏	XT437	'423'	Wasp HAS.1	ex Lee-on-Solent, *Diomede, Arethusa* and *Olna* Flts.		
				Del Boy.	➡	7-03
❏	XT597		Phantom FG.1	ex DERA, A&AEE.		4-02
❏	XV401	'I'	Phantom FGR.2	ex DERA, Wattisham, 74, 23, 29, 228 OCU, 56,		
				111, 41.		4-02
❏	XV784*		Harrier GR.3	ex DS&TL, Wittering 8909M, 233 OCU, 4, 1, 4.		
				Damaged 2-4-86. Nose. First noted 4-02.		4-02
❏	XW269*	'BD'	Harrier T.4	ex QinetiQ, Wittering, SAOEU, 233 OCU, 3, 1,		
				233 OCU, 4. Arrived by 3-04.		3-04
❏	XX343		Hawk T.1	ex DERA, ETPS. Crashed 8-4-97. Hulk.		4-02
❏	XX761*		Jaguar GR.1	ex airfield, Warton, 226 OCU, 14. *Pudsey*. Accident		
				6-6-78. Arrived 7-00, to museum by 4-02.		6-02
❏	XX919		BAC 111-402	ex DERA, RAE, D-AFWC ntu, PI-C-1121. Nose.		4-02
❏	XZ457*		Sea Harrier FA.2	ex Yeovilton, 899, 800, 801, 800, 899, 800, 899,		
				700A. Crashed 20-10-95. Arrived 7-03.	®	3-04
❏	ZD936*	'AO'	Tornado F.2	ex 'Manchester', Bedford, St Athan, 229 OCU.		
				Nose. Arrived during 2002.		3-04
❏	–*		Typhoon	ex Salisbury. Cockpit project.	off-site ADC	6-03
❏	[WV910]		Sea Hawk	ex DERA. Nose. Identity confirmed.		4-02
❏	–*		Scout CIM	ex Middle Wallop, AETW. *Possibly* XP859.		3-04
❏	A-533	ZD486 FMA Pucará		ex Salisbury, St Mary Bourne, Middle Wallop,		
				Boscombe Down, Abingdon, Finningley,		
				Stanley, Argentine AF. Nose.	ADC	6-03
❏	7708		MiG-21MF	ex airfield, Fairford, Slovak AF, Czech AF.	[3]	4-02
❏	–	'4001'	Alpha Jet SIM	–		3-02

Defence Science and Technology Laboratory (DS&TL) / **QinetiQ**: The 'Chippax' is with **1011 Squadron, ATC** [1]. Hunter T.8C XL612 was put up for tender during February 2004 [2]. The nose of Harrier GR.3 XV784 moved to the museum, above, by April 2002 and was followed by Harrier T.4 XW269 by February 2004. BAC 111 XX105 - the oldest survivor of the type - flew its last 'MinTech' (sorry, old habits die hard!) sortie on 5th June 2003 and is stored [3].

❏	WP863		Chipmunk T.10 PAX	8360M, ex Bournemouth, Marlborough, Chippenham, Shawbury, CoAT Hamble G-ATJI, RAFC, 664, RAFC.	[1] 1-03
❏	XF358	'870'	Hunter T.8C	ex Shawbury, Yeovilton, FRADU, 112. Stored.	4-02
❏	XL612		Hunter T.7	ex ETPS, 8, 1417 Flt, APS Sylt. Last flight 10-8-01.	[2] 2-04
❏	XL629		Lightning T.4	ex ETPS, A&AEE. Gate guardian.	8-03
❏	XV806	'E'	Harrier GR.3	ex Culdrose, A2607 [3], A2606, Cosford, 4, 3, 233 OCU.	8-98
❏	XW902	'H'	Gazelle HT.3	ex Shawbury, 2 FTS, 18, CFS.	11-01
❏	XW906	'J'	Gazelle HT.3	ex Shawbury, 2 FTS, CFS. Apprentice school.	8-01
❏	XX105*		BAC 111-201	ex RAE, G-ASJD BCAL, BUA. Last flight 5-6-03.	[3] 6-03
❏	XX705*	'5'	Bulldog T.1	ex S'ton UAS, Birm UAS. Inst since 4-01.	1-03
❏	XZ101	'D'	Jaguar GR.1A	9282M, ex St Athan, Coltishall, 41, 2, 6, 2.	4-02
❏	ZA804	'I'	Gazelle HT.3	ex Shawbury, 2 FTS, CFS.	11-01
❏	XZ933	'T'	Gazelle HT.3	ex Shawbury, 2 FTS, CFS.	11-01
❏	ZJ651		Alpha Jet	ex Furstenfeldbruck, Luftwaffe 98+42, 41+42.	8-01
❏	ZJ652		Alpha Jet	ex Furstenfeldbruck, Luftwaffe 41+09.	11-01
❏	ZJ653		Alpha Jet	ex Furstenfeldbruck, Luftwaffe 40+22.	11-01
❏	ZJ654		Alpha Jet	ex Furstenfeldbruck, Luftwaffe 41+02.	11-01
❏	ZJ655		Alpha Jet	ex Furstenfeldbruck, Luftwaffe 41+19.	11-01
❏	ZJ656		Alpha Jet	ex Furstenfeldbruck, Luftwaffe 41+40.	11-01
❏	–		Scout AH.1	Dump. Pod.	6-01
❏	162958		AV-8B Harrier II	ex St Athan, USMC, VMA-214. Fuselage, tests.	1-02

CHISELDON or Draycott, west of the A346, south of Swindon
A farm strip here holds a bent Scout and the fuselage of a 'plastic' Spitfire.

❏	G-BXSL*	Scout AH.1	ex XW799, Middle Wallop, GAAS, 657, 656, 658, Westland. Stored, damaged. Crashed 19-11-01.	2-04
❏	OO-MEL*	Piaggio P.149	stored, dismantled. First noted 6-03.	2-04
❏	*	Spitfire FSM	fuselage.	2-04

COLERNE west of Corsham, between the A420 and A4
By January 2003 the former recruiting Wessex HU.5, in 'split' Royal Navy 'commando' and ASR colours, had appeared on the airfield. It had been kept here during its mobile days. It was transferred to the fire crews in late 2003. A Bulldog arrived during mid-2002 for restoration.

❏	XS486*	'F'	Wessex HU.5	9292M, ex Bath, Wroughton 9292M, Lee-on-Solent.	
		and '524'		Union Jack painted nose. Dump.	2-04
❏	XX657*	'U'	Bulldog T.1	ex Andover, Newton, 2 FTS, Cam UAS. Overstressed 22-11-98. First noted 7-02.	® 7-02

KEEVIL AERODROME south of the A361, south-west of Devizes
Bannerdown Gliding Club: Cadet WT905 is an unfinished Motor Cadet conversion [1]. ARV Super 2 G-POOL departed by road to La Rochelle, France, in December 2002. Grob Astir DKV to the Swindon area by December 2002. Hutter H-17 EPR moved to Husbands Bosworth, Leics, on 14th February 2004. Cadet TX.3 XA310 was active in 2003 as KBP (BGA.4963).

❏	G-AKXP*	Auster 5	ex Hedge End, Hatfield, Claygate, NJ633, 29 EFTS, 22 EFTS, 659, HS. Crashed 9-4-70.	® 1-04
❏	–*	AYK T.21B	BGA.765, ex Spalding. Stored. First noted 8-02.	1-04

Wiltshire wends its merry way after the second photo-spread, on page 257.

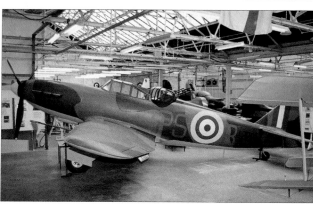

MERSEYSIDE
Jetstream 41 G-JMAC
Liverpool, July 2003. *Ken Ellis*

WEST MIDLANDS
Defiant 'L7005', Wolverhampton,
April 2003. *Ken Ellis*

NORFOLK
Jaguar T.2A XX830, Coltishall
(here at North Weald), August 2002
also Cadet TX.3 XN238
from Doncaster. *Hugh Trevor*

226

NORFOLK

Phantom FGR.2 XV420
Neatishead, June 2002
Don Nind

NORTHAMPTONSHIRE

T.67B G-BONU
Hinton-in-the-Hedges, October 2003
Brian Roffee

Stampe SV-4C G-AYZI (and Mini-N
Spanhoe Lodge, June 2003
David J Burke

NORTHAMPTONSHIRE

Hunter F.6A XF375
Spanhoe Lodge, August 2003
Alf Jenks

Autocrat G-AJDY
Spanhoe Lodge, September 2002
David J Burke

NORTHUMBERLAND
AND TYNESIDE

HS.125-3B 5N-AAN
and Boeing 737 C-GWJO
Newcastle, November 2003
Gareth Symington

NOTTINGHAMSHIRE

Hurricane FSM 'V7467'
Farnsfield, June 2002
Mark Whitnall

Harvard IIB KF532
Winthorpe, June 2003
Ken Ellis

Newark Air Museum
August 2002
Dave Allport

NOTTINGHAMSHIRE
MiG-23 '04'
Winthorpe, June 2003
Ken Ellis

CockpitFest, Winthorpe, June 2002
Hunter F.1 WT684, Lavendon
Hunter FGA.9 XE597, Bromsgrove
Ken Ellis

OXFORDSHIRE
MiG-19
Chalgrove, July 2002
Mark Harris

SHROPSHIRE

Tornado P.02 XX946
Cosford, June 2003
Alf Jenks

Dolphin REP D5329
Cosford, June 2002
Phil Hewitt

Mohawk G-AEKW
Cosford, June 2002
Phil Hewitt

SHROPSHIRE

Tempest TT.5 NV778
Cosford, June 2002
Phil Hewitt

Me 163B-1a 191614
Cosford, June 2002
Phil Hewitt

Gnat T.1 XR574
Cosford, April 2002
Mark Harris

SHROPSHIRE

Jaguar GR.1 XX818
Cosford, October 2003
Mark Harris

Horsa REP BAPC.279
Shawbury, October 2003
Mark Harris

Scout AH.1 XV123
Shawbury, October 2003
Mark Harris

SOMERSET

Widgeon 2 G-AOZE
Weston-super-Mare
(here at Fairford), July 2003
Roger Richards

Piper Pacer G-BHMO
Rooks Bridge, March 2003
Tony McCarthy

Trident 2E G-AVFM and
Varsity T.1 WF410
Bristol, February 2002
David S Johnstone

SOMERSET

SA.365N Dauphin F-WQAP
Weston-super-Mare, October 2003
Alf Jenks

Gyro-Boat BAPC.289
Weston-super-Mare, October 2003
John Phillips

WG.30-100 N112WG
Weston-super-Mare, November 2002
Stephen C Reglar

SOMERSET

Sea Harrier FA.2 XZ499
Yeovilton, November 2002
Bob Turner

Sea Hawk FGA.6 WV908
Yeovilton, September 2003
Mark Roberts

Harrier GR.3 XW630
Yeovilton, November 2003
Bob Turner

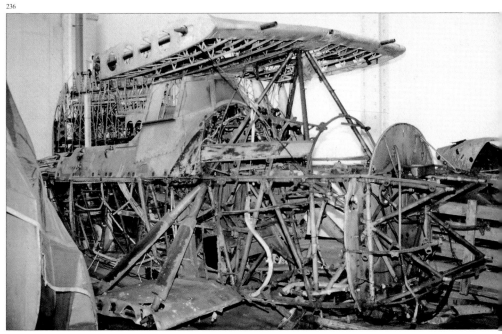

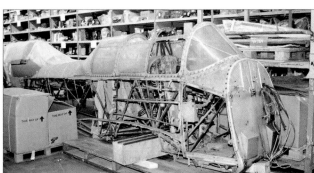

STAFFORDSHIRE

Swordfish IV HS503
Stafford, September 2002
Mark Harris

PT-19A Cornell 15195
Stafford, September 2002
Mark Harris

SUFFOLK

Buccaneer S.2 XK526
Honington, September 2003
Tony McCarthy

SURREY

Hunter F.51 E-421
Brooklands, August 2003
Mark Harris

Harrier GR.3 XV751
Charlwood, July 2003
Ian Haskell

Hunter F.6A XG196
Mytchett, April 2002
Mark Harris

WEST SUSSEX

Harrier T.4N XW268
Faygate, December 2003
Gareth Jones

Tomahawk G-BGRN
Goodwood, May 2003
Jon Wickenden

Wessex HC.2 XR517
Shoreham, March 2003
Anthony Mills

WARWICKSHIRE

Pou du Ciel G-AEGV
Coventry, January 2003
Brian Roffee

HS.125-1 G-ARYB
Coventry, August 2003
Ian Haskell

Hunter F.6A XF382
Coventry, March 2003
Roger Richards

WARWICKSHIRE

Shackleton AEW.2 WR963
Coventry, September 2003
Stephen C Reglar

CV-440 G-CONV
Coventry, August 2003
Ian Haskell

Sea Prince T.1 G-RACA
Long Marston, April 2003
Alf Jenks

WARWICKSHIRE
Bulldog T.1s XX634 and XX671
Wellesbourne Mountford,
April 2003
Tony McCarthy

WILTSHIRE
Supermarine 544 WT859
Boscombe Down, October 2002
David J Burke

Harrier GR.3 and Pucará A-533
Boscombe Down (here at
Winthorpe) June 2002
Ken Ellis

WILTSHIRE

Comet C.2 XK699
Lyneham, October 2003
Stephen G Robson

Scout AH.1 XP883
Oaksey Park, August 2002
Tony Wood

Wessex HU.5 XS486
Colerne, January 2003
Bob Vandereyt

WILTSHIRE
Cmelak G-AVZB
Wroughton, March 2003
Tony McCarthy

WORCESTERSHIRE
Meteor T.7 WH166
Birlingham, November 2003
Alf Jenks

EAST YORKSHIRE
OH-7 Coupe G-ARIF
Breighton, October 2002
Andy Wood

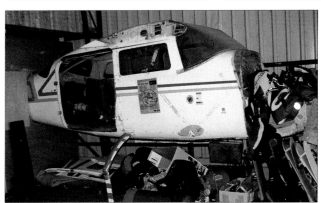

EAST YORKSHIRE

Gnome G-AXEI, 'Flea' 'F50',
and Elf G-MMUL
Breighton, June 2002
Andy Wood

Cessna U.206A G-BRID
Grindale, August 2002
David E Thompson

NORTH YORKSHIRE

Air Command 532 G-TFRB
Elvington, June 2003
Roger Richards

EAST YORKSHIRE

Wright Flyer REP BAPC.28
Elvington (here at Fairford),
July 2003
Roger Richards

SOUTH YORKSHIRE

Jetstream T.1 XX477
Askern, February 2003
Gareth Symington

Whirlwind HAS.7 XL840
Bawtry, September 2003
Gareth Jones

SOUTH YORKSHIRE

Chipmunk T.10 WB733
and Dove 8 G-ARHX
Doncaster, March 2003
Roger Richards

DC-3-201 N4565L
Doncaster, December 2003
Alf Jenks

Whirlwind HAS.1 XA870
Doncaster, December 2003
Alf Jenks

SCOTLAND

Jet Provost T.3A XM412
Balado Bridge, February 2002
David S Johnstone

Trislander fuselages
Cumbernauld, November 2002
David S Johnstone

Jetstream T.1 XX483
Dumfries, February 2003
David S Johnstone

SCOTLAND

Buccaneer S.2B XT280 and XX888
Dundonald, November 2002
David S Johnstone

Turbulent G-AVPC
East Fortune, July 2003
Ken Ellis

Beaufighter II
East Fortune, July 2003
Ken Ellis

SCOTLAND

Spitfire F.21 LA198
East Fortune, July 2003
Ken Ellis

Gannet T.5 XG882
Errol, August 2003
James Roffee

Buccaneer S.1 XK532
Inverness, May 2003
Tony McCarthy

SCOTLAND

Tornado GR.1B ZA475
Lossiemouth, May 2002
Don Nind

Boeing 747 N852FT
Prestwick, June 2003
David S Johnstone

Phantom FGR.2 XT852
West Freugh, April 2002
David S Johnstone

WALES

Anson T.21 VS562
Llanbedr, June 2002
David S Johnstone

Whirlwind HAR.10 XJ409
Llanbedr, June 2002
David S Johnstone

Canberra B.2 WK128
Llanbedr, November 2003
Mark A Jones

WALES

Phantom FGR.2 XV435
Llanbedr, November 2003
Mark A Jones

Phantom FGR.2 XV498
St Athan, September 2002
Roger Richards

Harrier GR.3 XZ993
St Athan, September 2002
Roger Richards

WALES

Tornado GR.1 ZA399
St Athan, September 2002
Tony Wood

Bulldog T.1 XX626
St Athan, September 2002
Roger Richards

UH-1H '998-8888'
Valley, October 2002
Tony McCarthy

NORTHERN IRELAND

Tucano G-BTUC
Langford Lodge, February 2004
Ken Ellis

Cessna 172A EI-BAC
Langford Lodge, February 2004
Ken Ellis

Jet Provost T.3A XM414,
Eurowing G-MJWS and
Robinson R-22 G-RENT
Langford Lodge, February 2004
Ken Ellis

IRELAND

Magister 34
Casement, June 2002
Mark Harris

Provost T.51 183
Casement, June 2002
Mark Harris

CM-170 219 and Avro XIX 141
Casement, May 2003
Seamus Mooney

IRELAND

Cessna 172B '98'
Casement, May 2003
Seamus Mooney

Douglas DC-7C G-AOIE
Dromod (here at New Ross),
August 2002
Philip S Bedford

Dove 6 G-ASNG
Casement, May 2003
Seamus Mooney

Wiltshire, Keevil, continued from page 224...

❑	–	BAA	T.8 Tutor	BGA.804, ex VM589, XE761. CoA 3-97.		1-04
❑	–	BJJ	T.45 Swallow	BGA.1003, ex Lasham. Wreck.		1-04
❑	–	CHM	Schleicher K.4	BGA.1556, ex Lasham, D-5015. Stored.		1-04
❑	–*	DWF	Grunau Baby	BGA.2433, ex AGA.16, RNGSA.1-13, VW743. Stored.		1-04
❑	–	EAZ	Schleicher K8B	BGA.2543, ex D-5256, D-KANO, D-5256.		
				Crashed 25-7-97. Wreck, stored.		1-04
❑	–	GEQ	SZD-12A Mucha	BGA.3776. Ex SP-2001, Bury St Edmunds,		
				Tibbenham. Stored.	®	1-04
❑	–*	FEZ	Eton TX.1	BGA.3214, ex RAFGSA R13, WP269. Stored.		1-04
❑	WB981	FFZ	Sedburgh TX.1	BGA.3238. Ex Aston Down, Sealand, 635 VGS.		
				Fuselage.	®	1-04
❑	–*	FRQ	Slingsby T.45	BGA.3469, ex XT653. Stored.		1-04
❑	WE992*		Prefect TX.1	BGA.2692. Stored.		1-04
❑	WT905*		Cadet TX.3	ex Stour Row. Stored. First noted 4-03.	[1]	1-04
❑	WZ793		Grasshopper TX.1	ex Croydon, Basingstoke, Taunton.	®	1-04
❑	XA240	JJS	Grasshopper TX.1	BGA.4556, ex Yeovilton, Locking, Radley. Stored.		1-04
❑	XA244		Grasshopper TX.1	ex Lasham, Cosford, Walsall. Stored.		1-04
❑	XA295		Cadet TX.3	BGA.3336, ex Fareham. Stored.		1-04
❑	XA310		Cadet TX.3	BGA.4963, ex Fareham. Stored.		1-04

LYNEHAM AIRFIELD west of the A3102, south-west of Wooton Bassett

RAF Lyneham: The Dakota outside 47 Air Despatch Squadron, Royal Logistics Corps, was dedicated on 21st June 2002. The dump is occupied by a large, all-steel 'DC-10' look-alike.

❑	'FZ625'	C-47B-30-DK	ex G-AMPO, Coventry, Air Atlantique, LN-RTO,		
	'YS-DH'		G-AMPO, KN566, Oakington SF, 77, 62, Waterbeach		
			SF, 1381 CU, 133 CU, 238, 44-76853. CoA 29-3-97.		
			271 Squadron colours. Displayed.		10-02
❑	XK699	Comet C.2	7971M, ex Henlow, Lyneham, 216. Gate.		2-02

MALMESBURY

Martin Painter: Moved to this general area in 2003. He continues on the restoration of the Nimrod cockpit. Spares from the scrapping of XV147 at Warton, Lancs, have helped with the task.

❑	XV148*	Nimrod proto	ex Guildford, Woodford, A&AEE, HSA. Cockpit.		
			Arrived 10-03.	®	2-04

MELKSHAM on the A350 south of Chippenham

Adrian Brimson and **John Phillips:** The pair seek original documents for this aircraft.

◆ Viewing by prior permission *only*. ☎ 01225 702485

❑	XL765	Skeeter AOP.12	ex Northants, Clapham, Leverstock Green, Leamington		
			Spa, Leeds, Rotherham, Wroughton, 17F, 654,		
			651, SARO.	®	3-04

NETHERAVON AIRFIELD on the A345 north of Amesbury

No.7 Regiment, AAC:

❑	XT150	Sioux AH.1	7883M, ex Middle Wallop, comp with 7884M. Gate.	1-04
❑	XV136	Scout AH.1	ex Almondbank, Wroughton. Gate.	1-04

OAKSEY PARK AERODROME south of Cirencester, east of the A429

❑	G-AZMN*	Airtourer T5	ex Kemble, Oaksey Park, Bristol, Glasgow.	
			Crashed 23-6-87. First noted 4-02.	9-03
❑	G-BZBD*	Scout AH.1	ex XT632. Crashed 23-8-00. Spares. First noted 4-02.	5-03
❑	XP883*	Scout AH.1	ex Boscombe Down Apps, 658, 655, 652. Spares.	5-03
❑	91	Wasp HAS.1	ex SAAF. Forward fuselage.	5-03

OLD SARUM AERODROME east of the A345 north of Salisbury

Tiger Moth G-ACDI had gone by August 2003, probably locally to continue rebuild. Yak-18T RA01370 had moved on by July 2002. Scout AH.1 XV130 (G-BWJW) was flying by 2002, as 'XW130', just to keep us on our toes!

❑ G-BJBY	PA-28 Warrior 161	ex N8415L. Crashed 23-11-97. Wreck.		2-03
❑ G-BKRL	Leopard 001	ex Cranfield. CoA 14-12-91.		7-00
❑ G-BRTK	PT-13D Kaydet	ex Swanton Morley, N16716, 42-17786.		
		CoA 24-4-93. First noted 3-00.	®	3-00

SALISBURY

Air Defence Collection (ADC): Tony Dyer is heavily involved in the Boscombe Down project. From this edition his Hurricane and Typhoon projects have been listed under that heading, see above.

SWINDON

Richard Galazka's restoration of the Harvard is *believed* to continue in the area. A Cadet glider is stored, possibly as spares for a motor conversion.

❑ KF435	Harvard IIB	ex Ottershaw, Wycombe AP, Camberley, Sandhurst,		
		1 FTS, 2 FTS, 22 SFTS, 20 FTS, 11 (P)AFU.	®	2-96
❑ WT899	Cadet TX.3	ex Rush Green, Benington, Syerston, 661 VGS,		
		643 VGS, Cosford, St Athan.		4-99

TROWBRIDGE on the A361 south-east of Bath

E J Shanley and Sons: The Lynx EMU (last noted in February 2002) has been cut up and is no more.

UPAVON AIRFIELD on the A342 south-east of Devizes

Wyvern Gliding Club: Evans VP-1 G-BICT had moved to <u>Wattisham</u>, Suffolk, by January 2004.

❑ D-4019	Bergfalke II	last flown 1996. Stored.	1-04
❑ XA225	Grasshopper TX.1	ex Keevil, Petersfield. Stored.	1-04

WARMINSTER on the A36 east of Frome

Restoration of the Stampe is *assumed* to continue, but this reference is well long-in-the-tooth.

❑ G-AYDR	SNCAN SV-4C	ex Raveningham, F-BCLG. CoA 27-3-75.	®	8-93

WROUGHTON AIRFIELD on the A4361 south of Swindon

Science Museum Air Transport Collection and Storage Facility (ScM):

♦ Occasional open days and special events. ✉ Science Museum, Wroughton Airfield, Swindon, SN4 9NS ☎ 01793 814466 **www.sciencemuseum.org.uk/wroughton**

❑ G-AACN	HP Gugnunc	ex Hayes and K1908.	3-04
❑ G-ACIT	DH.84 Dragon	ex Southend, Beagle, ANT Blackpool, BEA,	
		Scottish, Highland. CoA 25-5-74.	3-04
❑ G-AEHM	HM.14 'Flea'	ex Hayes, Whitchurch, Bristol.	3-04
❑ G-ALXT	Dragon Rapide	ex Strathallan, Staverton, 4R-AAI, CY-AAI,	
		G-ALXT, NF865, 5 MU, 18 MU, MCS.	3-04
❑ G-ANAV	Comet 1A	ex South Kensington. CF-CUM. Nose.	3-04
❑ G-APWY	Piaggio P.166	ex Southend, Marconi. CoA 14-3-81.	3-04
❑ G-APYD	Comet 4B	ex Dan-Air, Olympic SX-DAL, G-APYD,	
		BEA. CoA 3-8-79.	3-04
❑ G-ATTN	Piccard HAB	ex South Kensington, Hayes, South Kensington.	3-04
❑ G-AVZB	Z-37 Cmelak	ex Southend, OK-WKQ. CoA 5-4-84.	3-04
❑ G-AWZM	Trident 3B-101	ex Heathrow, BA, BEA. CoA 13-12-85.	3-04
❑ G-BBGN	Cameron A-375	ex South Kensington, Hayes, South Kensington.	
		Gondola. *Daffodil II.*	3-04

❑	G-BGLB	Bede BD-5B	ex Booker. CoA 4-8-81.	3-04
❑	G-MMCB	Pathfinder II	microlight.	3-04
❑	G-RBOS	Colt AS-105	hot air airship. CoA 6-3-87.	3-04
❑	EI-AYO	DC-3A-197	ex Shannon, N655GP, N65556, N225JB, N8695SE, N333H, NC16071.	3-04
❑	N18E	Boeing 247	ex Wings and Wheels, Orlando, Sky Tours, NC18E, NC18, NC13340 CAA, United/National A/T.	3-04
❑	N7777G	L-749A-79	G-CONI, ex Dublin, Lanzair, KLM PH-LDT, PH-TET.	3-04
❑	OO-BFH	Piccard Gas	ex South Kensington, Hayes, South Ken'. Gondola.	3-04
❑	VP975	Devon C.2/2	ex RAE Farnborough, A&AEE, CCCF, 19 GCF, CPE.	3-04
❑	XP505	Gnat T.1	ex South Kensington, RAE Bedford, MinTech, Dunsfold, CFS.	3-04
❑	100509	Fa 330A-1	ex South Kensington, Farnborough.	3-04
❑	–	BAPC.52 Lilienthal Glider	ex South Kensington, Hayes, South Kensington, Oxford. Original of 1895. Stored.	3-04
❑	–	BAPC.162 Manflier MPA	major parts.	3-04
❑	–	BAPC.172 Chargus Midas	powered hang glider.	3-04
❑	–	BAPC.173 Grasshopper	hang glider.	3-04
❑	–	BAPC.174 Bensen B.7	gyroglider.	3-04
❑	–	BAPC.188 Cobra 88	hang glider.	3-04
❑	–	BAPC.276 Hartman Orni'	ex Cranfield. Stored.	3-04

YATESBURY north of the A4, east of Calne
Meteor Flight: Having amassed a huge spares holding, including over a dozen engines, the group continues to make good progress towards the restoration of T.7 WA591.
◆ Visits possible by prior arrangement *only* to Max Tapper ☎ 01249 812557. General correspondence: ✉ Hal Taylor, Sunfield House, Townsend Road, Streatley, Berks, RG9LH ☎ / **fax** 01491 872205 **www.meteorflight.com**

❑	WA591 G-BWMF	Meteor T.7	ex Woodvale, St Athan 7917M, Kemble, CAW, 8 FTS, 5 FTS, CAW, 12 FTS, 215 AFS, 208 AFS, 203 AFS, 226 OCU, CFE.	®	3-04
❑	WF825	'A' Meteor T.7	ex Malmesbury, Monkton Farleigh, Lyneham 8359M, Kemble, CAW, 33, 603. Stored.		3-04
❑	WL360	'G' Meteor T.7	ex Staverton, Hucclecote, Locking 7920M, 229 OCU, 1, Wattisham SF, 211 AFS, 210 AFS, 215 AFS. Stored.		3-04
❑	WL405	Meteor T.7	ex Chalgrove, Farnborough, BCCS, 1 GCF, 231 OCU, Wittering SF, JCU, Hemswell CF. Stored.		3-04
❑	WS760	Meteor NF.14	ex Loughborough, Cranfield, Bushey, Duxford, Brampton, Upwood, 7964M, 1 ANS, 64, 237 OCU. Stored.		3-04

WORCESTERSHIRE

☛ From 1st April 1998 Worcestershire reverted to county status and is 'divorced' from Herefordshire.

BIRLINGHAM on the A4104, east of the B4080 to the west of Evesham
Graham Revill: This *private* collection is unchanged.

❑	[WF299]	Sea Hawk FB.3	WF299, ex 'WN105', Helston, St Agnes, Topcliffe, Catterick 8164M, Lee-on-Solent, A2662, A2509, Culdrose SAH-8, 802, 738, 736. Composite.	2-04
❑	WH166	Meteor T.7	ex Digby 8052M, CFS, 5 CAACU, CAW, 4 FTS, 205 AFS, 210 AFS, 208 AFS.	2-04

❑ WZ425	Vampire T.11	ex Cardiff-Wales, Woodford, Chester,	
		St Athan, 5 FTS, RAFC, 229 OCU, CGS.	2-04
❑ XE979	'54' Vampire T.11	ex Standish, Woodford, Chester, St Athan,	
		1 FTS, 8 FTS, RAFC.	2-04
❑ XF526	'78' Hunter F.6	ex St Athan, Halton 8679M, Laarbruch SF,	
and 'E'		4 FTS, 229 OCU, 56, 43, 56, 63, 66.	2-04
❑ XN632	Jet Provost T.3	ex Eaglescott, Chivenor, St Athan 8352M,	
		Kemble, Shawbury, 3 FTS.	2-04

BROMSGROVE on the A448 north-west of Redditch
Bob Dunn, Brian Barrett and Mick Boulanger of the **Wolverhampton Aviation Group** keep two cockpits locally. See also under Wolverhampton, W Mids, for Mick's 'JP'.

❑ WJ865	Canberra T.4	ex Stamford, Stock, Farnborough, ETPS. Nose.	3-04
❑ XE597	Hunter FGA.9	8874M, ex Moreton-in-Marsh, Halton, Bentley Priory,	
		Brawdy, 1 TWU, 2 TWU, TWU, 229 OCU, West	
		Raynham SF, 1, 54, MoA, 208, 56, 63, 66. Nose.	3-04

DEFFORD on the A4104 south-west of Pershore

❑ G-BOKW	Bö 208C Junior	ex G-BITT, F-BRHX, D-EEAL. CoA 3-11-95.	4-98
❑ G-BPAO	Air Command 503	CoA 8-8-91. Stored.	4-98
❑ G-MNAF	Pegasus XL-R	CoA 3-95. Stored.	4-98

ECKINGTON on the B4080 south of Pershore
A private owner keeps the cockpit of an Arrow in the general area. It is being turned into a simulator.

❑ G-TOBE*	Cherokee Arrow II	ex Lashenden, G-BNRO, N40979. Cr 6-3-92.	12-03

EVESHAM on the A435 south of Redditch
HMS *Explorer:* In Honeybourne Road, South Littleton, the Sea Cadets have a Wessex HAS.1.

❑ XS886	'27' Wessex HAS.1	ex Birmingham, Lee-on-Solent A2685, Wroughton, 771.	5-02

MALVERN WELLS on the A449 south of Great Malvern
Peter Ward: A 'Flea' is kept in the area.

❑ 'G-ADYV'	HM.14 'Flea'	BAPC.243, ex 'A-FLEA', Leigh-on-Sea.	8-03

PERSHORE on the A44 west of Evesham
John Morgan: Acquired a former Air UK F-27 and is busy restoring it. It was damaged beyond repair on landing at Guernsey and broken up there in January 1998. The nose clearly survived and came back to the mainland. Having got the 'bug' the cockpit of an Electra and then a Lightning soon followed!
◆ Viewable by prior arrangement *only* - jsmorgan@btconnect.com

❑ G-BNCY*	F.27-500F	ex Bournemouth, Guernsey, Air UK, VH-FCE,		
		PH-EXH. *Friendship Lilly Langtree.* Damaged		
		7-12-97. Nose. Arrived 7-6-03.	®	3-04
❑ G-CHNX*	Electra 188AF	ex Bournemouth, Channel Express, EI-CHO,		
		G-CHNX ntu, N5535. Nose. Arrived 1-10-03.		3-04
❑ XM144*	Lightning F.1	ex Wycombe AP, Eaglescott, Burntwood, Leuchars		
		8417M, Leuchars TFF, 23 Leuchars TFF, 226 OCU,		
		74. 74 Sqn c/s. Nose, trailer-mounted. Arr 28-11-03.		3-04

REDDITCH

❑ G-ARMD	Chipmunk 22A	ex WD297, 666, 1 BFTS. CoA 5-6-<u>76</u>. Stored.	2-04
❑ 'WZ868'*'H'	Chipmunk T.10	ex Wellesbourne, Twyford, WG322, 63 GCF,	
G-ARMF		Leeds UAS, 22 RFS. Damaged 19-6-96. Stored.	2-04

WORCESTER
John Hancock: *Should* still have his Canberra nose.

❏ WK118	Canberra TT.18	ex Stock, Wyton, 100, 7, 59, 103. Nose.	3-96

EAST YORKSHIRE

BEVERLEY
Museum of Army Transport (MoAT): Readers will remember that the museum suffered a financial problem in 1997 and was thankfully bailed out. A combination of problems arose early in 2003 and on August 19, 2003 the staff were made redundant and shortly afterwards the liquidators were called in. Much of the collection here was on loan and frenetic activity followed as exhibits returned to their original homes. The need to clarify ownership of Beverley C.1 XB259 delayed any sale of it and this breather was used by the Yorkshire Air Museum to dust off the 'rescue plan' it had prepared back in 1997 and to look for funding for the awesome project. The Beverley Association and later the London-based Centaur Group consortium stepped into the fray, both declaring if they were successful in acquiring the aircraft, it would go to Elvington. With the ownership problem resolved, the liquidators – Carrick Read Insolvency – invited sealed bids with a deadline of 26th January 2004. With a reported bid of £36,000, Brian Rushworth, the owner of Fort Paull Armouries, was successful and plan to move the aircraft before May. In the early days of the collapse of MoAT it looked as though XB259 was doomed to be scrapped on site. It is good that it has been saved but the new venue faces the steepest of learning curves in coming to grips with the move and re-assembly, let alone the conservation of the 'Bev'.

❏ XB259	Beverley C.1	ex Paull, Luton, RAE, Blackburn, G-AOAI.	2-04

BREIGHTON AERODROME in between Bubwith and Breighton, east of Selby
Real Aeroplane Company and **Museum**: Tony 'Taff' Smith was not without Jungmann G-TAFF for very long. It returned to the fold on 15th May 2002. Mew Gull G-AEXF was shipped to Reno, Nevada, during mid-2003 to compete in the famous air races, returning during the autumn [1]. Spitfire PR.XI PL965 (N965RF) is due back from the USA mid-2004.
  Mick Ward died of a heart attack at his home in North Scarle, Lincs, in June 2003, he was 83. I turn to Nigel Ponsford to pay tribute... Mick served with 214 Squadron as a rear gunner on Stirlings from 1942 until the unit disbanded in 1945. Mick was a well-known aeromodeller and he turned his hand to the full-sized. From the 8ft shed in his garden emerged Gnome G-AXEI, Elf G-MMUL and the Flea 'F50'. At the time of its first flight (4th August 1967) G-AXEI was the smallest powered aeroplane in the world. All three of Mick's creations can be found today 'flying' in the 'Superhangar' here.
  Notes: Aircraft owned and operated by 'Taff' Smith or Rob Fleming plus the collection assembled by Nigel Ponsford (NHP) and any other aircraft under long-term restoration are listed here. (See also under Wigan, Gtr Man, and Selby, N Yorks, for other elements of Nigel's collection.) Airframes marked ➡ attended the '100 Years of Flight Experience' static display at Fairford, Glos, July 2003.
  Departures: The wreck of Coyote II G-MWRK was removed in December 2003 for scrapping. OH-7 Coupe G-ARIF transited through here, coming in from Wigan, Gtr Man, and moving on to <u>Kington</u>, Hereford, on 22nd November 2003. Deleted are Ryan ST3-KR G-BYPY and Elster B 97+04 (G-APVF) which remain based but are not part of the 'collection'.
◆ Signed from Bubwith on the A163. Open 10.30am to 4pm, weekends and Bank hols, Easter to October. Other times by prior arrangement. Different admission rates apply to fly-ins/airshows.
  ✉ The Aerodrome, Breighton, Selby, YO8 7DH ☎ / fax 01757 228838 www.realaero.aol.com

❏ G-ABVE*	Active II	➡ ex Old Warden, Tiger Club. Arrived 15-6-02.		2-04
❏ G-AEVS	Aeronca 100	➡ Composite, inc parts from G-AEXD. *Jeeves.*	NHP	2-04
❏ G-AEXF*	Mew Gull	➡ ex Old Warden, Sudbury, Old Warden, ZS-AHM. Arrived 15-6-02.	[1]	2-04
❏ G-AMAW	Luton Minor	ex Batley, Old Warden, Hitchin. CoA 6-8-88.	NHP	2-04
❏ G-AOBG	Somers-K SK.1	ex Benington, Eaton Bray, Cranfield. CoA 6-6-58.	NHP	2-04
❏ G-AXEI	Ward Gnome	ex East Kirkby, Tattershall.	NHP	2-04

❏	G-BVGZ		Fokker Dr I REP➜	ex Netheravon.		2-04
❏	G-BWUE	'1'	HA-1112-M1L	ex Sandown, Breighton, Duxford, N9938,		
			Buchón	*Battle of Britain*, G-AWHK, Spanish AF C4K-102.		
				Werner Schroer, JG27 colours.		2-04
❏	G-MJLK		Dragonfly 250	Stored, dismantled.		2-04
❏	G-MMUL		Ward Elf	ex Newark area. Citroen Ami.	NHP	2-04
❏	G-TAFF*		CASA I-131E	ex Sherburn, Breighton, G-BFNE, SpanAF		
			Jungmann ➜	E3B-148. Arrived 15-5-02.		2-04
❏		'F50'	HM.14 'Flea'	taxiable. Built by Mick Ward. Citroen Ami.	NHP	2-04
❏	T9738		Magister I ➜	G-AKAT, ex F-AZOR, G-AKAT, T9738,		
				24 EFTS, 15 EFTS.	➥	2-04
❏	'52024'		Hurricane XII	G-HURR, ex Duxford, Brooklands, RCAF 5589.		
	'LK-A'		➜	87 Sqn, night-fighter, c/s.	➥	2-04
❏	97+04		Elster B ➜	G-APVF, ex D-EEQX, 97+04, D-EJUH. CoA 1-7-98.		2-04
❏	'18'-5395'		L-18C Cub ➜	G-CUBJ, ex PH-MBF, PH-NLF, RNethAF		
				R-43, 52-2436.		2-04
❏	U-99		Jungmeister ➜	G-AXMT, ex N133SJ, G-AXMT, HB-MIY,		
				Swiss AF U-99.		2-04

BROUGH AIRFIELD south of the A63 west of Hull

BAE Systems: Refer to *W&R18* (p262) for comments on the Hawk Fuselage Replacement Programme (FRP) detritus. Swordfish NF389 will be rebuilt to ASR.III status, complete with under-fuselage radome [1]. The end of an era came on 16th August 2002 when Blackburn B-2 G-AEBJ left its long term home here and crossed the Pennines to live at Warton, Lancs. Blackburn Lincock FSM 'G-EBVO' (BAPC.287) moved to Hull, E Yorks.

❏	NF389		Swordfish III	ex Yeovilton, Brough, Lee-on-Solent.	® [1]	3-02
❏	XV168		Buccaneer S.2B	ex Lossiemouth, 12, 208, 12, FAA. 12 Sqn c/s.		2-04
❏	XX736		Jaguar GR.1	9110M, ex Coltishall, Shawbury, Warton, G-27-327,		
				Indian AF JI013, 6, 226 OCU, JOCU. Fatigue tests.		3-02
❏	ZD353	'H'	Harrier GR.5	ex Dunsfold, Brough, Wittering, 233 OCU, 1.		
				Damaged 29-7-91. Undercarriage test rig.		3-02
❏	–		Jaguar GR.1	nose.		3-02
❏	–		Hawk	fatigue rig. T.1A life extension test.		3-02
❏	–		Hawk Mk.203	forward fuselage.		3-02
❏	–		Harrier GR.5	fatigue rig.		3-02
❏	–		Eurofighter 2000	fatigue rig, two-seater variant. Nose only.		3-02
❏	–		Eurofighter 2000	fatigue rig, single-seater cockpit only.		3-02
❏	LL-5313*		Hawk T.53	ex Bournemouth, Indonesian Air Force. Spares.		10-03

GRINDALE north-west of Bridlington

British Skysports: By March 2003 the former para-trainer was dumped out on the airfield.

❏	G-BRID	Cessna U.206A	ex N4874F. CoA 20-5-93. Para-trainer. Dumped.	2-04

HULL

Street Life Museum: In High Street, took the Brough-built Blackburn Lincock FSM in 2003.

❏	'G-EBVO'*	Lincock FSM	BAPC.287, ex Brough.	5-03

Anderson Antiques: In Wincolmlee, on the banks of the river. By August 2002 the hulk of Cessna 150E G-ATAT had moved on, reportedly to a flying club in the Norwich area.

LINLEY HILL AERODROME or Beverley, west of Leven, off A165 north-east of Beverley.

❏	G-AYBW	Cessna FA.150K	ex Perth. Crashed 8-10-72. Fuselage.	9-01
❏	G-BAIP	Cessna F.150L	Crashed 30-5-95. Dismantled.	9-01

MARFLEET on the A1033 east of Kingston upon Hull
Humbrol Ltd: The Hunter guards the factory.
❑ XF509   Hunter F.6   ex Chivenor 8708M, Thurleigh, 4 FTS, MoA, AFDS, 54. 7-03

OTTRINGHAM on the A1033 east of Hull
❑ G-AWLP* Mooney M.20F CoA 7-7-00. Stored.   7-99
❑ G-BRPG   Cessna 120 ex N72703, NC72703. CoA 29-8-94. Stored.   7-99

PAULL on minor road south of Hedon
Fort Paull Armouries: In February 2004 it was announced that this venue had been successful in bidding for Beverley XB259 at Beverley, E Yorks. The aircraft was due to make the move to its new home by May. The Paull in XB259's history was the now long-defunct aerodrome not far from its new resting place. Part of a set-piece scene from World War Two includes a Bulldog cockpit.
◆ Fort Paull, Battery Road, Paull, HU12 8F ☎ 01482 882655
❑ XB259   Beverley C.1 ex Beverley, Paull, Luton, RAE, Blackburns, G-AOAI. **due**
❑ [XX557] Bulldog T.1 ex Topcliffe, Linton-on-Ouse, St Athan, Gla UAS,
            CFS. Crashed 11-9-75. Cockpit.   7-03

POCKLINGTON AERODROME east of the A1079, west of the village
❑ –*   BPX T.45 Swallow BGA.1136. Ex XS859. CoA 5-7-98. Stored. 3-03

PRESTON on the B1239 north of Hedon
The Varsity nose is still kept at the filling station-cum-scrapyard.
❑ WL627   Varsity T.1 ex Hull, Newton 8488M, 6 FTS, 2 ANS, 1 ANS,
            BCBS. Nose.   12-02

SEATON ROSS north-west of Holme-on-Spalding-Moor
Hornet Aviation: Are restoring a Proctor for the Air Atlantique Classic Flight.
❑ G-AKIU* Proctor V   ex Coventry, Nottingham, Bedford, Houghton-on-
            the-Hill, North Weald, Southend, Edenbridge.
            CoA 24-1-65. Here since mid-2000. off site ® 2-04

STORWOOD south of the B1228, south-east of York
Melbourne Autos: The Yorkshire Helicopter Preservation Group keep a 'spares ship' here courtesy of the company - see under Doncaster, S Yorks.
❑ XD165* 'B' Whirlwind ex Wattisham, Netheravon, Halton 8673M, SARTS,
        HAR.10   202, 228, 22, 225, 155. Stored.   4-03

THWING east of the B1249/B1253 junction, north of Great Driffield
J/1N G-AHCK moved to Scarborough, N Yorks, in late 2003, along with former flyer J/1 G-AJRC.

WITHERNSEA on the A1033 east of Hull
Oblivion: Within the night-club can be found a 'crashed' Cessna.
❑ G-BDEW Cessna FRA.150M Crashed 13-8-96.   2-02

NORTH YORKSHIRE

BAGBY AERODROME on the A19 south-east of Thirsk

❏ G-BCUL*	Rallye 100ST	ex F-OCZL. CoA 8-5-00. First noted 7-03.	7-03
❏ G-BLLP*	T.67B Firefly	CoA 4-12-00. First noted 10-02.	10-02

CARLTON MOOR on minor road south-east of Carlton-in-Cleveland
Carlton Moor Gliding Club: The glider store is thought unchanged.

❏ BAC	Skylark 3B	BGA.806, ex RNGSA 'CU19', BGA.806. CoA 5-97.	3-00
❏ DUC	Carmam M.100S	BGA.2383, ex F-CCSA. CoA 5-88. Stored.	3-00
❏ EAL	Rhonlerche II	BGA.2530, ex PH-331. CoA 9-91. Stored.	3-00

CARTHORPE west of the A1, south-east of Bedale
Camp Hill Activity Centre:
◆ Access by prior arrangement *only*. ☎ 01845 567788 **fax** 01845 567065 **www**.camphill.co.uk

❏ G-BHXJ	Norecrin II	ex 'London', F-BEMX.	3-02

ELVINGTON off the A1079 south-east of York
Yorkshire Air Museum (YAM): Please refer to Beverley, E Yorks, for the story of the Beverley and attempts to bring it into the care of YAM. During the summer of 2002 a major refurbishment of the workshop, the Handley Page Restoration Hangar, was carried out and it is now an impressive open area allowing visitors a glimpse of work-in-progress.

    Notes: The PV.8 Eastchurch Kitten REP WAS built by Bill Sneesby [1]. The Spitfire FSM 'guards' the memorial room of the **609 (West Riding) Squadron Association** [2]. The Mosquito is on loan from **Tony Agar** and is a complex composite, using the nose section of HJ711; the rear fuselage of TT.35 RS715 from Elstree; the centre section from Mk XVI PF498 from Leyland; and the outer wings of T.3 VA878 from St Davids [3]. The Halifax re-creation is a complex composite: using the centre section from former 58 Squadron Mk II HR792 which came to grief in a take-off accident at Stornoway on 13th January 1945; the wings from Hastings C.1 TG536 from Catterick; myriad Halifax detail parts; Hercules engines courtesy of the French Air Force and ex-Noratlas, plus new-build nose and rear section and many other elements [4]. Buccaneer S.2B XX901 is owned by the **Buccaneer Aircrew Association** (Dave Herriott, 84 Lees Gardens, Maidenhead, SL6 4NT). BAA serves to link all former Buccaneer aircrew [5]. The original nose of the Hadrian is still to be found at Bacup, Lancs [6]. The Bf 109G FSM was built by Danny Thornton of Garforth, W Yorks [7]. Several airframes are on loan and are marked ±: the 'Flea' from Dave Allan; the Dragonfly from Ray McElwain; the Victor from André Tempest and team, which regularly taxies (they also have a Victor procedure trainer); and the Lightning from Peter Chambers. Airframes marked ➡ attended the '100 Years of Flight Experience' static display at the International Air Tattoo, Fairford, Glos, July 2003. Snowbird IV G-MVIM left the collection during 2003 - destination unknown.
◆ Signed from the A64 southern York ring, at the A64/A166/A1079 junction. Open late Oct to late Mar 10am to 3.30pm daily, summer 10am to 5pm daily.✉ YAM, Elvington, York, YO41 4AU ☎ 01904 608595 **fax** 01904 608246 **www**.yorkshireairmuseum.co.uk

❏ 'G-AAAH'	DH.60 Moth FSM	BAPC.270, *Jason*.		3-04
❏ 'G-AFFI'	HM.14 'Flea'	BAPC.76, ex Hemswell, Cleethorpes, Nostell, Rawdon.	±	3-04
❏ [G-AJOZ]	Argus II	ex Woodhall Spa, Tattershall, Wigan, Market Drayton, Wigan, Southend, Sywell, FK338, Kemble, ATA 2 FP, 42-32142. Cr 16-8-62. Stored.		3-04
❏ G-AVPN	Herald 213	ex Channel Express, I-TIVB, G-AVPN, D-BIBI, HB-AAK ntu. CoA 14-12-99.		3-04
❏ G-MJRA	Mainair Tri-Flyer	ex Wetherby. Demon 175 wing.		3-04
❏ G-TFRB	Air Command 532	ex Hartlepool. CoA 6-8-98.		3-04
❏ G-YURO	Europa 001	ex Wombleton. CoA 9-6-95.		3-04
❏ 'F943'	SE.5A REP	G-BKDT, ex Selby, Elvington, Selby.		3-04
❏ 'H1968'	Avro 504K REP	BAPC.42, ex St Athan, Halton.	➡	3-04

❏	[N540]	PV Kitten REP	ex Selby. Stored.	[1]	3-04
❏	'P3873''YO-H'	Hurricane I FSM	BAPC.265, 1 Sqn RCAF colours.		3-04
❏	'R6690''PR-A'	Spitfire I FSM	BAPC.254, 609 Sqn colours.	[2]	3-04
❏	HJ711 'VI-C'	Mosquito NF.II	ex Huntington. 169 Sqn c/s. *Spirit of Val.*	® [3]	3-04
❏	KN353	C-47B-30-DK	ex Coventry, Air Atlantique, SU-AZF, G-AMYJ,		
	G-AMYJ		XF747, G-AMYJ, KN353, 110, 96, 243,		
			44-76384. CoA 4-4-97. (Wings of G-ANAF.)	®	3-04
❏	'LV907'	Halifax II	ex Isle of Lewis. 'NP-F', *Friday 13th*, 158 Sqn c/s.	® [4]	3-04
❏	RA854	Cadet TX.1	ex Wigan, TAC, Woodford, RAFGSA,		
			Woodvale, 41 GS. Stored.		3-04
❏	'TJ704' 'JA'	Terrier 2	G-ASCD, ex Holme-on Spalding Moor, Nympsfield,		
			Blackbushe, PH-SFT, G-ASCD, Auster AOP.6		
			VW993, 651, 663. CoA 26-9-71.	®	3-04
❏	VV901	Anson T.21	ex Bacup, Burtonwood, Cosford, Irton Holme,		
			Leconfield, CFCCU, Dur UAS, 1 RFS.	®	3-04
❏	WH846	Canberra T.4	ex Samlesbury, St Athan, Laarbruch SF, 231 OCU.		3-04
❏	WH903	Canberra B.2	ex 100, 85, MoA, 85, W Raynham TFF,		
			228 OCU, 102, 617. Nose. Id confirmed.		3-04
❏	WH991	Dragonfly HR.5	ex Storwood, Tattershall Thorpe, Tattershall,		
			Wisbech, Taunton, Fleetlands, Culdrose SF, 705,		
			700, Eglinton SF, *Centaur* Flt, 705, *Illustrious* Flt.	➡ ±	3-04
❏	'WK864' 'C'	Meteor F.8	WL168 ex Finningley, 'WH456', St Athan, Swinderby,		
			Finningley, Heywood 7750M, Sylt, 604, 111. 616 c/s.		3-04
❏	WS788 'Z'	Meteor NF.14	ex Leeming 'WS844', Patrington 7967M,		
			1 ANS, 2 ANS, 152.		3-04
❏	XH278 '42'	Vampire T.11	ex Felton, Henlow 8595M, Upwood 7866M,		
			27 MU, RAFC. RAFC colours.		3-04
❏	XH767	Javelin FAW.9	ex Norwich, Monkton Farleigh, Worcester 7955M,		
			Shawbury, 228 OCU, 11, 25. 23 Sqn colours.		3-04
❏	XL231	Victor K.2	ex 55, 57, Witt Wing, Victor TF, Witt Wing,		
			139. *Lusty Lindy*.	±	3-04
❏	'XL571' 'V'	Hunter T.7	XL572 / G-HNTR, ex Brough, Bournemouth,		
			Cosford 8834M, 1 TWU, 2 TWU, TWU, 229		
			OCU. 92 Sqn, 'Blue Diamonds' colours.		3-04
❏	XN974	Buccaneer S.2	ex BAe Warton, Holme on Spalding Moor, A&AEE, 803.		3-04
❏	XP640 'M'	Jet Provost T.4	ex Halton 8501M, CATCS, 6 FTS, CAW,		
			CFS, 3 FTS. 6 FTS colours.		3-04
❏	XS903 'BA'	Lightning F.6	ex Binbrook, 11, 5-11 pool.	±	3-04
❏	XV748 '3D'	Harrier GR.3	ex Cranfield, Bedford, 233 OCU, 1, 233 OCU, 1.		3-04
❏	XX901	Buccaneer S.2B	ex Kemble, St Athan, Lossiemouth, 208, 12, 237		
			OCU, 208. *Kathryn - The Flying Mermaid*. Pink c/s.	[5]	3-04
❏	– '1'	Jet Provost T.3	ex Linton-on-Ouse. Procedure trainer.		3-04
❏	– '2'	Jet Provost T.3	ex Linton-on-Ouse. Procedure trainer.		3-04
❏	–	Victor	ex Navenby. Procedure trainer.	±	3-04
❏	21417	CT-133 S' Star	ex Sollingen, CAF.		3-04
❏	538 '3-QH'	Mirage IIIE	ex Chateaudun, 3 *Esc*, FAF.		3-04
❏	'N-2'	Hunter FGA.78	N-268. ex Bournemouth, Qatar AF QA-10, G-9-286,		
			Dutch AF N-268. Dutch colours.		3-04
❏	'237123'	CG-4A Hadrian	BAPC.157, ex Bacup, Ormskirk.	® [6]	3-04
❏	–	BAPC.28 Wright Flyer REP	ex Leeds, Eccleston, Cardington, Finningley.	➡	3-04
❏	–	BAPC.41 BE.2c REP	ex St Athan, '6232'. Halton.	➡	3-04
❏	–	BAPC.89 Cayley REP	ex Manchester, Hendon, Lasham. Rolled-out 12-8-99.		3-04
❏	–	BAPC.130 Blackburn 1911 R	ex Stoke, Helston, *Flambards*.	➡	3-04
❏	–	BAPC.240 Bf 109G FSM	ex Garforth.	[7]	3-04

Yorkshire Helicopter Preservation Group (YHPG): During 2002 YHPG decided to relocate its operation to AeroVenture at Doncaster, S Yorks. Dragonfly HR.5 WH991 remains with YAM and is listed above accordingly. Whirlwind HAR.10 XJ398 moved to temporary display at Benson, Oxon, before settling on <u>Doncaster</u>, S Yorks, on 1st April 2003. Whirlwind HAR.10 XP345 moved to Doncaster, S Yorks, earlier in the year. For Whirlwind HAR.10 XD165 see Storwood, E Yorks.

GREAT AYTON on the A173 south-east of Middlesbrough
In the general area is a private collection. Viewing is *not* possible.

❑ WM145	Meteor NF.11	ex Rotherham, Finningley, 5, 29, 151, 219. Nose.	11-03
❑ WZ557	Vampire T.11	ex Huntingdon, Acaster Malbis, Woodford, Chester, St Athan, 5 FTS, 16. Black colours.	11-03
❑ XM169	Lightning F.1A	ex Thirsk, Leuchars 8422M, Leuchars TFF, 23, Binbrook TFF, 111, A&AEE, MoA, EE. Nose.	11-03
❑ XN607	Jet Provost T.3	ex Leeds, 3 FTS. SOC 28-5-76. Nose. All grey c/s.	11-03
❑ XV867	Buccaneer S.2B	ex Leeming, 208, 12, 208, 237 OCU, FAA, 809, 736, 803. Nose.	11-03

HARROGATE on the A61 north of Leeds
The reference here is getting long-in-the-tooth and is on finals for LOST!

❑ XR726	Lightning F.6	ex Rossington, Binbrook, LTF, 11, LTF, 11, 5. 'TVI726'. Nose.	3-93

INGLEBY ARNCLIFFE between the A19 and A172 north east of Northallerton

❑ G-BHNV*	W-Bell 47G-3B1	ex F-GHNM, G-BHNV, XW180. CoA 28-5-<u>89</u>.	10-02
❑ G-MMKM*	Gemini/D Striker	CoA 11-6-99. Stored.	10-02

KIRKBYMOORSIDE AERODROME on the A170 west of Pickering, south of the town
Slingsby Aviation:

❑ –	T.67 Firefly	c/n 2006, static test airframe.	3-02
❑ ZE686	Viking TX.1	ex BGA.3099. Static test airframe.	1-03

LEEMING AIRFIELD east of the A1, west of Bedale
RAF Leeming: Lightning F.6 XR753 is displayed outside XI Squadron's headquarters – see under Tangmere, W Sussex, for its doppelgänger [1].

❑ XA634		Javelin FAW.4	7641M, ex Shawbury, Colerne, Melksham, Gloster. 228 OCU markings.	1-04
❑ XR753	'BP'	Lightning F.6	8969M, ex Binbrook, 11, 5-11 pool, 23, FCTU. [1]	1-04
❑ XV499		Phantom FGR.2	ex 74, 92, 228 OCU, 29, 23, 19, 92, 41, 6.	1-04
❑ ZD934	'AD'	Tornado F.2	ex St Athan, 229 OCU. Nose. ABDRT.	1-04

LINTON-ON-OUSE AIRFIELD west of the A19, north-west of York
RAF Linton-on-Ouse: JP T.3A XM372, last noted March 2002, is believed to have been scrapped.

❑ XN589	'46' Jet Provost T.3A	9143M, ex 1 FTS, RAFC. 1 FTS c/s. Gate.	5-03

MALTON off the A64 north of Malton at A169 junction
Eden Camp Modern History Theme Museum: Each hut in this former prisoner of war camp has a different theme and the level of presentation is breath-taking. There is much to fascinate the aviation follower, including a Link trainer display, plotting room, items on 617 Squadron, the Comete escape line and much more. The Hurricane was built by G B Moulders of Norfolk, the Spitfire and V-1 by TDL Replicas of Lowestoft.

◆ Daily 10am to 5pm, last admission 4pm. (Extended closure Xmas and New Year, call for details.)
✉ Eden Camp, Malton, YO17 6RT. ☎ 01653 697777 **fax** 01653 698243 **e-mail** admin@edencamp.co.uk **www**.edencamp.co.uk

❑ 'P2793''SD-M'	Hurricane FSM	BAPC.236. 501 Sqn colours.	1-04
❑ 'AB550''GE-P'	Spitfire FSM	BAPC.230, ex 'AA908'. 349 Sqn colours.	1-04
❑ –	BAPC.235 Fi 103 (V-1) FSM	–	1-04

NEWBY WISKE north-west of Thirsk, near South Otterington

❑	G-BGFK		Evans VP-1	Canx 7-4-99. Stored. First noted 11-99.		10-02
❑	E3B-369		Jungmann	G-BPDM, ex SpanAF. CoA 22-6-96.	®	10-02

RICHMOND west of the A1, north-west of Catterick
Avro 504L S-AHAA arrived here by March 2002 before settling upon <u>Woodford</u>, Gtr Man, in 2003.

RUFFORTH AERODROME south of the A1237, west of York
McLean's Sailplanes:

❑	G-ATSY		Super Baladou IV	ex Newcastle. CoA 23-11-91. Spares.	7-03
❑	G-BCHX		SF-23A Sperling	ex Netherthorpe, D-EGIZ. Damaged 7-8-82. Frame.	3-02
❑	–	AUJ	T.21B	BGA.668. Damaged 16-7-85. Stored.	3-02
❑	XA286		Cadet TX.3	ex Eaglescott, Syerston, 615 VGS. Fuselage. Stored.	3-02
❑	XA290		Cadet TX.3	ex Syerston, Dishforth, 661 VGS, 643 VGS. Fuselage.	3-02

Others:

❑	G-LUFT	Elster C	ex Humberside, North Coates, G-BOPY, D-EDEZ. Spares for G-APVF, stored.	2-04

SCARBOROUGH
Two Austers have moved into the area for restoration.

❑	G-AHCK*	J/1N Alpha	ex Thwing, Spilsby, Croft, Skegness. Damaged 14-9-91. Arrived 12-03.	®	12-03
❑	G-AJRC*	J/1 Autocrat	ex Thwing. CoA 14-7-02. Arrived 31-12-03.	®	12-03

SELBY on the A19 south of York
Anne Lindsay and **Nigel Ponsford**: See also under Breighton, E Yorks and Wigan, Gtr Man. Lafayette 1 G-MBWI moved to <u>Kington</u>, Hereford, on 22nd November 2003.
◆ Airframes listed held in deep storage or restoration in and around the area and visits are *not* possible.

❑	G-ADPJ		BAC Drone II	ex Breighton, Wigan, Bristol, Benson, Thetford. Damaged 3-4-55. Also parts from G-AEKU.	®	2-04
❑	G-AEFG		HM.14 'Flea'	BAPC.75, ex Breighton, Leeds, Harrogate, Kirkby Overblow, Accrington.	®	2-04
❑	G-APXZ		Knight Twister	ex Breighton, Tumby Woodside, Loughborough, Biggin Hill. Frame.		2-04
❑	–	ALX	Dagling	BGA.491, ex Leeds, Great Hucklow.		2-04
❑	–	AQY	EoN Primary	BGA.588, ex Breighton, Hemel Hempstead. Stored.		2-04
❑	–	BVM	Dart 17R	BGA.1269, ex Breighton, Rufforth.		2-04
❑	–		Hutter H.17a	ex Leeds, Accrington.		2-04
❑	–		Dickson Primary	ex Leeds, Harrogate.		2-04
❑	XK819		Grasshopper TX.1	ex Breighton, Warmingham, Stoke-on-Trent, Cosford, Malvern, 2 MGSP, Kimbolton.	®	2-04
❑	100502		Fa 330A-1	ex Breighton, East Kirkby, Tattershall, Wigan. TAC loan.		2-04
❑	–	BAPC.14	Addyman STG	ex Leeds, Harrogate, Wigan.		2-04
❑	–	BAPC.16	Addyman UL	ex Leeds, Harrogate, Wigan.		2-04
❑	–	BAPC.18	Killick Gyroplane	ex Leeds, Harrogate, Irlam.		2-04
❑	–	BAPC.39	Addyman Zephyr	ex Leeds, Harrogate. Substantial parts.		2-04

SHERBURN-IN-ELMET AERODROME on the B1222 east of the town, east of Leeds

❑	G-BNCZ	Rutan LongEz	damaged 12-2-94. Stored.	off-site ®	9-00
❑	G-SACU	Cadet 161	ex N9162X. Crashed 29-6-96.		9-02

THIRSK on the A19 north-east of Ripon
A pair of Evans 'Volksplanes' have arrived in the area.

❏ G-BEKM*	Evans VP-1	ex Eaton Bray. CoA 23-3-95. Stored.	11-03
❏ G-BFFB*	Evans VP-2	ex Eaton Bray. Unflown. Stored.	11-03

SOUTH YORKSHIRE

ARMTHORPE on the A630 north of Doncaster
No.1053 Squadron Air Cadets: Keep a 'Chippax' in Church Street. 'Parent' is Waddington.

❏ WG419	Chipmunk T.10	8206M, ex Finningley, MoA, Laarbruch SF, Gütersloh	
	PAX	SF, Ahlhorn SF, Oldenburg SF, CFS, Abn UAS, Bir	
		UAS, 15 RFS, 4 BFTS, 6 RFS.	11-02

ASKERN on the A19 north of Doncaster
For a long time a farm here has been the home of former Finningley Jetstream T.1 XX477. It was believed to have moved to Cranwell, Lincs, for use there but this was clearly not so. In its time, 6 FTS Finningley had two Jetstream cockpits for use as trainers. The prototype Jetstream G-ATXH was used as a cockpit procedures trainer and it is this that should be at Cranwell. It was only ever a very truncated cockpit area when at Finningley. XX477 was used not be the Jetstream element of 6 FTS at Finningley, but by the Dominie team. It was (and is) a full fuselage from forward bulkhead to close to, but ahead of, the pressure bulkhead. It was used as an escape trainer, hence the very confusing crew door immediately behind the cockpit on the port side and the Dominie placing of the roundel.

❏ XX477*	Jetstream T.1	ex Finningley 8462M, Little Rissington, CFS,	
		G-AXXS. Crashed 1-11-74. Fuselage, stored.	2-04

BAWTRY on the A638 south of Doncaster
No.216 Squadron Air Cadets:

❏ WK584	Chipmunk T.10	7556M, ex Church Fenton, Linton-on-Ouse,	
	PAX	Edzell SF, Ox UAS, Glas UAS, 11 RFS.	3-03

Bawtry Paintball: Located to the north of the town, the arena has a 'chopper'.

❏ [XL840]	Whirlwind	ex Long Marston, Norwich, Sibson, Blackpool,	
	HAS.7	Fleetwood, Wroughton, 705, Brawdy SF,	
		Culdrose SF, 705, 820.	9-03

DONCASTER
AeroVenture: Expansion of both airframes and facilities continues apace here. Arriving in August 2003 was Gannet AS.4 XA460. This is owned by the local **750 Squadron, Air Training Corps**, and is to be kept and restored in a co-operative arrangement with AeroVenture [1]. Working with AeroVenture and co-based on site is the **Yorkshire Helicopter Preservation Group** - see below.
  Notes: Several airframes are on loan to AeroVenture including: Dave Charles, marked DC; Bill Fern - BF; and those owned by AeroVenture curator Naylan Moore via his **Classic Aircraft Collection**, CAC. Naylan is also at work on a Typhoon or Tempest cockpit section acquired from Gloucestershire. The Cessna F.150G is a composite, including the cabin of F.152 II G-BISB (from Sturgate, Lincs) [2]. HS.125 nose G-BOCB is owned by Mike North [3]. The Tiger Moth fuselage will be restored to the colours of the locally-based 9 RFS [4]. The identity of the Venom is now confirmed [5]. Bill Fern's new Cadet glider is fitted with the wings of WT917 [6]. Venom NF.3 WX788 is on loan from Steve Hague [7]. Vampire T.11 XD459 incorporates the wings and tail feathers from XE872 and is owned by Dave Hardy [8]. Lightning F.6 XP703 is owned by Scott Clayton [9]. Lightning F.6 XS897 is owned by a consortium of six museum members [10]. The Valetta nose came from Cardington and presumably from Henlow before that and is said to have been with an ATC unit before joining the museum's stock. During strip-down it revealed a CFS badge [11].

Departures: Cadet BGA.972 left for a new owner 3-04. Auster AOP.9 XK421 to <u>Okehampton</u>, Devon, by 11-03; Sioux AH.1 XT242 to YHPG 13-12-03 - see below.

♦ At the Doncaster Lakeside Leisure Park. Access off the A638 beyond 'The Dome' or follow signs off the M18/ A6182 for 'Yorkshire Outlet'. Open Thu, Fri, Sat, Sun, 10am to 5pm. AeroVenture are happy to offer 'back lot' tours of the storage area - apply in advance. ✉ Sandy Lane, Doncaster, DN4 5EP ☎ 01302 761616 **www.syam.freehosting.net**

❑	'K-158'	Whippet REP	BAPC.207, ex Sunderland, Stoke-on-Trent.	DC 3-04
❑	G-ALYB	Auster 5	ex Firbeck, Bristol, White Waltham, RT520, 85 GCS, 84 GCS. CoA 26-5-63. Frame.	® 3-04
❑	G-AOKO	Prentice 1	ex Coventry, Southend, VS621, CFS, 2 FTS, 22 FTS. CoA 23-10-72. Stored.	3-04
❑	G-APMY	Apache 160	ex Firbeck, Connah's Quay, Halfpenny Green, EI-AJT. CoA 1-11-81.	3-04
❑	G-ARGI	Auster 6A	ex Newark-on-Trent, Chirk, Heathfield, VF530, 661. CoA 4-7-76. Frame, stored.	3-04
❑	G-ARHX	Dove 8	ex Sunderland, Booker, Southgate, Leavesden. CoA 8-9-78.	3-04
❑	G-AVAA	Cessna F.150G	ex Firbeck, Shobdon, Bournemouth. CoA 5-7-96. Fuselage, composite.	[2] 2-00
❑	G-AWCL*	Cessna F.150H	Canx 2-2-88.	CAC 3-04
❑	G-BOCB	HS.125-1B/522	ex Cardiff, Hatfield, G-OMCA, G-DJMJ, G-AWUF, 5N-ALY, G-AWUF, HZ-BIN. CoA 16-10-90. Nose.	[3] 3-04
❑	G-DELB	Robinson R.22B	ex Firbeck, Sherburn, Retford, N26461. Crashed 27-12-94. Stored.	3-04
❑	–*	Pup	ex Stamford. Unfinished cockpit.	3-04
❑	–*	Jetstream 41	ex Woodford, Prestwick. Unfinished cockpit.	3-04
❑	G-MJKP	Hiway Skytrike	—	3-04
❑	G-MJPO*	Goldwing	—	3-04
❑	N3188H*	Ercoupe 415C	ex Chislet, NC3188H. Damaged 7-92. F/n 6-03.	3-04
❑	N4565L*	DC-3-201A	ex Framlingham, Ipswich, Dublin, LV-GYP, LV-PCV, N129H, N512, N51D, N80C, NC21744. *Aisling*. Arrived 6-8-03.	3-04
❑	'NM145'*	Tiger Moth	fuselage.	CAC ® [4] 3-04
❑	WA662	Meteor T.7	ex Firbeck, Willington, Chalgrove, Llanbedr, Farnborough, FCCS, 3, Wildenrath SF, Gütersloh SF, 3.	® 3-04
❑	WB560	Chipmunk T.10 PAX	ex Firbeck, Fownhope, St Athan, Ox UAS, 242 OCU, 2 SoTT, South Cerney SF, ITS, 7 AEF, Nott UAS, 4 AEF.	CAC 3-04
❑	WB733	Chipmunk T.10	ex Firbeck, Sevenoaks, Shawbury SF, Hamble CoAT, Marham SF, 4 SoTT 'hack', Lyneham SF, Upavon SF, HUAS, 11 RFS.	3-04
❑	[WB969]	Sedbergh TX.1	ex Wroot.	3-04
❑	WD935*	Canberra B.2	ex Birdlip, Bridgnorth, Ottershaw, Egham, 8440M, St Athan, 360, 97, 151, CSE, EE, BCDU, RAAF A84-1 ntu. Nose. Arrived by 5-03.	CAC 3-04
❑	[WE987]	Prefect TX.1	BGA.2517, ex Newport Pagnell.	3-04
❑	WF122* '575'	Sea Prince T.1	ex Bruntingthorpe, Helston, Culdrose A2673, 750, Sydenham SF, Arbroath SF, Lossiemouth SF, 700Z Flt, Lossiemouth SF, FOFT, 750, Eglinton SF, 744. Arrived 20-8-03.	3-04
❑	WJ565*	Canberra T.17	ex Harrington, North Coates, Coventry, North Coates, Binbrook, Bruntingthorpe, Cosford 8871M, St Athan, 360, CA. Nose. Arrived 22-3-03.	3-04
❑	WJ903	Varsity T.1	ex Firbeck, Dumfries, Glasgow Airport, 6 FTS, AE&AEOS, 1 ANS, 2 ANS, 3 ANS. Nose.	3-04
❑	WK393	Venom FB.1	ex CGS, FWS, Silloth, Firbeck, Dumfries, Silloth. Pod.	BF [5] 3-04

❑	WK626		Chipmunk T.10	ex Firbeck, Salisbury, Welling, White Waltham, Bicester, 8213M, Odiham SF, Ox UAS, South Cerney SF, 1 FTS, Bicester SF, Odiham SF, FTCCS, Lon UAS, Cam UAS, Colerne SF, Leeds UAS, Nott UAS, 16 FRS, 18 RFS. Fuselage.	BF	3-04
❑	WL131		Meteor F.8	ex Firbeck, Guernsey 7751M, APS Sylt, 601, 111. Nose.	BF	3-04
❑	WN890		Hunter F.2	ex Firbeck, Robertsbridge, Stamford, Hedge End, Boscombe Down, A&AEE, AWA. Nose.	CAC	3-04
❑	WP255		Vampire NF.10	ex Haverigg, Firbeck, Ecclesfield, Bingley, Church Fenton, 27 MU, CNCS, 1 ANS, CNCS, 23. Pod.	CAC	3-04
❑	WT913*	FGA	Cadet TX.1	BGA.3239, ex Strubby. CoA 21-7-96. F/n 9-03.	BF [6]	3-04
❑	WX788		Venom NF.3	ex Elvington, Kenilworth, Long Marston, Cardiff-Wales, Bledlow Ridge, Connah's Quay, DH. Stored.	[7]	3-04
❑	[WZ822]		G'hopper TX.1	ex Firbeck, Robertsbridge, Halton, London. Stored.	BF	3-04
❑	XA460*	'768'	Gannet AS.4	ex Connah's Quay, Brawdy, 849. Arrived 8-03.	[1]	3-04
❑	XD377	'A'	Vampire T.11	ex Firbeck, Barton, Elvington, Cosford, B'ham, Shawbury 8203M, Hawarden, 66. Pod, stored.	BF	3-04
❑	XD459*	'63'	Vampire T.11	ex East Mids, B'thorpe, Long Marston, Bennington, Cranfield, Bushey, Keevil, 3/4 CAACU, 229 OCU, 233 OCU, 151, 253, 56. Arr 2-03.	® [8]	3-04
❑	XE317	'S-N'	Sycamore HR.14	ex Firbeck, Winthorpe, Portsmouth, CFS, 275, G-AMWO ntu.	®	3-04
❑	XE935	'30'	Vampire T.11	ex Firbeck, Sibson, Hitchin, Woodford, Chester, St Athan, 8 FTS.		3-04
❑	XG297		Hunter FGA.9	ex Firbeck, Newton-le-Willows, Bacup, Macclesfield, Bitteswell, HSA, 20, 28, 20, 4. Nose.	off-site BF	3-04
❑	XH584		Canberra T.4	ex Firbeck, Sunderland, Marham, 231 OCU. Nose.		3-04
❑	XL388*		Vulcan B.2	ex Walpole, Honington 8750M, 50, Wadd Wing, Scampton Wing,9. Nose. Arrived 7-4-03.		3-04
❑	XM350	'89'	Jet Provost T.3A	ex Firbeck, Church Fenton 9036M, 7 FTS, 1 FTS, RAFC, A&AEE.		3-04
❑	[XM411]	'X'	Jet Provost T.3	ex Firbeck, Otterburn, Halton 8434M, St Athan, Shawbury, Kemble, CFS. Nose section.		3-04
❑	XM561		Skeeter AOP.12	ex Firbeck, East Kirkby, Tattershall, Moston, Middle Wallop, Arborfield 7980M, Wroughton, HQ 1 Wing, HQ 2 Wing, 651.		3-04
❑	XN238		Cadet TX.3	ex Firbeck, Robertsbridge, St Athan, 622 VGS. Nose.	BF	3-04
❑	XN386	'435'	Whirlwind HAR.9	ex Lancaster, Blackpool, Heysham, Wroughton, Yeo'n A2713, Fleetlands, *Endurance* Flt, 846, 814. Cockpit.		3-04
❑	XN511	'12'	Jet Provost T.3	ex Firbeck, Robertsbridge, 'XM426', Lutterworth, Liversedge, Kemble, CFS, 1 FTS, CFS. Nose.	BF	3-04
❑	XN979*		Buccaneer S.2	ex Stamford, Croydon, Popham, Stanbridge, Henlow, Cranfield, 801.Ditched 9-6-66. Nose.	®	3-04
❑	XP190		Scout AH.1	ex Firbeck, Wroughton, Arborfield.		3-04
❑	XP706*		Lightning F.3	ex Hemswell, Strubby, Binbrook 8925M, LTF, 11, 5, LTF, 23, 111, 74. Arrived 19-11-02.	[9]	3-04
❑	XP902		Scout AH.1	ex Firbeck, Otterburn, Edinburgh, Dishforth, Netheravon, Wroughton, Garrison Air Sqn, 3 CBAS. Cockpit.		3-04
❑	XR754		Lightning F.6	ex Firbeck, Walpole, King's Lynn, Stock, Honington, Binbrook 8972M, 11, 5-11, 23, 5, A&AEE. Nose.	BF	3-04
❑	XS216*		Jet Provost T.4	ex Goole, Finningley, 6 FTS, CAW. Dam 7-5-73. Nose. Arrived by 9-03.		3-04
❑	XS481		Wessex HU.5	ex Firbeck, Dishforth, Wroughton, Yeovilton, Culdrose, Yeovilton, 771, 707.		3-04
❑	XS897		Lightning F.6	ex Firbeck, Rossington, Binbrook, 5, 11, 5, 11, 56, 74. Stored.	[10]	3-04
❑	XW666		Nimrod R.1	ex Long Marston, Warton, Woodford, Kinloss, 51. Crashed 16-5-95. Cockpit.		3-04
❑	XX411*		Gazelle AH.1	ex Chichester, 3 CBAS. Shot down 21-5-82, San Carlos. Arrived 5-02.		3-04

❑ E-424	Hunter F.51	ex Firbeck, East Kirkby, Tattershall, Cosford, Dunsfold, G-9-445, Aalborg, RDanAF, Esk.724.		3-04
❑ ET-273	Hunter T.53	ex Firbeck, Chelford, Macclesfield, Leavesden, Elstree, Hatfield, RDanAF Esk.724, RNethAF N-302. Nose.		3-04
❑ 333*	Vampire T.55	ex Barton, Chelford, Hadfield, Dukinfield, New Brighton, Chester, Iraqi AF. Pod. Arrived 2-03.	CAC	3-04
❑ –*	Tiger Moth	ex Spanhoe Lodge. Fuselage. First noted 6-03.	BF ®	3-04
❑ –	Vampire FB.5	ex Firbeck, Malmesbury, 229 OCU. Pod, stored.		3-04
❑ –	Valetta	ex Cardington, Henlow (?), ATC unit (?). Nose.	[11]	3-04
❑ –*	CG-4 Hadrian REP	ex Hatfield, *Saving Private Ryan*. Nose. F/n 6-03.	BF	3-04
❑ –	C-10A Jetstream EMU	ex Sunderland, Wycombe Air Park, Bushey, West Ruislip, Stanmore, St Albans, Radlett. Nose.		3-04

Yorkshire Helicopter Preservation Group: The group took the decision to relocate from the Yorkshire Air Museum to AeroVenture during late 2002. They have set to with gusto to establish themselves, with plans for their own restoration hangar. The removal and restoration of HAS.1 XA870 is a preservation epic! YHPG's Alan Beattie acquired the Sioux from The Aeroplane Collection (who had placed it on loan with SYAM/AeroVenture) on 13th December 2003. It is a composite, with parts of XW179 included [1]. The group produce an excellent newsletter to keep members and 'rotorheads' in general in touch. See also under Storwood, E Yorks.
✉ YHPG, Alan Beattie, 18 Marshall Drive, Pickering, YO18 7JT e-mail info@yhpg.co.uk www.helicopter-preservation-yhpg.org.uk

❑ XA870*	Whirlwind HAS.1	ex Helston, Predannack, Lee-on-Solent A2543, *Protector* Flt, 705, *Protector* Flt, 155, 848. Sectioned. Arrived 1-12-02.		3-04
❑ XJ398*	Whirlwind HAR.10	G-BDBZ, ex Elvington, Oxford, Luton, XJ398, Culdrose, RAE, ETPS, Weston-super-Mare, DH Engines, A&AEE, XD768 ntu. Arrived 1-4-03.		3-04
❑ XP345*	Whirlwind HAR.10	ex Elvington, Storwood, Tattershall Thorpe, Lee-on-Solent, 8792M, Cyprus, 84 'B' Flt, 1563 Flt, 202, CFS. Arrived 6-7-02.	®	3-04
❑ XT242*	'12' Sioux AH.1	ex Firbeck, Hooton Park, Warmingham, Long Marston, Wimborne, Middle Wallop, 'Blue Eagles'.	[1]	3-04

Museum and Art Gallery: The 'Flea' and the Bensen are displayed on the first floor.
◆ Open Mon-Sat 10am to 5pm and Sun 2pm to 5pm. ✉ Chequer Road, Doncaster, DN1 2AE ☎ 01302 734293 fax 01302 735409 e-mail museum@doncaster.gov.uk www.doncaster.gov.uk/museums

❑ 'G-AEKR'	HM.14 'Flea'	BAPC.121, ex Breighton, Firbeck, Nostell Priory, Crowle, Finningley.	1-04
❑ –	Bensen B.7	BAPC.275, built by S J R Wood, Warmsworth. Flew in the early 1960s. Volkswagen 1600.	1-04

NETHERTHORPE AERODROME north of the A619, west of Worksop

❑ G-ARJT*	Apache 160G	ex N10F. CoA 29-1-01. Stored.	9-03
❑ G-AYRG*	Cessna F.172K	CoA 26-7-00. Stored.	9-03
❑ G-AYXW*	Evans VP-1	CoA 15-8-01. Stored.	5-03
❑ G-BCBM*	Aztec 250C	ex N5854Y. CoA 15-5-01. Stored.	9-03

SHEFFIELD
Brimpex Metal Treatments: Work continues on the Campbell-Bensen and the 'Flea'. The former was involved in blade-tip propulsion experiments. The hunt is on for another gyroplane to restore.
◆ Visits by prior arrangement *only*. ✉ 5 Devonshire Close, Dore, Sheffield, S17 3NX ☎ 0114 2366484 fax 0114 2620184 e-mail brimpex@demon.co.uk

❑ –	BAPC.13 HM.14 'Flea'	ex Kirk Langley, Wigan, Peel Green, Styal, Urmston, Berrington, Tenbury Wells, Knutsford.	®	3-02
❑ –	C-Bensen B.7	–	®	3-02

WEST YORKSHIRE

BATLEY on the A652 north of Dewsbury
Northern Aeroplane Workshops (NAW): Make good progress with their Sopwith Camel, which will fly with the Shuttleworth Collection. The workshop is within the **Skopos Motor Museum**.
♦ At Alexander Mills in Alexander Road, signed. Visits to see work in progress are on a prior permission *only* basis. ✉ Skopos Motor Museum, Alexander Mills, Alexander Road, Batley, WF17 6JA. ☎ 01924 444423 NAW c/o C Page, 20 Lombard Street, Rawdon, near Leeds, LS19 6BW **e-mail** r.hendrie4@ukonline.co.uk **www**.shuttleworth.org/collection/naw.htm
❑ [G-BZSC]   Camel F1 REP   fuselage, project under construction.   3-04

BIRD'S EDGE on the A629 north-west of Penistone
❑ G-BKIR   SAN D.117   ex F-BIOC. CoA 28-8-92.   ® 10-02

HALIFAX
❑ G-AIBY   J/1 Autocrat   ex Sherburn, 'Halifax'. CoA 13-4-81. Stored.   7-00

HUDDERSFIELD AERODROME or Crosland Moor, south of the A670 west of the city
❑ G-AYKK   SAN D.117   ex F-BHGM. CoA 22-5-85.   ® 5-99
❑ G-BLYY   Archer II   ex OO-PAY, N9792K. Wreck, open store.   9-99
❑ C-GDQD   Thurston Teal   G-TEAL. Damaged 3-93. Fuselage.   5-00

LEEDS
A private owner *should* still keep a Bensen gyroglider in the area [1]. Another collector (or possibly the same one) took delivery of a pair of Skeeters in 2003. XL738 has the boom of XM565 [2].
❑ –   BAPC.200 Bensen B.7   ex Cheltenham, Long Marston, Stoke.   [1] 11-93
❑ XL738*   Skeeter AOP.12   ex Ivybridge, Middle Wallop, Fleetlands, Middle Wallop, Southampton, Middle Wallop 7860M, 651, HTF. Arrived by 12-03.   [2] 2-04
❑ XL763*   Skeeter AOP.12   ex Ivybridge, Ottershaw, Southall, Wroughton, 15/19 Hussars, 2 Div, 654, 1 Wing. Arr by 12-03.   2-04

LEEDS-BRADFORD AIRPORT or Yeadon, on the A658 north-east of Bradford
Bandeirante G-ODUB was scrapped early in 2003.
❑ G-ATND   Cessna F.150F   crashed 9-12-72. Engine test-rig.   3-02
❑ G-AWES   Cessna 150H   ex Blackpool, Glenrothes, N22933. Dam 2-10-81.   ® 3-02
❑ EI-BPD   Short 360-100   ex Southend, Aer Arran, Gill, G-RMCT, Aer Lingus EI-BPD, G-BLPU, G-14-3656. Dam 4-2-01.Fire crews.   2-04

Locally: The Avian is under restoration, but 'off-site'.
❑ G-ACGT   Avian IIIA   ex Linthwaite, EI-AAB. CoA 21-7-39.   ® 1-01

The 'regions' of Scotland work on a wholly 'single tier' unitary authority structure.
The regions are as follows:

Borders	–
Central	Clackmannan, Falkirk and Stirling.
Dumfries & Galloway	–
Fife	–
Grampian	Aberdeenshire, City of Aberdeen, Moray.
Highland	–
Islands	Argyll & Bute, Orkney, Shetland, Western Isles.
Lothian	City of Edinburgh, East Lothian, Falkirk, Midlothian, West Lothian.
Strathclyde	City of Glasgow, East Ayrshire, East Dumbartonshire, East Renfrewshire, Inverclyde, North Ayrshire (including the Isle of Arran), Renfrewshire, South Ayrshire, South Lanarkshire, West Dumbartonshire.
Tayside	Angus, Perth & Kinross.

ABERDEEN
HQ Aberdeen Wing, Air Cadets / 2489 Squadron Air Cadets: Within the TAVR Gordon Barracks, Bridge of Don. Restoration of the Phantom was completed in late 2002 and the nose was dedicated to F/L Martin Owens who was killed in a 43 Squadron Tornado F.3 in 1995.

| ❏ XV581 | Phantom FG.1 | ex Lossiemouth, Buchan 9070M, Wattisham, 43, 111, 43. Nose. 43 Squadron colours. | 1-03 |

Others: An ARV *may* still be in the area.

| ❏ G-BNHC | ARV Super 2 | Crashed 4-8-96. | ® 12-96 |

ABERDEEN AIRPORT or Dyce, off the A96 north-west of Aberdeen
The fire dump is occupied by a wholly 'synthetic' Sikorsky S-61 look-alike and an equally 'ersatz' Boeing 737-ish fuselage – the former for rescue/egress training, the latter for burning.

| ❏ G-TIGH | Super Puma | ex Bristow, F-WXFL. *City of Edinburgh*. Crashed 14-3-92. Fuselage, rescue training. | 2-04 |

ABOYNE AERODROME south of the A93 west of Banchory
Terrier 3 G-AVYK moved to Okehampton, Devon, circa 2001. J3C-65 G-BHVV was flying again by mid-2002.

| ❏ G-BAHP | Volmer Sportsman | CoA 18-10-93. Stored. | 1-01 |

ARBROATH
No.662 VGS: Stored inside the hangar is a former Portmoak Cadet.

| ❏ XE786* | HLR Cadet TX.3 | BGA.4033, ex Syerston, 643 VGS, 662 VGS. Stored. | 5-03 |

BALADO BRIDGE on the A91 west of Milnathort
A 'JP' has arrived at the former airfield to act as a 'gate guardian'.

| ❏ XM412* | '41' Jet Provost T.3A | ex Ipswich, North Weald, Binbrook, Colsterworth, | |
| and '49' | | Halton 9011M, 1 FTS, 3 FTS, 2 FTS. F/n 2-02. | 9-03 |

BANCHORY on the A93 west of Aberdeen
The nose of Vulcan B.2MRR XH563 moved to Bruntingthorpe, Leics, in May 2003. Both Airedales are under restoration in the general area.

| ❏ G-ARXD | Airedale | ex Netherley. CoA 13-6-86. | ® 2-02 |
| ❏ G-ASAI | Airedale | ex Dundee, Islay. CoA 20-5-77. | ® 2-02 |

BLAIRGOWRIE on the A923 north-west of Dundee
Last reported in May 1997, Cessna Agwagon G-AZZG appeared at Perth, Scotland, by February 2003.

BORGUE on the B727 west of Kirkcudbright
Brighouse Bay Caravan Park: Displayed inside the camp is the former Carlisle Meteor.

| ❏ WS792 | 'K' Meteor NF.14 | ex Carlisle, Cosford 7965M, 5 MU, 1 ANS, 2 ANS. | 5-03 |

BRIDGE OF WEIR on the A761 north-west of Paisley
Neil Geddes: XK820 has wings from WZ754 and WZ778 and its wings are at Kirton Lindsey.

| ❏ XK820 | Grasshopper TX.1 | ex Strathallan, Aberdeen, Lancing, Locking. Stored. | 10-02 |

CHARTERHALL south of Edinburgh, off the A697 near Greenlaw
Turbulent G-APOL moved by February 2003 to Morpeth, Northumberland.

CROSSHILL on the B7023 south of Maybole
A trailer-bound Prefect has been resident at the bowling green for over a decade.
| ❑ –* | CKJ T.30A Prefect | ex PH-197. CoA 14-4-90. Stored, in trailer. F/n 9-01. | 2-03 |

CRUDEN BAY on the A975 south of Peterhead
Hobson Home for Distressed Aeroplanes: Malcolm's three 'in-patients' are thought to remain.
❑ G-AVKM	Condor	ex Edderton. Damaged 3-3-82.	2-04
❑ G-AXBU	FR.172F	ex Bearsden, Kirknewton, Inverkeithing. Cr 13-10-74.	2-04
❑ G-BCIL	AA-1B Trainer	ex Auchnagatt, N6168A. Crashed 14-6-86.	2-04

CULLODEN north-east of Inverness
A Tipsy Belfair has moved to this general area for restoration.
| ❑ G-APOD* | Tipsy Belfair | ex Dundee, OO-TIF ntu. CoA 23-8-88. Arr 2001. | ® 2-01 |

CUMBERNAULD AERODROME north of the A80, north of Cumbernauld
Tipsy B G-AISC and Silvaire G-BNIP moved to <u>Prestwick</u>, Scotland, by 2003. By April 2003 the fuselage of Trislander G-BEVR had moved to <u>Bembridge</u>, Isle of Wight.
❑ G-BELF*	BN-2A-26	ex D-IBRA, G-BELF. CoA 12-3-01. Stored.	2-04
❑ G-BEVV*	Trislander	ex Bembridge, Cumbernauld, 6Y-JQK, G-BNZD,	
		G-BEVV. Fuselage, stored. First noted 2-03.	11-03
❑ G-BVER*	Beaver 1	ex G-BTDM, XV268, Middle Wallop. CoA 23-4-95.	8-03
❑ G-BWUC	PA-18-135	N719CS, ex SX-ASM, EI-1818, I-EIYB,	
		MM54-2369, 54-2369. Stored, dismantled.	2-02

CUPAR on the A91 west of St Andrews
W&R16 confined Cadet TX.3 XE802 to LOST! It has proven to be more resilient than that, and can still be found dismantled within a hangar at a local strip. An enthusiast keeps a Victor nose in the area.
❑ G-ARTJ	Bensen B.8M	ex East Fortune, Cupar, Currie, Cupar.	5-03
❑ XA917	Victor B.1	ex Crowland, Barnham, Marham 7827M,	
		A&AEE, HP. Cockpit.	8-95
❑ XE802	Cadet TX.3	ex Syerston, 624 VGS. Store - see above.	1-03

CURRIE on the A70 south-west of Edinburgh
A private collector still has a 'Chippax' here.
| ❑ WB670 | Chipmunk T.10 | 8361M, ex Southend, MoS, 5 FTS, LAS, | |
| | PAX | 12 RFS, 5 RFS. Rear of WG303. | 2-04 |

DUMFRIES off the A701 north-east of Dumfries on the former airfield
Dumfries and Galloway Aviation Museum (DGAM): Run by the Dumfries and Galloway Aviation Group, the restored watch tower that forms the centrepiece of the museum contains a huge array of artefacts, all well presented. The tower and grounds continue to be refined. The Trident fuselage is open to the public and includes an extensive interior display and 30-seat lecture hall.
 Notes: Chipmunk T.10 WD386 was fitted with the rear end of WD377. This project is being worked on off-site on behalf of the museum [1]. Canberra T.4 nose WJ880 is used as a travelling display [2]. Vampire XD547 has the wings of XD425 [3].
♦ Open Sat and Sun 10am to 5pm 1st Apr to Oct inclusive. Also Wed, Thu, Fri Jul and Aug, 11am to 4pm. Also open *most* Bank Holidays. Special visits by prior arrangement. Follow brown signs from A75 at the A701 roundabout. ☎ 01387 720487 **e-mail** info@dumfriesaviationmuseum.com www.dumfriesaviationmuseum.com

| ❑ G-AHAT | J/1N Alpha | ex Firbeck, Exeter, Taunton, Old Sarum, | |
| | | HB-EOK ntu. Crashed 31-8-74. Frame. | 3-04 |

❑ G-AWZJ	Trident 3B-101	ex Prestwick ,Heathrow, BA, BEA.		
		CoA 12-9-85. Forward fuselage.		3-04
❑ G-MMIX	Tiger Cub 440	ex Long Marston.		3-04
❑ P7540	Spitfire IIa	ex Loch Doon, 312, 266, 609, 66. Cr 6-7-41.	®	3-04
❑ WA576	Sycamore 3	ex East Fortune, Strathallan, Halton 7900M,		
		RAE, A&AEE, G-ALSS ntu.		3-04
❑ WD386 'O'	Chipmunk T.10	ex Firbeck, Cranfield, Tenby, St Athan, 1 FTS,		
		Ox UAS, 22 RFS , 2 BFTS. SOC 29-7-70.	[1]	3-04
❑ WJ880	Canberra T.4	ex Firbeck, North Weald, Halton 8491M, 7, 85,		
		100, 56, Laarbruch SF, RAE, 16, Laarbruch SF,		
		Gütersloh SF, 104. Nose.	[2]	3-04
❑ WL375	Meteor T.7(mod)	ex West Freugh, RAE. RAE Bedford colours.		3-04
❑ XD547 'Z'	Vampire T.11	ex Aberfoyle, Strathallan, Milngavie, Glasgow,		
		CATCS, 8 FTS, 1 RS, 263.	[3]	3-04
❑ 'XF506' 'A'	Hunter F.4	WT746, ex Saighton, Halton 7770M, St Athan,		
		AFDS. 'Black Arrows', 111 Sqn colour scheme.		3-04
❑ XT280*	Buccaneer S.2B	ex Dundonald, Birtley, East Fortune, Lossiemouth,		
		12, 208, 12, 16, 237 OCU. Nose. Arrived 2-03.		2-04
❑ XX483* '562'	Jetstream T.1	ex Welshpool, Weston-on-Trent, Shawbury, 750,		
		CFS, 5 FTS. Cockpit. Arrived by 12-02.		4-04
❑ FT-36	T-33A-1-LO	ex Sculthorpe, Belgian AF, USAF 55-3047.		
		Little Miss Laura.		3-04
❑ 318 '8-NY'	Mystère IVA	ex Sculthorpe, French Air Force.		3-04
❑ Q497	Canberra T.4	ex Warton, Samlesbury, frustrated Indian AF B.52,		
		Bracebridge Heath, Samlesbury, Kemble, WE191, 231		
		OCU, 237 OCU, 231 OCU, 245. Fuselage.		3-04
❑ 42163 '005'	F-100D-11-NA	ex Sculthorpe, FAF. USAF colours, *Shillelagh.*		3-04
❑ 68-0060	F-111E	ex 20 TFW. Escape pod. Crashed 5-11-75.		3-04
❑	'ZT-E' Spitfire FSM	ex Dundonald, Prestwick. Damaged 11-96.	off-site	3-04

DUNDEE
| ❑ G-REEK* | AA-5 Cheetah | ex Dundee. CoA 10-12-01. Stored. | 7-02 |

DUNDEE AIRPORT also known as Riverside, on the A85 to the south of the city
| ❑ G-BNCE | Gulfstream I | ex Aberdeen, Aberdeen Airways, N436M, N436, | |
| | | N436M, N43M, N709G. CoA 9-4-92. Dump. | 2-04 |

DUNDONALD south of the A759, north-east of Troon
Dundonald Aviation Centre: Sadly, the centre closed by early December 2002. Disposals were as follows: Canberra TT.18 WJ721 nose to <u>Oban</u>, Scotland; Whirlwind HAR.10 XP359 was scrapped on site; Buccaneer S.2B XT280 nose to <u>Dumfries</u>, Scotland, 2-03; Buccaneer S.2B XV161 nose unaccounted for, possibly to 'North Wales'; Buccaneer S.2B XX888 nose to <u>Barnstaple</u>, Devon 11-02.

EAST FORTUNE AERODROME north of the A1, west of East Linton
National Museums of Scotland – Museum of Flight (MoF): The museum was successful in 'bidding' for a Concorde from British Airways. This is G-BOAA, long out-of-use at London Airport. The aircraft was brought to East Fortune via a combination of road and sea transport, costing over £2 million. The plan is to unveil it in early July 2004 and to go on full exhibition in August 2004 [1]. *Alpha-Alpha* will go into the main exhibition hangar and – as these words were typed – it seems that very little else in terms of hardware will be displayed alongside it. Other exhibits will be redistributed through the other hangars on site. Some will be going into 'deep store', others leaving - see below. The opportunity to display the Pilcher alongside the Concorde is an incredible prospect - testament to the amazing variety of exhibits the museum boasts. Not content with ignoring this perfect possibility, the iconic Pilcher is now in deep store. This will rob visitors the world over of a chance to see a unique world aviation artefact - something that a production Concorde is not. (See Brooklands, Surrey, for some more Concorde viewpoints.)

The ultimate plan is to apply for a lottery grant for a new display building that will house Concorde, the Comet and other transport airframes, but this will not be until 2009 at the earliest. The writer hopes upon hope that this is not all a piece of Concorde-mania and the belief that it will improve visitor figures long-term all on its own. Accordingly, the status of several airframes below will be open to revision during 2004.

The restoration team finished Spitfire F.21 LA198 in November 2002, having produced an exceptional piece of work. It moved to Glasgow, Scotland, 23rd July 2003. Sadly the team did not get to move on to the Beaufighter as had been hoped. They were disbanded and the 'Beau' remains in store.

Working in support of all aspects of the museum is the **Aviation Preservation Society of Scotland** (APSS): The society started construction of a flyable Sopwith 1¹/₂ Strutter reproduction in April 2001, but it is too early to give it a 'formal' listing. Sadly, its workshop – Building 25 – was needed for storage following the onset of Concorde and the work on this project has had to be slowed down. To aid fundraising for the Strutter project, APPS put their Brantly B.2B G-ATFG up for sale in late 2003, it left on 21st January 2004, for Weston-super-Mare, Som. Other current work centres on the Bolingbroke and Anson restorations, several engine rebuilds and a radio and radar exhibition. APSS members receive copies of the excellent journal, *The Fortune Teller*. (✉ c/o Museum of Flight, see below. **e-mail** Jim Mattocks at j-f@jmattocks.freeserve.co.uk) During 2002 a stalwart of both APSS and East Fortune passed away, **Roy Corser**. From 1983 Roy was a major force within APSS, helping to broaden its activities and aiding considerably in the archiving and documenting of the Museum of Flight.

Notes: The Kay Gyroplane from Glasgow, Scotland, is on loan [2]. Fergus McCann donated the Eurowing Goldwing. Built as a kit by Eurowing at East Kilbride, assembled by a Scottish syndicate and operated in Scotland for 20 years, it is a highly appropriate item [3]. Slingsby Gull I BED is *possibly* the former VW912 [4]. The Buccaneer cockpit is thought to be XK533 [5]. The Catto CA-16 microlight 'trike' was donated by Robin Henderson in 1983 [6].

Departures: Whirlwind HAS.7 XG594 returned to Yeovilton, Somerset, on 11th December 2003.

♦ Open daily (except Xmas and New Year) 10.30am to 5pm. Weekdays only Oct to Mar. Parties by appointment. Guided tours of the storage hangar are possible, enquire prior to arrival. A series of regular events, including an airshow, are staged – SAE for details. There is also a gift shop and a cafe with food of great renown. ✉ East Fortune Airfield, near Haddington, East Lothian, EH39 5LF ☎ 01620 880308 **fax** 01620 880355 **e-mail** museum_of_flight@sol.co.uk **www**.nms.ac.uk/flight

❏	G-ACVA	Kay Gyroplane	ex Glasgow, Strathallan, Perth, Glasgow, Perth.	[2]	3-04
❏	G-ACYK	Spartan Cruiser	ex Hill of Stake, Largs. Cr 14-1-38. Fuselage, stored		3-04
❏	G-AFJU	Miles Monarch	ex York, Strathallan, Lasham, Staverton, X9306, G-AFJU. CoA 18-5-64.	APSS	3-04
❏	G-AGBN	GAL Cygnet II	ex Strathallan, Biggin Hill, ES915, MCCS, 52 OTU, 51 OTU, 23, G-AGBN. CoA 28-11-80.		3-04
❏	G-AHKY	Miles M.18-2	ex Perth, Strathallan, Blackbushe, HM545, U-0224, U-8. CoA 20-9-89.		3-04
❏	G-ANOV	Dove 6	ex CAFU Stansted, G-5-16. CoA 31-5-75.		3-04
❏	G-AOEL	Tiger Moth	ex Strathallan, Dunstable, N9510, 7 FTS, 2 GU, 11 RFS, 1 RFS, 7 RFS, 7 EFTS. CoA 18-7-72.		3-04
❏	G-ARCX	Meteor Mk 14	ex Ferranti, WM261. CoA 20-2-69.		3-04
❏	G-ASUG	Beech E.18S	ex Loganair, N575C, N555CB, N24R. CoA 23-7-75.		3-04
❏	G-ATOY	Comanche 260B	ex Elstree, N8893P. Crashed 6-3-79. *Mythtoo*, Sheila Scott's aircraft. Fuselage.		3-04
❏	G-AVPC*	Turbulent	first flown 8-9-73. Donated by Stephen Sharp 4-03.		3-04
❏	G-AXEH	Bulldog Srs 1	ex Prestwick, Shoreham. Prototype. CoA 15-1-77.		3-04
❏	G-BBVF	Twin Pioneer 2	ex Shobdon, XM961/7978M, SRCU, Odiham SF, 230, 21. Damaged 11-3-82.		3-04
❏	G-BDFU	Dragonfly MPA	ex Blackpool Airport, Warton, Prestwick. Stored.		2-00
❏	G-BDIX	Comet 4C	ex Lasham, Dan-Air, XR399, 216. CoA 11-10-81.		3-04
❏	G-BOAA*	Concorde 102	ex London, BA, G-N94AA, BOAC. CoA 24-2-01.	[1]	4-04
❏	G-JSSD	Jetstream 3100	ex Prestwick, N510F, N510E, N12227, G-AXJZ. CoA 9-10-90.		3-04
❏	G-MBJX	Super Scorpion	ex Halton. Acquired 1998. Canx 13-6-90.		3-04
❏	G-MBPM	EW-21 Goldwing	CoA 21-8-98.	[3]	3-04
❏	G-MMLI	Typhoon	BAPC.244. ex Glasgow. Canx 7-9-94. Stored		3-04
❏	– [BED]	Gull I	BGA.902, ex Newbattle, 'G-ALPHA'.	[4]	3-04
❏	– [BJV]	T.21A	BGA.1014, ex Feshiebridge, SE-SHK.		3-04

❏	W-2		Weir W-2	BAPC.85, ex Glasgow, East Fortune, Hayes,	
				Knockholt, Hanworth, Cathcart. On loan.	3-04
❏	–		Jetstream 1	ex Hatfield, East Midlands, N14234, N102SC,	
			(Super 31 EMU)	N200SC ntu, N1BE, G-BBBV, G-8-12. Fuselage.	3-04
❏	VH-SNB		Dragon I	ex Strathallan, VH-ASK, RAAF A34-13.	3-04
❏	VH-UQB		Puss Moth	ex Strathallan, Bankstown, G-ABDW.	3-04
❏	'B5577'*	'W'	Camel REP	BAPC.59, ex Cosford, St Athan 'D3419', St Mawgan,	
				'F1921', St Athan, Colerne. Arr 26-11-02. Stored.	3-04
❏	TE462		Spitfire XVI	ex Ouston 7243M, 101 FRS, Finningley SF.	3-04
❏	'TJ398'		Auster AOP.5	BAPC.70, ex 'TJ472'. Inverkeithing, Currie, Perth,	
				Hamble, 'G-ALES'. Stored.	APSS 3-04
❏	TS291		T.8 Tutor	BCB / BGA.852, ex Portmoak, TS291.	3-04
❏	VM360		Anson C.19	G-APHV, ex Strathallan, Kemps, BKS,	
				TRE, A&AEE. Stored.	by APSS ® 3-04
❏	VX185		Canberra B.5	ex Wroughton, South Kensington, 7631M, EE. Nose.	3-04
❏	WB584		Chipmunk T.10	7706M, ex Manston, Kilmarnock, Edinburgh,	
			PAX	Shawbury, Debden CF, 11 GCF, Tangmere SF,	
				Glas UAS, 8 FTS, Bri UAS, 12 RFS, 22 RFS.	3-04
❏	WF259	'171'	Sea Hawk F.2	A2483, ex Lossiemouth SF, 736.	3-04
❏	WV493	'29'	Provost T.1	G-BDYG, ex Strathallan, Halton 7696M,	
				6 FTS. CoA 28-11-80. Stored.	3-04
❏	WW145	'680'	Sea Ven FAW.22	ex Lossiemouth, 750, 891.	3-04
❏	XA109		Sea Vampire T.22	ex Lossiemouth, 831, JOAC.	3-04
❏	XA228		G'hopper TX.1	ex Glenalmond School. Stored.	APSS 3-04
❏	XL762		Skeeter AOP.12	ex Middle Wallop, Halton 8017M, 2 RTR,	
				9 Flt, 652, 22 Flt, 654, 651. Stored.	3-04
❏	XM597		Vulcan B.2	ex Waddington, 50, 35, 101, 9, 50, 35, Wadd W, 12.	3-04
❏	XN776	'C'	Lightning F.2A	ex Leuchars, 92, 19.	3-04
❏	XT288		Buccaneer S.2B	ex Lossie' 9134M, A&AEE, 208, 12, RN. Stored	3-04
❏	XV277		Harrier GR.1	ex Ipswich, Yeovilton A2602 [2], A2600 [2],	
				Filton, HSA.	3-04
❏	–		Beaufighter II	ex Hendon, Duxford, Hendon, Cranfield. Nose.	3-04
❏	–		Buccaneer S.1 CIM	ex Lossiemouth.	[5] 3-04
❏	9940		Bolingbroke IVT	ex Strathallan, RCAF 5 B&GS.	by APSS ® 3-04
❏	3677		MiG-15bis SB	ex Cáslav, Ostravian Air Regt, Czech AF. c/n 613677.	3-04
❏	309		MiG-15UTI	ex Polish AF. c/n 3309. Cockpit section.	3-04
❏	BF-10		Beaufighter	ex Swartkop, South Africa, Alverca, Lisbon,	
			TF.10	Port AF, RD220. Stored.	3-04
❏	591		Rhonlerche II	ex D-0359.	3-04
❏	–	'FI+S'	MS.505 Criquet	G-BIRW, ex Duxford, OO-FIS, F-BDQS.	
				CoA3-6-83. Luftwaffe colours. Stored.	3-04
❏	191659	'15'	Me 163B-1a	ex Cambridge, Cranfield, Brize Norton, RAE,	
				Husum, II/JG400.	3-04
❏	155848	'WT'	F-4S-MC	ex Yeovilton, VMFA-232, USMC. 'WT'.	3-04
❏	–		CG-4A Hadrian	ex Aberlady. Nose section. *The Bunhouse.*	3-04
❏	–	BAPC.49	Pilcher Hawk	ex Edinburgh. First flown at Eynsham 1896,	
				crashed at Stanford Hall, Leics, 30-9-1899.	off-site 3-04
❏	–	BAPC.160	Chargus 18/50 hg	ex Tranent. (Acquired 1975.)	3-04
❏	–	BAPC.195	Moonraker 77 hg	ex Edinburgh. Birdman-built, *circa* 1977.	3-04
❏	–	BAPC.196	Sigma II Metre hg	ex Penicuik. Southdown Sailwings-built c 1980.	3-04
❏	–	BAPC.197	Cirrus III hg	ex Edinburgh. Scotkites-built 1977.	3-04
❏	–	BAPC.245	Electra Floater hg	ex Edinburgh. Built 1979. Stored	3-04
❏	–	BAPC.246	Hiway Cloudbase	ex Edinburgh. Built 1978, acquired 1995.	3-04
❏	–	BAPC.247	Albatros ASG.21	ex Edinburgh. Built 1977, acquired 1995.	3-04
❏	–	BAPC.262	Catto CA-16	ex Gifford. Acquired 1983. No wings.	® [6] 3-04

Others:

❏	G-BEYN	Evans VP-1	Stored.	4-00
❏	G-BSNO	Denney Kitfox	crashed 9-7-97. Wreck, stored.	4-00
❏	G-MMBE*	Tiger Cub 440	ex 'Fat Sam's', Edinburgh. Stored by 6-02.	6-02

EDINBURGH
Ferranti: The factory in the South Gyle Estate is guarded by a dramatically-posed Lightning.
- ❑ ZF584   Lightning F.53   ex Turnhouse, Warton, RSAF 53-682, G-27-52. Gate.   12-03

EDINBURGH AIRPORT or Turnhouse, on the A8 east of Edinburgh
Noralpha The 603 (City of Edinburgh) Squadron Association Spitfire FSM was refurbished by RAF Leuchars during 2003 and remounted in a new position on the airport [1]. Cessna F.152 II G-BFFE was flying again by mid-2003.
- ❑ G-BWYE*   Cessna 310R II   ex F-GBPE, N26269 ntu. CoA 8-12-02. Stored.   10-03
- ❑ G-MALK   Cessna F.172N   ex PH-SVF, PH-AXF. Crashed 23-7-97. Dump.   2-04
- ❑ 'L1070'   Spitfire FSM   BAPC.227. 'XT-A', 603 Sqn colours. Displayed.   [1] 2-04

ELGIN on the A941 south of Lossiemouth and north of Elgin
Buccaneer Service Station: Ian Aitkenhead keeps the 'Brick' in excellent condition on the forecourt.
- ❑ XW530   Buccaneer S.2B   ex Lossiemouth, 208, 12, 208, 216, 16, 15, 16.   11-03

ERROL south of the A90, east of Perth
The Vampire and Gannet are kept by a private collector locally. The Gannet is a composite, including bits from XA463 and XG889 [1].
- ❑ G-ATIN*   SAN D.117   ex F-BHNV. CoA 18-4-96.   ® 2-04
- ❑ 'XE897'   Vampire T.11   XD403, ex Leuchars, Errol, Strathallan, Woodford, Chester, 4 FTS, 1 FTS, 7 FTS, 8 FTS, 5 FTS, 4 FTS.   8-03
- ❑ XG882 '771' Gannet T.5   ex Lossiemouth 8754M, 845.   [1] 8-03

FALGUNZEON on the A711 south-west of Dumfries
Dumfries and Galloway Gliding Club: The references here are getting close to their 'glide by' date! The T.45 is an amalgam of BGA.1041 and BGA.1032 [1].
- ❑ G-BFPA*   SF-25B Falke   ex D-KAGM. CoA 13-8-98. Stored.   9-01
- ❑ –   BRQ EoN 460 Srs 1C   BGA.1177. Ex G-ARFU. CoA 8-96. Stored.   9-01
- ❑ –   DCG Schleicher Ka 2B   BGA.2004. Ex D-7064. Stored.   7-97
- ❑ –   DGT Schleicher Ka 2B   BGA.2110. Ex D-5469. Stored.   9-01
- ❑ –   DHP T.45 Swallow   BGA.2130. CoA 10-89.   ® [1] 5-95

FORDOUN AERODROME on the A90 north-east of Brechin
Condor G-AWSS had moved by early 2002, very likely to Montrose, Scotland.

FORRES on the A96 west of Elgin
Christies Garden Centre: Buccaneer S.2B nose XX892 was sold during 2002 and moved to 'Perthshire'.

FYVIE on the B947 west of Peterhead
Mark Reeder: Mark is undertaking the construction of a full-size reproduction of a DH Hornet for the De Havilland Heritage Museum (see under London Colney, Herts). This will use as many original parts as possible and will include the tail section from Sea Hornet NF.21 VW957 '415' found at St Davids, Wales, and displayed at DHHM. (See also under Chelmsford, Essex.)

GIRVAN on the A77 north of Stranraer
The Flix: A 'fun pub' in Bridge Street should have a Tiger Cub 'flying' from the ceiling.
- ❑ G-MJUH   Tiger Cub 440   CoA 5-8-92.   4-98

GLASGOW
Museum of Transport: Spitfire F.21 LA198 arrived in July 2003 and was 'inaugurated' on 17th September 2003. The Spitfire will be here until late 2005 when it will move to the city's Kelvingrove Art Gallery and Museum. The Pilcher was built by 2175 Squadron ATC, Glasgow, and awaits restoration.
◆ Mon to Thu and Sat 10am to 5pm. Fri and Sun 11am to 5pm. Nearest underground is Kelvin Hall. ✉ Kelvin Hall, 1 Bunhouse Road, Glasgow, G3 8DP ☎ 0141 2872720 **fax** 0141 2872692 **e-mail** museums@cls.glasgow.gov.uk **www.glasgowmuseums.com**

❏	BAPC.48 Pilcher Hawk REP	Stored.	3-04
❏	LA198* 'RAI-G'	Spitfire F.21	ex East Fortune, Cardington, St Athan, Leuchars, Locking, Worcester, 7118M, 3 CAACU, 602, 1. 602 Sqn colours. Arrived 23-7-03.	3-04

No.2175 Squadron Air Cadets: Base a 'travelling' Bulldog at their Hillingdon HQ.
❏	'XX530'	'F'	Bulldog T.1	XX637, ex Cranwell, St Athan 9197M, North UAS, 2 FTS.	6-03

Others: Stored locally...
❏	G-AWJF	Nipper T.66	ex airport and local area. CoA 7-6-88.	® 12-01
❏	G-AZHT	Airtourer T3	ex airport and local area. Crashed 29-4-88.	6-95

GLASGOW AIRPORT or Abbotsinch, north of the M8 west of Renfrew
The end of an era. The nose of Trident 1C G-ARPL was scrapped by GJD Services on 20th June 2003. The complete G-ARPP was scrapped by the same concern on the same day. The nose was salvaged and moved to <u>Palnakie</u>, Scotland. The fire crews have a steel airliner shell to provide 'hot' training.

GLENROTHES on the A92 north of Kircaldy
❏	G-AREH	Tiger Moth	ex Bridge of Weir, Lochwinnoch, Kilkerran, G-APYV ntu, 6746M, DE241, 22 RFS, 22 EFTS. CoA 19-4-66.	® 8-01

GREENOCK west of Glasgow on the A8
James Watt College: Within the Aeronautical Eng Dept, Kingston Industrial Estate, in Port Glasgow.
❏	XX690	'A' Bulldog T.1	ex Shawbury, Lpl UAS, 3 FTS, CFS, York UAS, RNEFTS, EL UAS, RNEFTS, 2 FTS	2-03

INSCH AERODROME west of the B992 at Auchleve
❏	G-AISS	L-4H Cub	ex D-ECAV, SL-AAA, 44-79781. CoA 25-6-97. Stored.	4-02
❏	G-BALK	SNCAN SV-4C	ex Aboyne, 'Cheshire', Liverpool, Littleborough, F-BBAN, French mil No.387. Fuselage.	4-02

INVERNESS
Highland Aircraft Preservation Society: As the Hunter is due to move to the airport site during the summer of 2004, the opportunity has been taken to move it in this edition - see below. A Campbell Cricket has been stored in the area for a long time.
❏	G-AYHI*	Cricket	CoA 19-8-<u>86</u>. Stored.	8-03

INVERNESS AIRPORT or Dalcross, off the A96 north-east of Inverness
Highland Aviation Museum: Formerly the Highland Aircraft Preservation Society, which was founded by James Campbell. James acquired Buccaneer S.1 XK532 from Ken Charlton and moved it a short distance from the airport site to the Dalcross Industrial Estate for display on 22nd December 2002. The Valiant nose came from a private collector from the north-east of England [1]. The Hunter from James' home is due on site in the summer of 2004 so is best listed here.

◆ Due to open on a regular basis in April 2004. ✉ James Campbell, HAPS, 50 Newton Park, Kirkhill, Inverness, IV5 7QB ☎ 01463 831459 e-mail jamesacampbell@highlandaircraft.fsnet.co.uk

❑ WT660*	Hunter F.1	ex Inverness, Cullen, New Byth, Carlisle, 229 OCU, DFLS. 43 Sqn colours.		**due**
❑ XD875*	Valiant B.1	ex Winthorpe, Bruntingthorpe, Marham, Firbeck, Coventry, Cosford, 7, 138, 207, 49, 207. Nose.	[1]	2-04
❑ XK532 '632'	Buccaneer S.1	ex airport, Lossiemouth 8867M, Manadon, A2581, Lossiemouth, 736. Moved across 23-12-02.		2-04
❑ XT480* '468'	Wessex HU.5	ex Hixon, Fleetlands, A2603 [2], A2617, Wroughton, 847. Arrived 2-04.		2-04

Airport: See above for the Buccaneer's shuffle. Cessna 140 G-BTVG's status is unknown.

KILKERRAN AERODROME east of the B741, north-east of Girvan
Neither Condor G-ATAV (gone 'south'?) nor Bensen B.8M G-BIZT were to be found in May 2002.

KILMARNOCK north-east of Ayr
No.327 Squadron Air Cadets: In Aird Avenue, off Dundonald Road.

❑ WJ872	Canberra T.4	8429M, ex Halton, Wyton SF, 360, 13, Akrotiri SF, 231 OCU.	10-02
❑ –	Hunter CIM	—	1-98

KINNETTIES on the B9127 south of Forfar
A pair of Air and Space 18A gyroplanes are stored in the area.

❑ G-BVWK*	A&S 18A	ex SE-HID, N6108S. Stored. Arrived c.1998.	5-03
❑ G-BVWL*	A&S 18A	ex SE-HIE, N90588, N6152S. Stored. Arrived c.1998.	5-03

LEUCHARS AIRFIELD on the A919, north-west of St Andrews
RAF Leuchars: The Harrier cockpit is on charge with **2345 Squadron**, ATC [1]. Phantom FG.1s XT867 and XV577 were scrapped in mid-2001.

❑ XR713	'C'	Lightning F.3	8935M, ex LTF, 5, 11, 5, LTF, 11, LTF, 5, 111, Wattisham TFF, 111. Displayed, officially ABDR.	12-03
❑ XT864	'A''BJ'	Phantom FG.1	8998M, ex 111, 892, 767. Gate. 43 / 111 Sqn c/s.	12-03
❑ XV582	'M'	Phantom FG.1	9066M, ex WLT, 43. Black Mike. All black c/s.	9-03
❑ XV586	'AJ'	Phantom FG.1	9067M, ex 43, 893. 43 Sqn mascot.	12-03
❑ XW265*	'W'	Harrier T.4	ex St Athan, Cosford 9258M, Shawbury, 20, 233 OCU, A&AEE. Cockpit.	[1] 7-03
❑ ZD906		Tornado F.2	ex St Athan, 229 OCU. Nose. ABDRT.	9-01

LOCHEARNHEAD on the A85 west of Crieff

❑ G-DHCB	Beaver 1	ex G-BTDL, XP779. CoA 16-9-97. Stored.	9-03

LONGSIDE on the A950 west of Peterhead
With no physical sighting since December 1993, Cessna F.172K 'G-ASOK' (D-ECDU) has been confined to LOST! An S-61N is in long-term store here.

❑ G-BEJL*	S-61N Mk.II	ex CHC Scotia, EI-BPK, G-BEJL, N4606G. CoA 30-9-98. Store.	9-03

LOSSIEMOUTH AIRFIELD south of the B4090, west of Lossiemouth
RAF Lossiemouth:

❑ XV863	'S' Buccaneer S.2B	9145M, ex 9115M, 9139M, 16, 237 OCU, 208, 237 OCU, 208, 809. Pink c/s. Off gate 9-11-01.	12-01

❑	ZA324* 'TAY'	Tornado GR.1	ex 15, TTTE. BDRT by 8-01, well stripped down.	9-03
❑	ZA355*'TAA'	Tornado GR.1	ex 15, TTTE. WLT by 9-01.	3-02
❑	ZA362* 'TR'	Tornado GR.1	ex 15, TTTE. Withdrawn by 6-02. Spares.	1-03
❑	ZA474*'AJ-F'	Tornado GR.1	ex 617, 12, 27, 20, 16. Spares.	1-03
❑	ZA475 'FH'	Tornado GR.1B	9311M, ex 12, 27, 20, 17, 9, 16. Gate, from 19-12-01.	10-03
❑	ZD900	Tornado F.2	ex St Athan, Warton, A&AEE. Nose, junked by 9-03.	9-03

MAYBOLE on the A77 south of Ayr

❑	OO-NAT	MS.880B Rallye	ex G-BAOK. Fuselage.	8-99

MINTLAW on the A950 west of Peterhead

❑	G-MBFZ	Goldwing	CoA 5-9-00. Stored.	1-01
❑	G-MJUF	Tiger Cub 440	Canx 27-4-90. Stored.	1-01

MONTROSE on the A92 north of Arbroath

Montrose Air Station Museum (MASM): Within the museum site can be found arguably the oldest buildings designed for military flying extant in the UK - opened in 1913. MASM stalwart Ian McIntosh died in January 2003, aged 73. Ian was a founder member of the museum and a great enthusiast. The museum has established an amateur radio station, catch them on call-signs 'GM3KC' or 'GB2MAS'!

Notes: Vampire XE874 is fitted with the booms of XD528 (the rest of it is at Firbeck, S Yorks). The booms of XE874 are *also* present, just to confuse things! XE874 and the Sycamore are on loan from a private collector [1]. XE340 is on loan from the Fleet Air Arm Museum, Yeovilton, Somerset [2].

♦ At Waldron Road, north Montrose. Open Sun 12noon to 5pm, other times by prior arrangement.
✉ Waldron Road, Broomfield, Montrose, DD10 9BB ☎ 01674 673107 ☎ / fax 01674 674210
e-mail pd.mams@btopenworld.com www.rafmontrose.org.uk

❑	XD542	'N'	Vampire T.11	7604M, ex Edzell, Cranwell, 'XD429', Colerne, Melksham, FWS, CGS. Camo.	1-04
❑	XE340	'131'	Sea Hawk FGA.6	ex Strathallan, Wroughton, Staverton, Brawdy, 801, 898, 897, 800.	[2] 1-04
❑	XE874	'61'	Vampire T.11	ex New Byth, Valley 8582M, Woodford, Chester, Shawbury, 1 FTS, 4 FTS, 8 FTS, 4 FTS, 1 FTS, 4 FTS, 7 FTS.	[1] 1-04
❑	XJ380		Sycamore HR.14	ex New Byth, Drighlington, Finningley 8628M, Catterick, CFS, MoA, HS, 275.	[1] 1-04
❑	XJ723		W'wind HAR.10	ex OPITB, Wroughton, 202, 228, 155.	1-04

Neil Butler: Work continues on the Prentice.

❑	G-AWSS*	Condor	ex Fordoun. CoA 19-10-94. Stored.	4-02
❑	VS356	Prentice T.1	G-AOLU, ex Stonehaven, Perth, Strathallan, Biggin Hill, EI-ASP, G-AOLU, VS356, CFS, 2 FTS. CoA 8-5-76.	® 4-02

Oil Petroleum Training Industry Board:

❑	N116WG	WG.30-160	ex Weston-super-Mare, Yeovil, PanAm.	7-03

OBAN
In the general area a collector has taken on the nose of a Canberra.

❑	WJ721*	Canberra TT.18	ex Dundonald, Bacup, Samlesbury, 7, 50, 40. Nose.	4-03

ORPHIR near Kirkwall, Orkney Islands
It has been a long time - understandably - since there was a *physical* report of this one.

❑	G-ASRP	SAN DR.1050	ex F-BITI. Ditched 17-3-86. Stored.	10-94

PALNACKIE on the A711 south of Dalbeattie, south west of Dumfries
James Halliday: Keeps the nose of the former Glasgow Airport Trident and is restoring it in the area.
❏ G-ARPP*   Trident 1C   ex Glasgow, Heathrow, BA, BEA. CoA 16-2-86.
    Nose. Arrived 6-03.   2-04

PATHHEAD on the A68 south-east of Edinburgh
❏ G-BOHN   Tomahawk 112 II ex Edinburgh, Cardiff-Wales, N23593.
    Crashed 13-8-93. Cockpit, plaything.   1-97

PERTH AIRPORT or Scone, on the A94 north-east of Perth
Perth College: Using some of the former AST buildings and four of its airframes, airframe and aero engine skills are still taught at Perth. A previously unlisted Auster frame from here had moved to Manston, Kent, by March 2003.

❏ G-ASVO	Herald 214	ex Shoreham, Alton, Bournemouth, Channel Express,	
		PP-SDG, G-ASVO, G-8-3. Damaged 8-4-97. Cockpit.	11-03
❏ G-AYGB	Cessna 310Q	ex N7611Q. CoA 23-10-87.	11-03
❏ G-AZZG*	Cessna 188-230	ex Blairgowrie, Lairg, Inverness, Southend, OY-AHT,	
		N8029V. CoA 1-5-81. First noted 2-03.	11-03
❏ G-BCIE	Warrior 151	ex N9588N. Crashed 27-5-99. Dump.	3-04
❏ G-BEWP	Cessna F.150M	crashed 4-10-83.	11-03
❏ G-BTIN	Cessna 150C	ex N7805Z. Damaged 12-98.	11-03
❏ EI-APF*	Cessna F.150G	ex Sligo. CoA 8-98. Arrived 5-03. Stored.	11-03
❏ XL875	Whirlwind HAR.9	ex Wroughton, Lee SAR Flt, CU SAR Flt, 847, 848, 815.	11-03
❏ [XT140]	Sioux AH.1	ex Middle Wallop.	11-03

Others: By September 2003, Auster 5 G-AOFJ had moved to Spanhoe Lodge, Northants.
❏ G-APXU   Tri-Pacer 150   ex Rochester, Bredhurst, N1723A. CoA 20-2-85.   ® 5-03

PETERHEAD on the A90 south of Fraserburgh
Score Energy Ltd: The Lightning will 'guard' the GLEN Test Facility, which includes an overhaul facility for industrial Rolls-Royce Avons. The aircraft is due to be unveiled in May 2004.
❏ XR749* 'DA' Lightning F.3   ex Tees-side, Chop Gate, Leuchars 8934M, 11, LTF,
    11, LTF, Binbrook pool, 29, 226 OCU, 56, EE.
    Overstressed 17-2-87. LTF colours.   **due**

PORTMOAK AERODROME west of Glenrothes
The old Nissen hut that contained several glider hulks was demolished during 2002. The contents were scrapped at the same time: K-8Bs DFQ and EFP (as listed in *W&R*) and Pirat CBN and K-8 DPB.

PRESTWICK AIRPORT east of the A79 north of Ayr
HMS *Gannet*:
❏ XL497 '041' Gannet AEW.3   ex Lossiemouth, 849. Gate of RN enclave.   1-04

Others: Belfast G-HLFT arrived from Southend, Essex, on 13th November 2002. It became 9L-LDQ and left for the trip to Australia on 16th September 2003. The hulk of Jetstream 61 c/n 2069 has all but perished by February 2004. The Luscombe Silvaire is for rebuild by local apprentices [1].

❏ G-ATDB*	Noralpha	ex Edinburgh, Skelmorie, Prestwick, F-OTAN-6,	
		Fr mil 186. CoA 22-11-78. First noted 10-03.	® 10-03
❏ G-BNIP*	Silvaire 8A	ex Cumbernauld, N77820, NC77820. CoA 10-2-93.	[1] ® 6-03
❏ N250TB	Aztec 250D	ex G-VHFA, G-BZFE, G-AZFE, EI-BPA,	
		G-AZFE, N13962. Stored. First noted 5-01.	2-04
❏ N852FT*	Boeing 747-122	ex Polar Air Cargo, N4712U. Arrived 16-3-02.	
		Fire crews, non-destructive by 3-02.	2-04
❏ –	ATP/J61	fuselage. c/n 2068. Fire crews. c/n 2068.	2-04

Locally: A Tipsy has arrived for restoration.
❏ G-AISC*   Tipsy B   ex Cumbernauld, Henstridge, Yeovil. CoA 23-5-79.   ®   6-03

SKELMORLIE on the A78 north of Largs
By late 2003, Noralpha G-ATDB (last noted here in August 1993) had moved briefly to Edinburgh, before settling upon <u>Prestwick</u>, Scotland, for restoration.

STONEHAVEN on the A90 north of Montrose
Pete Morris: Is working on the restoration of a Terrier 2 with another for spares.
❏ G-ASAX   Terrier 2   ex Auster AOP.6 TW533, 652, LAS, AOPS,
                                   663. CoA 1-9-96.   ®   1-00
❏ G-ASBU   Terrier 2   ex Netherley, Auster T.7 WE570, LAS, CFS,
                                   2 FTS, CFS. Crashed 12-8-80.   1-00

STRATHALLAN AERODROME west of the B8062, north of Auchterarder
With the 'arrival' of the Cessna 206 as jump trainer, the fuselage of Islander G-AXHE was turned into a small square box of metal care of a JCB and removed.
❏ G-BAGV*   Cessna U.206F   ex N9667G. Crash 5-5-02. Para-trainer.   11-03
❏ G-STAT*   Cessna U206F   ex Hibaldstow. A6-MAM, N8732Q. Crashed 24-8-03.
                                     Stored.   12-03
❏ R1914   Magister I   G-AHUJ, ex Aboyne, Balado, Kemble, 137, 604,
                                     Middle Wallop SF, 604. CoA 9-7-98. Stored.   12-01

STRATHAVEN AERODROME on the A71 south-east of East Kilbride
The Grasshopper is a composite with the one at Carlisle, Cumbria - qv. Quicksilver G-MJUO and Blanik DCL (BGA.2009) were not to be seen in June 2002.
❏ –   Skycraft Scout   fuselage. Stored, unflown. Possibly G-MJDM.   6-02
❏ –   Skycraft Scout   fuselage. Stored, unflown.   6-02
❏ –   DMJ   Schleicher K-8B   BGA.2221. Ex PH-290. Stored.   6-02
❏ WZ824   Grasshopper TX.1   ex Ringmer, Dishforth, St Bees.   11-03

STRATHDON on the A97 north of Ballater
❏ N15750   Beech D.18S   ex Corgarff, 'CF-RLD', Lasham, G-ATUM,
                                     D-IANA, N20S. Cockpit section.   2-97

SUMBURGH AIRPORT Shetland Islands, on the A970 south of Lerwick
❏ F-BMCY   Potez 840   wheels-up landing 29-3-81. Fire dump.   2-01

TAIN north of Inverness
❏ G-ATWS   Luton Minor   CoA 26-3-69.   ®   7-01

THORNHILL AERODROME on the A873 north-west of Stirling
The parachute school is no longer here and para-trainer Cherokee Six G-ATES (last noted in August 1999) is also believed to be no more.

WEST FREUGH AIRFIELD on the A715 south-east of Stranraer
Defence Science and Technology Laboratory (DS&TL) The airfield technically closed on 28th March 2002, but does still see traffic.
❏ XN817   Argosy C.1   ex A&AEE, MinTech, MoA. Fuselage, dump.   1-04

❑ XT852   Phantom FGR.2   ex BAe Scampton, A&AEE, HSA, A&AEE,
HSA, A&AEE, McDD. Dump, poor shape.   1-04

YARROW on the A708 west of Selkirk
❑ G-ANOK   Safir   ex Strathallan, East Fortune, SE-CAH ntu.
CoA 5-2-73. Stored.   10-01

PART THREE
CHANNEL ISLANDS

ALDERNEY AIRPORT
The overall yellow Aztec continues to provide the fire crews with practice.
❑ G-ASHV   Aztec 250B   ex Guernsey, N5281Y ntu. CoA 22-7-85. Dump.   12-99

GUERNSEY
Mooney G-ASTH at Sausmarez Park is now known to be only small parts and is best deleted. The EAA
Biplane is also at Sausmarez Park, while the Noralpha is stored within St Peter Port.
❑ G-ATEP   EAA Biplane   CoA 18-6-73. Stored.   5-03
❑ G-ATHN   Noralpha   ex F-BFUZ, French mil No.84. CoA 27-6-75. Stored.   5-03

GUERNSEY AIRPORT
❑ G-BAZJ   Herald 209   ex Air UK, Alia 4X-AHR, G-8-1. Fire crews.   2-04
❑ G-BBYO   Trislander   ex ZS-KMH, G-BBYO, G-BBWR. CoA 1-5-92.
Fuselage.   10-01
❑ G-BDTN   Trislander   ex S7-AAN, VQ-SAN, G-BDTN. CoA 10-6-98.
Stored, dismantled.   6-01
❑ N32625   Seneca 200   dump.   10-01
❑ N97121   Bandeirante   ex City-Line, PT-SDK. Withdrawn by 4-97.   10-01
❑ XM409   Jet Provost T.3   ex Firbeck, Moreton-in-Marsh, Halton 8082M,
Shawbury, 2 FTS. Nose.   10-01
❑ XS888   '521' Wessex HAS.1   ex Lee-o-S, Wroughton, Fleetlands. Dump.   10-01

JERSEY AIRPORT
The fire service compound, located north of the Runway 09 threshold, has a steel airliner mock-up for
'burning' exercises. Viscount 802 G-AOJD and Herald 203 G-BBXJ were scrapped in spring 2003.
Tomahawk G-BMTP was last noted in use for spares in November 1995 and is thought to have expired.
❑ XP573   '19' Jet Provost T.4   ex Halton '8236M', Kemble, Shawbury, R-R,
1 FTS, CFS. Really 8336M. Fire crews.   9-03

The 'regions' of Wales work on a wholly 'single tier' unitary authority structure.
The regions are as follows:

Clwyd	Denbighshire, Flintshire, Wrexham.
Dyfed	Carmarthenshire, Ceredigion, Pembrokeshire.
Gwent	Monmouthshire, Newport, Torfaen.
Gwynedd	Anglesey, Conwy, Gwynedd.
Powys	–
Mid Glamorgan	Blanau Gwent, Bridgend, Caerphilly, Merthyr Tydfil, Rhondda, Cynon and Taff.
South Glamorgan	Cardiff, Vale of Glamorgan.
West Glamorgan	Neath Port Talbot, Swansea.

ABERGAVENNY on the A40 west of Monmouth

❑ N9191	Tiger Moth	G-ALND, ex Shobdon, Shipdham, N9191, 5 SoTT, 19 EFTS, Duxford CF, 6 CPF. Crashed 8-3-81.	®	3-96

ABERPORTH AIRFIELD north of the A487, east of Cardigan

Defence Science and Technology Laboratory: This site is believed to be closing, in line with the ending of flying at Llanbedr. The airfield is now being actively traded as 'West Wales Airport'. The Hunter is kept by **1429 Squadron Air Cadets** and is 'parented' by St Athan.

❑ WT680	'J' Hunter F.1	7533M, ex Weeton, DFLS, West Raynham SF.	1-03
❑ A92-255*	Jindivik 3	ex DRA, RAE. Gate, first noted 5-02.	5-02

AMMANFORD on the A483 north of Swansea

No.2475 Squadron Air Cadets: Still keep a Canberra nose.

❑ WH739	Canberra B.2	ex St Athan, 100, 85, 45, 75 RNZAF, Upwood SF, 50, 101. Nose.	7-03

BRAWDY north of the A487 east of St David's

No.14 Signals Regiment: Cawdor Barracks. Hunter FGA.9 XE624 moved to Bruntingthorpe, Leics, on 18th April 2002.

BRIDGEND on the A473 west of Cardiff

De Havilland Aviation Ltd: Maintain a workshop here. See also under Bournemouth, Dorset. One of the anonymous Vampire FB.6 pods is believed to have gone to New Zealand.

◆ The workshop is *not* available for inspection.

❑ WL505	Vampire FB.9	G-FBIX, ex Bruntingthorpe, Cranfield, St Athan, Ely, 19, RAFC, 73.	[1]	1-01
❑ 'WL505'*	Vampire FB.6	G-MKVI, ex 'VZ304', Bruntingthorpe, Cranfield, Swiss AF J-1167. 614 Squadron colours. Stored.		12-03
❑ XE956	Vampire T.11	G-OBLN, ex St Albans, Hatfield, CATCS, 1 FTS, 8 FTS, 3 CAACU, APS, 67.	®	1-01
❑ XE985	Vampire T.11	ex London Colney, Woodford, Chester, St Athan, 5 FTS.		2-00
❑ –	Vampire FB.6	ex Switzerland. Pod, unflown.		2-00

CAERNARFON AERODROME or Caernarfon airparc, or Llandwrog north of the A487, south-west of Caernarfon

Caernarfon Air Museum: The museum tells the story of aviation in general and aviation in North Wales in particular. The mountain rescue exhibit is a graphic story of wartime crashes, both Allied and Luftwaffe. The Weedhopper may be G-MJSM [1]. The Flea from St Athan is currently on show in uncovered form, but there are plans to restore it to taxiable condition [2].

◆ Open Mar 1 to end of Oct, 10am to 5pm. ✉ Caernarfon airparc, Dinas Dinlle, Caernarfon, LL54 5TP ☎ 08707 541500 **fax** 08707 541510 **e-mail** info@caeairparc.com **www**.caeairparc.com

❑ G-ALFT	Dove 6	ex Higher Blagdon, Stansted, CAFU. CoA 13-6-73.		3-02
❑ G-AMLZ	Prince 6E	ex Coventry, VR-TBN ntu, G-AMLZ. CoA 18-6-71.		3-02
❑ G-AWUK	Cessna F.150H	ex Shobdon, Stansted, Oaksey Park, Bristol, Biggin Hill. Crashed 4-9-71. Cockpit. Stored.		3-02
❑ G-MBEP	Eagle 215B	first noted 1-97. On loan from R W Lavender.		3-02
❑	Weedhopper	loaned from Ray Bancroft, Prestatyn.	[1]	3-02
❑ WM961	'J' Sea Hawk FB.5	ex Higher Blagdon, Culdrose A2517, FRU, 802, 811.		3-02
❑ WN499	'Y' Dragonfly HR.3	ex Higher Blagdon, Blackbushe, Culdrose SF. Plaything.		3-02
❑ WT694	Hunter F.1	ex Newton, Debden 7510M, 229 OCU, DFLS, 54.		3-02
❑ WV781	Sycamore HR.12	ex Finningley, Odiham, Digby 7839M, HDU, CFS, ASWDU, G-ALTD ntu. Forward fuselage.		3-02

❏	XA282		Cadet TX.3	ex Syerston, 635 VGS.	3-02
❏	XH837		Javelin FAW.7	ex Northolt, Ruislip 8032M, 33. Forward fuselage.	3-02
❏	XJ726	'F'	W'wind HAR.10	ex Sibson, Wroughton, 2 FTS, CFS, ME SAR Flt, 22.	3-02
❏	XK623	'56'	Vampire T.11	ex Bournemouth 'G-VAMP', Moston, Woodford, Chester, St Athan, 5 FTS.	3-02
❏	XL618	'05'	Hunter T.7	ex Cottesmore 8892M, Shawbury, Kemble, 1 TWU, 229 OCU, Jever SF, Gütersloh SF.	3-02
❏	–	BAPC.201	HM.14 'Flea'	ex Talysarn. Fuselage, rudder, wing spars. Modded u/c.	3-02
❏	–*	BAPC.286	HM.14 Flea	ex St Athan, 'local area'. Scott A2S. Arrived 12-02. ® [2]	9-03
❏	–		Tiger Moth	ex Shobdon, Fownhope. Frame in 'workshop' scene.	3-02
❏	–		Varsity T.1 EMU	ex Higher Blagdon.	3-02

CARDIFF
National Museum and Galleries of Wales: The Watkins moved to Nantgarw, Wales.

CARDIFF AIRPORT or Rhoose, on the A4226 west of Barry
Airport: The fire crews here have a three-engined synthetic fire trainer as well as the real airframes.

❏	G-AVGH	Cherokee 140	CoA 5-12-91. Fuselage. Fire crews.	2-01
❏	–	Jetstream 41 EMU	ex WAM, Hatfield, Prestwick. Based on Srs 200 G-ATXJ. CoA 8-2-71. Fire crews.	2-02

International Centre for Aerospace Training (Barry Technical College): Within the industrial and business park on the airport perimeter.

❏	G-BDAX		Aztec 250C	ex 5B-CAO, N6399Y. CoA 12-11-93.	2-04
❏	XX672	'E'	Bulldog T.1	ex Shawbury, Birm UAS.	2-04
❏	XX687	'F'	Bulldog T.1	ex Shawbury, EM UAS, Lpl UAS.	2-04

CHESTER AIRFIELD or Hawarden or Broughton, on the B5129 west of Chester
BAE Systems: The references for this section are getting dated.

❏	–		HS.748	ex Hatfield. Forward fuselage. Dump.	11-97
❏	–		ATP	ex Chadderton. Fuselage. c/n 2075.	4-98
❏	'WE275'		Venom FB.50	G-VIDI, ex Dunsfold, Cranfield, Swiss AF J-1601. 45 Sqn c/s. Damaged 7-7-96. Fire dump.	5-97

Hawarden Air Services and **North Wales Military Aircraft Services**: Strikemaster G-FLYY was flying by late 2003. On 22nd May 2002 MiG-23ML '04' and MiG-27K '71' moved to Winthorpe, Notts, on loan. Mil Mi-24V 'Red 06' moved to Redhill, Surrey, on 28th March 2003 for fitting out before it moved to its new home at Rochester, Kent, on 25th June 2003. By November 2003, MiG-23MF '50' had moved to Foulness Island, Essex.

❏	G-ASXH	Bensen B.8M	CoA 22-8-73.	3-96
❏	G-BHXB	Bulldog 120	ex Botswana DF OD2, G-BHXB. CoA 23-4-98. Stored.	2-99
❏	G-BYED*	Jet Provost T.5A	ex Londonderry, N166A, XW302, 6 FTS, 3 FTS, RAFC, 1 FTS. Crashed 12-2-01. Arrived 7-01. ®	2-04
❏	G-OJCM	Rotorway Exec 90	crashed 25-9-95. Wreck.	8-96
❏	G-UPCC	Robinson R-22	ex G-MUSS. Crashed 5-6-94.	8-96
❏	CCCP-07268	An-2 *Colt*	YL-LEV, Latvia, USSR.	5-02
❏	CCCP-17939	An-2 *Colt*	YL-LFC, Latvia, USSR. Dumped outside.	5-02
❏	CCCP-19731*	An-2 *Colt*	YL-LEU, ex Hooton Park, Chester, Latvia, USSR. Arrived 2002.	5-03
❏	CCCP-19733	An-2 *Colt*	YL-LEZ, Latvia, USSR. Dumped outside.	5-02
❏	CCCP-20320	Mi-2 *Hoplite*	YL-LHN, Latvia, USSR.	5-02
❏	CCCP-20619	Mi-2 *Hoplite*	YL-LHO, Latvia, USSR.	5-02
❏	CCCP-40748	An-2 *Colt*	YL-LFA, Latvia, USSR.	5-02
❏	CCCP-40749	An-2 *Colt*	YL-LFD, Latvia, USSR.	5-02
❏	CCCP-40784	An-2 *Colt*	YL-LEY, Latvia, USSR.	5-02
❏	CCCP-40785	An-2 *Colt*	YL-LFB, Latvia, USSR.	5-02

❑	CCCP-54949	An-2 *Colt*	YL-LEX, Latvia, USSR.	5-02
❑	CCCP-56471	An-2 *Colt*	YL-LEW, Latvia, USSR.	5-02
❑	–	Tucano T.1	ex Waverton, Belfast City. c/n S45/T42. Dam 1990. ⓇR	2-04
❑	'03' r	Mi-24 *Hind-D*	ex Latvia, USSR. (3532461715415).	5-02
❑	'05' b	Yak-50	YL-CBH, ex Latvia. (832507).	11-97
❑	'05' r	Yak-50	YL-YAK, ex Strathallan, CIS. (832507?)	11-95
❑	'09' g	Yak-52	YL-CBI, ex Wrexham, Chester, Latvia. (811202).	11-96
❑	'20' b	Yak-52	YL-CBJ, ex Strathallan, CIS. (790404).	5-02
❑	'23' r	MiG-27 *Flogger*	ex Latvia, USSR. (83712515040). Dumped outside.	5-02
❑	'35' r	Su-17M-3 *Fitter*	ex Latvia, USSR. ('25102')	2-00
❑	'54' r	Su-17B *Fitter*	ex Latvia, USSR. (69004/5). Dumped outside.	5-02
❑	'56' r	Yak-52	ex Strathallan, CIS. (811506)	5-02
❑	–	Mi-24V *Hind*	ex Latvia, USSR. (3532424810853).	5-02

No.2247 Squadron Air Cadets: 'Parented' by Sealand, in Manor Lane to the east of the airfield.
❑ XE852 'H' Vampire T.11 ex Woodford, Chester, Shawbury, 1 FTS, 4 FTS. 2-04

CHIRK on the A5 north of Oswestry

❑	G-AJBJ	Dragon Rapide	ex Coventry, Blackpool, NF894, 18 MU, HQ TCCF. CoA 14-9-61.	10-01
❑	'G-AJCL'	Dragon Rapide	G-AIUL, ex Southend, British Westpoint, NR749, Kemble, 2 RS. CoA 29-9-67. Stored.	10-01
❑	G-AKOE	Dragon Rapide	ex Booker, X7484, PTS. CoA 25-2-82. Stored.	10-01
❑	G-ATFV	Bell 47J-2A	ex 9J-ACX, G-ATFV, It AF MM80417. CoA 8-8-92.	10-99
❑	G-BAYL	Norecrin VI	ex Ivychurch, Solihull, Bodmin, F-BEQV. Fuselage.	10-01
❑	G-BEDB	Norecrin	ex Liverpool, Chirk, F-BEOB. CoA 11-6-80.	10-01

CONNAH'S QUAY on the A548 west of Chester
North East Wales Institute, Dee-side College: (See also under Wrexham, Wales.) The college presented Gannet AS.4 XA460 to 750 Squadron, Air Training Corps, and it was moved in August 2003 to Doncaster, S Yorks. A Jet Provost T.5 and a Cessna 340 have arrived.

❑	G-AZMX	Cherokee 140	ex Chester, Half' Green, SE-FLL, LN-LMK. CoA 9-1-82.	8-03
❑	N66SW*	Cessna 340	ex N5035Q.	**due**
❑	XR658	Jet Provost T.4	ex Bournemouth, Wroughton, Abingdon 8192M, RAFEF, 6 FTS, CAW, 7 FTS.	8-03
❑	XW423* '14'	Jet Provost T.5A	ex Little Snoring, RAF, Shawbury, 3 FTS, RAFC, 1 FTS, 3 FTS. CoA 14-2-02. Arrived by 9-03.	9-03

Terry Parker: Has taken delivery of a former Swiss Air Force Venom pod. Vampire and Venom 'guru' Alan Allen is not convinced about its identity. Another possible is J-1711.
❑ 'J-1712'* Venom FB.54 ex Charnock Richard, Bournemouth, Swiss AF. Arrived 15-8-03. Pod. 2-04

COWBRIDGE on the A48 west of Cardiff
Task Force Paintball: The Whirlwind still battles it out at the paintball wargames park.
❑ XG592 Whirlwind ex Cardiff, Wroughton, 705, 846, 705, 700, HAS.7 C(A), HS, Westland. 5-02

CWMBRAN on the A4051 north of Newport
A collector in the general area has a Hunter nose.
❑ QA-12 Hunter FGA.78 ex B'mouth, Qatar AF, G-9-284, RNethAF N-222. Nose. 12-03

HAVERFORDWEST
A 'JP' nose is stored on a farm south of the town.

❏ XN503*   Jet Provost   ex Milford Haven, Salisbury, Firbeck, Coventry, Bicester,
                             Kemble, RAFEF, 4 FTS, 2 FTS, 6 FTS, A&AEE. Nose.4-03

HAVERFORDWEST AERODROME or Withybush, on the A40, north of Haverfordwest

Terrier 2 G-ASEG was cancelled as sold in Denmark in April 2002. Auster J/1 G-AHAP was sold in the 'Southampton' area in mid-2003.

❏ G-ACZE	Dragon Rapide	ex Dorchester, G-AJGS, G-ACZE, Z7266, 3 FP,		
		6 AONS, G-ACZE. CoA 11-8-95.	®	7-03
❏ G-ASAN	Terrier 2	ex Auster T.7 VX928, 661, HCEU, 661. CoA 28-6-96.	®	4-01
❏ G-BPGK	Aeronca 7AC	ex Llanelli, N4409E. Crashed 7-5-91.	®	10-99
❏ G-BTWU	Tri-Pacer 135	ex N3320B.	®	10-99

HOLYWELL on the A5026 north west of Queensferry,

Stored in the area is a Hobbycopter. It was built in the mid-1960s and flew, albeit unofficially!

❏ –*   Adams-Wilson   Stored.   7-01

KENFIG HILL north of the B4281 east of Pyle

No.2117 Squadron Air Cadets: Off Main Street, and behind Pwll-y-Garth Street. The Hunter, 'parented' by St Athan, is hard to find! When found, it is overall grey and unmarked.

❏ WT569   Hunter F.1   ex St Athan 7491M, A&AEE, Hawkers trials.   5-02

LLANBEDR on the A496 south of Harlech

Maes Artro Village: This delightful location re-opened during late 2002. It is hoped to be able to expand the aviation content in due course. The Hunter nose is on loan from local 2445 Squadron, ATC.

◆ Open daily 10am to 5.30pm (last admission 4pm). Closed January and February. ✉ Maes Artro,
  Llanbedr, LL45 2PZ. ☎ 01341 241467 **www.maesarto.co.uk**

❏ 'MAV467''RO'Spitfire V FSM	BAPC.202, ex *Piece of Cake*.		10-02
❏ [VS562]	Anson T.21	ex Portsmouth, Llanbedr 8012M,	
		A&AEE, AST Hamble, CS(A).	10-01
❏ WN957	Hunter F.5	ex Llanbedr, Stafford, North Weald 7407M, RAE. Nose.	10-01
❏ XJ409	Whirlwind	ex Grangetown, Cardiff-Wales, Wroughton,	
	HAR.10	Warton SAR Flt, 1310F, 228, 155, XD779 ntu.	10-02
❏ A92-664	Jindivik 3	ex DRA, RAE. Composite.	10-02

LLANBEDR AIRFIELD west of Llanbedr and the A496 on the road to Shell Island

Defence Science and Technology Laboratory: Another crying waste of an airfield, the base is due to close in June 2004. In February 2004, Canberras WH734 and WK128 were offered for tender [1].

❏ WH453	'L'	Meteor D.16	ex 5 CAACU, 72, 222. Engine test-bed, stored.	11-03
❏ WH734*		Canberra B.2	ex FRL. Spares recovery.	[1] 11-03
❏ WH887	'847'	Canberra TT.18	ex St Athan, FRADU, Upwood SF, 21, 542, 1323F.	11-03
❏ WK128*		Canberra B.2	ex FRL. Spares recovery.	[1] 11-03
❏ XV435	'R'	Phantom FGR.2	ex 92, 228 OCU, 92, 228 OCU, 23, 228 OCU, 14. Dump.	11-03
❏ 'A92-LLAN1'		Jindivik 3	A92-480, gate guard.	11-03

LLANWRTYD WELLS on the A483 west of Builth Wells

❏ XM358   Jet Provost T.3A   ex Twyford, North Scarle, Colsterworth, Halton 8987M,
                               1 FTS, 3 FTS, 1 FTS, CFS, RAFC, CFS, 7 FTS, 2 FTS.   2-00

MILFORD HAVEN on the A4076 south of Haverfordwest

No.1284 Squadron Air Cadets: By April 2003 'JP' XN503 had moved to <u>Haverfordwest</u>, Wales.

MOLD on the A494 west of Chester.
Derek Griffiths: There are now three cockpits held in the general area. Derek runs the **International Cockpit Club** which serves to unite and inform anyone who owns, would like to own, or just likes the idea of cockpit collecting.
◆ Visits by prior arrangement *only.* ✉ 21 Bryn-Y-Foel, Rhosemor, near Mold, CH7 6PW e-mail dgg.icc@btinternet.com www.internationalcockpitclub.org.uk

❑ G-AYFA*	Twin Pioneer 3	ex Carlisle, Hooton Park, Warmingham, Sandbach, Shobdon, Prestwick, G-31-5, XM285, SRCU, 225, Odiham SF, 230. Nose.	3-04
❑ WH984	Canberra B.15	ex Bruntingthorpe, Hinckley, Bruntingthorpe, Cosford 8101M, HS, 9, Binbrook SF, 9. Nose.	3-04
❑ XW541*	Buccaneer S.2B	ex Welshpool, Ingatestone, Stock, Foulness, Honington, 8858M, St Athan, 12, 16, 15. Nose. Due to arr 4-04.	**due**

NANTGARW on the A470 north-west of Cardiff
The Collection Centre: (Note name change.) Large object store, visits by prior appointment *only.* The Watkins is stored; destined for the Industrial Museum of Wales which will be set up in Swansea.

❑ XM300	Wessex HAS.1	ex Cardiff, Cardiff-Wales, Farnborough, RAE, Westlands. SAR colours. Stored.	2-04
❑ –*	BAPC.47 Watkins CHW	ex Cardiff, St Athan, Cardiff. Stored.	2-04

NEWPORT
No.210 Squadron Air Cadets:

❑ WD293	Chipmunk T.10 PAX	7645M. ex Caerleon, Cwmbran, QuB UAS, StA UAS, G&S UAS, StA UAS, Chatham Flt, SMR, 1 BFTS.	10-98

PENDINE RANGES on the A4066 east of Tenby
Proof and Experimental Establishment: No news from the ranges.

❑ XV373	SH-3D	ex Foulness, A&AEE, RAE.	2-02

PETERSTONE on the B4239 north-east of Cardiff

❑ N5834N	Commander 114	force-landed 23-10-98. Hulk.	1-04

ROSEMARKET north-east of Milford Haven
The Cub was/is in external store, on a local golf course! The others are stored elsewhere and are also getting very dated.

❑ G-AYCN	J3C-65 Cub	ex F-BCPO. CoA 27-1-89. Stored.	8-95
❑ G-BBKR	Scheibe SF-24A	ex D-KECA. CoA 30-3-79. Stored.	5-95
❑ G-BHPM	PA-18-95 S' Cub	ex F-BOUR, ALAT, 51-15501. Stored.	5-95
❑ G-BJNY	Aeronca 11CC	ex CN-TYZ, F-OAEE. CoA 9-8-90. Stored.	1-95

RUTHIN on the A494 south-west of Mold
Phantom Preservation Group: See also under Nantwich, Cheshire, for the group's 'showcase'.
◆ Visits by prior arrangement only. ✉ Mark A Jones, Tyn Yr Erw, Llanfair Road, Ruthin, LL15 1BY e-mail mark3045@freeuk.com

❑ –	Phantom FGR.2	Nose section. Stored.	2-04

ST ATHAN AIRFIELD on the B4265 west of Barry
RAF St Athan: During December 2002, the **University of Wales Air Squadron** delivered the anonymous HM.14 Flea to Caernarfon, Wales.

❑ 'XV498'	Phantom FGR.2	XV500 / 9113M, ex 56, 29, 23, 56, 111, 43, 54. 92 Sqn colours. Displayed.	1-04

Defence Aviation Repair Agency (DARA): The scenery is rapidly changing here with the 'Super Hangar' dominating the skyline. This can hold as many as 80 fastjets should the workload dictate. *W&R18* (p293) noted Islander AL.1 ZG994 coming here. Sleuthing has proved this not to be so – largely because it remains very prominently stored within the main 'production' hangar at Bembridge, IoW! The hulk here is a civilian Islander, last used at Bembridge as an engineering mock-up for the Defender 4000 programme. It may have come here as early as 1994 - 'special fit' trials? [1]. The arrival of the VFW-614 was a major surprise. It is being used by DARA and Lufthansa - the latter have a residential training college at Cwmbran [2].

The last of 80 Fuselage Replacement Programme (FRP) Hawk T.1/T.1As was delivered back to the RAF on 27th August 2003 when XX242 flew to Scampton to rejoin the 'Red Arrows'. See page 292 in *W&R18* for further details. Redundant Hawk rear fuselages can be found as teaching aids at several points on the base. Others have been distributed to other bases for similar purposes.

Departures: **Gazelle** HT.2 XZ938 to Cosford, Shropshire - follow this through for a good plot!; **Harrier** T.4 XW265 arrived from Cosford 6-1-03, its cockpit was removed and sent to <u>Leuchars</u>, Scotland while the remainder was dumped; **Jaguar** T.2B XX839 was scrapped 5-02 with the hulk going to Clay Cross, Derbys; T.2 XX847 left by 10-02 returning to service; **Jet Provost T.4** XS180 departed 17-7-02 and has not returned - where is it now?; **Sea Harrier** FA.2 ZD580 to <u>Ipswich</u>, Suffolk, by October 2002; **Tornado GR.1** XZ630 prepared for display then to <u>Halton</u>, Bucks, 3-2-04; ZA319 to <u>Bicester</u>, Oxon, 5-12-02; ZA320 to <u>Cosford</u>, Shropshire, 8-4-02; ZA321 was shipped to the China Lake ranges in the USA in 2002 and is reported to have been destroyed in a missile test; ZA323 arrived 16-4-02, to <u>Cosford</u>, Shrop, 18-8-03; ZA325 to <u>Cosford</u>, Shrop, 13-8-03; ZA356 dumped out 9-02 with the nose going to <u>Marham</u>, Norfolk, and the remainder to Clay Cross, Derbys; ZA357 first noted 3-03, to <u>Cosford</u>, Shrop, 18-8-03; and the following to be 'fragmentised' at Clay Cross, Derbys: ZA352 17-12-02; ZA358 dumped out by 9-02, left 10-1-03; ZA360 dumped out by 9-02, left 17-12-02; ZA455 dumped out by 9-02, left 14-10-02; ZA466 dumped out by 9-02, left 14-10-02; ZA490 to the dump 25-4-02, left 14-10-02; **Tornado F.2** ZD903 to Clay Cross, Derbys, 17-12-02; ZD905 to Clay Cross, Derbys, 17-12-02; ZD933 to Clay Cross, Derbys, 27-2-03; ZD940 to Clay Cross, Derbys, 9-9-02; **Tornado F.3** ZE163 left 9-5-02 for return to service; ZE253 to EADS at Munich, Germany, 14-1-03, for use in the F.3 MLU programme for spares; ZE296 to EADS at Munich, Germany, 19-1-03 for use in the F.3 MLU programme, to be used for spares; **VC-10** C.1K XV103 reduced to sections by 11-02 and removed; **Wessex** HU.5 XT773 to <u>Cosford</u>, Shropshire, 8-9-03; K.4 ZD235 scrapping started 1-03, gone by 1-04.

❏	G-BCWR*		BN-2A-20	ex Bembridge, OY-RPZ, G-BCWR. Fuse. stored. [1]	5-03
❏	D-ASDB*		VFW-614	ex Luftwaffe 17+03, D-BABS. Arrived 15-4-03. [2]	1-04
❏	WJ717	'841'	Canberra TT.18	9052M, ex 4 SoTT, FRADU, 61, 15. Stored.	1-04
❏	XV643*	'262'	Sea King HAS.6	ex Gosport, Culdrose, 819, 849, 819, 814, 820, 824, 814, WHL, A&AEE. ABDRT. Arr 4-7-02.	12-02
❏	XX254		Hawk T.1A	ex Brough, Chivenor, 7 FTS, 1 TWU, 2 TWU. Front fuselage. Stored.	1-04
❏	XX326		Hawk T.1A	ex Brough, 19, 92, 2 TWU. Front fuselage.	1-04
❏	XX722	'EF'	Jaguar GR.1	9252M, Shawbury, Warton, Shawbury, 6, 54, JOCU. Fuselage. ABDRT.	1-04
❏	XX723*	'GQ'	Jaguar GR.3A	ex Coltishall, 54, 226 OCU, 6, 54, 20, 54, JOCU. Arrived 1-8-03.	2-04
❏	XX977	'DL'	Jaguar GR.1	9132M, ex Abingdon, Shawbury, 31. ABDRT	1-04
❏	XZ322	'N'	Gazelle AH.1	9283M, ex Shawbury, 670, ARWS, 6 Flt. ABDRT	1-04
❏	XZ439*		Sea Harrier FA.2	ex 809. Arrived 25-4-02.	1-04
❏	XZ459*		Sea Harrier FA.2	ex 809. Arrived 11-4-03.	1-04
❏	XZ941	'B'	Gazelle HT.2	ex Shawbury, 2 FTS, Odiham hack, CFS. ABDRT	1-04
❏	XZ991	'3A'	Harrier GR.3	9162M, ex 233 OCU, 4, 1417F, 233 OCU, 1, R-R, 1, 3, 1. ABDRT	1-04
❏	XZ993*	'M'	Harrier GR.3	9240M, Laarbruch, St Athan, 4, 1, 1453F, 3.	2-04
❏	ZA140		VC-10 K.2	ex 101, A40-VL, G-ARVL. Cockpit.	2-04
❏	ZA142	'C'	VC-10 K.2	ex 101, A40-VI, G-ARVI. Scrapping.	1-04
❏	ZA399	'AJC'	Tornado GR.1	ex 617, 20, TWCU. Arrived 11-12-01. BDRT by 8-03.	1-04
❏	ZA411*	'TT'	Tornado GR.1	ex 617, 15, 617, 2, 20, 16. Stored. Arr 25-7-02.	1-04
❏	ZD350	'A'	Harrier GR.5	9189M, ex Wittering, 1. Cr 7-8-92. Nose. ABDRT.	1-04
❏	ZD412*		Harrier GR.5	ex Dunsfold, Brough, 3. Cr 30-9-01.NDT. F/n 9-02.	1-03
❏	ZD462*		Harrier GR.7	9302M, ex Cosford, St Athan, 1. Ditched 25-1-97. Arrived 30-1-04. ABDRT.	1-04

❑	ZD607*		Sea Harrier FA.2	ex Warton, 800, 801, 800, 801, 800, 801, 800, 899.	
				Crashed 17-7-00. Arrived 13-3-01. ABDRT by 12-02.	1-04
❑	ZD611*	'719'	Sea Harrier FA.2	ex 899, 801, 899, 800, 899, 800, 899, 899, 800, 899,	
				801. Arrived 16-9-03.	1-04
❑	ZD901	'AA'	Tornado F.2	ex 229 OCU. F.2-F.3 exchange. Dump 4-02.	4-02
❑	ZD932	'AM'	Tornado F.2	ex 229 OCU. F.2-F.3 exchange. ABDRT.	1-04
❑	ZE252*		Tornado F.3	ex ItAF MM7225, RAF. Arrived 28-5-03. Stored.	1-04
❑	ZE290	'AG'	Tornado F.3	ex 56. Spares reclaim.	1-04
❑	ZE339		Tornado F.3	ex 56, 5, 56, 25, 5. Cockpit.	1-04
❑	ZG706*	'E'	Tornado GR.1A	ex SAOEU. Arrived 24-1-00.	11-03
❑	ZG734*		Tornado F.3	ex ItAF MM7231, RAF. Arrived 5-6-03.	1-04
❑	162730*		AV-8B Harrier II	ex Wyton, St Athan, USMC. Fuselage. ABDRT	1-04

No.4 School of Technical Training / Civilian Technical Training School: Not part of DARA - see under Cosford, Shrop, for a glimpse of the future. Bulldog T.1 XX710 was scrapped in March 2001.

❑	XM419	'102'	Jet Provost T.3A	8990M, ex 7 FTS, 3 FTS, CFS, RAFC, CFS,	
				3 FTS, RAFC, 6 FTS, RAFC, 2 FTS.	9-02
❑	XN551	'100'	Jet Provost T.3A	8984M, ex 7 FTS, RAFC, 1 FTS, 3 FTS, 6 FTS, RAFC.	9-02
❑	XS735*	'R'	Dominie T.1	ex Sealand, Cranwell, 55, 6 FTS, RAFC, CAW.	
				Arrived 1-5-02.	9-02
❑	XW404	'77'	Jet Provost T.5A	9049M, ex 1 FTS.	9-02
❑	XW409	'123'	Jet Provost T.5A	9047M, ex 7 FTS, 1 FTS.	9-02
❑	XX626	'W'	Bulldog T.1	9290M, ex Wales UAS, CFS. (Also coded '02')	9-02
❑	XX635		Bulldog T.1	8767M, ex Ems UAS.	9-02
❑	XX686	'5'	Bulldog T.1	9291M, ex CFS, 3 FTS, Gla UAS, Ox UAS,	
				Gla UAS, Lpl UAS, 2 FTS.	9-02
❑	XX763	'24'	Jaguar GR.1	9009M, ex Shawbury, 226 OCU.	9-02
❑	XX764	'13'	Jaguar GR.1	9010M, ex Shawbury, 226 OCU, 14.	9-02

SEALAND on the A550 south-west of Ellesmere Port
Defence Aviation Repair Agency (DARA): Dominie T.1 XS735 moved to St Athan, Wales, on 1st May 2002. The RAF element 'parents' a series of ATC airframes (eg Birkdale, Hawarden, Royton).

| ❑ | 'WT720' | 'B' | Hunter F.51 | 8565M, ex Cranwell 'XF979', Brawdy, Dunsfold, | |
| | | | | G-9-436, Esk.724, Dan AF E-408. 74 Sqn c/s, Gate. | 2-04 |

SWANSEA AIRPORT (or Fairwood Common), on the A4118 west of Swansea
De Havilland Aviation Ltd (DHA): Having relocated to Bournemouth, Dorset (qv), the operation here was closed by mid-2003. Vampire FB.6 'WL505' (G-MKVI) is believed to have moved to the DHA store at Bridgend, Wales. Sea Vampire T.22 N6-766 (G-SPDR) moved to East Grinstead, W Sussex in October 2003. Vampire T.11 WZ507 (G-VTII) flew again on 26th May 2002 after nearly six years of restoration. It ferried to Bournemouth, Dorset, the following month. **Others**:

❑	G-MJAZ		Ultravector 627	ex PH-1J1, G-MJAZ. CoA 23-9-93. Stored.	5-98
❑	D-5084		Schleicher K.8b	BGA.2688. Stored.	5-98
❑	'FT323'		Harvard II	EX884, ex 'Exeter', Cranfield, Bushey, East Ham,	
	G-CCOY			Port AF 1513, SAAF 7426, EX884, 41-33857.	® 3-97

VALLEY AIRFIELD south of the A5, south-east of Holyhead
RAF Valley: The Hawk Composite Servicing School have a Hawk nose for instruction. A 'synthetic' Hawk fire training aid serves on the dump. The **Search and Rescue Training Unit** (SARTU) have two training airframes, the newly-arrived 'Huey' playing the role of a Griffin.

❑	WV396	'91'	Hunter T.8C	9249M, ex Yeovilton, FRADU, 229 OCU, 20.	
				4 FTS red/white c/s. Gate	2-04
❑	XT772		Wessex HU.5	8805M, ex Wroughton, 781. SARTU inst.	11-01
❑	XX300		Hawk T.1	8827M, ex Chivenor, 2 TWU, 1 TWU.	
				Crashed 2-10-82. Nose.	4-98

❑ '998-8888'*   UH-1H 'Huey'   ex Middle Wallop, Greenford, Middle Wallop,
Fleetlands, Stanley, Argentine Army AE-406, 72-21491.
US Army colours. SARTU. Arrived 17-9-02.   9-02

WELSHPOOL on the A483 west of Shrewsbury
Military Aircraft Cockpit Collection: Run by Sue and Roy Jerman. The collection has been thinned
down to a more manageable size. The Whirlwind HAR.10 cockpit is on loan from Dave Higgins [1]. The
Harrier GR.1 nose is a 'spare' from the huge store at Stafford, marked '4 Spare Ser 41H-769733',
which falls within the 'XW' range [3].
     Departures: Canberra B.2 nose WP515 (12th March 2004) and Hunter FGA.9 nose IF-68 (mid-
2003) moved to Market Drayton, Shrop. Sea Vixen FAW.2 XN650 nose moved to Newton Abbot,
Devon, in mid-2002. Buccaneer S.2B XW541 to Mold, Wales, *due to move* 4-04. Tornado GR.1 cockpit
ZD710 to Barnstaple, Devon, 10-12-02. Vampire T.11 XD534 pod arrived from Barton, Gtr Man, 1-03,
but moved to Nottingham East Midlands, Leics, by 2-04. The cockpit of Jetstream T.1 XX483 arrived
from Weston-on-Trent, Staffs, in 2002, but moved on to Dumfries, Scotland, by 4-03.
♦ *Private* collection, visits possible by prior arrangement *only*.

❑	WH775	Canberra PR.7	ex Bruntingthorpe, Cosford 8868M/8128M, 100, 13, 31, 17, 31, 13, 82, makers.		3-04
❑	WK102	Canberra T.17	ex Bruntingthorpe, Cosford 8780M, 360, 45, RNZAF, 207.		3-04
❑	XJ758	Whirlwind HAR.10	ex Oswestry, Shrewsbury, Shawbury 8464M, CFS, 230, CFS, 217, 1360F, 22.	[1]	3-04
❑	XM652	Vulcan B.2	ex Burntwood, Sheffield, Waddington, 50, 35, 44, 9. Nose.		3-04
❑	XS923	'BE' Lightning F.6	ex Bruntingthorpe, Cranfield, Binbrook, 11, LTF, 5-11 pool.		3-04
❑	XT277	Buccaneer S.2A	ex Bruntingthorpe, Cosford 8853M, Shawbury, 237 OCU, 12.		3-04
❑	–	Harrier GR.1	ex Market Drayton, Stafford, Abingdon, Hamble.	[2]	3-04

WELSHPOOL AERODROME or Trehelig, south of the town at the A493/A490 junction
Tiger Moths G-ALWS, G-BXMN and T8191 (G-BWMK) had moved on by mid-2002.

| ❑ | G-BKCY | Tomahawk 112 | ex OO-XKU. CoA 7-11-94. Fuselage. | 7-98 |
| ❑ | G-BPER | Tomahawk 112 | ex N91465. Fuselage. | 10-01 |

WREXHAM
North East Wales Institute: Located next to the football ground, see under Connah's Quay for another
NEWI site. The forward fuselage of the HS.125 prototype G-ARYA moved to London Colney, Herts, on
13th February 2004. NEWI at Connah's Quay had the wing box, tail and parts of the mid-fuselage for
structures teaching, it is not known if these moved as well. Cherokee 140 G-AVLC was in use as an
instructional airframe from circa 2001 until it was put up for disposal in early 2004. It moved to Spanhoe
Lodge, Northants, on 12th March 2004.

| ❑ | XP585 | '24' Jet Provost T.4 | 8407M, ex Halton, St Athan, RAFC, 6 FTS, RAFC. | 10-02 |

YSTRAD MYNACH on the A472 south of Merthyr Tydfil
A private owner has a 'JP'.

| ❑ | XP638 | 'A' Jet Provost T.4 | 9034M, ex Waddington, Halton, Shawbury, CATCS, CAW, 6 FTS. | 2-02 |

PART FIVE
IRELAND

Northern Ireland
Antrim
Armagh
Down
Fermanagh
Londonderry
Tyrone

Ireland
Carlow
Cavan
Clare

Cork
Donegal
Dublin
Galway
Kerry
Kildare
Kilkenny
Laois
Leitrim
Limerick
Longford
Louth

Mayo
Meath
West Meath
Offaly
Roscommon
Sligo
Tipperary
Waterford
Wexford
Wicklow

NORTHERN IRELAND

BALLYKINLER BARRACKS, Down
Exact location of the barracks is uncertain, but the hulk of a long-lost Wessex is to be found within the grounds. It was last reported, in *W&R14*, as having perished on the dump in 1998.
❑ XS865*   Wessex HAS.1   ex Lee-on-Solent, A2694, Wroughton, 771. Camo.   4-03

BALLYMENA, Antrim
❑ G-ARDV*	Tri-Pacer 160	ex EI-APA, G-ARDV, N10F. CoA 2-1-99.	®	1-04
❑ G-BPMM*	7ECA Citabria	ex N5132T. CoA 25-2-97. Stored.		1-04

BALLYMONEY on the A26 south-east of Coleraine, Antrim
Super Cub 95 G-BPJH was flying by early 2001.

BANN FOOT north-west of Craigavon, Armagh
❑ G-PFAL	FRED II	CoA 27-7-88.	1-04
❑ EI-AUT	F.1A Aircoupe	ex Cork, G-ARXS, D-EBSA, N3037G. CoA 30-7-76.	1-04

BELFAST, Down
No.817 Squadron Air Cadets should still have their Devon fuselage [1]. The **Flight Experience Workshop** is believed to be moribund and the Sunderland forward fuselage project is thought to have been shelved. Canberra T.4 nose WT486 is believed to have gone to an ATC unit - 817 Squadron is Lisburn?Jet Provost XM414 (which had been in store in Dundonald) moved on 23rd December 2003 to Langford Lodge, N Ireland, and the care of the Ulster Aviation Society. At **Campbell College** the Vampire 'pod' has long since gone and relocated to the REME at Kinegar Camp [2].
❑ VP957	Devon C.2/2	8822M, ex Bishop's Court, Belfast Airport, Northolt, 207, 21, WCS, SCS, NCS, SCS, WCS, SCS, Andover SF, 38 GCF, AAFCE, 2 TAF CS, BAFO CS. Forward fuselage.	[1] 10-00
❑ XD525	Vampire T.11	ex Holywood, Belfast, Aldergrove 7882M, 1 FTS, 4 FTS, 5 FTS, 7 FTS. Pod.	[2] 1-04

BELFAST AIRPORT or Aldergrove, on the A26 west of the city (Antrim)
❑ G-AVFE	Trident 2E	ex BA, BEA. CoA 6-5-85. Fire crews.		2-04
❑ G-BBSC	Sierra 200	CoA 3-6-99. Stored.		1-04
❑ G-BCBX	Cessna F.150L	ex F-BUEO. CoA 19-2-95. Stored.		1-04
❑ G-BFWK*	Warrior 161	ex N9589N. CoA 8-12-99. Stored.		1-04
❑ G-BNMK	Dornier Do 27A-1	ex OE-DGO, 56+04, BD+397, BA+399. Stored.		1-04
❑ G-KNAP	Warrior II	ex G-BIUX, N9507N. Crashed 13-7-99.	®	3-02
❑ XT456 'XZ'	Wessex HU.5	ex 8941M ABDR, Wroughton, 847, 846, 845. Dump.		1-04

RAF Aldergrove: The trailer-mounted nose sections are used by RAF Careers and do 'the rounds'.
❑ XE643	Hunter FGA.9	8586M, ex Abingdon, 208, 56, 63, 66, 92. Nose.		1-04
❑ XR529 'E'	Wessex HC.2	ex 72, SARTU, 2 FTS, 18, 78, 72. Gate, put into position 14-3-03.	®	1-04
❑ XR700	Jet Provost T.4	8589M, ex Abingdon, Shawbury, CATCS, 3 FTS, 1 FTS. Nose.		1-04

CASTLEROCK
Two Cessna 337s are used for spares.
❑ G-RORO*	C.337B	ex G-AVIX, N5454S. Crashed 25-6-99. Spares, hulk.	1-04
❑ EI-AVC	F.337F	ex Abbeyshrule, N4757. Spares, hulk.	1-04

DROMORE on the A1 south west of Belfast, Down

An amazing 'discovery' hanging in the roof of a large shed here is the fuselage of an Argus.

❏ G-AJSN*	Argus II	ex Cork, HB612, ATA, 43-14885. Crashed 10-6-67.		
		Barbara Ann. Fuselage, stored. First noted 2-02.		1-04
❏ EI-ACY*	J/1 Autocrat	ex G-AIBK. Crashed 6-4-67. Dism. First noted 2-02.		1-04

FIVEMILETOWN on the A4 east of Enniskillen, Tyrone

Blessingbourne Carriage Museum: The museum has a Scout on permanent loan.

◆ Open by prior appointment *only*. ✉ Blessingbourne, Fivemiletown, Co Tyrone, BT75 0QS.

❏ XW795	Scout AH.1	ex Middle Wallop, Almondbank, Wroughton,	
		659, 655, 669.	1-04

HOLYWOOD on the A2 east of Belfast, Down

Ulster Folk and Transport Museum: The 'original' Ferguson REP, the Short SC.1 and the Sherpa cockpit are in a 'hands-on' gallery known as 'The Flight Experience', staged in association with Bombardier Aerospace (FE). McCandless G-ATXX is displayed in an adjacent section showing achievements of local engineers and designers. Other than those mentioned above, all other airframes are in store and not available for inspection. See under Dromod, Ireland, for a possible insight into Gemini G-AKEL [1]. The registration G-ARTZ has been used twice, both times on Rex McCandless' products, see under St Merryn, Corn, for the second use [2].

◆ Open daily, closed three days at Xmas. Telephone for details of opening times. ✉ Cultra Manor, Holywood, BT18 0EU ☎ 028 9042 8428 **fax** 028 9042 8728 **www**.nidex.com/uftm

❏ G-AJOC	Messenger 2A	ex East Fortune, Strathallan, Dunottar. CoA 18-5-72.		1-04
❏ G-AKEL	Gemini 1A	ex Kilbrittain Castle. CoA 29-4-72. Stored.	[1]	1-04
❏ G-AKGE	Gemini 3C	ex Kilbrittain Castle, EI-ALM, G-AKGE. CoA 7-6-74.		1-04
❏ G-AKLW	Sealand	ex Bradley Air Museum, Connecticut, Jeddah,		
		RSaudiAF, SU-AHY, G-AKLW. Stored.		1-04
❏ G-AOUR	Tiger Moth	ex Belfast, NL898, 15 EFTS. Cr 6-6-65. Stored.		1-04
❏ G-ARTZ (1)	McCandless M-2	ex Killough. Stored.	[2]	1-04
❏ G-ATXX	McCandless M-4	ex Killough. wfu 9-9-70. Stored.		1-04
❏ G-BKMW	Short Sherpa	ex Belfast City, CoA 14-9-90. Cockpit section.	FE	1-04
❏ – ALA	Nimbus I	BGA.470, ex Bishop's Stortford, Duxford. Stored.		1-04
❏ VH-UUP	Scion I	ex East Fortune, Strathallan, G-ACUX,		
		VH-UUP, G-ACUX. Stored.		1-04
❏ XG905	Short SC.1	ex Shorts, Sydenham, Thurleigh, RAE.	FE	1-04
❏ – IAHC.6	Ferguson Mono	REP, ex Dublin.	FE	1-04
❏ – IAHC.9	Ferguson Mono	REP, ex Belfast Airport, Holywood. Stored.		1-04

LANGFORD LODGE AIRFIELD on the shores of Lough Neagh, west of Belfast, Antrim

Ulster Aviation Society Heritage Centre: The former parachute packing shed near the entrance to the airfield serves as a visitor centre. As well as the display hangar, the control tower of rare design has been restored. Special events are held, including fly-ins. All of this has been made possible thanks to Langford Lodge Engineering, who operate on the site. As *W&R* closed for press, UAS may well have clinched their long-held requirement for a Wessex - see Shoreham, W Sussex.

The Eurowing Goldwing is a very relevant exhibit, having made its first flight from Langford Lodge [1]. The Robinson is on loan from Harold Hassard [2] and the Cessna 172 from Andy Allen [3].

◆ Open Sat 1pm to 6pm, Feb to Nov, other times by prior appointment. ✉ 33 Old Mill Meadows, Dundonald, BT16 1WQ ☎ on-site / info-line 028 9445 4444 **www**.ulsteraviationsociety.co.uk

❏ G-BDBS	Shorts 330	ex Belfast City, Shorts, G-14-3001. CoA 2-9-92.		2-04
❏ G-BTUC	Tucano	ex Belfast City, Shorts, G-14-007, PP-ZTC.		
		CoA 20-8-91.		2-04
❏ G-MJWS	Goldwing	donated by Jeff Salter.	[1]	2-04
❏ G-RENT*	R.22 Beta	ex Newtownards, N2635M. Damaged 30-9-92.		
		Arrived 28-2-03.	[2]	2-04

❑	EI-BAG		Cessna 172A	ex Upper Ballinderry, Portadown, Enniskillen, Abbeyshrule, G-ARAV, N9771T. CoA 26-6-79.	® [3]	2-04
❑	EI-BUO		Sea Hawker	ex Newtownards. Damaged 9-91.		2-04
❑	JV482		Wildcat V	ex Newtownards, Castlereagh, Lough Beg, 882. Crashed 24-12-44.	®	2-04
❑	WN108	'033'	Sea Hawk FB.3	ex Newtownards, Belfast City, Shorts Apps, Sydenham AHU, Bournemouth, FRU, 806, 895, 897, 800.		2-04
❑	WZ549	'F'	Vampire T.11	ex Newtownards, Coningsby, Tattershall, Coningsby 8118M, CATCS, 1 FTS, 8 FTS, FTU, C(A).		2-04
❑	XM414*	'101'	Jet Provost T.3A	ex Dundonald, Binbrook, Colsterworth, Halton 8996M, 7 FTS, RAFC, 1 FTS, RAFC, 2 FTS. Arr 23-12-04.		2-04
❑	XV361		Buccaneer S.2B	ex Lossiemouth, 208, 15, 208, 12, 15, 809, 800.		2-04
❑	–	BAPC.263	Chargus Cyclone	ex Ballyclare. Built 1979. Last flight 4-4-88.		2-04
❑	–	BAPC.266	Rogallo h-glider	donated by Charles Linford. Last flown 1978.		2-04
❑	–		Tucano EMU	ex Belfast City, Shorts. Test rig, stored.		2-04

LISBURN on the A3 south west of Belfast
A Terrier is under restoration in the area and Billy Lester took delivery of a Rallye during mid-2003.

❑	G-AVCS*	Terrier 1	ex WJ363, Odiham SF, AAC, 1900F. Cr 18-10-81.	®	1-04
❑	EI-BGB*	Rallye Club	ex Upper Ballinderry, Abbeyshrule, G-AZKB. CoA 18-5-91. Arrived 6-03.		1-04

LONDONDERRY
Champion 7DC G-BRFI moved to the East Midlands by mid-2003.

❑	G-ARAP	7EC Traveler	ex Eglinton. Crashed 22-9-81.	®	1-04

LONDONDERRY AIRPORT or Eglinton, north-east of the town
Jet Provost T.5A G-BYED moved to Chester, Wales, in July 2001.

LOUGH FOYLE Londonderry
Just off shore can be seen the hulk of Corsair II JT693:R, ex 1837 Squadron.

MONEYMORE on the A29, north of Cookstown, Londonderry

❑	G-BANF*	LA-4A Minor	CoA 5-6-92. Stored.	1-04
❑	G-NORD*	SNCAC NC.854	ex F-BFIS. CoA 27-5-82. Stored.	1-04

MOVENIS AERODROME near Garvagh, Londonderry

❑	G-AWJA	Cessna 182L	ex N1658C. Crashed 12-9-84. Fuselage.	off-site	1-04
❑	G-BBRZ*	AA-5 Traveler	ex Mullaghmore, EI-AYV ntu, G-BBRZ. CoA 30-4-99. Stored, dismantled.		1-04
❑	G-BIEW	Cessna U.206G	ex OO-DMA, N7344C. Crashed 31-12-88. Fuselage.		1-04
❑	G-EESE	Cessna U.206G	ex N6332U ntu. Cr 29-8-89. Forward fuse.	off-site	1-04

MULLAGHMORE AERODROME south-west of Ballymoney, Down

❑	G-BDRL*	SA-3 Playboy	ex N730GF. CoA 17-6-98. Stored.	1-04
❑	EI-BGA*	Rallye 100ST	ex G-BCXC, F-OCZQ. CoA 7-01. Stored.	1-04

NEWTOWNARDS AERODROME south of the town, between the A20 and A21, Down

❑	G-AJIH*	J/1 Autocrat	CoA 19-11-94. Stored.	1-04

❏ G-ARCT	PA-18-95	ex EI-AVE, G-ARCT. Damaged 29-3-87.	®	1-04
❏ N80B<u>A</u>	Pitts S-2A	stored. Crashed 11-7-99.		12-99

Locally: A Bensen is stored in an attic.
❏ G-BSNY*	Bensen B.8M	CoA 6-9-01. Stored.	1-04

RATHFRILAND on the A25, north-east of Newry, Down
❏ G-AVDT*	7AC Champion	ex N3594E, NC3594E. CoA 10-7-<u>90</u>. Stored.	2-03

UPPER BALLINDERRY on the A26 west of Belfast, near Crumlin, Antrim
Whitney Straight G-AERV moved to Southampton, Hants, in April 2002. The reference to **Andy Allen**'s Rallye in *W&R18* (p299) being restored to flying condition was a classic example of editorial optimism! In Andy's own words EI-BGB "had been my equivalent of a garden gnome"! It was passed on to Billy Lester at Lisburn, Northern Ireland, in June 2003. Andy owns Cessna EI-BAG at Langford Lodge, Northern Ireland - qv.

IRELAND

ABBEYSHRULE AERODROME Westmeagh, north-west of Mullignar
Some of the references here are a little dated now, but the hulks at this aerodrome do have a track-record of considerable longevity!

❏ EI-ANN	Tiger Moth	ex Dublin, Kilcock, G-ANEE, T5418, 63 GCF, 24 EFTS, 19 EFTS, 12 EFTS. Crashed 18-10-64. Spares for EI-AOP.		11-93
❏ EI-AOP	Tiger Moth	ex Dublin, G-AIBN, T7967, 18 EFTS, 1667 CU, 1 GCF, 16 PFTS. Crashed 5-5-74.	®	11-93
❏ EI-ARW	SAN DR.1050	ex F-BJJH. Crashed 28-7-86. Wreck.		8-98
❏ EI-ATK	Cherokee 140	ex G-AVUP. Crashed 14-2-87. Wreck.		4-03
❏ EI-AUJ	Rallye Club	ex Birr, G-AXHF, F-BNGV. Wreck.		6-97
❏ EI-AUP	Rallye Club	ex Coonagh, G-AVVK. Crashed 1-9-83. Wreck.		5-99
❏ EI-AWE	Cessna F.150L	Fuselage, stored.		4-03
❏ EI-AYS	PA-22 Colt 108	ex G-ARKT. Stored.		5-99
❏ EI-AYT	Rallye Minerva	ex G-AXIU. Crashed 12-11-89. Stored.		4-03
❏ EI-BCW	Rallye Club	ex G-AYKE.		6-97
❏ EI-BDP*	Cessna 182P	ex G-AZLC, N9327G. Damaged 1998. Stored.		4-03
❏ EI-BFI	Rallye 100ST	ex F-BXDK. Crashed 14-12-85. Spares.		4-03
❏ EI-BGD	Rallye Club	ex F-BUJI, D-EKHD ntu.		8-98
❏ EI-BGS	Rallye 180GT	ex F-BXTY. Crashed 20-7-90. Spares.		5-96
❏ EI-BGU	Rallye Club	ex F-BONM.		8-98
❏ EI-BHB	Rallye 125	ex F-BUCH. Stored, dismantled.		5-99
❏ EI-BIC	Cessna F.172N	ex OO-HNZ ntu. Crashed 13-4-95.		4-03
❏ EI-BIM	Rallye Club	ex F-BKYJ.		6-97
❏ EI-BJJ	Aeronca Sedan	ex G-BHXP ntu, EI-BJJ, N1214H.		6-97
❏ EI-BKU	Rallye C'dore	ex F-BRLG. Wreck.		5-99
❏ EI-BMV	AA-5 Traveler	ex G-BAEJ. Crashed 21-3-93.		8-98
❏ EI-BNR	AA-5 Traveler	ex N9992Q, CS-AHM. Crashed 21-2-88.		5-00
❏ EI-BOP	Rallye C'dore	ex Coonagh, G-BKGS, F-BSXS. Crashed 29-3-86.		5-99
❏ EI-BPJ	Cessna 182A	ex G-BAGA, N4849D. *The Hooker*. Wreck.		4-03
❏ EI-BUJ	Rallye C'dore	ex G-FOAM, G-AVPL.		6-97
❏ EI-CAA	Cessna FR.172J	ex G-BHTW, 5Y-ATO. Damaged 12-93. Wreck.		4-03
❏ G-BSUH	Cessna 140	ex N89088, NC89088. Damaged 6-93.		4-03
❏ G-SKYH	Cessna 172N	ex A6-GRM, N76034. Crashed 21-7-91. Stored.		4-03

BALLYJAMESDUFF on the R194 south of Cavan, Cavan
N Reilly: No news on either the Plus D or the Cadet.
❑	EI-ANA	Taylorcraft Plus D	ex G-AHCG, LB347, 657, 655.	® 4-92
❑	XE808	Cadet TX.1	ex Syerston, 617 VGS, 645 VGS. Stored.	4-92

CARLOW on the N9 south-west of Dublin, County Carlow
Carlow Institute of Technology:
❑	220	CM-170-1	ex Casement, IAC. Inst.	8-01

CASEMENT AIRFIELD or Baldonnel, west of Dublin, County Dublin
Irish Air Corps (IAC):
❑	34		Magister	ex Dublin, Casement, N5392.	9-03
❑	141		Avro XIX	ex Dublin, Casement.	9-03
❑	164		Chipmunk T.20	stored.	9-03
❑	172*		Chipmunk T.20	stored.	9-03
❑	183		Provost T.51	ex Dublin, Casement.	9-03
❑	191*		Vampire T.55	ex Gormanston, Dublin, Casement. Dismantled.	9-03
❑	198		Vampire T.11	ex 'gate', XE977, 8 FTS. Unflown by IAAC.	9-03
❑	199		Chipmunk T.20	ex Gormanston. Dismantled.	9-03
❑	202		Alouette III	ditched 20-10-95. Stored, dismantled.	12-03
❑	215		CM-170-1	stored.	12-03
❑	217		CM-170-1	stored.	9-03
❑	218		CM-170-1	stored.	1-02
❑	219		CM-170-1	stored.	9-03
❑	221	'3-KE'	CM-170-2	ex French Air Force No.79. Inst. Dismantled.	9-03
❑	233		SF-260MC	ex I-SYAS. Fuselage. Stored.	9-03
❑	237*		Gazelle	crashed 16-8-02. Wreck, first noted 4-03.	12-03
❑	'98'		Cessna 172B	ex Southend, G-ARLU, N8002X. Dam 30-10-77. Rig.	4-02
❑	[EI-BMM]*		Cessna F.152 II	ex Weston. IAAC roundels.	
❑	[G-ASNG]		Dove 6	ex Waterford, Cork, (EI-BJW), Coventry, HB-LFF, G-ASNG, HB-LFF, G-ASNG, PH-IOM. Stored.	4-03
❑			Alouette III	instructional, non-flying, rig. c/no 1012	9-03

CELBRIDGE on the R403 west of Dublin, Kildare
The Proctor is due to move to Dromod, Ireland, in due course.
❑	G-AHWO	Proctor V	ex Whitehall, Dublin, (EI-ALY). Cr 5-5-59. Stored.	4-03

CHURCHTOWN south of Dublin city centre, Dublin
Nutgrove Shopping Centre: A Grob Astir 'flies' over the bargains.
❑	EI-124	G.102 Astir CS	displayed since 1993.	6-03

CORK
Technical College: Their Magister was delivered to the airport not here – see below.

CORK AIRPORT
The local Technical College keeps their CM-170 Magister at the airport.
❑	–*	Rallye	Fuselage.	4-03
❑	216	CM-170-1	ex Casement. Stored.	4-03

DELGANY east of the N11, south of Dublin, Wicklow.
Mick Donohoe: Is thought to still be at work on restoring the 'Flea'.
❑	IAHC 3	HM.14 'Flea'	ex Carbury.	® 4-96

DROMOD on the N4 north of Longford, Leitrim

South East Aviation Enthusiasts Group (SEAEG): During 2002, the mammoth task of relocating the collection from New Ross, Ireland, to the exceptional **Cavan and Leitrim Railway** was carried out. It will still be some time before the airframes are on regular public view, and for the moment prior appointment is the best plan. The railway is superb, with steam trains in action April to September.

Notes: See under New Ross, Ireland, for the remainder of the collection. See under Celbridge, Ireland, for Proctor G-AHWO which will also make the move. Leading light of the group is Phil Bedford. His collection of aircraft are marked ¶. The identity of Gemini G-ALCS is in doubt. Markings indicate it *may* be from G-AKEL (see Holywood, Northern Ireland) [1]. Phil is restoring T.8 Tutor CBZ to its original 1944 condition as a long-span Cadet TX.2. CBZ was converted into a motor glider with an enclosed cockpit and will use the cockpit of RA881 in the rebuild [2]. The Chipmunk, Provost and Vampires are on loan from the Ministry of Defence [3].

◆ On the R202 out of Dromod village, east of the N4 Dublin-Sligo main road and alongside the mainline railway station. Open Sep to Jun 10am to 2.30pm; Jul to Aug10am to 5.30pm; Sun all year, 1pm to 5.30pm. ✉ Cavan and Leitrim Railway, Station Road, Dromod, Leitrim, Ireland ☎ 00 353 7838599 **e-mail** dromod@eircom.net **www.cavanandleitrimrailway.com For SEAEG:** ✉ Phil Bedford, 10 Walled Gardens, Castletown, Celbridge, Kildare, Ireland. **e-mail** pbedford@tcd.ie

❏	EI-BDM*	Aztec 250D	ex New Ross, Waterford, Kildimo, G-AXIV, N6826Y. Arrived 14-9-02.		4-04
❏	G-ALCS*	Gemini 3C	ex New Ross, Waterford, Kilbritain. Cockpit. Arrived 24-3-02.	[1]	4-04
❏	G-AOIE*	Douglas DC-7C	'EI-AWA', ex New Ross, Waterford, Shannon, PH-SAX, G-AOIE Caledonian, BOAC. Forward fuselage. Arrived 24-8-02.	¶	4-04
❏	NC285RS*	Navion	ex New Ross, Naas, Abbeyshrule, N91488. Cr 11-6-79. *My Way*. Cockpit. Arrived 24-3-02.		4-04
❏	VP-BDF*	Boeing 707-321	ex New Ross, Waterford, Dublin, N435MA, G-14-372, G-AYAG, N759PA. *Spirit of 73*. Nose. Arrived 24-8-02.		4-04
❏	EI-100*	SZD-12 Mucha	ex New Ross, OY-XAN. CoA 1-7-97. Arr 29-12-02.		4-04
❏	EI-139*	T.31B	ex New Ross, Gowran Grange, BGA.3485, G-BOKG, XE789. CoA 2-8-97. Arr 3-3-02.	¶	4-04
❏	–* CBK	Grunau Baby III	BGA.1410, ex New Ross, Naas, Breighton, Stoke-on-Trent, Firbeck, RAFGSA.378, D-4676. Arrived 26-5-02.	¶	4-04
❏	–* CBZ	T.8 Tutor	BGA.1424, ex New Ross, Naas, Gowran Grange, Jurby, RAFGSA.214, RA877. Arr 3-3-02.	¶ [2]	4-04
❏	173*	Chipmunk T.20	ex New Ross, Waterford, Gormanston, IAAC. Arrived 3-7-02.	[3]	4-04
❏	184*	Provost T.51	ex New Ross, Waterford, Casement, IAAC. Arrived 14-7-02.	[3]	4-04
❏	192*	Vampire T.55	ex New Ross, Waterford, Casement, IAAC. Arrived 25-8-02.	[3]	4-04
❏	RA881*	Cadet TX.1	ex New Ross, Breighton, Halfpenny Green, RAFGSA 163. Nose.	[2]	4-04
❏	– IAHC.1	HM.14 'Flea'	ex New Ross, Waterford, Dublin, Coonagh. *St Patrick.* Arrived 26-5-02.		4-04

DUBLIN

Institute of Technology: In Bolton Street, should still have its instructional airframe.

❏	EI-BHM	Cessna F.337E	ex Farranfore, Weston, OO-PDC, OO-PDG. CoA 9-7-82.	9-01

Former **Irish Aviation Museum** (IAM): Both references getting close to their 'sell by' date!

❏	EI-AOH	Viscount 808	ex Dublin Airport, Aer Lingus, PH-VII. Nose section.	10-97
❏	G-ANPC	Tiger Moth	ex Edinburgh (?), Strathallan, Portmoak, R4950, 2 GS, Kirton SF, Hemswell SF, Oakington SF, 28 EFTS, 25 PEFTS, 17 EFTS, Benson SF. Crashed 2-1-67.	4-96

Area: No news on the status or location of the Brewster Buffalo.
❑ BW-372   Buffalo   ex Finnish Air Force. Shot down 25-6-42. Stored.   11-00

DUBLIN AIRPORT or Collinstown, on the R122, north of the City, Dublin
❑ EI-ABI	DH.84 Dragon ✈	ex EI-AFK, G-AECZ, AV982, EE, 7 AACU, 110	
		Wing, G-AECZ. *Iolar*. Aer Lingus 'Historic Flight'.	12-03
❑ EI-BEM	Short 360-100	ex ALT, East Midlands, G-BLGC, G-14-3642.	
		St Senan. Crashed 31-1-86. Cabin trainer.	9-93
❑ EI-BSF	HS.748-1/105	ex Ryanair, EC-DTP, G-BEKD, LV-HHF, LV-PUM.	
		Spirit of Tipperary. CoA 21-5-87. Fire crews.	1-04

FOYNES on the N69 west of Limerick, Limerick
Foynes Flying-Boat Museum: Located in the original transatlantic flying-boat terminal on the River
Shannon, the museum recalls the era of the great 'boats 1937-1945. Among other items at this nascent
museum are the engines and other remains from BOAC Sunderland III G-AGES, which came to grief off
Kerry on July 28, 1943. The museum is also a shrine to Irish Coffee, invented here by chef Joe Sheridan
and first served up to revive passengers in 1942!
♦   Open March 31 to October 31, 10am to 6pm – last visit 5pm ◙ Flying-Boat Museum, Foynes,
    Limerick, Ireland. ☎ / **Fax** 00 353 69 65416 **e-mail** famm@eircom.net **www**.webforge.net

GALWAY
Eyre Square Centre: Ireland's oldest extant registered glider is displayed here.
❑ VM657 1GA.6 T.8 Tutor   ex County Wicklow.   4-99

GALWAY AIRPORT on the N64 east of the city
| ❑ G-AFNG | Moth Minor | ex AW112 EAAS, Wyton SF, Binbrook SF, | |
| | | G-AFNG. CoA 21-10-98. | 4-03 |

GORMANSTON AIRFIELD on the N1 north of Dublin, Meath
IAAC: The last aircraft flew out of here on 24th April 2001 and the formal shut-down was held 9th
August 2001. Vampire T.55 191 had moved to <u>Casement</u>, Ireland, by 9-03. The status of the Chipmunk
168 is therefore in doubt.

GOWRAN GRANGE near Dublin, Kildare
Dublin Gliding Club:
❑ EI-102	Kite 2	ex IGA.102, IAC.102. Stored.		6-03
❑ EI-128	Schleicher Ka 6CR —		®	5-99
❑ WZ762	Grasshopper TX.1	EI-135, ex Cosford, Rugby. (Wings of WZ756.)		6-03

NEW ROSS on the N25 north-east of Waterford, Wexford
South East Aviation Enthusiasts Group (SEAEG): The collection moved to <u>Dromod</u>, Ireland, during
2002. Departing were: Aztec 250D EI-BDM (14-9); Gemini 3C 'G-ALCS' (24-3); Douglas DC-7C G-
AOIE (24-8); Navion NC285RS (24-3); Boeing 707 cockpit VP-BDF (24-8); T.31B EI-139 (3-3);
Grunau Baby III CBK (26-5); T.8 Tutor CBZ and the cockpit of Cadet TX.1 RA881 (3-3); Chipmunk
T.20 173 (3-7); Provost T.51 184 (14-7); Vampire T.55 192 (25-8); HM.14 'Flea' IAHC.1 (26-5).
Additionally, SZD-12 Mucha EI-100 joined the collection at New Ross. It moved to Dromod 29-12-02.
The Aries (held off-site) and Vampire T.55 187 have yet to make the trek [1]. The Dove 6 is not owned
by SEAEG and is up for sale [2]. No reports on the status of the Hawker Hector frame [3].
❑ G-AOGA	Aries 1	ex Casement, Dublin, Kilbrittain Castle,		
		EI-ANB, G-AOGA. Damaged 8-8-69.	off-site [1]	4-03
❑ '176'	Dove 6	VP-YKF, ex Waterford, Cork, 3D-AAI,		
		VQ-ZJC, G-AMDD. For sale.	[2]	4-04

| ❏ | 187 | Vampire T.55 | ex Waterford, Casement, IAAC. | [1] | 4-04 |
| ❏ | – | Hector | frame | of-site [3] | 3-02 |

POWERSCOURT, Wicklow
| ❏ | EI-AUS | J/5F Aiglet Tnr | ex G-AMRL. CoA 2-12-75. Stored. | 4-95 |

RATHCOOLE, Cork
| ❏ | EI-AFN* | BA Swallow 2 | ex G-AFGV. Stored, off-site. | 4-03 |
| ❏ | G-AXVV | L-4H-PI | ex F-BBQB, 43-29572. CoA 16-6-73. Stored. | 4-03 |

SHANNON AIRPORT on the N19, south of Ennis, Clare
W&R16 (p326) declared Boeing 707-123B YN-CCN as being scrapped in June 1996. This was not the case, it has proved to be made of sterner stuff. It was 'parted-out' and then relocated on the airport [1]. Boeing 707-351C EL-AKL was in stored here by 2-02 but was scrapped by July 2003.

❏	N285F*	L.188CF Electra	ex N5012K. Damaged 1-3-99. Hulk.		8-02
❏	TN-AEE*	Boeing 737-2Q5C	ex F-GFVR, TN-AEE, EL-AIL. Arrived 14-6-<u>98</u>. Stored.		9-03
❏	YN-CCN*	Boeing 707-123B	Aeronica, 5B-DAO, G-BGCT, N7526A. Derelict.	[1]	8-02

SLIGO, Sligo
Gerry O'Hara: Gerry's homegrown aircraft are *believed* to be still stored here.
| ❏ | – | IAHC.7 Sligo Concept | single seat low wing monoplane. Unflown, stored. | 8-91 |
| ❏ | – | IAHC.8 O'Hara Gyro | on Bensen lines. Unflown. Stored. | 8-91 |

TRIM on the R154 north-west of Dublin, Meath
| ❏ | EI-ASU | Terrier 2 | ex Rathcoole, G-ASRG, Auster T.7 WE599, LAS, HCCS. | ® | 4-03 |

WATERFORD AIRPORT south-east of Waterford, Waterford
❏	EI-BFE	Cessna F.150G	ex G-AVGM. Dismantled.	4-99
❏	EI-BKK	JT.1 Monoplane	ex G-AYYC. Dismantled.	4-99
❏	207	Cessna FR.172H	ex Casement, IAAC. Fire crews.	6-01

WESTON AERODROME near Leixlip, Kildare
❏	EI-ALP	Avro Cadet	ex Castlebridge, G-ADIE. CoA 6-4-78. Stored.	6-01
❏	EI-BBG	Rallye 100ST	CoA 1-12-83. Fuselage, stored.	1-02
❏	EI-BCU	Rallye 100ST	Derelict by 8-01.	4-03
❏	EI-BEA	Rallye 100ST	CoA 10-5-86. Fuselage, stored.	1-02
❏	EI-BFP	Rallye 100ST	ex F-GARR. CoA 1-10-87. Stored.	6-01
❏	EI-BKN	Rallye 100ST	ex G-GBCK. CoA 5-98. Stored.	1-02
❏	EI-BUG	ST-10 Diplomate	ex G-STIO, OH-SAB. CoA 8-98. Stored.	4-03
❏	EI-BVK	Tomahawk 112	ex OO-FLG, OO-HLG, N9705N. CoA 5-98. Stored.	1-02
❏	EI-CGG	Aircoupe 415C	ex N2522H, NC2522H. CoA 10-00. Stored.	4-03

PART SIX
RAF OVERSEAS

An ever-dwindling listing of all British military aircraft in the *W&R* categories on Crown territory or property. Please note that this section does *not* appear in any index.

CYPRUS – AKROTIRI AIRFIELD

RAF Akrotiri: Wessex HU.5 XT479 and Whirlwind HAR.10 XJ437 were removed by mid-2002, having been acquired by a diving club. They will be sunk somewhere off the coast and as such leave the concern of *W&R*. (Although they were still in a boatyard at Paphos in November 2003!)

❑	XD184	W'wind HAR.10	8787M, ex 84 'A' Flt, 1563F, 228, 155. SAR c/s. Gate	9-02
❑	XR504	Wessex HC.2	ex 84, 22, SARTS, 18, 1 FTU. Spares.	5-02
❑	XS929	'L' Lightning F.6	ex Binbrook, 11, LTF, 11, 56, 11. 56 Sqn c/s. Gate	9-02
❑	XV470	'BD' Phantom FGR.2	9156M, ex 56, 228 OCU, 19, 228 OCU, 92, 56, 92, 56, 17, 14, 2.	9-02

FALKLAND ISLANDS – MOUNT PLEASANT AIRPORT

RAF Enclave: The Phantom stands guard over the Tornados.

❑	XV409	'H' Phantom FGR.2	9160M, ex 1435 Flt, 29, 228 OCU, 56, 111, 56, 111. *Hope*. Displayed.	7-01

Appendix A
AUCTIONS

For the first time since we have been covering these as a separate item, we are reduced to just one sale! This was the contents of the Museum of D-Day Aviation at Shoreham, West Sussex, on 17th May 2003 and covered on pages 214 and 215. I blame David Dickenson! Here's hoping for better days in the next edition!

Appendix B
EXPORTS

Within the text, all known exports are of course listed, but not highlighted as such. The table here should help to tie all of this activity together. Column 4 gives the location under which it was to be found within *W&R* and Column 5 the destination, new identity etc.

G-AKEK		Gemini 3A	Hatch, Beds	Iceland 8-03
G-AMCA		Douglas C-47B	Coventry, Warks	Netherlands 10-10-03
G-ARDG		Prospector	Washington, West Sussex	New Zealand 4-02
G-ASEG		Terrier 1	Haverfordwest, Wales	Denmark 4-02
G-AVMY		BAC 111-510ED	Bournemouth, Dorset	Switzerland 25-5-03
G-AWHB		CASA 2-111	North Weald, Essex	USA 2002*
G-BNNI		Boeing 727-276	Southend, Essex	Denmark 22-9-03
G-BTGA		Boeing PT-17	Duxford, Cambs	New Zealand 1-03
G-BWOE		Yak-3U	Duxford, Cambs	New Zealand 12-03
G-POOL		ARV Super 2	Keevil, Wilts	France 12-02
CLJ	BGA.1625	EoN Primary	Bicester, Oxford	France by 3-04
N999PJ		MS Paris 2 ✈	North Weald, Essex	USA 9-03
PH-NLH		Hunter T.7 nose	Eaglescott, Devon	Netherlands 2001
VT-DPE	G-BUJY	Tiger Moth	St Leonards, E Sussex	Belgium 11-02
A1325	G-BVGR	RAF BE.2e	Sudbury, Suffolk	New Zealand 6-02
'D8781'	G-ECKE	Avro 504K REP	Duxford, Cambs	New Zealand 9-02
FE992	G-BDAM	Harvard IIB ✈	Duxford, Cambs	Canada 11-9-03
MK912	G-BRRA	Spitfire IX ✈	Duxford, Cambs	Canada 11-9-03
SM832	G-WWII	Spitfire XIV ✈	Duxford, Cambs	USA 1-04
TB252	G-XVIE	Spitfire XVI	Audley End, Essex	USA (via New Zealand) 2003

TV959		Mosquito T.3	Duxford, Cambs	USA 12-6-03*
XE327		Sea Hawk FGA.6	Bruntingthorpe, Leics	Germany 23-10-02
XR588		Wessex HC.2 ✈	Shawbury, Shrop	New Zealand 6-1-04
XR670		Jet Provost T.4	Ipswich, Suffolk	Germany 4-03
XS101	G-GNAT	Gnat T.1 ✈	North Weald, Essex	Australia 3-10-03
XS675		Wessex HC.2 ✈	Shawbury, Shrop	New Zealand 8-1-04
XT680		Wessex HC.2 ✈	Shawbury, Shrop	New Zealand 6-1-04
XV730		Wessex HC.2 ✈	Shawbury, Shrop	New Zealand 6-1-04
XW986	ZU-NIP	Buccaneer S.2B ✈	Kemble, Glos	South Africa 7-8-02
OJ4	G-UNNY	Strikemaster 87 ✈	Duxford, Cambs	Ivory Coast 3-03
OJ9	G-BXFR	Strikemaster 87	North Weald, Essex	USA N604GV 1999
NZ3009	ZK-RMH	P-40E-CU ✈	Duxford, Cambs	New Zealand 11-12-03
NZ5648	G-BXUL	FG-1D Corsair ✈	Duxford, Cambs	New Zealand 12-12-03
'28'	ZK-LIX	Lavochkin La-9 ✈	Duxford, Cambs	New Zealand 1-04
1121	G-CCAI	Strikemaster 80A	North Weald, Essex	USA 12-02
'122351'	G-BKRG	Beech C-45G	Bruntingthorpe, Leics	Netherlands 10-03
92399	G-CCMV	Vought FG-1D ✈	Duxford, Cambs	USA 9-02, becoming N451FG
474008	G-SIRR	P-51D-25-NA ✈	Duxford, Cambs	USA 2-03

* Delivered to a workshop in Norfolk for preparation, may have taken / might take some time to cross the 'Pond'.

Appendix C
'COCKPITFEST'

Following suggestions from several readers, we thought it was about time that this quintessentially *'W&R'* event was put on the map! Now being flattered by imitators, the event was conceived by Bill O'Sullivan of the Newark Air Museum and I'm proud to say that its potential was recognised and *FlyPast* threw in its support. It has flourished ever since – No.5 will be staged at the Newark Air Museum on June 12/13, 2004. The 'Best Cockpit' and 'Special' awards come from the judging team, while the 'Cockpiter's Cockpit' award is voted for by the attending 'cockpiters'. The *FlyPast* Readers Award is a vote from the attending public.

We've four events to catch up on. Information is given as follows: Column 1 type and identity; Column 2 owner/keeper at that time; Column 3 location at that time; Column 4 awards, notes etc. Some of the very sophisticated and challenging cockpits that attend *CockpitFest* are instrumentation clusters and as such would not get a mention in the main text and are equally not given here.

CockpitFest I, Winthorpe, 17th-18th June 2000

Avro Anson C.19 VP519	{ Alan Hulme { Iain Forster	Wolverhampton, West Mids	
Canberra B.2 WE113	Chris Cannon	Woodhurst, Cambs	
Canberra T.17 WH863	Aaron Braid	Resident	Best Cockpit - runner-up
Hunter F.2 WN890	Naylan Moore	Firbeck, Notts	
Jet Provost T.3 XN511	Bill Fern	Firbeck, Notts	
Jet Provost T.3 XP642	Nikki Collins	Lavendon, Bucks	Best Cockpit
Jet Provost T.4 XR654	Ian Starnes	Sealand, Wales	
Meteor F.8 WL131	Bill Fern	Firbeck, Notts	
Pucará A-533	Tony Dyer	Boscombe Down, Wilts	
Venom FB.1 WK393	South Yorks AM	Firbeck, Notts	

CockpitFest II, Winthorpe, 16th-17th June 2001

Canberra B(I).6 WT319	Tony Collins	Lavendon, Bucks	Cockpiters' Cockpit
Canberra PR.7 WT536	Frank Lund	Southampton, Hants	Best Cockpit
Canberra PR.9 XH177	Frank Millar	Resident	
Canberra T.4 WJ865	Bob Dunn	Wolverhampton, W Mids	ex Stamford, Lincs
Canberra T.4 XH584	Bill Fern	Doncaster, S Yorks	
Canberra T.17 WH863	Aaron Braid	Resident	
Chipmunk T.10 WB626	Stewart Thornley	Aylesbury, Bucks	ex Barnstaple, Devon
Chipmunk T.10 WZ876	Mick Long	Yately, Bucks	ex Twyford, Bucks
Hunter F.2 WN890	Naylan Moore	Doncaster, S Yorks	
Hunter F.6 XG290	Tony Dyer	Boscombe Down, Wilts	
Hunter FGA.9 XG297	Bill Fern	Doncaster, S Yorks	
Jet Provost T.3 XN511	Bill Fern	Doncaster, S Yorks	Best Cockpit - runner-up

Jet Provost T.4 XP642	Nikki Collins	Lavendon, Bucks	
Phantom FGR.2 XV426	Mick Jennings	Coltishall, Norfolk	*FlyPast* Readers' Best Cockpit
WACO CG-4A	Bill Fern	Doncaster, S Yorks	

CockpitFest III, **Winthorpe, 15th-16th June 2002**

Buccaneer S.2 XN979	David Burke	Stamford, Lincs	ex Croydon, Gtr Lon
Cadet TX.3 XN238	Bill Fern	Doncaster, S Yorks	Best Cockpit, runner-up
Canberra T.4 WH850	Bill Fern	Doncaster, S Yorks	
Canberra T.4 WJ880	Dumfries & Galloway	Dumfries, Scotland	
Canberra PR.7 WT536	Frank Lund	Southampton, Hants	
Canberra PR.7 XH177	Frank & Lee Millar	Resident	
Canberra T.17 WH863	Aaron Braid	Resident	
Chipmunk T.10 WB560	Naylan Moore	Doncaster, S Yorks	
Harrier GR.3	{ AeroVenture	Doncaster, S Yorks	Best Cockpit
	{ Roy Jerman		
Harrier GR.3 XV806	Roy Hudson	Boscombe Down, Wilts	
Hunter F.1 WT684	Tony Collins	Lavendon, Bucks	Cockpiters' Cockpit
Hunter F.2 WN890	Naylan Moore	Doncaster, S Yorks	
Hunter FGA.9 XE584	NW Aviation Heritage	Hooton Park, Cheshire	
Hunter FGA.9 XE597	{ Bob Dunn	Bromsgrove, Worcs	ex Moreton-in-Marsh, Glos
	{ Mick Boulanger		
Jaguar T.2A XX830	Mick Jennings	Coltishall, Norfolk	*FlyPast* Readers' Best Cockpit
Meteor F.8 WL131	Bill Fern	Doncaster, S Yorks	
MiG-21SPS 764	Murray Jacobsen	Northampton, Northants	ex Wycombe Air Park, Bucks
Pucará A-533	Tony Dyer	Boscombe Down, Wilts	
Scout AH.1 XP902	AeroVenture	Doncaster, S Yorks	Special Award
Sea Hawk F.1 WF145	Stuart Gowan	Chelmsford, Essex	
Shackleton T.4 VP293	Shackleton Assoc	Resident	
Valiant B.1 XD875	North-east owner	Resident	

CockpitFest IV, **Winthorpe, 17th-18th June 2003**

Canberra B.2 WJ676	Simon Pulford	Hooton Park, Cheshire	Best Cockpit and Cockpiters' Cockpit, joint winner
Canberra PR.7 WT536	Frank Lund	Southampton, Hants	
Hunter F.1 WT684	Tony Collins	Lavendon, Bucks	Cockpiters' Cockpit, joint winner and *FlyPast* Readers' Best Cockpit
Hunter F.2 WN890	Naylan Moore	Doncaster, S Yorks	
Meteor F.8 WL131	Bill Fern	Doncaster, S Yorks	
McDD Phantom SIM	Mike Davey	Hooton Park, Cheshire	ex Norway
Scout AH.1 XP902	AeroVenture	Doncaster, S Yorks	
Tiger Moth	AeroVenture	Doncaster, S Yorks	
Vampire T.11 XD599	Stuart Gowans	Ingatestone, Essex	Best Cockpit, runner-up

---

Appendix D
LOST and FOUND!

This section seeks to get readers scratching around to solve some of the many 'unfinished' stories within the pages of *W&R*. Listed below are aircraft that have been shunted into the LOST! column from the pages of this edition. The ultimate aim is to 'find' these, and this mostly takes the form of a confirmed scrapping, or similar. Note that, as with all of the book, the criterion for an aircraft entering LOST! or FOUND! is a *physical* input and not an assumption or interpretation of registration changes etc. Over to YOU!

Lost! **G-ARTY** Cessna 150B, last at Popham, Hants, 8-96; **'G-ASOK' (D-ECDU)** Cessna F.172F, last at Longside, Scotland, 12-93; **G-ATGZ** Griffiths GH.4, last at Shardlow, Derbyshire, 7-91; **XG544** Sycamore HR.14, last at Tremar, Conrnwall, reported as sold in 'Wales' 11-00.

Found! **G-BCAC** Rallye Minerva last at Trafford Park, Gtr Man (5-92), confirmed scrapped on site circa 1997/1998.

Appendix E
ABBREVIATIONS

Without the use of abbreviations for the 'potted' histories of the aircraft listed in *W&R*, the book would perhaps be twice the size. Readers should face few problems, especially if they have previous editions to refer to. There follows a decode of abbreviations to help readers wend their way through the individual histories. Footnotes have been added to go into greater depth with some entries. To save repetition, abbreviations that are clearly combinations of others are not listed in full, eg MEAFCS, breaks into MEAF and CS, ie Middle East Air Force Communications Squadron.

A&AEE	Aeroplane and Armament Experimental Establishment. From the late 1980s became the Aircraft and Armament Evaluation Establishment. Now QinetiQ!
AAC	Army Air Corps
AACU	Anti-Aircraft Co-operation Unit
AAFCE	Allied Air Forces Central Europe
AAIU	Air Accident Investigation Unit
ABDR	Aircraft Battle Damage Repair
ACC	Allied Control Commission
ACSEA	Allied Command, South East Asia *Note 1*
ACU	Andover Conversion Unit
ADS	Air Director School
AE&AEOS	Air Engineers and Air Electronic Operators School
AEF	Air Experience Flight
AES	Air Engineers School
AES	Air Engineering School
AETW	Air Engineering Training Wing
AFDS	Air Fighting Development Squadron,
AFDU	Air Fighting Development Unit
AFEE	Airborne Forces Experimental Establishment
AFN	Air Forces North
AFNE	Air Forces Near East
AFS	Advanced Flying School
AFTS	Advanced Flying Training School
AFU	Advanced Flying Unit
AFWF	Advanced Fixed Wing Flight
AIU	Accident Investigation Unit
ALAT	Aviation Legere de l'Armee de Terre
AMARC	Aerospace Maintenance& Regeneration Center, Arizona, USA
AMIF	Aircraft Maintainance Instruction Flight
AMS	Air Movements School
ANG	Air National Guard
ANS	Air Navigation School
AONS	Air Observer and Navigator School
AOTS	Aircrew Officers Training School
APS	Aircraft Preservation Society
APS	Armament Practice Station
arr	arrived, denotes airframe arrived at location by surface transport.
AR&TF	Aircraft Recovery and Transportation Flight, St Athan – tri-service 'mover' of fixed-wing airframes. (See MASU)
ARWF	Advanced Rotary Wing Flight,
AS	Aggressor Squadron
AS&RU	Aircraft Salvage and Repair Unit
ASF	Aircraft Servicing Flight
ASS	Air Signals School
AST	Air Service Training
ASWDU	Air-Sea Warfare Development Unit
ATA	Air Transport Auxiliary
ATAIU	Allied Technical Air Intelligence Unit
ATC	Air Training Corps (Air Cadets)
ATDU	Air Torpedo Development Unit
ATE	Army Training Estate

ATF	Airframe Technology Flight	
Att	Air Attache	
AuxAF	Auxiliary Air Force	
aw/cn	AWaiting CollectioN	*Note 2*
AWFCS	All Weather Fighter Combat School	
AWOCU	All Weather Operational Conversion Unit	
AWRE	Atomic Weapons Research Establishment,	
BA	British Airways	
BAAT	British Airways Airtours	
BAC	Bristol Aero Collection	
BAC	British Aircraft Corporation	
BAe	British Aerospace	
BAF	British Air Ferries	
BAFO	British Air Forces of Occupation	
BAH	British Airways Helicopters	
BAM	Booker Aircraft Museum	
BANS	Basic Air Navigation School	
BAOR	British Army of the Rhine	
BAPC	British Aviation Preservation Council	
BATUS	British Army Training Unit, Suffield (Can)	
BBMF	Battle of Britain Memorial Flight	
BBML	British Balloon Museum and Library	
BC	Bomber Command.	
BCAL	British Caledonian Airlines	
BCBS	Bomber Command Bombing School	
BDRF	Battle Damage Repair Flight	
BDTF	Bomber Defence Training Flight	
BDU	Bomber Development Unit	
BEA	British European Airways	
BEAH	British European Helicopters	
BEAS	British Executive Air Services	
BFTS	Basic Flying Training School	
BFWF	Basic Fixed Wing Flight	
B&GS	Bombing & Gunnery School (RCAF)	
BG	Bomb Group	
BIH	British Independent Helicopters	
BLEU	Blind Landing Experimental Unit	
BMA	British Midland Airways now bmi	
BOAC	British Overseas Airways Corporation	
BPPU	Bristol Plane Preservation Unit	
BRNC	Britannia Royal Naval College	
BSE	Bristol Siddeley Engines	
B&TTF	Bombing & Target Towing Flight	
BTF	Beaver Training Flight	
BTU	Bombing Trials Unit	
BUA	British United Airlines	
BW	Bomb Wing	
C(A)	Controller (Aircraft) see also CS(A) *Note 3*	
CAA	Civil Aviation Authority	
CAACU	Civilian Anti-Aircraft Co-operation Unit	
CAF	Canadian Armed Forces.	
CAFU	Civil Aviation Flying Unit	
Cam Flt	Camouflage Flight,	
CATCS	Central Air Traffic Control School	
CAW	College of Air Warfare	
CBE	Central Bombing Establishment	
CC	Coastal Command.	

CCAS	Civilian Craft Apprentices School,
CCF	Combined Cadet Force
CF	Communications Flight as suffix with other unit, or for an airfield.
CFCCU	Civilian Fighter Control and Co-op Unit
CFE	Central Fighter Establishment see CFE-EAF.
CFE-EAF	Central Fighter Establishment - Enemy Aircraft Flight
CFS	Central Flying School
C&TTS	Communications and Target Towing Sqn
CGS	Central Gliding School
CGS	Central Gunnery School
CIFAS	Centre d'Instruction des Forces Aeriennes Strategiques
CIT	Cranfield Institute of Technology
CNCS	Central Navigation and Control School
CoA	Certificate (or Permit) of Airworthiness.
Cott	Cottesmore, in relation to V-Bomber wings
CPF	Coastal Patrol Flight
cr	crashed, or other form of accident
CR	Crash Rescue, training airframe.
CRD	Controller, Research and Development
C&RS	Control and Reporting School
CS	Communications Squadron, as a suffix with other units, or for an airfield.
CS(A)	Controller, Supplies (Air), see also CA *Note 3*
CSDE	Central Servicing Development Es.
CSE	Central Signals Establishment
CSF	Canberra Servicing Flight
CTE	Central Training Establishment
CTTS	Civilian Technical Training School
C&TTS	Communications & Target Towing Squadron
CU	Communications Unit, as suffix
CU	Conversion Unit, as suffix
DARA	Defence Aviation Repair Agency, Fleetlands, St Athan, Sealand
dbr	damaged beyond repair, to distinguish an aircraft that was written off but did not crash
deH	de Havilland
del	delivered, an airframe that arrived by air.
DERA	Defence Evaluation and Research Agency — replaced DRA and DTEO.
Det	Detachment, flight or other unit detached from main base
DFLS	Day Fighter Leader School
DLO	Defence Logistics Organisation
DPA	Defence Procurement Agency replaced MoD(PE)
DRA	Defence Research Agency – see DERA
DSA	Disposal Sales Agency
DSDA	Defence Storage and Distribution Agency tri-service unit with the following sites: Ashchurch, Aston Down, Bicester (not the airfield), Donnington, Llangenneach, Stafford, West Moors
DTEO	Defence Test and Evaluation Organisation – see DERA
DU	Development Unit, as suffix
EAAS	East Anglian Aviation Society
EASAMS	European avionics consortium
ECTT	Escadre de Chasse Tous Temp
EE	English Electric
EFTS	Elementary Flying Training School
EOD	Explosive Ordnance Disposal

EP&TU	Exhibition, Production and Transport Unit
ERFTS	Elementary & Reserve Flying Trng School
ERS	Empire Radio School
Esc	Escadre, French squadron
ETPS	Empire Test Pilots School
ETS	Engineering Training School
ETU	Experimental Trials Unit
EWAD	Electronic Warfare and Avionics Detachment
EWE&TU	Electronic Warfare Experimental and Training Unit
F	Flight, suffix to number
FAA	Fleet Air Arm
FAA	Fuerza Aerea Argentina
FAAHAF	Fleet Air Arm Historic Aircraft Flight
FAAM	Fleet Air Arm Museum
FAF	French Air Force.
FAH	Fuerza Aerea Hondurena
FC	Fighter Command.
FC&RS	Fighter Control and Reporting School
FCS	Fighter Control School
FEAF	Far East Air Forces *Note 1*
FECS	Far East Communications Flight
FF	Ferry Flight
FF&SS	Fire Fighting and Safety School
FGF	Flying Grading Flight
FLS	Fighter Leader School
FOAC	Flag Officer, Aircraft Carriers
FOCAS	Friends of Cardington Airship Station
FOFT	Flag Officer, Flying Training
FONA	Flag Officer, Naval Aviation
FONAC	Flag Officer, Naval Air Command
FP	Ferry Pool
FPP	Ferry Pilots Pool
FRADU	Fleet Requirements and Direction Unit
FRL	Flight Refuelling Ltd
FRS	Flying Refresher School
FRU	Fleet Requirements Unit
FSM	Full Scale Model
FSS	Ferry Support Squadron
FSS	Flying Selection Squadron
FTC	Flying Training Command
FTS	Flying Training School
FTU	Ferry Training Unit
FU	Ferry Unit
FWS	Fighter Weapons School
GAM	Groupe Aérien Mixte
GCF	Group Communications Flight
GE	Groupement Ecol
GIA	Ground Instructional Aircraft
GS	Glider School
GSU	Group Support Unit
GTS	Glider Training School
GU	Glider Unit
GWDS	Guided Weapons Development Squadron
HAB	Hot air balloon
HAM	Historic Aircraft Museum, Southend
HC	Home Command
HCEU	Home Command Examining Unit
HCF	Hornet Conversion Flight
HDU	Helicopter Development Unit
HGSU	Heavy Glider Servicing Unit
HMTS	Harrier Maintenance Training School
HQ	Headquarters
HS	Handling Squadron
HSA	Hawker Siddeley Aviation
HTF	Helicopter Training Flight

IAAC	Irish Army Air Corps
IAF	Indian Air Force
IAM	Institute of Aviation Medicine
IGN	Institut Geographique National
IHM	International Helicopter Museum
ITF or 'S	Instrument Training Flight / Squadron
IWM	Imperial War Museum
JASS	Joint Anti-Submarine School
JATE	Joint Air Transport Establishment - see JATEU
JATEU	Joint Air Transport Evaluation Unit – replaced JATE
JCU	Javelin Conversion Unit
JEHU	Joint Experimental Helicopter Unit
JMU	Joint Maritime Unit
JOCU	Jaguar Operational Conversion Unit
JTU	Joint Trials Unit (Nimrod AEW)
JWE	Joint Warfare Establishment
LAS	Light Aircraft School
LC	Logistics Command
LCS & 'U	Lightning Conversion Squadron / Unit
LTF	Lightning Training Flight
LWRE	Long Range Weapons Research Est
MAM	Midland Air Museum
MASL	Military Aircraft Spares Ltd
MASU	Mobile Aircraft Support Unit – DARA Fleetlands, tri-service 'mover' of helicopters. See AR&TF
MBA	Museum of Berkshire Aviation
MC	Maintenance Command
MCS	Metropolitan Communications Squadron
MEAF	Middle East Air Force Note 1
MECS	Middle East Communications Squadron
MGSP	Mobile Glider Servicing Party
MinTech	Ministry of Technology, see also MoA, MoS Note 3
MoA	Ministry of Aviation, see MinTech, MoS Note 3
MoD	Ministry of Defence
MoD(PE)	Ministry of Defence (Procurement Executive) – see DPA
MoS	Ministry of Supply, see MinTech, MoA Note 3
MoTaT	Museum of Transport & Technology, NZ
MOTU	Maritime Operational Training Unit
MPA	Man-powered aircraft
MU	Maintenance Unit Note 4
NAAS	Navigator and Airman Aircrew School
NACDS	Naval Air Command Driving School
NASA	National Aeronautical and Space Admin
NASU	Naval Aircraft Servicing Unit
NBC	Nuclear, Bacteriological and Chemical
NCS	Northern Communications Squadron
nea	Non effective airframe Note 2
NECS	North Eastern Communications Squadron
NIBF	Northern Ireland Beaver Flight
NSF	Northern Sector Flight
ntu	Not taken up, registration applied for, but not worn, or paperwork not concluded
(O)AFU	(Observers) Advanced Flying Unit
OCTU	Officer Cadet Training Unit
OCU	Operational Conversion Unit
OTU	Operational Training Unit
(P)AFU	(Pilot) Advanced Flying Unit
PAX	Passenger, as used in Chipmunk PAX trainer
PCSS	Protectorate Comms and Support Squadron

PEE	Proof & Experimental Establishment
PFA	Popular Flying Association
PFS	Primary Flying School
PFTS	Primary Flying Training School
PP	Pilots' Pool
PPS	Personal Plane Services
PRDU	Photo Reconnaissance Development Unit
PRU	Photographic Reconnaissance Unit
PTC	Personnel and Training Command
PTF	Phantom Training Flight
PTS	Primary Training School
QF	Queen's Flight
RAAF	Royal Australian Air Force
RAE	Royal Aircraft / Aerospace Establishment
RAeS	Royal Aeronautical Society
RAF	Royal Air Force
RAFA	Royal Air Force Association
RAFC	Royal Air Force College
RAFEF	Royal Air Force Exhibition Flight
RAFG	Royal Air Force Germany
RAFGSA	Royal Air Force Gliding & Soaring Assoc
RAFHSF	Royal Air Force High Speed Flight
RAFM	Royal Air Force Museum
RAN	Royal Australian Navy
RC	Reserve Command
RCAF	Royal Canadian Air Force
RCN	Royal Canadian Navy
RCS	Rotary Conversion Squadron
Regt	Regiment
RFS	Reserve Flying School
RHK	Royal Hong Kong
RMAF	Royal Malaysian Air Force
RNAY	Royal Naval Aircraft Yard
RNEC	Royal Naval Engineering College
RNGSA	Royal Navy Gliding and Soaring Association
RNHF	Royal Navy Historic Flight
RNoAF	Royal Norwegian Air Force
RNZAF	Royal New Zealand Air Force
ROC	Royal Observer Corps
RPRE	Rocket Propulsion Research Establishment
RRE	Royal Radar Establishment
RRF	Radar Reconnaissance Flight
RRHT	Rolls-Royce Heritage Trust
RS	Radio School
RSRE	Radar and Signals Research Establishment
RSS & 'U	Repair & Servicing Section / Unit
RTR	Royal Tank Regiment
RWE	Radio Warfare Establishment
SAAF	South African Air Force
SAC	School of Army Co-operation
SAF	School of Aerial Fighting
SAH	School of Aircraft Handling
SAR	Search and Rescue
SAREW	Search and Rescue Engineering Wing
SARTS	Search and Rescue Training Squadron
SC	Signals Command
Scamp	Scampton, to distinguish a V-Bomber wing
SCBS	Strike Command Bombing School
SCS	Southern Communications Squadron
SEAE	School of Electrical and Aeronautical Engineering
SF	Station Flight, usually with an airfield name
SFDO	School of Flight Deck Operations
SFTS	Service Flying Training School
ShF	Ship's Flight
SHQ	Station HQ

SLAW	School of Land/Air Warfare		TMTS	Trade Management Training School	
SMR	School of Maritime Reconnaissance		toc	Taken on charge	Note 2
soc	Struck off charge	Note 2	TRE	Telecommunications Research Establishment	
SoRF	School of Refresher Training		TS	Training Squadron	
SoTT	School of Technical Training	Note 5	TTC	Technical Training Command	
SRCU	Short Range Conversion Unit		TTU	Torpedo Training Unit	
SRW	Strategic Reconnaissance Wing		TWU	Tactical Weapons Unit	
SS	Signals Squadron		UAS	University Air Squadron	Note 6
SS	Support Squadron		UNFICYP	United Nations Forces In Cyprus	
SU	Support Unit		USAAC	United States Army Air Corps	
SVAS	Shuttleworth Veteran Aeroplane Society		USAAF	United States Army Air Force	
TAC	The Aeroplane Collection		USAF	United States Air Force	
TAF	Tactical Air Force		USMC	United States Marine Corps	
TAW	Tactical Airlift Wing		USN	United States Navy	
TC	Transport Command		VAFA	Vintage Aircraft Flying Association	
TEE	Trials and Experimental Establishment		VAT	Vintage Aircraft Team	
TEU	Tactical Exercise Unit		VGS	Volunteer Gliding School	
TF	Training Flight		Wadd	Waddington, denoting a V-Bomber wing	
TFF	Target Facilities Flight		WAP	Wycombe Air Park	
TFS	Tactical Fighter Squadron		WCS	Western Communications Squadron	
TFTAS	Tactical Fighter Training Aggressor Squadron		wfu	Withdrawn from use	
			Witt	Wittering, denoting a V-bomber wing.	
TFW	Tactical Fighter Wing		WLT	Weapons Loading Trainer	
TGDA	Training Group Defence Agency		WSF	Western Sector Flight	
Thum Flt	Temperature and HUMidity Flight				
TMS	Tornado Maintenance School				

Notes

1   RAF 'Holding Units': For administrative purposes, the history cards of some RAF aircraft become fairly vague when transferred to either Middle East or Far East theatres of operations. Accordingly, the following abbreviations denote the 'operator' for the segment of an aircraft's life in that theatre, even though it may have been used by several front-line units : ACSEA, FEAF, MEAF.

2   History Card 'milestones': There are several RAF aircraft history card 'milestones' referred to in the main text. Essentially an aircraft starts off as AWaiting Collection (Aw/cn) - a signal from the manufacturer that the aircraft is ready for issue to service; it is then taken on charge (toc) and becomes a part of the RAF; after service life, it may eventually to be declared a non-effective airframe (nea) and down-graded to instructional or fire-training use; the final act is for it to be struck off charge (soc), either being written-off in an accident, scrapped, sold to another user etc etc.

3   Government 'owning' bodies: Technical 'owner' of UK military machines is the C(A) or CS(A) and at times these are noted within the aircraft history cards instead of a unit, although it may well be a pointer to the aircraft being operated at that time of its life by a test or trials unit. In similar manner, MinTech, MoA or MoS can appear, frequently meaning operation by the RAE, or DRA.

4   Maintenance Unit (MU): Frequently mentioned in the text are: 4 Stanmore Park (detachment); 5 Kemble; 6 Brize Norton, 7 Quedgeley; 8 Little Rissington; 9 Cosford; 10 Hullavington; 12 Kirkbride; 14 Carlisle; 15 Wroughton; 16 Stafford; 19 St Athan (also 32); 20 Aston Down; 22 Silloth; 23 Aldergrove; 27 Shawbury; 29 High Ercall; 32 St Athan (also 19); 39 Colerne; 44 Edzell; 46 Lossiemouth; 47 Sealand; 48 Hawarden; 54 Cambridge; 57 Wig Bay; 60 Leconfield; 71 Bicester.

5   School of Technical Training (SoTT): The following are mentioned in the main text: 1 Halton; 2 Cosford; 4 St Athan; 8 Weeton; 9 Newton; 10 Kirkham; 12 Melksham.

6   University Air Squadron (UAS): Prefixed with a university name: Abn Aberdeen, Dundee & St Andrews; Bir Birmingham; Bri Bristol; Cam Cambridge; Dur Durham; Edn Edinburgh; Elo East Lowlands; Ems East Midlands; G&S Glasgow & Strathclyde; Lee Leeds; Liv Liverpool; Lon London; Man Manchester & Salford; Nor Northumbrian; Not Nottingham; Oxf Oxford; QUB Queens University Belfast; Stn Southampton; Wal Wales; Yor Yorkshire.

We hope you enjoyed this book . . .

Midland Publishing titles are edited and designed by an experienced and enthusiastic team of specialists.

Our associate, Midland Counties Publications, offers an exceptionally wide range of aviation, military, naval and transport books and videos for sale by mail-order around the world.

For a copy of the appropriate catalogue, or to order further copies of this book, and any of many other Midland Publishing titles, please write, telephone, fax or e-mail to:

Midland Counties Publications
4 Watling Drive, Hinckley, Leics, LE10 3EY, England

Tel: (+44) 01455 254 450
Fax: (+44) 01455 233 737
E-mail: midlandbooks@compuserve.com
www.midlandcountiessuperstore.com

Index I
TYPES

Note that two broad types have been 'bundled' into 'families' for ease of reference: Balloons and Airships and Hang-gliders (modern examples only, classics, Lilienthals, Pilchers etc are listed separately).

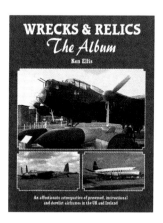